Crusades
Volume 11, 2012

Crusades

Edited by
Benjamin Z. Kedar, Jonathan Phillips
and Jonathan S. C. Riley-Smith with William J. Purkis

Crusades is published annually for the Society for the Study of the Crusades and the Latin East by Ashgate. A statement of the aims of the Society and details of membership can be found following the Bulletin at the end of the volume.

Manuscripts should be sent to either of the Editors in accordance with the guidelines for submission of papers on p. 369.

Subscriptions: Crusades (ISSN 1476–5276) is published annually.

Subscriptions are available on an annual basis and are £65 for institutions and non-members, and £25 for members of the Society. Prices include postage by surface mail. Enquiries concerning members' subscriptions should be addressed to the Treasurer, Dr. Jon M. B. Porter (see p. 292). All orders and enquiries should be addressed to: Subscription Department, Ashgate Publishing Ltd, Wey Court East, Union Road, Farnham, Surrey, GU9 7PT, U.K.; tel.: +44 (0)1252 331600; fax: +44 (0)1252 736736; email: journals@ashgatepublishing.com

Requests for Permissions and Copying: requests should be addressed to the Publishers: Permissions Department, Ashgate Publishing Ltd, Wey Court East, Union Road, Farnham, Surrey, GU9 7PT, U.K.; tel.: +44 (0)1252 331600; fax: +44 (0)1252 736736; email: journals@ashgatepublishing.com. The journal is also registered in the U.S.A. with the Copyright Clearance Center, 222 Rosewood Drive, Danvers MA 01923, U.S.A.; tel.: +1 (978) 750 8400; fax: +1 (978) 750 4470; email: rreader@copyright.com and in the U.K. with the Copyright Licensing Agency, 90 Tottenham Court Road, London, W1P 9HE; tel.: +44 (0)207 436 5931; fax: +44 (0)207 631 5500.

Crusades

Volume 11, 2012

Published by ASHGATE *for the*
Society for the Study of the Crusades
and the Latin East

Published by
Ashgate Publishing Limited
Wey Court East
Union Road
Farnham
Surrey GU9 7PT
England

Ashgate Publishing Company
110 Cherry Street
Suite 3-1
Burlington, VT 05401–3818
USA

Ashgate website: http://ashgate.com

ISBN: 978-1-4094-4666-8

ISSN 1476–5276

Typeset by N²productions

The paper used in this publication meets the minimum requirements of the American National Standard for Information Sciences – Permanence of Paper for Printed Library Materials, ANSI Z39.48-1984

Printed and bound in Great Britain by the MPG Books Group, UK

CONTENTS

REVIEWS

SHORT NOTICES

A Note to Our Readers

When we launched *Crusades* in 2002 we were far from certain whether we would obtain a sufficient number of submissions and whether the journal would become a going concern. Indeed, in the early years we had to plead with scholars, especially those who delivered promising papers at conferences, to submit articles for publication. But this was to change rapidly. We are now a first choice for scholars wishing to publish articles on the many topics we cover; our contributors range from doctoral students to senior academics. Consequently, over the past few years it has become possible to subject all submissions to a thorough if time-consuming scrutiny. Not only are all articles read by us editors, but they are also being examined by at least two outside readers. This peer reviewing process has brought forth helpful comments and suggestions in almost all instances.

A comparison of the Editors' Statement appearing at the outset of Vol. 1 with the content of the journal's first ten volumes is quite instructive. "It is not a dogmatic 'pluralistic' point," we wrote in that statement, "but a fact that scholars who perceive themselves to be working in the field of crusade history include not only those studying expeditions to the eastern Mediterranean and the settlements of westerners established there, but also those writing on the Iberian peninsula, the Baltic region, crusades against heretics and opponents of the church ..." All these subjects have indeed been dealt with, yet a breakdown of the 98 articles and reports published over the past ten years shows that 31 dealt with the crusades to the eastern Mediterranean and 42 with the Frankish states of the Levant and their Muslim adversaries, while eight were devoted to the crusade idea, propaganda and plans before 1291. As only six articles discussed pre-1291 crusading in other theatres, and ten dealt with post-1291 events, we may conclude that the breakdown reflects a de facto compliance of most articles with what Giles Constable labelled as the "traditionalist" view of the crusade.

The Editors' Statement announced also that "there would be an emphasis on the publication of source-material in original languages, including Arabic, Armenian and Syriac, accompanied, if need be, by translations." Although we have not yet published a Syriac text, the journal's record on this count is quite satisfactory. Volume 1 contains the edition and translation of the treatise by Diya' al-Din al-Maqdisi, which sheds abundant light on Muslim life in the Nablus area under Frankish rule; Shaykh Muhammad al-ʿAlami's seventeenth-century poem, which proves that Saladin was not forgotten by Jerusalem's Muslims, is edited and translated in Vol. 10; a translation of Ibn al-ʿArabi's observations made during visits to Palestine in the 1090s appears in Vol. 3. The same volume contains an Armenian colophon of 1181 and its translation. A Hebrew poem written in the wake of the Second Crusade is re-edited and translated in Vol. 6. As for Latin texts, the account of the "Inventio Patriarcharum" in Hebron is re-edited in Vol. 4 (the commentary is to appear in a future issue), while the poem rendering in verse the Books of

Maccabees, composed by Prior Geoffrey of the Lord's Temple, is edited in Vol. 9, and an early guide to Frankish Jerusalem is re-edited in Vol. 10. Other Latin and vernacular texts appear in the appendices of several articles.

While most articles are based on western source material and describe events mainly from a western standpoint, 11 articles present a Muslim, Oriental Christian or Jewish perspective; only in a very few cases has an attempt been made to view issues from more than a single point of view. As for the language of publication, the great majority of articles – 84 in all – are in English, with nine in French, three in Italian and two in German; no author has, as yet, made use of the option to write in Spanish.

Ten years ago we mentioned military orders and trade, as well as literature, art history, science, archaeology and numismatics as subjects that crusade historians are studying, and implied that all these topics would be discussed in our journal. Of these, archaeology has been represented in *Crusades* with nine articles and reports; eight articles discuss the military orders; four – medicine; three – epigraphy; two – literature, and one – numismatics. None of the articles has dealt specifically with art history or trade.

Our intention to host discussions among contributors yielded just one result: the exchange of views in Vol. 1 on fiefs and vassals in the kingdom of Jerusalem, followed by a contribution on the same issue in Vol. 8.

Thus, the comparison between the original Editors' Statement and the journal's actual content leads to the conclusion that we have met our objectives only in part. We hope that in its second decade *Crusades* will attract more scholars working on issues that have been scantly represented, or neglected, in the first ten volumes. We shall also encourage comparative studies, whether of relatively traditional issues – such as relations between crusaders and indigenous populations in different theatres – or of facets of the crusader phenomenon in a world-historical perspective, and thereby render the journal more significant for a wider academic community.

Benjamin Kedar
Jonathan Riley-Smith
Jonathan Phillips

Abbreviations

AA	Albert of Aachen, *Historia Ierosolimitana. History of the Journey to Jerusalem*, ed. and trans. Susan B. Edgington. Oxford, 2007
AOL	*Archives de l'Orient latin*
Autour	*Autour de la Première Croisade. Actes du colloque de la Society for the Study of the Crusades and the Latin East: Clermont-Ferrand, 22–25 juin 1995*, ed. Michel Balard. Paris, 1996
Cart Hosp	*Cartulaire général de l'ordre des Hospitaliers de Saint-Jean de Jérusalem, 1100–1310*, ed. Joseph Delaville Le Roulx. 4 vols. Paris, 1884–1906
Cart St Sép	*Le Cartulaire du chapitre du Saint-Sépulcre de Jérusalem*, ed. Geneviève Bresc-Bautier, Documents relatifs à l'histoire des croisades 15. Paris, 1984
Cart Tem	*Cartulaire général de l'ordre du Temple 1119?–1150. Recueil des chartes et des bulles relatives à l'ordre du Temple*, ed. Guigue A.M.J.A., (marquis) d'Albon. Paris, 1913
CCCM	Corpus Christianorum. Continuatio Mediaevalis
Chartes Josaphat	*Chartes de la Terre Sainte provenant de l'abbaye de Notre-Dame de Josaphat*, ed. Henri F. Delaborde, Bibliothèque des Écoles françaises d'Athènes et de Rome 19. Paris, 1880
Clermont	*From Clermont to Jerusalem: The Crusades and Crusader Societies 1095–1500. Selected Proceedings of the International Medieval Congress, University of Leeds, 10–13 July 1995*, ed. Alan V. Murray. International Medieval Research 3. Turnhout, 1998
Crusade Sources	*The Crusades and their Sources: Essays Presented to Bernard Hamilton*, ed. John France and William G. Zajac. Aldershot, 1998
CS	*Crusade and Settlement: Papers read at the First Conference of the Society for the Study of the Crusades and the Latin East and Presented to R. C. Smail*, ed. Peter W. Edbury. Cardiff, 1985
CSEL	Corpus Scriptorum Ecclesiasticorum Latinorum
EC, 1	*The Experience of Crusading 1: Western Approaches*, ed. Marcus G. Bull and Norman J. Housley. Cambridge, 2003
EC, 2	*The Experience of Crusading 2: Defining the Crusader Kingdom*, ed. Peter W. Edbury and Jonathan P. Phillips. Cambridge, 2003

FC   Fulcher of Chartres, *Historia Hierosolymitana (1095–1127)*, ed. Heinrich Hagenmeyer. Heidelberg, 1913

GF   *Gesta Francorum et aliorum Hierosolimitanorum*, ed. and trans. Rosalind M. T. Hill and Roger Mynors. London, 1962

GN   Guibert of Nogent, *Dei gesta per Francos*, ed. Robert B. C. Huygens, CCCM 127A. Turnhout, 1996

Horns   *The Horns of Hattin*, ed. Benjamin Z. Kedar. Jerusalem and London, 1992

Kreuzfahrerstaaten *Die Kreuzfahrerstaaten als multikulturelle Gesellschaft. Einwanderer und Minderheiten im 12. und 13. Jahrhundert*, ed. Hans Eberhard Mayer with Elisabeth Müller-Luckner. Schriften des Historischen Kollegs, Kolloquien 37. Munich, 1997

Mansi. *Concilia* Giovanni D. Mansi, *Sacrorum conciliorum nova et amplissima collectio*

MGH   Monumenta Germaniae Historica

MO, 1   *The Military Orders: Fighting for the Faith and Caring for the Sick*, ed. Malcolm Barber. Aldershot, 1994

MO, 2   *The Military Orders, vol. 2: Welfare and Warfare*, ed. Helen Nicholson. Aldershot, 1998

MO, 3   *The Military Orders, vol. 3: History and Heritage*, ed. Victor Mallia-Milanes. Aldershot, 2008

Montjoie   *Montjoie: Studies in Crusade History in Honour of Hans Eberhard Mayer*, ed. Benjamin Z. Kedar, Jonathan Riley-Smith and Rudolf Hiestand. Aldershot, 1997

Outremer   *Outremer. Studies in the History of the Crusading Kingdom of Jerusalem Presented to Joshua Prawer*, ed. Benjamin Z. Kedar, Hans E. Mayer and Raymond C. Smail. Jerusalem, 1982

PG   Patrologia Graeca

PL   Patrologia Latina

PPTS   Palestine Pilgrims' Text Society Library

RHC   *Recueil des Historiens des Croisades*
  Darm   *Documents arméniens*
  Lois   *Les assises de Jérusalem*
  Oc   *Historiens occidentaux*
  Or   *Historiens orientaux*

RHGF   Recueil des Historiens des Gaules et de la France

RIS   Rerum Italicarum Scriptores
  NS   New Series

ROL   *Revue de l'Orient latin*

RRH   Reinhold Röhricht, comp., *Regesta regni hierosolymitani*. Innsbruck, 1893

RRH Add	Reinhold Röhricht, comp., *Additamentum*. Innsbruck, 1904
RS	Rolls Series
Setton, *Crusades*	*A History of the Crusades*, general editor Kenneth M. Setton, 2nd edn., 6 vols. Madison, 1969–89
SRG	Scriptores Rerum Germanicarum
WT	William of Tyre, *Chronicon*, ed. Robert B. C. Huygens, with Hans E. Mayer and Gerhard Rösch, CCCM 63–63A. Turnhout, 1986

The Relationship Between the *Gesta Francorum* and Peter Tudebode's *Historia de Hierosolymitano Itinere*: The Evidence of a Hitherto Unexamined Manuscript (St. Catharine's College, Cambridge, 3)

Marcus Bull

University of North Carolina at Chapel Hill
mgbull@email.unc.edu

One of the most seemingly intractable and long-running problems in the study of the contemporary historiography of the First Crusade has been the relationship between two of the so-called "eyewitness" accounts of that expedition, the anonymous text generally known as the *Gesta Francorum et aliorum Hierosolimitanorum* (hereafter *GF*) and the *Historia de Hierosolymitano Itinere* attributed to a priest, probably from Civray in Poitou, named Peter Tudebode (hereafter the text that bears his name will be referred to as *PT*).[1] Within the tangled and still imperfectly understood web of relationships between the many histories of the First Crusade that were written soon after the event, both the eyewitnesses and what might be termed the "second generation" texts, the nexus between the *GF* and *PT* is self-evidently the single closest. Lexically, syntactically, substantively in terms of the propositional content of each text, and globally in their respective plot architectures, a particularly close affinity is immediately evident. Although each text contains passages absent from the other – this is more the case in *PT*, which is generally the more expansive – sequences in which there are close correspondences predominate. In the closeness of the two texts something more is at stake than the patterns of borrowings and influences that can be detected between other narratives of the First Crusade. More particularly, the relationship between the *GF* and *PT* differs from those between the *GF* and its adaptations by Robert the Monk, Guibert of Nogent, and Baldric of Bourgueil, who were able to express the *GF*'s plot content in more elevated literary registers.[2] In contrast, the difference in the historiographical ambitions evidenced by the *GF* and *PT* in those portions in which they directly overlap resides very precisely in what might sometimes appear to be trivial lexical preferences and

---

[1] *GF*; Peter Tudebode, *Historia de Hierosolymitano Itinere*, ed. John H. Hill and Laurita L. Hill (Paris, 1977). Although the edition of the *GF* bears Rosalind Hill's name, the editorial work on the manuscripts and Latin text was largely carried out by one of the general series editors, Sir Roger Mynors, in line with the then standard practice of the Nelson (subsequently Oxford) Medieval Text series.

[2] Robert the Monk, *Historia Iherosolimitana*, in *RHC Oc* 3:717–882; GN; Steven J. Biddlecombe, "The *Historia Ierosolimitana* of Baldric of Bourgueil: A New Edition in Latin and an Analysis" (PhD thesis, Bristol, 2010).

sentence-building habits that do not usually translate into the sorts of variations in substantive detail with which historians of the First Crusade reading these texts are typically concerned. Indeed, analysis of the differences between the two texts has tended to focus on those points where there is substantive variation, in other words where one text makes statements not parallelled in the other. This has been the approach taken in a recent study by Jean Flori, for example.[3] But, as will emerge more fully below, an itemization of differences in the texts' respective propositional contents is of limited hermeneutic value: it bypasses the rich textuality of the material in favour of limiting one's attention to the cruder measure of the texts' paraphraseable factual content. In fact, there is much more analytical purchase in a close comparison of the lexical and syntactical textures of the *GF* and *PT* at the points where they most closely correlate. A new discovery, a text preserved in a manuscript in St. Catharine's College, Cambridge, reinforces the value of such a textuality-centred approach, as this paper will demonstrate.

It is first necessary to review in outline the debate about the status of the *GF* and *PT*. This debate emerged in the formative years of crusade scholarship in the seventeenth century, resurfaced with the increase in scholarly attention to the First Crusade narratives in the nineteenth century, and has been renewed since the 1970s. In his great anthology of crusade texts, the *Gesta Dei per Francos* (1611), Jacques Bongars printed the text of the *GF*, which he stated he derived from two manuscripts: one borrowed from Paul Petau, which is almost certainly to be identified with what is now Vatican, Biblioteca Apostolica, Reg. Lat. 572; and a second lent to him by William Camden.[4] This second manuscript, which has not been identified, must have been the source of several additional readings, typically comprising one or more clauses expanding on an action or character utterance, that Bongars inserted within the text of his edition, which otherwise follows the readings of the Petau manuscript very closely. (These additions are to be found in the version of the *GF* presented in his 1890 edition by Heinrich Hagenmeyer, who was persuaded that the expanded text in Bongars represented an early stage in the *GF*'s composition and thus functioned as an appropriate base text.)[5]

Bongars did not include the *PT* in his compendium. It did not appear in print until its publication in the fourth volume of André Duchesne's *Historiae Francorum*

---

[3] See Jean Flori, "De l'Anonyme normand à Tudebode et aux *Gesta Francorum*: l'impact de la propagande de Bohémond sur la critique textuelle des sources de la première croisade," *Revue d'Histoire Ecclésiastique* 102 (2007), 717–46. Flori states that he has identified about one hundred ("centaine") differences between the *GF* and *PT*, and he cites individual instances by number, but curiously the article does not provide a key to the numbering system, not does it explain the principles according to which the differences were identified.

[4] *Gesta Dei per Francos, sive Orientalium Expeditionum, et Regni Francorum Hierosolimitani Historia a Variis, sed illius Aevi Scriptoribus, Litteris Commendata*, ed. Jacques Bongars, 1 vol. in 2 (Hanau, 1611), 1:1–29. In the prefatory note (s.p.) Bongars notes of his sources: "Igitur primum sine nomine scriptorem debemus Paulo Peteavio, et Guill. Camedeno … Cambdeni Codex librum claudit tribus verbis: Explicit via bona."

[5] *Anonymi Gesta Francorum et aliorum Hierosolymitanorum*, ed. Heinrich Hagenmeyer (Heidelberg, 1890), esp. pp. 97–98.

Scriptores in 1641.[6] The appearance of the text in this series was largely the work of the Poitevin historian Jean Besly, who discovered the manuscript upon which the edition was based and whose local patriotism informed his belief that the *PT*, seemingly the work of a priest from his own part of France, was the original from which the *GF* derived. This was the view subsequently enshrined within the *Receuil des historiens des croisades*; significantly, Wallon and Regnier, the editors of the *GF* in volume three of the *Historiens occidentaux* series, chose to qualify the title of the text with the coda "seu Tudebodus abbreviatus."[7] In contrast to this position, nineteenth-century German-speaking scholarship, most influentially in the person first of Heinrich von Sybel and then Heinrich Hagenmeyer, argued for the opposite view, asserting the priority of the *GF*.[8] It is the latter position that has generally commanded assent in modern scholarship. The question of the relationship between the texts was reopened, however, by the editorial work on the *PT* of John and Laurita Hill, which followed up on their study of a third eyewitness account of the First Crusade, that by Raymond of Aguilers. The Hills argued for the existence of what they termed the "common source," a now-lost account of the First Crusade that stood behind both the *GF* and *PT* in the forms in which they survive (as well as Raymond of Aguilers's text) and explains their many affinities.[9] Unfortunately, however, the Hills did not adequately develop their ideas about the form that the hypothetical common source took, nor the precise configurations of its respective influences upon the texts believed to derive from it. This same imprecision extends in the Hills' edition of *PT* to the absence of a discussion of the interrelationships between the four manuscripts that were consulted, even though this question is self-evidently important for the development of the common source thesis, especially in light of the fact that the Hills' critical apparatus itself reveals shifting permutations of proximity to readings in the *GF* among the various *PT* manuscripts.

For all its apparent imprecision, however, the common source thesis has been revisited by two recent scholars. In much the more nuanced discussion of the relationship between the *GF* and *PT*, Jay Rubenstein has argued for a variant of the common source hypothesis, according to which the text of the *PT* as we now have it is the result of a two-stage process of composition: a reworking of a now-lost aboriginal account of the First Crusade, which Rubenstein labels the "Jerusalem History," was added to by the former crusader Peter Tudebode drawing upon his own memories of the crusade. The "Jerusalem History," in this view, was also the ancestor of the *GF* in the form in which it now survives: certain non sequiturs and breaks in the story logic that it can be argued are present within the *GF* may then be

---

[6] *Historiae Francorum Scriptores ab ipsius Gentis Origine usque ad R. Phillip IV. Dicti Pulchri Tempora*, ed. André Duchesne, 5 vols. (Paris, 1636–49), 4:773–815.

[7] *RHC Oc* 3:119–63.

[8] Heinrich von Sybel, *Geschichte des ersten Kreuzzugs* (Düsseldorf, 1841), pp. 22–32; *Anonymi Gesta Francorum*, ed. Hagenmeyer, pp. 80–89.

[9] *PT*, pp. 21–22. See also the same authors' introduction to their earlier translation of the *PT*: *Historia de Hierosolymitano Itinere*, trans. John H. Hill and Laurita L. Hill (Philadelphia, 1974), pp. 4–12.

explained as the result of faulty copying at some point in the transmission of the text anterior to the surviving manuscript witnesses.[10] A somewhat less economical and less convincing model has been suggested by Jean Flori: a common source, itself possibly derived from an antecedent account of the crusade, was subject to multiple rewrites to arrive at the text of the *GF* as it now survives, while Peter Tudebode adapted a copy of the redaction that emerged from an early – the second – stage in this morphology. The text of the *PT* is thus closer to the common source than the extant, much-revised, *GF*.[11] The principal weakness of Flori's approach is the elaboration of its suggested multi-stage process of composition (none of which has manuscript warrant, incidentally), a schema devised, it seems, to accommodate a narrow and anachronistic *a priori* assumption that the *GF*, like all the narratives of the First Crusade, primarily emerged and mutated in order to subserve political propagandist agendas.[12] The common source thesis, then, requires further scrutiny: as it stands it does not do full justice to the many different shades of commonality between texts that are potentially subsumed within the term "common," nor does the notion of "source" fully accommodate the nuances within the multiplicity of ways in which one text can act upon another. A different methodological approach is in order.

A new route into the problem is opened up by the evidence of a manuscript that has not hitherto been factored into the debate: St. Catharine's College, Cambridge, 3. The origins of St. Catharine's small collection of medieval manuscripts are obscure, and the provenance of the manuscript in question is thus uncertain. It does not correspond to any of the entries in the list of books that formed part of the college's endowment when it was founded in the 1470s, and it is not attested until 1710, the date that also appears on a probably nineteenth-century *ex libris*.[13] The manuscript dates from around the middle of the thirteenth century (its wooden-board binding is quite possibly original), and on palaeographical grounds it is almost certainly English, an origin further suggested by some of its contents.[14] The manuscript is a collection of texts in a small number of hands, including a *Historia Alexandri* (fols.

---

[10] Jay Rubenstein, "What is the *Gesta Francorum*, and who was Peter Tudebode?," *Revue Mabillon* 16 (2005), 179–204.

[11] Flori, "De l'Anonyme normand," *passim*; Jean Flori, *Chroniqueurs et propagandistes: Introduction critique aux sources de la première croisade* (Geneva, 2010), pp. 9, 19, 25–28, 47, 61–62, 67–103, 167–69.

[12] Recent studies are moving towards a more finely nuanced understanding of the propagandistic loading of First Crusade narratives: Marc Carrier, "Pour en finir avec les *Gesta Francorum*: une réflexion historiographique sue l'état des rapports entre Grecs et Latins au début du XIIe siècle et sur l'apport nouveau d'Albert d'Aix," *Crusades* 7 (2008), 13–34; Nicholas L. Paul, "A Warlord's Wisdom: Literacy and Propaganda at the Time of the First Crusade," *Speculum* 85 (2010), 534–66. More work is needed on the question whether "propaganda" is an adequate usage in the context of the illocutionary range of medieval texts, medieval manuscript culture, the mechanisms of textual reception, and habits of communication.

[13] *A Descriptive Catalogue of the Manuscripts in the Library of St. Catharine's College, Cambridge*, ed. Montague Rhodes James (Cambridge, 1925), pp. 1, 4–7.

[14] Ibid., pp. 10–12. The manuscript formerly bore the pressmark L. v. 87.

1r–45v), extracts of geographical interest from Henry of Huntingdon's *Historia Anglorum* (fols. 96r–105v), an important witness to Gerald of Wales's *Topographia Hiberniae* (fols. 105v–167v), and works on physiognomy and *mirabilia* (fols. 168r–186v, 190r–203r). The binding and the somewhat eclectic range of the contents, as well as the rather unpolished effect of the presence of blank folios between some of the texts, suggest that the codex was not originally devised to assume its present form. On the other hand, its various parts are almost certainly the work of a single scriptorium and were produced close in time to one another; very close similarities in the decoration of majuscules emerge across texts in different hands, and all the texts are ruled at 26 lines to the page (as are several of the interjacent blank folios).[15] For our purposes the salient part of the manuscript is the text that appears at fols. 48r–90v under the rubricated title "Peregrinatio Antiochie per Urbanum papam facta." In a brief note in his 1925 catalogue of St. Catharine's manuscripts, M. R. James identified this as a copy of the *GF*, most probably on the basis of the incipit, but he did not delve deeper.[16] For, although the incipit does indeed correspond to that of the *GF* (as well as to that in three of the four manuscripts of the *PT*), the text as a whole is something subtly but significantly different.

As noted above, there are broadly two modes, or registers, in which differences between the *GF* and *PT* may be identified: in terms of their substantive content; and at the lexical and syntactical level. With respect to the latter register, a close side-by-side reading of the two texts reveals consistent and sustained patterns in their respective forms of expression: at the lexical level, for example, pairs of preferred near-synonyms emerge such as (the *GF*'s preference placed first) *urbs–ciuitas, mox–continuo/confestim/extimplo, donec–usque, cursores–curritores, penuria–paupertas, mittere–mandare, explorare–inuestigare,* and *capere–apprehendere.* Another repeated contrast is that the *GF* favours the construction of subordinate clauses expressing purpose or consequence by means of *ut* + subjunctive, whereas the *PT* generally prefers *quod* + indicative. As noted above, it is precisely in such individually minor but recurrent variations in the clause-by-clause textures of the *GF* and *PT* that the differences between them principally emerge. The text in St. Catharine's 3 (hereafter cited as the *Peregrinatio Antiochie*) is more closely akin to the *PT* with respect to the latter's signature lexis and grammatical rhythms. Indeed, there are numerous passages in which, to all intents and purposes, one is presented with a version of the *PT* well within the range of variance evidenced by the readings of the manuscripts in the Hills' critical apparatus.

It is important to note, however, that these close correspondences only occur in those passages that also directly overlap with equivalent sequences in the *GF*. For in terms of its plot content the *Peregrinatio Antiochie* almost entirely matches the *GF*. Virtually all the propositional content found in the *GF* but not in the *PT*

---

[15] See, for example, the decoration of the letter T at fols. 41r and 69r, and of D at fols. 74v and 183r.

[16] *Descriptive Catalogue*, p. 11: "It is the anonymous Gesta Francorum: ed. Bongars, *Gesta Dei,* p. 1."

is present within it. In contrast, very little of the substantive content in the *PT* but not in the *GF* appears.[17] This latter category includes material which, if we follow Rubenstein's two-stage composition thesis, we would expect to have been the work of Peter Tudebode himself, such as the mention of himself at the siege of Jerusalem, references to the deaths on crusade of kinsmen, and possibly other details with a specifically south-western French resonance such as the presence of Archbishop Amatus of Bordeaux in the entourage of Pope Urban II during his tour of France preaching the crusade, and the fact that the Gascon lord Gaston of Béarn had command of a body of troops identified by their hailing from the territory of the count of Poitou (and duke of Aquitaine), even though Count William did not himself participate in the 1096–99 phase of the First Crusade.[18] This category expands, however, substantially beyond this autobiographical and regionally-oriented material to include almost all the points at which there is divergence between the propositional contents of the *GF* and the *PT*, both discrete statements to be found in one text but not the other and passages in which substantially the same idea is expressed with different nuances of emphasis and at different lengths.

Examples of material to be found in the *PT* but absent from the *Peregrinatio Antiochie* include: the account of the passage of Raymond of Saint-Gilles and Adhemar of Le Puy through the Balkans to Constantinople;[19] details of Raymond of Saint-Gilles's supervision of the siege castle outside Antioch and the martyrdoms of Rainald Porchet and captive pilgrims;[20] the longer list of names of those who flee Antioch with William of Grandmesnil;[21] and details of the penitential regime enjoined upon the crusaders when they were trapped within Antioch.[22] Only the *PT* explicitly states that the person who discovered the Holy Lance during the excavations in Antioch cathedral was Peter Bartholomew, whereas the *GF* and *Peregrinatio Antiochie* use deixis to point to his identity (*homo ille*).[23] The *PT*'s reference to the quality of the water from the springs in Antioch is not present in the equivalent passages in the *GF* and the *Peregrinatio Antiochie*, nor its total – 1,200 – for the number of churches within that city. The *PT* alone refers to the princes ordering the heaping up into mounds and the burning of the bodies of the Muslim slain in Ma'arrat as a reaction to the sight of desperate crusaders

---

[17] One rare exception is the mention at fol. 51v of the lake adjacent to the castle of heretics in the Balkans attacked by Bohemond's forces, a detail present in *PT*, p. 41, but absent from *GF*, p. 8. The construction in the *Peregrinatio Antiochie* is "Nos undique aggredientes illud in lacum ubi edificatum fuerat." The account at fol. 62r of Bohemond's haranguing of those who had failed on a foraging raid includes a sentence specifying that the targets of his anger were those who had found nothing and were hurrying back: "Illi namque qui inuenire non poterant statim reuerti festinabant." The same formulation appears at *PT*, p. 67, but is absent from *GF*, pp. 32–33. Rubenstein, "What is the *Gesta Francorum*," p. 193, argues that the sentence was present in the supposed common source.

[18] *PT*, pp. 31–32, 97, 110, 116, 136.

[19] *PT*, pp. 43–47.

[20] *PT*, pp. 78–81.

[21] *PT*, p. 97.

[22] *PT*, p. 100.

[23] *PT*, p. 108; cf. *Peregrinatio Antiochie*, fol. 76v; *GF*, p. 65.

mistreating and eating the corpses.[24] It alone gives the names of some of the fourteen knights who engage a force of sixty Saracens near Tripoli.[25] And it alone mentions the capture and elaborate execution of a spy during the siege of Jerusalem.[26] Many more such examples could be adduced.[27]

Likewise, the *Peregrinatio Antiochie* includes details absent from the *PT* but present in the *GF*, such as the list of names of the southern Italian Normans who join Bohemond's *famulatus* at the start of their crusade, certain of Bohemond's measures to prevent depredations while his force moved through Byzantine territory, and Tancred's efforts to find provisions for that army in Bohemond's absence before its arrival at Constantinople.[28] The *Peregrinatio Antiochie*, like the *GF*, has the count of *Russignolo* stranded on the wrong bank of the river Vardar with two or more unidentified brothers (*cum fratribus suis*), whereas the *PT* places him in this predicament with one brother, qualified as a bishop (*cum fratre episcopo*).[29] The *Peregrinatio Antiochie* shares with the *GF* the narratorial apostrophe reflecting on the pressures that led the crusade leaders to swear oaths of submission to the Byzantine emperor and the rectitude of their actions; this is absent from the *PT*.[30] Similarly, the *Peregrinatio Antiochie* and the *GF* but not the *PT* mention the attempt by Tancred and Richard of the Principality to evade taking the oath to Emperor Alexius by slipping across the Bosphorus; and the provision by Bohemond of relief

---

[24] *PT*, pp. 124–25; cf. *Peregrinatio Antiochie*, fol. 83r; *GF*, p. 80.

[25] *PT*, pp. 128–29; cf. *Peregrinatio Antiochie*, fol. 84r; *GF*, p. 83. See also the inclusion of the name of Pons of Balazun among those martyred during the siege of ʿArqah in *PT*, p. 131; cf. *Peregrinatio Antiochie*, fol. 85r; *GF*, p. 85.

[26] *PT*, p. 139.

[27] For instance: Kerbogha's mockery of captured crusader arms is expanded by the statement that these items were brought from the western, third part of the world, namely Europe, *PT*, p. 91; four emirs in the citadel of Antioch wearing golden armour and with golden trappings on their horses engage the crusaders, *PT*, p. 103; the crusaders trapped within Antioch flock to the cathedral to venerate the recently unearthed Holy Lance, and are joined in their devotions by Greek, Armenian, and Syrian Christians, *PT*, p. 108; the footsoldiers of the forces of Hugh of Vermandois and Robert of Flanders are the first to emerge from Antioch before the decisive battle on 28 June 1098, *PT*, p. 111; Bohemond does not arrive at the agreed rendezvous in November 1098 because he is seriously ill, *PT*, p. 118; the description of the city of Antioch includes a long list of the names of its ancient kings, *PT*, p. 120; standards flutter as the crusaders launch an assault on Maʿarra, *PT*, p. 122; in the Bukeia valley the crusaders come upon an additional castle, which the enemy has burned, *PT*, p. 127; the emir of Tripoli promises to honour Raymond of Saint-Gilles's diplomatic demand that he convert, *PT*, p. 128; during the siege of Jerusalem, Raymond of Saint-Gilles's siege tower is built of timber carried by 50 or 60 Saracen captives, *PT*, p. 138; this siege tower breaks at its upper levels just before Raymond learns of Godfrey of Bouillon's entry into Jerusalem, *PT*, p. 140; fuller details are given of the spoils of the battle of Ascalon and the effects on the prices of foodstuffs, *PT*, p. 149.

[28] Fols. 51r, 52r, 52v, corresponding to *GF*, pp. 7–8, 10–11.

[29] Fol. 51v; *GF*, p. 9; *PT*, p. 41. For discussion of the problematic identity of this count, see Evelyn Jamison, "Some Notes on the *Anonymi Gesta Francorum*, with Special Reference to the Norman Contingent from South Italy and Sicily in the First Crusade," in *Studies in French Language and Literature Presented to Professor Mildred K. Pope* (Manchester, 1939), pp. 205–7; Jonathan S. C. Riley-Smith, *The First Crusaders, 1095–1131* (Cambridge, 1997), pp. 93–94, 204, 207, 208.

[30] Fol. 53r; *GF*, p. 12.

supplies for the forces besieging Nicaea.[31] The *Peregrinatio Antiochie* and the *GF* but not the *PT* mention that it is Italians (*Longobardi*) who inform the Muslim commander of the citadel of Antioch that the Frankish banner he first secures in surrendering after the battle of Antioch belongs to Raymond of Saint-Gilles, not Bohemond as he intends.[32] The same pattern applies to the mention of the sending of Hugh of Vermandois on an embassy to Emperor Alexius Comnenus soon after the defeat of Kerbogha outside Antioch.[33] The *Peregrinatio Antiochie* follows the *GF* in having Tancred upset by the massacre in the Temple area during the taking of Jerusalem because he and Gaston of Béarn had given their banners to, that is taken the surrender of, those on the Temple platform, whereas the *PT* contrastively has Tancred actively encouraging the slaughter.[34] Again, instances of this pattern could be multiplied.[35]

As these examples reveal, the *Peregrinatio Antiochie* may be characterized as substantively cognate with the *GF* as against the *PT*. But its idiom more closely resembles the latter. Prima facie, therefore, the *Peregrinatio Antiochie* represents an intermediate form lying between the *GF* and the *PT*. It might be argued, contrary to this, that the text is a later confection, a blend of the *GF* and *PT*; but it is extremely difficult to see why a scribe would have undertaken such a hugely intricate and laborious, not to say rather pointless, operation involving the clause-by-clause recasting of the *GF* in language inspired by the *PT*. If this had been the case, we should also expect substantive detail that is present in the *PT* but absent from the *GF* to have migrated into the *Peregrinatio Antiochie* in the interests of greater amplitude. The importance of the *Peregrinatio Antiochie* thus lies in its occupying some interjacent point in the sequence of textual morphologies that produced the *GF* and *PT* in their surviving forms. As will also become evident, there is a clear linear directionality in the relationship between the three texts, as opposed to separate, collateral descent from a common point of origin. But in which direction: *GF* > *Peregrinatio Antiochie* > *PT*, or *PT* > *Peregrinatio Antiochie* > *GF*? As we shall see, at numerous points in the three texts one can track lexical, syntactical, and substantive morphologies that point to the anterior status of the *GF*. No one instance can definitively establish this point, for the reverse morphology *PT* > *Peregrinatio Antiochie* > *GF* can never be excluded in strict logic. But the cumulative weight of the

---

[31] Fols. 53v, 54r; *GF*, pp. 13, 14.

[32] Fol. 78v; *GF*, p. 71; *PT*, p. 113.

[33] Fol. 79r; *GF*, p. 72.

[34] *Peregrinatio Antiochie*, fol. 88r; *GF*, pp. 91–92; *PT*, p. 141. Note that here, as elsewhere in the manuscript, Tancred is described in the *Peregrinatio Antiochie* in more fulsome language than that in the equivalent passage in the *GF*: "uidens Tancredus *uir sapiens et prudens* iratus est nimis [*nimis fuit*]."

[35] The *Peregrinatio Antiochie* follows the *GF* in its account of the bringing of ships onto the lake next to Nicaea, a sequence that the *PT* omits: *GF*, p. 16; *Peregrinatio Antiochie*, fols. 54v–55r; *PT*, p. 50. The *Peregrinatio Antiochie* resembles the *GF* but not the *PT* in its account of Bohemond's peroration to Robert fitz Girard before the battle of Antioch Lake and includes the leonine simile absent from the *PT*: *GF*, pp. 36–37; *Peregrinatio Antiochie*, fol. 64r; *PT*, p. 72.

evidence is compelling, establishing a pattern of textual and propositional change across the three works that can be patterned in the form ABC > BCD > CDE, with the *Peregrinatio Antiochie* representing an essential intermediate, the BCD, stage of adaptation. The *GF* tends to offer the more compressed and allusive formulations, while the *PT* tends towards the more expansive and padded, sometimes to the point of redundancy; the *Peregrinatio Antiochie* occupies an intermediate ground in this respect. It is much easier to imagine a textual morphology resulting from successive stages of scribal expansiveness than the reverse, which would require that there were at least two stages of textual contraction leading to the *GF* as we now have it. This is difficult to credit as a possibility. In short, the dynamics within the morphology that we can observe across the three texts shade in the direction of the impulses towards improvement of style and expansion of substantive content that were taken much further by Robert the Monk, Baldric of Bourgueil, and Guibert of Nogent vis-à-vis the *GF* as their point of textual departure.

How does this morphology manifest itself? One important point about the illustrative examples that follow is in order. The manuscript evidence does not permit us to isolate and compare definitive or "pure" forms of the *GF* and *PT*, even if such forms ever existed as discrete, aboriginal compositions. Instead we must rely on what amount to "least worst" approximations as made available by the extant manuscript witnesses. In the case of the *GF*, the single most authoritative point of reference is the text preserved in Vatican, Biblioteca Apostolica, Reg. Lat. 572, which is the best witness to the earliest surviving recension. The version of the text in this manuscript (with a few revisions) supplied the base for Rosalind Hill and Sir Roger Mynors's 1962 edition, which can thus be conveniently cited as a point of comparison with the *Peregrinatio Antiochie* and the *PT*.[36] In the case of the *PT*, the absence that we have already noted of any analysis of the relationships between the four manuscripts in the Hills' edition means that, for the purposes of comparison, the most secure option is to limit oneself to those cases in which those four manuscripts are in close agreement; in other words, where their readings probably reflect their common ancestor, the point in the morphology of the *PT* at which it assumed substantially its present form. The *Peregrinatio Antiochie* in St. Catharine's 3, it should be remembered, is a thirteenth-century copy which, to judge from several omissions and lexical confusions evident in the copying process, is probably more than one remove from the original. When we compare the three texts, therefore, we should look for patterns that emerge *grosso modo* across multiple instances to offset our necessary reliance on articulations of the texts that are themselves the products of morphologies within the textual transmission of each of the three works. (In the examples that follow, punctuation other than full points is omitted for ease of comparison, and use of upper case is standardized.)

---

[36] Reg. Lat. 572 serves as the base text for my edition of the *GF* in the Oxford Medieval Texts series (in press).

What, then, are these patterns? First, there are instances of lexical connections between the *GF* and the *Peregrinatio Antiochie* in constructions that also reveal grammatical and/or lexical shifts in the latter that are likewise evidenced by the *PT*:

GF, p. 5:	Christiani igitur qui in castro erant miserunt ignem in ligna congregata
PA, fol. 49v:	Christiani igitur qui in castello erant miserunt ignem in lignis congregatis
PT, p. 37:	Christiani igitur qui in castello erant miserunt ignem in lignis adunatis

GF, p. 33:	quia libenter ad hostem redirent
PA, fol. 62v:	quia libenter redissent ad hostem
PT, p. 68:	quod libenter redissent ad exercitum

GF, p. 34:	qui auditis his uerbis uoluntarie concessit
PA, fol. 62v:	qui statim auditis his uerbis uoluntarie concessit
PT, p. 69:	qui statim auditis his sermonibus libenter concessit

GF, p. 63:	uehementique captus timore recessit fugitque festinanter cum suo exercitu
PA, fol. 75v:	uehementer captus timore una cum suo exercito turpiter fugit cum magna festinatione
PT, p. 105:	nimio correptus timore una cum suo exercito turpiter fugiuit cum magna festinatione

A further category comprises the progressive expansion of a single idea, including the substitution or addition of close synonyms that have an intensifying effect:

GF, p. 7:	Deus uult Deus uult Deus uult una uoce conclamant
PA, fol. 51r:	Deus leuolt Deus leuolt Deus leuolt simul una uoce conclamant
PT, p. 40:	Deus hoc uult Deus hoc uult Deus hoc uult simul omnes una uoce conclamant

GF, p. 15:	trahentes secum funes quibus nos ligatos ducerent
PA, fol. 54r:	ducentesque secum funes unde nos ducerent ligatos
PT, p. 49:	ducentesque secum funes unde nos ligatos in captiuitatem ducerent

GF, p. 24:	quia uolumus et petimus dominari et regnare super nos illum
PA, fol. 58v:	quia illum uolumus et petimus dominari et super nos regnare
PT, p. 59:	quia nos illum flagitamus et petimus dominari et regnare super nos

GF, p. 37:	nostri itaque persecuti sunt illos et detruncauerunt
PA, fol. 64r:	nostri itaque eos persequentes ac detruncantes
PT, p. 72:	nostri itaque illos persequentes ac superantes et detruncantes

GF, p. 40:	Sed Deus omnipotens hoc illis non permisit
PA, fol. 65v:	Sed omnipotens Deus hoc illis permittere noluit
PT, p. 75:	Sed omnipotens Deus hoc illis permittere nullatenus uoluit

GF, p. 57:	Cum nocte una iacerem
PA, fol. 73r:	Dum uero una nocte iacerem
PT, p. 98:	Dum uero in hac nocte iacerem

In a similar vein, note the layering of the parataxis of the *GF* in the following:

GF, p. 9:	[Bohemond approached] cum sua gente sed non tota. Remansit enim ibi comes de Russignolo
PA, fol. 51v:	cum gente sua, partim perrexit et partim remansit. Remansit enim ibi comes de Russuignolo
PT, p. 41:	cum una parte gentis sue; alia uero pars remansit simul cum comite de Rosignolo

GF, p. 76:	Hoc totum laudauit Boamundus et promiserunt ambo in manibus episcoporum quod nullo modo per se uia Sancti Sepulchri deturbaretur
PA, fol. 81r:	Hoc totum laudauit Boamundus et promiserunt ambo in manibus episcoporum quod Sancti Sepulchri uia nullomodo fieret deturbata
PT, p. 119:	Quod laudauit Boamundus et annuit. Et ita promiserunt ambo in manibus episcoporum uidentibus peregrinis quod Sancti Sepulchri uia nullomodo fieret deturbata

Another recurrent category, overlapping with those already cited, involves the introduction of synonyms or related ideas in the *PT* in addition to correspondences with constructions or grammatical forms present in the *Peregrinatio Antiochie* but not in the *GF*. For example:

GF, p. 35:	Itaque tali modo inerat
PA, fol. 63r:	Sic itaque tali modo inerat
PT, p. 70:	Sic itaque tali modo uenerat

GF, p. 48:	et mersi sunt in unam domum
PA, fol. 69r:	et mersi sunt in quandam domum
PT, p. 87:	et intrauerunt in quandam domum

GF, p. 48:	confestim apprehenderunt eum truncaueruntque caput illius
PA, fol. 69r:	confestim apprehenderunt illum et truncauerunt caput eius
PT, p. 87:	confestim apprehenderunt illum et ceciderunt caput eius

GF, p. 60:	tam acriter ut nequirent suffere pondus eorum
PA, fol. 74r:	tam acriter quod illi nequibant iam suffere pondus illorum
PT, p. 102:	tam acriter quod illi nequibant iam suffere uirtutem illorum [var. eorum]

GF, pp. 68–9:	ut … protinus preconari faceret omnem exercitum redire sciens Turcos amisisse bellum
PA, fol. 77v:	ut … protinus preconare fecisset omnem exercitum retro redire scientes Turcos amisisse bellum
PT, p. 111:	ut … protinus preconiare fecisset suum exercitum et redisset retro scientes Turcos amisisse campum

GF, p. 72:	donec peragerent iter Sancti Sepulchri
PA, fol. 79r:	usque dum peragant Sancti Sepulchri iter
PT, p. 114:	usque dum uiam Sancti Sepulchri incipere potuissent

GF, p. 80:	quomodo honeste possent tenere uiam Sancti Sepulchri
PA, fol. 83r:	quomodo honeste potuissent tenere uiam Sancti Sepulchri
PT, p. 125:	quomodo incipere potuissent uiam Sancti Sepulchri

GF, p. 89:	Sarraceni namque in cunctis fontibus et aquis latentes
PA, fol. 87r:	Sarraceni namque cunctis fontibus <et> uniuersis aquis erant latentes
PT, p. 136:	Sarraceni quoque cunctis fontibus et uniuersis puteis erant latentes

GF, p. 92:	ut unusquisque faceret elemosinas cum orationibus
PA, fol. 88r:	ut unusquisque faciat orationes et elomosinas
PT, p. 142:	ut unusquisque faciat orationes et elemosinas atque ieiunium

Another pattern involves the express clarification and scenic expansion of actions and elements otherwise left to be implied within the story logic:

GF, p. 13:	[Bohemond] dixit quia si aliquid iniustum imperatori faceret
PA, fol. 53v:	dixit quod si aliquid iniustum imperatori fecisset
PT, p. 47:	dixit quod si aliquod iniustum comes imperatori fecisset

GF, p. 46:	Motus est ille cum aliis
PA, fol. 68v:	Motus est autem ille cum aliis

PT, p. 86:   Motus est autem ille uir cum aliis

GF, p. 58:   Statim cecidi ad pedes eius rogans humiliter ut subunerit nobis in oppressione illa quae super nos erat

PA, fol. 73r: Tunc statim cecidi ad pedes eius rogans eum humiliter ut nobis subueniret in oppressione illius execrate gentis que super nos erat

PT, p. 99:   Tunc statim cecidi ad pedes eius lacrymando rogansque humiliter eum ut nobis subueniret in obsessione illius execrate gentis que tenebat nos inclusos in ciuitati

GF, p. 61:   Quod uidentes illi qui erant in ciuitate

PA, fol. 74v: Videntes enim illi qui erant in ciuitate hoc

PT, p. 102:   Videntes enim [var. uero] illi qui erant in ciuitate ignem ardere et uentum surgere

GF, p. 62:   ab illis quorum numerus fuit innumerabilis

PA, fol. 75r: ab illis paganis inimici [sic] Dei et sancte Christianitatis quorum numerus fuit innumerabilis

PT, p. 103:   ab aliis [var. illis] paganis inimicis Dei et sancte Christianitatis qui fuerunt numero ccc^{ti}. lx^{ta}. v^{que}. milia

GF, p. 82:   Quod castrum aggressi sunt nostri idque fortiter superassent nisi …

PA, fol. 83v–84r: Quod aggrediuntur nostri peregrini idque fortiter superassent nisi …

PT, p. 127:   Illudque aggrediuntur tam fortiter nostri peregrini quod in sua potestate habuissent nisi …

GF, p. 84:   secesserunt in quemdam angulum

PA, fol. 84v: recesserunt se in quodam angulo

PT, p. 129:   recesserunt nostri in quodam angulo iuxta siluam

GF, p. 89:   peruenerunt usque ad illos preliando

PA, fol. 86v: uenerunt usque ad illos adhuc preliantes

PT, p. 136:   uenerunt usque ad illos quos inuenerunt adhuc preliando

GF, p. 91:   Tunc consiliati sunt nostri ut implerent foueam

PA, fol. 87v: Consiliati sunt in illa hora quod implere fecissent illam foueam

PT, p. 140:   Consiliatus est Raimundus in illa hora quod implere fecisset illam foueam

GF, p. 97:   Conduxi omnia armorum genera et omnia machinamenta

PA, fol. 90r: Ego namque hic conduxi omnia armorum genera et omnia
                           instrumenta siue machina
PT, p. 148:   Ego namque conduxi omnia armorum genera et omnia
                           instrumenta siue machina et multa ferrea uincula cum quibus
                           putaui eos ducere ligatos Babiloniam

Among other morphologies that relate to the differences between the *GF* and *PT*
that have long been familiar to students of the First Crusade, mention may be made
of the following:

- A lexical item in the *GF* is present at a different point within an expanded
  formulation in the *Peregrinatio Antiochie*, but is then absent from the further
  expanded equivalent construction in the *PT*:

GF, p. 6:   mox mala cogitatio cor eius tetigit illosque apprehendit
PA, fol. 50r: continuo mala cogitatio in corde eius ascendit moxque illos
                           apprehendit
PT, p. 38:   continuo mala cogitatio in eius corde ascendit et iussit illos
                           apprehendi

- An amplification of meaning or effect is achieved by means of verbs with shared
  roots:

GF, p. 9:   et quicquid nobis imperat nos oportet implere
PA, fol. 52r: et quicquid nobis imperat illud oportet implere
PT, p. 42:   et quicquid nobis imperat oportet illud adimplere

GF, p. 96:   ascendebant in arbores in quibus putabant se abscondere
PA, fol. 90r: ascendebant in arbores in quibus putabant se recondere
PT, p. 146:   ascendebant in arbores in quibus recondebant se

- And the *Peregrinatio Antiochie* shares the use of the first-person plural with the
  GF, whereas the *PT* has the third person, but is closer to the *PT* in terms of the
  organization of the syntax:

GF, p.14:   ut etiam foderemus
PA, fol. 54r: quod etiam fodere fecimus
PT, p. 49:   quod fodere quoque fecerunt

GF, p. 68:   exiuimus per portam
PA, fol. 77v: cepimus exire extra ciuitatem ad portam
PT, p. 111:   ceperunt exire extra ciuitatem per portam

GF, p. 85:   quia in medio Martio comedebamus nouellas fabas
PA, fol. 85r: quoniam in medio Martio manducabamus nouellas fabas
PT, p. 132:   quoniam in medio Marcio manducabant nouellas fabas

GF, p. 88:   In illa autem obsidione panes ad emendum inuenire non poteramus

PA, fol. 86v: Fuimusque in illa oppressione quod nichil panis ad emendum inuenire poteramus

PT, p. 135:   Fueruntque in illa obsessione quod nichil panis ad edendum inuenire poterant

The cumulative weight of these examples is to establish the intermediate position of the ancestor of the copy of the text that appears in St. Catharine's 3 along a continuum of lexical, syntactical, and propositional mutations. Jay Rubenstein's suggestion that the *PT* is the product of more than one effort at revision and expansion is thus broadly confirmed. But the number of such stages must be increased. In addition to the extra stage represented by the ultimate exemplar of the text preserved in St. Catharine's 3, there may well have been further stages in the transmission either side of it. Unless we posit that all the substantive changes present in the *PT* relative to the *Peregrinatio Antiochie* (and by extension the *GF*) were the work of the actual Peter Tudebode, not just those details of autobiographical and regional pertinence to himself, one or more further stages in the text's morphology must be supposed to account for all the additions and omissions found in the *PT*. There is also the question of the readings of the manuscript that William Camden lent to Jacques Bongars. As noted above, Bongars's edition of the *GF* follows his guide text, that found in Vatican, Biblioteca Apostolica, Reg. Lat. 572, very closely apart from a series of additions of mostly clause- or sentence-length. These are in the nature of discrete, "bolt-on" locutions dropped into the readings of the guide manuscript, typically acting as glosses or expansions upon ideas and scenes that are already present within the narration, rather than supplying new plot matter. These additions, in closely similar formulations, are also present in the *Peregrinatio Antiochie*; and most likewise appear in the *PT*, sometimes with fairly minor lexical and syntactical variations. The likelihood is that the presence of this extra material in the St. Catharine's text originates in one or more stages anterior to the ultimate exemplar of the *Peregrinatio Antiochie* in the chain of textual transmission and mutation that we have identified. But we cannot be certain about precisely how it so relates in the current state of the evidence.

The critical problem is the form of the text in the Camden manuscript. If it was a copy of the version that is now known to us from St. Catharine's 3, Bongars would have immediately spotted the lexical and grammatical differences that we have noted between it and the *GF* of his guide manuscript, although he would also have realized that the plot content and action-by-action sequencing were predominantly the same in the two texts. Reading the two manuscripts side by side, Bongars could then have easily noticed the additional formulations and transposed them into the readings of his base text, thereby creating a blended version. Not all the extra material in the *Peregrinatio Antiochie*, and thus on this hypothesis likewise present in the Camden manuscript, finds its way into the Bongars edition; but we do not know enough about Bongars's working methods and editorial strategies to say with certainty what principles of selection he applied, only that he was selective in his inclusion of variant forms and comfortable with creating hybrid readings, to the extent that he sometimes finessed the syntax to accommodate the sutures in his blended text. An alternative hypothesis is that the text that Bongars saw in the Camden manuscript was much closer in its lexis and locutionary texture to the *GF*. If this were the case, it would have been more straightforward for Bongars to isolate the additional elements, in the manner of laying one transparency over another; and it would have been correspondingly easier for him to be persuaded that the additional readings represented appropriate insertions into his edited version.

If this latter hypothesis is followed, the question then arises of the origin of the additional readings. It is possible, but unlikely, that these readings were present in the *GF* in, if not its aboriginal form, a recension that was anterior to the extant witnesses to this text. In this view, this material would have been omitted at some point in the transmission that leads to the surviving forms of the *GF*, while the chain of adaptation that would eventually lead to the *PT* began with a copy in which this material remained present. The problem with this suggestion, however, is that it is difficult to see why this material in particular would have been excised by a copyist. The additions in Bongars's text often read as "padding," expansions and circumlocutions that are much more likely to have been added at a subsequent stage in the transmission of the *GF*.[37] Further research into these additional elements in Bongars, their wording and the manner in which they are sutured into the surrounding text, will help to clarify this issue.[38]

In the meantime, the larger point to be drawn from St. Catharine's 3 is this: that the patterns of textual morphology that the *Peregrinatio Antiochie* reveals explode the notion of the "common source." The essential linear directionality of the stages by which the *PT* assumed its extant forms is made clear, even if some uncertainty still surrounds the number and character of all the stages in that process. How many individual copyist-revisers were involved and where they were working are unclear. But one can glimpse in the morphology of the *PT* the same sorts of impulses to enhance a base text by means of substantive and stylistic alteration that

---

[37] For example, *GF*, p. 3, "in festo sancti Michahelis" becomes "in die dedicationis S. Mikahelis qui est in Kal. Octob." in *Gesta Dei*, p. 2. *GF*, p. 8, "combussimus castrum cum habitatoribus suis" is glossed by means of "scilicet haereticorum congregatione" in *Gesta Dei*, p. 3. *GF*, p. 14, "Turci quippe" becomes "Turci quippe licet gens barbara" at *Gesta Dei*, p. 5. *GF*, p. 29, "referebantque omnia his" becomes "referebantque omnia his excommunicatis" at *Gesta Dei*, p. 10. Robert fitz Girard is additionally exhorted to recall the prowess of his and Bohemond's brave forebears: *GF*, p. 37; *Gesta Dei*, p. 12. *Gesta Dei*, p. 13, adds to *GF*, p. 41, the idea that the Christian women of Antioch's applause of the crusaders' success was a habit, "sicut mos erat illarum." *GF*, p. 55, "Quae ait" becomes "Quae respondens ait" at *Gesta Dei*, p. 17. On several occasions the content of speeches and other utterances rendered indirectly by the *GF* is enhanced by passages of direct speech, or direct speech is expanded: *Gesta Dei*, pp. 2, 3, 4, 12, 16, 29. References to Bohemond and other leaders are sometimes glossed by additional use of the honorific locutions such as *uir sapiens*, *doctus* and *egregius* routinely deployed by the *GF*: *Gesta Dei*, pp. 4, 5, 6, 7, 8, 21.

[38] See Marcus G. Bull, "The Nature and Significance of the Readings Supplied by William Camden's Manuscript in Jacques Bongars's Edition of the *Gesta Francorum*" (forthcoming).

also subtended, to a much greater extent, the crusade histories of Robert the Monk, Baldric of Bourgueil, and Guibert of Nogent. There was a "common source," but only to the extent that there was a shared point of origin for the extant forms of the *GF*, the *Peregrinatio Antiochie*, and the *PT*. And this point of origin was, effectively, the *GF*, not necessarily entirely as it now survives but very substantially so. There is no value in parking the uncertainties that attend the *GF* and the texts closely related to it in an imprecise, and ultimately unknowable, space marked "common source." How and why the *GF* came into being and whether even earlier written narratives and other sources fed into it are matters for debate.[39] But the morphology of the *PT* can only be explained by the anteriority of the *GF*, as St. Catharine's 3 makes clear. In other words, the *GF* is exactly what it has often been taken to be, the earliest surviving narrative telling of the course of the First Crusade.[40]

---

[39] Matters addressed in my forthcoming monograph, *Eyewitness and Narration: The Narratology of the Earliest Accounts of the First Crusade.*

[40] I am extremely grateful to Dr. Samu Niskanen, who brought the existence of St. Catharine's College, Cambridge, 3 to my attention and has been very generous in sharing his ideas, and to Mr Colin Higgins, Librarian of St. Catharine's College, who made the manuscript available to me and provided ideal conditions in which to study it.

The First Crusade and the Kingdom of Jerusalem in an Unpublished Hebrew Dirge

Avraham Gross
(Ben-Gurion University in the Negev; agross@bgu.ac.il)
and *Avraham Fraenkel*
(Independent Scholar; avrahamf@gmail.com)

Sixty years ago, when S. D. Goitein published the *Geniza* letters on the crusader conquest of Jerusalem in 1099, he contrasted the discrepancy between the existence of Hebrew reports and dirges on the 1096 persecutions in the Rhineland with the absolute lack of a Jewish literary or poetic response to the conquest of Jerusalem three years later.[1] However, this discrepancy was less pronounced than Goitein assumed. The present paper will draw attention to an unpublished Hebrew dirge that alludes to the call for the crusade, the 1096 persecutions, the conquest of Jerusalem, and its subsequent Christianization. This dirge appears (as of now) only in a single source: the famous Nuremberg *Mahzor*, written in 1331, now in The Dr. David and Jemima Jeselsohn Collection, Zurich.[2]

The fact that the poet describes the peaceful life of the crusaders in their new kingdom, noting that they have been "ruling in the Land for a number of years," indicates that he wrote it at some point after 1099. It also appears that he was acquainted with some of the 1096 dirges.[3] Memories about the massacre of the Jews during the conquest of Jerusalem seem fresh. Since the poet does not mention the Second Crusade and does not hint at any repetition of the First Crusade persecutions, one may posit 1147 as the *terminus ad quem*.[4]

We would like to thank Professor Shulamit Elizur for her important comments, and Mr Gabriel Wasserman for the poem's English translation.

[1] S. D. Goitein, "New Sources on the Fate of the Jews during the Crusaders' Conquest of Jerusalem," *Zion* 17 (1952), 129 [Hebrew]. See also idem, "Contemporary Letters on the Capture of Jerusalem by the Crusaders," *Journal of Jewish Studies* 3 (1952), 162; idem, "Geniza Sources for the Crusader Period: A Survey," in *Outremer*, p. 308.

[2] Fol. 205b. We hereby thank Dr. David and Jemima Jeselsohn for their gracious permission to publish the poem.

[3] The expression בוקקים (line 4) appears in the poem *zedim qamu* (זדים קמו) by Eliezer bar Nathan. In the same poem we have also the term שוחות (line 28) as referring to the Holy Sepulcher. The phrase עוללה זאת בעפרה להתעפרה (line 31) could have been influenced by Qalonymos bar Judah's poem *mi yiten* (מי יתן): כי שקולה הריגתם להתאבל ולהתעפרה. Another point for consideration is the fact that our poem appears in the manuscript after the 1096 dirges. In many instances this indicates a chronological order; namely, that additional poems were inserted after those that had become part of the canon. Yet this is only a rule of thumb to which there are many exceptions.

[4] Many churches were constructed, extended, or renovated in Jerusalem throughout the twelfth century. However, we do not possess precise dates that can aid us in dating the relevant part of our dirge (lines 25–28). For example, the Holy Sepulcher was significantly extended and the ceremony of dedication took place in 1149, however, the construction started and ended many years before and after this date.

The dirge was designed to be recited on the Ninth of Av, the day on which according to Jewish tradition both Temples of Jerusalem were destroyed. Each stanza opens with the word *Ekhah*, the first word of the biblical Scroll of Lamentations recited in synagogues the world over on the eve of the Ninth of Av. The poem consists of a double alphabetical acrostic, with the signature "Samuel" – the poet's name – figuring in the last stanza. The stanzas have four lines, and the rhythm is of four words per line.

Location of Composition

During the decades that followed the destruction of 1096, German Jewry was occupied with the rehabilitation of local communities. From the middle of the twelfth century, these communities suffered other persecutions, such as those witnessed during the Second Crusade and subsequently throughout the rest of that century. This can account for the fact that liturgical poetry with historical contents written in Ashkenaz during this period deals primarily with occurrences and the general situation within the Ashkenazic world itself. This phenomenon characterizes West Ashkenaz (Rhine area) liturgical poetry much more than that of their counterparts in East Ashkenaz (Regensburg, Austria, and Bohemia). The Hebrew chroniclers, those who recount the 1096 events and those who tell about the later persecutions, also focus on Ashkenaz. Very rarely do we read about a battle in which the crusaders were defeated, and when we do it is mainly in order to show that God is avenging the blood of the Ashkenazic martyrs. There is almost no mention of the situation in the Holy Land. In the post-1096 heated atmosphere of Jewish–Christian religious rivalry and polemics, mentioning the success of the First Crusade in conquering Jerusalem would have been self-defeating for the Jews.

The inward perspective of Ashkenazic poetry is even more conspicuous if posed against contemporary Sephardic and French sources, especially the poetry of Judah Halevi and his followers. The latter very often mourn the current situation of the conquest of Zion by the hands of the kingdom of Edom, the medieval "code name" for Christianity. Our poem seems to reflect a similarly broader Jewish view which distinguishes it from the above-mentioned self-centered Ashkenazic concerns. Indeed, though dirge it is, it does not follow the structure of classic Ashkenazic dirges.[5]

The *Nuremberg Mahzor*, the only manuscript in which this poem survives, systematically reflects the Ashkenazic liturgical tradition in Eastern Ashkenazic communities.[6] The contents of the dirge seem to point in the same direction. The

---

[5] This structure is of three-line stanzas in which the third line is a part of a biblical verse, and the end of the dirge calls on God to take revenge on the enemies.

[6] On the *Nuremberg Mahzor*, the liturgical tradition it reflects, and the poetical treasures it holds, see Jonah and Avraham Fraenkel, *Prayer and Poem in the Nuremberg Mahzor*, http://jnul.huji.ac.il/dl/mss-pr/mahzor-nuremberg/intro.html

description of the 1096 catastrophe is missing some of the hallmark motifs of Western Ashkenazic poems, notably, the active martyrdom and the abuse of the carcasses of the martyrs. On the other hand, it does contain a reference to a motif which was entirely ignored in the 1096 poems (in contra-distinction to the Hebrew chronicles), namely, forcible conversion (lines 15–20). This subject, we assume, was a highly sensitive one in the two generations following 1096, the span of time during which our poem was in all probability composed. It is plausible to suggest that only a geographically remote poet could refer to the forced converts without being inhibited by the social sensitivities of the survivors in the Rhine communities. All of this seems to indicate that the author of our poem is indeed East Ashkenazi.

Content

The poem is written as a comprehensive dirge on the actual situation of the city of Jerusalem and on the Temple site, which amounts to a new chapter and continuation of the historical destruction of the Temples. It is not a "persecution poem" dealing with specific persecutions, a genre that developed rapidly in the twelfth century. Rather, it is a poem that focuses on the profundity of the actual destruction of Jerusalem. However, though the dirge is Jerusalem-centered with an emphasis on the present, the poet chose to include also a summary of persecutions associated with the First Crusade, starting with the events in Germany in 1096, the massacre of the Jews during the crusader conquest of Jerusalem in 1099, and the contemporaneous repression of the Jews in the Land of Israel.

At the outset (lines 1–4) the poet bemoans the conquest of the Land of Israel by the crusaders, the servitude of the "remnant" – the few Jews who remained in the Land – and the permanent settlement of the crusaders in parts of the Land which were intended for the Tribes of Israel. At this point, he returns to briefly describe the plan and intention of the crusade (5–8). In more detail, he mourns the destruction of the important communities by the crusaders (9–20). The bulk of the poem is devoted to the conquest of Jerusalem and to the actions of the crusaders within the city (21–44). He ends in a conventional manner by asking God to remember His people, to hasten their redemption, and to rebuild the Temple (45–48). In this manner, the poem is connected to an additional and central motif of the Ninth of Av liturgy: the request and hope for the rebuilding of the Temple.

Christianity is described using derogatory terms reserved for idolatry, as we find in contemporary Ashkenazic literature, poetry and prose alike.[7] When he describes the present situation in the Land of Israel and in Jerusalem, the poet mentions the fact that the crusaders filled the city with "idols." He inserts there a stanza which

---

[7] חמנים = idols (originally, pagan worship-items devoted to the sun); טינוף = filth; אלילים = idols, godlets; מבואות טמאות = profane alleyways; פסילים = idols; בתי גילולים = "houses of dung," a term used for pagan idols throughout the Book of Ezekiel (see 6.4 *et passim*); שוחות קלקולים = "pits of perversion," i.e., the Holy Sepulcher; יקר נתעב = "abominable glory."

deals with the tearing and burning of sacred books by the crusaders (29–32). Such acts are known to us from the 1096 Hebrew chronicles and poetry, but the present description may well refer to the doings of the crusaders in the Levant.[8] Indeed, the burning of the books of the huge Muslim library of Tripoli by the crusaders upon their conquest of that city in 1109 is well known.[9] We may have here a testimony about a specific occurrence, brought to our poet's attention by a Jew who visited the Land of Israel.

The poem may be regarded as a concise history of the First Crusade from a Jewish perspective. The poet sees the entire period – the call for the crusade, the 1096 persecutions in Germany, the conquest of *Eretz Zvi* (most beautiful land) and Jerusalem, and the continuous situation there under Christian rule – as one historical unit.[10] Conventional dirges mourn the historical destruction of Jerusalem and the Temples. Twelfth-century Ashkenazic dirges bemoan the destruction of their own communities. Our poet "covers" the entire destruction, physical and religious, caused by the First Crusade in the past – in Germany and during the conquest of Jerusalem – and the continuous occupation of Jerusalem and the entire Land of Israel at present. The process of the physical Christianization of Jerusalem by building churches and monasteries, and by placing Christian "idolatry" all over the holy city, serves to indicate the dismal state of Exile that has reached, with the First Crusade, its lowest point since the destruction itself. This Christian campaign is, according to this view, but another phase in broadening the destruction of the Second Temple; in this way our poet has no need to refer to the destruction that took place more than one thousand years earlier. The expression *Ekhah,* which opens the Book of Lamentations, and is often used in conventional dirges, is here applied with ease to the widespread destruction of the First Crusade.

The Poet's Historical Sources

Jews in western Europe were not entirely ignorant of what took place in the Land of Israel. Most information probably reached them by Christian travelers or pilgrims who returned to Europe and brought news from the Holy Land to anyone ready to listen. They might have been informed also by circulating Latin descriptions of crusader Jerusalem. Some of the information could have been brought from the

---

[8] On crusaders pillaging Jewish sacred books, and on Jewish efforts to redeem them, see Joshua Prawer, *The History of the Jews in the Latin Kingdom of Jerusalem* (Oxford, 1988), pp. 29–30.

[9] See, for instance, Youssef Eche, *Les bibliothèques arabes publiques et semi-publiques en Mésopotamie, en Syrie et en Égypte au Moyen Age* (Damascus, 1967), pp. 117–21.

[10] It is interesting to note, inter alia, that "persecution poets" from the second half of the twelfth century express a similar view with respect to their own history, namely, that late persecutions, starting with the Second Crusade, are but a part of a historical unit that started with the First Crusade and the 1096 persecutions. On this subject see the introduction to our critical edition of the 1096 poems in the MGH Hebrew series (forthcoming).

East by Jewish travelers and pilgrims. The sources for specific descriptions of the fate of Jews in the Land of Israel were probably Jewish.[11]

---

[11]   Though much later, this seems to have been the case with an Ashkenazi Jew who knew that Acre fell on Friday, 18 Sivan [50]51 – which is the precise Hebrew date for Acre's fall on Friday, 18 May 1291. See Benjamin Z. Kedar, "Jews and Samaritans in the Crusading Kingdom of Jerusalem," *Tarbiz* 53 (1983/84), 407 [Hebrew].

קִינָה

אֵיכָה   אֶרֶץ צְבִי נִמְסְרָה לְאוֹיְבִים
         אִיבְּדוּ הַשְּׁאֵרִית בָּהּ יוֹשְׁבִים
         בּוֹקְקִים מַדִּיקִים כָּל הַסּוֹבְבִים
         בְּנַחֲלַת שְׁבָטִים הֵם מִתְרַבִּים

5   אֵיכָה   גָּבַהּ לֵב עָרִיצִים לְהָבִינָה
         גּוֹרוּ מִכָּל צַד בְּתוֹאֲנָה
         דָּרְשׁוּ יְקַר נִתְעָב לְהַדְלְיָנָה
         דַּרְכָּם הִסְלִילוּ לְאֶבֶן פִּנָּה

    אֵיכָה   הִשְׁחִיתוּ בְּלֶכְתָּם בְּקָרוֹב הַקְּהִילוֹת
10   הָאֲנָשִׁים וְהַנַּשִׁים בַּחוּרִים וּבְתוּלוֹת
         וְאַלוּפִים בַּעֲלֵי חֲמוּרוֹת וְקַלּוֹת
         וְתַלְמִידִים הַמְשַׁמְּשִׁים רוֹבְצִים עֲגוּלוֹת

    אֵיכָה   זָדוּ כֹּהֲנִים וּלְוִיִם לְחַבֵּל
         זָמְמוּ שֵׁם קוֹדֶשׁ לְנַבֵּל
15   חוּלַל יִחוּם פֶּרֶץ וְאַשְׁבֵּל

         חַמָּנִים לַעֲבוֹד עֲלֵיהֶם לְקַבֵּל

    אֵיכָה   טָפְשׁוּ לְהַגְאֵיל צֵאוּי יְקָרִים

         טִינוּף הִרְגִּילוּ בְּכָל עֲבָרִים
         יָחִיד הֶחֱזִיר לִשְׁמוֹ מַמְרִים
20   יַחְדָּיו מִלִּטְמַע בֵּין הַבְּתָרִים

---

1   **lovely land** = the Land of Israel; cf. Jeremiah 3.19, and see Tractate Megillah 6a: ארץ צבי גידלה 'שעשועיה'

2   **the remnant**: cf. for instance II Kings 21.14.

3   For בוקקים in the sense of "destroy," see Nahum 2.3. For מדיקים in the sense of "crush," see אכלה 'ומדקה' in Daniel 7.7, referring to the Fourth Beast that "devoured and brake." Jewish tradition identifies this beast with the Roman Empire and western Christendom, and thus with the crusaders.

7   **abominable precious**. This term refers not only to the Holy Sepulcher, as indicated in the translation here, but also to Jesus himself.

to raise it up. Cf. Ecclesiastes 20.5. Or, possibly, "to ascend to it."

8   **cornerstone.** Cf. אבן בחן פנת יקרת (Isaiah 18:16).

12   **sitting in circles.** Seated like the Sanhedrin in a semicircle. Cf. Mishnah Sanhedrin 4.3, and Bereshith Rabbah 98.12 (p. 1262).

15   **The seed of Perez [a sub-tribe of Judah] and Ashbel [a sub-tribe of Benjamin].** See Numbers 26.21, 38. Of the twelve tribes of Israel, only Judah and Benjamin (and the priestly tribe, Levi) survived into the post-biblical period, so the sub-tribes Perez and Ashbel here are a synecdoche for the entire Jewish people.

Translation

The meaning of some of the lines is not certain; their proposed translation is approximate only (see lines 3, 19, 28).

1   **How is it** that the lovely land hath been given over to enemies,
    Who have destroyed the remnant [of Jews] living there!
    [The crusaders] destroy and crush all those who surround them,
    And they have become numerous in the inheritance of the Tribes [of Israel].

5   **How is it** that the heart of the tyrants hath become too haughty to act with comprehension!
    Tremble ye from every side, [when they make their] claim!
    They seek their abominable precious [goal, the Sepulcher], to raise it up,
    And they have made their path to [Jerusalem], the cornerstone [of the universe].

    How is it that in their treks through the many [Jewish] communities, they have destroyed
10 Men and women, youths and maidens,
    Scholars, experts in both small and great [precepts of the law],
    And students, serving [these scholars], sitting in circles!

    How is it that they have acted wantonly, to harm priests and Levites,
    And have conspired to profane the Holy Name!
15 The seed of Perez [a sub-tribe of Judah] and Ashbel [a sub-tribe of Benjamin] hath been violated,
    [By having been forced] to accept upon themselves to serve idols.

    How is it that [the foes] have foolishly befouled the honorable [Jews] with their filth [baptismal water]!
    They have made grime common on all sides.
    Yet the Unique One hath restored to His name those [forced] apostates,
20 Together, so that they not be absorbed by the nations.

---

hath been violated. Probably referring to the forced conversions, as can be surmised from the following lines. References to those forced converts, which can be found abundantly in the Hebrew chronicles (e.g. below, lines 19–20), are extremely rare in the 1096 *piyyutim*.

16   **idols** = the cross.

17   **grime.** Another Jewish derisive term for baptismal water common in Ashkenaz.

honorable [Jews]. Cf. בני ציון היקרים (Lamentations 4.2).

19–20   Meaning of Hebrew uncertain. The lines may mean that God ensured that the apostasy of these Jews to Christianity would be only temporary, for eventually they would safely return to Judaism. See, for example, Eva Haverkamp, ed., *Hebräische Berichte über die Judenverfolgungen während des Ersten Kreuzzugs*, MGH. Hebräische Texte aus dem mittelalterlichen Deutschland 1 (Hanover, 2005), pp. 481–83.

20   **by the nations.** Literally, "between the pieces." In Genesis 15.9 ff., Abraham cuts up the corpses of various animals into pieces. According to rabbinic tradition (Bereshith Rabba 44.9, p. 437), these pieces of animals represent the kingdoms of the gentile nations.

אֵיכָה כָּבְשׁוּ שָׁלֵם קִרְיַת חָנָה
כָּלוּ דְּרָכֶיהָ בְּחֶרֶב שְׁנוּנָה
לְוִיֵּם שָׂמוּ לְמָשָׁל וְלִשְׁנִינָה
לִינַת הַצֶּדֶק הָיְתָה כְּאַלְמָנָה

אֵיכָה 25 מָלְאָם לִבָּם לַעֲשׂוֹת אֱלִילִים
מָבוֹאוֹת טְמֵאוֹת טִמְּאוּ בִּפְסִילִים

נוֹצְרִים בָּנוּ בָתֵּי גִילּוּלִים
נָדְבוּ לְהִתְהַלֵּל בְּשׁוּחוֹת קִילְקוּלִים

אֵיכָה שָׂרְפוּ כִּתְבֵי יִרְאָה טְהוֹרָה
סָחוֹב וְהַשְׁלֵךְ נִיתְּקוּם בְּעֶבְרָה 30
עוֹלְלָה זֹאת בַּעֲפָרָה לְהִתְעַפְּרָה
עָלֶיהָ כָּל עַיִן נִגְרָה

אֵיכָה פָּשְׁטוּ לַהֲלֵךְ בְּהֵיכָל וּבַעֲזָרוֹת

פּוֹסְעִים בְּמָקוֹם הַלְּשָׁכוֹת וְהַכִּיּוֹרוֹת
צוֹעֲדִים בָּאוּלָם וּבִדְבִיר הַחֲדָרוֹת 35
צְפִירַת תַּלְפִּיּוֹת נִשְׁחַת בְּהַעֲבָרוֹת

אֵיכָה קִידְּמוּ מְלָכִים לְשַׁעֲרֵי הָעִיר
קָם אֲרִי מִסֻּבְּכוֹ הֵעִיר
רֵיקִים עַתָּה פָּחֲזוּ לְהַכְעִיר
רָצוּ וְהִגִּיעוּ בְּחֶרֶץ לְהַגְעִיר 40

אֵיכָה שׁוֹלְטִים בָּאָרֶץ כַּמָּה שָׁנִים
שְׁקֵטִים שׁוֹכְנִים דְּשֵׁנִים רַעֲנַנִּים
תַּחְתֵּיהֶם דּוֹרְכִים כָּל הֲמוֹנִים
תְּמִימִים מִתְפַּחְדִים בְּשַׁלְוַת עוֹיְנִים

---

21   **Salem.** That is, Jerusalem; cf. Genesis 14.18 and Psalms 76.3.
23   **Levites.** Should probably be understood as a synecdoche for Jews in general. Cf. הנלוים על ה' לשרתו (Isaiah 56.6).
24   **the city where justice dwelt.** Jerusalem, at the time of its glory. Cf. Isaiah 1.21.
widow. Cf. Lamentations 1.1.
28   **And have donated [money] in order to engage in self-praising prayers in the profane Sepulcher.** Hebrew uncertain; this translation is merely one way to understand the words. שוחה is a common "code name" for the Holy Sepulcher in the 1096 *piyyutim*. Cf., for example, הצלוב הקבור ונתון

How is it that they have conquered the city of Salem, where [David] camped,
And they have finished off its inhabitants, with a sharp sword!
They have made its Levites into objects of scorn and ridicule,
And the city where justice dwelt hath become like a widow.

25 **How is it** that their heart hath inspired them to make idols,
And they have contaminated alleyways, making them contaminated with graven images!
Christians have built idolatrous temples,
And have donated [money] in order to engage in self-praising prayers in the profane Sepulcher.

How is it that they have burned writings of pure reverence [i.e., of Scripture],
30 Dragged them around and hurled them, and cut them up in rage!
This [the Torah] hath been abused, rolled around in the dust,
And every eye hath shed tears for her.

How is it that they have spread out to walk in the [places of the] Temple and its courtyards!
They trod upon the place of the chambers and the lavers,
35 They march around the rooms of the Temple hallways and the sanctum,
And the crowning glory to which all [Jews] turn hath been destroyed by their passing through.

How is it that kings have hastened to the gates of the city,
And the lion hath arisen from his lair, whom [God] hath aroused!
Empty men have now become wanton, to do ugly deeds,
40 They have run, and arrived, to terrorize [the city] with utter destruction.

How is it that they have now been ruling in the [Holy] Land for a number of years,
Dwelling quietly, calmly, and happily!
Beneath them, they trod upon the nations,
And the pure [Jews] are terrified by the stability of the hostile [conquerors].

בשוחה עמוקה (Eliezer bar Nathan, *elohim zedim qamu*, line 19).

35 **sanctum.** Cf. אל דביר הבית אל קדש הקדשים (I Kings 8.6).

36 **And the crowning glory to which all [Jews] turn.** That is, the city of Jerusalem. In Song of Songs 4.4, Jerusalem is called "built unto *talpiyyoth*." This last word is extremely obscure, but the Babylonian Talmud (Berakhoth 30a) explains it as meaning: "The hill (*tel*) to which all [Jewish] mouths [*piyyoth*] turn."

38 **And the lion hath arisen from his lair.** Cf. Jeremiah 4.7.

42 **calmly and happily.** Cf. Psalms 92.15 (translated as "fat and flourishing" in the King James Bible).

45 אֵיכָה **שָׁ**כַחַת מָרוֹם אֱמוּנֶיךָ לְעוֹלָמִים
מפוֹאר וְנֶחְמָד בְּנֵה בַּנְּעִימִים
וְאוֹרך תַּזְרִיחַ לְמעוטי עַמִּים
וחוּשׁ לְנַחֲמֵם בְּאַחֲרִית הַיָּמִים

---

46 **Build thou the glorious and delightful [Temple].** Cf. נחמד כרך ראה לא בתפארתה ירושלים ראה שלֹא מי
מעולם מפואר בנין ראה לא בבנינו המקדש בית ראה שלֹא מי .מימיו (Tractate Sukkah 51b).

47 **smallest of nations.** Cf. העמים מכל המעט אתם כי (Deuteronomy 7.7).

48 **the Final [Redemption].** Literally, "the End of Days."

45   **How is it** that Thou hast forever forgotten, O lofty One, Thy faithful ones!
     Build Thou the glorious and delightful [Temple],
     And shine Thy light upon the smallest of nations [= the Jews],
     And hasten to comfort them, by means of the Final [Redemption].

Alexios, Bohemond, and Byzantium's Euphrates Frontier: A Tale of Two Cretans

John H. Pryor
(University of Sydney, john.pryor@sydney.edu.au)
and Michael J. Jeffreys
(Oxford University, michael.jeffreys@mod-langs.ox.ac.uk)

Introduction

The First Crusade contingents of Hugh of Vermandois and Godfrey of Bouillon arrived in Constantinople earlier but all of the others came together in the spring of 1097. Alexios I Komnēnos invited each of the major leaders to an audience in the Blachernai palace and all those of the first rank accepted sooner or later, either eagerly or reluctantly. At these audiences commitments were made, mutual guarantees were exchanged, and Alexios gave them splendid gifts. Their first attempts to collaborate and to take collective decisions occurred in the context of establishing relations with the Byzantine emperor.

The audience that had the widest ramifications later was undoubtedly the one in early April 1097 with Alexios's most dangerous former enemy, Bohemond of Taranto, who had been his father's, Robert Guiscard's, lieutenant in his assault on the Balkans early in Alexios's reign. He would later seize Antioch, the major focus of Byzantine policy in the East, and found a dynasty that would hold it until 1268. In 1104 he would return to the West, make a triumphal journey around Italy and France, systematically blacken Alexios's name, and persuade Pope Paschal II to authorize a new crusade, which he would turn against the Empire. In 1107 he would invade Albania but be fought to a standstill and compelled to agree to the Treaty of *Deabolis*,[1] in September 1108. Unsurprisingly, both the Greek and Latin accounts of their audience are dominated by mutual suspicions and attempts to allay them. Discussions seem to have gone well, nevertheless, and ended with agreement and rich rewards for Bohemond, who subsequently helped Alexios to negotiate with other leaders. We argue that the keystone of the relations established between

---

We thank John France, John Haldon, Jonathan Shepard, Christopher MacEvitt, and Jean-Claude Cheynet for their comments. We also thank Tara Andrews for the Armenian transliterations, Judith Ryder for her paper on John the Oxite, and Tom Madden for a copy of the verses in praise of Bohemond in Rome, Biblioteca Apostolica Vaticana, MS Reg. Lat. 572, fol. 68r. In view of recent advances that have only lately come to our attention, readers should consult the Postscript first.

[1]   We have followed throughout the principle of italicizing place names whose medieval forms we have used when the places no longer exist, as in this case, or when we have a preferred a medieval form to a modern one; e.g. *Dyrrachion* rather than Durrës. Many people and places had multiple names in Greek, Turkish, Armenian, Frankish, and Arabic. We have used Greek and Armenian forms for Greeks and Armenians and places in Byzantine and Armenian regions, with modern Turkish or Arabic in parentheses the first time, except in the case of well known places, for example Edessa.

Alexios and Bohemond was Alexios's grant to him of a marcher lordship in the East and the office of the *Domestikaton of the East*.

The *Alexiad* (correctly *Alexias*) of Anna Komnēnē and her husband Nikēphoros Bryennios is the only Greek source for the audience. It agrees in part on the discussions with some important Latin sources, although perspectives differ. The *Alexiad* reports Bohemond requesting the *Domestikaton of the East* and Alexios then obfuscating on the grounds that the office might enable Bohemond to manipulate other "counts" and threaten the Empire, although he leaves the prospect dangling enticingly. This office was that of commander of the Empire's eastern military forces. It transcended local commands and had been held previously by Alexios himself and two of his brothers. It would have made Bohemond one of the most powerful men in the Empire.

The Latin sources do not mention this but rather that Alexios granted Bohemond vast lands: a huge region fifteen days' march in length and eight in width, defined with reference to Antioch. After the capture of Nicaea, however, imperial policy throughout the crusade and afterwards was to recover Antioch for the Empire. Alexios cannot, therefore, have granted the city itself to Bohemond.

For the most part, historians have dismissed the ideas both that Bohemond requested an imperial command and also that Alexios granted him a marcher lordship. The passage in the *Alexiad* has been considered an extended encomium of Alexios showing the Byzantine hero mastering the dangerous crusader. The passage in the Latin sources has for over 80 years been considered a later interpolation designed to justify Bohemond's refusal to return Antioch to the Empire and his campaign of 1107.

A request for the *Domestikaton of the East* has never made sense. Why would Bohemond want to abandon the crusade, submit to imperial authority, and probably have to reside in regions under Byzantine control? How could he use such a command to manipulate other leaders and what aspirations to threaten the Empire might it facilitate? Moreover, since he did not do so, if he did make such a request, he meant something else. Furthermore, the Latin sources are clear that Antioch was excluded from the marcher lordship.

Despite their differences, coincidences in the Greek and Latin reports give them a credibility that has been dismissed too easily. By 1097 there was in fact a context for the office of *Domestikos of the East* that would have been attractive to Bohemond and would have brought with it large territories: a marcher lordship on the Euphrates frontier in the lands of ancient *Kommagēnē*.[2] We argue that Alexios actually granted these to Bohemond but that because of the later history of

---

[2] John France has detected an "Armenian strategy" that may have been discussed with Alexios in Constantinople. See *Victory in the East: A Military History of the First Crusade* (Cambridge, 1994), p. 368 and pp. 116, 167–68, 190–96; idem, "La stratégie arménienne de la Première Croisade," in *Les Lusignans et l'Outremer. Actes du Colloque (Poitiers, Université de Poitiers, 1994)*, ed. Claude Mutafian (Poitiers, 1995), p. 144. His inquiry was not the same as ours, however, and he did not make a connection to the *Domestikaton of the East* and a marcher lordship for Bohemond.

relationships between the Empire and the principality of Antioch the *Alexiad* turned the grant into a request because its authors did not wish to preserve the memory of such a fundamental political mistake as the emperor granting a high office and lordship to a man who became an implacable foe of the Empire. The implications affect understanding of the ways in which relations were established between the emperor and the leaders, the playing-out of the crusade, and subsequent relations between the Empire and the Frankish states.

The *Domestikaton of the East*

The *Alexiad* reads as follows:

> The emperor, knowing of his [Bohemond's] hostility and ill intentions, was careful to dispel without difficulty all that was designed to serve the plans that he nourished secretly. So when Bohemond asked for the position of *Domestikaton of the East*, he did not gain his wish, playing the Cretan to a Cretan. For the emperor was afraid that, if he [Bohemond] gained this authority and used it to bring all the counts under his control, he would easily be able to manipulate them in any way he wished. But not wanting Bohemond to realise at all that his plans were already understood, he flattered him with positive hopes, saying: "It is not yet the time for this, but through your energy and loyalty, this too will come about in a short time."[3]

Anna Komnēnē was not the sole author of the *Alexiad*. Her husband, the *Kaisar* Nikēphoros Bryennios, gathered material for it and wrote much of it. His style has been discerned in many passages, especially those referring to events in which he participated himself. The text "had reached the form of connected compositions at a more or less advanced stage of drafting by the time of his death."[4] In some places Anna's role was limited to arranging or revising what Nikēphoros had written or to writing up his notes or those of others. Bohemond's audience with Alexios took place in the Blachernai palace, where both Anna and Nikēphoros may equally well have witnessed it or heard about it from Alexios. The *Alexiad*'s account does, however, centre on a classical tag, "playing the Cretan to a Cretan,"[5] which is more characteristic of Anna's style than Nikēphoros's. He may well have penned the passage originally and Anna rewritten it.

---

[3] *Annae Comnenae Alexias*, ed. Diether R. Reinsch and Athanasios Kambylis (Berlin and New York, 2001) [hereafter *Alexias*], X.xi.7 (1:320), alternatively, *Anne Comnène Alexiade (règne de l'empereur Alexis I Comnène 1081–1118)*, ed. and trans. Bernard Leib, 3 vols. (Paris, 1937–45); tome IV, Index, Paul Gautier (Paris, 1976) [hereafter *Alexiade*], 2:234. The texts are identical here.

[4] On the authorship of the *Alexiad*, see James Howard-Johnston, "Anna Komnene and the *Alexiad*," in *Alexios I Komnenos. I: Papers*, ed. Margaret Mullett and Dion Smythe (Belfast, 1996), p. 300. Varied reactions to Howard-Johnston's thesis may be found in *Anna Komnene and Her Times*, ed. Thalia Gouma-Peterson (New York and London, 2000).

[5] That is, as one dissembler to another. The skill of Cretans as dissemblers was proverbial. The quotation, perhaps from Plutarch, was a learned way of referring to it. See *Alexiade*, 2:234, n. 2.

Many scholars have accepted that Bohemond asked for the *Domestikaton of the East* and some have suggested that Alexios may have intended to use Bohemond and other crusaders to create buffer states between the Empire and the Turks, but, to the best of our knowledge, only Paul Magdalino has suggested that the *Domestikaton of the East* may actually have been granted to him.[6]

The offices of *Domestikos of the East*, *Domestikos of the West*, and *Megas* (great) *domestikos* were first created in the East over local commands out of need for unified action against the Muslims and then became the highest offices in the Byzantine armies from the mid-tenth century.[7] A *domestikos* often commanded an army if the emperor was absent or was his lieutenant when he was present. The three did not function as a college, however, and the links between them are not immediately obvious. Men moved between the offices with apparent ease. "Of the East" was sometimes assumed, while "of the West" was not and had to be added when necessary. "*Megas*" may have indicated that only one *domestikos* was in post.

"The East" shrank greatly as a result of Turkish incursions before and after 'Aḍud al-Dawla Alp Arslan's defeat of Rōmanos IV Diogenēs at *Mantzikert* in 1071 and there were few holders of the office between then and the crusade. What then did the *Alexiad* mean by the title? Leaving aside problems of translation, did

---

[6] We say to the best of our knowledge advisedly. No doubt we have overlooked someone. Rudolf Hiestand's paper came to our attention only at the last moment. In a thought-provoking paper to the Canadian Institute of Balkan Studies in 1996, Paul Magdalino asked: "Is it not just as likely that Alexios offered Bohemond the position, and that Bohemond refused it because it would hamper his freedom of action?" See *The Byzantine Background to the First Crusade* (Toronto, 1996), p. 8.

John France also suggests that there may have been something lying behind the reports of the *Alexiad* and the *Gesta Francorum* but does not consider that Alexios may have offered Bohemond the office rather than the latter asking for it; see "The Departure of Tatikios from the Crusader Army," *Bulletin of the Institute of Historical Research* 44 (1971), 141. Peter Charanis also suggests that Alexios intended to use Bohemond to create "a Latin state in the Orient under his suzereinty which might serve as a buffer between his empire as he hoped to reconstitute it and the Islamic world"; see "Aims of the Medieval Crusaders and how they were Viewed by Byzantium," *Church History* 21 (1952), 129. He makes no connection, however, to the *Domestikaton of the East*. Pasquale Corsi does the same; see "Boemondo a Constantinopoli," in *Boemundo: storia di un principe Normanno. Atti del convegno di studio su Boemondo, da Taranto ad Antiochia e Canosa: Normanno, Taranto–Canosa, maggio–novembre 1998*, ed. Franco Cardini et al. (Università degli Studi di Lecce, 2003), p. 20. Giuseppe Morea argues that Bohemond wanted the leadership of the crusade and that since Urban had not offered it to him he sought the *Domestikaton of the East* from Alexios so as to allow him to direct operations and, as an imperial official, to receive any lands conquered for the Empire; see *Marco Boemondo d'Altavilla* (Canosa, 1986), pp. 45–46. Rudolf Hiestand does connect the grant of lands to Bohemond's request for the *Domestikaton of the East* and argues that Bohemond sought a permamenent arrangement for himself within Byzantine structures. See Rudolf Hiestand, "Boemondo I e la Prima Crociata," in *Il Mezzogiorno normanno-svevo e le Crociate*, ed. Giosuè Musca (Bari, 2002), pp. 80–81. Ralph Yewdale also thought that the story that Bohemond asked for the *Domestikaton of the East* was "not impossible." He rejected, however, the grant of lands and did not put the two together; see *Bohemond I, Prince of Antioch* (Princeton, 1924), p. 43.

[7] Hélène Glykatzi-Ahrweiler, "Recherches sur l'administration de l'empire byzantine aux IXe–XIe siècles," *Bulletin de correspondance hellénique* 84 (1960), 52–67; Rodolphe Guilland, *Recherches sur les institutions byzantines*, 2 vols. (Berlin and Amsterdam, 1967), 1:405–68; Hans Joachim Kühn, *Die byzantinische Armee im 10. und 11. Jahrhundert: Studien zur Organisation der Tagmata* (Vienna, 1991), pp. 135–57.

Anna or Nikēphoros use it in its traditional sense or rather in a new one because of new circumstances created by the Turkish occupation of most of the East? Was the role proposed for, or requested by, Bohemond – one that two old enemies would have considered worth pursuing, each for their own reasons?

Consideration of men named as *domestikoi* elsewhere in the *Alexiad*, and also in Nikēphoros Bryennios's *Hyle Historias*,[8] provides the key. In chronological order, these were: John Komnēnos, Alexios's father; the Armenian Philaretos Brakhamios;[9] Andronikos Doukas, the conqueror of Rōmanos Diogenēs; Isaac Komnēnos, Alexios's elder brother; John Bryennios, brother of the rebel Nikēphoros; the Armeno-Georgian Grigor son of Bakuran, known to the Byzantines as *Gregorios Pakourianos*; and Alexios's younger brother Adrian, first attested as *Megas domestikos* in 1087. Alexios himself also held each of the three offices at various times. When Adrian died or retired as *Megas domestikos* is unknown, raising the question of whether Alexios could have made Bohemond *Domestikos of the East* while he was still in office. Guilland asserts that Bohemond's office would have been independent of Adrian's whereas Frankopan argues that Alexios's discussion with Bohemond confirms that Adrian was by then no longer *domestikos*, which is indeed probable on other grounds.[10]

The four Komnēnoi cannot have provided a model for Bohemond's office, neither in the minds of those involved nor for Anna or Nikēphoros later. Since Andronikos Doukas also belonged to an imperial family and John Bryennios and his brother Nikēphoros planned to establish one, they also may be ruled out.

The Georgian and Armenian *domestikoi* are much more probable models. Grigor son of Bakuran was a Georgian landowner with Armenian connections. He began serving the Empire with a band of followers and fought on various frontiers, becoming a *domestikos* under Michael VII and *Megas domestikos of the West* under Alexios I, with whom he fought against Robert Guiscard. Bohemond would have been familiar with his office and title.

Philaretos Brakhamios was a Greek orthodox Armenian who was both a brigand and in Byzantine service from the 1050s.[11] First appointed *doux* and *stratēgos*

---

[8] Details conveniently available in *Alexias*, 2:116–17, *Alexiade*, 4:39; Nikēphoros Bryennios, *Hyle historias*, ed. and trans. Paul Gautier, as *Nicéphore Bryennios histoire* (Brussels, 1975) [hereafter Nikēphoros Bryennios, *Hyle*] under δομέστικος μέγας and δομέστικος τῶν Σχολῶν. On the *Hyle historias*, see Leonora Neville, "A History of the Caesar John Doukas in Nikephoros Bryennios' *Material for History?*," *Byzantine and Modern Greek Studies* 32 (2008), 168–88.

[9] Philaretos was always known by his Greek name and we have retained it.

[10] Guilland, *Recherches*, 1:407; Peter Frankopan, "Kinship and the Distribution of Power in Komnenian Byzantium," *English Historical Review* 122 (2007), 20. See also Jonathan Shepard, "When Greek meets Greek: Alexius Comnenus and Bohemond in 1097–98," *Byzantine and Modern Greek Studies* 12 (1988), 219, n. 113.

[11] On Philaretos see Michael Attaleiatēs, *Historia: introducción, edición, traducción y comentario*, ed. Inmaculada Pérez Martín, Nueva Roma 15 (Madrid, 2002) [hereafter MA (Pérez Martín)], pp. 99–100, 215; Michael Attaleiatēs, *Historia*, ed. C. M. Wladimir Brunet de Presle and Immanuel Bekker, Corpus scriptorum historiae Byzantinae 34 (Bonn, 1853) [hereafter MA (Bonn)], pp. 132, 301; Bar Hebraeus, *The Chronography of Gregory Abū 'l Faraj the son of Aaron, the Hebrew physician commonly*

autokratōr at *Khlat'* (Ahlat) on the northwest shore of Lake Van, he was made *Domestikos of the East* by Rōmanos IV according to the *Alexiad*.[12] This could only mean that he was appointed before *Mantzikert*. He refused to accept Rōmanos's deposition and spurned Michael VII. The imperial government tried to replace him with more amenable Armenians,[13] but despite that he established an extensive realm stretching from *Honi* (Arıtaş) and *Lykandos*[14] in the north-west to *Kharberd* (Kharput) and *Rōmanoupolis* (Bingöl) in the north-east, south to *Samusat* (Samsat) on the Euphrates and west to Maraš and the River *Jahan* (Ceyhan) (see Map 1). At his height he ruled most of the later Frankish states of Antioch and Edessa. Matthew of Edessa said that his forces included 800 Latins led by a certain "Rmbarat," Raimbaud perhaps.[15] His career would also have been known in Norman circles.

---

known as *Bar Hebraeus*, trans. Ernest A. Wallis Budge, 2 vols. (Oxford, 1932) [hereafter Bar Hebraeus, *Chronography*], 1:227–29, 231; Ἡ συνέχεια τῆς Χρονογραφίας τοῦ Ἰωάννου Σκυλίτζῃ, ed. Eudoxos Tsolakes, Εταιρεία Μακεδονικῶν σπουδῶν 105 (Thessalonike, 1968) [hereafter *Skylitzēs continuatus*], pp. 136–37, 184; Matthew of Edessa, *Armenia and the Crusades, Tenth to Twelfth Centuries: The Chronicle of Matthew of Edessa*, trans. Ara E. Dostourian (Lanham, 1993) [hereafter ME], II.60, 62, 66, 71, 74 78, 82, 84 (pp. 137–43, 145, 147–52); Vardan Arewelc'i, *Historical Compilation*, trans. R. W. Thomson, "The Historical Compilation of Vardan Arewelc'i," *Dumbarton Oaks Papers* 43 (1989), 125–226 [hereafter Vardan Arewelc'i, *Compilation*], §60 (p. 196); John Zōnaras, Ἐπιτομὴ ἱστοριῶν/*Epitome historiarum*, ed. Ludovicus [Ludwig] Dindorf, 6 vols. (Leipzig, 1868–75) [hereafter Zōnaras, *Epitomē*], XVIII.xii (4:209); Michael the Syrian, *Chronique de Michel le Syrien patriarche Jacobite d'Antioche (1166–1199)*, ed. and trans. Jean-Baptiste Chabot, 4 vols. (Paris, 1899–1910) [hereafter MSyr], XV.iv, vi, viii (3:173, 179, 187–88); *Alexias*, VI.ix.2 (1:186–87), *Alexiade*, 2:64; Nikēphoros Bryennios, *Hyle*, II.28 (pp. 200–3); *Anonymi auctoris chronicon ad A.C. 1234 pertinens*, trans. Albert Abouna, Corpus scriptorum Christianorum orientalium 354; Scriptores Syri 154 (Louvain, 1974) [hereafter *Anonymi auctoris chronicon*], §§237, 239 (pp. 35, 36).

See also Christopher MacEvitt, *The Crusades and the Christian World of the East: Rough Tolerance* (Philadelphia, 2008), pp. 41–43 and *passim*; Werner Seibt, "Philaretos Brachamios – General, Rebel, Vasall," in Καπετάνιος και Λόγιος/Captain and scholar: Papers in Memory of Demetrios I Polemis (Andros, 2009), pp. 281–95; Claude Mutafian, *La Cilicie au carrefour des empires*, 2 vols. (Paris, 1988), 1:370–72; Gérard Dédéyan, *Les Arméniens entre Grecs, Musulmans et Croisés: étude sur les pouvoirs Arméniens dans le proche-Orient Méditerranéen (1068–1150)*, 2 vols. paginated continuously (Lisbon, 2003), pp. 5–357, esp. pp. 17–73, 97–99, 195–206; Nicolas Adontz, "La famille de Philarète," in "Notes arméno-byzantines III," in *Études armeno-byzantines* (Lisbon, 1965), pp. 147–52, originally published in *Byzantion* 9 (1934), 377–82; Jean-Claude Cheynet, *Trois familles du duché d'Antioche*, in idem and Jean-François Vannier, *Études prosopographiques*, Byzantina Sorbonensia 5 (Paris, 1986), pp. 66–73; idem, *La société byzantine. L'apport des sceaux*, Bilans de recerche 3, 2 vols. (Paris, 2008), 2:390–410; Friedrich Hild and Hansgerd Hellenkemper, *Kilikien und Isaurien*, Tabula imperii Byzantini 5, 2 vols. (Vienna, 1990), 1:62–64; idem and Marcell Restle, *Kappadokien (Kappadokia, Charsianon, Sebasteia und Lykandos*, Tabula imperii Byzantini 2 (Vienna, 1981), pp. 105–8; Joseph Laurent, "Byzance et Antioche sous le curopalate Philarète," *Revue des études arméniennes* 9 (1929), 61–72; idem, "Des Grecs aux Croisés: étude sur l'histoire d'Édesse entre 1071 et 1098," *Byzantion* 1 (1924), 387–95, 397–99; C. J. Yarnley, "Philaretos: Armenian Bandit or Byzantine General," *Revue des études arméniennes*, n.s. 9 (1972), 331–53.

[12]   *Alexias*, VI.ix.2 (1:186), *Alexiade*, 2:64.

[13]   Jean-Claude Cheynet, "Les Arméniens de l'empire en Orient de Constantin X à Alexis Comnène," in *L'Arménie et Byzance: histoire et culture*, ed. Bernadette Martin-Hisard et al., Byzantina Sorbonensia 12 (Paris, 1996), pp. 67–78.

[14]   Now ruined, about 8 kilometres west of *Aplast'a* (Elbistan).

[15]   ME, II.60 (p. 138).

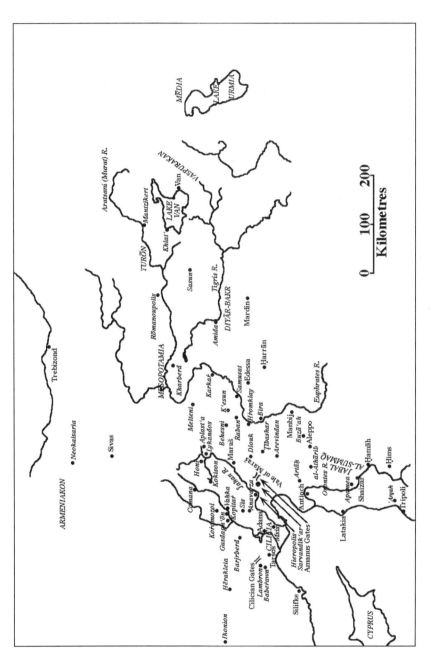

Map 1   The Armenian lands at the time of the First Crusade

Philaretos was awarded the highest dignities: first *sebastos*, soon to be restricted to the imperial family, then the dizzying *prōtosebastos*, testifying to how highly he was valued and which he must have obtained under Alexios, who created it. He occupied Antioch in 1078 but lost it to the Saljūqid of Rūm, Sulaymān ibn Qutalmïsh, in 1084, who in turn lost it in 1086 to Tāj al-Dawla Tutush, a brother of the Saljūqid sultan Jalāl al-Dawla Malik-Shāh. He continued to control lands and towns south and east from *Aplast'a* to Maraš and *Melteni* (Malatya), *K'esun* (Keysun), *Karkař* (Gerger), and Edessa until he submitted to Malik Shāh in 1086 and was left with only Maraš. He died sometime before 1097, when Maraš was already governed by a successor: T'at'ul. He was the last to hold the office of *Domestikos of the East* before the crusade and his realms fragmented after him.

Philaretos's seals make the *Alexiad*'s claim that he was *Domestikos of the East* before 1071 unlikely,[16] but they confirm beyond dispute that he was by the 1080s. They show a rise in his offices' importance and his dignities' heights from beginning to end of his career. Another Armenian, Khač'atur, was *doux* of Antioch from 1068–72, followed by Joseph Tarchaneiōtēs and Isaac Komnēnos.[17] Philaretos took it from Isaac in 1078 and was appointed *doux* and probably *domestikos* when he was reintegrated into the Byzantine system under Nikēphoros III Botaneiatēs. Michael Attaleiatēs said he was already a *kouropalatēs* at the time.[18]

Most confusion over his seals concerns those on which he has the dignity of *kouropalatēs*, which was appropriate to 1070 when Rōmanos IV entrusted Byzantine forces to him. It is assumed that he continued to hold this dignity during the reign of Michael VII. From 1078, however, both his dignities and offices rose spectacularly, indicating the important role that he played in the policies of Nikēphoros III and Alexios.[19] Being relics of a two-way correspondence, his seals show that Constantinople was concerned to keep alive imperial influence in his lands behind the main Turkish lines of penetration, where the invaders' presence was limited.[20] There is a strong context for a grant to Bohemond of his office and lands.

In practice, Philaretos was independent and at different times his realms looked like an Armenian principality or a rebel Byzantine regime. But after 1078 he returned to Byzantine political orthodoxy. Both Nikēphoros III and Alexios seem to have been generous with subsidies and neither was ever able to reach so far afield militarily. Philaretos's former office would have appealed to both Alexios and Bohemond in 1097, for their own different and particular reasons of course.

---

[16] See Appendix. Cheynet concludes that the *Alexiad* was mistaken; see *La société byzantine. L'apport des sceaux*, 2:406.

[17] MA (Pérez Martín), pp. 127–28, 215–16, idem (Bonn), pp. 172–74, 301; Nikēphoros Bryennios, *Hyle*, II.28 (p. 201). See Joseph Laurent, "Le duc d'Antioche Khatchatour 1068–1072," *Byzantinische Zeitschrift* 30 (1929–30), 405–11.

[18] See Cheynet in Cheynet and Vannier, *Études prosopographiques*, pp. 66–73.

[19] Cheynet, *La société byzantine. L'apport des sceaux*, 2:407–9.

[20] See Cheynet, "Les Arméniens de l'empire en Orient."

Turkoman bands moving west dominated the map of Anatolia in the 1080s. Imperial strategy was limited to stopgap defence, with little long-range action or long-term planning. Nikēphoros III denuded the East of troops for his bid for the throne and Alexios did so even more for his struggles with Robert Guiscard and the Pechenegs.[21] By 1097 the view south-east from Constantinople was bleak. Most of Anatolia was in Turkish hands. Further afield there were more promising areas for imperial recovery in Philaretos's old realms now in the hands of Armenian princes but, with Cilicia and Antioch in Turkish hands, these were inaccessible.

The imperial government would have desired very much to strengthen those princes east of the Orontes and Maraš by a man to replace Philaretos in a marcher lordship against the Turks and thus to give the Empire a chance to recover Cilicia and Antioch. The *Alexiad* specified as Bohemond's office precisely that which Philaretos had held a few years before. The Empire would not surrender Cilicia and Antioch but it could probably never recover lands further east in any case.

Bohemond was the obvious choice because he needed status and titles. In 1059 Robert Guiscard had repudiated his mother Alberada and married Sichelgaita of Salerno. When he left for Albania in 1081, he designated her son Roger as heir to the duchy and took Bohemond with him. He seems to have intended Roger to inherit Italy and Bohemond Balkan lands to be conquered. William of Malmesbury said that Bohemond induced Urban II to preach the crusade because he wanted to recover "*Illyricum et Macedoniam*," which his father had taken from Alexios and which were his since Roger had been given Apulia. This may well reflect Norman memory of the objective of the campaign of 1081–83. Analysis suggests that this was, in fact, the conquest not of Constantinople but rather of Balkan lands.[22]

Bohemond motive (margin annotation)

In 1074 Michael VII had granted to Robert the dignity of *nōbelissimos* and authority to grant that of *kouropalatēs* to one of his sons in return for an alliance and the marriage of Michael's son Constantine to one of Robert's daughters. Did Robert intend *kouropalatēs* for Bohemond? If so, that would have been known in Constantinople. Bohemond had fought Roger for years and had taken Apulia but could not become duke because their uncle, Roger of Sicily, was backing Roger.[23]

---

[21]   Nikēphoros Bryennios, *Hyle*, III.15 (p. 239); *Alexias*, III.ix.3 (1:110–11), *Alexiade*, 1:131.

[22]   William of Apulia, *Gesta Roberti Wiscardi*, in MGH SS 9:239–98, II.416–43 (p. 262); William of Malmesbury, *Gesta regum Anglorum: The History of the English Kings*, ed. and trans. Roger A. B. Mynors, completed by Rodney M. Thomson and Michael Winterbottom, 2 vols. (Oxford, 1998) [hereafter WM], IV.344 (1:594–95). See William B. McQueen, "Relations between the Normans and Byzantium 1071–1112," *Byzantion* 56 (1986), 441–42; Richard Upsher Smith, "*Nobilissimus* and Warleader: The Opportunity and the Necessity behind Robert Guiscard's Balkan Expeditions," *Byzantion* 71 (2001), 510–11, 515–16.

[23]   *Alexias*, I.x.2, (1:35), *Alexiade*, 1:37; Amatus of Monte Cassino, *L'ystoire de li Normant*, ed. Jacques-Joseph Champollion-Figeac, *L'ystoire de li Normant et la chronique de Robert Viscart* (Paris, 1835) [hereafter Amatus, *Ystoire*], VII.xxvi (p. 214); idem, *Chronique de Robert Viscart, loc. cit.*, II.i (pp. 301–2); Gaufredus Malaterra, *De rebus gestis Rogerii Calabriae et Siciliae comitis et Roberti Guiscardi ducis fratris eius*, ed. Ernesto Pontieri, RIS NS 5.1 (Bologna, 1928), III.xlii, IV.iv (pp. 82, 87). See also Hélène Bibicou, "Une page d'histoire diplomatique de Byzance au XIe siècle: Michel VII Doukas, Robert Guiscard et la pension de dignitaires," *Byzantion* 19–20 (1959–60), 43–75; Jonathan Harris, *Byzantium and the Crusades* (London and New York, 2003), pp. 27, 38–41; McQueen, "The Normans and Byzantium," pp. 429–32, 447–49; Jonathan Shepard, "'Father' or 'Scorpion'? Style and

To dangle a prestigious imperial office before Bohemond would be an obvious ploy for Constantinople, perhaps with the hope that the crusade would push aside the Turks of Anatolia and then to use Bohemond in its interests in Armenian lands.[24] It would not want him to gain Antioch but to use him further east would be another matter.

Moreover, the Saljūqids of Syria were in chaos. Malik-Shāh had died in 1092 leaving only minor sons. One of his wives, Turkān-Khātūn, persuaded the 'Abbāsid caliph to proclaim her own son, Nāṣir al-Dīn Maḥmūd, sultan, at the expense of his eldest son, Rukn al-Dīn Berk-yaruq. Tāj al-Dawla Tutush tried to take advantage of the resulting civil war but Berk-yaruq's troops defeated and killed him near *Rayy* in 1095. His son Riḍwān managed to seize Aleppo the next year, however, and his younger brother Duqāq then fled to their father's city of Damascus. The brothers were hostile and in Antioch Tutush's governor Yaghi-Siyan was resisting both. Moreover, the populace of Antioch was mostly Christian and that of Aleppo mostly Shī'ah. East of Edessa, Diyār-Bakr and *Amida* (Diyarbakir) and Mardin were held in fief from Berk-yaruq by Sökman ibn Artuq.

For Alexios, there was a chance to revitalize an ancient attachment to the lands of *Kommagēnē*. For Bohemond, there was a chance to replace a recent predecessor in a familiar office backed by imperial authority and riches. According to the *Alexiad*, Alexios offered exactly that: very large sums of gold and riches.[25]

Even if Bohemond requested it, rather than Alexios offering it as we believe, that would not influence the argument. The imperial government would have seized the moment rather than prevaricating. If Bohemond did make some such request, it would surely have been for the *Domestikaton of the West* rather than that of the East. No one else held that office in 1097 and it would have carried with it the lands for which he and his father had fought in the 1080s. Constantinople would no doubt have refused such a request by a potentially dangerous Norman, but surely he would have sought precisely that, even if he were savvy enough to know that it would be refused. Why seek an office and lands far off in eastern Anatolia and Mesopotamia rather than in the Balkans? If Bohemond were the initiator, he would surely have sought the *Domestikaton of the West*. But if the imperial government were the initiator, it would surely have offered the *Domestikaton of the East*.

We need not see the negotiations of 1097 as yet another example of those "artful ruses" common to both Byzantines and Normans.[26] Both parties could have entered into them in perfectly good faith, each in their own interests. But which Cretan would outwit the other? Whose interests would prevail?

Substance in Alexios's Diplomacy," in Mullett and Smythe, eds., *Alexios I Komnenos. I: Papers*, pp. 69, 76–79.

[24] Cf. France, "La stratégie Arménienne de la Première Croisade," p. 144: "Le rétablissement d'un tel territoire [the lands of Philaretos] attirait beaucoup Alexis, pour qui il servirait de base pour miner le sultanat de Nicée-Iconium et cela a été manifestement entrepris avec son consentement et son accord."

[25] *Alexias*, X.xi.5–6 (1:318–19), *Alexiade*, 2:232–33.

[26] See Emily Albu, "Bohemond and the Rooster: Byzantines, Normans, and the Artful Ruse," in *Anna Komnene and Her Times*, pp. 157–68. Albu does not discuss Alexios's and Bohemond's negotiations of 1097 as an example.

The Empire and "Barbarian" Generals   Balliol

Byzantinists will know well but crusade historians may not that it was perfectly in accordance with imperial practice to offer a renowned warrior such as Bohemond the *Domestikaton of the East*. Many "barbarians" from Armenia and Georgia, the steppes beyond the Danube, the Latin West, and elsewhere, some of whom had opposed the Empire previously, had been recruited regularly to fight for it.

As early as 1049 Hervé Frangopoulos commanded a Latin regiment sent against the Pechenegs. He demanded the dignity of *magistros* from Michael VI and retired to domains in the *thema* of *Armeniakon* when refused. From there he crossed into Muslim territory in *Mēdia* and was captured by the Marwānid *amīr* Naṣr al-Dawla Aḥmad. He was released later and a surviving seal is inscribed: "Hervé, *magistros*, *vestēs*, and *stratelatēs* of Anatolia, *Frangopoulos*," *stratelatēs* being a dignity for a military commander. Another seal discovered recently has been interpreted to suggest that he played a role regrouping Byzantine forces after *Mantzikert*.[27]

Also drawn to the Empire by military service, Robert Crispin rebelled and took refuge in the *thema* of *Armeniakon* when dissatisfied with dignities and gifts that Rōmanos IV gave him. After *Mantzikert* Michael VII granted him those sought and he served against Rōmanos after his release. He died, probably in 1073.[28]

Roussel de Bailleul, *Oursel* to the Byzantines, joined Robert Crispin around 1069–70. A seal bears the inscription: "Mother of God, lend help to your servant Oursel, *vestēs*, *Frangopoulos*." He became leader of the Normans in Anatolia after *Mantzikert* and tried to carve out a principality in *Armeniakon*. Captured by the

---

[27] John Skylitzēs, *Ioannis Scylitzae synopsis historiarum*, ed. Ioannes (Hans) Thurn, Corpus fontium historiae Byzantinae 5 (Berlin, 1973) [hereafter JS], Κωνσταντῖνος ὁ Μονομάχος.22 (pp. 467–69), Μιχαὴλ ὁ Γέρων.4 (p. 486); ME, II.17–19 (pp. 100–101). On Hervé, Robert Crispin, and Roussel de Bailleul, see also Gustave Schlumberger, "Deux chefs normands des armées byzantines au onzième siècle," *Revue historique* 16 (1881), repr. in *Récits de Byzance et des Croisades*, 2e série (Paris, 1922), 65–91; idem, *Sigillographie de l'Empire byzantin* (Paris, 1884), pp. 656–64; Jean-Claude Cheynet, "L'implantation des Latins en Asie Mineure avant la Première Croisade," in *Migrations et diasporas méditerranéenes (Xe–XVIe siècles)*, ed. Michel Balard and Alain Ducellier (Paris, 2002), pp. 117–22; idem, "Le rôle des Occidentaux dans l'armée byzantine avant la Première Croisade," in *Byzanz und das Abendland im 10. und 11. Jahrhundert*, ed. E. Konstantinou (Cologne, 1997), pp. 111–28; Raymond Janin, "Les Francs au service des Byzantins," *Echos d'Orient* 29 (1930), pp. 63–67; Jonathan Shepard, "The Uses of the Franks in Eleventh-Century Byzantium," *Anglo-Norman Studies* 15 (1992), 296–302; Alexander Kazhdan, "Latins and Franks in Byzantium: Perception and Reality from the Eleventh to the Twelfth Century," in *The Crusades from the Perspective of Byzantium and the Muslim World*, ed. Angeliki E. Laiou and Roy P. Mottahedeh (Washington, D.C., 2001), pp. 92–95; G. A. Leveniotis, *Το στασιαστικό κίνημα του Νορμανδού Ουρσελίου (Ursel de Bailleul) στην Μικρά Ασία (1073–1076)*, Εταιρεία Βυζαντινών Ερευνών 19 (Thessalonike, 2004); Werner Seibt, "Übernahm der französische Normanne Hervé (Erbebios Phrangopoulos) nach der Katastrophe von Mantzikert das Kommando über die verbleibende Ostarmee?" *Studies in Byzantine Sigillography* 10 (2010), 89–96.

[28] Amatus, *Ystoire*, I.viii–ix (p. 12); *De nobili Crispinorum genere*, in PL 150:735–44, col. 737; MA (Pérez Martín), pp. 93–95, 126–28; idem (Bonn), pp. 122–25, 170–73; Michael Psellos, *Chronographie ou histoire d'un siècle de Byzance (976–1077)*, ed. and trans. Émile Renauld, 2 vols. (Paris, 1926–28) [hereafter MPChr], ʹΡωμάνος Δʹ.xxxix–xl (2:169–70); Nikēphoros Bryennios, *Hyle*, I.24 (p. 134); *Skylitzēs continuatus*, pp. 134, 153; Zōnaras, *Epitomē*, XVIII.xv (4:217).

Turks and handed over to the Byzantines, but released in 1077, he helped the young Alexios Komnēnos put down John Bryennios's revolt but then joined Nikēphoros Botaneiatēs and perished mysteriously the following year, probably poisoned.[29]

The careers of many other Latin military leaders in the Empire did not involve rebellion and some are known only from their seals.[30] According to the *Alexiad*, Alexios lured Bohemond's half-brother Guy into imperial service during Robert Guiscard's campaigns. He was with Alexios at Philomēlion in 1098 but by 1107–8 was back in the West and joined Bohemond on the *Dyrrachion* campaign.[31]

Not only Latins held such commands. The Armenian Grigor Pahlawuni, known to the Byzantines as *Gregorios magistros*, was given the dignity of *magistros* by Constantine IX in 1044. He held it until his death in 1058 and became *doux* of *Vaspurakan* and *Tarōn* and later of *Mesopotamia*.[32]

The Greek orthodox Armenian Vasil son of Apuk'ap defended *Mantzikert* successfully against the Saljūqid Toghrïl I in 1054–55. After 1072 he became Philaretos's lieutenant and captured Edessa in 1078, becoming *doux* until his death in 1083. Because of his status and the traditional subordination of Edessa to Antioch and the *Domestikaton of the East*, dignities on his seals were arranged neatly one step below Philaretos's at any one time. They show a similar rapid inflation, from *vestarchēs* to *sebastos*.[33]

---

[29] MA (Pérez Martín), pp. 111–12, 136–42, 146–47, 151–52, 182–83, 192–95, 206–7; idem (Bonn), pp. 148–50, 184–93, 198–200, 206–7, 252–55, 268–72, 288–89; *Skylitzēs continuatus*, pp. 144, 147, 157–61, 175–76, 178, 180, 186; Nikēphoros Bryennios, *Hyle*, II.4, 14–25, 28, III.26 (pp. 146–49, 166–97, 200–201, 254–55); Zōnaras, *Epitomē*, XVIII.xiii–xiv, xvi, xviii, xix (4:212–13, 220–23, 226, 231); *Alexias*, I.i.1–iii.4, x.1, II.1.2 (1:11–17, 34, 55), *Alexiade*, 1:10–16, 36, 63; Amatus, *Ystoire*, I.ix–xvi (pp. 12–15). See also Jean-Claude Cheynet, "Sceaux de la collection Khoury," *Revue numismatique* 159 (2003), N° 20 (pp. 436–37).

[30] For some others, see Cheynet, "L'implantation des Latins," pp. 117–19.

[31] *Alexias*, VI.v.2, XIII.iv.5 (1:176, 395–96), *Alexiade*, 2:51, 3:102; *Gesta Francorum et aliorum Hierosolimitanorum*, ed. Louis Bréhier as *Histoire anonyme de la Première Croisade* (Paris, 1924) [hereafter *GF* (Bréhier)], IX[27] (pp. 142–45); Peter Tudebode, *Petri Tudebodi seu Tudebovis sacerdotis sivracensis, historia de Hierosolymitano itinere*, in *RHC Oc* 3:9–117 [hereafter PT (*Recueil*)], XI.iii (pp. 75–76); idem, *Historia de Hierosolymitano itinere*, ed. John H. and Laurita L. Hill, Documents relatifs à l'histoire des Croisades 12 (Paris, 1977) [hereafter PT (Hill)], XI (pp. 105–6); Tudebodus *imitatus et continuatus ex codice bibliothecæ casinensis, qui inscribitur Historia peregrinorum euntium Jerosolymam ad liberandum Sanctum Sepulcrum de potestate ethnicorum*, *RHC Oc* 3:165–229 [hereafter *HBS*], §LXXVIII (pp. 203–4); Ralph of Caen, *Gesta Tancredi in expeditione Hierosolymitana*, in *RHC Oc* 3:603–716 [hereafter RC], c. LXXII (pp. 658–59); Robert of Reims, *Historia Iherosolimitana*, in *RHC Oc* 3:717–882 [hereafter RR], VI.xvi (pp. 816–17). See also McQueen, "The Normans and Byzantium," pp. 445–47.

[32] ME, I.64, 77, 87 (pp. 56, 67–68, 74); Aristakēs Lastivertc'i, *History of Armenia*, trans. Marius Canard and Haïg Berbérian, *Récit des malheurs de la nation arménienne* (Brussels, 1973) [hereafter AL], §§X, XIII (pp. 51, 68); Vardan Arewelc'i, *Compilation*, §55 (pp. 193–94). See also Victor Langlois, "Grégoire Magistros," in *Collection des historiens anciens et modernes de l'Arménie*, 2 vols. (Paris, 1867–69), 1:401–3; idem, "Mémoire sur la vie et les écrits du prince Grégoire Magistros duc de la Mésopotamie, auteur arménien du XIe siècle," *Journal Asiatique*, 6ème série 13 (1869), 5–64.

[33] AL, §XVI (pp. 81–87); ME, II.3, 24, 71, 77 (pp. 87, 105, 142–43, 146); MA (Pérez Martin), pp. 35, 63; idem (Bonn), pp. 46, 83; JS, Βασίλειος καὶ Κωνσταντῖνος.43 (p. 363), Κονσταντῖνος ὁ Μονομάχος.19 (pp. 462–64); *Skylitzēs continuatus*, pp. 113–14. See also Michael Grünbart, "Die Familie Apokapes im

Even Turks entered imperial service.[34] A brother-in-law of Alp Arslan, called *Chrysoskoulos* by the Byzantines, defeated and captured Manuel Komnēnos but then entered Byzantine service and was given the dignity of *proedros*. He was with Rōmanos IV at *Mantzikert*, survived, and was still in Byzantine service in 1078.[35] The later Turkish corsair *amīr Tzachas*, or Çaka, was in Byzantine service during the reign of Nikēphoros III and was given the dignity of *prōtonobellisimos*.[36]

Alexios actually increased the use of "barbarian" warlords. Constantine Humbertopoulos may have been the Constantine Oumpertopoulos whose surviving seals bear the dignities of *nōbellissimos*, *prōtonōbellissimos*, *prōtoproedros*, *vestēs*, and *sebastos*, and the offices of *doux*, *stratēgos*, and *domestikos of the Uzes*.[37] Another was Roger, son of Dagobert, a Norman who revealed Robert Guiscard's invasion plans to the Byzantines. He remained in Alexios's service, was given the dignity of *sebastos*, and founded a noble Byzantine family: the *Rogerioi*. A seal that may be his survives.[38] Grigor son of Bakuran fought with Alexios in the Balkans against Robert Guiscard and the Pechenegs.[39] *Monastras*, who spoke Turkish, and the Oghuz Turk called *Ouzas* were two others.[40] The most famous such Turk was Tatikios, who became close to the young Alexios and was made *megas primikērios* after he seized the throne. He fought the Normans in the Balkans, the rebel Nikēphoros Diogenēs, commanded the regiment that went with the crusade to Antioch, and may have had a naval command against the Pisans.[41]

Lichte neuer Quellen," *Studies in Byzantine Sigillography* 5 (1998), 29–41; Ivan Jordanov, *Corpus of Byzantine Seals from Bulgaria. Vol. 2: Byzantine Seals with Family Names* (Sofia, 2006), pp. 56–59.

[34] See Charles M. Brand, "The Turkish Element in Byzantium, Eleventh–Twelfth Centuries," *Dumbarton Oaks Papers* 43 (1989), 1–25.

[35] MA (Pérez Martín), pp. 105–6; idem (Bonn), pp. 139–40; Nikēphoros Bryennios, *Hyle*, I.11–12, III.15–16 (pp. 100–104, 236–41); *Skylitzēs continuatus*, p. 141; Zōnaras, *Epitomē*, XVIII.xii (4:211). See also Joseph Laurent, "Byzance et les origines du sultanat de Roum," in *Mélanges Charles Diehl* (Paris, 1930), 1:177–82, p. 178; Brand, "Turkish Element in Byzantium," p. 2.

[36] *Alexias*, VII.viii.7 (1:225), *Alexiade*, 2:114. See Brand, "Turkish Element in Byzantium," pp. 2–3.

[37] *Alexias*, II.iv.7, IV.iv.3, VI.xiv.4, VIII.v.5, X.ii.6 (1:64, 127, 201, 247, 286), *Alexiade*, 1:74, 152; 2:83, 141, 146, 193; Jordanov, *Corpus of Byzantine Seals from Bulgaria. Vol. 2*, Nos 529–32 (pp. 312–15). See Janin, "Les Franks," pp. 68–69; Shepard, "Father or Scorpion," pp. 116–17; Marquis de la Force, "Les conseillers latins du basileus Alexis Comnène," *Byzantion* 11 (1936), 164–65.

[38] *Alexias*, I.xv.5, XIII.iv.4, ix.1, ix.8 (1:50, 395, 407–8, 410), *Alexiade*, 1:55, 3:101, 117, 120; AA, II.9 (pp. 74–75); Nicholas Kalliklēs, *Nicola Callicle Carmi*, ed. and trans. Roberto Romano (Naples, 1980), N° 19 (pp. 93–94), trans. pp. 141–42; Jordanov, *Corpus of Byzantine Seals from Bulgaria. Vol. 2*, N° 696 (pp. 395–97). See Janin, "Les Franks," p. 68; de la Force, "Les conseillers latins," pp. 161–62.

[39] *Alexias*, II.iv.6–7, IV.iv.1, vi.2, V.iii.2, VI.xiv.3–4 (1:63–64, 126, 132–33, 146–47, 200–1), *Alexiade*, 1:73–74, 150–51, 159, 2:14, 82–83. See Shepard, "Father or Scorpion," p. 116.

[40] *Alexias*, V.vii.3, VII.iii.6, ix.7, x.2, VIII.v.5, X.ii.7, iv.10, XI.ii.7–10, ix.4, xi.5, XII.ii.1, XIV.iii.1, v.7 (1:160, 211, 229, 230, 247, 287, 294–95, 327–29, 350, 358, 362, 435), *Alexiade*, 2:31, 97, 120, 121, 141, 194, 204, 3:14–16, 41, 48, 49, 56, 154–55, 168–69.

[41] Nikēphoros Bryennios, *Hyle*, IV.20 (pp. 287–88); *Alexias*, IV.iv.3, VI.x.2–xi.1, xiv.4–7, VII.iii.6, vii.3, IX.v.5, vii.1, ix.3, X.ii.6, XI.ii.4–5, iii.3–4, iv.3, ix.1–x.8 (1:126–27, 189–93, 200–2, 211, 221, 269–70, 272, 277–78, 286, 326, 330–33, 348–52), *Alexiade*, 1:151; 2:67–72, 83–86, 97, 109, 171, 175, 182, 193, 3:12–13, 17–18, 20, 40–45. See Brand, "Turkish Element in Byzantium," pp. 3–4. The naval

Alexios offering such a command to Bohemond in 1097 would have been nothing unusual but it would have embarassed Nikēphoros Bryennios or Anna Komnēnē writing later. Their hero offered imperial authority and resources to the Empire's most implacable foe. We suggest that they distorted an offer too well known to suppress completely by having Bohemond ask for the post and Alexios obfuscate, just as the *Gesta Francorum* distorted Peter Tudebode, or the text that it used, to paint a more hostile picture of Alexios,[42] and Ralph of Caen also distorted Bohemond's relations with Alexios in 1097.[43]

A Marcher Lordship East of Antioch

The *Alexiad* survives in only a few related manuscripts but the Latin sources are a world of multiple works, recensions, and versions. Editions of the various works are possible but the manuscript traditions are so fluid that variant readings often give important status to particular versions.

The *Gesta Francorum* said of the audience of 1097:

> After he had been lodged, the [malevolent] emperor sent for him {… lodged, he sent for him …} that he should come to talk (to talk, om.) together with him in private. … However, to the most valiant warrior Bohemond, whom he feared greatly since in the past he had often (often, om.) driven him with his army from the battlefield, he said that provided that he would swear to him freely, he would grant fifteen days' journey in extent and eight in width of land beyond Antioch.[44]

The grant is in all known manuscripts, including the oldest twelfth-century ones: Biblioteca Apostolica Vaticana, MSS *Reg. Lat.* 572 and 641. There are only small variants. Bongars supplied "*malignus*" to "*imperator*," presumably from the manuscript loaned to him by William Camden, which has never been identified; "*imperator*" is omitted in the abbreviated version of Cambridge, Corpus Christi, MS 281; and "*loqui*" and "*sepe*" are omitted in Vatican, MS *Reg. Lat.* 641.[45]

---

command against the Pisans is most improbable; see John H. Pryor, "A View from a Masthead: The First Crusade from the Sea," *Crusades* 7 (2008), 98.

[42] See Jean Flori, "De l'anonyme normand à Tudebode et aux *Gesta Francorum*: l'impact de la propagande de Bohémond sur la critique textuelle des sources de la première croisade," *Revue d'histoire ecclésiastique* 102 (2007), 717–46.

[43] See below p. 52 and n. 83.

[44] *GF* (Bréhier), II[6] (pp. 28–31): "Quo hospitato, imperator [*malignus imperator*, Bongars] misit pro eo {… *hospitato, misit pro eo*, … Cambridge, Corpus Christi, MS 281}, ut veniret loqui (*loqui*, om. Vatican MS *Reg. Lat.* 641) simul secreto secum. … Fortissimo autem viro Boamundo, quem valde timebat, quia olim eum sepe [*sepe*, om. Vatican MS *Reg. Lat.* 641] cum suo exercitu ejecerat de campo, dixit quoniam, si libenter ei juraret, XV dies eundi terre in extensione ab Antiochia retro daret et VIII in latitudine; …."

[45] Hagenmeyer claimed that "*loqui*" and "*sepe*" were omitted in Vatican, MS *Reg. Lat.* 572 also, but this was because he thought that the *Recueil* edition was of 572, when in fact it was of *Reg. Lat.* 641.

Peter Tudebode's *Historia de Hierosolymitano itinere* has two versions of the grant on two occasions. His account is fractured, repetitive, and inconsistent whereas that of the *Gesta Francorum* is unitary, elegant, and simple. Here at least, a compiler of the *Gesta* more probably reworked Tudebode rather than the reverse.[46] In three of the four extant manuscripts Tudebode wrote on the first occasion: "And when he [Bohemond] had been happily lodged, then the emperor enjoined on him that he prepare to talk privately with him. They both agreed with each other. The emperor in truth granted to Bohemond fifteen days' journey in length and eight in width of land of *Romania*."[47] The *Romaniæ*, "of *Romania*," included here referred to lands either under imperial control or known to have been so in the past and, as Jamison pointed out, could be used for lands as far east as the Euphrates.[48] We argue that those granted to Bohemond included lands east of the Euphrates and suggest as far east as the Tigris. Alexios's invitation to a private meeting was replicated in the *Gesta Francorum* but the grant of lands was not, at this point.

Later, Tudebode repeated the grant in the different terms of the *Gesta Francorum*:

However, to the most valiant warrior (reading *Fortissimo autem viro* with MS A) Bohemond, who he feared greatly in his heart because [previously] he had often driven him [with his army] from the battlefield, the emperor said that if he would freely swear

---

In fact *Reg. Lat.* 572 has both words (fols. 8v, l. 21 and 9r, l. 23) and reads as in n. 44. *Reg. Lat.* 641 omits both words (fols. 6v, l. 20 and 7r, l. 17) and reads as indicated in n. 44.

[46]   On Peter Tudebode and the *Gesta Francorum*, see most recently Susan Edgington, "The First Crusade: Reviewing the Evidence," in *The First Crusade: Origins and Impact*, ed. Jonathan Phillips (Manchester, 1997), pp. 57–77; Flori, "De l'anonyme normand"; John France, "The Anonymous *Gesta Francorum* and the *Historia Francorum qui ceperunt Iherusalem* of Raymond of Aguilers and the *Historia de Hierosolymitano itinere* of Peter Tudebode: An Analysis of the Textual Relationship between Primary Sources for the First Crusade," in *Crusade Sources*, pp. 39–69; idem, "The Use of the Anonymous *Gesta Francorum* in the Early Twelfth-Century Sources for the First Crusade," in *Clermont*, pp. 29–42; Jay Rubenstein, "What is the *Gesta Francorum* and who was Peter Tudebode?," *Revue Mabillon*, n.s. 16 (2005), 179–204. See also Evelyn Jamison, "Some Notes on the *Anonymi Gesta Francorum*, with Special Reference to the Norman Contingent from South Italy and Sicily in the First Crusade," in *Studies in French Language and Medieval Literature presented to Professor Mildred K. Pope* (Manchester, 1939), pp. 183–208, repr. in her *Studies on the History of Medieval Sicily and South Italy*, ed. Dione Clementi and Theo Kölzer (Aalen, 1992), pp. 275–300; Kenneth B. Wolf, "Crusade and Narrative: Bohemond and the *Gesta Francorum*," *Journal of Medieval History* 17 (1991), 207–16.

[47]   PT (*Recueil*), II.ii (p. 18), manuscript variants in square brackets: "Cumque feliciter hospitatus esset [taliter receptus fuisset, MS B], tunc [tunc, om. MS B acc. PT (Hill), p. 43] imperator mandavit pro eo [mandavit illi, MS D; mandavit ille, MS D acc. PT (Hill), p. 43] ut iret locutum secrete [secrete om. MS C acc PT (Hill), p. 43] cum eo. [ut veniret loqui cum eo, MS D] Concordaverunt se ambo. Imperator quidem permisit [ambo ita quod imperator permisit, MS C] Boamundo XV dietas terrae [om. terrae, MS C] in longitudine Romaniæ et octo in latitudine; ...." The second sentence is omitted in Paris, Bibliothèque nationale, MS Lat. 5135 from "... cum eo."

According to PT (*Recueil*), MS B (Paris, Bibliothèque nationale, MS Lat. 4892) turns the approach around to Bohemond: "Quumque taliter receptus fuisset (Bohemond), mandavit imperatori quatinus insimul colloquerentur. Tunc concordaverunt se ambo. Nam imperator promisit Boamundo quindecim dietas terræ in longitudinem Romaniæ et octo in latitudinem." The Hills read "*Cumque*" for "*Quumque*," "*imperator mandavit*" for "*imperatori mandavit*," and "*permisit*" for "*promisit*."

[48]   See Jamison, "Notes on the *Anonymi Gesta Francorum*," p. 287.

to him, he would grant fifteen days of riding in length and eight in width of land [of his] from beyond Antioch.[49]

Addition of *suae*, "of his," in Paris, Bibliothèque nationale, MSS Lat. 4892 and 5135 suggests that scribes understood that the emperor could dispose of all lands of *Romania*. The word is not in the London, British Library, MS Harley 3904 and Montpellier, Faculté de médicine, MS H142 manuscripts.

Ralph of Caen said that Bohemond was constrained to pay homage to Alexios, "but granted, however, as much of *Romania* in extent on which a horse would expend for crossing fifteen days in length and eight in width."[50] His use of "*per longum*" and "*per transversum*" for the "*in extensione*" or "*in longitudinem*" and "*in latitudine(m)*" of the *Gesta Francorum* and Peter Tudebode suggests that he was not using them at this point. He is said to have used no written sources.[51] He did use *Romania* three other times, however, referring to lands in Asia Minor lost to the Empire,[52] which raises the issue of whether he did know Tudebode. Comparison of all passages of the *Gesta Tancredi* referring to events also reported by Tudebode has, however, shown no other instances where Ralph used him.[53] His independent testimony to the grant to Bohemond therefore suggests that Norman circles in Antioch knew that Alexios had made it. Ralph had spoken with both Bohemond and Tancred and either or both of them may have told him about it. The grant is reported in all works associated with the Normans but by no one else except for Guibert of Nogent, who copied it but changed it.

The choice of words and word order of the compiler of the *Historia Belli Sacri* or *Historia peregrinorum euntium Jerusolymam* contained in Monte Cassino, MS 300 make it clear that at this point he was using Tudebode.[54] Realizing that Tudebode had repeated himself, however, he deleted the first version and retained only the second:

---

[49] PT (*Recueil*), II.viii (p. 22), manuscript variants in square brackets: "Fortissimo autem viro Boamundo dixit [*Facturum Boamundo dixit*, MS C; *Itaque dixit*, MS D] imperator, quem valde timebat in corde suo quia sæpe eum [*in corde quia jam sæpe eum*, MSS C, D] ejecerat [*cum suo exercitu ejecerat*, MSS C, D] de campo, quod si libenter ei jurasset, quindecim dies eundi terrae suae [om. *suae*, MSS C, D] in [om. *in*, MSS A, C] extensione ab Antiochia retro daret, et octo in latitudine." PT (Hill), p. 48, has no other variants. MS B (Paris, Bibliothèque nationale, MS Lat. 4892) has an abbreviated text: "Boamundo itaque dixit imperator, quem valde timebat (nam sæpe eum cum suo exercitu devicerat) quod si libenter jurasset, ei quindecim dietas terræ in extensione ab Antiochia daret, et octo in latitudine."

[50] RC, c. X (p. 612): "sed tamen tanta Romaniæ dimensione donatus, in qua equus dies quindecim per longum, octo autem expenderet per transversum." Ralph's translators thought that the grant was "not repeated in other crusade accounts," but have overlooked the other reports. See *The Gesta Tancredi of Ralph of Caen: A History of the Normans on the First Crusade*, trans. Bernard S. Bachrach and David S. Bachrach (Aldershot, 2005), p. 32, n. 27.

[51] RHC Oc 3:xli.

[52] RC, cc. CXXIII, CXLI, CXLVII (pp. 691, 705, 709).

[53] Cf. below, n. 83, where the report that Tancred crossed the Bosporos in secret in order to avoid taking an oath may have been derived from the *Gesta Francorum*.

[54] See also Rubenstein, "What is the *Gesta Francorum*," pp. 181–82.

However, to the most valiant man Bohemond, whom he feared greatly in [his] heart because previously he had often driven him with his army from the battlefield, the emperor said that if he would swear freely to him, he would grant [him] fifteen days land from beyond Antioch in length and eight in width.[55]

Peter the Deacon then incorporated the grant into his chronicles, interpreting it as to be made from the region of Antioch.[56]

Guibert of Nogent knew some version of the *Gesta Francorum*. All manuscripts of his *Gesta Dei per Francos* contain the grant with one very significant change: "He [Alexios] therefore promised to him that he would grant him land on this side of Antioch fifteen days in journey in length and eight no less in width."[57] Guibert changed "*ab Antiochia retro*" to "*citra Antiochiam*," probably having in mind Tancred gaining possession of Cilicia. In doing so, however, he made the passage useless for justifying Bohemond's attack on the Empire.

Only one of the seven manuscripts used for the *Recueil* edition of Baudri of Bourgueil's *Historia Jerosolimitana* has the grant:[58] "Also, to Bohemond, who he feared more than the others, he promised to grant land fifteen days journey in length and eight in width from Antioch beyond if he would freely make homage and an oath to himself." This is in Paris, Bibliothèque nationale, MS Lat. 5513, a manuscript compiled by a later twelfth-century reworker associated with the family of the lords of Amboise who put back into the text some material in the *Gesta Francorum* that Baudri had omitted.[59] Baudri either omitted the grant or he had a manuscript of the *Gesta* that did not contain it.

As we have them, all editions of Robert of Reims,[60] Raymond of Aguilers, and Fulcher of Chartres do not contain the grant.

The old and thorny question of relationships between texts and manuscripts of the *Gesta Francorum* and Peter Tudebode, and whether the *libellus* that Ekkehard of Aura saw in Jerusalem was an *Ur-Gesta*, as John France calls it, confronts us again. Whatever the case, there was not just one single text of the *Gesta*. Baudri of

---

[55] *HBS*, §XVIII (pp. 179–80).

[56] Peter the Deacon, *Chronica monasterii Casinensis IV*, ed. Hartmut Hoffmann, in MGH SS 34:458-6-7, c. 11 (p. 478): "…, insuper et Boamundo quindecim dierum terram in longitudine, octo autem in latitudine ex ista parte Antiochie daret."

[57] GN, III.iv (p. 142). Huygens signals no manuscript variations of any significance.

[58] At the Seventh Conference of the Society for the Study of the Crusades and the Latin East in Avignon, 27–31 August 2008, Stephen Biddlecombe, who is preparing a new edition of Baudri of Bourgueil, reported that 14 extant manuscripts are known. We do not know whether any of the seven new manuscripts have the grant of lands.

[59] Baudri of Bourgueil, *Historia Jerosolimitana*, RHC Oc 4:9–111 [hereafter BB], I.xx (p. 25, n. 8): "Boamundo etiam, quem plus quam ceteros metuebat, si libenter hominium et juramentum faceret, promisit ab Antiochia deinceps quindecim dietas terræ in longum et octo in latum dare." See also Préface, pp. xii–iii. On the manuscript, see Nicholas L. Paul, "Crusade, Memory and Regional Politics in Twelfth-Century Amboise," *Journal of Medieval History* 31 (2005), 127–41; Neil Wright, "Epic and Romance in the Chronicles of Anjou," *Anglo-Norman Studies* 26 (2004), 177–89, p. 182.

[60] At Avignon, Damien Kempf reported preparing a new edition of Robert of Reims. We do not know whether new manuscripts have been found.

Bourgueil's characterization of the author as a "*compilator*" rather than an "*auctor*" suggests that he knew that different versions were circulating.[61] That contained in Biblioteca Apostolica Vaticana, MS *Reg. Lat.* 641 and in other manuscripts derived from it has an emphasis on Robert of Normandy.[62] As Rubenstein says, "we might observe more guardedly that a text, or three very similar texts, in the *Francorum* tradition served as the source material for the later writers."[63] That some authors who used the *Gesta* or Peter Tudebode included the grant when others did not, but that all known surviving manuscripts of the *Gesta* and Tudebode did, makes it clear that there were other versions that did not. That Baudri of Bourgueil, Ekkehard of Aura, and Robert of Reims, as well as Fulcher of Chartres and his adaptator Bartolf of Nangis, all deliberately cut the grant, but that Guibert of Nogent included it but changed it, is impossible to believe. Versions of the *Gesta* and Peter Tudebode without the grant must have existed.[64]

This oft-repeated western report of the extent of lands granted to Bohemond by Alexios complements the *Alexiad*. We suggest that Alexios or one of his counsellors invented the phraseology to define the territories from the realms of Philaretos Brakhamios to be attached to the office of *Domestikos of the East*.[65] We will return below to the question of which directions were meant by "in length" and "in width." One objection must be disposed of first, however.

August Krey, 1928

In 1928, August Krey argued that the grant of lands was interpolated into the *Gesta Francorum* as propaganda for Bohemond's crusade against the Byzantine Empire. Peter Tudebode, Guibert of Nogent, and Baudri of Bourgueil used the *Gesta* and copied the passage. He did not consider why Tudebode gave it at two different times in somewhat different terms, why Guibert changed the terms, or why only the one Amboise manuscript of Baudri included it. Krey knew that the *Historia Belli Sacri* had it but drew no conclusions from that. He either did not know of, or else ignored, Ralph of Caen. We summarize his argument as follows:[66]

---

[61]   BB, Prologus (p. 10).

[62]   *GF* (Hill), Introduction, pp. xxxix–xl.

[63]   Rubenstein, "What is the *Gesta Francorum*," pp. 189, 194: "No one would deny that an earlier draft must lie behind the *Gesta*." Rubenstein's conclusion, p. 197, that the versions of the *Gesta* and of Peter Tudebode were derived from the *libellus* seen by Ekkehard of Aura is unnecessary.

[64]   See also Flori, "De l'anonyme normand," esp. pp. 740–42, who believes that there were at least two versions before Peter Tudebode's, which was then reworked for the *Gesta Francorum*. At Avignon, Marcus Bull, who is preparing a new edition of the *Gesta Francorum*, stated that for various reasons there must have been at least two versions of the *Gesta* prior to the extant one.

[65]   John France has suggested that the "interpolation" may have been based on Bohemond's own understanding of the reply to his request for the office. See his "Departure of Tatikios," p. 142.

[66]   August C. Krey, "A Neglected Passage in the *Gesta* and its bearing on the Literature of the First Crusade," in *The Crusades and other Historical Essays presented to D. C. Munro*, ed. Louis J. Paetow (New York, 1928), pp. 57–78. Paraphrase and quotation of Krey is tacit here.

The interpolated passage referred to Bohemond alone and was inserted between one referring to all the leaders and lamenting that they swore oaths to Alexios and another doing the same that seems to run on naturally from the first.[67]

There was heated disagreement over Antioch later but the *Gesta* never again referred to the grant. Hugh of Vermandois was sent to Constantinople to offer possession to Alexios and Bohemond presumably acquiesced, which was strange for someone who had been offered Antioch and its surrounds.

Ekkehard of Aura, who saw a *libellus* on the crusade in Jerusalem in 1101, which Krey accepted was the *Gesta*, mentioned negotiations between the emperor and the leaders but not lands. When he wrote (wrongly) that the leaders returned Nicaea to Alexios after its conquest and "had affirmed their oaths thus, [to the effect] that they would, if they should conquer [them], restore to its original rule whatever cities [had been] cut off from his empire; and they, in their turn, were in no doubt that they were succoured as much by royal forces as by [royal] finances within the same frontier [of the Empire],"[68] this may have come from the *Gesta* and have been cut to insert the "interpolation."

Bohemond advanced his claim to Antioch not on the grounds of the grant but rather on possession being granted to he who gained entry. The agreement to return conquered towns was null and void because Alexios had not met his commitments. Bohemond did not march on Jerusalem with the others for fear that Alexios would come to take Antioch since he had no right to it.

When Raymond of Saint-Gilles, Robert of Flanders, and Robert of Normandy forced Bohemond in September 1099 to abandon the siege of Latakia, which would certainly have lain within lands fifteen by eight days around Antioch, he did not attempt to assert rights under the grant.

The letter of Bohemond, Raymond, Godfrey, and others to Urban II from Antioch dated 11 September 1098 had in its final paragraph Bohemond's plea for Urban to confirm his title to Antioch; in Krey's translation: "Moreover, most holy father, you ought to separate us, sons obedient to you in all things, from the unjust Emperor who has made us many good promises, but has not at all carried

---

[67] The two passages are as follows, with the "interpolated" passage marked "…". *GF* (Bréhier) II[6] (p. 30): "Novissime vero congregati omnes maiores natu (natu, om. MS C²) qui Constantinopoli erant, timentes ne sua privarentur patria, repererunt in suis consiliis atque ingeniosis schematibus quod nostrorum duces, comites, seu omnes maiores imperatori sacramentum fideliter (fidelitatis MSS C², C³) facere deberent *(Reg. Lat. 641: debent)*. Quod [qui MS A¹, Bongars] omnino prohibuerunt, dixeruntque: 'Certe indigni sumus, atque justum [injustum, Bongars] nobis videtur nullatenus [ullatenus, MS C¹, Bongars] ei sacramentum jurare.' Forsitan adhuc a nostris majoribus sepe delusi erimus *(Reg. Lat. 641: eximus)*; ad ultimum quid facturi erunt? *(Bongars: erant)* Dicent quoniam necessitate compulsi volentes nolentesque [nolentes volentesque MS A¹, Bongars] humiliaverunt se ad nequissimi imperatoris uoluntatem. … Tam fortes et tam duri milites, cur hoc fecerunt? Propterea igitur *(MS C²: scilicet)*, quia multa [multi, MS C²] coacti erant necessitate."

[68] Ekkehard of Aura, *Hierosolymita*, RHC Oc 5:7–40 [hereafter EA], c. XIV (p. 22). Cf. Ekkehard of Aura, *Chronica. Recensio I*, ed. Franz-Josef Schmale and Irene Schmale-Ott, *Frutolfi et Ekkehardi chronica necnon anonymi chronica imperatorum*, Ausgewählte Quellen zur Deutschen Geschichte des Mittelalters 15 (Darmstadt, 1972), p. 148.

them out. For he has caused us all the ill and hindrance which he could."[69] As Krey put it: "Bohemond is not holding Antioch by virtue of a grant from Alexius. He is holding it by a breach of the general agreement which all the leaders had made with that emperor, and he is seeking to justify it by accusing the latter of an antecedent breach of contract."[70]

That Alexios did not instruct Greek garrisons of towns within the bounds of the grant, specifically Latakia, to surrender them to Bohemond suggests that there was no grant. Byzantine envoys sent to take over Antioch complained bitterly to the crusaders at *'Arqah* when Bohemond rejected them. Alexios then launched a determined assault on Cilicia and Antioch by land and sea in 1104.

All sources agree that Antioch was within lands to be returned to the Empire. The only issue was whether the crusaders could breach their obligations because Alexios had not fulfilled his.

By 1105 hostility to Alexios in the West had intensified and conditions were ripe to create a story of a grant to justify attacking the Empire on the grounds that Alexios had not kept his grant to Bohemond. It was interpolated into the *Gesta Francorum* as part of Bohemond's recruiting campaign in France and was taken from there by Peter Tudebode, Guibert of Nogent, and Baudri of Bourgueil. Krey did not explain Robert of Reims's failure to do so and merely observed that he did express anti-Byzantine sentiments.

Krey's argument has remained almost unchallenged for 80 years and even recently scholars have accepted that the passage's intent was to bolster Bohemond's claims to Antioch, although Lilie thinks that it was original and not a later interpolation.[71]

To the best of our knowledge,[72] only Ferdinand Chalandon, and René Grousset following him, and Evelyn Jamison long ago, Peter Charanis, David Douglas, and more recently Jonathan Shepard, Emily Albu, Jean Flori, Gennaro Maria Monti, and Rudolf Hiestand have suggested that Alexios may have made a grant to Bohemond. Marc Carrier and William McQueen argue that Krey's analysis was faulty but are not concerned with our issues.[73] Hans-Joachim Witzel and Hans Oehler argue on stylistic grounds that the passage was not interpolated, although

---

[69] August C. Krey, *The First Crusade: The Accounts of Eye-Witnesses and Participants* (Gloucester, MA, 1958), p. 195.

[70] Krey, "A Neglected Passage in the *Gesta*," pp. 63–64. Our own translation is below, p. 54.

[71] Thomas S. Asbridge, *The Creation of the Principality of Antioch, 1098–1130* (Woodbridge, 2000), p. 92; Harris, *Byzantium*, p. 64; Ralph-Johannes Lilie, *Byzantium and the Crusader States 1096– 1204*, rev. ed. (1988; Eng. trans., Oxford, 1993), pp. 9–10; idem, "Der Erste Kreuzzug in der Darstellung Anna Komnenes," in *VARIA II: Beiträge von A. Berger et al.*, Poikila Byzantina 6 (Bonn, 1987), pp. 49–148, at pp. 120–27; France, *Victory in the East*, p. 16, n. 48; Hiestand, "Boemondo I e la Prima Crociata," p. 68.

[72] We say so advisedly. No doubt we have overlooked someone.

[73] Marc Carrier, "Pour en finir avec les *Gesta Francorum*: une réflexion historiographique sur l'état des rapports entre Grecs et Latins au début du XIIe siècle et sur l'apport nouveau d'Albert d'Aix," *Crusades* 7 (2008), 22–31; McQueen, "The Normans and Byzantium," p. 453.

the author may have revised the text.[74] Rosalind Hill, John France, and Albu argue that the manuscript evidence does not support a case for a later interpolation.[75] If Bohemond's campaign lay behind it, the *Gesta Francorum* would not have distinguished between lands beyond Antioch and the city itself and would not have referred to his oath. Flori thinks it possible that Alexios granted Bohemond lands lost to the Muslims since the seventh century and no longer considered part of the Empire and Monti that Bohemond was promised that in the event of victory he would be entrusted with lands beyond Antioch.[76] Pasquale Corsi considers it possible that the imperial government sought to establish a series of buffer states on the eastern frontiers bound to the Empire by the oaths of the leaders.[77] Chalandon and Grousset considered the land grant a sop to Bohemond for denying him the *Domestikaton of the East*. Charanis thinks it quite possible that Alexios thought to create a Latin buffer state in the East under imperial suzerainty between the empire and Muslim territories. Hiestand argues that Bohemond sought to obtain lands and an office within the Byzantine structures. Douglas asks the rhetorical question whether it is conceivable that Alexios contemplated setting up Bohemond in a frontier "fief" to buttress Antioch against Turks to the East.[78] Most recently, Nicholas Paul has also registered scepticism.[79] We return to Jamison, below. Shepard's purpose is different to our own but we agree with his argument and summarize it as follows:[80]

> Bohemond's request for the *Domestikaton of the East* as reported by the *Alexiad* and the *Gesta Francorum*'s offer of a land grant have a comparable essence,

---

[74] Hans-Joachim Witzel, "Le problème de l'auteur des *Gesta Francorum et aliorum Hierosolymitanorum*," *Le Moyen Age* 61 (1955), 319–28; Hans Oehler, "Studien zu den «Gesta Francorum»," *Mittellateinisches Jahrbuch* 6 (1970), pp. 74–76.

[75] *GF* (Hill), p. x, n. 3; Emily Albu, *The Normans in their Histories: Propaganda, Myth and Subversion* (Woodbridge, 2001), p. 178; France, "The Departure of Tatikios," p. 142.

[76] Jean Flori, *Bohémond d'Antioche: chevalier d'aventure* (Paris, 2007), p. 107; Gennaro Maria Monti, *L'Italia e le crociate in Terra Santa*, 2nd ed. (Genoa, 1988), p. 73. In "De l'anonyme normand," pp. 737–38, Flori argues that the "interpolation" was meant to include Antioch: "Qu'elle [Alexios's promise] soit ou non plausible, la mention de cet engagement sert évidemment la propagande de Bohemond: Antioche lui appartient à la fois *de facto*, par droit de conquête et *de iure* par suite d'une promesse d'Alexis."

[77] Corsi, "Boemondo a Constantinopoli," p. 20.

[78] Ferdinand Chalandon, *Essai sur le règne d'Alexis Ier Comnène (1081–1118)* (1900; repr. New York, n.d.), p. 186; René Grousset, *Histoire des Croisades et du royaume Franc de Jérusalem*, vol. 1 (Paris, 1934), pp. 22–23; Charanis, "Aims of the Medieval Crusaders," pp. 128–29; Hiestand, "Boemondo I e la prima Crociata," pp. 80–81; D. C. Douglas, *The Norman Fate, 1100–1154* (Berkeley and Los Angeles, 1976), pp. 175–76, and cf. his *The Norman Achievement, 1050–1100* (London, 1969), p. 164.

[79] Nicholas L. Paul, "A Warlord's Wisdom: Literacy and Propaganda at the time of the First Crusade," *Speculum* 85 (2010), 541–42.

[80] Shepard, "When Greek meets Greek," pp. 219–27. Paraphrase and quotation of Shepard is tacit here.

even though they differ on initiation and detail.[81] Alexios may have dangled before Bohemond a high command or lands, or both.

Krey's thesis is at best unproven and needs modifying because: an interpolation would be expected to have Alexios swearing to a grant rather than merely saying that he would give one; "lands beyond Antioch" is equivocal and need not necessarily have included Antioch and an interpolation trying to establish Bohemond's title to the city would surely have specified it; that by 11 September 1098 Bohemond was not using the offer to bolster his claim to Antioch is inconclusive;[82] and Peter Tudebode representing Alexios making two successive grants may mean that he had two different sources and thought that there were two grants, one in *Romania* and one of lands beyond Antioch.

The author of the *Gesta* was not present at the private meeting and the report of an offer of lands beyond Antioch probably reflected rumours generated by Bohemond's long stay at Constantinople and familiarity with Alexios.[83]

Ralph of Caen contrasting Bohemond's cooperation to Tancred's intransigence may also reflect rumour of an offer of lands beyond Antioch.

In the *Gesta Francorum* laments over the oaths and the report of the offer are in a general description of the oath taking. The section can be criticized as a whole on both literary and historical grounds. It is ill-proportioned and the report of the offer is not glaringly out of place.

---

[81] Hiestand also considers the two accounts not irreconcilable. They may reflect two solutions proposed or two aspects of a single one. See Hiestand, "Boemondo I e la prima Crociata," p. 80.

[82] Referring to the letter from the leaders to Urban II; see below pp. 54–55.

[83] Shepard's judgement is based on Ralph of Caen; see RC, cc. X–XIII (pp. 612–14). Bohemond goes ahead to Constantinople and performs homage to Alexios. Tancred (and Ralph) lament over the leaders brought low by their oaths. Tancred crosses the Bosporos secretly to avoid swearing an oath and joins others heading for Nicaea. Bohemond is still in Constantinople. Tancred sends messengers to rebuke him. Bohemond follows when they return to Tancred.

Ralph's scenario elevated Tancred at Bohemond's expense. No crusader could cross the Bosporos without Alexios's knowledge. The report that Tancred crossed secretly to avoid taking an oath and joined others advancing on Nicaea may have been derived from *Gesta Francorum*, II [vii] (pp. 13–14). Peter Tudebode has nothing of this and has all forces crossing together after Tancred arrives; see PT (*Recueil*), II.i–ix (pp. 18–22); idem (Hill), pp. 43–48. The *Historia Belli Sacri* followed the *Gesta Francorum* because its compiler found nothing about this in Tudebode; see *HBS*, §XIX (p. 180). Albert of Aachen also said that Tancred crossed with his and Bohemond's forces but kept it secret from the emperor and also from Bohemond and Godfrey, which was obviously impossible; see AA, II.19 (pp. 90–91). Significantly, William of Tyre altered Albert's account to say merely that Tancred carefully avoided the presence and audiences of the emperor. WT, 2.15 (p. 181).

No evidence supports Ralph's assertion that Tancred crossed without Bohemond's knowledge or that Bohemond lingered on in Constantinople, except to organize supplies. The only explanation is that some sources interpreted Tancred's avoidance of Alexios as keeping his presence "secret." He certainly did avoid swearing an oath to Alexios but, according to the *Alexiad*, did so later at *Pelekanos* (Pendik) after the conquest of Nicaea. See *Alexias*, XI.iii.1–2 (1:329–30), *Alexiade*, 3:16–17. Of the Latin sources, only Ralph of Caen recorded this meeting with Alexios but it is confirmed by Stephen of Blois's first letter to Adela. See RC, cc. XVII–XVIII (pp. 618–20); *Epistulæ et chartæ ad historiam primi belli sacri spectantes/Die Kreuzzugsbriefe aus den Jahren 1088–1100*, ed. Heinrich Hagenmeyer (Innsbruck, 1901; repr. Hildesheim, 1973) [hereafter Hagenmeyer, *Epistulæ*], N° IV (p. 140).

That both the *Alexiad* and the *Gesta* represent Alexios giving Bohemond special treatment is suggestive and: "Somewhere behind the smoke of the rumour related by the *Gesta* there may lurk fire of a sort."

These are telling points but the argument may be taken farther. Krey was a pioneer in the history of the crusades and a fine historian. Yet, apart from evidence that we adduce in due course, his argument is so obviously riddled with errors and inconsistencies that it is hard to understand how it has remained unchallenged.

All sources except Guibert of Nogent and Peter the Deacon clearly specified lands "beyond" Antioch – that is, somewhere east across the Orontes. Together with others we reject Krey's assumption that the grant included Antioch and his entire argument collapses.[84] Why did he think that it did, when all the first-generation sources said clearly that it did not? This explains why Bohemond did not advance the grant in his claim to Antioch, why he did not raise it against sending Hugh of Vermandois to Constantinople, why the *Gesta Francorum* did not raise it again in the context of Antioch, why all agreed that Antioch was promised to be returned to the Empire, and why Alexios did not instruct the garrison of Latakia to hand it over to Bohemond and sought to gain possession of Antioch.

Moreover, if the grant was interpolated to justify attacking the Empire, why did the interpolator weaken his own argument by retaining statements about Alexios trying to ensnare the leaders by oaths and they being compelled to agree from desperate need? Presenting the grant as made without ulterior motive and accepted freely would have been far more effective.[85]

That Ekkehard of Aura, Baudri of Bourgueil, and Robert of Reims do not mention the grant is explained by the *libellus* seen by Ekkehard in Jerusalem, and the texts that Baudri and Robert had, not being the *Gesta Francorum* as we have it. Krey understandably thought there was only one original text of the *Gesta*, the now-extant text without the interpolation, but scholars have since revealed that other versions were circulating early in the twelfth century. That some contained the grant but others did not makes later interpolation impossible. Peter Tudebode's *Historia de Hierosolymitano itinere*, or its source, was certainly written originally before such an interpolation could have been made, rather than afterwards as Krey

---

[84] See Jamison, "Notes on the *Anonymi Gesta Francorum*," p. 286; Charanis, "Aims of the Medieval Crusaders," p. 129; Flori, "De l'anonyme normand," p. 719.

In *Bohémond d'Antioche*, pp. 108–9, Flori argues ingeniously that "*retro*" is an adverb governed by "*daret*," rather than a locative adjective governed by "*ab Antiochia*," and that the phrase "... quindecim dies eundi terrae in extensione ab Antiochia retro daret, et octo in latitudine" should read: "... he would give him in return lands ...." This forces the meaning to allow the possibility that Antioch may have been included. It also ignores the "*ab*" of "*ab Antiochia*" and Peter Tudebode's first reference and Ralph of Caen's, neither of which can be read to include Antioch since they do not mention the city. We consider that the traditional reading of the text should stand.

[85] Pointed out by Susan Palmieri in "Heroes and Villains: Bohemond, Alexius and the Question of Antioch in Propaganda and Myth" (IV-Honours thesis, Sydney, 2006), pp. 9–10.

assumed.[86] Versions without the grant used by Ekkehard, Baudri, Robert of Reims and others were circulating before it could have been made. Ekkehard's narration of the crusade's passage through Constantinople containing the reference to the *libellus* is so different to the now-extant *Gesta* and Peter Tudebode that he cannot have seen anything related to them.[87]

The supposed request in the letter to Urban II of 11 September 1098 ("you should separate us, sons obedient to you in all things, most pious father, from the unjust Emperor who promised to us many benefits but did the very least. For he did to us all the mischiefs and whatever hindrances he was able to do"),[88] can not be a request by Bohemond to legitimize his rule in Antioch both because the grant never included Antioch and also because of the manuscript tradition.[89]

The request is in a final paragraph, clearly appended to the letter because the person changes from third to first, in only one surviving manuscript. In 1901 Hagenmeyer said that he had edited the letter, with the appendix, from two manuscripts and a number of editions. The manuscripts are Florence, Biblioteca Medicea Laurenziana, MS Plut. LXV, 35, fol. 3 and Rome, Biblioteca Apostolica Vaticana, MS *Reg. Lat.* 547, fols. 189v–190r, neither of which contains the appendix, as Hagenmeyer said.[90] In fact he must have added it from Paris, Bibliothèque nationale, MS Lat. 2827, fol. 129, as he said in 1913 in his edition of Fulcher of Chartres's *Historia Iherosolymitana*.[91] This manuscript does not contain the *Historia*. Krey did not use Hagenmeyer's edition of the letter in the edition of Fulcher. The letter is also found without the appendix in all first recension manuscripts of the *Historia*, except for London, British Library, MS Reg. 5 B XV, but in no second recension manuscripts.[92] It is Book I.xxiv, sandwiched between Adhemar of Le Puy's death and the sending of Hugh of Vermandois to Constantinople and the forces' recovery of their strength.

There are two other versions of Fulcher's *Historia*, the first attributed to Bartolf of Nangis and known as the *Gesta Francorum Iherusalem expugnantium*. It ended in 1106 at II.xxxiii and is thought to have been compiled in the Holy Land at that

---

[86]   Even if one accepts that the *Gesta* and Peter Tudebode were based on a now-lost common source, rather than Tudebode being based on the *Gesta* or vice versa, that does not affect the argument. Note that in his report of the siege of Jerusalem Tudebode wrote: "Credendus est qui primus hoc scripsit, quia in processione fuit et oculis carnalibus vidit, videlicet Petrus [sacerdos] Tudebovis Sivracensis." See PT (*Recueil*), XIV.vi (p. 106); idem (Hill), p. 138. The very idea that Tudebode, who was on the crusade and at Jerusalem, did not write his text until after the *Gesta Francorum* had been revised and interpolated and then used it as his source for the land grant is absurd.

[87]   EA, c. XIII (p. 21).

[88]   Hagenmeyer, *Epistulæ*, N° XVI (pp. 161–65). On the letter, see also Paul, "A Warlord's Wisdom," pp. 555–56.

[89]   Hiestand also considers the paragraph a later interpolation, on some of the same grounds as we: see "Boemondo I e la prima Crociata," pp. 84–85.

[90]   Hagenmeyer, *Epistulæ*, pp. 161 and 165, n. d. Also pointed out by Hiestand, "Boemondo I e la prima Crociata," p. 68, n. 6.

[91]   FC, I.xxiv.14 (p. 258, n. m). The two texts in the *Epistulæ* of 1901 and Fulcher's *Historia* of 1913 are absolutely identical, all the way down to the punctuation.

[92]   FC, I.xxiv.1 (p. 258, n. h).

time. The other, Codex L (Cambridge University Library, MS Kk. 6. 15, fols. 1r–76r), continued to 1124.[93] Both proceed directly from the death of Adhemar and sending Hugh to Constantinople to the forces' recovery, and do not have the letter.[94] Fulcher's original chronicle cannot have contained it since Bartolf of Nangis and Codex L did not replicate it. He must have added it in the first recension completed in 1124 but the compiler of Codex L used a manuscript like London, British Library, MS Reg. 5 B XV that did not have it. Fulcher must have realized that it was not genuine and deleted it from the second recension. The request to Urban to release the leaders from their obligations cannot be true.

Krey also ignored evidence that Alexios and Bohemond did indeed develop a special relationship.[95] Only Bohemond is reported to have had a private audience.[96] The *Alexiad* said that he submitted readily to Alexios and swore an oath. Albert of Aachen said that he needed little coaxing and swore not to retain imperial lands conquered except with Alexios's favour and consent, something not said of any others. The *Gesta Francorum*, Peter Tudebode, and Raymond of Aguilers all said that he threatened to take Alexios's part if Raymond refused to swear and, according to Tudebode and Raymond, Alexios offered him to Raymond as a pledge. The *Gesta*, followed by Baudri of Bourgueil, Robert of Reims, the *Historia Belli Sacra*, the *Historia Nicæna*, and Orderic Vitalis all said that he did stay on in Constantinople to organize supplies. The *Alexiad* said that he persuaded the others to wait upon Alexios at *Pelekanos* (Pendik), and Ralph of Caen that he induced Tancred to swear. The reports are somewhat contradictory but so many suggest a special relationship that it is difficult to believe that nothing lay behind them.[97]

Moreover, the foundations of this relationship were probably laid before Bohemond even began his march. The *Gesta Francorum*, followed by the *Historia Belli Sacra*, has a curious passage in which Bohemond's men want to attack a town full of provisions but Bohemond forbids it both for the sake of the jurisdiction of the land and for that of the "*fiducia*" of the emperor.[98] One common medieval

---

[93] Not used by Hagenmeyer and found only in the notes to the edition of Fulcher in *RHC Oc* 3:311–485 [hereafter FC²], esp. p. 466, n. 13.

[94] FC², I.xiii (p. 350, n. e); Bartolf of Nangis, *Gesta Francorum Iherusalem expugnantium*, in *RHC Oc* 3:487–543 [hereafter BN], c. XXIV (p. 506).

[95] Also pointed out by Palmieri in "Heroes and Villains," pp. 49–50.

[96] The *Gesta Francorum*'s claim that Godfrey and Baldwin of Boulogne were also present at this private audience is obviously ridiculous. It would hardly be private if they were; see *GF* (Bréhier), II[6] (p. 28). Peter Tudebode does not say they were; see n. 47 above. The *Historia Belli Sacra* follows the *Gesta Francorum*; see *HBS*, §XIII (p. 178). No other source reports a private meeting.

[97] *Alexias*, X.xi.5, XI.iii.1 (1:318–19, 329), *Alexiade*, 2:232–33, 3:16; AA, II.18 (pp. 88–91); BB, I.xxi (p. 25); *GF* (Bréhier), II[6–7] (32–34); RR, III.i (p. 755); *Balduini III Historia Nicæna vel Antiochena*, in *RHC Oc* 5:133–85 [hereafter HN], c. XIV (p. 146); PT (*Recueil*), II.ii, vii (pp. 18, 21); idem (Hill), pp. 43, 46–47; *HBS*, §XIX (p. 180); Raymond of Aguilers, *Historia Francorum qui ceperunt Iherusalem*, in *RHC Oc* 3:231–309 [hereafter RA], c. II (p. 238); RC, c. XVII (p. 618); Orderic Vitalis, *The Ecclesiastical History*, ed. and trans. Marjorie Chibnall, 6 vols. (Oxford, 1968–78) [hereafter OV], IX.6 (5:51).

[98] *GF* (Bréhier), II[5] (p. 10): "...; sed vir prudens Boamundus noluit consentire, tantum pro justicia terre quantum [tam ... quam, MSS C] pro fiducia imperatoris."; *HBS*, §XI (p. 178): "Sed vir

meaning of *fiducia* was a solemn promise, even an oath of fealty. It suggests that Bohemond already had an agreement with Alexios, as Guibert of Nogent thought because he turned the *Gesta's* "*fiducia*" into "agreements made with him recently through messengers." Baudri of Bourgueil also said that Bohemond had sent envoys to Alexios and prohibited the attack so that Alexios "would not decide anything against him by mistake."[99] William of Tyre reported much later that a legation from Bohemond had reached him and that he knew that Bohemond was en route.[100] Given the two men's past history, it only makes sense that Bohemond would have sent to Alexios announcing his coming, requesting provision of markets, and undertaking to keep his forces under control and to avoid pillaging.[101]

Finally, if we are correct and Bohemond decided to take his crusade to the Balkans rather than to Antioch only after he returned from France to Italy in August 1106,[102] then Krey's scenario for an interpolation collapses completely.

Krey's argument that the passage granting Bohemond lands fifteen days' journey in length and eight in width was "interpolated" in 1105–6 to portray Alexios breaking his word in trying to recover Antioch cannot be sustained. He distorted the evidence of the *Gesta* and other sources that the lands lay beyond Antioch, misdated Peter Tudebode, and ignored Ralph of Caen. His thesis falls apart at every turn and its own arguments can be turned against it. Moreover, the Treaty of *Deabolis* of 1108, which only Evelyn Jamison and Jonathan Shepard have considered in this context,[103] provides clear evidence that the Byzantines knew that Bohemond and Alexios had concluded a "treaty" of their own in 1097.

---

sapiens Boamundus noluit consentire pro justitia terræ et fiducia imperatoris, …." The clause does not occur in Peter Tudebode.

[99] GN, III.iii (p. 140): "At vir ille illustris id vetuit, partim ne terrae iura turbaret, partim ne imperatoris tenerum adhuc animum offenderet, immo ne pacta cum eo per internuntios recens facta cassaret"; BB, I.xix (p. 24): "Boemundus enim suos [legatos] jam ad eum [Alexios] direxerat. … Boamundus autem illud viriliter prohibuit, ne forte imperator in eo aliquid [aliquem MS G] inveniret perperam; …."

[100] WT, 2.11 (p. 174): "Imperator igitur cum suis familiaribus et domesticis anxius plurimum, … tum quia domini Boamundi affuisse legationem eumque in proximo venturum cognoverat, …." William's authority for this is unknown but he did know the *Gesta Francorum*, Baudri of Bourgueil, and the *Historia Belli Sacri* and may well have put two and two together.

[101] *Li estoire de Jerusalem et d'Antioche*, which survives in a single manuscript dated to the second half of the thirteenth century, reports a meeting of the Norman barons at Bari deciding to send envoys to Alexios to seek safe conduct for Bohemond and Tancred. As it stands the report is a fantasy, but it may well reflect a memory of this actually having been done. See *Li estoire de Jerusalem et d'Antioche*, in *RHC Oc* 5:621–48, §V (pp. 627–28).

[102] See below, pp. 54–55.

[103] See Jamison, "Notes on the *Anonymi Gesta Francorum*," p. 287. Jamison thought that the "pact" of 1097 referred to in the treaty was "the agreement by which imperial territory was to be handed back to the emperor on its conquest by the Crusaders." She made no connection to the *Domestikaton of the East* and did not notice that the treaty referred to a written document in 1097. Shepard also considers the treaty but with reference to the oaths rather than the grant. He considers that the *Alexiad's* reference to a written treaty was to a written version of Bohemond's oath and that the other leaders would also have had them. He does point to a special relationship between Bohemond and Alexios in 1097 and to Bohemond alone performing liege homage in 1097 but does not make the connection to a written

The Treaty of *Deabolis*

The Dānishmendid *amīr*, Amīr Ghāzī Gümüshtigin, captured Bohemond in August 1100 when he raced to relieve the Armenian ruler of *Melteni*, Khawril or Gabriel, which suggests some special relationship between the two. He was taken into captivity far to the north at *Neokaisaria* (Niksar), together with Richard of the Principate. Albert of Aachen said that Alexios offered Amīr Ghāzī 260,000 bezants for Bohemond, "wishing him to perish either in eternal exile or in perpetual damnation, so that he could no longer harm his realm by any machination." The offer failed, supposedly because the Saljūqid sultan of Rūm was refused a share and the Dānishmendids and Saljūqids then came to blows. Bohemond then persuaded Amīr Ghāzī to accept 100,000 bezants and sent messages to relatives and friends in Antioch, Edessa, and Sicily to raise the money and send it to *Melteni*.[104] The kernel of all this does make sense. Alexios would surely have tried to take advantage by gaining posession of Bohemond and compelling him to surrender Antioch. The *Alexiad* would not mention his imprisonment since neither Nikēphoros nor Anna would want to record his failure. Orderic Vitalis, however, had the same story and said explicitly that Alexios's motive was that Bohemond had seized Antioch.[105] He is not known to have used Albert of Aachen and this may reflect Norman memories. So also may be the story in the "miracle of Richard the Norman," Richard of the Principate, that he was ransomed into the emperor's custody in Constantinople and the later tirade against the emperor attributed to Richard in the "miracle of Bohemond."[106] Moreover, the Latin sources are confirmed by Theophylakt of Ochrid's letter of May–September 1103 to Gregory Taronitēs saying that Alexios

---

treaty and the *Domestikaton of the East*. See Shepard, "When Greek Meets Greek," pp. 236–41. Jean Flori affirms that there is no evidence that Alexios and Bohemond had a "pacte particulier" in 1097, overlooking the evidence of the Treaty of Deabolis, which he later says "annule donc totalement le traité antérieur conclu en 1097." See *Bohemond d'Antioche*, pp. 111, 284.

[104] AA, IX.33–36 (pp. 680–87). On Bohemond's captivity and release, see also Yvonne Friedman, "Miracle Meaning and Narrative in the Latin East," in *Signs, Wonders, Miracles: Representations of Divine Power in the Life of the Church*, ed. Kate Cooper and Jeremy Gregory, Studies in Church History 41 (Woodbridge, 2005), pp. 123–34. Claudio Carpini accepts that Alexios did offer the 260,000 bezants for Bohemond; see "La prigionia di Boemondo," in *Boemundo: storia di un principe Normanno*, pp. 67–73, at p. 69. So also does Giuseppe Morea; see *Boemondo d'Altavilla*, p. 80.

[105] OV, X.24 (5:354–55).

[106] *Vita et miracula S. Leonardi Nobiliacensia*, in *Acta sanctorum*, 6 November (November, Tomus III), (Brussells, 1910), pp. 160, 164. Matthew of Edessa reported that Richard was given to Alexios in return for a great sum of money when Bohemond was released; see ME, III.14 (p. 192).

The story of Richard of the Principate's release to Alexios and his subsequent release by him upon the intervention of St Leonard cannot be true but may well reflect a story of Alexios trying to ransom Bohemond into his hands. See A. Poncelet, "Boémond et S. Léonard," *Analecta Bollandiana* 21 (1912), 35–36, n. 5. George Beech has tried to reconcile the stories of Richard's release into Alexios's custody but in our opinion they cannot be reconciled; see "A Norman-Italian Adventurer in the East: Richard of Salerno, 1097–1112," *Anglo-Norman Studies* 15 (1992), 25–40, esp. p. 33. Orderic Vitalis, who has his own fantastic tale about how Bohemond was released, is clear that Richard was released with Bohemond and that they went to Antioch together. See OV, X.24 (5:377). Moreover, why would Alexios want to buy Richard? He would have wanted Bohemond. And why would Amīr Ghāzī let Bohemond go free with

had tried to ransom an unnamed Frank, probably Bohemond, with a view to reducing him to servitude.[107]

Bohemond was released in May 1103 at *Melteni* after the ransom was paid. Albert said that it was raised in Antioch, Edessa and Sicily but Matthew of Edessa and Vardan Arewelc'i that it was was raised by Goł Vasil and that Goł contributed 10,000 *dahekans* himself. Michael the Syrian and Ibn al-Athīr reckoned it at 100,000 dinars. Ralph of Caen, however, said that it was only 10,000 *Michaels*, Byzantine *hyperpyroi* of the reign of Michael VII but meaning simply *hyperpyroi*, and that Baldwin II of Edessa and Patriarch Bernard of Valence of Antioch gathered it. The *Miracula S. Leonardi* said that it was only 5,000 bezants and concocted a fantastic story about how it was paid. The *Historia Belli Sacri* said that it was 100,000 *Michaels* and that it was raised in Antioch.[108] Most probably it was indeed gathered in Edessa, the Armenian lands, and Antioch. It was certainly paid over by Khawril at *Melteni* and his involvement and that of Goł Vasil again underlines a special relationship between Bohemond and these Armenian princes.

In the autumn of 1104 Bohemond left Antioch for the West. On 7 May 1104 Shams al-Dawla Jokermish of Mosul and Sökmen ibn Artuq of Mardin had defeated Bohemond, Tancred, Baldwin II of Edessa, and Joscelin of Courtenay, count of *Turbessel* (Ṭlbashar), at Ḥarrān and captured Baldwin and Joscelin. Riḍwān of Aleppo had then invaded the eastern parts of the principality and forced its garrisons to evacuate back to the Orontes. At the same time Alexios had sent *Monastras* to occupy Cilicia and a fleet under Kantakouzēnos to occupy Latakia. Ralph of Caen said that Bohemond left to raise forces amongst "the Gauls" and that he stripped Antioch of its wealth for the purpose and handed the city to Tancred. Then he has Bohemond add: "The intercessions of the blessed Leonard have set me free: either I shall fulfill the vow of visiting him or I shall die aforetime."[109]

---

only a small ransom but release Richard to Alexios for a great deal when he could have got ten times what he would for Richard?

[107] The letter is one of three problematic letters by Theophylakt to the rebel Gregory Taronitēs and the Frank referred to is unnamed; but Bohemond fits the bill. Theophylakt of Ochrid, *Theophlacti Achridensis Epistulae*, ed. Paul Gautier, Corpus fontium historiae Byzantinae 16/2 (Thessalonike, 1986), Nº 81 (p. 430). See also Alice Leroy-Molinghen, "Les lettres de Théophylacte de Bulgarie à Grégoire Taronite," *Byzantion* 11 (1936), 589–92; Margaret Mullett, "The Madness of Genre," *Dumbarton Oaks Papers* 46 (1992), 239–43.

[108] AA, IX.36 (pp. 686–87); ME, III.14 (pp. 191–92); MSyr, XV.viii (3:189); Vardan Arewelc'i, *Compilation*, §65 (p. 200); Ibn al-Athīr, *The Chronicle of Ibn al-Athīr for the Crusading Period from al-Kāmil fī'l-ta'rīkh. Part 1: The Years 491–541/1097–1146, The Coming of the Franks and the Muslim Response*, trans. Donald S. Richards (Aldershot, 2006) [hereafter Ibn al-Athīr, *Al-Kāmil*], A.H. 495 (p. 60); RC, c. CXLVII (p. 709); *Vita et miracula S. Leonardi Nobiliacensia*, p. 168; *HBS*, §CXXXIX (p. 228).

[109] RC, cc. CXLVIII–CLIII (pp. 710–14). See also *Alexias*, XI.x.9–xi.7 (1:352–55), *Alexiade*, 3:45–49; AA, IX.38–47 (pp. 688–703); WT, 11.1 (p. 495); FC, II.xxvi–xxvii, (pp. 464–77); *HBS*, c. CXL (p. 228); ME, III.20 (p. 194); A. S. Tritton, "The First and Second Crusades from an Anonymous Syriac Chronicle," *Journal of the Royal Asiatic Society* 65 (1933), 69–101, 273–305 [hereafter *Anonymous Syriac Chronicle*], pp. 78–80; Ibn al-Qalānisī, *Dhayl ta'rīkh Dimashq*, trans. H. A. R. Gibb as *The Damascus Chronicle of the Crusades* (London, 1967) [hereafter Ibn al-Qalānisī, *Dhayl*], pp. 60–61;

The right-hand door of Bohemond's tomb at Canosa cathedral has two panels in the middle. The upper shows two figures in oriental robes kneeling in prayer to a now-effaced figure above. The lower shows three figures, again in oriental robes. The middle one holds the left hand of the left-hand one and gestures farewell with his right. The right-hand figure is separated from them and is half turning around to look back and waving goodbye with his right hand. Flori argues convincingly that the upper scene represents Bohemond and Richard of the Principate praying to St. Leonard in prison and the bottom one Bohemond departing and confiding Antioch to Tancred while Richard of the Principate goes ahead to prepare the way,[110] as indeed Guibert of Nogent said that he saw him do.[111]

After landing in Apulia at Bari, Bohemond crossed into France and went first to Noblac to offer silver chains to St. Leonard,[112] after which he went north and married Constance, the daughter of Philip I of France and Berta of Holland, at Chartres around the end of April 1106. At the same time Philip's daughter by Bertrada of Montfort, Cecilia, was betrothed to Tancred. She sailed for the East later in the year and became princess of Antioch.[113]

The primary purposes of Bohemond's return to the West were to offer thanks to St. Leonard and to cement political relations between France and Antioch. During his journey he promoted constantly a new crusade. He visited Paschal II in Rome and was given a papal banner and a renowned crusade preacher, Bishop Bruno of Segni, to accompany him as papal legate. He complained incessantly about the Byzantines throughout his travels and returned to Apulia with Constance in August 1106.[114] He certainly sought help against the Byzantines because "Bartolf of Nangis" said that he did and his adaptation of Fulcher of Chartres breaks off in 1106, before Bohemond's assault went in.

His assault would eventually be directed against the Balkans, but when that objective was decided upon is unclear. Everything suggests that when he left Antioch it was to raise help for the principality in the East. Only that explains why Paschal II supported him. Historians have either accepted that Paschal supported a

---

Kamāl al-Dīn Abū 'l Qāsim 'Umar ibn al-'Adīm, *Zubdat al-ḥalab fī ta'rikh Ḥalab*, extracts in *RHC Or* 3:571–690, p. 592; Ibn al-Athīr, *Al-Kāmil*, A.H. 497 (pp. 79–80).

[110]   Flori, *Bohémond d'Antioche*, pp. 294–99.

[111]   GN, III.2 (p. 138). See also OV, X.24 (5:377).

[112]   *HBS*, c. CXL (p. 228); BN, c. LXV (p. 538); OV, XI.12 (6:68–69).

[113]   GN, VII.xxxvii (p. 337), a passage added to Guibert's *Gesta Dei* by a later scribe, preserved only in MS F, Florence, Biblioteca Medicea Laurenziana, Ashburnham (Libri) 1054, fol. 90v. See also FC, II.xxix (pp. 482–83); *HBS*, c. CXLI (pp. 228–29); *Narratio Floriacensis de captis Antiochia et Hierosolyma et obsesso Dyrrachio*, in *RHC Oc* 5:356–62 [hereafter *NF*], §XII (p. 361); OV, XI.12 (6:70–73); WM, IV.387 (1:693); Suger of Saint-Denis, *Vita Ludovici grossi regis*, in *Oeuvres complètes de Suger*, ed. A. Lecoy de la Marche (1867; repr., Hildesheim and New York, 1979), pp. 1–149, c. IX (pp. 29–30); WT, 11.1 (p. 495). ME, III.20 (p. 194) has Bohemond marrying Adela of Blois, who was instrumental in arranging the marriage.

[114]   *HBS*, c. CXL (p. 228); BN, c. LXV (p. 538); Caffaro de Caschifelone, *Annales Januenses*, in *Annali genovesi di Caffaro e de' suoi continuatori dal MXCIX al MCCXCIII*, vol. 1, ed. L. T. Belgrano (FStI) (Rome, 1890), p. 14; EA, c. XXXIII (pp. 37–38); Ekkehard, *Chronica. Recensio I*, p. 202.

crusade against the Byzantine Empire or have thought that Bohemond hoodwinked him.[115] But neither of these views is necessary. A change of direction is perfectly comprehensible. Bohemond was in Apulia from August 1106 until September 1107, and must have then received news of events in the East, where Tancred had been remarkably active and spectacularly successful.

With Baldwin II of Edessa in captivity, Tancred was regent of Edessa and won a great victory over Riḍwān of Aleppo at *Artāḥ* around 20 April 1105, consolidating the eastern frontiers and securing a truce that lasted until 1110. In 1106 he gained possession of *Apamea* (Qal'at al-Muḍīq) and took control of the entire Jabal al-Summāq. Aleppo and Shaizar became tributaries.[116] Once that news reached the West, Bohemond would know that only the Byzantine forces of *Monastras* and Kantakouzēnos now threatened the principality. An assault in the West might force Alexios to withdraw forces from Cilicia and Latakia, thus allowing Tancred to mop up any Byzantines remaining there, and allow him himself to use the crusaders who had flocked to him to establish the Albanian lordship that had been a Norman objective since 1081. Moreover, the Albanian assault was surely presented as merely a means to an end since after Bohemond's defeat and return to Italy many of the crusaders did in fact go on to the Holy Land.

It was quite brilliant. The *Alexiad* said that rumours of an assault in the West forced Alexios to withdraw *Monastras* and Kantakouzēnos and to replace them at Tarsos and Latakia by the Armenian prince Ōshin of *Lambron* (Çamlıyayla) and a certain Petzeas respectively. Tancred swept Ōshin aside, recovered Cilicia, and turned on Latakia, which he recovered by August 1108 at the latest.[117]

Bohemond's assault was successful initially and he occupied *Avlona* (Vlorë) but he was outmanœuvred and outfought by Alexios at *Dyrrachion* and forced to accept the "Treaty" of *Deabolis*. The only surviving version of this is in the *Alexiad* and was the work of Nikēphoros Bryennios, who was with Alexios at *Dyrrachion* and played a role in bringing Bohemond to terms.[118] The various Latin sources reported merely that Alexios promised to allow "pilgrims," meaning either Bohemond's forces at *Dyrrachion* or also other pilgrims or crusaders, to pass through the Empire peacefully, or gave Bohemond many gifts, or adopted him as a son, and

---

[115] See Brett E. Whalen, "God's Will or Not? Bohemond's Campaign against the Byzantine Empire (1105–1108)," in *Crusades – Medieval Worlds in Conflict*, ed. Thomas F. Madden et al. (Farnham, 2010), pp. 111–12.

[116] RC, cc. CLIV–VI (pp. 714–15); AA, IX.47 (pp. 702–5); FC, II.xxx.2–5 (pp. 485–88); Ibn al-Athīr, *Al-Kāmil*, A.H. 498 (pp. 92–93); ME, III.33 (p. 199); Ibn al-'Adīm, *Zubdat al-ḥalab fī ta'rikh Ḥalab*, pp. 593– ; Ibn al-Qalānisī, *Dhayl*, pp. 69–70.

[117] *Alexias*, XII.ii (1:362–64), *Alexiade*, 3:56–59; AA, XI.40 (pp. 816–17); WT, 10.23 (24) (pp. 481–82). Tancred issued a privilege to Pisa for its help in the recovery of Latakia dated to the first Indiction, which ended on 31 August 1108. See *Documenti sulle relazioni delle città toscane coll' Oriente Cristiano e coi Turchi fino all'anno MDXXXI*, ed. Giuseppe Müller (Florence, 1879), N° I (p. 3).

[118] *Alexias*, XIII.xi.2 (1:412–23), *Alexiade*, 3:124–39; ME, III.14 (pp. 191–92); MSyr, XV.viii (3:189). See Howard-Johnston, "Anna Komnene and the *Alexiad*," p. 280. John Zōnaras reports Bohemond's attack and making peace but adds nothing. See Zōnaras, *Epitomē*, XVIII.xxv (4:247–48).

that Bohemond swore peace or friendship or "*fidelitas*" to the emperor, or was "reconciled" to him, or became his "subject." None contains any details.[119]

The treaty stipulated that Bohemond should instruct Tancred to hand over Antioch to imperial officials. Then he was said to have declared:

> The former treaty that was made with your majesty, crowned by God, when I arrived in the imperial city with that numerous army of Franks on the way from Europe to Asia to deliver Jerusalem, and which has been cancelled in consequence of unforseen events, should be considered void and henceforth without effect, abrogated and without value because of the change of circumstances. Your majesty should no longer have any right over me, nor consequently assert anything from what was settled in that and written down.[120]

The word for "treaty," συμφωνία, is used only twice in the first twelve books of the *Alexiad*, both times with the sense of a general agreement.[121] It appears suddenly seventeen times in book XIII in the context of the negotiations at *Deabolis* and twice more in book XIV.[122] It still refers to general agreements but on twelve occasions it refers specifically to the Treaty of *Deabolis*, on another three to the agreement of 1097, and in book XIV to a treaty with the Saljūqid sultan of Rūm, Malik-Shāh.

Nikēphoros Bryennios knew that the two had made a previous political treaty. That it was written down means that it was different to the oral oaths sworn by both Bohemond and the others.[123] It was also different to the obligation to hand back former imperial lands since the Empire always saw that as remaining in force.

---

[119] FC, II.xxxix.2 (p. 524); AA, X.45 (pp. 758–59); WT, 11.6 (p. 504); *NF*, §XIV (p. 362); *HBS*, §CXLII (p. 229); *HN*, c. LXXII (p. 181); *Secunda pars Historiæ Iherosolimitanæ*, in *RHC Oc* 3:545–85, c. XXII (p. 568); OV, XI.24 (6:100–5); Rodulphus Tortarius, *Epistula VII ad Gualonem*, in Rodulphus Tortarius, *Carmina*, ed. M. B. Ogle and D. M. Schullian (Rome, 1933), pp. 315–16. But see below p. 64 and n. 132.

[120] *Alexias*, XIII.xii.1 (1:413), *Alexiade*, 3:125 [the editions are identical].

[121] *Alexias*, III.x.5, VII.viii.7 (1:113, 225), *Alexiade*, 1:134, 2:114.

[122] *Alexias*, XIII.ix.4, xi.1 and 2 (twice), xii.1 (twice), xii.2, 4, 5, 9, 11, 13 (three times), 15, 23 (twice), XIV.i.1, iii.8 (twice) (1:408–9, 412–18, 420–21, 424, 437–38), *Alexiade*, 3:119, 124–32, 135, 141, 158.

[123] To the best of our knowledge, only Joshua Prawer alludes to this written agreement. Without citing his source, which was no doubt the *Alexiad*, he wrote that in 1097: "Il semble bien qu'il [Bohemond] ait dès ce moment conçu un projet de longue haleine: apparaître à la tête de l'armée franque, non comme un de ses chefs, mas comme investi d'un commandement émanant directement de l'empire byzantin." Prawer thought, however, that Bohemond did not get the written agreement for which he had hoped: "… Bohémond ne reçut pas l'acte écrit de privilège qu'il avait espéré, …." See *Histoire du royaume latin de Jérusalem*, trans G. Nahon, 2nd ed. (Paris, 1975), 1:198.

Shepard reads the *Gesta Francorum* as referring later to a written version of Raymond's agreement with, and oath to, Alexios. See Jonathan Shepard, "Cross-Purposes: Alexius Comnenus and the First Crusade," in *The First Crusade: Origins and Impact*, ed. Jonathan Phillips (Manchester, 1997), p. 110. See *GF* (Bréhier), X[31] (p. 168): "Boamundus autem querebat cotidie conventionem quam omnes seniores olim habuerant ei [olim erga illum habuerant, MSS C] in reddendam civitatem [reddenda civitate, MSS C]; … Boamundus recitavit suam conventionem suumque ostendit compotum. Comes Sancti Egidii similiter sua patefecit verba et jusjurandum quod fecerat imperatori per consilium Boamundi." Cf. PT (*Recueil*), XIII.vi (p. 94); idem (Hill), p. 125. But this "*conventio*" was the agreement Bohemond reached with the other leaders before Antioch was taken. See *GF* (Bréhier) VIII[20] (p. 102)

The treaty was referred to again when Bohemond was made to declare that its only clause to be retained was that by which he had become the emperor's subject (δοῦλος) and liege man (λίζιος ἄνθρωπος).[124] Δοῦλος was common in Greek for an imperial subject by this time,[125] and λίζιος ἄνθρωπος is a Graecization of Latin "*ligius homo*," the first known use in Greek of the term used commonly in the West. No evidence corroborates anyone becoming Alexios's liege man in 1097 under the terms of the oaths. The *Alexiad* did not record the terms of the request for, or offer of, the *Domestikaton of the East* in 1097 and had no context to use the term. Scholars have tried to make sense of it in terms of the oaths,[126] but none have considered that if Bohemond was given the *Domestikaton of the East*, he would have become exactly this: in Byzantine terms the δοῦλος of the emperor as all imperial subjects were, and in western terms his "*ligius homo*."

Then he was made out to agree to never again hold imperial lands except for those enumerated in the treaty. Should he acquire others, they would be imperial.[127] Cilicia and Latakia and its coast south were to be detached from Antioch and excluded from his lands.[128] The first group allowed to him were enumerated in a chrysobull. They were Antioch and its port Σουετίος (Süveydiye) and a number of fortresses and military districts in what had been the *doukaton* of Antioch,[129] including Δούξ (*Dūqsā*, probably derived from the ancient *Daphnē* a few kilometres south-west of Antioch but applied to the Orontes valley downstream from Antioch), Καυκᾶς (the Jabal al-Aqra' on the coast south of the Orontes), Λοῦλον (the Jabal Lailūn east of Hārim), Θαυμαστὸν Ὄρος (the Jabal Mār Sim'ān, north-east of that), Φέρσια (perhaps *al-Athārib* to the south), the military districts of Ἅιος Ἡλίας (perhaps Qala'at al-'Aido, south of Antioch), Βορζὲ (Qala'at Berze), Σέζερ (Shaizar), the military districts of Ἀρτὰχ (*Artāḥ*), Τελούχ (*Dlouk*), Γερμανίκεια (Maraš), Μαῦρον Ὄρος (the southern Amanus Range), the *stratēgata* of Παγρᾶς (Baghrās) and Παλατζά (the valley of the al-Aswad River), and the *thema* of Ζοῦμε (the valley of the 'Afrīn River). Most of these places are known, although some are questionable. They constituted territories around Antioch to the south along the Orontes valley,

---

and cf. PT (*Recueil*), IX.iii (p. 55); idem (Hill), p. 84. Raymond simply made clear, "*patefecit*," the terms of his oath.

[124] *Alexias*, XIII.xii.2 (1:414), *Alexiade*, 3:126.

[125] See John H. Pryor, "The Oaths of the Leaders of the First Crusade to Emperor Alexius I Comnenus: Fealty, Homage – πίστις, δουλεία," *Parergon: Bulletin of the Australian and New Zealand Association for Medieval and Renaissance Studies*, n.s. 2 (1984), 120–24.

[126] For instance, Pryor, "The Oaths of the Leaders of the First Crusade," pp. 130–32. Views expressed there must now be modified.

[127] *Alexias*, XIII.xii.7, 11 (1:416–17), *Alexiade*, 3:128, 129–30.

[128] *Alexias*, XIII.xii.12, 21 (1:417, 420), *Alexiade*, 3:130, 134–35.

[129] Attempts to identify the various places were made by René Dussaud, *Topographie historique de la Syrie antique et médiévale* (Paris, 1927), *passim*, and Ernst Honigmann, *Die Ostgrenze des Byzantinischen Reiches von 363 bis 1071 nach griechischen, arabischen, syrischen und armenischen Quellen* (Brussels, 1935) [= Aleksandr Vasiliev (Vasil'ev), *Byzance et les Arabes*, tome III], pp. 126–29. See also Klaus-Peter Todt, "Antioch and Edesssa in the so-called Treaty of *Deabolis* (September 1108)," *ARAM Periodical* 11–12 (1999–2000), 485–501.

Map 2   The Treaty of *Deabolis*

east towards the Euphrates, north to the foothills of the Tauros Mountains, and west to the frontiers of Cilicia (see Map 2). They represented the extent of the principality in 1108 plus Shaizar.

The treaty then enumerated the districts of Cilicia and the Latakian coast to be cut off and then territories that Bohemond had requested should be allowed to him to counterbalance those. These included the *thema* of Κασιώτις, whose capital was Βέρροια (Aleppo), the *thema* of Λαπάρα, an alternative name for the old *thema* of *Lykandos*,[130] and its dependent towns, and the *themata* of the *Limnii* (north-east of Edessa) and of *Aetos* (Karākoūsh, north of *Samusat*). He was also given authority to give Edessa to anyone he chose, subject to acknowledging imperial suzerainty.[131] This was a belt of territory from *Lykandos/Lapara* in the Tauros, south-east to the Euphrates at *Bira* (Birejik), east to Edessa and towards the Tigris, and then back

---

[130]   See Hild and Restle, *Kappadokien*, pp. 41 n. 2, 93, 111, 225, 272, 277.
[131]   *Alexias*, XIII.xii.24–25 (1:421), *Alexiade*, 3:136–37.

south-west as far as Aleppo. The distances were around 250 kilometres from north to south and around 150 from the longitude of Aleppo-*Lykandos* to Edessa, for which fifteen and eight days' journey respectively makes sense. Surely that was what was meant in 1097. In Constantinople, "length" would be reckoned from north to south and "width" from west to east. In 1108 Bohemond asked for the lands of the grant of 1097 as compensation for territories cut off from what had been the old *doukaton* of Antioch. That Aleppo was included shows clearly that imperial intent in 1097 had been to use a marcher lordship for Bohemond to push the Muslims back as far as Aleppo itself, making a re-established Byzantine *doukaton* of Antioch much more secure.

This is virtually confirmed by the *Narratio Floriacensis*.[132] In giving the terms of the Treaty of *Deabolis*, it said that Alexios promised to hand to Bohemond lands that his father had claimed by arms, which was obviously not true. But it continued with an offer of other lands from his possessions in *Romania* to be reconquered that had been seized by the Turks, lands that could be covered in journeys of fifteen days in length and breadth.[133] This reflects the terms of the offer of 1097, with fifteen days by eight days now turned into fifteen days by fifteen days, perhaps reflecting the addition of the lands of Antioch as far as Cilicia and Latakia.

An offer of old Byzantine *themata* around Aleppo and Edessa to Bohemond at *Dyrrachion* in 1108 was not unrealistic. Nor would it have been in 1097.

The Empire and the Lands of *Kommagēnē*

The Empire had never abandoned hope of recovering its ancient *themata* in the East and emperors had been active on the Euphrates frontier.[134] Nikēphoros Phōkas took Aleppo in 962 and conquered Cilicia after he became emperor in 963. His generals Michael Bourtzēs and the Armenian Sahak Varažnuni stormed Antioch in

---

[132] We say "virtually" because it is an unreliable text. That being said, its editors date it to ca. 1110–14, so it is very nearly contemporary. It is part of a chronicle of France from 879–1110. The same text was published by Bouquet; see "Ex historiæ Francicæ fragmento," in RHGF 12, ed. Léopold Delisle (1877; repr., Farnborough, 1968), pp. 1–8, at p. 7.

[133] *NF*, §XIV (p. 362): "Duci quas pater armis vindicaverat terras redditurum. Praebiturum quoque ex suis supplementum copiis ad conquirendum in Romania, quam Turci obtinuerant, quantum itineris diebus XV confici possit longitudinis et latitudinis: ...."

[134] The Euphrates was considered a natural frontier. See Jean-Claude Cheynet, "La conception militaire de la frontière orientale (IXe–XIIIe siècle)," in *Eastern Approaches to Byzantium: Papers from the Thirty-third Spring Symposium of Byzantine Studies, University of Warwick, Coventry, March 1999*, ed. Antony Eastmond (Aldershot, 2001), pp. 57–69. For earlier periods see Jonathan Shepard, "Constantine VII, Caucasian Openings and the Road to Aleppo," and Catherine Holmes, "'How the East was Won' in the Reign of Basil II," both in *Eastern Approaches to Byzantium*, pp. 19–40, 41–56; Jonathan Shepard, "Byzantium's Eastern Frontier in the Tenth and Eleventh Centuries," in *Medieval Frontiers: Concepts and Practices*, ed. David Abulafia and Nora Berend (Aldershot, 2002), pp. 83–104. Shepard points to a new desire to recover frontier provinces, especially in the East, from the mid-tenth century and the reign of Constantine VII. See his "Emperors and Expansionism: From Rome to Middle Byzantium," in *Medieval Frontiers*, pp. 55–82, esp. pp. 72–77.

969. Matthew of Edessa said that after a successful campaign in Syria in 974 John I Tzimiskēs sent a letter to the Armenian king Ašot III claiming that: "We also were intent on delivering the Holy Sepulchre of Christ our God from the bondage of the Muslims." A *doukaton* of Antioch was created and successive emperors returned to Syria to defend it against the Fāṭimids and later the Saljūqids. Rōmanos III Argyros led a campaign against Aleppo in 1030 that ended in fiasco but George Maniakēs recovered Edessa the following year. The campaigns of Rōmanos IV that ended in disaster at *Mantzikert* in fact began with a formidable attempt to reinforce Antioch and the Euphrates frontier in 1068. Some outstanding generals and/or later emperors were *doux* of Antioch: Michael Bourtzēs, Leo Melissēnos, Bardas Phōkas, Nikēphoros Ouranos, Rōmanos Sklēros, Katakalon Kekaumenos, Nikēphoros Botaneiatēs, and others.[135]

Aleppo was lost to Asad al-Dawla Ṣāliḥ ibn Mirdās of the Banū Kilāb in 1023. His family held it until 1079, when it was surrendered to Muslim ibn Quraysh, who was killed in 1085, after which Tāj al-Dawla Tutush occupied it. The Byzantines tried to re-establish imperial suzerainty over it several times during the late-tenth and eleventh centuries. Rōmanos III Argyros had intended to attack it in 1030 and as recently as 1068 Rōmanos IV had occupied Manbij to its north-east.[136]

In 1091 Alexios attempted to bolster imperial influence by having John the Oxite appointed patriarch of Antioch. He could no longer appoint imperial officials to the city but an empathetic ecclesiastic may have been able to look after imperial interests quite effectively. Judith Ryder argues that, far from John being exiled to Antioch as punishment for an attack on Alexios's government, his appointment reflected Alexios seeing a use for him in this important role. He remained in Alexios's favour even after he abdicated and returned to Constantinople in 1100.[137]

Kommagēnē was farther away than other regions lost to the Turks but the Empire had a long and deep attachment to it. Its partial reconquest in the tenth century confirmed the religious importance of Edessa, the city of Abgar and source of the Mandylion of Christ and Christ's letter authenticating it, two of Byzantium's most venerated relics, taken to Constantinople in 944 and 1032 respectively.[138] Its religious prestige was unaffected by the populace being anti-Chalkēdōnian.

---

[135] ME, I.7, 18–19, 58–59, II.53 (pp. 21, 28–30, 51–55, 128–29); MSyr, XIII.vi (3:136); Yaḥyā ibn Saʿīd, al-Anṭāki, *Histoire de Yaḥyā ibn Saʿīd d'Antioche continuateur de Saʿīd ibn Biṭrīq*, ed. and trans. Ignatii Kratchkovsky and Aleksandr Vasiliev, Patrologia Orientalis XVIII.5, XXIII.3, 2 vols. (Paris, 1957; Paris, 1932, repr. Turnhout, 1988), XXIII.3, pp. 353–54, 268–69; AL, §VI (pp. 30–31); JS, Ρωμανὸς ὁ Νέος.10 (pp. 252–53), Νικηφόρος ὁ Φωκᾶς.17 (pp. 271–73), Ἰωάννης ὁ τζιμισκὴς.21 (p. 311), Ρωμανὸς ὁ Ἀργυρός.4-6, 13 (pp. 378–82, 387); MP*Chr*, Ρωμανὸς Γ´, VII–XI (1:35–40); Ῥωμάνος Δ´, XIII (2:159); MA (Pérez Martín), pp. 80–82, 91–2, idem (Bonn), pp. 105, 107–8, 120–21; *Skylitzēs continuatus*, pp. 120, 125–32; Zōnaras, *Epitomē*, XVII.xi, XVIII.xi (4:129–31, 207–9).

[136] ME, I.57, II.53 (pp. 50–51, 128–29); MSyr, XV.iii (3:168); AL, §VI (pp. 28–29); MA (Pérez Martín), pp. 83–84, idem (Bonn), p. 110; JS, Ῥωμανός ὁ Ἀργυρός.4–6 (pp. 377–82); *Skylitzēs continuatus*, p. 139.

[137] Judith R. Ryder, "John the Oxite and Alexios I Komnenos: Friends or Foes" (forthcoming).

[138] On the religious importance of Edessa and the two relics, see Judah B. Segal, *Edessa, "The Blessed City"* (Oxford, 1970); Holger Klein, "Sacred Relics and Imperial Ceremonies at the Great

The reconquest's longest-lasting effect was to bring into the Byzantine orbit the epic of Digenēs Akritēs,[139] the "double-born borderer," an epic of a pre-Turkish mixed Muslim and Christian society with local loyalties that transcended those to distant Muslim and Christian capitals. The poem was probably preserved orally initially since its nuggets of earlier frontier history are strung together in a non-historical way, but it was written down in the mid-twelfth century.[140]

The importance of the Euphrates frontier to Byzantium may be judged by the fact that the Digenēs story appeared in both of the earliest poetic works in Greek vernacular; many would call them the first works of modern Greek literature. As well as the epic itself, there are the *Ptochoprodromika*, four clever and funny satirical poems probably written by Theodore Prodromos (ca. 1100–57) and addressed to John II, Manuel I, and others.[141] Poem IV, addressed to Manuel, twice calls him a second *Akritēs* and pictures him as dressed and armed in terms referring unmistakably to Digenēs. Poem I, addressed to John II, parodies a lion hunt from the epic.[142] Digenēs retained his importance in Greek popular culture and most rural Greeks in the nineteenth century would still know folk-songs mentioning Digenēs or Akritēs or explicitly set on the Euphrates, where there had been no direct contact with Greek-speakers since the twelfth century.

The oral poem was written down in the twelfth century probably because Greek-speakers finally had to accept that its geographical locus on the Euphrates frontier was lost forever and its survival was threatened.[143] Brief adventures on the Euphrates frontier by John and Manuel Komnēnos were reported in Constantinople in terms of the return of imperial heroes to the heartland of the epic, disregarding completely the actual facts. John's great expedition of 1137–38, which failed to capture Shaizar or secure Antioch, was reported by Theodore Prodromos in two poems and by Michael Italikos and Nikēphoros Basilakēs in two speeches delivered to John around the same time.[144] Antioch and Shaizar are ignored or barely mentioned in these texts. The central event is a cavalry raid in which imperial forces briefly crossed the Euphrates, an unimportant detail in the campaign itself but not in reliving the epic. According to William of Tyre, in 1150 Manuel offered to purchase the surviving fortresses of the county of Edessa from Beatrice of Courtenay, the wife of Count Joscelin captured earlier that year. This Byzantine return to the Euphrates was brief

---

Palace of Constantinople," *Byzas* 5 (2006), 91–92.

[139] *Digenis Akritis: The Grottaferrata and Escorial Versions*, ed. and trans. Elizabeth Jeffreys (Cambridge, 1998).

[140] See *Digenis Akritis*, pp. xlvii–xlviii.

[141] *Ptochoprodromos*, ed. Hans Eideneier, Neograeca medii aevi V (Cologne, 1991).

[142] *Ptochoprodromika*, IV.116, 189–90, 1058; I.155–57.

[143] Roderick Beaton, "Cappadocians at Court: Digenes and Timarion," in *Alexios I Komnenos. I: Papers*, pp. 329–38.

[144] Theodoros Prodromos, *Historische Gedichte*, ed. Wolfram Hörandner, Wiener Byzantinistische Studien 11 (Vienna, 1974), XI.54, 101–10, 161–70; XII.35–6. Michael Italikos, *Lettres et discours*, ed. Paul Gautier, Archives de l'Orient Chrétien 14 (Paris, 1972), N° 43 (pp. 239–70); Nicephoros Basilaca, *Orationes et epistulae*, ed. A. Garzya (Leipzig, 1984), N° B3 (pp. 48–74), esp. p. 65.13–31.

and the garrisons were soon starved into submission,[145] but it was the motivation for calling Manuel a second *Akritēs* in *Ptochoprodromika* IV, written about the same time. It is used increasingly to date and explain the writing down of the epic.

These literary reflections add another dimension to the scenario. In seeking to use Bohemond to maintain influence over the Tauros and middle Euphrates, Alexios was following a longstanding historical and cultural imperative as well as seizing an opportunist moment.

The Armenian Princes and the Empire

In the 1040s the Empire finally conquered old Armenia. Armenian kings and nobles were given lands and offices to the west and south-west in return for their domains and, accompanied by retainers in a great population movement,[146] many settled in the Tauros Mountains. An arc of Armenian territory formed south-west through the mountains towards Cilicia and the upper Euphrates. The Turkoman incursions of 1065–80 aimed at more fertile regions of central Anatolia farther north and bypassed these Armenian lands.[147] The Empire could exploit Armenian traditions of both independence and also a degree of loyalty to the Empire.

In the chaos following *Mantzikert* other Armenian princes as well as Philaretos Brakhamios seized power.[148] To the west, they were Ōshin, son of Het'um, and Rubēn. Ōshin, religiously Greek orthodox, appeared in 1073 and was granted the fortress of *Lambron* by the Armenian governor of Tarsos, Apłarib Arcruni. He married Apłarib's daughter and was awarded the dignity of *stratopedarchēs*, thereafter obtaining numerous dignities at various times. He acquired the fortress of *Baberawn* (Çandır Kalesi), south of *Lambron*, and Tarsos itself after Apłarib died in 1078, only to lose it and the Cilician plain to the Saljūqids of Rūm in 1084. During the crusade he dominated the mountains west of the Cilician Gates.[149]

---

[145]   WT, 17.16–17 (pp. 781–85).

[146]   Gérard Dédéyan, "L'immigration arménienne en Cappadoce au XIe siècle," *Byzantion* 45 (1975), 41–117; MacEvitt, *Crusades and Christian World of the East*, pp. 38–39.

[147]   As Cheynet has pointed out; see his "Conception militaire de la frontière orientale," p. 64.

[148]   We have researched the major sources ourselves but acknowledge the work of other scholars. We have not attempted to reinvent the wheel. See Dédéyan, *Arméniens entre Grecs, Musulmans et Croisés*; idem, "Les princes Arméniens de l'Euphratèse et l'empire byzantin (fin XIe – milieu XIIe S.)," in *L'Arménie et Byzance*, ed. Martin-Hisard et al., pp. 79–86; Sirarpie Der Nersessian, "The Kingdom of Cilician Armenia," in Setton, *Crusades*, 2:630–59; James H. Forse, "Armenians and the First Crusade," *Journal of Medieval History* 17 (1991), 13–22; Jacob G. Ghazarian, *The Armenian Kingdom in Cilicia during the Crusades: The Integration of Cilician Armenians with the Latins, 1080–1393* (Abingdon, 2000; repr. London and New York, 2005). Ludwig Buisson, *Erobererrecht, Vasallität und byzantinisches Staatsrecht auf dem ersten Kreuzzug* (Hamburg, 1985), adds little. On Armenian historiography see Tim Greenwood, "Armenian Sources," in *Byzantines and Crusaders in Non-Greek Sources, 1025–1204*, ed. Mary Whitby, Proceedings of the British Academy 132 (Oxford, 2007), pp. 221–52.

[149]   ME, II.76, 87, 114 (pp. 66–67, 74, 167); *Alexias*, XII.ii.1–7 (1:362–64), *Alexiade*, 3:56–59 [the identification with the "Aspietes" of the *Alexiad* is disputed]; AA, XI.40 (pp. 816–17); RC, c. XL (p. 634). Samuel of Ani, *Tables chronologiques*, trans. Marie-Felicité Brosset, in *Collection d'historiens*

Michael VII had made Apłłarib *stratēgos* of Tarsos in 1072 with the dignity of *magistros* to counterbalance Philaretos. He held Adana, *Msis* (Misis), *Baberawn* and *Lambron*, until he ceded it to Ōshin. He lost Tarsos to Philaretos in 1078 and died some time before 1081. In contrast to most other Armenians, half of his known seals were found in or near the area he administered. As a Byzantine governor, he would have been sending messages to regional subordinates whereas other Armenians would not have been.[150]

The Apłłarib Pahlawuni who held *Bira* with his brother Likos from before the crusade until 1110 was a different man, a grandson of Grigor Pahlawuni.[151]

Rubēn, perhaps an officer of the last Armenian king, Gagik II of Ani, seized the region of *Kopitar* (Bostan Kalesi) east of the Cilician Gates some time before 1073 and then the fortress of *Barjrberd* (Meydan Kalesi) around 1073–74. Armenian orthodox by religion, he was virulently anti-Byzantine. He eventually ruled over lands from *Barjrberd* east to *Gasdagh'ōn* (Karakilise) and *Kopitar*, north to *Koromozol* (Gürümze), and south to *Sis* (Kozan). At times he held parts of the coastal plain also, including Tarsos, Silifke, and Adana. His son Kostandin succeeded him around 1093, seized the fortress of *Vahka* (Eski Feke), and controlled the region as far south as *Anavarza* at the time of the crusade.[152]

T'ornik, lord of the region of *Sasun* (Sason), far to the east on the upper reaches of the Batman Su tributary of the Tigris, was also a Byzantine client. Grigor Pahlawuni had given him his lands and he had obtained the office of *stratēgos*. Philaretos Brakhamios attacked T'ornik but was defeated; later, after T'ornik was slain his skull was presented to Philaretos.[153]

After submitting to Malik Shāh, Philaretos left as governor of Edessa an unnamed *parakoimōmenos* who was murdered by one of his officers called Barsaumā, probably a Jacobite Syrian, who then became *doux* of Edessa. He was overthrown

---

arméniens, 2 vols. (St. Petersburg, 1874–76), 2:339–483, at p. 453. See Dédéyan, *Arméniens entre Grecs, Musulmans et Croisés*, pp. 660–80 and *passim* under Ochin; Hild and Hellenkemper, *Kilikien und Isaurien*, 1:65; Joseph Laurent, "Arméniens de Cilicie: Aspiétès, Oschin, Ursinus," in *Études d'histoire arménienne* (Louvain, 1971), pp. 51–60.

[150] ME, II.74 (pp. 144–45); AL, §X (pp. 46, 50, 56). See also Dédéyan, *Arméniens entre Grecs, Musulmans et Croisés*, pp. 308–11, 318–19; Hild and Hellenkemper, *Kilikien und Isaurien*, 1:63–64.

[151] ME, III.46, 74 (pp. 205, 220); See also Dédéyan, *Arméniens entre Grecs, Musulmans et Croisés*, pp. 430, 433, 489, 1209.

[152] ME, II.113–14 (pp. 166–68); MSyr, XV.viii (3:187); Samuel of Ani, *Tables chronologiques*, pp. 453, 455–57; Vahram of Edessa, *Chronique rimée des rois de la Petite Arménie*, in *RHC Darm* 1:493–533, at pp. 497–98; *Extrait de la Chronique de Sempad, seigneur de Babaron, Connétable d'Arménie*, trans. Victor Langlois, Mémoires de l'Académie impériale des sciences de St.-Pétersbourg, VIIe série, tome IV, N° 6 (St. Petersburg, 1862) [hereafter Smbat Sparapet, *Chronique*], p. 7; *Alexias*, XII.ii.1–7 (1:362–64), *Alexiade*, 3:56–59; AA, XI.40 (pp. 816–17). See also Mutafian, *La Cilicie au carrefour des empires*, 1:368; Dédéyan, *Arméniens entre Grecs, Musulmans et Croisés*, pp. 365–417; Adontz, "L'aïeul des Roubéniens," in "Notes arméno-byzantines VI," in *Études armeno-byzantines*, pp. 177–95 [originally published in *Byzantion* 10 (1935), 185–203]; Hild and Hellenkemper, *Kilikien und Isaurien*, 1:64.

[153] ME, II.60–61 (pp. 137–39). See also Dédéyan, *Arméniens entre Grecs, Musulmans et Croisés*, pp. 319–29.

early in 1087 by one of Malik Shāh's *amīrs*, Buzan, who held the citadel of the town until his death in 1094.[154]

Goł Vasil was another Armenian and relative of Philaretos, who made him governor of *Kommagēnē*. Whether he was Orthodox or Armenian by religion is unclear. He had lands and castles at *K'esun* (Keysun), *Ṙaban* (Raban), *Behesni* (Besni), and *Kokison* (Göksun), and for a time *Ḣromklay* (Rum Kalesi), until his death in 1112. He acquired the dignity of *sebastos* and office of *doux*.[155]

According to Albert of Aachen, Goł Vasil's brother Bagrat, known to the crusaders as Pakrad, had been in Byzantine armies but was held by Baldwin of Boulogne at Nicaea. Baldwin entrusted *Arevindan* (Ravanda) to him after he took it but two Armenian princes – named by Albert as *Fer*, the commander at *Ṭlbashar* (Tell Bashir), and a certain *Nicusus* – reported to Baldwin that Bagrat was planning to seize it himself. After torture and under threat of execution Bagrat ordered his son to surrender *Arevindan* and was himself "estranged from Baldwin's company." *Fer* and *Nicusus* are not known otherwise but Armenians did surrender *Ṭlbashar* to Baldwin and these two were probably its lords before 1097.[156]

Two other lieutenants of Philaretos established themselves at Edessa and *Melteni*. T'oros, son of Het'um, was at first *doux* of *Melteni*. Only his name suggests that he was Armenian and he may in fact not have been. Malik Shāh appointed him governor of Edessa when it was captured in 1087, with Buzan commanding the citadel. After Tutush was killed the Turkish garrison abandoned the citadel and T'oros became independent. His last known seal bears the title of "*amēr*" as well as *kouropalatēs*. An inscription over Edessa's Ḥarrān gate dated to 1094 records Roman rule being saved from the Turks and confirms that T'oros considered himself an imperial subject. The *Anonymous Syriac Chronicle* claimed that in 1098 he intended to hand over Edessa to Alexios.[157] After Baldwin reached Edessa T'oros adopted him as his son but was then murdered by the populace. All sources agree

---

[154] ME, II.85, 88 (pp. 152–54); Vardan Arewelc'i, *Compilation*, §61 (p. 197). See also Dédéyan, *Arméniens entre Grecs, Musulmans et Croisés*, pp. 156–59.

[155] ME, III.14, 25, III.37–38, 46, 56–57 (pp. 191–92, 196, 200–1, 205, 211–12); MSyr, XV.viii (3:187); AA, IV.6, V.14, XI.40 (pp. 256–57, 354–57, 816–17); Bar Hebraeus, *Chronography*, 1:237; Samuel of Ani, *Extrait de la Chronographie de Samuel d'Ani*, in *RHC Darm* 1:445–68, *Annus* 561 (p. 449); *Anonymous Syriac Chronicle*, p. 72; *Anonymi auctoris chronicon*, §249 (p. 44). See also Mutafian, *La Cilicie au carrefour des empires*, 1:369–70; Werner Seibt, "Vasil Goł – Basileios der 'Räuber' – Βασίλειος σεβαστὸς καὶ δούξ," *Jahrbuch der Österreichischen Byzantinistik* 58 (2008), 153–58; MacEvitt, *Crusades and the Christian World of the East*, pp. 84–87; Joseph Laurent, "Les croisés et l'Arménie," in *Études d'histoire arménienne*, p. 132.

[156] AA, III.17–18 (pp. 164–67). Bagrat is not otherwise known.

[157] ME, II.104–6, 113 (pp. 161–63, 166–67); *Anonymi auctoris chronicon*, §§ 238, 241 (pp. 35–36, 37–39); MSyr, XV.iv, vi (3:173–74, 179). See also Jean-Claude Cheynet, *Sceaux de la collection Zacos (Bibliothèque national de France) se rapportant aux provinces orientales de l'Empire byzantin* (Paris, 2001), pp. 67–68; *Anonymous Syriac Chronicle*, p. 69; William Saunders, "The Greek Inscription on the Harran Gate at Edessa: Some Further Evidence," *Byzantinische Forschungen* 21 (1995), 301–4.

that he was hated.[158] Did the Armenians detest his Greek orthodoxy, Byzantine dignities, and close relationships with the imperial government?

Further north T'oros's client, Kostandin son of David, held *Karkaṙ* on the west bank of the Euphrates. T'oros's father-in-law Khawril, another Greek orthodox Armenian, established himself at *Melteni* some time after Malik Shāh's death in 1092, recognizing Saljūqid suzerainty. Bohemond's attempted rescue of him from the Dānishmendids led to his capture and his relationships with these Armenian princes seem to have reached back to Constantinople. Baldwin II saved *Melteni* for the moment but it soon fell and Khawril was killed.[159]

Further west Alexios appointed an Armenian named T'at'ul, probably one of Philaretos's lieutenants, governor of Maraš some time after Philaretos died. Whether he was Orthodox or Armenian religiously is unclear. Matthew of Edessa said that his title was Prince of Princes, "*Iškhan iškhanac*," which is confirmed by a seal with the title "archon of archons" and the dignity *protonobellisimos*. When the crusade reached Maraš, Tatikios confirmed him in office but he abandoned it to Joscelin of Courtenay in 1104 and retired to Constantinople.[160]

In 1097 Armenian princes with imperial dignities and offices, except for the anti-Byzantine Kostandin of *Vahka*, held the whole region from *Lambron* in the west to *Sasun* in the east and from *Melteni* in the north to *Ṭlbashar* in the south. The only Muslim rulers north of Ḥarrān were an *amīr* named Balak ibn Bahrām who held *Sarūj* and one named Balduk, a son of Amīr Ghāzī, who held *Samusat* and surrendered it to Baldwin of Boulogne in 1098.[161] The seals and other evidence make it clear that the imperial government was communicating with many of these princes and considered their lands part of the Empire.

From *Dorylaion* to Antioch, Cilicia, and Edessa

After the battle of *Dorylaion* the forces advanced into Turkish territory to *Ikonion* (Konya) and *Hērakleia* (Ereğli). Unless Tatikios's regiment had carrier pigeons no

---

[158] *Anonymous Syriac Chronicle*, pp. 70–71; ME, II.117–18 (pp. 168–70); *Anonymi auctoris chronicon*, §§245–46 (pp. 41–42); MSyr, XV.viii (3:187); AA, III.22–23 (pp. 172–77); FC, I.xiv.13 (pp. 213–14).

[159] AA, III.19–24, 31, V.18, VII.27–29 (pp. 168–77, 188–89, 360–61, 524–27); Bar Hebraeus, *Chronography*, 1:233–34, 236–37; ME, II.104–5, 108, 113, 117–18, 134 (pp. 161–64, 166–70, 176); MSyr, XV.vi, vii, viii (3:179–80, 185–86, 188–89); *Anonymous Syriac Chronicle*, pp. 74, 78; *Anonymi auctoris chronicon*, §§239, 252, 260 (pp. 36, 45, 49–50). On T'oros and Khawril see Laurent, "Des Grecs aux Croisés," pp. 405–10; Cheynet, *Sceaux de la collection Zacos*, pp. 80–82.

[160] ME, II.133, III.24, 74 (pp. 176, 195, 220). See Jean-Claude Cheynet, "Thatoul, archonte des archontes," *Revue des études byzantines* 48 (1990), 233–42; George T. Beech, "The Crusader Lordship of Marash in Armenian Cilicia, 1104–1149," *Viator* 27 (1996), 38–39; MacEvitt, *Crusades and the Christian World of the East*, pp. 82–84.

[161] AA, III.21, IV.8, 50, VIII.23 (pp. 170–73, 260–61, 328–29, 616–17); ME, II.105, 117 (pp. 162–63, 168–69); *Anonymous Syriac Chronicle*, p. 78; *Anonymi auctoris chronicon*, §260 (p. 49).

one in their rear can have known where they were until they reached Antioch.[162] What happened and when after *Dorylaion* is unclear. The sources conflict and none give dates.[163] Albert of Aachen, followed by William of Tyre, said that Tancred and Baldwin of Boulogne went ahead soon after *Dorylaion* and Tancred left the "royal road" after *Hērakleia* and took the road to the Cilician Gates. Baldwin followed. Bohemond was to follow Tancred and Godfrey Baldwin. Ejected from Tarsos by Baldwin, Tancred then took Adana, probably from Ōshin, and then *Msis* from the Turks. They came to blows again at *Msis* but reached terms and Baldwin headed east to "Armenia" on Bagrat's advice.[164]

The *Gesta Francorum* and Peter Tudebode, followed by the *Historia Belli Sacri*, reported that Tancred and Baldwin did not go ahead until after *Ikonion* and that they entered Cilicia together. Neither mentioned expecting Bohemond or Godfrey to follow. Both had essentially the same story of the conflict in Cilicia, in which Baldwin took Tarsos from Tancred, who then took Adana and *Msis*. Beyond that they had no more information and did not mention Baldwin going east.[165]

Raymond of Aguilers did not mention the Cilician expedition at all and Fulcher of Chartres only in explaining what Baldwin had done before he headed for the Euphrates.[166] Robert of Reims, Baudri of Bourgueil, and Guibert of Nogent merely repeated the *Gesta Francorum* and Peter Tudebode.[167]

Only Ralph of Caen added more. He repeated Tancred's strike for Cilicia, his capture of Tarsos, his being forced to surrender it to Baldwin, Ōshin surrendering Adana to him, and his capturing *Msis*. Then a legation, presumably Armenian, reached Tarsos and invited Baldwin to take possession of Ṭlbashar. Baldwin then disappears from view to reappear only at *Artāḥ* shortly before the opening of the siege of Antioch. The only other sources, Matthew of Edessa and the *Anonymous Syriac Chronicle*, reported respectively that an embassy from T'oros reached Baldwin at *Ṭlbashar* and that it reached Godfrey, who then sent Baldwin. Michael the Syrian adopted the latter report. Ibn al-Athīr observed simply that the Franks occupied Edessa by treaty with its Armenian population.[168]

---

[162] On carrier pigeons and the crusaders' apparent unfamiliarity with them, see Susan B. Edgington, "The Doves of War: The Part Played by Carrier Pigeons in the Crusades," in *Autour*, pp. 167–75. To the best of our knowledge, the Byzantines did not use carrier pigeons.

[163] For some estimates see France, *Victory in the East*, pp. 188–89, n. 119.

[164] AA, III.3–13, 15–17 (pp. 140–65); WT, 3.18(17), 20(19)–23(22), 25(24)–26(25) (pp. 218–26, 228–30).

[165] *GF* (Bréhier), IV[10] (pp. 56–60); PT (*Recueil*), IV.ii–iii (pp. 30–31); idem (Hill), pp. 58–59; *HBS*, §XXXI (pp. 184–85).

[166] FC, I.xiv.3 (pp. 206–8); BN, c. IX (pp. 496–97).

[167] RR, III.xx–xxii (pp. 767–68); BB, II.v–vi (pp. 37–38); GN, III.xiii (p. 164). The Amboise MS G of Baudri of Bourgueil, Paris, Bibliothèque nationale, MS Lat. 5513, has an insert later, after the defeat of Kerbogha, discussing Baldwin's expedition into "*terra gentilium*," his arrival at Edessa, and his adoption by its old Armenian ruler. There is no mention of him being summoned there, however. See BB, III.xx (p. 80).

[168] RC, cc. XXXIII–XLV (pp. 629–40); ME, II.117 (p. 168); *Anonymous Syriac Chronicle*, p. 70; MSyr, XV.vii (3:184); Ibn al-Athīr, *Al-Kāmil*, A.H. 494 (p. 47). The *Gesta Tancredi* is now known solely

The Cilician campaign has been presented almost invariably as private adventures of two younger leaders.[169] But surely it was not. The main forces would not have allowed them to leave with considerable numbers of men on private adventures.[170] Moreover, some important crusaders accompanied them, who would not have done so if these were private adventures.[171] Albert of Aachen said that the decision was made with common goodwill and William of Tyre attempted a better explanation, writing that:

> The design of all those [with Tancred and Baldwin], however, was one and the same, to search out the routes, to explore the surrounding regions and to put to the test fortune and the lot of events which might occur both in place and time [and] to send back a report to those of the princes who had sent [them] so that the army might advance with better knowledge and more without danger.[172]

Clearly, they did not go off on their own since Bohemond sent Tancred 300 reinforcements.[173] Albert, followed by William, referred to Bohemond being about to follow Tancred and Godfrey Baldwin in the context of threats to make Turks and Armenians submit.[174] Neither Bohemond nor Godfrey did so, of course, but the point is that Albert and William thought that Tancred and Baldwin would hold conquests in Cilicia in the names of their lords.

Baldwin overcame Tancred because by every account he had superior forces, yet he did not take advantage of this and struck east for the Euphrates. He is often said to have headed for Maraš but that is based on erroneous reading of the sources,

in the twelfth-century manuscript from the monastery of Gembloux, Brussels, Bibliothèque Royale, MS 5373. At a critical point, Edmund Martène and Ursin Durand in 1717 were able to decipher only partially some eight lines of it and they were illegible by the time of the *Recueil* edition. From where the legation came is missing. In the *Chanson d'Antioche*, the only other source, the legation is from "Li Vius de la Montagne," identified by Paulin Paris as T'oros of Edessa, even though the offer included the hand of his daughter and Baldwin actually married the daughter of T'at'ul of Maraš. See *Chanson d'Antioche*, ed. Paulin Paris, 2 vols. (Paris, 1832–48; repr. Geneva, 1969), III.446–47 (1:181).

Matthew of Edessa said that the crusaders announced their coming in letters to Kostandin of *Vahka* and to T'oros of Edessa; see ME, II.113 (p. 166). An embassy from T'oros may have been a response to such a letter but this must be doubted given the distances and the limited time available.

[169] See Stephen Runciman, *A History of the Crusades*, 3 vols. (1951–54; repr., Harmondsworth, 1965), 1:197ff.; MacEvitt, *Crusades and the Christian World of the East*, pp. 56–58 and n. 14; Flori, *Bohemond d'Antioche*, p. 126. Many others could be added. For dissenting views, see Robert L. Nicholson, *Tancred: A Study of his Career and Work in their Relation to the First Crusade and the Establishment of the Latin States in Syria and Palestine* (Private ed., Chicago, 1940), pp. 5, 38–39.

[170] As John France has pointed out: see *Victory in the East*, p. 194; idem, "La stratégie arménienne de la Première Croisade," p. 145. See also Asbridge, *Creation of the Principality of Antioch*, pp. 17–18.

[171] Richard of the Principate and Robert of Anzi went with Tancred. Baldwin was accompanied by Baldwin of le Bourcq, Peter of Dampierre-le-Château, count of Astenois, Count Rainald III of Toul and his brother Count Peter of Stenay, Count Gilbert of Clermont-sur-Meuse, Gilbert of Montclair, and Count Cono of Montaigu. See AA, III.6, 15–16 (pp. 148–49, 162–63); WT, 3.18(17), 25(24) (pp. 219, 229); RC, cc. 37, 43 (pp. 632, 638).

[172] AA, III.3 (p. 140); WT, 3.18(17) (p. 219).

[173] AA, III.11 (pp. 154–57); WT, 3.23(22) (p. 226).

[174] AA, III.5, 7, 8, 9 (pp. 147, 148, 150, 152); WT, 3.20(19).23–32, 24(23).17–23 (pp. 222, 227).

which did not actually say that he did.[175] Maraš is over 150 kilometres away up the river *Ĵahan*, even as the crow flies, and he would not have gone that way in any case. Its upper reaches wind through precipitous gorges and there was no Roman road following it from *Msis* (cl. *Mopsuestia*) to Maraš (cl. *Germanicia*). After leaving *Msis*, he would have followed the Roman road north-east to Kara Kaya (cl. *Hieropolis/Kastabala*) and then east past *Sarvandik'ar* (Saruvan) through the Amanus Gates to the vale of Maraš.[176] If he then went north to Maraš, it would have been a march of around 185 kilometres but once through the Gates *Ṭlbashar* lay ahead. Fulcher of Chartres said that he and Baldwin left the main forces for the Euphrates one day's march from Maraš and three from Antioch, which is about right if Baldwin met them east of the Gates, which are around 50 kilometres south of Maraš and 125 kilometres north of Antioch.[177] The proportions are right, although the number of day's march should probably be doubled.

Baldwin did not head for Maraš but rather for *Ṭlbashar*, the Euphrates, and Edessa. Albert of Aachen, followed by William of Tyre and indirectly supported by Ralph of Caen, was no doubt right. He headed for Armenian territory either on Bagrat's advice or on the invitation of an Armenian legation, or both.[178] But this lay in lands granted to Bohemond by Alexios, raising the issue of whether Baldwin went with Bohemond's blessing and would hold lands he might conquer from him. Moreover, he left Cilicia to Tancred, who must have known about the grant. Leaving Cilicia to Tancred, Bohemond allowing him to strike for *Ṭlbashar* and Edessa, and there being no disputes later makes it clear that they were all in it together.

The lands granted to Bohemond did not include *Comana* and *Kokison* to the West in the Tauros Mountains. They began further to the East at *Lykandos*. The crusaders installed Peter of Alifa, a Norman in imperial service, as governor of *Comana* and

---

[175] Albert of Aachen said that Baldwin went to Armenia and *Ṭlbashar*; Fulcher of Chartres that he set out for the Euphrates and *Ṭlbashar*; Raymond of Aguilers that he headed towards the Euphrates for Edessa; "Bartolf of Nangis" that he headed for the Euphrates and *Ṭlbashar* on the advice of native scouts; Guibert of Nogent that he headed for Edessa on the advice of one of T'oros's household "knights"; and the Amboise manuscript of Baudri of Bourgueil that he headed for the Euphrates lands and Edessa. William of Tyre was confused. He first said that Baldwin returned to the main army "which had reached Maraš some time ago," and where he had earlier said, following Fulcher of Chartres, that the forces stayed for three days. Then, in an attempt to explain away Baldwin's reprehensible conduct in Cilicia, which he attributes to the suggestion of others, he said that he went to see Godfrey, who was sick, at Maraš, was reconciled, and then left with Pakrad towards the North. All of this is either simply erroneous or impossible. Since the forces were at Maraš for only three days, Baldwin cannot possibly have learned that they were there and have reached them in the time. See AA, III.17 (pp. 164–65); WT, 3.19(18), 21(20), 26(25), 4.1 (pp. 221, 224, 229, 233); FC, I.xiv.4 (p. 208); RA, c. XIV (p. 267); BN, c. IX (p. 496); GN, III.xiv (p. 165); BB [MS G], III.xx (p. 80).

[176] See N. H. H. Sitwell, *Roman Roads of Europe* (London, 1981), pp. 194–95; *Barrington Atlas of the Greek and Roman World*, ed. Richard J. Talbot (Princeton, 2000), map 67: *Antiochia*.

[177] FC, I.xiv.2 (p. 206).

[178] See also ME, II.117 (p. 168); *Anonymous Syriac Chronicle*, p. 70; *Anonymi auctoris chronicon*, §245 (pp. 41–42). See also Laurent, "Des Grecs aux Croisés," pp. 410–38; Dédéyan, *Arméniens entre Grecs, Musulmans et Croisés*, pp. 666–77.

left *Kokison* to Goł Vasil. But they must have included Maraš, later identified in the Treaty of *Deabolis*. Yet they left T'at'ul in place there.[179] Bohemond was with them at Maraš but apparently made no protest. Surely he himself already had eyes on a far more glittering prize: Antioch! He would have known perfectly well what Alexios's intentions had been in granting him the lordship and the *Domestikaton of the East*. But what was sauce for the goose was sauce for the gander. He allowed Baldwin to swap Cilicia, which Tancred and he would contest in any case, for the lands of *Kommagēnē* that Alexios had offered to him. Which Cretan outwitted the other? This does not imply necessarily that Bohemond had Antioch in mind as far back as Constantinople. He could have accepted the imperial grant in all good faith. But when other opportunities became apparent, why not pursue them? An imperial offer of lands beyond, but not including Antioch, would surely set anyone to thinking: "Why not?"

Tatikios would also have known his master's intentions. Raymond of Aguilers said that before leaving Antioch next year he granted to Bohemond "two or three cities, Tarsos, *Mamistra* (*Msis*), Adana." No other evidence supports this and, since the Byzantines returned to Cilicia as early as 1104 and never abandoned their claim to it, Raymond's assertion must be rejected.[180] But why did Tatikios leave the siege and why does nothing suggest that Alexios was in any way displeased? This has intrigued many but no one has given a satisfactory explanation.

The *Alexiad* claimed that Bohemond told Tatikios that other leaders were plotting to kill him because they thought that Kerbogah's approach (chronologically out of place) was the emperor's doing. The *Gesta Francorum* and Peter Tudebode, followed by the *Historia Belli Sacri*, said that he abandoned the siege on the approach of Riḍwān of Aleppo to arrange supplies and left his equipment behind. Albert of Aachen also said that he left to arrange supplies. Raymond of Aguilers said that he informed the crusaders that Alexios was approaching but feared to come further because of previous skirmishes with them and that he left to join Alexios.[181] All tried to make sense of what did not make sense. But it does make sense. Bohemond did not deceive Tatikios at Antioch but rather had deceived both him and his master long before. Tatikios's position became untenable once Bohemond abandoned the lands of *Kommagēnē* to Baldwin and his designs on Antioch became obvious. He returned to Alexios to report.

---

[179] ME, II.133, III.24 (pp. 176, 195); *GF* (Bréhier), IV[11] (pp. 60–64); PT (*Recueil*), IV.iv–vi (pp. 32–34); idem (Hill), pp. 60–61. Matthew of Edessa alone names T'at'ul. The Latin sources do not mention him but neither do they mention appointing anyone to govern the town and he was still there after the crusade. On Peter of Alifa, see de la Force, "Les conseillers latins du basileus Alexis Comnène," pp. 158–60; Kazhdan, "Latins and Franks in Byzantium," pp. 94–95.

[180] RA, c. VI (p. 246). Hiestand accepts Raymond's evidence and argues that the territories offered to Bohemond included Cilicia. See "Boemondo I e la prima Crociata," p. 82. This flies in the face of the terms of the grant and of the Empire's claims to Cilicia, which it never abandoned.

[181] *Alexias*, XI.iv.3 (1:332–33), *Alexiade*, 3:20; *GF* (Bréhier), VI[16] (pp. 78–80); PT (*Recueil*), VI.v (pp. 41–42); idem (Hill), pp. 69–70; *HBS*, §XLIII (p. 189); AA, IV.40 (pp. 310–13); RA, c. VI (p. 245).

Bohemond was not concerned by Baldwin's possession of Edessa thereafter. Indeed, they were quite close. They completed their pilgrimages by going to Jerusalem together in autumn 1099 and when Bohemond was captured Baldwin tried to rescue him.[182] We must conclude that Baldwin struck east for the Euphrates and beyond with the blessing of Bohemond, who swapped his Euphrates lordship for the glittering prospect of Antioch. Both would have to be conquered in any case. Why did he not have Tancred rather than Baldwin take over the lands of *Kommagēnē*? Because Tancred was left with the already conquered and very attractive Cilicia, equally as important to a new Norman principality of Antioch. When Tancred left Cilicia to join the forces at Antioch, he left garrisons behind. The Cilicians expelled them in 1104 after the Frankish defeat at Ḥarrān.[183]

Baldwin did acknowledge Bohemond as his lord. When he raced to rescue Bohemond, Bartolf of Nangis called Bohemond Baldwin's "lord and friend of his." William of Tyre also referred to Bohemond as Baldwin's "lord prince": "*domino principi.*" He did not qualify "*dominus*" with "*suus*," but the suggestion is there. Tancred's intervention in Edessa in 1104 after the capture of Baldwin II and Joscelin of Courtenay reflected this. Matthew of Edessa's claim that after their release Tancred wanted to make them his vassals also does so, as does Albert of Aachen's report that in 1110 Tancred claimed before Baldwin of Jerusalem that Edessa and many other cities of the county had formerly been dependent on Antioch. Albert used "*ante hos dies*" and "*hactenus*," which could refer to any time before the present. He did not know that Edessa was part of the *doukaton* of Antioch in pre-Frankish times and attributed to Baldwin's rejection of Tancred's claims an interpretation pertaining to then.[184]

William of Tyre later wrote that, at the siege of Shaizar in 1138, Joscelin II of Edessa poisoned John II's mind against "his lord, namely the prince": Raymond of Poitiers, prince of Antioch. In audience after return to Antioch, he put into Joscelin's mouth: "It is proper that he [Raymond] should deliberate very thoroughly about this with the counsel of his [men], namely of me and of his other *fideles*."[185] He clearly understood Joscelin to be Raymond's vassal.

All evidence suggests that Baldwin held Edessa from Bohemond, that Tancred's claims to lordship over it were justified, and that that continued until the end of the county; all of which argues that Baldwin formed the county with Bohemond's permission from lands that Alexios had granted to him.

The Empire always claimed suzerainty over Antioch by the oaths of 1097. Princes of Antioch acknowledged that many times. But what about Edessa? The

---

[182] RC, c. CXLI (pp. 704–5); FC, I.xxxv.2–5 (pp. 344–48); BN, c. XLI (p. 519); AA, VII.27–29 (pp. 524–27); WT, 9.21 (pp. 447–48); ME, II.134 (pp. 176–77); Ibn al-Athīr, *Al-Kāmil*, A.H. 493 (p. 32).

[183] RC, c. CLI (p. 712).

[184] ME, III.39 (p. 201); AA, XI.21–22 (pp. 794–97). See also Asbridge, *Principality of Antioch*, pp. 104–23.

[185] WT, 15.2 (p. 676), 15.3 (p. 678). See also Monique Amouroux-Mourad, *Le Comté d'Edesse, 1098–1150* (Paris, 1988), pp. 80–81, 110–11. Paul Gindler, *Graf Balduin I von Edessa* (Halle, 1901), does not discuss the issue.

Treaty of *Deabolis* allowed Edessa and its lands to Bohemond, reflecting a clear Byzantine claim to them. Then, when John II attacked Syria in 1137 and captured *Buzā'ah*, he delivered it to Joscelin II of Edessa according to Nikētas Chōniatēs and the *Anonymous Syriac Chronicle*. Of all the sources for this campaign, however, only the *Anonymous Syriac Chronicle* said that Joscelin paid homage to the emperor together with Raymond of Poitiers.[186] Was it simply assumed that Antioch included Edessa?[187]

Finally, Fulcher of Chartres and William of Tyre reported that Godfrey and Bohemond received their lands, or investiture of their lands, at Christmas 1099 from Daimbert of Pisa after he became patriarch of Jerusalem. Both put this in the context of Bohemond and Baldwin going south to Jerusalem with Daimbert to complete their pilgrimages. Albert of Aachen confirms the journey of the three to Jerusalem and Daimbert's installation, but not the investiture.[188] Other issues that lie behind these reports need not concern us here, but it is glaringly obvious that all three sources agree that Baldwin was in Jerusalem but neither Fulcher nor William mentioned him also receiving investiture of his lands. Why not? Because neither Godfrey nor Bohemond had any title to rule except by election and conquest respectively but Baldwin did, under the terms of Alexios's grant to Bohemond. The lands of Edessa were not for the patriarch of Jerusalem to dispose of.

Conclusion

We argue that in 1097 the imperial court hit upon a strategy to use Bohemond and the crusade to recreate the *Domestikaton of the East*, reoccupy Philaretos Brakhamios's lands, and use them to assault the Turks in Anatolia and Syria.

Upon his accession, Alexios reorganized the system of dignities to base the government of the Empire on his own family. Yet Philaretos Brakhamios, an Armenian from a family of no great distinction on the south-east frontier, continued to hold a dignity and office virtually identical to those of his brother Adrian. His lieutenants had only slightly lesser ones. The seals recording them are unexpectedly varied and numerous, suggesting intense negotiations by the imperial government to preserve influence in the lands of the Tauros and Euphrates.

But from the mid-1080s Philaretos's power declined sharply and after his death his realm fragmented into petty principalities. Alexios needed another Philaretos and he cast Bohemond in that role. Following long Byzantine tradition and without

---

[186] *Anonymous Syriac Chronicle*, pp. 275–79.

[187] Amouroux-Mourad, *Le Comté d'Edesse*, pp. 111–12; MacEvitt, *Crusades and the Christian World of the East*, p. 64.

[188] FC, I.xxxiii.1–21, III.xxxiv.16 (pp. 322–34, 741–42); WT, 9.14–15 (pp. 438–40); AA, VII.6–8 (pp. 494–99).

regard for past hostilities he sought to lure into imperial service the most renowned warrior of the age, as Jonathan Shepard has also argued.[189]

The *Alexiad* portrayed the meeting in the Blachernai palace as a contest between two Cretans, two dissemblers: its hero, Alexios, who won the contest, and Bohemond. With malice aforethought Bohemond asked to be made *Domestikos of the East* but Alexios obfuscated, dangling before him the prospect of the office at some time in the future if he was energetic and loyal. But this account was false. That Bohemond would have asked for the *Domestikaton of the East* rather than that of the West makes no sense in any case. Moreover, the *Alexiad* itself gave the game away in making a slip in the Treaty of *Deabolis* referring to a written treaty in 1097 and to Bohemond having become at that time a δοῦλος, subject, and λίζιος ἄνθρωπος, liege man, of the emperor. A treaty in writing was different to the oral oaths sworn by all the leaders, including Bohemond. Moreover, that it was a response to an improbable request from Bohemond rather the brainchild of the imperial government is not credible.

The post had a historical context that accords so well with Byzantine strategy in the East and Alexios's priorities that he must have taken the initiative and offered it. He asked Bohemond to become Philaretos Brakhamios's successor. The history of the decades after the crusade made this something to be suppressed but perhaps because of its dual authorship the *Alexiad* allowed a contradiction to remain. Anna Komnēnē probably reworked Nikēphoros Bryennios's account of the audience of 1097 to spare her father posthumous blushes by turning his offer into Bohemond's request. But she overlooked reworking the passage in Nikēphoros's account of the Treaty of *Deabolis* and left a trace of what was there originally.

Latin sources associated with the Normans, and their derivatives, attributed the initiative to Alexios in inviting Bohemond to a private meeting and granting him a huge tract: land of *Romania* fifteen days' journey in length and eight in width. They reflect a well-known Norman report of the negotiations rather than a later interpolation. August Krey was wrong. He assumed that the offer included Antioch when it clearly did not. Not one original source said that it did. The appendix to the Treaty of *Deabolis* that listed the *themata* that Bohemond asked to be added to the *doukaton* of Antioch in compensation for Cilicia and the coast from Latakia south being cut off makes it clear that those lands ran in a wide swathe from *Lykandos* in the north, south-east to Edessa, and then back south-west across the Euphrates towards Aleppo. They were Philaretos's lands east of the *doukaton* of Antioch.

To Alexios and the imperial government, the region in question was of great emotional importance. He would have heard in his native Paphlagonia and in Constantinople epic songs from the Euphrates sung among refugees. These would later have a role in the first modern Greek writings.

Bohemond surely accepted. What was there to lose? The crusaders were only just coming together and their leadership's dynamic was unclear. He knew probably

---

[189] Shepard, "When Greek Meets Greek," *passim*.

better than anyone else how unpredictable the outcome might be. Perhaps he was flattered by his old enemy's offer. He certainly would have been attracted to the Byzantine gold that accompanied it. He would have had some idea of the office's history and at the very least it would be a good fall-back position. Later, however, he saw the possibility of an infinitely more glittering prize and gave up Edessa for Antioch. Baldwin overcoming Tancred in Cilicia but then abandoning it to him and heading for the Euphrates reflected knowing all about the grant to Bohemond. Raymond of Saint-Gilles, between Bohemond and whom there was antagonism from the outset,[190] denied Bohemond's claims to Antioch until the bitter end because he knew well that the grant to him did not include Antioch.

Which Cretan outwitted the other? Bohemond did. But he was outmanoeuvred and outfought by Alexios at *Dyrrachion*. Nicholas Paul has drawn attention to Bohemond's later reputation after the crusade for "*sapiens*," or in the particular case for being "*sapientissimus*," which, as he points out, could have either positive or negative connotations.[191] As well as "wisdom," it could also mean "shrewdness," or "cunning," or even "wiliness" in the sense of his father's sobriquet, "*guiscard*." Paul has also drawn attention to Bohemond's reputation for ruses and it is not difficult to see why he acquired it. His career was studded with them. Some verses in praise of Bohemond added on folio 68r to Rome, Biblioteca Apostolica Vaticana, MS *Reg. Lat.* 572 include the following lines: "Glory be through all the years to the Normans; who this world fears, a *sapiens* like Bohemond teaches."[192] His reputation for cunning was well established.

Bohemond was buried in a mausoleum constructed for him alongside the cathedral at Canosa.[193] Under the cornice of the cupola there is an inscription in verse:

---

[190] This explains why Raymond took his forces through the wilds of the east coast of the Adriatic rather than through Norman South Italy. The reasons are tied up with Raymond's history of marriage and marriage relations with the daughters of Roger the Great, count of Sicily. The Normans hated him.

[191] Paul, "Crusade, Memory and Regional Politics," p. 141: "Boamundus princeps sapientissimus et modestus"; idem, "A Warlord's Wisdom," esp. pp. 534–35, 538

[192] The verses are in several hands. Since they have never been published, we transcribe them here. The original poem in six lines is a declension poem on the name Boamundus. The lines that concern us are 7–8. They are in a second hand, probably of the later twelfth century. The last three lines, not reproduced here, are in later third (ll. 9–10) and fourth (l. 11) hands.

N.	Nunc reboat mundus; quia fecit tot Boamundus
G.	Facta Boamundi; resonant per clymata mundi
D.	Ergo Boamundo; sit laxi et gloria mundo
acc.	Per totum mundum; fert fama boatis boamundum
V.	Vixisti munde; mundo mundus boamunde
a.	In monacho mundo sit lax . decus in Boamundo
	Gloria Normanis in cunctis redditur annis;
	Quos timet hic mundus . sapiens docet ut Boamundus

[193] See Ann W. Epstein, "The Date and Significance of the Cathedral of Canosa in Apulia, South Italy," *Dumbarton Oaks Papers* 37 (1983), 79–90; Heinrich W. Schulz, *Denkmäler der Kunst des Mittelalters in Unteritalien*, vol. 1 (Dresden, 1860), pp. 59–62; Émile Bertaux, *L'art dans l'Italie*

The magnanimous prince of Syria lies under this vault, than whom no one better will after be born in the world. Greece conquered four times, Parthia, the greatest part of the world, felt long ago the spirit and strength of Bohemond. In ten battles he subdued by the reins of his valour hosts of thousands, which indeed the city of Antioch knows.[194]

Another consisting of verses in praise of Bohemond is on the panels of the bronze doors below the reliefs discussed above. All of the verses need not detain us but some are relevant:

> How the world bellows, how great was Bohemond,
> Greece bears witness, Syria reckons up.
> This he destroyed, that he defended from the enemy;
> Henceforth the Greeks mock your misfortunes, Syria.
> Since the Greek mocks, since the Syrian mourns, each of them
> with reason, may it be for you, Bohemond, true salvation.[195]

Unlike the anonymous verses of MS Reginenis 572, which represent views of Bohemond held popularly abroad, the inscription and verses on his tomb reflect his own propaganda, views of him that he wanted to be propagated after his death. The claim that he conquered Greece four times and destroyed it is an obvious exaggeration, to say the least. His "conquests" in the Balkans were ephemeral, to say the best. But that he would see the Greeks mocking Syria's loss at his death and Syria mourning it, fits perfectly with the scenario we have presented of a man who first attempted a conquest of lands in the Balkans during his father's lifetime, who then turned a Byzantine offer of lands and an office in the East against the emperor, and who finally used his own crusade against the Empire in the Balkans. Well indeed might the Greeks mock the death of such a man, or at least well might Bohemond perceive them doing so.

---

méridionale. Tome premier: De la fin de l'Empire Romain à la conquête de Charles d'Anjou (Paris, 1904), pp. 312–16; Flori, *Bohémond d'Antioche*, pp. 294–96.

[194] "Magnanimus Sirie iacet hoc sub tegmine princeps / Quo nullus melior nascetur in orbe deinceps. / Grecia victa quater, pars maxima Partia mundi / ingenium et vires sensere diu Boamundi. / Hic acie in dena vicit virtutis abena / agmina millena, quod et urbs sapit Antiocena."

[195] "Unde boat mundus, quanti fuerit Boamundus / Graecia testatur, Syria dinumerat. / Hanc expugnavit, illam protexit ab hoste; / hinc rident Graeci, Syria damna tua. / Quod Graecus ridet, quod Syrus luget, uterque / iuste, vera tibi sit, Boamunde, salus."

Appendix:
Titles and Careers of Some Armenian Rulers According to their Seals

More than 70,000 Byzantine lead sealings or "seals" survive.[1] Unlike coins, usually struck in ideal conditions by experts in mints, seals authenticating documents were stamped on lead blanks from matrices in harder metals whenever and wherever needed. They are often difficult to read. Perhaps half of those preserved are duplicates and poor examples already published are often replaced by better versions, which may change readings dramatically.

Bad readings may result from damage when seals are unearthed, from lead blanks being too small for the matrices stamped on them, from stamping being too faint or not properly centred, from damage on removal from documents to which they were attached by twine fed through channels in the blank, or from deformation of the lead by heat when archives were burnt. Despite such problems, a high percentage are deciphered satisfactorily, although many require several attempts, gradually building up a core of certainty in the reading.

Identification of seals of individuals below is facilitated by unusual non-Greek names. We may then attempt skeleton biographies. Byzantine dignities relevant here are in ascending order: *hypatos – anthypatos – prōtospatharios – vestēs – vestarchēs – magistros – proedros – prōtoproedros – kouropalatēs – prōtokouropalatēs – prōtonōbelissimos – sebastos – prōtosebastos.* The other titles marked on seals are offices. Dignities and offices are used for skeletal biographies in different ways. Dignities help most in arranging seals in chronological order within careers since the order of promotion was fixed. When individuals had the same dignity for a time but changed offices, the offices may also assist, although their order was less regular than that of dignities. Systems of both dignities and offices were in flux. The ladder of dignities was gaining new rungs above and between the old at the same time as civil wars and their aftermath made progress up the ladder unusually haphazard. Offices were destabilized by Turkish conquests and roles that holders were expected to play cannot always be assumed. Uncertainty creates particular problems when seals are hard to read.

The number of seals surviving for individuals varies. Philaretos Brakhamios has more different ones preserved than any Byzantine non-emperor and the total number of his seals is rivalled only by a few long-serving emperors. Other contemporary Armenians also have unexpectedly large numbers of seals for men on or beyond the frontiers of the Empire.

Finding a seal in a particular place indicates most probably that a communication from its owner was received there. Most surviving seals were found in or near Istanbul. Thus most of the seals of the Armenians below show that they were writing to Constantinople, though there will be some, especially those sold at auction, that will have been found in southern Turkey and exported illegally. In some cases there must have been a lively correspondence. The imperial bureaucracy is assumed to have sent out at least as many letters as it received but unstable peripheral archives were much less likely to preserve them and their seals. Recently, however, increasing numbers of seals have been found in provinces and deposited in museums there, thus allowing categorization by provenance. Seals of Armenians in this category are likely to derive from local business done by the owners for themselves or as imperial representatives. Seals probably found in the provinces are marked below with an asterisk.

---

[1]   Although generally referred to as seals, the lead stampings attached to documents were actually "sealings." The "seals" were the matrices used to stamp them.

Most seals are owned, or have been owned, by individual collectors, although collections do generally end up in libraries and museums. Groups of finds or whole collections may, however, disappear or be sold to unknown buyers, with the result that the only record of a seal may be a collection list or auction catalogue of doubtful accuracy. *Studies in Byzantine Sigillography* (*SBS*) now scans auction catalogues and suggests improvements in reading and dating, especially where there are good photographs. *SBS* also records and comments on publications of small collections, particularly in local periodicals and/or languages not widely known in the western scholarly community. It sometimes establishes reference numbers for seals that may have none.

The relationship of collectors to sigillographers is ambiguous. Collectors usually need sigillographers to decipher and identify their seals but typically are unwilling to permit publication of detailed catalogues of their collections. They will sometimes allow a statement that a further copy of a seal published elsewhere has been preserved in their private collection but this often remains unconfirmed by reference, location, or even the collector's name. Gaps in documentation for seals listed below are often due to this.

Two excellent, well-documented studies of Philaretos Brakhamios's seals have been published recently and are given below. The many less accurate publications they replace are ignored. Of the other Armenians here, some are discussed in other recent articles or a key set of Spink auction catalogues.[2] Details of some other Armenians have been examined but not included here for various reasons: attribution being contested, unpublished seals rumoured to be in prominent collections, and a badly understudied group of seals in Armenian or with bilingual inscriptions. For similar reasons, we have not listed Armenians with no preserved seals. Further development depends on more fundamental research.

References begin with the museum, library, or collection if the current owner is known, including an identification number if available. This is followed by a bibliographical reference. In the few cases where the current location is unknown, the only reference is bibliographical.

"Private collection" without a collector's name means that the collectors owning the seals have chosen to remain anonymous and are identified by the cities or countries where they live. Collections not asterisked as local or provincial may have been formed, wholly or in large part, from seals found in Istanbul. Many of the auctioned seals may have been found, however, in Eastern Europe and smuggled west. Abbreviations are in square brackets. Distinctions between ε and η, and o and ω are ignored.

[*AdM]:	*Adana Museum. Largely found near Adana.
[*AnM]:	*Antioch Museum. Generally found near Antioch.
[ANM]:	Athens, Numismatic Museum / Νομισματικό Μουσείο Αθηνών.
[BKC]:	Brussels, Bibliothèque royale de Belgique, Kimps collection.
[*BMM]:	*Bucharest Military Museum / Muzeul Militar National. Mostly found in Romania.
[*CM]:	*Cyprus Museum, Nicosia (Lefkosia). Mostly found in Cyprus but there is a minority of seals from other sources, doubtless including Istanbul.
[DC]:	Diamantis collection. Whereabouts now unknown but recorded by Vitalien Laurent, the greatest sigillographer of his day.

---

[2] Catalogues for the three Spink sales in 1998–99 were prepared by Jean-Claude Cheynet, which gives them an unusually high credibility for auction catalogues.

[DO]:   Dumbarton Oaks Research Library and Collection, Washington DC.
[DTC]:   Theodorides collection. Private collection of D. Theodorides, Munich.
[FAM]:   Fogg Art Museum, Cambridge, Massachusetts. Published with the DO collections.
[*GM]:   *Gaziantep Museum. Seals generally found near Gaziantep, Turkey.
[GZC]:   Zacos collection, Bibliothèque nationale de France. Donated by Mrs. Janet Zacos, widow of the collector George Zacos.
[HM]:   The State Hermitage Museum, St. Petersburg.
[IAM]:   Istanbul Archaeology Museum.
[IFEB]:   Institut Français d'Etudes Byzantines, Paris.
[*KC]:   *Khoury collection. Largely acquired in Antioch and preserved as a distinct collection in the Antioch Museum.
[*MF]:   *Jerusalem, Museum of the Flagellation. Found in the area, not well published.
[PC]:   Private collection of Haluk Perk, Istanbul.
[*SC]:   *Seyrig collection, Bibliothèque nationale de France. Mainly assembled by purchase in Antioch and Beirut.
[*ShHM]:   *Shumen, Historical Museum; [*ShMA]: *Shumen, Museum of Archaeology. Generally found near Shumen (Bulgaria).
[*SMA]:   *Sofia, Museum of Archaeology. Mostly found in Bulgaria.
[*SMH]:   *Silistra, Museum of History. Generally found near Silistra (Bulgaria).
[TC]:   Private collection of Mr. Tatiš, Istanbul.
[*TM]:   *Tarsos museum. Generally found near Tarsos, Turkey.
[VM]:   The Medagliere of the Vatican Library.
[ZC]:   Zarnitz Collection. The collection of M.-L. Zarnitz, now held mainly in the Staatliche Münzsammlung, München.

Aplﬁarib Arcruni of Tarsos
References: Jean-Claude Cheynet, Cécile Morrisson, Werner Seibt, *Sceaux byzantins de la collection Henri Seyrig* (Paris, 1991), N° 40; D. Michael Metcalf, *Byzantine Lead Seals from Cyprus* (Nicosia, 2004), N° 227. Identification of the Apnelgaripes of these seals is uncertain, based in part on the spots where they were found.
* *Vestes*. [*AdM, N° 647]. The wording of the seal is unknown to us.
* *Lord aid Apnelgaripes, magistros*. [*SC, N° 192; *AdM, N° 1021; *TM, N°ˢ 972-10-4; *CM, N°ˢ 1951/V-3/4B; GZC, 2 copies; IFEB, N° 1031; *Lanz auction 62 (1992), N° 969; *SBS* 6 (1999), p. 139.]

Khawril (Gabriel) of Melitene
References: (Cheynet, Zacos) Cheynet, *Sceaux de la collection Zacos*; *SBS* 8 (2003).
* *I seal the writings you see, those of Gabriel, emir, doux and protokouropalates*. [GZC, 3114] (Cheynet, Zacos, N° 41).
* *I seal the writings of the protonobelissimos doux Gabriel of the black-named city*. Two types. [(a) Spink auction 132 (1999), 127; (b) Gorny auction 96 (1999), 708; *SBS* 8 (2003), p. 221.]

Philaretos Brakhamios

References: (Cheynet) Cheynet, *La société byzantine. L'apport des sceaux*, 2:390–410, has photographs and a fuller list of Turkish seals; (Seibt) Seibt, "Philaretos Brachamios," pp. 281–95, has a somewhat more critical discussion.

- *Lord aid your servant Philaretos Brachamios, taxiarches.* [DO, 58.106.5670] (Cheynet, pp. 391–92; Seibt, p. 282).
- *Philaretos Brakhamios, protospatharios, hypatos and topoteretes of the Cappadocians.* [Classical numismatic group auction XI (2008); HM, M-5515] (Cheynet, pp. 392–93; Seibt, p. 283).
- Private seal (no dignity or office) *St Demetrios, aid your servant Philaretos Brakhamios.* [HM, M-8002] (Cheynet, p. 391; Seibt, pp. 282–83).
- *Lord aid Philaretos Brakhamios, magistros and doux.* [DO, 55.1.3396; GZC, 633; HM, M-6696; IAM, 122, 852; ZC, 575] (Cheynet, pp. 393–95; Seibt, pp. 283–84).
- *Philaretos Brakhamios, kouropalates and doux.* [ANM, 387γ; HM, M-3090] (Cheynet, pp. 395–96; Seibt, pp. 286–87).

[Probable gap for the reign of Michael VII].

- *Lord aid Philaretos Brakhamios, kouropalates and doux of Antioch.* [BKC] (Cheynet, p. 397; Seibt, p. 287).
- *Philaretos Brakhamios, kouropalates and stratopedarches of Anatolikon (or of the whole East).* Two types. [(a) Spink auction 132 (1999), 122; (b) IFEB, 764] (Cheynet, pp. 396–97; Seibt, p. 286).
- *Philaretos Brakhamios, kouropalates and domestikos of Anatolia.* [DC, 12] (Cheynet, p. 398; Seibt, p. 286, does not accept the reading of this seal).
- *Lord aid Philaretos Brakhamios, (proto)kouropalates and megas domestikos.* In a bad state of preservation. [ZC, 406] (Cheynet, pp. 399–400; Seibt, p. 290).
- *Philaretos Brakhamios, protokouropalates and domestikos of the scholai of the East.* At least three different types. [GZC, 632; HM, M-9916; Lanz auction 64 (1993), 1013; Sternberg auction 26 (1992), 506; VM, 113] (Cheynet, pp. 391–92; Seibt, p. 289).
- *Philaretos Brakhamios, protokouropalates and megas domestikos.* [GZC, 631; PC] (Cheynet, pp. 400–401; Seibt, p. 289).
- *Philaretos Brakhamios, sebastos and megas domestikos.* [Peuss auction 29 (2003), 1388] (Cheynet, p. 399; Seibt, p. 289).
- *Martyr, bestow victories on Philaretos Brakhamios, sebastos and domestikos of the East.* Two types. [(a) Spink auction 132 (1999), 123; (b) *TM, 974-23-41] (Cheynet, pp. 401–2; Seibt, p. 290).
- *Martyr, may you protect Philaretos Brakhamios, protosebastos and domestikos of the East.* Four types. [(a) DTC (probably two examples); *SC, 646; *Sofia, private collection; (b) GZC, 1127, 1128, 1139; (c) *MF, 13?; Spink auction 132 (1999), 124, 125, 126; Sternberg auction 25 (1991), 505; (d) TC, 2804] (Cheynet, pp. 402–5; Seibt, pp. 291–92 divides the types in a different way).

T'at'ul of Maraš

Reference: (Jordanov) Jordanov, *Corpus of Byzantine Seals from Bulgaria. Vol. 2*, pp. 318–19.

- *Tatoules protonobelissimos, archon of the archons.* [Spink auction 132 (1999), 128; IFEB, 11].

- *Tatoules Pakourianos protonobelissimos, archon of the archons.* [Spink auction 132 (1999), 129; *Batak (Bulgaria), private collection of V. Stankov] (Jordanov, N° 536A).

T'oros, son of Het'um, of *Melteni* and Edessa

Reference: V. S. Šandrovskaja and Werner Seibt, *Byzantinisches Bleisiegel der Staatlichen Eremitage mit Familiennamen I (A bis I)* (Vienna, 2005), N° 62.

- *May you assign grace to Chetames, anthypatos.* [Spink auction 132 (1999), 114]. Identification with T'oros is doubtful because of the much lower dignity than those of the seals below.
- *I am the seal of Chetames, Kouropalates.* [GZC, 3 seals].
- *Martyr [Theodoros], may you protect your namesake Chetames, kouropalates and doux of Melitene.* Two types. [(a) Spink auction 132 (1999), 130; (b) HM, M-8008].
- *Lord aid Theodoros Chetames, Emir and kouropalates.* [GZC, 72 (Cheynet, Zacos, N° 34).

Vasil Goł (Kogh Vasil)

Reference: Seibt, "Vasil Goł."

- *May you protect Basileios, sebastos and doux.* [*KC, 47].
- *May you protect, oh Word (of God), Basileios, sebastos and (nephew?) of the megas domestikos.* [FAM, 412].

Vasil, son of Apuk'ap

References: (Grünbart) Grünbart, "Die Familie Apokapes"; (Cheynet, Khoury) Cheynet, "Sceaux de la collection Khoury," pp. 425–27; (Cheynet, Zacos) Cheynet, *Sceaux de la collection Zacos*; Ivan Jordanov, "Molybdobulles nouvelements découverts de Basile Apokapes," *Études balkaniques* 1 (1983), 103–7; idem, (Jordanov), pp. 56–59.

- *Lord aid Basileios Apokapes, vestarches and katepano of Vaspourakhan.* Two types. [(a) HM, M-2897; *ShHM, 15051; *ShMA, 394; Spink auction 132 (1999), 116; *Bulgaria, private collection; *SMH, 77; (b) Spink auction 135 (1999), 275] (Grünbart, p. 36, is uncertain whether to ascribe the seal to this Vasil or to a homonym).
- *Lord aid Basileios Apokapes, magistros, vestes and doux.* [*BMM; *Bulgaria, private collection; *SMH, 54; *SMA, 191] (Grünbart, pp. 37–38).

[Probable gap during the reign of Michael VII].

- *Lord aid Basileios Apokapes, proedros and doux.* [*GM; *KC, 7; Münz Zentrum auction 76 (1993), 1390] (Grünbart, p. 39; Cheynet, Khoury, N° 7).
- *Lord aid Basileios Apokapes, protoproedros and doux of Edessa.* Two types. [(a) GZC, 8; (b) DO, 58.106.4763] (Grünbart, pp. 39–40).
- *Lord aid Basileios Apokapes, protonobilissimos and doux of Edessa.* [GZC, 6, 7] (Grünbart, p. 40; Cheynet, Zacos, N° 30).
- *Thrice-blessed saint, may you protect Basileios Apokapes, sebastos and doux of Edessa.* [*AnM, 2349] (Grünbart, p. 40).
- *May you protect Basileios Apokapes, sebastos and doux.* [*KC, 47] (Cheynet, Khoury, N° 8).

Postscript

As this volume was in final stages of editing, I became aware of new editions of the *Historia Belli Sacri* and of Ralph of Caen by Edoardo d'Angelo: *Hystoria de via et recuperatione Antiochiae atque Ierusolymarum (olim Tudebodus imitatus et continuatus): I Normanni d'Italia alla prima Crociata in una cronaca cassinese*, ed. Edoardo d'Angelo [Edizione nazionale dei testi mediolatini, 23 - Serie I, 14] (Florence, 2009); *Radvlphi Cadomensis Tancredvs* [CCCM, 231] (Turnhout, 2011).

The first of these is important for two reasons. First, it incorporates variants from the partial text in the Paris, Bibliothèque nationale de France, MS. Lat. 6041A, that John France drew attention to in 1968 but did not publish: John France, "Note sur le ms. 6041A du fond Latin de la Bibliothèque nationale: un nouveau fragment de l'historia belli sacri," *Bibliothèque de l'Ecole des Chartes* 126 (1968), 413–16. Secondly, erroneous readings of the Monte Cassino MS 300 by Mabillon have been corrected, including one massive homoeoteleuton of some eleven lines. Unfortunately, they have been corrected tacitly. The Paris manuscript is more faithful to the *Gesta Francorum* than the Monte Cassino one. All passages we have used here, however, occur either before it commences or after it ends.

The text of the *Gesta Tancredi* published by d'Angelo is virtually identical to that of Wallon and Regnier in the *Recueil*. There are no new manuscripts. In particular the maculated passage referred to at note 168 is the same.

I have checked all references to, and quotations from, the *Historia Belli Sacri* and the *Gesta Tancredi* against these editions.

This study was written before I acquired copies of manuscripts of the *Gesta Francorum* and Peter Tudebode for other purposes, when I was dependent on editions and unaware of how bad most of those of Tudebode and the *Gesta Francorum* are.

Fortunately, it was decided to use both editions of Tudebode – that of Philippe le Bas in the *Recueil* and that of John and Laurita Hill – because they were considered to be equally available to scholars. For other reasons, I had compiled a database of 158 variants in Jacques Bongars's version of the *Gesta Francorum* and the *Belli Sacri Historia* for which there are corresponding readings in manuscripts of Peter Tudebode. Comparing the readings of the *Recueil* and the Hills to MS A of Peter Tudebode (BnF, MS Lat. 5135A), of which Samu Niskanen kindly provided a copy, I found that the *Recueil* was in error 34 times but the Hills only 6 times. I also performed a spot check of 47 readings differing between the *Recueil* and the Hills' editions for four separate sections of the text against MS. A and found that the Hills were erroneous only twice but the *Recueil* was erroneous 45 times. The Hills' edition is infinitely preferable.

The *Gesta Francorum* situation is worse. I decided to use Louis Bréhier's edition here because it purported to notice all manuscript variants, whereas the Hill/Mynors edition noticed, with rare exceptions, only the *Reginenses Latini* MSS 572 and 641. Research into the manuscript and editorial traditions of the *Gesta Francorum* showed beyond doubt, however, that Bréhier never saw any manuscript. His "edition" was compiled from Bongars, the *Recueil*, and Hagenmeyer. Moreover, neither Le Bas in the *Recueil*, nor Hagenmeyer ever saw a manuscript either. Le Bas had a transcript of *Reg. Lat.* 641 made by someone in Rome, which was attributed erroneously to *Reg. Lat.* 572. The transcription must have been appalling because there are hundreds of errors. Hagenmeyer had a collation of *Reg. Lat.* 641 made by someone for Comte Paul Riant but thought that the *Recueil* edition was of *Reg. Lat.* 572. Bréhier, using the two, repeated their errors over and over again. He cannot possibly have seen either manuscript. There is in fact no satisfactory edition of the *Gesta Francorum* and Marcus Bull's new edition is needed desperately.

Production of the present volume was so far advanced by the time that this was known that it was not possible to rewrite all the notes. I have checked, however, all references to the *Gesta Francorum* and Peter Tudebode against the two *Reginenses Latini* manuscripts, the Escorial D.III.11 manuscript (again thanks to Samu Niskanen), and the Corpus Christi 181 manuscript for the *Gesta Francorum* and the BnF 5135A manuscript for Peter Tudebode. In the case of the *Gesta Francorum*, this necessitated adding some variants in note 67 that are given in *italics*. In the case of notes 44, 98, and 123, and in all references to Peter Tudebode, minor manuscript variants can be ignored for our purposes.

John Pryor
19 April 2012

Conquest, Conversion, and Heathen Customs in Henry of Livonia's *Chronicon Livoniae* and the *Livländische Reimchronik*

Shami Ghosh

Magdalen College, Oxford
shami.ghosh@magd.ox.ac.uk

Henry of Livonia's *Chronicon Livoniae* (*HCL*),[1] a narrative of the mission to Livonia[2] between the last decades of the twelfth century and ca. 1227 (when Henry wrote), and the *Livländische Reimchronik* (*LR*),[3] covering Baltic history until ca. 1290 (when the chronicle was probably composed), are the sole contemporary, locally written narrative works for the history of this region during this period. Henry's chronicle was composed within the first generation of conversion, while the authority of the bishop of Riga was still dominant, and before the Teutonic

---

A version of this paper was presented to the Medieval German Seminar at the University of Oxford on 1 December 2010, and I am very grateful to the members of the seminar for their feedback. I should also like to thank Michael Gervers at the University of Toronto for discussing some of this material with me many years ago; the two anonymous readers of this journal for their comments; and Helen Buchanan at the Taylor Institution Library for her efforts in obtaining otherwise unavailable scholarship for me.

[1] *Heinrici Chronicon Livoniae*, ed. Leonid Arbusow and Albert Bauer, MGH SRG 31, 2nd ed. (Hanover, 1955), cited as *HCL* by page and line numbers. All translations are my own. On Henry's life and the background to and date of his chronicle, see Vilis Biļķins, "Die Autoren der Kreuzzugszeit und das Milieu Livlands und Preussens," *Acta Baltica* 14 (1974), 231–54; James A. Brundage, "The Thirteenth-Century Livonian Crusade: Henricus de Lettis and the First Legatine Mission of Bishop William of Modena," *Jahrbücher für Geschichte Osteuropas* n.s. 20 (1972), 1–9; idem, "Introduction," in *The Chronicle of Henry of Livonia*, trans. James A. Brundage (New York, 2003), pp. xi–xliii; Robert Holtzmann, "Studien zu Heinrich von Lettland," *Neues Archiv der Gesellschaft für ältere Deutsche Geschichtskunde* 43 (1922), 161–212; Paul Johansen, "Die Chronik als Biographie: Heinrichs von Lettland Lebensgang und Weltanschauung," *Jahrbücher für Geschichte Osteuropas* n.s. 1 (1953), 1–24; and Marek Tamm, Linda Kaljundi, and Carsten Selch Jensen, eds., *Crusade and Chronicle Writing on the Medieval Baltic Frontier: A Companion to the Chronicle of Henry of Livonia* (Farnham, 2011). This volume appeared some months after the present article had been accepted for publication and it was no longer possible to make use of the material contained therein.

[2] I use Livonia to refer to the region later under the diocese of Riga and the Livonian branch of the Teutonic Order, not just to the areas inhabited by Livs and Livonians.

[3] *Livländische Reimchronik*, ed. Leo Meyer (Paderborn, 1876), cited as *LR* by line number. On the chronicle's date, genre, and audience, see Edith Feistner, Michael Neecke, and Gisela Vollmann-Profe, *Krieg im Visier: Bibelepik und Chronistik im Deutschen Orden als Modell korporativer Identitätsbildung*, Hermaea 114 (Tübingen, 2007), pp. 79–104, and Alan V. Murray, "The Structure, Genre, and Intended Audience of the *Livonian Rhymed Chronicle*," in *Crusade and Conversion on the Baltic Frontier 1150–1500*, ed. Alan V. Murray (Aldershot, 2001), pp. 235–59; see further the introductory paper of Hartmut Kugler, "Über die *Livländische Reimchronik*: Text, Gedächtnis und Topographie," *Jahrbuch der Brüder-Grimm-Gesellschaft* 2 (1992), 85–104.

Order arrived on the scene in Livonia.[4] At this point in time, Livonia had only very recently become (nominally) Christian.[5] By the time the *LR* was written, Christianity was no longer a new import, and the Teutonic Order had long been the

---

[4]   The first serious attempts at conversion in Livonia from the west had started in the 1180s under Meinhard; the crusading indulgence for Livonia was issued in 1199; the town (later also diocese) of Riga was established as a Christian foundation in 1201; and the Order of the Sword-Brothers was founded in 1202, subordinate to Riga. On papal policies regarding the Baltic, the work of Iben Fonnesberg-Schmidt is now fundamental: *The Popes and the Baltic Crusades, 1147–1254*, The Northern World 26 (Leiden, 2007). On the Sword-Brothers, see Friedrich Benninghoven, *Der Orden der Schwertbrüder: Fratres Milicie Christi de Livonia*, Ostmitteleuropa in Vergangenheit und Gegenwart 9 (Cologne, 1965); idem, "Zur Rolle des Schwertbrüderordens und des Deutschen Ordens im politischen Gefüge Altlivlands," *Zeitschrift für Ostforschung* 41 (1992), 161–85; Enn Tarvel, "Livländische Chroniken des 13. Jahrhunderts als Quelle für die Geschichte des Schwertbrüderordens und Livlands," in *Werkstatt des Historikers der mittelalterlichen Ritterorden: Quellenkundliche Probleme und Forschungsmethoden*, ed. Zenon Hubert Nowak, Ordines Militares 4 (Toruń, 1987), pp. 175–85. For a survey of research and an overview of recent approaches and methods applied by scholarship with regard to the Baltic crusades, see Sven Ekdahl, "Crusades and Colonization in the Baltic," in *Palgrave Advances in the Crusades*, ed. Helen Nicholson (Basingstoke, 2005), pp. 172–203.

[5]   On the early contact between the Christian world and Livonia, see Nils Blomkvist, *The Discovery of the Baltic: The Reception of a Catholic World-System in the European North (AD 1075–1225)*, The Northern World 15 (Leiden, 2005), pp. 505–63; Eric Christiansen, *The Northern Crusades: The Baltic and the Catholic Frontier, 1100–1525*, 2nd ed. (Harmondsworth, 1997), pp. 43–49; 93–104; Tiina Kala, "The Incorporation of the Northern Baltic Lands into the Western Christian World," in *Crusade and Conversion*, pp. 3–20; and two fundamental collections of essays: *Gli inizi del cristianesimo in Livonia–Lettonia: atti del colloquio internazionale di storia ecclesiastica in occasione dell'viii centenario della chiesa in Livonia (1186–1986)*, Atti i Documenti 1 (Vatican, 1989); and *Studien über die Anfänge der Mission in Livland*, ed. Manfred Hellmann, Vorträge und Forschungen, Sonderband 37 (Sigmaringen, 1989). Of the specialized studies on the early process of Christianization, see in particular: Sven Ekdahl, "Die Rolle der Ritterorden bei der Christianisierung der Liven und Letten," in *Gli inizi del cristianesimo*, pp. 203–44; Fonnesberg-Schmidt, *Popes and the Baltic Crusades*, pp. 65–75, 83–105, 122–28; Manfred Hellmann, "Bischof Meinhard und die Eigenart der kirchlichen Organisation in den baltischen Ländern," in *Gli inizi del cristianesimo*, pp. 9–30; idem, "Die Anfänge der christlichen Mission in den baltischen Ländern," in *Studien über die Anfänge*, pp. 7–38; Bernd Ulrich Hucker, "Der Zisterzienabt Bertold, Bischof von Livland, und der erste Livlandkreuzzug," in *Studien über die Anfänge*, pp. 39–64; Carsten Selch Jensen, "The Nature of the Early Missionary Activities and Crusades in Livonia, 1185–1201," in *Medieval Spirituality in Scandinavia and Europe: A Collection of Essays in Honour of Tore Nyberg*, ed. Lars Bisgaard et al. (Odense, 2001), pp. 121–37; Michele Maccarrone, "I Papi e gli inizi della cristianizzazione della Livonia," in *Gli inizi del cristianesimo*, pp. 31–80; Ēvalds Mugurēvičs, "Die Verbreitung des Christentums in Lettland vom 11. Jahrhundert bis zum Anfang des 13. Jahrhunderts," in *Rom und Byzanz im Norden: Mission und Glaubenswechsel im Ostseeraum*, ed. Michael Müller-Wille (Stuttgart, 1997), 2:81–96. A recent volume of conference papers has much of interest: Alan V. Murray, ed., *The Clash of Cultures on the Medieval Baltic Frontier* (Aldershot, 2009); see in particular: Ekdahl, "How to Convert a Landscape: Henry of Livonia and the *Chronicon Livoniae*" (pp. 151–68); Eva Eihmane, "The Baltic Crusades: A Clash of Two Identities" (pp. 37–51); Tiina Kala, "Rural Society and Religious Innovation: Acceptance and Rejection of Catholicism among the Native Inhabitants of Medieval Livonia" (pp. 169–90); and Andris Šnē, "The Emergence of Livonia: The Transformations of Social and Political Structures in the Territory of Latvia during the Twelfth and Thirteenth Centuries" (pp. 53–71).

dominant military power in Livonia, albeit theoretically subordinate to the diocese of Riga.[6]

HCL was written by a cleric, in Latin, possibly for the papal legate William of Modena.[7] The *LR*, a verse chronicle in Middle High German, was composed by an anonymous author, probably associated in some way with the Teutonic Order, and covers extensively the Order's involvement in the eastern Baltic in the thirteenth century. It has been argued that it was intended as mealtime reading for the brothers of the Teutonic Order, or perhaps for the seasonal crusaders from Germany, or both.[8] The two works, therefore, are not only chronologically quite far apart; despite uncertainties about their audiences (and for the latter work also the author), it is clear that their political, cultural and intellectual milieux were also very different.

In the present paper, I examine the depiction of the conquest of the non-Christian population of the Baltic, in particular, explicitly stated religious or secular motivations for battle; the effects of war on the native population; and the presentation of the customs and character of the heathens.[9] It must be acknowledged at the outset that differences or similarities between the chronicles do not actually present solid ground for a comparison of real changes, or lack thereof, in the processes of Christianization, given that the sources were produced by representatives of two very different institutions: it is entirely possible that the attitude of the see of Riga did not change between 1227 and 1290, even if it might have diverged from that of the Teutonic Order. Furthermore, while it is likely that both works, in particular the later chronicle, have some representative value with regard to the attitudes of the larger institutions with which their authors were affiliated, it should be stressed that the focus of this study is on establishing how these individual chroniclers presented

---

[6]   This subordinate status was inherited from the Sword-Brothers when the latter were absorbed into the Teutonic Order in 1237. On the Sword-Brothers' relationship with the Livonian branch of the Teutonic Order, see, in addition to the works cited in n. 4: Manfred Hellmann, "Die Stellung des livländischen Ordenszweiges zur Gesamtpolitik des Deutschen Ordens vom 13. bis zum 16. Jahrhundert," in *Von Akkon bis Wien: Studien zur Deutschordensgeschichte vom 13. bis zum 20. Jahrhundert*, ed. Udo Arnold, Quellen und Studien zur Geschichte des Deutschen Ordens 20 (Marburg, 1978), pp. 6–13; see also Christiansen, *Northern Crusades*, 79–92; Klaus Militzer, *Die Geschichte des Deutschen Ordens* (Stuttgart, 2005), pp. 78–83.

[7]   Brundage, "Thirteenth-Century Livonian Crusade." William was present in Livonia in 1225–26 and in the Baltic at various points in the next decade. On his activities and their relationship to papal policies in Livonia, see Fonnesberg-Schmidt, *Popes and the Baltic Crusades*, pp. 170–82.

[8]   Murray, "*Livonian Rhymed Chronicle*," suggests – against the general consensus – that the work was intended for mealtime reading, and that its audience was primarily the visiting crusaders; but there is no reason why the chronicle could not have been composed with both types of audience in mind: thus Feistner et al., *Krieg im Visier*, pp. 101–2.

[9]   Note that I study the depiction of all the non-Christian peoples presented here, not specifically the Livs or Livonians. I make no claim to provide a study of pre-Christian religion and custom, but rather attempt to show how the chroniclers depict local customs that they see as particularly contrary to their own practices. For a study of pre-Christian religion in the region based primarily on Henry of Livonia, see Anzelm Weiss, "Mythologie und Religiosität der alten Liven," in *Gli inizi del cristianesimo*, pp. 81–96. For discussions of the actual processes of contact, see primarily the works referred to above in nn. 4 and 5; the present paper is a study solely of how contact was depicted, rather than of what really took place.

the themes of war, conquest, and the religion and behaviour of the native population; this is not a study of the attitudes of the Church of Riga or the Teutonic Order as corporate bodies. Similarities of views between the two authors are as significant as differences, as they show, I will argue, that even the narrative presented by a clerical writer not affiliated with any military order presents a high level of non-religious motivation as a background to conflict.[10]

secular motives

The Motivations for War and Its Effects[11]

Both Henry and the *LR* depict the beginnings of the mission to Livonia under Meinhard as being peaceful in intent, although it is apparent that Meinhard did indeed have some military (and probably also institutional) support.[12] Unlike Henry, the *LR* makes explicit the economic motives for Christian expansion: while Henry mentions merchants with whom Meinhard journeys to Livonia, their activities are not described, whereas the *LR* states specifically that the merchants were able to "sell [their wares] to greater advantage there than elsewhere."[13] The first contact of the merchants with the heathens brings about a brief armed conflict, which the heathens, wounded, seek to end in a truce, readily granted by the merchants with no mention of conversion; the description of this first encounter ends with what seems to be harmonious commerce,[14] and indeed after this, we are told that the merchants "often returned again"[15] and "were well-received, as beloved guests ought to be."[16] The settlement (*burc*) where Meinhard first establishes a base for his mission is said to be built by merchants, who were then able to remain and pursue in peace their trade with the heathens.[17] Henry states that only a few of the people were baptized before the building of the *castrum* there, and all the local people promise to be baptized after the castle is built.[18] He does not give the merchants a major

---

[10]   I should note also that, although I distinguish, for the purpose of this analysis, between religious motives (the defence or spread of Christianity, and less prominently, the promise of heavenly reward) and secular ones (gaining land, money, honour), there is no necessary opposition between the two. My distinctions are thus between motivations that are explicitly religious on the one hand, and those that are not explicitly presented as having a religious value, on the other; these distinctions are not meant to suggest incompatibility between two motivations, but rather what is, I believe, a perceptible and significant difference of emphasis.

[11]   For an analysis of the techniques and technologies of warfare (not discussed in the present paper), see Stephen Turnbull, "Crossbows or Catapults? The Identification of Siege Weaponry and Techniques in the Chronicle of Henry of Livonia," in Murray, *Clash of Cultures*, pp. 307–19.

[12]   This is argued by Jensen, "Missionary Activities," to my mind convincingly; much previous scholarship thought that Meinhard lacked military support: cf. Hellmann, "Bischof Meinhard"; idem, "Anfänge."

[13]   *LR* 185–86: "daz vorkouften sie aldar / ein teil baz denne anderswar."

[14]   *LR* 159–200.

[15]   *LR* 201: "quâmen dicke sider."

[16]   *LR* 205–6: "sô wurden sie entpfangen wol, / als man liebe geste sol."

[17]   *LR* 215–24.

[18]   *HCL* 3,11–14.

role in building Ikšķile (Üxküll), nor does he state that their trade was especially profitable; although he mentions merchants many times, they feature primarily as providers of transport for the missionaries. Interestingly, Henry mentions that "the German merchants were joined by family ties to the Livs,"[19] a detail omitted by the *LR*. Henry tells us further that Bishop Albert of Riga obtained from the pope an interdiction on merchants mooring anywhere else apart from Riga, thus ensuring that the Rigan merchants' support (financial and military) was guaranteed for the mission;[20] this also meant that long-distance trade had to be routed through Riga, a Christian town. Furthermore, Rasa Mažeika has shown that the Teutonic Order eagerly maintained friendly trade links even with its (heathen) enemies, and this trade was probably a source of a good part of the Order's wealth.[21] By linking the interests of the episcopal see to those of the merchants, the local populace was also given a reason to look favourably to Christianity: as Eric Christiansen notes, one of the reasons for the adherence of the local people to the crusading army later on was "the fact that the bishop was in partnership with everybody's best customers, the German merchants";[22] this is equally true for the first fifteen years of the mission as "everybody's best customers" were now under the wing of the episcopate.[23]

Henry states that the papal authorization of crusade was specifically to ensure that the baptized could be forced to remain Christian: "[the pope] decreed that they were not to be deserted, but ought to be compelled to observe the faith that they had voluntarily promised."[24] The key word in this statement, of importance for our consideration of later conflict, is *sponte*: those who had voluntarily accepted baptism were to be coerced to maintain the faith, but no mention is made of conversion by the sword. The report of the indulgence follows immediately after this passage: "[the pope] granted a remission of all sins to all those who made the journey in order to resuscitate the original faith."[25] The choice of the word *resuscitandam* implies that the indulgences are for crusaders who go to aid in maintaining the faith already accepted (*illam primitivam*, referring to *fide[m]* of the previous sentence),

---

[19] *HCL* 2,6–7: "Theutonici enim mercatores, Lyvonibus familiaritate coniuncti."

[20] *HCL* 15,1–16.

[21] Rasa J. Mažeika, "Of Cabbages and Knights: Trade and Trade Treaties with the Infidel on the Northern Frontier, 1200–1358," *Journal of Medieval History* 20 (1994), 63–76.

[22] Christiansen, *Northern Crusades*, p. 101.

[23] On the place of merchants and trade in the Baltic crusades, see further Carsten Selch Jensen, "Urban Life and the Crusades in Northern Germany and the Baltic Lands in the Early Thirteenth Century," in Murray, *Crusade and Conversion*, pp. 75–94; and Mark R. Munzinger, "The Profits of the Cross: Merchant Involvement in the Baltic Crusade (*c.* 1180–1230)," *Journal of Medieval History* 32 (2006), 163–85. Ekdahl ("Ritterorden," pp. 212–14) argues that the merchants would have been especially interested in Christian conquest in order to establish a safe venue of trade (he is followed by Munzinger, "Profits of the Cross"); while the suggestion is in itself plausible, it does not explain why such an enterprise should have become important at this moment in time and not earlier, considering that there had been peaceful and profitable trade with this region for at least two centuries previously.

[24] *HCL* 7,2–4: "non eos deserendos censuit, sed ad observationem fidei, quam sponte promiserant, cogendos decrevit."

[25] *HCL* 7,4–6: "Remissionem quippe omnium peccatorum indulsit omnibus, qui ad resuscitandam illam primitivam accepta cruce transeant."

rather than to force anyone to accept baptism. This episode is not present in the *LR*. *HCL*'s next mention of a papal indulgence, in the context of the next mention of battle, concerns *perfidos Lyvones*, with the adjective "treacherous" possibly here also intended to indicate apostasy.[26] This indulgence is granted in the episcopate of Bertold, who (perhaps unwisely) arrives in Livonia "without an army" according to Henry.[27] Bertold's episcopate (and life) did not last long, and his successor Albert, bishop for over two decades, did not repeat the mistake, taking crusaders with him on his first journey into Livonia.[28] Perhaps unsurprisingly, the *LR* gives rather more prominence to Albert's military men than does Henry, stating not only that the pope authorized the establishment of a military order ("found a spiritual life according to the rule of the Temple, those who are called 'God's knights'"[29]), but also that the pope explicitly says that the Order "should be given a third of the men and land to have as their own forever";[30] this establishes at the outset the relatively greater emphasis on the military nature of the narrative in the later work, as well as the relatively greater prominence afforded to secular gain (in this case of land).

We should note that, although there seems to have been a really coordinated effort at military conquest only after the appointing of Albert, even before a permanent military presence was established, it is at the very least debatable that the Baltic peoples who accepted Christianity did so wholly voluntarily.[31] Even when they did, it was often the case that "baptism became the consequence, not the cause, of adherence to the crusading army. The adherence came about because of material inducements"[32] – not least the provision of support against other enemies (who included, at various points, the Russians, Lithuanians, and Estonians), but also the benefits of trade with the Christian merchants. Even in Henry's presentation, the heathens repeatedly agree to accept baptism out of fear that the Christians will bring an army against them (this is characterized by Henry as treacherous, for they do not really wish to become Christian), and it is likely that, with perhaps some exceptions, the earliest converts might have chosen to accept the new faith either because of the presence of an armed force with Meinhard (which would have cowed

---

[26] *HCL* 9,9. The papal letters mentioned here by Henry are no longer extant, and it seems likely that he did not have access to them himself: Fonnesberg-Schmidt, *Popes and the Baltic Crusades*, pp. 68–71.

[27] *HCL* 8,12: "sine exercitu."

[28] *HCL* 12,6–8.

[29] *LR* 597–99: "stifte ein geistlîchez leben / nâch dem tempil ûz gegeben, / die gotes ritter heizen dâ."

[30] *LR* 601–4: "den gebe man lûte und lant / daz dritte teil in die hant / nâch rechte vrîlichen / vor eigen êwiclîchen." The *LR* gets the chronology wrong, for although crusaders did come with Albert, an Order following the rules of the Templars was not established until 1202/3, and the grant of a third of the land did not take place until 1204.

[31] On this issue, see the works cited in n. 5. There seems to be little evidence to suggest that papal policy initially supported the use of force for the conversion of pagans; but force was sanctioned with regard to apostates, and Innocent III might have become more favourable to forcible conversion from 1209, although even after this point, force was primarily intended to be used against heretics and apostates: see Fonnesberg-Schmidt, *Popes and the Baltic Crusades*, pp. 67–75 (on Celestine's policies and Henry's reporting of his letters), 95–98, 105–11 (on Innocent III's policies).

[32] Christiansen, *Northern Crusades*, p. 101.

them into submission, and also offered assistance against their enemies), or because of his association with the merchants – the heathens' trading partners.[33]

In the second year of his episcopate, Albert demanded and received hostages from the Livs to ensure their keeping the peace;[34] this became standard procedure after successful battle against all the local heathen groups. The taking of hostages after battle is similarly mentioned on many occasions in the *LR*.[35] Notably, the *LR* does not in any of these passages link the taking of hostages to the assumption of Christianity among the newly conquered.[36] In contrast, baptism and maintaining Christianity are most often (but not always) linked to the taking of hostages in Henry's chronicle; and in two instances the hostages are expressly said to have been sent to Germany (where they would have received a Christian and German education/indoctrination).[37]

The concern to maintain both peace and the subordinate status of the conquered would have always been one of the primary motives for taking hostages, even if in Henry's account this is not always explicitly stated. In most instances where Henry says hostages are taken this is immediately followed by a promise to accept Christianity; given the close connection of the two acts (giving hostages and promising to become Christian), the taking of hostages was clearly, in Henry's presentation, a method of ensuring both peace and conversion. In some cases, the chronicle expressly states that hostages are given "in order that they [the conquered] accept the sacrament of baptism and pay a tax to the Livonian Church."[38] Even

---

[33] These matters are fully examined by Jensen, "Missionary Activities," and therefore not rehearsed here; I expand his argument only by the suggestion of an economic motive to conversion in the early period, drawing on Christiansen's suggestion for the later one. On the secular and religious significance of baptism in *HCL*, see also Kala, "Rural Society," pp. 176–80.

[34] *HCL* 14,3–4.

[35] *LR* 888; 1259; 1684; 2419; 5988; 6297; 7344–45; 11524–25.

[36] *LR* 2350–425 states that the master wishes to wage war on the heathen because they are still heathen; after victory, hostages are taken, but there is no mention of conversion or a promise to convert – even though in this instance Mary is praised as being a *helferîn* of the knights (*LR* 2427–28)!

[37] Instances where the taking of hostages is followed by baptism, or the promise of accepting Christianity, or is described as a means to ensure the converts' remaining Christian: *HCL* 30,23–24; 32,2–4; 44,18–19; after hostages are taken, priests are sent to preach: 54,13–14; 85,15–18; 96,20–22; 102,7–9; 106,26–107,26; the bishop demands hostages to prevent the Livs reverting to paganism; the Livs refuse and declare that they will drive out Christianity and the Germans: 133,25–27; 138,33–34; 144,17–18; the hostages are taken to ensure that the defeated maintain "all laws of Christianity" ("omnia christianitatis iura"); this probably implies religious as well as secular laws: 145,22–25; 145,31–33; 159,26–29; 162,8–10; 165,6–7; 167,18–21; 170,4–5; 199,4–7; 220,20–25.

Instances where the taking of hostages is not explicitly linked to baptism, but rather to maintaining peace: *HCL* 10,3–4; 26,20–22; 82,3; 121,1; 204,33–37.

Hostages sent to Germany: *HCL* 14,6–9; 15,19–20. Later on in his chronicle (*HCL* 37,1–10), Henry tells us about an Estonian priest who had been educated at Segeburg (where Henry himself was probably trained), and it is quite possible that hostages sent to Germany mentioned earlier were also sent to the same monastery.

[38] *HCL* 145,31–32: "ut et ipsi baptismi mysterium acciperent et ecclesie Lyvonensi censum ministrarent" (note the conjunction of conversion with the economic benefit of the tithe); a similar formulation is at 145,19–26: after plundering the Livonians and taking women and children captive, the

in Henry's chronicle, therefore, conversion is almost invariably the consequence of military defeat, is coerced and maintained by military force and the taking of hostages, and often occurs in conjunction with the establishment of payments to the Church. While in some cases in Henry's account, the conquered peoples from whom hostages are taken had earlier promised to convert, normally there is no mention of such a prior promise. The stipulation of the papal indulgence for crusade as reported by Henry – that those who had voluntarily accepted the faith could be coerced to maintain it – is therefore, in his own work, largely ignored by the Christians. The *LR*, in contrast to *HCL*, is clearly rather less interested in conversion than military subjugation, given that the conversion of the defeated is rarely mentioned; as Hartmut Kugler has pointed out, the process of Christianization seems not to be a theme the author is concerned with at all.[39]

In both chronicles plunder and the taking of captives including women and children are characteristics of almost all descriptions of battle (in many instances it is also specifically mentioned that both women and children are killed).[40] This was, of course, not an uncommon feature of medieval warfare, but the fact that there are so many instances of plunder in Henry's chronicle (some of which he himself takes part in), and that successful pillage and the capture of women and children is often praised as the work of God, indicates that in the mind of the chronicler the purpose of battle was far from solely the defence of the faith; war was equally an offensive matter, which, although aided by God, provided gains that had no explicit religious value (in a number of instances it is Christian Russians whose villages are plundered and whose women are taken captive).[41] The *LR* in fact contains fewer

Christians offer peace in return for conversion, and we are told that "with hostages having been given they subjugated themselves to the Livonian Church, agreeing to receive the sacraments of baptism and pay an annual tax" ("positis obsidibus ecclesie Lyvonensi se subdiderunt, ut et baptismi sacramenta reciperent et censum annuatim persolverent").

[39]   Kugler, "Text, Gedächtnis und Topographie," p. 93; idem, "Die 'Livländische Reimchronik' des 13. Jahrhunderts," *Latvijas Zinātņu Akadēmijas Vēstis* 9 (1993), 22–30, p. 24.

[40]   There seems to be no justification for Ekdahl's remark ("Ritterorden," p. 223, n. 100) that "die christlichen Heere haben diese Art der Kriegführung übernommen." Henry makes no such statements, and treats warfare of this sort as normal, not exclusively a characteristic of the Baltic peoples, later adopted by Christians. Indriķis Šterns shows that there are in fact far more instances of Germans than any of the converted Christians taking women captive: "Female Captives in Henry's 'Livonian Chronicle'," in *Civitas et castrum ad mare Balticum: Baltijas arheoloģijas un vēstures problēmas dzelzs laikmēta un viduslaikos*, ed. Ēvalds Muguvēričs and Ieva Ose (Riga, 2002), pp. 610–15. In his first report of females (here *puellae*) being captured, Henry states specifically that normally "the armies were accustomed to spare them [the *puellae*] alone in these lands" (*HCL* 65,2–3: *quibus solis parcere solent exercitus in terris istis*). This would seem to imply in fact that the native custom was to spare girls (this does not, or need not, include adult women).

[41]   Instances of plunder on the part of Christians (though not necessarily "Germans") where the capture of women and children is not mentioned (though the taking of captives without specification of age or gender often is): *HCL* 28,19–24; 40,24; 41,5–9; 70,9–22; women and children are explicitly stated to be spared: 91,8–10; 96,5; 97,24–29; 114,1–5; 117,16–18; 120,33–36; 122,9; 133,27–30; 136,6; 143,33–34; 144,18–21; 152,13–15; 153,24–36; 184,30–185,1; the plunder of a Russian Orthodox church: 185,21; 192,8–10; 192,14–15; 192,35–193,7; 194,36; 196,3–7; 196,12–13; 197,26; 198,30–32; 199,28–29; 219,33–34; 220,8–9.

instances of the capture of women and children, although it covers a greater length of time; the cause, however, is probably the greater detail in Henry's chronicle rather than fewer actual occurrences of such captures after Henry's time.[42] The later chronicler often states that a large amount of booty was taken; the damage wrought by the Christians is clearly seen as praiseworthy.[43] In both texts, plunder by the enemy is also often described, and it is apparent that Christian conduct did not, at least in this respect, differ from that of the heathens. It is worth noting that while in Henry's chronicle, when the booty is divided up amongst the Christians after the

Women and children taken captive: 65,1; 70,10–15; 72,2–4; 78,12; 82,12; 86,18–19; 88,21–22; 94,24–30; 95,7; 95,26–27; 96,18; 97,5–6; 97,31–32; 119,21–22; 125,17–18; 125,26–28; 126,6–12; 126,23; 133,3–4; 134,3; 138,9–12; 138,24–25; 145,11; 158,32–159,6; Russian women taken captive: 159,19–21; 160,13–15; 167,9; 185,7; 185,27; 205,14–19. Although significant portions of both *HCL* and *LR* concern battles against Russians, these are not examined in the present paper; on relations between Livonia and Russia in the thirteenth century, the fundamental works are: Anti Selart, *Livland und die Rus' im 13. Jahrhundert*, Quellen und Studien zur baltischen Geschichte 21 (Cologne, 2007); idem: "Der Livländische Deutsche Orden und Russland," in *L'Ordine Teutonico tra Mediterraneo e Baltico: incontri e scontri tra religioni, popoli e culture*, ed. Hubert Houben and Kristjan Toomaspoeg, Acta Theutonica 5 (Galatina, 2008), pp. 253–87; idem, "Orthodox Churches in Medieval Livonia," in *Clash of Cultures*, pp. 273–90. For analyses of how Henry portrays Russians, cf. Torben K. Nielsen, "Sterile Monsters? Russians and the Orthodox Church in the Chronicle of Henry of Livonia," in *Clash of Cultures*, pp. 227–52; and Christoph Schmidt, "Das Bild der 'Rutheni' bei Heinrich von Lettland," *Zeitschrift für Ostmitteleuropa-Forschung* 44 (1995), 509–20. On papal policies regarding Russian campaigns in the Baltic, cf. also Fonnesberg-Schmidt, *Popes and the Baltic Crusades*, pp. 214–24; 231–32. Kugler notes that there is no indication in the whole of the *LR* that the Russians were also Christians: "Text, Gedächtnis und Topographie," p. 99.

[42] Women and children taken captive in *LR*: 674–79; 1215–16; 1721–23; 4256–60: here we are told that "what they were unable to drive or carry was killed" ("was man trîben und tragen / nich enmochte, daz wart geslagen"); it is not clear whether this refers only to the cattle mentioned in the previous line, or also to the women and children; 5964–76: the Rhymer tells us that the women "had to offer their hand to the brothers for the sake of their lives; many a hand was given there" ("mûsten ire hande / den brûderen bieten umme daz leben. / daz wart vil mancher dâ gegeben") – surely this cannot refer to marriage, but if not, what exactly does it mean? – 6840–43; 7290–93; 7381–90; 8041–43; 9165–67.

[43] Plunder on the part of the knight-brothers (and their allies) in *LR*: 1215–16; 1550; 1721; 1796; 1841–43; 1902; 3343; 3390; 3430; 3617; 3997–99; 4275–77; 4256–60; 5964–65; 6187–91; 6237–39; 6300–6301; 6312–14; 6843; 7276–79; 7290–93; 7430–35; apart from plunder, the land is completely razed with fire: 8041–43; 8357–59; 9153; 9160; 9168; 11352; 11365; God praised immediately after plunder: 7381; 8140–48; 8357–59; 9153; 9160; 9168; 11352; 11365.

Four passages state that God received his part of the booty: 2669–75; 3399–404; 11776–81; 11990–95. It is not entirely clear what is meant when, for example, the chronicler states that "he [namely, the Lord] was given weapons and horses" (3404: "man gap im [sc. unserm herren] wâpen unde pfert"). Kugler ("Text, Gedächtnis und Topographie," p. 94; "Livländische Reimchronik," p. 24) is certainly right in stating that this description of Christian behaviour makes the Christians similar to their enemies, who, we are told, "took much plunder and gave a significant part to their gods" ("nâmen roubes vil ... und gâben schônen teil / iren goten" (*LR* 6085–89; similarly 4873–76), but the actions of the Christians must surely refer to donations made to monasteries or some sort of ecclesistical institutions rather than sacrifice – though there is no explicit indication that this is the case. Mary Fischer states that the kind of "direct correlation to God's praiseworthiness with material gain" found in *LR* is "totally alien" to the later Prussian chronicles (on which see briefly below): *"Di himels rote": The Idea of Christian Chivalry in the Chronicles of the Teutonic Order*, Göppinger Arbeiten zur Germanistik 525 (Göppingen, 1991), p. 186. Kugler finds that there are roughly twice as many instances of Christians taking the initiative to go on a plundering expedition: "Text, Gedächtnis und Topographie," p. 93.

end of the battle, in almost all instances the author states that they did so offering thanks to God; the *LR* reports praise of God in this context relatively rarely.

Plundering the enemies' fields and property would have had a primarily, probably solely, non-religious justification; the women and children captured were probably forced into some form of slavery – at any rate, they would not have posed a direct military threat, so the reason for taking them captive was most likely economic.[44] In other words, despite the ostensible purpose of the Christian forces – the defence and expansion of Christianity – both chronicles show the army operating out of motives that appear to be primarily economic, and in the case of plunder and the capture of women and children do not even have purely military justifications, far less religious ones. (There is, of course, no necessary opposition between economic or military and religious motives; what is interesting is the extent to which the latter remain unstated.) However, as with the taking of hostages, Henry often mentions that after plunder or the capture of women and children, the enemies requested peace, agreeing to be baptized in return (freeing the captive women and children is never mentioned); this is a form of forced conversion and thus might be seen to provide a religious motivation for warfare. Even if conversion is one of the conditions of peace, however, it certainly does not seem to be the explicit motivation for the plunder in any of the instances cited above. The *LR* never associates plunder with baptism, and is in this respect too more secular than is *HCL*. On one occasion, Henry explicitly makes the connection between military subjugation and religion, in words ascribed to the conquered Estonians, who say that they "recognize that your [the Christians'] God, who by conquering us inclined our mind to his cult, is greater than our gods."[45] Despite this, a solely religious motive cannot be ascribed, even in Henry's presentation, to the capture of women and children or the plunder of land.

It is also worth noting that, in both chronicles, there seems often to be no explicitly stated immediate ideological motivation for the battles at all. Henry does not always give conversion as the cause for fighting, although he is clearly very concerned with this issue and often mentions conversion following the battle.[46]

---

[44] Sven Ekdahl, "The Treatment of Prisoners of War during the Fighting between the Teutonic Order and Lithuania," in *MO, 1*, pp. 263–69, provides a convincing argument, with regard to fourteenth-century warfare against Lithuania, that the numerous captives (women and children) were forced into slavery; I believe that this suggestion could be equally applicable to the many instances of such captures cited above. Šterns, "Female Captives," suggests, apart from slavery, rape and abandonment, forced marriage, or concubinage as other possibilities regarding the fate of captured women, as well as being forced into prostitution in the brothels of Riga.

[45] *HCL* 85,6–8: "cognoscimus Deum vestrum maiorem diis nostris, qui nos superando animum nostram ad ipsius culturam inclinavit."

[46] We are often told that the converted people seek help from the Rigans or the Sword-Brothers in defending themselves against attacks from Russians or non-Christian enemies. While defence of the faith could conceivably be a motive here (and is not easy to separate from defence of land, goods and life), conversion certainly is not (not all calls for help are answered, and when they are, all the Rigans or knights seem to get is plunder and captives, not converts): *HCL* 48,14–15; 59,5: here the Rigans deny help because of their own meagre number; 62,16; 87,5: fearing treachery, the Rigans choose not

The *LR* has even less to provide us in the way of religious motivation. I have found only one instance in which we are told that the knight-brothers were spreading Christianity (though this is not explicitly called a reason for war); the *LR* says that "they constantly spread the faith and the proper custom."[47] In addition, in one episode we are told that the master of the Order is saddened by the fact that the Curonians are still heathen: "he then became aware that the people were still heathen in Kurland; he began to suffer greatly because of this."[48] He thus decided that "he wanted to lay waste to that land,"[49] but the *LR* does not explicitly state elsewhere that war is motivated by the desire to convert – and even in this episode, there is no mention of conversion after the Christians win the battle, but rather of the taking of land and hostages.[50] Every season, the Christians go out on campaign, sometimes in response to an attack, often with no apparent provocation. In many instances there seems to be no motive for battle beyond revenge for earlier damage caused by the enemy, or conquest and the economic gains of land, plunder, and capturing prisoners.[51] Despite the initial ideological statements in both works, from the depictions of warfare it is apparent that the battles are motivated at least as much (if not more) by a desire to plunder and acquire land (and perhaps slaves), as by any need for defence of the faith or effort to proselytise. Unlike *HCL*, in which, although it is clear that secular rewards do accrue from battle, these are not given as the motivations to fight, the *LR* does explicitly state that seeking honour, land, and riches was a reason to go into battle.[52] It even provides an example of

---

to assist; 94,13–14; 136,15–16; 137,11–12; 156,15–157,10: the Semigallians seek help, and the bishop agrees on condition that they accept baptism, and when they do, he posts a detachment of Sword-Brothers with them.

[47] *LR* 2598–99: "sie breiten stêteclîche / den gelouben und die rechte ê"; *ê* here probably refers to religious practice rather than secular law.

[48] *LR* 2349–52: "dô wart im wol bekant, / daz dannoch in Kûrlant / die lûte wâren heiden. / daz begunde im sêre leiden."

[49] *LR* 2357: "er wolde heren Kûrlant."

[50] *LR* 2391–425. This does not mean, however, that there is no religious incentive to fight: conversion is rarely mentioned, but the possibility, even certainty, of heavenly reward often is, though generally after rather than before the battles: *LR* 538–52; 1164–66; 4519–26; 9344–48. On these passages, see also Horst Wenzel, *Höfische Geschichte: Literarische Tradition und Gegenwartsdeutung in den volkssprachigen Chroniken des hohen und späten Mittelalters*, Beiträge zur älteren deutschen Literaturgeschichte 5 (Bern, 1980), pp. 37–38; 46. We are also told repeatedly after battles are won that this happened with God's or Mary's help – even if there is no mention of any new converts being won for Christianity (*LR* 1150–52; 1702; 2427–28; 2683–84; 5997–99; the cult of the Virgin so prominent in the Order later on is certainly also in evidence in this chronicle (though less so than in later Prussian works), in which the knights are not just aided by, but also often seem to fight for Mary; see on this point Christiansen, *Northern Crusades*, pp. 95–96 ("The Virgin ... is here a war-goddess"); Fischer, *"Di himels rote"*, pp. 186–89.

[51] Thus also Kugler, "Text, Gedächtnis und Topographie," pp. 92–95, with regard to *LR*: the motivation on both sides is primarily plunder.

[52] *LR* 612–13: "without shame they wanted to acquire honour and wealth" ("sie mochten âne schande / irwerben êre und gût"); 1915–16: the master tells his knights: "Now fight, it is time! All our honour depends on it" ("nû strîten, des ist zît! / al unser êre dar an lît"); there are numerous instances of the chronicler stating that the Christian warriors achieved honour, *êre*, in battle, though that is not

repeated plunder and devastation of fields forcing the heathens off their land, thus leaving it free for the Christian knight-brothers.[53] This incident is perhaps the most blatant case of warfare conducted solely for political motives: the harassed peasants are forced to flee their land, escaping to still-heathen Lithuania, and are therefore obviously not converted. The sole motives for this action are the desire for land and the destruction of a fortification (that could admittedly have been used against the Christians).[54]

Although both chronicles show quite explicitly that completely secular motives lay behind many of the battles, Henry of Livonia also often links conquest with conversion; while he might not always portray this as the primary motive for war, it is clear that the conversion of the heathen is of far greater importance to this chronicler than to his vernacular successor. Moreover, Henry includes, in addition to the many instances of conquest and hostage-taking followed by baptism cited above, a lengthy chapter (XXIV) describing the activities of some priests who travel through newly conquered territories baptizing and preaching.[55] Meinhard, the first bishop of Riga, is characterized primarily as a preacher.[56] Preaching the word of God is also mentioned elsewhere before the chapter devoted to this subject, and it is apparent that Henry does give some importance to this aspect of the conquest of the heathens (though preaching is not necessarily divorced from fighting even in his account).[57]

---

the same as stating it was their motivation to fight. Note that seeking fame is also a motivation ascribed to the heathens: *LR* 534; 1122; 1564. *êre* can also, of course, have a religious connotation, though in the language of courtly literature used by the Rhymer such a significance is rarely explicitly intended.

[53] *LR* 11343–408.

[54] Note in this context Henryk Łowmiański, "Anfänge und politische Rolle der Ritterorden an der Ostsee im 13. und 14. Jahrhundert," in *Der Deutschordensstaat Preussen in der polnischen Geschichtsschreibung der Gegenwart*, ed. Udo Arnold and Marian Biskup, Quellen und Studien zur Geschichte des Deutschen Ordens 30 (Marburg, 1982), pp. 36–85, who argues that the Order's policies in the Baltic were, from the start, concerned with expansion and securing a base for survivial in the light of the increasingly dim prospects in the Holy Land; the economic motivation was, therefore, always of greater importance than spreading the faith. See however Klaus Militzer, "From the Holy Land to Prussia: The Teutonic Knights between Emperors and Popes and their Policies until 1309," in *Mendicants, Military Orders and Regionalism in Medieval Europe*, ed. Jürgen Sarnowsky (Aldershot, 1999), pp. 71–81, for some reservations regarding this view.

[55] *HCL* 169,8–177,20.

[56] *HCL* 2,5; 2,12; 3,3; 14; 4,5.

[57] Apart from chapter XXIV, preaching, or peaceful conversion efforts involving instruction in the faith, is mentioned in the following passages: 31,28–32: the Christian voices are not stopped by the killing of their coreligionists, and in fact "grow stronger and stronger both in fighting and in preaching" ("tam preliando quam predicando magis ac magis invalescere"); 32,13–26: a description of the play performed in Riga that expounded the rudiments of the faith (on this incident, see Reinhard Schneider, "Straßentheater im Missionseinsatz: Zu Heinrichs von Lettland Bericht über ein grosses Spiel in Riga 1205," in *Studien über die Anfänge*, pp. 107–21); 44,17–19: priests are sent "to preach after hostages have been received" ("acceptis obsidibus … sacerdotes mittit ad predicationem"); 44,19–47,2: describes the activities of some of the aforementioned priests in *peaceful* baptism of the conquered; 61,6–11; 99,6–7. Chapter XXIX also mentions the preaching of the papal legate (*HCL* 209,1–212,14; 213,1–214,14), though this is probably best not considered a part of the conversion effort.

Apart from plunder, the enslavement of captives, and the acquisition of land that could be settled and cultivated by the Christians, a further economic gain from the conversion to Christianity was the payment of the tithe or a church tax, often a matter of contention between the newly converted and the Church. A number of passages in Henry's chronicle mention that the converts were oppressed by the tithes.[58] In many instances, agreeing to become Christian is also explicitly an agreement to pay the Christian tithe (*decima*) or tax (*censum*), expressed in formulations like: "they subjugated themselves to the Livonian Church, agreeing to receive the sacraments of baptism and pay an annual tax";[59] as noted above, this agreement was often sealed by giving hostages to the Christians, and was made in conjunction with the promise of accepting Christianity.[60] From the admonishments of the papal legate to the Sword-Brothers to ease the tithe payments,[61] it is apparent that heavy burdens were indeed placed on the converts. Furthermore, there is a reference to converts who "assert that the yoke of faith was intolerable,"[62] probably referring to the tithes and/or labour services. This grievance is addressed to a Russian king in a plea for help against the Christian overlords and is therefore characterized as treachery by Henry; but this need not mean that there was no truth in the complaint, given that Latin Christians such as the papal legate and Henry himself also made similar statements.[63] The *LR* also mentions oppressive taxes, though not in a sympathetic manner at all, and is in general far less concerned with tithes and the complaints of the converts. Taxes are often paid to the Christians as the price of peace (but

---

[58] *HCL* 92,26–93,2: "the Livs begged that the Christian laws and particularly the tithe should be made less burdensome to them" ("[Lyvones] petentes iura christianorum et maxime decimam sibi alleviari"); 103,16–21: the Livs are oppressed because they have to pay taxes to both the church and the Russian king, their secular overlord; 210,1–5: the papal legate admonishes the *fratres milicie* not to oppress the Estonians with tithes "lest by such a cause they are forced to return again to paganism" ("ne per talem occasionem iterum ad paganismum redire cogantur"); similarly 211,1–6: the legate here admonishes not only the knight-brothers, but also *alios Theutonicos*).

[59] *HCL* 145,23–25: "ecclesie Lyvonensi se subdiderunt, ut et baptismi sacramenta reciperent et censum annuatim persolverent."

[60] Other instances where baptism and tithes (*decima*) or taxes (*censum*) are explicitly linked: *HCL* 110,21–111,20: this passage includes a speech in which the Livs are told, among other things, that their prosperity will increase with the new faith if they also pay their tithes; 138,30–33; 145,32–146,1; 165,6–7; 205,26–28; 206,16–18.

[61] *HCL* 210,1–5: "he instructed them [*sc.* the Sword-Brothers] that they should not be exceedingly harsh to those subjugated to them, those dull Estonians, either in taking tithes or in any other matters" ("docebat eos ne subditis suis, stultis Estonibus illis, aut in decimis accipiendis aut in aliis quibuscunque causis nimium graves existerent"); similary *HCL* 211,1–6.

[62] *HCL* 33,11: "intollerabile iugum fidei asserebant."

[63] Henry appeals to the rulers of the land not to oppress the Livs and Letts with excessive taxes: "take care ... not to oppress the poor too much, namely the Livs and Letts and any other converts ... For the Blessed Virgin is not delighted by the heavy tithe, which the converts are accustomed to pay, nor pleased by other taxes collected from them, nor by a heavy yoke" (*HCL* 181,10–24: "attendite ... ne pauperes nimium opprimatis, pauperes dico Lyvones et Lettos sive quoscunque neophytos ... Non enim beata Virgo censu magno, quem dare solent neophyti, delectatur, non diversis exactionibus ipsis ablata placatur, neque iugum grave"). Henry's concerns here mirror those of the popes Innocent III and Honorius III: see Fonnesberg-Schmidt, *Popes and the Baltic Crusades*, pp. 117–19; 177–79.

baptism is not mentioned in conjunction with this in the *LR*, in contrast to *HCL*).[64] It is likely that these payments were at least one of the reasons why many converts frequently lapsed, and also why the Church was so eager to maintain firm control over its converts as well as gain more.

The Depiction of Heathen Customs

Both texts provide some descriptions of heathen customs, as well as some indications of how these customs or manners were retained (in the view of the chroniclers) even after conversion.[65] Although the various heathen groups appear to be differentiated according to political or ethnic boundaries, neither chronicle distinguishes between the religious beliefs of any of these groups. Both show the heathens as polytheistic. Henry describes the unconverted population as idolaters, and names one of their gods (Tharaphita).[66] He presents them as repeatedly trying to wash off the Christian faith very literally, by bathing in the river.[67] Henry also provides many examples of the heathens consulting oracles; in a number of cases, the oracles appear to go against the wishes of the heathens, and seem more favourable to the Christians, and they are also presented as predicting correctly the outcome of battle.[68]

The *LR* is less concerned specifically with the idolatry of the Baltic peoples, though it often states that they are led by the Devil and refers to their false gods.[69]

---

[64] *LR* 1396–99 (the Estonians have to pay increasing taxes, regardless of whether this might do them damage); 1406–12 (the converts are forced to build churches, and their reluctance is chided); 2439–41 (the Curonians have to pay a heavy tax). Other passages mention the payment of taxes in order to maintain peace: *LR* 3441–50; 8066–71; 9609; 9639–42. In one instance the chronicler explicitly links the *zins* and Christianity, stating that the Oselians remained free of both for many years: *LR* 1622–23.

[65] On the following, see also Rasa J. Mažeika, "Granting Power to Enemy Gods in the Chronicles of the Baltic Crusades," in *Medieval Frontiers: Concepts and Practices*, ed. David Abulafia and Nora Berend (Aldershot, 2002), pp. 153–71; Weiss, "Mythologie und Religiosität." Note that I do not examine here depictions of political or social structures, or indeed how the narratives of my two chronicles match up with any other independent evidence. On the portrayal of political and social structures in Henry, see most recently Andris Šnē, "The Image of the Other or the Own: Representations of Local Societies in *Heinrici Chronicon*," in *The Medieval Chronicle VI*, ed. Erik Kooper (Amsterdam, 2009), pp. 247–60, as well as idem, "Emergence of Livonia," and Eihmane, "Baltic Crusades."

[66] References to idolaters: *HCL* 2,1; 37,10; 45,13; 54,8; 109,35–36; 133,24; 176,32; 212,6; the god Tharaphita: *HCL* 220,30. On this deity, see the comprehensive study of Urmas Sutrop: "Taarapita – The Great God of the Oeselians," *Folklore: Electronic Journal of Folklore* 26 (2004), 27–64 (available online at http://www.folklore.ee/folklore/vol26/sutrop.pdf). One should note that, with the exception of Jews, the reference to non-Christian peoples (even Muslims) as idolators is commonplace in medieval writings, and does not necessarily say much about actual religious practice.

[67] *HCL* 4,7–8; 29,18–20; 191,16–18.

[68] *HCL* 4,15–21: the oracle says a Christian priest should live; 55,9–14: the oracle says the Letts should join the Latin Christians rather than the Russians, and accept baptism; *HCL* 59,7–8: the oracles predict a good outcome to battle, and the battle is indeed later won; 190,33–36: the lot favours the sacrifice of an ox rather than a Christian priest.

[69] Idols and the devil in *LR*: 339: "the heathens have many false gods" ("sie haben abgote vil"); 1363–64: "they pray to the false gods because of the Devil's scorn" ("daz sie die valschen apgot / an

Like Henry, the *LR* provides many examples of the heathens consulting oracles; the *LR* might grant somewhat more credence to the efficacy of these oracles and to the enemy's gods. A heathen god has the power to freeze water so that the Lithuanian army can cross over the ice;[70] the oracles' view of the future for the heathens proves correct on two occasions.[71] The Teutonic Knights even appear to believe in the oracle of their heathen allies, apparently becoming confident because of what it says, and it turns out that the oracle's prediction is in fact fulfilled.[72] Similarly, one episode depicts the conquered heathens casting lots which predict that their battle, alongside the Teutonic Knights, will end favourably; while the Christians are not shown to be affected in any way by this, it is apparent that the oracle was actually correct – something the chronicler need not have included at all.[73]

Henry states that the heathens sacrifice humans to their gods (or at least plan to do so).[74] He also describes them as cruel on a number of occasions. Even after conversion, Henry depicts the new converts as being especially bloodthirsty,[75] and the heathens are sometimes depicted as killing their victims after torturing them, or burning them alive (Henry also does state that the heathens receive a cruel death at the hands of the Christians – deservedly, in his view).[76] This was, of course, hardly uncommon practice for Christians too, but the adjective *crudelis* and the adverb *crudeliter* are rarely used to refer to the Christians in *HCL*. It is also worth noting that in most of the instances when Christians torment their enemies or burn

---

beten durch des tûvels spot"); 1427: they are led by the *tûvel*; 3881–89: the heathens cremate their dead, along with armour and weapons, "to satisfy the devil in the otherworld" ("dar mite solden sie stillen / den tûvel in jener werlde dort"); the chronicler says of this at 3890 that "such great foolishness was unheard of" ("sô grôze tôrheit wart nie gehôrt").

[70] *LR* 1435–57.

[71] *LR* 3019–45: an oracle correctly predicts a death; 4680–876: an oracle correctly predicts victory, and the heathen allies of the knight-brothers "gave thanks to their gods for the fact that they were successful in battle" ("saiten iren goten danc, / daz an deme strîte in gelanc").

[72] *LR* 7229–80.

[73] *LR* 2478–572; see also Feistner et al., *Krieg im Visier*, pp. 87–88.

[74] *HCL*, 4,12–13; 31,27–28; 190,33–36.

[75] *HCL* 119,4–8.

[76] *HCL* 80,15–19: "they roasted some [Christians] alive" ("alios vivos assaverunt"); of others we are told that "crosses are cut into their backs before they slit their [the Christians'] throats" ("in dorsi eorum crucibus factis iugulaverunt"); 121,17–30: a priest is tortured in various ways before being killed; 124,35–36: a Christian is burnt alive; 190,12–17: the heart of a Christian is removed while he is alive, then roasted and eaten.

The heathens receiving a cruel death: 58,22–24: "They killed all of them with the harsh death as they deserved" ("omnes crudeli morte sicut meruerunt interfecerunt"); 96,10–12: a recently converted Christian roasts some of his victims; 126,31–38: the sons of a recent convert killed by heathens take revenge by torturing their enemies and burning them alive. Chapter XXV,2 (*HCL* 179,1–181, 25) justifies the cruel fate of many of the opponents of the Church saying they deserved it for their persecution of the Christians; some of these adversaries are Christians – even Latin Christians – and they are exhorted to fear the "gentle mother of mercy," who is equally the "harsh avenger" ("ipsam tam mitem matrem misericordie timete ... ipsam tam crudelem vindicatricem"). This speech seems to be aimed as much at the Christian lords who are harsh to their subjects as at the heathen and Christian opponents of the Livonian Church.

them alive, those doing so are recent converts, not Germans. The *LR* seems far less concerned with depicting the cruelty of the heathens.[77]

Both texts also often depict the local populace (before and after conversion) as foolish and cowardly, with a number of instances of them deserting in battle when fighting alongside the Christians;[78] the *LR*, however, does also show the converts as being extremely brave in battle on other occasions.[79] Henry does not seem inclined to ascribe their lack of constancy in Christianity or obstinacy in their own religion to stupidity (as do later chronicles from Prussia),[80] but rather to deceit and treachery (*dolum* or *perfidia*).[81] The treachery of the Livs and Livonians is also mentioned in the *LR*, though less often, and here it lacks any specific religious context.[82]

Unlike Henry's chronicle, the *LR* devotes a fair amount of space to depicting the secular honours of battle and the armour and trappings of the warriors and their mounts. The heathens are depicted quite on par with the Christians: their armour, like that of the Christians, is often described as gleaming, shining in the sun, and so on, and there are actually more instances of enemy armies being described as mighty with gleaming armour than of Christians.[83] The heathen warriors, like the Christians, are also often presented in entirely positive terms as brave or mighty

---

[77] *LR* 7013–14: a captured knight-brother "is placed on a spit" ("sie satzten in ûf einen rôst"); 10700–709: one knight-brother is clubbed to death, another is roasted.

[78] Foolishness in Henry: *HCL* 3,18–21; 210,3.

Converts fleeing the battlefield in Henry: *HCL* 51,1–4; 60,10–11; heathen allies of the Christians flee from the battle: 80,1–4; 88,8–9; 122,19–20; 149,22–28. Converts fleeing in *LR*: 5601–7; 6050–53; 7490–91; 8441–43; 10274–75; 10579–85; 10632–33.

[79] *LR* 1149; 8107–20.

[80] The two most significant works of Prussian historiography are Peter von Dusburg, "Chronicon terrae Prussiae," ed. Max Töppen, in *Scriptores rerum prussicarum* (Frankfurt am Main, 1965), vol. 1, pp. 3–219, and the vernacular adaptation of this by Nikolaus von Jeroschin, "Die Krônike von Prûzinlant," ed. Ernst Strehlke, in *Scriptores rerum prussicarum* (Frankfurt am Main, 1965), vol. 1, pp. 291–624. How *HCL* and the *LR* relate to these will be discussed briefly below; on the stupidity (and other qualities and practices) ascribed to the heathens in these works, see "Chronicon terrae Prussiae," pp. 53–55, and "Krônike von Prûzinlant," ll. 3983–4264. For discussion, see Feistner et al., *Krieg im Visier*, pp. 38–39; Edith Feistner, "Vom Kampf gegen das 'Andere': Pruzzen, Litauer und Mongolen in lateinischen und deutschen Texten des Mittelalters," *Zeitschrift für deutsches Altertum* 132 (2003), 281–94; eadem, "Die (Ohn-)Macht des 'Anderen': Pruzzen und Mongolen in mittelalterlichen Texten," in *Germanistik im Kontaktraum Europa II: Beiträge zur Literatur*, ed. Mira Miladinovic Zalaznik (Ljubljana, 2003), pp. 81–99.

[81] Deceit and treachery mentioned as qualities of the native peoples of Livonia: *HCL* 3,23–24; 5,13–6,4; 13,12–14; 14,2; 18,2; 19,10–14; 30,4; 33,7–9; 41,20; 42,17–18; 46,13–14; 75,10–11; 75,18–20; 77,14; 82,4; 86,30; 102,11–15; 110,6–20; 120,28–32; 133,17; 152,35–36; 155,5–7; 163,23–24; 180,12–21; 189,31–32; 189,37; 201,23; 201,29. The terms *dolum/dolose* and *perfidus/perfidia* are frequently used to describe the Russians and their actions as well, though these instances are not cited here.

[82] *LR* 1287–1307; 5671–77; 9612–16.

[83] Descriptions of the Christian army in shining armour: *LR* 2374–83; 3281–86; 7178–79; 10410–11. Descriptions of the enemy's equipment as impressive: *LR* 1084–87; 1578–80; 1594–97; 2107–9; 2216–19; a description of the excellence of the Russian army's equipment: 5016–21; 5449–50; 8340–42.

warriors or heroes (*helt*), who happen to be the enemy.[84] In this respect, the *LR* treats both parties far more equitably than does Henry's chronicle, which is inclined to consider the heathens almost exclusively in negative terms.

It seems that Henry was more concerned than the vernacular chronicler with the religious customs of the heathens, and specifically with their idolatry and human sacrifice; these are not issues of particular importance for the Rhymer. Henry, while far more sympathetic to the converts and in fact critical of the knight-brothers for oppressing their subjects, nevertheless generally depicts all the native peoples as more cruel in their ways than the Germans, and seems to be far more interested in showing this cruelty than is the *LR*, which has far fewer mentions of such incidents. Both chroniclers consistently differentiate between the converts and the Germans; while they are sometimes collectively referred to as Christians, most often they are broken up into ethnic groups (Henry also frequently refers to the converts as *neophiti*). It is apparent throughout both chronicles that the authors clearly identify themselves with the Germans (in Henry's case the Church at Riga rather than the Sword-Brothers), more than with all Christians, including the recent converts to Christianity.[85] Henry's chronicle displays the heathens more consistently in a negative light, whereas in the *LR*, "the predominant characteristic of the portrayal of the heathen is the knight's respect for the fighting abilities of the enemy";[86] Michael Neecke has recently concluded that not only is there in this text "weder eine subtstantielle Überlegenheit der Ordensritter noch eine umfassende 'Verteufelung' der Feinde," but also that the similarity between heathens and Christians "geht in der Reimchronik tatsächlich über das hinaus, was die Heldenepik traditionell an demonstrativer Wertschätzung der Kombattanten kennt."[87]

Conclusions

The preceding analysis of the two primary narrative sources for Baltic history in the thirteenth century provides somewhat mixed results. While Henry of Livonia clearly presents an ideological viewpoint and stresses the importance of conversion – a theme almost completely lacking in the later vernacular work – he does not shy away from describing the material gains and battle techniques of the Christians,

---

[84] Thus also Fischer, *"Di himels rote"*, pp. 183–84; Kugler, "Text, Gedächtnis und Topographie," p. 92, and "Livländische Reimchronik," p. 24; citing, however, only five of the following instances between them: *LR* 2722–29; 3731–35; 4087 (an enemy is called a *vil vromer helt*); 5378–81; 5524–25 (mighty warriors on both sides); 6044–48; 6216–19; 7780; 8397–407 (both sides have brave heroes); 8992; 9197; 11744; 11753.

[85] On this aspect of Henry's work, see also Bilķins, "Autoren," and Holtzmann, "Studien." On the discourse of German identity in the Baltic, see also Len Scales, *The Shaping of German Identity: Authority and Crisis, 1245–1414* (Cambridge, 2012); this important work appeared when the present article was already at proof stage and its findings could thus not be properly incorporated into this paper.

[86] Fischer, *"Di himels rote"*, p. 183.

[87] Feistner et al., *Krieg im Visier*, p. 87.

and shows that they are identical to those of their enemies. He does, however, often try to link warfare to the theological justification for it by describing the baptism of the conquered after their defeat – though he does not by any means do this consistently throughout. Furthermore, Henry is more consistent in portraying the practices and character of the heathens negatively, highlighting their human sacrifices and treachery, with few positive images of them; although he is willing to see them more sympathetically, deserving to be sheltered (to some extent) from fiscal exploitation, he is incapable of valorizing their martial prowess.

The later German chronicle views things far more from the point of view of the battleground rather than the pulpit. The heathens are described primarily in terms of their military abilities, which compare favourably to those of the Christians. Unlike Henry, although the Rhymer is more willing to portray the heathen warriors positively as warriors, he is less sympathetic to the plight of the conquered, ignoring the oppression of tithes and so on. Moreover, little consideration is given to baptism: the *LR* is concerned almost exclusively with military matters, and after the opening lines, it appears almost as an incidental detail that the opponents are not Christian. The more secular nature of the *LR* is also perhaps the reason why even church taxes are not frequently mentioned; in contrast to this, Henry, patently concerned with the upkeep of the nascent church, very frequently mentions in the same sentence the promise of conversion and the payment of tithes. However, it is apparent that Henry has sympathy for the recent converts (even if none at all for the heathens), for he does speak out against excessive demands made on them. This does not prevent him from portraying them as inferior and cowardly when compared to the Germans.

The fundamental divergences appear to stem from the fact that Henry, a priest, gives an important place to baptism and tithes, whereas the later chronicle, probably written both by and for military men, gives more room to secular issues, and provides hardly any consideration of religious matters. It is likely that the differences between the chronicles are caused by the author and audience, rather than by a change in the way the crusades were conducted. The policy of the see of Riga probably remained much the same with regard to the importance given to conversion and preaching, whereas the attitude of the military orders was always more concerned with battle and conquest, leaving the proselytizing to the priests.[88]

The difference in focus is a reflection of a real change in the situation only insofar as the Teutonic Order at the end of the thirteenth century was in a far stronger position with regard to the archbishopric of Riga than it or its predecessor, the Order of the Sword-Brothers, had been at the century's beginning. From the middle

---

[88] Similarly Marie-Luise Favreau-Lilie, "Mission to the Heathen in Prussia and Livonia: The Attitudes of the Religious Military Orders Toward Christianization," in *Christianizing Peoples and Converting Individuals*, ed. Guyda Armstrong and Ian N. Wood, International Medieval Research 7 (Turnhout, 2000), pp. 147–54; Ekdahl, "Ritterorden," p. 232, with regard to the Sword-Brothers: "die Aufgabe des Ordens bei der Christianisierung im Baltikum bestand nicht darin, die Heiden durch Predigt zu bekehren, sondern sie gemäß seines Kampfauftrages mit Machtmitteln zu befriedigen."

of the thirteenth through much of the fourteenth century, the Teutonic Order was effectively the primary and often the sole military power in Livonia, and was by no means under the political control of Riga; it was also a landowner on a massive scale.[89] For this reason only, it is likely that there was in fact relatively less emphasis placed on conversion and fair demands in tithes and the like in the chronicle from the end of the century. Given the lack of an equivalent to Henry's narrative from this period, it is not easy to determine whether the Church would have chosen a mode of self-representation closer to that of the Teutonic Order (I suspect that this is unlikely), but it seems logical that the *LR* reflects the real situation at the end of the thirteenth century more accurately than would a latter-day Henry of Livonia, given that the balance of power was now on the side of the Teutonic Order, and the thrust of Christian efforts in the area is therefore more likely to have been primarily military, political, and economic, rather than religious.

I would like to stress, however, that there is very little fundamental divergence between the two works in the depiction of the Christian conflict with the heathens: in both chronicles, the Christians fight just as brutally as the heathens, not sparing women and children, devastating the land, and taking much plunder. In both chronicles, the immediate motives for battle are often unstated, and frequently do not appear to stem either from any imminent threat or the possibility of conversion. While Henry, unlike the *LR*, does not explicitly state that there were economic motives for conflict, his narrative makes it clear this was indeed the case. Although it is true that Henry does not, unlike the Rhymer, seem to be particularly bloodthirsty or take pleasure in gory depictions of slaughter, and therefore that the "the voice which came from Livonia at the end of the century was much harsher"[90] than its earlier counterpart appears to have been, the Christians had always been conquerors and plunderers, and it is obvious – despite Henry's apparent sympathy for his flock – that as far as conversion were concerned, even a priest such as he completely supported the brutal modes of conquest that preceded conversion. The nature of the process of Christianizing the Baltic, therefore, was probably in essence much the same at both ends of the century: in both periods, it was characterized by vicious warfare, economic exploitation and secular politics; and in both periods, secular motives were just as important, if not more so, than religious ideals (though the religious motivation of heavenly reward, rather than the expansion of Christendom, should not be discounted). In both periods too, the evidence of these chronicles suggests that conversion was more often a result of conquest than of conviction

---

[89] On relations between the Order and other authorities in Livonia, see Christiansen, *Northern Crusades*, 146–51; Manfred Hellmann, "Der Deutsche Orden und die Stadt Riga," in *Stadt und Orden: das Verhältnis des Deutschen Ordens zu den Städten in Livland, Preussen und im Deutschen Reich*, ed. Udo Arnold, Quellen und Studien zur Geschichte des Deutschen Ordens 44 (Marburg, 1993), pp. 1–33; idem, "Die Stellung des livländischen Ordenszweiges"; Juhan Kreem, "The Teutonic Order as Secular Ruler in Livonia: The Privileges and the Oath of Reval," in *Crusade and Conversion*, pp. 215–32; Militzer, *Geschichte des Deutschen Ordens*, pp. 82–86.

[90] Christiansen, *Northern Crusades*, p. 95; see also Murray, "*Livonian Rhymed Chronicle*," pp. 243–45.

brought about by preaching. Given the emphasis placed on preaching in Henry's work, this might seem surprising but, as we have seen, this conclusion emerges from Henry's own narrative, thus making it, I suggest, rather more similar in tone to the *LR* than is generally thought.

What emerges from the analysis of these two works with regard to modes of self-representation is that, although Henry was a priest and representative of the Church at Riga (though this does not by any means imply that his work embodies some sort of official position of the see), he could nevertheless present quite prominently the secular motives of conflict; his affiliation with the see of Riga also does not mean that Henry even desired to show Christians as shunning the use of force and excessive violence. To the contrary, while the representation of the Church is primarily religious, it is equally apparent that the Church's mission, in the eyes of Henry, was also a military one.[91] Henry saw the end result as beneficial to the local populace as well, not just the conquerors: the consistently negative portrayal of heathen customs and manners highlights the gains brought to the converts by Christianity, which could lead them to a virtuous life and salvation (the possible economic benefits are hinted at, but not given much room in his chronicle).

The consensus of the scholarship suggests that the *LR* may be seen as a work representing the position of a larger group, the Teutonic Order, as it was almost certainly composed for the Order, though possibly as a means of external self-representation. In contrast to *HCL*, the Order's chronicle is concerned with religion only insofar as the warriors who lose their lives are presented as martyrs for the faith; throughout the text, the role of the military order is indeed almost solely military, and the maintenance or spread of Christianity in the land are of little importance. Even the fact that the enemies are religious "others" seems of less significance than that they are enemies; moreover, in the interests of military gains, the Rhymer does not mind ignoring religion and benefits to Christianity altogether. It is also notable that, unlike the later Prussian chronicles of the Teutonic Order (and unlike Henry), the *LR* uses largely secular language, style, and imagery, with very little material drawn from religious sources; while this might be because its audience was partly secular (visiting crusaders), it sheds an interesting perspective on the self-representation of the Order in Livonia at this time. Neecke has found that, while some biblical epic was cultivated within the Prussian branch of the Teutonic Order in thirteenth century, there appears at this point to have been little interaction between religious literature and historiography, and between the ideologies and modes of self-identification they could each furnish.[92] It is apparent that in fact the Order in

---

[91] For this reason, Simon Gerber's argument that Henry essentially preaches a theology of peace seems to me somewhat overstating the case; Simon Gerber, "Heinrich von Lettland – ein Theologe des Friedens: 'Nichts Bessers weiß ich mir an Sonn- und Feiertagen, Als ein Gespräch von Krieg und Kriegsgeschrei'," *Zeitschrift für Kirchengeschichte* 115 (2004), 1–18, e.g. p. 15: "Die Mission, auch wenn sie zu kriegerischen Mitteln greift, ist ja nichts anders als die Ausbreitung des Friedens."

[92] Feistner et al., *Krieg im Visier*, pp. 49–79; 104. On the function of religious literature in this regard, see in addition Danielle Buschinger, "Literatur und Politik in der Deutschordensdichtung," and Michael Neecke, "Strategien der Identitätsstiftung: Zur Rolle der Bibelepik im Deutschen Orden

Livonia had also a more secular role, one less concerned with religious affairs; if we accept that the *LR* was composed for the Order, then it is clear that it manifestly also did not mind presenting itself in a largely non-religious light: the vernacular work "präsentiert ein ausschließlich militärisches Selbstbild der *brûdere*."[93] This was to change within the next few decades: the official chronicles of the Teutonic Order from the first half of the fourteenth century have a far more explicitly religious character, stressing the religious role of the Order, with other motives and attitudes certainly still present, but receding significantly in importance.[94]

The *LR* occupies a rather anomalous position, even with regard to its treatment by modern scholarship: although used by historians as a source of facts (albeit often with some reluctance, and understandably so), it has not received as much attention as a cultural and historical artefact in and of itself as have either Henry's chronicle or the later works from Prussia. I cannot go into the causes for the greater ideological sophistication of the Prussian works here;[95] Henry has seemed more

---

(13/14. Jahrhundert)," both in *Mittelalterliche Kultur und Literatur im Deutschordensstaat Preussen: Leben und Nachleben*, ed. Jarosław Wenta, Sieglinde Hartmann, and Gisela Vollmann-Profe, Sacra bella septentrionalia 1 (Toruń, 2008), pp. 449–60 and pp. 461–71 respectively.

[93] Feistner et al., *Krieg im Visier*, p. 104. There is absolutely no parallel in *HCL* or *LR* to the passages in the Prussian chronicles on religious and corporeal weapons, in which the real battles fought are allegorized in terms of spiritual struggle: "Chronicon terrae Prussiae," pp. 40–46; "Krônike von Prûzinlant," 2274–3392; see Fischer, *"Di himels rote"*, pp. 165–70. Nevertheless, Fischer has suggested that in *LR* there could be a (very cursory) indication of a concept of suffering in battle as some sort of *imitatio Christi* (*"Di himels rote"*, p. 185).

[94] On the more explicitly religious position of the later chronicles, see most recently Feistner et al., *Krieg im Visier* (with references to many useful earlier works by the same authors); and the important works of Mary Fischer: *"Di himels rote"*; eadem, "Biblical Heroes and the Uses of Literature: The Teutonic Order in the Late Thirteenth and Early Fourteenth Centuries," in *Crusade and Conversion*, pp. 261–75; eadem, "The Books of the Maccabees and the Teutonic Order," *Crusades* 4 (2005), 59–71; eadem, "Des tûvils kint? The German Order's Perception of its Enemies as Revealed in the Krônike von Prûzinlant," *Archiv für das Studium der neueren Sprachen und Literaturen* 244 (2007), 260–75. For a broader view of the historiography of the Teutonic Order in Prussia, see also Jarosław Wenta, *Studien über die Ordensgeschichtsschreibung am Beispiel Preußens* (Toruń, 2000). Note that, according to Fischer, while the use of typological imagery and other religious devices was certainly very sophisticated in some of the later Prussian chronicles, the non-Christian opponents are, especially in the latter part of Nikolaus von Jeroschin's chronicle, often granted some legitimacy, and in particular their prowess as warriors is often described in positive terms. For an interpretation that stresses the fact that the heathens could also be portrayed positively in Peter von Dusburg's chronicle, and could in fact have a function similar to that of the Germans in Tacitus (simple virtue vs. one's own people's decadence), cf. Rasa J. Mažeika, "Violent Victims? Surprising Aspects of the Just War Theory in the Chronicle of Peter von Dusburg," in *Clash of Cultures*, pp. 122–37, at pp. 127–31. Nevertheless, the extensive use of various kinds of religious literature, particularly Scripture, in the Prussian works is quite apparent; in contrast, there seems to be only one clear derivation from Scripture in the *LR* (Fischer, *"Di himels rote"*, p. 185, with reference to *LR* 476–80, quoting Matt. 25.40). Note also that "in contrast to the 'Krônike von Prûzinlant' the depiction of warfare in the chronicle [*sc. LR*] is detailed and precise," and similarly, the description of the splendour of the Christian army found in *LR* is lacking in the later vernacular work from Prussia (Fischer, *"Di himels rote"*, pp. 175, 184).

[95] Among the causes were the collapse of the Order in the Holy Land and its consequently greater commitment to and need for legitimacy in its Baltic lands, as well as the rising chorus of complaints against it, which, viewed in conjunction with the arrest and dissolution of the Templars, probably gave

interesting not least because of his chronicle's status as the first work to emerge out
of this region. I hope to have shown, though, that Henry has rather more in common
with the later vernacular history than is often appreciated – a fact that suggests
that there was relatively little difference between the beginning and the end of the
thirteenth century with regard to the forms of contact between (German) Christians
and the non-Christian or recently converted inhabitants of Livonia, and certainly
less divergence in self-representation between works by members of two different
Christian corporate groups, the secular clergy at Riga and the Teutonic Order. From
around 1200, contact was (and was presented as) predominantly violent, and fuelled
at least equally (if not more) by secular as by religious motives; the representation
of this contact throughout the thirteenth century makes little effort, in Latin or the
vernacular, to conceal or apologize for this fact.

---

the Order good reason to express itself in more religious rather than secular terms. On these issues, see in
brief Christiansen, *Northern Crusades*, pp. 147–51; see also Mažeika, "Violent Victims?". On the effects
of these developments on literary production, see the works of Feistner et al.; Fischer; and Wenta, cited
in the previous note; and in addition, for the broader context, see the essays collected in Wenta et al.,
Mittelalterliche Kultur und Literatur im Deutschordensstaat Preussen.

Wilbrand of Oldenburg's Journey to Syria, Lesser Armenia, Cyprus, and the Holy Land (1211–1212): A New Edition

Denys Pringle

Cardiff University
pringlerd@cardiff.ac.uk

Wilbrand of Oldenburg's account of his journey to the eastern Mediterranean in 1211–12 constitutes a significant source of information relating to the political, military and ecclesiastical state of affairs in the recently formed Christian kingdoms of Lesser Armenia and Cyprus and in those parts of the former Frankish-held territories in Syria and Palestine that remained divided between the Franks and the Ayyubids some two decades after the fall of the first kingdom of Jerusalem.[1] Wilbrand was the son of Henry II, count of Oldenburg (1167–98), and of Beatrix of Hallermund. When he set out for the East in 1211 he was a canon of the church of Hildesheim; and following his return he was made prior in 1218. In 1225 he was appointed to the see of Paderborn and between 1226 and 1227 he also administered the sees of Münster and Osnabrück. In 1227 he became archbishop of Utrecht. He died in Zwolle in July 1233 and was buried in the abbey church of St. Servaas.[2]

Wilbrand's eastern travels were undertaken for two specific purposes and his account of them falls into two parts. The first part, beginning with his landing in Acre on 25 August 1211 and ending the following spring, involved his participation in a diplomatic mission to King Levon I of Armenian Cilicia on behalf of the German emperor Otto IV, in the company of Hermann of Salza, grand master of the Teutonic Order, and the envoys of Leopold VII, duke of Austria. In 1195 the Rubenid Baron Levon II (as he then was) had requested a royal crown from the emperor Henry VI and Pope Celestine III. After protracted negotiations while a suitable formula was agreed to describe the relationship of the Armenian church to the papacy, Levon was finally crowned King Levon I on 6 January 1198 in the

---

[1] See discussion by Marc Delpech and Jean-Claude Voisin, "La mission en Cilicie de Wilbrand von Oldenburg 1211–1212: journal de route de Wilbrand," *Mélanges de l'Université Saint-Joseph* 56 (1999–2003), 291–345; Arieh Graboïs, "Terre sainte et Orient latin vus par Willebrand d'Oldenbourg," in Michel Balard, Benjamin Z. Kedar, and Jonathan Riley-Smith, eds., *Dei gesta per Francos: Études sur les croisades dédiées à Jean Richard, Crusade Studies in Honour of Jean Richard* (Aldershot, 2001), pp. 261–68; Peter Halfter, "Eine Beschreibung Kilikiens aus westlicher Sicht: Das Itinerarium des Wilbrand von Oldenburg," *Oriens Christianus* 85 (2001), 176–203.

[2] Delpech and Voisin, "Mission," pp. 294–95; Graboïs, "Terre sainte," p. 261; Halfter, "Beschreibung," p. 177; B. U. Hucker, "Wilbrand von Oldenburg-Wildeshausen: Administrator der Bistümer Münster und Osnabrück, Bischof von Paderborn und Utrecht (†1233)," *Jahrbuch für das Oldenburger Münsterland* (1994), 60–71; J. C. M. Laurent, *Peregrinatores Medii Aevi Quatuor* (Leipzig, 1864), pp. 161, 191.

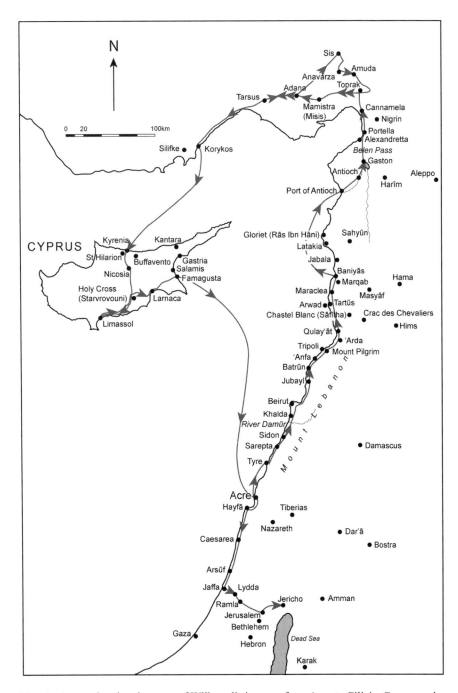

Map 1   A map showing the route of Wilbrand's journey from Acre to Cilicia, Cyprus and
        the Holy Land

Drawn by Ian Dennis

presence of the papal legate, Conrad of Querfurt, archbishop of Mainz, with a crown brought to the East by the imperial chancellor, Conrad, bishop of Hildesheim.[3] Although the precise purpose of Wilbrand's mission in 1211–12 is not stated, it was evidently intended to assist in cementing relations between Levon I and the new German emperor, Otto IV, who had been invested with the imperial crown by Pope Innocent III in 1209. Levon at this time was involved in a continuing dispute with the pope and the Templars over the succession to the principality of Antioch and was in need of support. In 1211 his envoys returned from the West with a new crown from Otto IV, which on 15 August Levon placed on the head of his heir, his great-nephew Raymond Rupen.[4] His favour towards the Teutonic Order is shown by a charter of April 1212, in which he identified himself as a confrater of the order and granted to it the castle of Amuda along with a number of villages in the Cilician plain.[5] It seems, however, that some of the places included in this grant would already have been in the Order's possession at the time of Wilbrand's visit, for he describes Amuda as a castle belonging to the German Hospital in January 1212 and *Cumbetefort* (*Cumbethfor*), which he calls a house and residence of the Order, was already in their hands in June 1209.[6] Wilbrand returned to Acre in the spring of 1212, taking ship from Korykos to Kyrenia and travelling across Cyprus by way of Nicosia, Limassol, and Stavrovouni monastery to Famagusta, where he took ship once again for the mainland.

The second part of Wilbrand's itinerary was a pilgrimage to Jerusalem and the Holy Places. No dates are given for this portion of his account, though they evidently occurred in the first part of 1212. The text breaks off abruptly, however, at the Mount

[3] Smbat the Constable, in *Chronique* 34, trans. G. Dédéyan, DRHC 13 (Paris, 1980), pp. 72–73; cf. *RHC Darm* 1:634–38; Sirapie Der Nersessian, "The Kingdom of Cilician Armenia," in Setton, *Crusades* 2:630–59 (at pp. 645–48); Thomas S. R. Boase, ed., *The Cilician Kingdom of Armenia* (Edinburgh and London, 1978) p. 19; Bernard Hamilton, "The Armenian Church and the Papacy at the Time of the Crusades," *Eastern Churches Review* 19 (1978), 61–87; repr. in idem, *Monastic Reform, Catharism and the Crusades (900–1300)* (London, 1979), ch. XII; idem, *The Latin Church in the Crusader States: The Secular Church* (London, 1980), pp. 335–36; Halfter, "Beschreibung," pp. 177–79.

[4] The embassy to Otto IV and the coronation are described by one of the participants, Het'um, abbot of St. Mary of Trazarg: see Ghewond M. Alishan, *Léon le Magnifique, premier roi de Sissouan ou de l'Arméno-Cilicie*, trans. G. Bayan (Venice, 1888), p. 281; cf. Reinhold Röhricht, *Geschichte des Königreichs Jerusalem (1100–1291)* (Innsbruck, 1898), pp. 712–13; Halfter, "Beschreibung," p.179; Claude Cahen, *La Syrie du Nord à l'époque des croisades et la principauté franque d'Antioche*, Inst. français de Damas, Bibl. orientale 1 (Paris, 1940), p. 618; Der Nersessian, "Kingdom of Cilician Armenia," p. 649. There appears to be no basis for the claim made by Marie-Anna Chevalier, in *Les Ordres religieux-militaires en Arménie cilicienne* (Paris, 2009), pp. 48, 120–22, 169–70, 471, that Wilbrand brought the crown with him and attended Raymond Rupen's coronation, still less that the coronation took place in Tarsus at Epiphany (6 January) 1212; the Epiphany celebrations, which Wilbrand did attend and describes in full, took place in Sis, whereas the coronation had already taken place before his arrival in Cilicia.

[5] *Tabulae Ordinis Theotonici ex Tabularii Regii Berolinensis Codice Potissimum*, ed. Ernst Strehlke (Berlin, 1869); repr. with Preface by Hans Eberhard Mayer (Toronto, 1975), pp. 37–39, no. 46; Cahen, *La Syrie du Nord*, p. 618; Jonathan S. C. Riley-Smith, "The Templars and the Teutonic Knights in Cilician Armenia," in Boase, ed., *Cilician Kingdom*, pp. 92–117 (at p. 111).

[6] *Tabulae Ordinis Theotonici*, pp. 266–69, no. 298.

of Temptation (*Quarennia*) on his return journey from Jericho, following his visit to Jerusalem. From remarks made earlier in the text, it appears that the missing portion would have included descriptions of Rama (ar-Ram) in Judæa and Capernaum in Galilee; but it is uncertain whether this abrupt ending was the result of Wilbrand's failure to complete the text or – as seems more likely – of the accidental loss of the final pages of the exemplar on which the surviving manuscript tradition is based.

The earliest surviving manuscript (*P*) is a thirteenth-century one, now in the Bibliothèque nationale de France in Paris but originally from the Premonstratensian abbey of Saint-Yved in Braisne, near Soissons.[7] In this, Wilbrand's *Itinerarium* (fols. 19vb–30vb) is wedged between other texts: on the one hand, an abbreviated chronicle of the kings of France to the end of the twelfth century (fols. 1ra–8va), followed by one concerning the dukes of Normandy to 1135 (fols. 8va–19vb), both in French; and on the other, a Latin chronicle of Fécamp, to which is appended in other hands some historical events of the years 1218–46 relating solely to Braisne (fols. 31ra–38vb). The manuscript appears to have been copied around 1220–30 and until the early seventeenth century it represented the final 38 folios of a composite collection comprising 140 folios in all. The *Itinerarium* starts at the top of fol. 20ra, with the heading at the bottom of the preceding column (19vb), and ends two and a half lines before the bottom of fol. 30vb.[8]

The Bibliothèque nationale also contains another manuscript of the *Itinerarium*, which was copied along with other texts from the abbey of Saint-Yved for Nicolas de Beaufort, canon of Saint-Jean in Soissons, in the sixteenth century.[9] During the seventeenth century, when this manuscript formed part of the library belonging to the descendants of the humanist Claude Dupuy (1546–94), it was itself copied by or for Lucas Holstein on behalf of Leo Allatius, who in 1653 published an edition of it.[10] Another manuscript version, now in Hanover, appears to be no more than an eighteenth-century copy of Allatius's text, made in preparation for a new edition, which never materialized, by Johann Daniel Gruber, the director of the Hanover library from 1729 to 1748.[11]

When J. C. M. Laurent prepared a new edition (*L*) of Wilbrand in the mid-nineteenth century, he based it on Allatius's edition (*E*) and on Holstein's copy (*B*),

---

[7] Paris, Bibliothèque nationale de France, MS fr. 10130, fols. 19vb–30vb; cf. Gillette Labory, in *Maria Careri et al., Album de manuscrits français du xiiie siècle* (Rome, 2001), pp. 111–14.

[8] Dominique Baron, "Note sur les manuscrits du voyage de Wilbrand d'Oldenbourg," *Le Moyen Âge* 81 (1975), 499–506, at pp. 500–505; Labory, pp. 110–13.

[9] BnF lat. 3088, fols. 52r–61v; cf. Baron, "Note," pp. 500, 503–4; Laurent, *Peregrinatores*, p. 161; "Inventaire sommaire des manuscrits relatifs à l'histoire et à la géographie de l'Orient latin," *AOL* 2.2, 131–204 (at p. 135).

[10] Leo Allatius (Allacci), Σύμμικτα *sive opusculorum Graecorum et Latinorum, vetustiorum ac recentiorum*, ed. N. Nihus, 2 vols. (in one) (Cologne, 1653), 1:122–52.

[11] Hanover, MS 1805, fol. 36ff.; cf. Reinhold Röhricht, *Bibliotheca Geographica Palaestinae: chronologisches Verzeichniss der auf die Geographie des Heiligen Landes bezüglichen Literatur von 333 bis 1878* (Berlin, 1890), p. 46; Baron, "Note," p. 505.

which was by then in Berlin.[12] His edition was published with a German translation and notes in Hamburg in 1859,[13] and was reprinted with just the Latin text and footnotes in a collection of pilgrim texts in 1864,[14] and again in 1873.[15] Laurent's text was again reprinted, with a facing Italian translation, by Father Sabino de Sandoli OFM in 1983.[16]

More recently a French translation of Laurent's edition has been published by Marc Delpech, with an introduction and notes by Jean-Claude Voisin.[17] Delpech, however, appears to have made no use of the version of Wilbrand's text existing in manuscript *P*, even though Voisin's introduction refers to the study of it made by Dominique Baron in 1975, which had clearly demonstrated it to be the version from which all the other surviving manuscripts were derived.[18] It is possible that they – and others too, perhaps – were misled by Baron's somewhat dismissive assessment of the historical value of the manuscript when comparing it to Laurent's edition:

> En comparant ces textes, nous avons pu relever des différences, nombreuses, mais portant sur des points de détail: variations de l'ordre des mots, de l'orthographie de noms communs et de noms propres, remplacement d'un adverbe ou d'un mot de liaison par un autre de même signification. Il arrive également qu'un substantif ait été modifié par les copies successives, ou que des phrases ou des propositions aient disparu. L'examen du manuscrit de Saint-Yved a permis dans ce cas de rétablir un sens que l'on peut supposer originel. Mais ces variations n'intéressent que des points particuliers. La forme et le sens général du texte restent les mêmes, ainsi que son intérêt historique.[19]

As an example of a particular point of detail of supposedly insignificant historical interest Baron cites Wilbrand's description of the mountain-top monastery of Stavrovouni (Holy Cross) in Cyprus. The versions in BnF fr. 10130 and in Laurent's edition may be compared thus:

BnF fr. 10130 (*P*)
In cuius cacumine est quoddam parvum cenobium monachorum nigrorum edificatum, quorum vita venerabilis nostrorum monachorum vite, ut in pace ipsorum dicam, est dissimillima.[20]

Laurent (*L*)
In cuius cacumine est quoddam parvum cenobium. Monachorum vita, ut pace ipsorum dicam, est dissimillima.[21]

---

[12]   Berlin, Staatsbibliothek, MS Diez C fo. 60, fols. 39r–58v; Baron, "Note," pp. 499–500, 503–4; Laurent, *Peregrinatores*, p. 161.

[13]   *Wilbrands von Oldenburg, Reise nach Palästina und Kleinasien* (Hamburg, 1859).

[14]   *Peregrinatores Medii Aevi Quatuor* (Leipzig, 1864), pp. 159–91.

[15]   *Peregrinatores Medii Aevi Quatuor, accessit Mag. Thietmari peregrinatio* (Leipzig, 1873), pp. 159–91.

[16]   *Itinera Hierosolymitana Crucesignatorum (saec. XII–XIII)* 3, Studium Biblicum Franciscanum, Collectio Maior 24.3 (Jerusalem, 1983), pp. 195–249.

[17]   Delpech and Voisin, "Mission en Cilicie," pp. 300–342.

[18]   Baron, "Note," pp. 499–506.

[19]   Baron, "Note," p. 506.

[20]   BnF fr. 10130, fol. 27va; cf. Baron, "Note," p. 506, n. 23.

[21]   Laurent, *Peregrinatores Medii Aevi Quatuor*, p. 181

Evidently this is a case of omission by homeoteleuton, in which the copyist's eye has accidentally jumped from *monachorum* to the same word repeated a little further on. The missing passage, however, appears to confirm that by 1212 the monastery had already passed from the Orthodox to the Benedictine monks from the monastery of St. Paul in Antioch, who are otherwise first recorded in possession of it in 1254.[22] Use has been made of manuscript *P*, however, by Lorenzo Calvelli in his discussion of Wilbrand's references to antiquity in describing places in Cyprus.[23]

While preparing an English translation of Wilbrand's Journey for a volume of translations of thirteenth-century Jerusalem pilgrim texts,[24] I made my own comparison of manuscript *P* with Laurent's edition (*L*) and found a number of significant differences, in addition to the examples already published by Baron and Calvelli. Besides allowing more accurate readings of the placenames and other descriptive details recorded in the text, they also include the following new pieces of information:

- The duke of Austria had taken the cross (*crucem*), rather than the sword (*ensem*) (fol. 20vb).
- While describing the double walls of Acre, Wilbrand explains that lower outer walls of the type existing there are known as barbicans (*barbacanas*) (fol. 20r).
- The Templar castle in Tortosa was not enclosed with walls and towers like a crown (*coronatum*), but rather horned like a tiara (*cornutum*) (fol. 22vb). While perhaps less poetic, this does in fact describe the shape of the castle more accurately.
- The Armenian king's "black castle" (*castrum regis nigrum*) was actually the castle of *Nigrin* (fol. 25ra). This was evidently associated with the *casale* of

---

[22] Nicholas Coureas, *The Latin Church in Cyprus, 1195–1312* (Aldershot, 1997), pp. 187–88; Christopher Schabel, "Religion," in Angel Nicolaou-Konnari and Christopher Schabel, eds., *Cyprus: Society and Cuture 1191–1374* (Leiden–Boston, 2005), pp. 157–218 (at p. 175); idem, "The Status of the Greek Clergy in Early Frankish Cyprus," in Julian Chrysostomides and C. Dendrinos, eds., *"Sweet Land ...": Lectures on the History and Culture of Cyprus* (Camberley, 2006), pp. 165–207, at pp. 175–76; repr. in idem, *Greeks, Latins, and the Church in Early Frankish Cyprus* (Aldershot, 2010), ch. I. It could of course be argued that the black monks seen by Wilbrand were Greeks rather than Benedictines. However, although a French pilgrim text of ca. 1229–39 describes the Greeks in the abbey of St. Margaret on Mount Carmel as "moines noirs" (*Itinéraires à Jérusalem et descriptions de la Terre Sainte rédigés en français*, ed. Henri Michelant and Gaston Raynaud (Geneva, 1882), p. 104³), western writers of this period more usually identify Greek monks as "Greek," as indeed Wilbrand himself does elsewhere. If the monks at Stavrovouni had been Greek, there would also have been no need for Wilbrand to remark in such deferential terms how different their way of life was to that of "our monks," particularly in view of the forthright description that he gives elsewhere of the behaviour of the Greeks who participated in the Epiphany celebrations at Sis. It seems more likely therefore that the monks were indeed Benedictines, but ones whose way of life differed somewhat from that normally followed in contemporary German Benedictine houses, quite possibly as a result of traits that they had picked up during their time in Antioch.

[23] *Cipro e la Memoria dell'Antico fra Medioevo e Rinascimento*, Memorie 133 (Venice, 2009), pp. 6–9, 257–64.

[24] Denys Pringle, *Pilgrimage to Jerusalem and the Holy Land, 1187–1291*, Crusade Texts in Translation 23 (Farnham, 2012).

Nigrinum, which was one of a number of *casalia* granted to the Hospital for two years by Levon I in April 1214.[25]

• Manuscript *P* states that the Armenians *did* eat meat on the Fridays between Easter and Whitsun, honouring the feast in that way: *Inter Pascha et Pentecostem sextis feriis utuntur carnibus, eodem modo festum honorantes* (fol. 24va). The *non* introduced by Laurent appears unjustified, especially as James of Vitry also remarks that the Armenians also ate meat on certain Fridays during Lent.[26]

• When Wilbrand arrived in Nicosia in spring 1212, the castle there was still being built (*In qua nunc temporis forte castrum elaboratur*), rather than already finished (*elaboratum*) (fol. 27rb)

• Wilbrand states that, although Caesarea of Palestine had been reoccupied by the Franks, its walls were still in ruins (fol. 28rb), thus confirming that they had been destroyed by Saladin after the fall of Acre to the Franks in July 1191.[27]

The present edition of Wilbrand's *Itinerarium* is based principally on manuscript *P*.[28] Since all the other surviving manuscripts are ultimately derived from this one manuscript, there has seemed little point in noting exhaustively all the variant readings which appear in them. Where the reading of a word given in *L* appears to make better sense, however, it is adopted and the reading in *P* is given in the apparatus. The apparatus also contains some other alternative readings from *L*, included for general interest. In order to facilitate comparison with and reference to Laurent's edition, however, the same book and chapter divisions have been adopted. General footnotes have been kept to a minimum, as a fuller commentary accompanies the published English translation.[29] The notes given here are therefore restricted to identifying quotations from or allusions to biblical, literary, and ecclesiastical texts, as well as people and places referred to in the text.

---

[25] *Cart Hosp* 2, pp. 165–66, no. 1426.

[26] *Histoire orientale: Historia orientalis*, ed. and Fr. trans. Jean Donnadieu (Turnhout, 2008), ch. 79, p. 320.

[27] Harry W. Hazard, "Caesarea and the Crusades," in *The Joint Expedition to Caesarea Maritima* 1: *Studies in the History of Caesarea Maritima*, ed. Chartes T. Frith, Bulletin of the American School of Oriental Research, supplemental series 19 (Missoula, 1975), pp. 79–122, at pp. 86, 104 n. 72.

[28] I am most grateful to my colleague Massimiliano Gaggero for checking some passages that were difficult to read from the digitized microfilm provided by the Bibliothèque nationale against the manuscript itself in Paris.

[29] Pringle, *Pilgrimage to Jerusalem*, pp. 61–94; cf. pp. 24–27.

The Text

[**19vb**] *Incipit itinerarium Willebrandi de Aldembore, canonici Hildesemensis, in quo agitur de situ terre sancte.*

[**20ra**] Presentis operis materia, suis terminis nimirum contenta, stilum grandiloquum[a] abhorrens, mediocri, immo humili non indebite describitur, quippe ne, si montes forte in ea parturirent, ridiculus mus nasceretur.[1] Quam ideo describere et in medium vestri deducere decrevi, ne ille hostis antiquus, *leo rugiens et querens quem devoret*,[2] non solum me peregrinum, verum etiam aliquibus operibus non vitiosis intentum inveniret et occupatum. Nullius itaque tumoris vana et pernitiosa inductus arrogantia, sed tamen predicta habita consideratione de locis sanctis et de civitatibus, quas in transmarinis partibus et in terra promissionis cum viris providis et honestis nuntiis[b] ducis Austrie,[3] nec non cum venerabili magistro domus Alemannorum, fratre Hermanno de Salza, diligenter perlustravi, et de incidentibus earum hystoriis, quas etiam predictorum virorum auxilio curiose disquisivi, et de statu et de munitionibus ipsarum, prout nunc sunt, scribere propono,[c] eum in dicendo ordinem et successionem, quam in videndo, observans. Quapropter favorabilem attentionem illorum humiliter deposco, qui qualibetcumque prepediti negotiis terram sanctam et eius loca et civitates non visitaverunt, amore tamen et desideratione illius inducti de eis, que[d] nondum senserunt nec viderunt, legere delectantur et intelligere. Gratiam vero et correctio[**20rb**]nis lineam illos appendere imploro, qui iam sepe pretacta loca aliquando visitantes et profundius[e] considerantes me in ipsorum descriptione animadvertunt et sciunt peccavisse; quia *pluribus intentus minor est ad singula sensus.*

[I.] De civitate Acharon et situ eius

1. Igitur post multa pericula et post multas quassationes, quas in mari vi septimanis sustinueramus, anno Dominice Incarnationis m°cc°xi°, consecrationis gloriosi regis Romanorum Ottonis iii°,[4] pontificatus domini Innocentii pape iii° xiii°, viii° kalendas Septembris,[5] Nachon, vel secundum vulgus Akers, pervenimus. Hec est civitas bona, dives et fortis, in littore maris sita, ita ut, dum ipsa in dispositione sit quadrangula, duo eius latera angulum constituentia a mari cingantur et muniantur; reliqua duo latera fossa bona et larga et profunda funditus murata et dupplici muro turrito pulcro ordine coronantur, eo modo, ut prior murus suis turribus ipsam matrem non excedentibus a secundo et interiore muro, cuius turres alte sunt et validissime, prospiciatur[f] et custodiatur. Unde et huiusmodi muros inferiores barbacanas consuevimus appellare, quia licuit semperque licebit signatum presente nota producere nomen. Hec civitas bonum et firmum habet portum, pulcra turre custoditum,

---

[1] Horace, *Ars poetica*, line 139: *parturient (parturiunt) montes, nascetur ridiculus mus.*
[2] 1 Peter 5.8.   [3] Leopold VII.   [4] I.e. the third year since the consecration of Otto IV.
[5] 25 August 1211.

---

[a] grandiloquum *L*] grandiloquium *P*.   [b] nuntiis] nunciis *L*, munitus *P*.   [c] prout nunc sunt, scribere propono *L*] prout nunc scribere sunt propono *P*.   [d] que *L*] qui *P*.   [e] profundius] profundiori *P*, profundiora *L*.   [f] prospiciatur *L*] prospitiatur *P*.

in qua olim apud gentiles errores deus muscarum, quem nos Beelzebud, ipsi vero Akaron appellabant, colebatur. A quo et ipsa civitas Hakon [**20va**] vel Akaron est nominata.[1]

Que post perditionem terre sancte multis laboribus nostrorum recuperata reliquias sancte Iherusalem, sue matris, videlicet dominum patriarcham, dominum regem, templarios et alios viros religiosos, episcopos et abbates, sicut fidelis filia in se fovet et enutrit. Unde et ipsa nunc temporis inter alias civitates, quibus nostri in Suria dominantur, principalis et capitanea reputatur. Plurimos enim et valde divites in se habet habitatores: Francos et Latinos, Grecos et Surianos, Iudeos et Iacobinos, quorum quilibet suas leges observant et colunt. Reliquis tamen ipsi Franci et Latini dominantur. Et sciendum, quod hoc nomen Franci large sumitur in transmarinis pro omnibus eis, qui romanam legem observant. Suriani vero dicuntur illi, qui de Suria nati sarraceno utuntur pro ydiomate et greco pro latino. Christiani sunt et servant legem Pauli, sicut Greci.

Usque in hanc civitatem fere protenditur Lybanus, et incipit Carmelus mons, in quo Helyas per corvum alebatur, quod melius suo loco expediemus. In terminis et huius civitatis situm est quoddam casale, de quo, ut dicitur, nata fuit Maria Magdalena, exemplum penitentie. Et notandum, quod Dominus noster, cum deambularet maritima Syrie, hanc civitatem, ut dicunt, non intravit, sed cuidam eius turri maledixit, que hodie Maledicta a populo nuncupata. Sed potius credo, quod aliunde nomen acceperit. Cum enim nostri hanc civitatem obsidissent, hec turris pre omnibus aliis se maxime deffendit: unde nostri eam Maledictam appellaverunt. Domina vero nostra intravit, et ubi ipsa requievit, illic ecclesia [**20vb**] pulcra est edificata, que in magna habetur veneratione. In hac vero civitate magna est episcopatus.

2. Inde in navi descendentes versus septentrionem, ad agendum negotia domini imperatoris Ottonis et ducis Austrie, qui tunc crucem[a] acceperat, pervenimus Surs, quam nos Latini Thyrum appellamus. Hec est civitas bona et fortis, maximum Christianorum solatium, quia inter omnes seculi civitates ipsa, ut creditur, vero nomine fortissima nuncupatur; ex una enim parte munitur muro bono et mari, in quo latentes scopuli longe sub aquis protenti insultum navium ex muro deffendunt; ex alia parte deffenditur fossa bona murata et quinque muris turritis et validissimis, in quibus disposite et transposite sunt quinque porte, que introitum civitatis adeo intricant et observant, ut, qui eas intraverint, in domo Dedali errare et laborare videantur. Hec est illa Thirus, de qua Apollonium de Thyro appellamus, in qua hodie eius palatium monstratur.[2] In hac etiam illa infelix et misera Dido Thyris et Sydoniis imperabat. Iuxta muros huius civitatis sunt tres lapides magne venerationis, in quibus Dominus dicitur cum discipulis requievisse, cum transiret per medios fines Thyri et Sydonis. Et nota, quod hec civitas, ut ante tactum est, iacet in littore maris. Quam etiam ipsum mare ex omni sua parte cinxisset, si suavem dulcedinem ortorum, qui iuxta muros sunt, sua amaritundine non abhorreret. Lybanus enim supra civitatem extenditur, qui, dum in suis cedris, quas [**21ra**] etiam Cantica commendant, lascivit, aquam dulcem et limpidissimam ad irrigandum ortos in pede suo iuxta muros pulcre elaboratos in ammirabili quantitate transmittit. In medio enim illorum habetur ille fons, de quo dictum est per typum in Canticis, *Fons ortorum, puteus aquarum viventium, que fluunt inpetu de Lybano.*[3] Et vere impetu, quia infra iactum teli

---

[1]   In the Middle Ages, Acre was commonly confused with Ekron, a city of the Philistines (cf. 2 Kings 1.1–16).   [2]   Apollonius of Tyre, the hero of a medieval romance, which ca. 1191 Godfrey of Viterbo included in his *Pantheon* (18.15–22 rubric, ed. G. Waitz, *MGH SS*, pp. 120, 147).   [3]   Song of Solomon 4.15.

---

[a]   crucem] ensem *L*.

ix molendina ad commodum ipsius civitatis propellit. Super quem nos vesperas et ipsam antiphonam *Fons ortorum* et cetera decantavimus. Huic tamen fonti, ut infra patebit, Tripolis civitas contradicit. Hec civitas multos habet inhabitatores, quibus rex de Hacon dominatur; et est in ea dives archiepiscopatus. Ispa distat ab Hacon parvam dietam.

3. Abhinc procedentes transivimus Sarfente, quam nos Sareptam vocamus. Et quia alia habetur Sarepta in Iudea, ut post scietis, ad differentiam illius dictum secundum librum Regum dictum est ad Helyam Tesbitem:[a] *Surge et vade ad Sareptam Sidoniorum.*[1] Hec est illa. Et est civitas parva, non multum munita, iuxta mare iacens, in mediis finibus Thiri et Sidonis, cui etiam nostri dominantur. Extra muros illius Helyas, videns viduam duo ligna colligentem, petiit ab ea aliquid, quod manducaret; quam dum ex ipsius professione pauperem intelligeret, ditavit oleo et farina.[2] Ob cuius rei memoriam ecclesiuncula in eo loco, in quo mulier loquebatur, est edificata, in qua hodie sua apparent vestigia. Hec civitas distat a Thyro quatuor milia [21rb] gallicana.

4. Inde venimus Saget, quam evvangelia Sydonem appellant. Que licet nunc temporis inter suas coetaneas civitates ferme sit minima, tamen in Sacra Scriptura non est minime[b] recitata. Paucos enim habet inhabitatores, quibus nostri – pro dolor! – inimici dominantur, aliquantulos redditus nostris ex ea pro pace servanda solventes; muri etenim et munitiones civitatis sunt destructe. Plurimos ortos et fertilissimos habet fines, qui nimirum, ut credo, a creatore suo et datore totius boni totiens superambulante de rore celi et de pinguedine terre habundanciam sibi attraxerunt. Forsitan et ipsa civitas, que nunc sedet in tristitia, dolet, et non est, qui consoletur eam, aliquid sibi attraxisset, si saltem eum, quem corporaliter se visitantem recipere recusavit, postmodum pectoris hospitio et fide receptum caste reservasset. Iuxta illam pugnavit aliquando Lippoldus senior, dux Austrie,[3] cum inimicis ecclesie, et devictos captivavit et occidit. Ubi etiam tunc nostri gratiam et fertilitatem predictis finibus collatam in multis spoliis – Deo gratias! – senserunt et gratanter acceperunt. De quibus quondam egressa est mulier chananea, clamans: *Fili David!* et cetera.[4] Hec distat a Sarepta duo milia, a Thyro sex.

5. Procedentes ab illa transivimus Flumen Amoris[5] et quoddam casale bonum Slaudie[6] vocatum, de quo natus fuit dux Hospinel,[7] vir bellicosus, de quo multa virilia facta leguntur, et, ut qui volunt, maximus ille poetarum Virgilius, qui postmodum in Longobardiam et Apuliam transfretavit, et pervenimus Baruth, quam Latini Beritum appellant. Hec est civitas admodum magna, super mare sita, fines [21va] habens amenissimos. Cuius muros Sarraceni, nimio timore nostrorum perculsi et ad fugam se disponentes, destruxerunt, in castro ipsius civitatis, quod fortissimum est et tunc erat, ad defensam [se][c] recipientes; superveniente autem pie memorie Conrado cancellario[8] cum omni exercitu Alemannorum et illos filios iniquitatis tantus timor invasit, ut, furorem teutonicum fugientes, castrum cum omnibus suis contentis nostris post tergum relinquerent illesum. Quod nunc a quodam Iohanne,[9] viro valde christiano et strenuo, possidetur. Et, ut tactum est, castrum fortissimum est. Ex una enim parte munitur mari et alti rupis precipitio; ex alia enim parte ambitur quadam[d] fossa murata et adeo profunda, ut in ea[e] plures captivos tamquam in alto carcere videremus

---

[1] 1 Kings 17.9.   [2] 1 Kings 17.8–24; cf. Luke 4.25–26.   [3] Leopold V.   [4] Matthew 15.22.
[5] Nahr al-Damūr, *Rivière Damor*.   [6] Khalda.   [7] Otherwise unknown.   [8] Conrad of Querfurt,
archbishop of Hildesheim, who accompanied Henry of Brabant at the fall of Beirut in October 1197.
[9] John of Ibelin, who received Beirut from King Aimery sometime after October 1200.

---

[a] Tesbitem] Tesbiten *P*.   [b] minime] *scribal correction from* minima.   [c] se] *added by L*.
[d] quadam *L*] quedam *P*.   [e] ea *L*] eo *P*.

detrusos. Hanc fossam prospiciunt[a] duo muri fortes, in quibus contra machinarum insultus eriguntur turres validissime, cum quarum iuncturis lapides magni ferreis vinculis et duris amplexibus internectuntur. In una illarum, que de novo construitur, vidimus quoddam palatium ornatissimum, quod pro mea insufficientia[b] breviter describo vobis. Funditus est forte, bene situm, ex una parte mare et naves illic discurrentes, ex altero latere prata, pomeria[c] et loca amenissima prospiciens.[d] Pavimentum habet subtile marmoreum, simulans aquam levi vento agitatam, ita ut, qui super illud incesserit, vadare putatur, cum tamen arene illic depicte summa vestigia non impresserit. Parietes vero domus marmoreis tabulis, que sui operis subtilitate diversas cortinas illic mentiuntur, undique conteguntur. Cuius testudo adeo [21vb] proprie et aerio colore depingitur, ut illic nubes discurrere, illic Zephirus flare et illic sol annum et menses, dies et ebdomadas, horas et momenta suo motu in zodiaco videatur distinguere. In quibus omnibus Suriani, Sarraceni et Greci in magistralibus suis artibus quadam delectabili operis altercatione gloriantur. In medio vero palatii loco centri est quedam cisterna diversissimo marmore consternata, in qua ipsum marmor ex diversis coloris tabulis compactum et tamen ductum pollicem non offendens innumerabiles florum ostentant varietates, quas cum oculi videntium distinguere laborant, disgregantur et illuduntur. In cuius medio quidam draco, qui animalibus illic depictis inhiare videtur, cristallinum quemdam fontem parturit et in habundanti quantitate profundit, ita ut alte dissiliens aerem, quem fenestre pulcro ordine ex omni latere amministrant, tempore caloris humectet et frigidet. Ipsa etiam aqua, ex omni parte cisterne perstrepens et in subtilissimos poros se recipiens, sompnum suis dominis assidentibus blando murmure inducit; cui omnibis diebus meis libenter assiderem.

Ipsa vero civitas, que huic castro adiacet, pauperem habet episcopatum et clerum valde religiosum. Extra muros illius monstratur sepulcrum Symonis et Iude.[1] In quo loco aliquando erat claustrum dives in honore ipsorum constructum; quod ipsi infideles penitus divulserunt; pro quo facto nostri eorum oratorio sive *mahoumerie* [22ra] condignam reddiderunt talionem.

In hac civitate primo vidimus poma Adam, et post sensimus cannamelam, de quo excoquitur zucarum. Item in hac aliquando yconia Domini a Iudeis crucifixa effudit sanguinem et aquam. Hec civitas distat a Sydone vi milia gallicana.

6. [I]nde post requiem duorum dierum venimus Gibeleth, quam episcopus loci illius Biblionem appellat, asserens Biblum in ea primo hebraico stilo fuisse compilatam. Hec est civitas parva, habens turrim quandam amplam et munitissimam, unicum sue defensionis[e] solatium; in qua Sarraceni, cum ipsam avellere laborarent, multos sudores sepius perdiderunt et expensas, qui tamen omnem murum ipsius civitatis destruxerunt. Portum habet parvis navibus satis commodum, raro frequentatum, quia eius tamquam *pauperis est numerare pecus.*[2]

In ea dominatur quidam Francigena, Guido nomine,[3] et, ut iam tetigi, in ea est sedes episcopalis, licet paupercula. Hec civitas distat a Beritho viii milia parva.

7. Eadem nocte, que semper a me nigro lapide computabatur, precessimus Boterun, quod est castellum bonum a nostris possessum, et transivimus Neffin, cuius situm et munitiones diligentius considerassem, si quedam validissima tempestas, que nos miseros illic invasit

---

[1] The Apostles Simon the Zealot and Jude Thaddaeus.   [2] Ovid, *Metamorphoses* 13, line 824.
[3] Guy I Embriaco, whose mother, the widow of Hugh III, regained Jubayl from the Muslims in 1197.

---

[a] prospiciunt *L*] prospitiunt *P*.   [b] insufficientia] insuffitientia *P*, insufficiencia *L*.
[c] pomeria] pomaria *L*.   [d] prospiciens *L*] prospitiens *P*.   [e] sue defensionis *L*] sue defendere *P*.

et quassavit, omnes sensus meos non impedivisset. Quantum vero contritis procellis permittentibus considerare potuimus, hec est civitas admodum parva, bene munita, surianos [**22rb**] fovens inhabitatores, nostris subdita et tributaria, cuius fines sunt fertilissimi, optima et multum commendata vina afferentes. Hec distat a Biblione quatuor milia.

8. Illa propter impellentem tempestatem breviter relicta Tripolim applicuimus que nos desperatos et quasi naufragos non sine multorum spectaculo, nostrum naufragium expectantium, recepit et refecit resolutos. Hec est civitas valde dives, plurimos habens inhabitatores, Christianos, Iudeos et Sarracenos, quibus omnibus comes,[1] vir notre fidei, sicut toti terre illi dominatur. Ipsa vero civitas in omni sua dispositione Thyro simillima fere undique mari cingitur et munitur; sed ipsa natura, suis naturatis, commoda, pratum quoddam amenum et fertiles ortos interiecit. Circa quem locum ipsa munitur duobus muris validis et turritis, duas fossas largas et profundas inter se capientibus, quorum portas et introitus speciales[a] quondam sinuose barbacane intricant et observant.

Et nota quod Libanus, qui illic, ut volunt, altissimus est, directe ipsi civitati superponitur,[b] ita ut large ad unum campum distet. Inter quem et civitatem iacet quidam monticulus, qui hodie *Monpelerin*, id est Mons Peregrinorum, appellatur. In quo comes sancti Egidii,[2] vir bellicosus, et alii peregrini castrum quoddam[c] edificaverunt et per illud filios iniquitatis, nostros inimicos, qui tunc Tripolim manutenebant, multis annis sicut viri laboribus infracti obsederunt. Quorum constantiam nimiam illi Sarraceni ammirantes et timentes a manibus eorum liberari desiderabant; et auxilium Soldani et suorum invocabant. Qui maximo [**22va**] exercitu apparato litteras consolatorias ipsis per columbam nunciam more illius terre remiserunt. Quam nostri casu comprehendentes (si etiam vere casus dici[d] possit, quod ex divina providentia sic accidit), litteris et secretis illorum perspectis alias sub nomine Soldani illi alligaverunt. Que sic dimissa suis dominis quasi in archa inclusis et exspectantibus pro ramo litteras, pro consolatione desolationem reportavit. Qui nimio timore vite perterriti vel attoniti et huiusmodi divinum dolum ignorantes ipsam civitatem nostris – Deo gratias! – illesam reddiderunt, salvis suis personis per conditionem preordinatam recedentes. Que nunc in eis, que nostre fidei sunt, vigens et exultans *fontem* se *ortorum, puteum* se *aquarum viventium, que fluunt impetu de Lybano*,[3] et cetera, gloriatur habere, multa super eo pro se contra[e] Thirum, sicut supra tetigi, allegans; cui tamen sufficeret,[f] quia prope suis finibus in pede Lybani oriuntur duo fontes, Ior et Dan, qui in unum confluentes Iordanem constituunt. Ex predictis scire potestis, quia Lybanus est mons altus et longus, qui usque ultra Thyrum protenditur. Item in summo illius supra Tripolim monstratur quidam sarcofagi, in quibus Noe et filii sui dicuntur requiescere, quia, ut etiam volunt, archa Noe in illo loco fuit edificata. In hac civitate est dives episcopus, curiam habens amenissimam, de qua vobis multa scriberem, si prolixitatem non timerem. Hec civitas distat a Neffin duo milia, que nobis in tempestate videbantur longissima, quia ut sortis desideranti animo nichil satis festinatur.

9. [A]liquot igitur diebus recreati et in equis [**22vb**] procedentes transivimus Culicath[4] et Manacusine,[5] que sunt duo castella a Sarracenis destructa. Iuxta que vidimus agros plenos feniculo et fructibus lanam afferentibus, quem nos lanam arborum vocamus.

---

[1] Bohemond IV, prince of Antioch and count of Tripoli.   [2] Raymond I of Tripoli.
[3] Cf. Song of Solomon 4.15.   [4] Qulay'āt.   [5] Unidentified.

---

[a] speciales *L*] spetiales *P*.   [b] superponitur] *scribal correction from* opponitur.
[c] castrum quoddam] castrum quoddam ~~castrum~~ *P*.   [d] dici *L*] dicit *P*.   [e] contra *L*] circa *P*.
[f] sufficeret *L*] sufficere *P*.

Et reliquimus ad dexteram Crac, quod est castrum Hospitum[a] maximum et fortissimum, Sarracenis summe dampnosum. De cuius situ et munitionibus, cum ipsum non viderim, scribere non presumo; sed, quod dictu mirabile est, tempore pacis a duobus milibus pugnatorum solet custodiri; quod Hospitalarii sub magno asserunt iuramento.

Ad eandem manum[b] vidimus Casteblans,[1] quod est castrum bonum et forte, situm in montanis et in terminis Antiqui *de la Montaigne*,[2] qui cultellis principes nostros per nuntios occidere consuevit. De cuius vita et paradyso, quam sibi paravit, satis audivistis,[3] unde ea tamquam nota pertranseo. Hoc castellum est sue terre valde nocuum, quia a Templariis est possessum et custoditum.

10. Inde venimus Tortose. Hec est civitas parva, non multum munita, super mare sita, in capite habens castrum fortissimum, optimo muro et xi turribus sicut xi pretiosis lapidibus cornutum.[c] Nec mirum si duodena turris ei subtrahatur, cum illa turris, quam rex Francie[4] ad subsidium terre edificavit, sua pulcra fortitudine illius suppleat defectum.[d] Hoc castrum a Templariis, quia ipsorum est, optime custoditur. Civitatem vero istius Latini Taradensem appellant. Et est in ea ecclesia parva maxime ve- **[23ra]** venerationis, quam beatus Petrus et Paulus, cum in Antiochiam[e] properarent, ex angelica ammonitione propriis manibus ex incultis lapidibus ad honorem sancte Marie tunc primo composuerunt; ac si dicerent: *Flebile principium melior fortuna sequetur.*[5]

Hoc erat prima ecclesia, que[f] in honore domine nostre semperque virginis Marie fuit edificata et dedicata. Et est in ea hodie sedes episcopalis. Ubi domina nostra, Dei genitrix, semper virgo Maria etiam ipsis infidelibus Sarracenis multa prestat beneficia. Hec civitas distat a Tripolim dietam.[g]

11. Hinc procedentes transivimus castellum quoddam,[6] cuius dominum Soldanus de Halaph pro fide nostra decollavit, et in altum scandentes ascendimus Margath,[7] quod est castrum amplum et fortissimum, dupplici muro munitum, multas in se turres ostentans, que potius ad sustentationem celi, quam ad defensam proficere videntur. Mons enim, in quo situm est castrum, altissimus est, ita ut ipse altum Athlas humeris suis celum sustentet.[h] Qui in pede latissimus et paulatim in altum conscendens annuatim large quingenta plaustra commendati novem suis dominis ministrat. Quod inimici suis laboribus, quamvis sepe attemptaverint, impedire non possunt.

Hoc castrum est Hospitalariorum, et est maximum totius terre illius solacium. Opponitur enim fortibus et multis castris Antiqui de Montanis et Soldani de Halaph, quorum tyrannidem et insultus in[i] tantum refrenavit, ut ab eis pro pace servanda singulis annis in valore duo milia marcarum recipiat. Et quia cavetur, quod accidere potest, ne aliqua traditio superveniat, singulis noctibus per **[23rb]** quatuor milites, fratres Hospitalis, et per alios viginti octo vigiles custoditur. Hospitalarii enim tempore pacis preter alios cives castri in suis expensis ad tutelam castri mille personas sustentant,[i] ita ut eis in omni commodo et habendo providerint

---

[1] Chastel Blanc, S̱āfīt̲ha. [2] The Old Man of the Mountains, leader of the Assassins.
[3] Cf. Arnold of Lübeck, *Chronica Slavorum*, ed. H. Pertz, in *MGH SS* 21, pp. 235–41; WT 20.29, pp. 953–54. [4] Presumably Louis VII, who would have passed through Tortosa on his way from Antioch to Jerusalem in late spring 1148. [5] Ovid, *Metamorphoses* 7, line 518: *flebile principium melior fortuna secuta est.* [6] Probably Maraclea (Khrab Marqiyya). [7] Qal'at Marqab.

---

[a] Hospitum] hospitalariorum *L.* [b] manum *L*] magnum *P.* [c] cornutum] coronatum *L.*
[d] defectum] *scribal correction from* defu … [e] Antiochiam] *scribal correction from* Anthiochiam.
[f] que *L*] quem *P.* [g] dietam *L*] dietem *P.* [h] sustetet *L*] substentet *P.* [i] in] *deleted and rewritten above the line, apparently for clarity.* [i] sustentant] substentant *P.*

quinque annis in necessariis castri. In pede illius montis sita est quedam civitas, Valenie[1] nuncupata. Que cum aliquando, ut dicitur et sicut apparet, fuerit maxima, per divinam vindictam modo est destructa[a] et desolata. Cuius sedes episcopalis in castrum Margat est translata et hoc propter timorem Sarracenorum. Hoc castrum distat a Tortosa vi milia parva.

Quoniam vero propter timorem Sarracenorum per terram et in equis procedere non audebamus, navi et mari, licet inviti, nos commissimus, ac transivimus Gibel,[2] quod castrum bonum, habens civitatem parvam, sed multum munitam, nostris valde inimicam. Cuius dominus et possessor filiam Soldani de Halaph sibi duxit in uxorem, ut ex illis duobus turpitudinis extremis nascatur tercium, utrumque extremorum sua turpitudine excedens, et illi duo filii Mahomet vel Mammone producant ex se vii spiritus nequiores. Hec civitas distat a Margat quatuor milia.

12. Inde transivimus Sahaun, castrum Soldani,[3] et iuxta illam Lizam.[4] Que est civitas fortis, bono muro et multis turribus munita, portum habens valde bonum, nostris summe dampnosum, qui, dum in mari tempestate quassantur, timore mortis inducti, illuc confugiunt et captivantur; et sic illi miseri – pro dolor! – cum Scillam effugere laborant, incidunt in Caribdin. Hec est illa, que in nostris libris Laodicia appellatur. Que nunc temporis *in arcum pravum conversa*[5] illud amenum et quondam securum iter de Hacon usque in Antiochiam sua [**23va**] crudelitate interrupit. Que etiam maiorem servitiam in nostros exerceret, si illam[b] nostra fidelis Margat[6] non oppugnaret, a qua distat vi milia gallicana.

13. Inde transivimus quoddam casale bonum, Gloriet[7] appellatum, et quosdam fines aut montana a Turcis inhabitata. Isti sunt homines silvestres, habitu et moribus Boideuoinis, quos nos vocamus Arabes, similes, non habitantes sub tectis, fundas tantum pro armis habentes. Et sic multo labore intravimus portum sinuosum Antiochie, quem Franci gulfas Antiochie[c] appellant. In quibus vidimus quoddam antrum summe horribile, quod tanto magis abhorruimus, quanto ibi maiorem fetorum senseramus. Et dicit vulgus beatum Petrum illic diabolum cathenatum detrusisse. Et nota, quod Antiochia distat a mari quinque milia, et tunc iste portus ad ea est denominatus, cum naves propius accedere non possunt.

14. Nunc tandem, hoc est in nocte Cecilie,[8] in qua etiam vidimus eclipsim diutissime durantem, ad desideratam venimus Antiochiam. Que civitas bona est et firma, ipsi Rome in sanctitate vix secunda. Que in uno suo latere munitur duobus muris turritis et quodam flumine admodum magno, quod suis civibus molendinorum prestat beneficia. Et illius *fluminis impetus letificat civitatem Dei.*[9] Ex altero sui latere munitur precipitio magno et muro bono, multis turribus geometrica distantia coronato. Ispa vero civitas adeo ampla est, ut, qui eam peragraverit, pulverulentos habens[d] pedes tota die erravisse putetur.

Et habet infra muros tres montes magnos et asperimos, quorum medius adeo altus est, ut suo [**23vb**] cacumine nubibus innitens cursum planetarum putetur impedire. Quem, ut puto, ipsa natura suis usibus preparaverat, ut, dum sabbatum ager et a laboribus requiesceret, illic per amenissima loca, que circum latent, reficeretur et ab alto prospiciens[e] defectum sui naturati consideraret et repararet. Que sue Antiochie ipsum montem uberrimos fontes

---

[1] Baniyas.   [2] Jabala, which fell to Saladin on 16 January 1188.   [3] Saladin took Saḥyūn in July 1188 and granted it to the ʿamīr Nāṣir al-Dīn Manguwirish, who held it until his death in 1229.
[4] Latakia, then in Muslim hands.   [5] Cf. Psalms 77.57 (*RSV* 78.57): *conversi sunt in arcum pravum.*
[6] Marqab, held by the Hospitallers, as mentioned above (I.11).   [7] Rās Ibn Hānī.   [8] The evening before 22 November.   [9] Psalms 45.5 (*RSV* 46.4).

---

[a] destructa] *scribal correction from* destructam.   [b] illam] illa *P.*   [c] Antiochie] *scribal correction from* Anthiochie.   [d] habens] *scribal correction from* habet.   [e] prospiciens *L*] prospitiens *P.*

mandavit profundere et parturire, in tantum, ut per omnia pomeria et ortos, qui illic sine numero habentur, aqua dulcis et bona largissime diffundatur, quam etiam ipsi cives per subterraneas et minusculas[a] venas in medium suorum hospiciorum et ad ipsa penetralia deduxerunt. Et nota, quod domus et palacia Antiochie foris luteam monstrant apparentiam, et infra aurea et delectabili vigent existencia. Qui, ut tetigi, in ortis varios fructus afferentibus et in aquis salientibus maxime gloriantur et solent lascivire. Ipsa etiam civitas divites et plurimos habet inhabitatores: Francos et Surianos, Grecos et Iudeos, Hormenos et Sarracenos; quibus omnibus Franci dominantur, et quilibet eorum suas leges observant.

In medio ipsius est ecclesia summe ornata, in qua olim beatus Petrus sicut patriarcha presidebat. Ubi et hodie patriarcha solet presidere et sue Asie, que sibi subicitur, imperare. Unde in consistorio ipsius isti versus aureis litteris sunt inscripti:

Sit procul hinc Iezi, tonus[b] hic sit iuris et equi:
Terciaque pars mundi iure tenetur ei.

In hac ecclesia monstratur cathedra beati Petri et carcer, in quo etiam ipse vinculatus tenebatur. Illic etiam requiescit in marmoreo sarcofago caro pie [**24ra**] memorie Frederici Imperatoris.[1]

Item non longe ab illa est quedam ecclesia tota rotunda, supra modum ornata, in qua habetur ymago domine nostre genitricis Dei semper virginis Marie. Que tante sanctitatis est, ut pluviam prestet dum movetur.[c] Quam Greci, sicut ipsam ecclesiam, in magno et laudando timore observant.

Item in uno montium, de quo supra dixi, est cenobium monachorum dives, in honore sancti Pauli fundatum, in quo monstratur parva cripta aureis picturis non plurimum, sicut decet, ornata, vel caverna, in qua sanctus Paulus facta predicatione in villa solebat requiescere et epistolas scribere. Et habetur in pulcra veneratione. Ante cuius fores sepulti sunt nobiles isti: Burchardus, madeburgensis bragravius;[2] Ogerus iuvenis, comes de Woldenborg;[3] Wilbrandus, comes de Halremunt,[4] avunculus Wilbrandi de Aldenborch, qui hunc libellum conscripsit; quorum anime requiescant in pace. Amen.

In pede illius montis est ecclesia super mansionem beati Luce ewangeliste edificata.

In medio vero monte, de cuius altitudine vobis scripsi, est castrum in medio edificatum. Sub cuius pede vidimus clusam, in qua beata Maria Magdalena egit per tempus penitentiam, et, sicut ipsa animo celestia concupivit, ita et tunc corpore terrena transcendit. Iuxta illam etiam est parva capellula, a qua beata Margareta, cum ad martyrium duceretur, fuerit extracta. Ad pedes illius in descensu montis vidimus ecclesiam super mansionem Iohannis Chrisostomi edificatam.

In tercio monte, qui reliquis inferior, est ecclesia ad honorem beate Barbare edi[**24rb**]ficata, que,[d] ut dicunt, ipsa de hac civitate fuit oriunda.

Et nota, quia Simon Magus, qui postmodum apostatavit, de Antiochia fuit oriundus. Multe vero hystorie, quas hic dici non opportet, in actibus apostolorum et in vitis sanctorum et in passionibus martium de hac Antiochia inveniuntur.

---

[1] Frederick I, who drowned in a river near Silifke in Asia Minor on 10 June 1190, on his way to participate in the Third Crusade. [2] Burchard III of Querfurt, who died in Antioch in 1189.
[3] Hoyer II, son of Hoyer I, commonly referred to as count of Woldenberg. [4] Wilbrand II, count of Hallermund, the brother of Wilbrand's mother Beatrix, who followed the emperor Frederick I on crusade and died in Antioch in 1191.

---

[a] minusculas L] musculos P.   [b] tonus] thronus L.   [c] movetur L] monetur P.   [d] que L] qui P.

Hic primo vidimus rosas albas totas rubeas et croceas et pomum vocatum Iesupubeledemis, quod talis est nature: In die Parasceves[a] seminantur sui nuclei, qui processu temporis sui in herbam consurgentes pariunt primo flores albos, qui postmodum in viridem, deinde in ruffum et ultimo in croceum variantur colorem. Qui in poma transsubstanciantur; quorum aliquod si aliquis super sua pulcritudine redarguerit, dicens se pulcriorem [vidisse],[b] ipsum pomum qua indignans turgescit et pre indignatione in minuta dirumpitur. Quod dictu mirabile est, cum ipsum sit quoddam insensatum; sed quod vidimus, hoc testamur, et testimonium nostrum verum est.

15. Ab illa post aliquot dies descendimus versus Hormeniam. Et reliquimus ad dextram terram Soldani et suam civitatem Halaph et quoddam suum castellum Haringc,[1] et venimus Gastun.[2] Hoc est quoddam castrum fortissimum, tres habens muros circa se fortissimos et turritos, situm in extremis montibus Hormenie, illius terre introitus et semitas diligenter observans; et possidetur a rege illius terre, scilicet a rege Hormenie. In cuius possessione Templarii conqueruntur se spoliari. Ipsum vero directe et de vicino prospicit Antiochiam, et distat quatuor milia.

16. Inde procedentes intravimus Hormeniam. Et sciendum, quod dominus terre illius Leo de Montanis consue[24va]verat appellari. Quem nostris diebus Henricus, gloriosus Romanorum imperator, qui semper rempublicam et romanum imperium augere laboravit, regem constituit et coronavit, unde postmodum rex Hormenie est appellatus, et deinceps terram suam a romano imperio recipere consuevit.[3] Cuius nepotem Otto[c] imperator ad peticionem Leonis, senioris regis, Henricus[d] coronavit. Quia heredem non habuit, de novo coronavit.[4]

17. Hec est terra firmissima: ex una enim parte cingitur mari; ex alia vero munitur altis montanis et asperimis, que paucos habent introitus et multum custoditos, ita ut hospes, si terram intraverit, absque regia bulla exire non possit. Ipsa vero in medio sui est plana et valde fertilis, multa fovens animalia venationi competencia. In longitudine sui protenditur ad XVI dietas, in latitudine exceptis montanis ad duas. Et inhabitatur a Francis et Grecis, Surianis, Turcis et Hormenis; reliquis tamen ispi Hormeni dominantur. Qui sunt homines valde religiosi et optimi Christiani, legem a minore Gregorio[5] sibi traditam observantes. In fide non errant.[e] Materna lingua recitant psalmos et alia divina officia. Duos habent calices dum celebrant, unum ad panem, in quem conficiunt, unum ad vinum, ex quo conficiunt.[f] Evvangelia et epistolas recitantes vertunt se ad populum et ad occidentem. Epiphaniam Domini pre omnibus festis agunt celeberrimam, de quo suo loco expediemini. Inter Pascha et Pentecostem sextis feriis utuntur carnibus,[g] eodem modo festum honorantes. Specialem habent papam, quem ipsi sua [lingua][h] Katelcose[6] appellant. Et sciendum, quod quidam sunt,

---

[1] Hārim.   [2] Baghras.   [3] Levon I, formerly Baron Levon II, was crowned on 6 January 1198; by this time, however, the emperor, Henry VI, who had entrusted Conrad, bishop of Hildesheim and imperial chancellor, with the crown and royal insignia a year before, was already dead.

[4] Raymond Rupen, Levon I's great nephew and named heir, was crowned on 15 August 1211 with a crown sent by Emperor Otto IV.   [5] Patriarch Gregory the Illuminator, ca. 300–ca. 332.
[6] I.e. catholicus.

---

[a] Parasceves L] Parasceven P.   [b] vidisse] *supplied by L.*   [c] Otto] Orto P.   [d] Henricus P, *apparently inserted here in error, omitted in L.*   [e] errant] erant P.   [f] conficiunt ... conficiunt] confitiunt ... confitiunt P.   [g] utuntur carnibus] non utuntur carnibus L.   [h] lingua] *added by L.*

qui dicunt istam Hor[**24vb**]meniam, in cuius montibus archa Noe post diluvium requievit,[1] hos versus pro se inducentes:

> Corvum perfidie dampnant animalia queque,
> Nuntius inclusis quia[a] noluit esse salutis.
> Ore columba suo ramum viridentibus ultro
> Detulerit foliis, superest Armenia testis.

Isti tamen, ut verius inquisivi, decepti sunt in equivoco, quia alia est Hormenia in oriente melius sita, que altissima habet montana, de qua fuerunt et egressi sunt illi Hormeni, qui hanc terram preocupaverunt, Grecos ab ea expellentes. A quibus ista minor Hormenia est appellata.

18. In prima planitie huius terre et in exitu montium, quos uno die cum magna transivimus difficultate …[b] Et venimus Alexandrete, que erat civitas murata, in littore maris sita, modo destructa. Istam, ut dicunt indigene, magnus Alexander ad custodiam sui equi Bucefali, qui tunc infirmabatur, laboribus unius diei composuit et a suo nomine denominavit. Iuxta etiam illam sunt prata equis commodissima.

Primo die venimus ad Portellam.[2] Hoc est casale bonum, prope se habens portam, a qua ipsum denominatur. Hec sola sita est in strata publica, in ripa maris, et est ornatissima albo et valde polito marmore composita, in cuius summitate, ut dicitur, ossa Alexandri prenominati requiescunt, qui illic se, ut volunt, poni mandavit, ut reges vel principes per illam portam transeuntes eum etiam mortuum super sua capita sustinerent, quem aliquando vivum super se sustinuerant. [**25ra**] Hoc casale distat ab Alexandrete quatuor milia.

Deinde relinquentes ad destram castrum regis Nigrin[3] et transeuntes castellum quoddam, Cannamelam[4] videlicet, venimus Mamistere.[5] Hec est civitas bona, supra flumen sita satis amene, murum habens circa se turritum, sed antiquitate corrosum, paucos in quodam respectu habens inhabitatores, quibus omnibus rex illius terre imperat et dominatur. Et est in ea episcopatus Hormenorum. Et sciendum, quia dominus rex, sicut ante tetigi, postquam a romano imperio coronam suscepit, in hac civitate et in aliis quibusdam latinos episcopos ordinaverat. Quos postmodum abiecit, asserens se iniuste a romana ecclesia gravari et excomunicari. Iuxta hanc civitatem situm est quoddam castrum, quod erat de patrimonio beati Pauli, qui de hac terra, ut iam audietis, fuit oriundus, et beatus Servacius;[6] sed nunc temporis possidebatur a Grecis. In hac civitate habetur sepulcrum beati Pantaleonis. Ipsa vero distat a Cannamela magnam dietam.

19. Abhinc transeuntes Cumbetefort,[7] ubi domus est et mansio bona Hospitalis Allemannorum, venimus Tursolt. Hec est illa Tharsis, de qua natus fuit beatus Paulus tempore Grecorum. In qua hodie eius apparet palacium, unde a loco sue nativitatis vocat eum Dominus Saulum tarsensem, ubi ait ad Ananiam: *Surge et vade in vicum, qui dicitur rectus, et quere in domo Iude Saulum nomine, tarsensem; iam enim orat.*[8] Quidam etiam sunt, qui dicunt hanc illam esse Tharsim, de qua venit unus magorum adora[**25rb**]re Dominum; et isti

---

[1] Genesis 8.4: *requievitque arca mense septimo vicesima septima die super montes Armeniae* (*RSV* mountains of Ararat).   [2] Bāb Iskandarūn.   [3] Probably Mancilik Kalesi, north-east of Payas.
[4] Hisn al-Tīnāt, north of Alexandretta (İskenderun).   [5] Misis.   [6] St. Servatius, or Aravatius, bishop of Tongeren (Tongres) and later of Maastricht, died during the Hun invasions ca. 384.
[7] Unidentified.   [8] Acts 9.11.

---

[a] quia] qui *L.*   [b] *There is evidently some text missing from here, though P continues without a break.*

sunt in equivoco decepti, quia non a septentrione sed ab oriente venerunt magi. Verumptamen hic dicendum occurrit, quod magi ammoniti, ut per aliud iter redirent de Bethleem, in Iopeam pervenerunt, ubi navem, quam sine omnibus suis necessariis invererant, intrantes sine remis et velo in portum huius Tharsis appodiaverunt; et inde reversi sunt in regiones suas. Quod dum audisset Herodes, qui eos persequebatur,[a] misit et combussit in nimio furore omnes naves Tharsis. Quod psalmista innuit, ut puto, ubi dicit: *Ibi dolores ut parturientis. In spiritu vehementi conteres naves Tharsis.*[1] Volunt etiam quidam ipsum Herodem, dum de Roma venit, tempestate ad hunc portum fuisse deiectum et in propria persona naves illic combussisse. Hec civitas multos habens inhabitatores; muro cingitur per[b] antiquitate mutilato, sed castrum habet in capite sui firmum et bonum, in quo sanctus Theodorus captus fuit et martirizatus; et est ibi ecclesia in eodem loco ad honorem ipsius edificata. In medio vero civitatis est ecclesia principalis, in honorem beati Petri et beate Sophie dedicata, multum ornata, tota strata marmore, in fine sui habens quandam statuam, cui imago domine nostre angelicis manibus est inpicta, que in maxima ab hominibus illius terre habetur veneratione. Sicut enim multi et omnes videre consueverunt, hec imago, dum aliquod grave periculum illi terre iminet, coram omnibus et in magna quantitate solet lacrimari. Hec est illa, ut dicitur, que Theophilum[2] reformavit; grate sane intelligatis, quia illam hystoriam tanquam notam pertranseo. In angulo quodam extra fores ecclesie sepulta est soror Mahummet, [**25va**] cuius tumbam Sarraceni in multo petunt timore et devotione. In hac ecclesia, ut supra tetigi, ordinaverat dominus rex de consilio episcopi Conradi maguntini,[3] quem imperator illuc transmiserat, archiepiscopatum latinum, quem nunc, sicut et alios, immutaverat. Illic dominus rex occurrit nobis et nunciis ducis Austrie, quos honestissime recepit et detinuit nos in terra xviii septimanis. Hec civitas distat a Mamistere duas dietas.

20. Ab illa post aliquot dies venimus Adene,[4] que est civitas regis in amenis locis supra flumen a se denominatum[c] sita, et non divites habet cives; que tamen infra muros largissima est. Quidam dicunt Medeam hinc fuisse oriundam, de qua Ovidius:

> Tune duos una, sevissime vippera, cena?
> Tune duos?[5]

Verum est, quod hec civitas multas et abhorrendas fovet incantatrices; quod quidam nostrum experimento didicerunt. Hec distat a Tharsi unam dietam.

21. In die[d] vero – hoc est in festo – Epiphanie, quod Hormeni Baptisterium appellant, pervenimus Sis, ad quam dominus rex nos ad celebrandum suum festum invitaverat. Hoc est capitanea civitas domini regis, infinitos et divites fovens inhabitatores. Nullis munitionibus cingitur. Unde potius eam villam, quam civitatem nuncuparem, si sedem archiepiscopalem Hormenorum in se non haberet. In qua etiam Greci suo obediunt patriarche. Castrum vero habet super se situm in monte valde munitum, a cuius pede ipsa civitas ordinate et gradatim descendere videtur. Et, ut dicunt, hec aliquando a Dario rege, quem Alexander devicit, possidebatur.

---

[1] Cf. Psalms 47.7–8 (*RSV* 48.6–7). Wilbrand, following the Vulgate, here confuses Tarsus (*Tarsis*) with Tarshish (Tartessos), a Phoenician colony in Spain.   [2] Cf. Luke 1.3; Acts 1.1.
[3] Conrad, archbishop of Mainz, the papal legate; not to be confused with Conrad, bishop of Hildesheim, the imperial chancellor.   [4] Adana.   [5] Not Ovid, but Juvenal, *Satires* 6, lines 641–42: *tune duos una, saevissima vipera, cena? / tune duos? septem, si septem forte fuissent!*

---

[a] persequebatur] persequebantur *P*.   [b] per] pre *L*.   [c] denominatum] denominato *P*.
[d] In die] *mistakenly changed by copyist to* Inde.

22. Festum Epiphanie, de quo me supra promisi dicturum, ad quod etiam dominus rex nos invitaverat, in hunc modum ab Hormenis agebatur. Duode[**25vb**]cim dies precedentes, quos nos in gaudio et epulis, ispi ab honoratione sui festi in penitencia egerunt et ieiuniis, a piscibus, vino et oleo abstinentes. Ipsa vero sacra vigilia toto die ab his abstinuerunt, ita ut post crepusculum missarum officia celebrarent et totam illam noctem in divinis insompnes deducerent. Ipso enim die agunt festum Dominice Nativitatis, dicentes Dominum uno et eodem etiam superiore[a] die fuisse natum et post anno tricesimo baptizatum.[1] Mane vero facto omnes ad quoddam flumen ipsi ville vicinum festinabant, ad quod dominus rex hoc ordine descendebat. Alto equo insidebat, et magistrum domus Allemannorum et castellanum de Seleph,[2] Hospitalarium, cum eorum sociis, viris religiosis militaribus,[b] suo lateri adiungebat. Quem dominus Ruppinus, iunior rex, quem, ut ante dixi, Otto Romanorum imperator ad petitionem senioris regis nuper coronaverat, cum nobilibus terre illius et cum multis militibus pulchre indutis subsequebatur. Quorum servi singula vexilla et baneras in manibus gestantes et eorum equos faleratos deducentes seniorem regem precedebant. Inter quos et ipsum multi sarganti pedites cum armis suis ad custodiam regis discurrebant. Qui ab omnibus hinc astantibus *Subtacfol!* – id est *Sacer rex!* – cum ingenti clamore salutabatur. Et sic ipse in magna [pompa][c] ad territorium suum in ripa fluminis predicti preparatum descendebant. Deinde Greci et eorum patriarcha pedites et preparati cum multis sanctuariis subsequebantur. Qui in tanto clamore buccinarum et aliorum instrumentorum musicorum incede[**26ra**]bant, ut pocius pompam quam processionem ducere viderentur. Isti etiam in loco eis deputato super flumen reliquos expectabant. Tunc tandem Hormenorum clerus crucem quandam baptizandam baiulans decenter cum suo archiepiscopo descendebat. Quorum humilitatem et decentem processionem satis laudavissem, si quidam sacerdos longa barba, ut reliqui, insignitus eam malo omine ne[d] interrupisset. Qui dum minus caute parvum rivulum ad sepedictum flumen decurrentem transiret, calceum pedi suo elapsum perdidit, ad cuius comprehensionem, cum ab aqua deduceretur, adeo incuriose laboravit, ut episcopum et alios detineret. Huiusmodi negligentiam Hildenshemenses, si forte in ipsorum processione accidisset, correxissent severissime. Isti etiam suam stationem et residentiam supra predictum flumen acceperunt. Processionibus igitur in unum convenientibus hinc inde discantari et longas ipsorum barbas, que illorum pectora sicut quedam plenaria contegebant, multo hiatu vidimus laborare. Qui evvangelia et epistolas grece et hormenice recitantes et illum simulatum Iordanem benedicentes crucem, quam illuc apportabant, baptizabant, et columbam a vertice illius emiserunt. Tunc quidam in asino in medium fluminis descendens et stans erectus zucarato gurgite, proclamabat: *Vivat rex noster in eternum!* Et rursus: *Valeat et confortetur omnis christianitas!* Omnibus autem ab ore illius dependentibus et respondentibus: *Amin!*, ille preceptor[e] in aquam detrudebatur. Quod non sine multorum risu est effectum. De[**26rb**]inde rex et alii ipsa aqua aspergebantur. Suriani vero toti nudi lavabantur. His ergo rite peractis clerici ad monasteria, rex vero et milites ad campos festinabant, ubi illi in faleratis equis discurrentes et hastas disrumpentes egerunt ludos militares. Et sic totum illum diem in leticia multa expenderunt, postero die omnibus ad sua remeantibus.

---

[1] Cf. Luke 3.23.   [2] Silifke, which was granted to the Hospitallers by Levon I in 1210.

---

[a] superiore] sperie *P*, specie *L*.   [b] militaribus] milibus *P*.   [c] pompa] *added by L; an alternative might be* turba.   [d] omine ne] omini ve *P*, omine *L*.   [e] preceptor] precentor *L*.

Illud etiam scitote, quia dominus rex iuxta hanc civitatem ortum deliciarum sibi preparavit, ad cuius delicias describendas meam confiteor insufficienciam.

23. Festo celebrato et licentia a domino rege, qui multo honore nos dimisit, nobis concessa venimus Naversan,[1] quod est castrum optimum in alto monte situm, quem natura in media planicie illius terre ad totam commodum domini regis ordinavit. A quo rex ipse signum suum *Naversa* solet proclamare. In pede huius montis sita fuit quedam civitas, cuius auctoritatem[a] fuisse magnam quidam mirabilis aqueductus illuc super altas columpnas ad spatium duorum miliariorum productus hodie contestatur. Iuxta quam beatus Gregorius[2] vermen, qui sub equo suo depingitur, occidit; qui dum fugeret, ipsum montem transivit, qui, ne virum sanctum insequentem impediret, in duo equalia se dividens transitum satis largum patefecit. In cuius facti memoriam ecclesia in eodem loco est edificata. Hoc castrum distat a predicta civitate Sis quatuor milia.

24. Inde venimus ad Amodanam,[3] quod est castrum hospitalis sive domus Allemannorum. Quod dominus rex, qui semper Allemannos dilexit, eis pro remedio anime sue cum quinque villis attinentibus donavit. In pede huius castri decurrit [**26va**] quidam fluvius, qui maximo gurgite oritur in montanis Hormenie et vicinis. Qui tribus diebus ante Palmas et tribus post et in ipso die festo ab ore suo, ubi oritur vel egreditur, tantam emittit piscium multitudinem, ut ab omnibus ex omni provincia illuc confluentibus carrucis et somariis deducantur. Inde nuper accidit, ut Latinis et Hormenis de Adventu, Quadragesime et Pace disputantibus et diversa putantibus verus dies Palmarum per effluxionem predictorum piscium monstraretur. Unde rex et Hormeni tali suo victi experimento nostrorum sentencie crediderunt, cum ad doctrinam suorum Palmas VIII diebus pervenissent. Hoc flumen et tale miraculum dicunt beatum Ioannem baptistam eis concessisse, quia ipse percussit petram, et fluxerunt aque. Hoc castrum distat a Naversan duo milia.

25. Abhinc revertebamur versus Cannamelam, de qua supra dixi, et venimus ad Thilam,[4] quod est castrum valde bonum cuiusdam nobilis. Iuxta illud situs est quidam mons satis amenus, quem Montem de Aventuris appellant. Sicut enim ex veridica relatione audivimus, quicumque VI septimanis ieiunaverit et penitencialibus illis diebus peractis communicaverit, et sic ieiunus dictum montem intraverit, procul dubio boni eventus et fortunati sibi occurrunt. Quod multorum compertum est experimento. Inter que illud pro magno reputo, quod quidam miles, quem et nos vidimus in Antiochia, illic huiusmodi casu bono invenit quoddam manutergium,[b] quod sue familie [**26vb**] et hospitibus, quotquot vocare consuevit, omnia necessaria in victualibus ministravit, ita ut in mensa et super se parata inveniantur. Utinam etiam huiusmodi minister hodie mee occurreret indigentie!

26. Hieme igitur iam recedente dum ad exitum terre istius intenderemus, per Tharsim, quam supra descripsi, versus occidentem descendimus, et invenimus circa illas partes ipsam Hormeniam in silvis, in recentibus aquis et bono aere nostre Teutonie simillimam. Quam in tribus diebus peragrantes venimus Cure,[5] que est civitas in mari sita, bonum habens portum. In qua hodie mirabiles, quamvis dirute, apparent structure, ita ut nimirum eas romanis structuris et ruinis comparaverim.

---

[1] Anavarza.   [2] Presumably St. Gregory the Illuminator (ca. 257–ca. 331), who converted King Trdat (Tiridates) III to Christianity in 301; however, as below (II.3), it is also possible that Gregory has become confused with St. George, the dragon slayer.   [3] Amuda.   [4] Toprak.   [5] Korykos.

---

[a] auctoritatem] auctoritate *P*.   [b] manutergium] manuterium *P*.

Iuxta illam ad duo milia situm est Seleph castrum, iuxta quod in flumine, a quo ipsum castrum denominatur, submersus fuit – pro dolor! – piissime memorie Fredericus Romanorum imperator,[1] cum recuperatione Terre Sancte laboraret.

27. Inde navigio nobis preparato in Cyprum descendimus. Que est insula summe fertilis, optima habens vina. Que licet sita sit prope Ciclades, tamen non est una illarum,[a] quia tantum LIII esse describuntur.[2] Hec in longitudine protenditur ad quatuor dietas, in latitudine amplius quam ad duas. Et habet in se alta montana. In qua unus est archiepiscopus, tres habens suffraganeos. Et sunt Latini. De quibus suis locis expediemini. Greci vero, quibus Latini per totam hanc terram dominantur, [**27ra**] XIII habent[b] episcopos, quorum unus est archiepiscopus, qui omnes ipsis Francis obediunt, tributum tanquam servi persolventes. Ex istis scire potestis, qui domini huius terre Franci sint,[c] quibus Greci et Hormeni ut coloni obediunt. Qui omni sua dispositione informes et paupere habitu incedentes plurimum luxurie deserviunt; quod vino illius terre, in quo multa est luxuria, vel pocius ipsis bibentibus imputabitur. Hac[d] etiam consideratione habita Venus in Cipro coli dicebatur. Unde et ipsa Cipris est appellata, ubi dicitur: *Cipris eo Marte vel ea devincitur arte.*[3] Vina etenim huius insule adeo spissa et pinguia sunt, ut aliquando, cum ad hoc decoquuntur, more mellis cum pane comedantur.[e] Hec etiam insula multos fovet silvestres asinos et arietes, cervos et damas; ursos et leones vel lupos vel aliqua nociva animalia in se non habens. Qui autem plenius de hac terra scire voluerit, qualiter primo facta fuerit habitabilis, et quomodo virgines in hac terra a demonibus fuerint corrupte et impregnate, et in quantum ipsi demones homines primos[f] huius terre colonos infestaverint, ille requirat librum prepositi Hermanni de Lugowe,[4] in quo ipse vir nobilis et piissime memorie omnia et multo plura de statu huius terre plene et ad unguem descripsit. Cuius anime nostra[g] caritativa oratio dignetur reminisci.

28. Primo introitu Scherins[5] applicuimus. Que est civitas parva et munita, castrum habens in se munitum et turritum. [**27rb**] Que maxime in suo bono portu gloriatur. In finibus huius rex Cypri habet IIII bona castra. Et notate, quia imperator Henricus dominum huius terre primum regem constituit et per manus Conradi cancellarii coronavit.[6] Hinc[h] est, quod rex huius terre romano imperatori[i] dominio tenetur et fidelitate.

Inde prodentes venimus Nicossiam. Hec est capitalis civitas domini regis, fere in media planicie illius terre sita, nullam habens munitionem. In qua nunc temporis forte castrum elaboratur. Innumerabiles et valde habet predivites inhabitatores, quorum hospicia intrinseco ornatu et picturis hospiciis Antiochie sunt simillima. In hac civitate est sedes archiepiscopi. Et est in ea curia et palacium domini regis, in qua primo vidimus strutionem. Hec civitas

---

[1] Frederick I drowned on 10 June 1190.   [2] The Cyclades are also numbered at 53 by Orosius, *Historiae adversus paganos* 1.2.98; cf. *Liber de Existencia Riverarum et Forma Maris Nostri Mediterranei*, ed. P.G. Dalché, *Carte marine e portulan au XIIe siècle* (Collection de l'École Française de Rome 203), pp. 133–34.   [3] *Polythecon* 8.244–45, ed. A. P. Orbán, in CCCM 93 (Turnhout, 1990), p. 196: *Qua specie Martis cedit uictoria Parthis, / Cipris eo Marte, uel ea deluditur arte.* Gerald of Wales, *Speculum ecclesiae* 3.8, ed. J. S. Brewer, RS 21.4, p. 170: *Cypris ea Marte, vel ea deluditur arte.* Cf. L. Calvelli, *Cipro e la Memoria dell'Antico fra Medioevo e Rinascimento*, Memorie 133 (Venice, 2009), p. 8.   [4] Hermann of Lüchow in Lower Saxony, an otherwise unknown author: cf. Calvelli, *Cipro e la Memoria*, pp. 8–9.   [5] Kyrenia.   [6] Aimery of Lusignan did homage to the emperor Henry VI's chancellor, Conrad, bishop of Hildesheim, and was crowned king of Cyprus by him in Nicosia in 1197.

---

[a] illarum *L*] illa *P*.   [b] habent *L*] habens *P*.   [c] qui ... sint] quod ... sunt *L*.   [d] Hac] Hanc *P*.
[e] comedantur] comedatur *P*.   [f] primos] *corrected by copyist from* primu ...   [g] nostra] vestra *L*.
[h] Hinc] Hin *P*.   [i] imperatori] imperator *P*.

distat a Scherins quinque milia. In cuius vie transitu multas incidimus cipressus, que illic in multa crescunt discreta quantitate. A quibus, ut puto, ipsa insula Ciprus est appellata.

29. Ab illa procedentes in peregrinatione ad visitandam crucem latronis ad dextram Domini crucifixi processimus Lemezun.[1] Que est civitas non multum munita, iacens in littore maris, portum habens frequentatum. In qua est prima sedes suffraganea episcopalis domini nicossensis.

Iuxta illam site sunt vinee Engadi, de quibus in Canticis: *Botrus Cypri, dilectus meus mihi in vineis Engadi.*[2] In quibus aliquando etiam inveniebatur balsamum, sed modo non invenitur. Vina autem illarum optima sunt; expertis credendum est, quia probavimus et gustavimus, quoniam suave est.

30. [I]nde conscendimus montem Sancte Crucis appellatum,[3] [**27va**] qui[a] omnia montana Cypri supereminet. In cuius cacumine est quoddam parvum cenobium monachorum nigrorum edificatum, quorum vita venerabilis nostrorum monachorum vite, ut in pace ipsorum dicam, est dissimillima.[b] In ipso cenobio est capella parva, in qua illa honorabilis crux multo reservatur honore. Que etiam, ut dicunt, nullo innitens amminiculo in aere pendet et fluctuat; quod tamen non videtur de facili. Que hoc modo et tali de causa illic fuit collata. Invisor omnium bonorum diabolus colonos et inhabitatores huius terre tanta infestavit malicia, ut [c] corpora suorum mortuorum, que de die humo imposuerunt, nocte de sepulcris evelleret et ad penetralia suorum carorum reportaret. Unde ipsi indigene mortuos suos non poterant sepelire. Quorum cladem Helena, Constantini mater, illi tunc imperans, est miserata, et eandem crucem, quam integram, sicut hodie est, a Iherosolima secum apportans, in predicto monte collocavit, et sic non solum illos hostes malignos a terra, verum etiam ab inferiore aere, qui carcer demonum putatur, potenter expulit, ac si diceret illud verbum Dominicum: *Sinite mortuos sepelire mortuos suos.*[4] Et sic *ille hostis antiquus, qui in ligno vincebat, in ligno quoque isto vincebatur.*

31. Ab hoc[d] monte vidimus Bafos,[5] que etiam sita iuxta mare habet in se secundam sedem episcopalem suffraganeam domini nicossensis. Et est civitas parva, in qua hodie mostratur turris illa, super quam apud gentilium errores Venus a suis amatoribus [**27vb**] colebatur.

Inde peregrinatione nostra persoluta versus Famagustam laboravimus, et quia pedes incessimus, asinos conducere pre lassitudine cogebamur, quibus nos cibo pariter et vino refecti insedimus, et in eis sicut in equis fortibus discurrere putabamus. Tunc quidam nostrum, quem nominare non presumo, quem etiam *fecundi calices nimis fecerant disertum,*[6] cum equitare putaret, pedibus suis in diversa tendentibus de asino occidit,[e] et dum surgere laboraret, aliquot ictus ab ipso asino recepit. Et iam verus[f] Sillenus calce feritur aselli! Qui tamen omnem casum suum vino imputabat, cum pocius istud documentum Catonis observare deberet:

> Qui potu peccas, tibi tuque ignoscere noli;
> Nulla etenim vini culpa est, sed culpa bibentis.[7]

---

[1] Limassol.   [2] Song of Solomon 1.13 (*RSV* 1.13); cf. Calvelli, *Cipro e la Memoria*, pp. 6–7.
[3] Stavrovouni.   [4] Luke 9.60.   [5] Paphos, though it is not visible from Stavrovouni.
[6] Cf. Horace, *Epistulae* 1.5, line 19: *fecundi calices quem non fecere disertum?*   [7] *Distichs of Cato*
2.21: *Quae potus peccas, ignoscere tu tibi soli; / Nam crimen vini nullum est, sed culpa bibentis.*

---

[a] qui *L*] quia *P*.   [b] dissimillima *L*] disimillima *P*.   [c] *Here the copyist accidentally inserted* si, *probably representing the beginning of* suorum, *before correcting the mistake.*   [d] hoc] *corrected by the copyist from* hac.   [e] occidit] cecidit *L*.   [f] verus] versus *L*.

Huiusmodi homo, ut puto, deinceps testimonium perhibere non potest.

32. Hinc venimus Famagustam, que est civitas sita iuxta mare, portum habens bonum, non multum munita. In qua est sedes episcopalis tercia suffraganea domini nicossensis. Iuxta illam sita est quedam civitas destructa, de qua, ut dicunt, fuit beatus ille et magnus Epiphanius,[1] cuius memoria habetur in canone.

Ab hac civitate post moram [a] trium ebdomadarum, quibus ventum commodum expectavimus, vela tendentes in altum multo labore et in magna tempestate in Hakon sumus reversi.

[II]

1. [N]unc primo ad cor redeuntes et principali voto nostro intendentes, licen[**28ra**]cia et benedictione domini patriarche[2] accepta, versus Ierosolimam ascendentes transivimus Cayphan. Que est civitas parva, destructos habens muros, sita iuxta mare. Cui nostri dominantur. Que nomen a Caypha fundatore accepit, qui cum esset pontifex anni illius, prophetavit, ut Dominus traderetur.[3]

Super istam directe iacet mons Carmelus, in quo hodie monstratur mansio Helye et honoratur. In quo et ipse Helyas per corvum alebatur.[4] Ubi etiam postmodum mulier sunamitis Heliseum invenit.[5] In quo loco cotidie missarum sollempnia celebrantur. Iuxta istam etiam sita est Galilea, casale bonum.[6] Et hec distat ab Hacon quatuor milia.

2. Inde transivimus Capharnaum,[7] quod est castellum parvum, supra mare situm. Et sciendum, quod quidam dicunt istud esse Capharnaum, ubi Dominus filium reguli curavit et alia plura signa fuit operatus. Et hii in equivoco decipiuntur, quia illud Capharnaum situm est in Galilea. De quo suo loco expediemini.[8] A quibus si forte opponitur auctoritas Luce, qui ait in evangelio: *Quanta audivimus in Capharnaum facta! fac et hic in patria tua signum!*[9] Et [contra argumentum]: *Domini patria fuit Galilea: igitur illa facta fuerunt extra Galileam et in Capharnaum*, respondeo, quia *patria* ponitur ibi pro sua Nazareth, de qua Dominus etiam Nazarenus et non Galileus vocabatur.

Et relinquentes ad sinistram Sareptam Iudee,[10] ad cuius differentiam altera Sarepta, de qua supra vos expedivi, Sydoniorum est appellata, venimus Cesa[**28rb**]ream. Hec non est Cesarea Philippi, sed Stratonis,[11] in qua beatus Petrus, cum in visione de omni immundo et reptili terre manducare iuberetur, sedem episcopalem ordinavit, et in illa presidens verbum fidei gentibus predicare incepit, per quod sua visio, de qua iam tetigi, adimplebatur.[12] In hac hodie est sedes episcopalis. Ipsa vero civitas destructos habet muros. Tantum tempore treugarum inhabitabatur et tunc nostris obedire consuevit. In hac, ut quidam volunt, vidit Iesus hominem sedentem in thelonio, nomine Matheum, et dixit illi: *Sequere me! etc.*[13] Hec distat ab Hakon spatio unius magne diete.

---

[1] St. Epiphanius (ca. 310/20–403), bishop of Salamis from 376 onwards.   [2] Albert of Vercelli (1205–14).   [3] Cf. John 11.51, though Caiaphas had no known connection with Haifa.
[4] But 1 Kings 17.3–6 locates this event by the Cherith brook, east of the Jordan.   [5] 2 Kings 4.25.
[6] Khirbat al-Tinʿama, referred to in Frankish sources as *Tymini* or *Galgala*.   [7] Khirbat al-Kanisa.
[8] In a part of the book now missing.   [9] Luke 4.23.   [10] Al-Ṣarafand.   [11] The city was called Strato's Tower until 9 BC, when Herod renamed it Caesarea in honour of Caesar Augustus.
[12] Acts 10.   [13] Matthew 9.9, which, however, places the event in Galilee.

---

[a] *Here the copyist wrote* d, *perhaps intending to write* duarum, *but then substituted* trium.

Ab illa magno timore transivimus Arsun,[1] que est civitas parva et destructa, tempore treugarum a nostris inhabitata, multos in finibus suis habens latrunculos sarrecenos.

Et notate, quod hec civitates et dicte et dicende in perditione Terre Sancte a Sarracenis fuerunt destructe, preter Iaf, quam nostri tempore Henrici imperatoris – pro pudor! – perdiderunt.[2] In qua filii Mammone nostris peccatis exigentibus xii milia Christianorum occiderunt et captivaverunt. Hec est illa Iopea, in qua beatus Petrus visionem supra tactam accepit, scilicet vas de celo missum, plenum omni reptili terre, quod angelus ipsum manducare precepit.[3] Hec est etiam illa, in cuius portu magi adorato Domino per aliam viam redeuntes navem nec velo nec remis munitam intraverunt. Qui illinc, ut supra plene scripsi, ad portum Tharsis miraculose sunt perducti. Hec civitas, sicut et relique, a nostris pace [28va] a paganis eis indulta inhabitari consuevit. Et distat a Cesarea unam dietam.

3. Illic ducatu nobis concesso relinquentes maritimam et incedentes versus meridiem transivimus terram verissime lacte et melle fluentem, et peragravimus Rammam. Que civitas destructa, a Sarracenis inhabitata. De qua tempore Grecorum, qui tunc terram manutenebant, beatus Georgius[a] oriundus fuit; unde et hodie a Gallicis *San Iorge de Ramnis* solet appellari. Cuius corpus in quodam cenobio Surianorum iuxta illam sito requiescit. Qui etiam aliquando post mortem carnis in eisdem finibus cum Boldewino rege ierosolimitano visibiliter contra Turcos [pugnavit][b] et nostris victoriam concessit.[4] Alia est Rama Iudee, de qua[c] suo loco expediemini.[5]

4. Ipso die venimus Bettenobele,[6] quod est casale, cuius munitiones sunt destructe, inhabitatum a Sarracenis. Et distat a Iopea vel Iaf vii milia gallicana.

Postero die, qui inter omnes dies mee felicitatis felicissimus nimirum computabitur, conscendimus montana Iherusalem. Que sunt admodum alta, lapisosa et asperrima et, quod mirabile est, multum vini, olei [et][d] frumenti afferentia. In quibus vidimus multa casalia et cenobia, quorum nomina mihi sunt ignota, destructa et desolata, in quibus religiosi[e] viri prope suam matrem habitabant.

5. Igitur sole oriente desiderata illa Iherusalem nostro aspectui oriebatur. Ubi tanto perculsi sumus gaudio et ammiratione, ut etiam illam celestem Iherusalem nos videre putaremus. Ad quam accedentes curiam quandam iuxta muros civitatis sitam [28vb] intrare compellebamur. In hoc loco fuit martirizatus beatus Stephanus, in cuius honore nostri fideles ecclesiam, sicut adhuc apparet, et archiepiscopatum fundaverant.[7] Ubi nunc temporis asini Soldani compelluntur. *Quomodo igitur obscuratum est aurum, mutatus est color optimus,*[8] quia de ecclesia materia,[f] de loco reliquiarum locus stercorum est ordinatus? Et nota, quia

---

[1] Arsūf, Crusader *Arsur*.   [2] Although Jaffa had been in Muslim hands between July 1187 and September 1191, it fell a second time to al-ʿĀdil just after the death of Henry of Champagne on 10 September 1197 and before that of the emperor Henry VI (1191–97) on 28 September, returning to Christian control again in September 1204.   [3] Acts 10.9–16.   [4] An allusion to the battle of Montgisart, near Ramla, on 25 November 1177, in which St. George was observed participating on the Frankish side: cf. *Chronique d'Ernoul et de Bernard le Trésorier*, ed. L. de Mas Latrie (Paris, 1871), p. 43.   [5] In a part of the book now missing.   [6] Bayt Nūbā.   [7] The reference to an archbishopric is obscure, though the abbot of St. Mary Latin, to whom the church belonged, was a suffragan of the patriarch of Jerusalem: see John of Ibelin, *Le Livre des Assises*, ed. Peter Edbury (Leiden and Boston, 2003), p. 592.   [8] Lamentations 4.1.

---

[a] Georgius] Gregorius *P, evidently in error.*   [b] pugnavit] *added by L.*   [c] qua *L*] quo *P.*
[d] et] *added by L.*   [e] religiosi] *corrected by the copyist from* religiosa.   [f] materia *L*] anateria *P.*

iste locus extra muros est, quia secundum Actus Apostolorum *eicientes eum extra portam lapidabant.*[1]

6. Situs ipsius civitatis, quem bene ab illo considerare potuimus, talis est. Ipsa civitas, quamvis sita sit in alto, respectu montium, qui adiacent, in valle iacere videtur.[a] Super quam ex una parte versus orientem extenditur Mons Oliveti, ex alia parte erga meridiem Mons Syon, qui nunc temporis muris civitatis includitur. Ipsa enim civitas post passionem Domini funditus a Tito et Vespasiano eversa in sua restitutione in tantum situm mutavit priorem, ut Mons Calvarie, qui tunc extra muros fuerat, ipsis modo includitur. Et quod extra fuerit, testatur Iohannes, ubi ait:[2] *Et baiulans sibi crucem exivit in eum, qui dicitur Calvarie, locum.*[b]

Turris etiam David, que tunc super portam[c] erat, nunc infra civitatem et suo loco antiquo est reedificata, a qua et nunc una portarum Porta David nominatur. Quam nos sicut oves quedam computati intrantes, inclinatis capitibus ad atria ecclesie sancti Sepulcri per nuntium Soldani deducebamur. Que desolata non habens, qui consoletur eam, adeo facta est sub tributo, ut ante fores ipsius VIII dragmas et dimidiam dare co[**29ra**]geremur. Quam nos eo, quo oportebat, timore et gaudio intrantes adoravimus vere in loco sancto, ubi steterunt pedes Eius. In cuius medio, quia tota rotunda est, intravimus monumentum dominicum, quod ad modum ample et quadrate ciste dispositum, ex omni latere albo et polito marmore contectum, in se habet ipsam petram, cui illud sacrosanctum corpus Domini *in ara crucis torridum*, fuit inpositum. Que etiam integra et marmore contecta in tribus locis patet tactui et osculis peregrinarum.[d] De quo Marcus ait: *Et posuerunt in monumento de petra exciso.*[3] In illo etiam vidimus locum ad dextram, in quo angelus apparuit tribus Mariis. Quod et tangit Marcus, dicens: *Et introeuntes in monumento viderunt iuvenem a dextris sedentem, coopertum stola candida.*[4] Et nota, quia erga monumentum ipsa ecclesia nec habet nec unquam habuit tectum, ita ut ipsum tectum ad dispositionem et formam clericalis corone sit abrasum, una, ut puto, habita consideratione: clericus enim raditur, ut inter rationem, que in capite manere dicitur, et suum creatorem nullum sit medium vel mundana superfluitas, que nimirum per pilos vel crines designatur. Sic et predictum tectum est abrasum, ut inter ipsum monumentum et suum aliquando contectum nullum medium esse videatur, et semper celesti gratia custodiatur. Quod etiam annuatim ex eo considerare possumus, quia nocte Pasche sacer ignis per celestem nuncium illic apportari consuevit.

Et sciendum, quia Mons Calvarie, qui modicus est ut quidam colliculus, infra parietes ecclesie [**29rb**] continetur, quia ipsum monumentum Domini erat in orto tempore passionis. Ortus autem iacebat in pede huius colliculi sive montis Calvarie, unde nimirum dictus mons et monumentum multum vicini sunt. De quibus Iohannes omnibus ait sic: *Erat autem in loco, ubi crucifixus est Iesus, ortus: et in orto monumentum novum, in quo nondum quisquam positus fuerat. Ibi ergo propter parasceven Iudeorum, quia iuxta erat monumentum, posuerunt eum.*[5] Ex istis veritatem predictorum perpendere potestis. Hunc montem etiam nos indigni ascendentes vidimus foramen in petra excisum, cui ipsa crux, *arbor decora et fulgida, ornata regis purpura*, dum *secli* ferret *precium*, fuit infixa.[6]

---

[1] Acts 7.58: *Et eiiciens eum extra civitatem lapidabant.*   [2] John 19.17.   [3] Mark 15.46: *et posuit eum in monumento, quod erat excisum de petra.*   [4] Mark 16.5.   [5] Cf. John 19.41–42.
[6] From the office hymn, *Vexilla regis prodeunt*, sung at Vespers from Passion Sunday to the Wednesday of Holy Week.

---

[a] videtur *L*] vindentur *P*.   [b] locum] locus *P*.   [c] portam *L*] portum *P*.   [d] peregrinarum] peregrinorum *L*.

Iuxta quem locum apparet sanguis Domini, qui de latere Ipsius in petram vicinam defluxit, quia teste Iohanne: *unus militum lancea latus eius apperuit, et sanguis et aqua continuo exivit.*[1] Hec petra magnam habet scissuram, quia, ut dixit Matheus: *petre scisse*[a] *sunt et monumenta aperta.*[2]

Circa hunc locum *stabant iuxta crucem Iesu mater eius et soror matris eius, Maria Cleophe, et Maria Magdalene.*[3] Item in eodem loco vidimus partem illius columpne, cui alligatus fuit Dominus, dum flagellaretur. Et notate, quia ipsa ecclesia et sanctum Sepulcrum, et omnia, que intus sunt contenta, a quatuor sacerdotibus surianis, qui exire non permittuntur, in bona devotione custodiuntur. Que omnia ipsi Sarraceni reliquerunt illesa; quod pocius ex divina voluntate, quam ex ipsorum accidit benivolentia. Ipsa vero ecclesia marmoreis tabulis et aureis picturis valde est ornata, in capite suo habens chorum largum et pulcrum, in cuius [**29va**] habitu ossa regum fidelium in marmoreis sarcofagis requiescunt.[4] In medio chori ostenditur quidam circulus, per quem dicunt centrum mundi illic verissime esse descriptum, quod tamen secundum astrologos pocius et verius sub torrida zona, si habitabilis esset, inveniretur.

Istis omnibis perspectis vidimus in atrio de longe ipsius capellam quandam ornatam, quam beata Helena, Constantini mater, in eo loco edificavit, in quo Iudas, fratre Stephani, monstrante ipsam crucem meruit invenire.[5] Et tunc ab ipsis infidelibus exire compulsi reliquimus ipsam ecclesiam et preciosas illas margaritas coram porcis – pro dolor! – manducandas et ipsum locum, in quo Tu, Pater Sancte, ut servum redimeres, Filium tradidisti. Et per eam Portam David, per quam intraveramus,[b] exire permittebamur reliquis locis sanctis in civitate nondum perspectis.

7. Inde prope muros civitatis, qui turriti et novi et fortissimi sunt,[6] descendentes transivimus portam beati Stephani, et vidimus Portam Auream, que directe opponitur Monti Oliveti. In cuius foribus est quedam cisterna, aliquando adeo fecunda, ut ex ea quidam torrens parvus per medium vallis Iosaphat et in pede Oliveti decurrat. Iste est, quem Iohannes evvangelista torrentem Cedron appellat.[7] Iuxta quem hodie sita est quedam ecclesia in eo loco edificata, in quo, in tempore passionis Domini erat ortus, in quem Dominus frequenter cum suis discipulis convenit, in quo ipse etiam osculum a Iuda traditore accepit. De quibus omnibus testatur Iohannes, ubi dicit: *Egressus est Iesus trans torrentem Cedron, ubi erat ortus, in quem introivit ipse et discipuli eius. Sciebat autem et Iudas hunc locum, quia frequenter Iesus convenit etc.*[8] Et vocatur ista ecclesia a populo Sanctum Pater Noster, et dicunt Dominum in eo loco illam orationem suos discipu[**29vb**]los primo docuisse.

8. Scire autem debetis, quia vallis Iosaphat incipit inter muros Iherusalem et Montem Oliveti. Que in principio sui arta et strictissima, in fine vero, qui extenditur fere usque ad

---

[1] John 19.34.   [2] Matthew 27.51–52.   [3] John 19.25.   [4] The tombs of Godfrey of Bouillon and the kings of Jerusalem from Baldwin I to Baldwin V, which lay before Calvary in the south transept of the church.   [5] On the legend surrounding the revelation of the burial place of the True Cross to Helena by Judas, brother of Stephen, see J. W. Drijvers, *Helena Augusta: The Mother of Constantine the Great and the Legend of her Finding of the True Cross* (Leiden, 1992), pp. 165–80.
[6] The city wall between St. Stephen's Gate and the Golden Gate had been rebuilt by Saladin's son, Malik al-Afdal, in 1191–92: see M. K. Hawari, *Ayyubid Jerusalem (1187–1250): An Architectural and Archaeological Study*, BAR International Series 1628 (Oxford, 2007), pp. 22–23.   [7] John 18.1.
[8] Cf. John 18.1–2.

---

[a] scisse] cisse *P*.   [b] intraveramus *L*] intraveras *P, probably a copyist's error, as Jesus is not recorded as having entered the city through David's Gate.*

miliare gallicum in terminos Bethleem, ipsa est latissima. In cuius capite vidimus ecclesiam optime ornatam et in medio sui monumenum undique albo et nimirum virgineo marmore contectum, in quod aliquando apostoli immaculatum corpus beate Virginis deposuerant, ita si illud, quod *repente fit templum Dei*,[1] illo in parte poterat templi contineri. In quo ipsi postmodum manna celeste loco corporis invenerunt. Quod nunc temporis suriani sacerdotes Sarracenis tributarii[a] in condigna veneratione observant. O mira circa nos, Sancte Pater, Tue pietatis dignatio, ut uno eodemque die sepulcrum sancte Matris et sui Filii, Tui scilicet Verbi incarnati, videre mereremur! Iuxta parietes ipsius ecclesie iacet Ager Figuli, quem Iudei triginta argenteis a Iuda reiectis in sepulturam peregrinorum comparaverunt. Qui licet non sit longus, protenditur tamen a muris Iherusalem usque ad Montem Oliveti. Ex quo consideretis, quia ille mons directe est situs super. De hoc agro dicit beatus Matheus[b] in hunc modum: *Consilio autem inito, emerunt ex illis agrum figuli in sepulcrum[c] peregrinorum. Propter hoc vocatus est ager ille Acheldemach, hoc est ager sanguinis, usque in hodiernum diem.*[2] In quo nunc temporis Christiani, Sarrace[**30ra**]norum captivi, sepeliuntur. Nec[d] mirum, si domina nostra, exemplum tocius humilitatis, in terminis illius agri locum sue sepulture elegit, cum Filius eius, *quem terra, pontus, ethera colunt, adorant, predicant*,[3] in orto dignatus fuerit sepeliri.

9. Inde conscendentes Montem Oliveti vidimus castellum Betphage,[4] de quo Matheus ait: *Cum appropinquaret Iesus Iherosolimam et venisset Betphage ad Montem Oliveti, misit duos etc.*[5] In summo montis vidimus duo claustra destructa, quorum unum edificatum est in eo loco, in quo Dominus oravit. *Et factus est illic sudor eius tanquam gutte[e] sanguinis decurrentis in terram.*[6] Aliud vero edificatum est super illum locum, de quo Dominus *ascendens in altum captivam duxit captivitatem.*[7] In quo nunc temporis quidam Sarracenus[f] infidelis ad honorem Mahummet suum oratorium preparavit. De hoc monte ipsam civitatem perfecte inspicientes[g] vidimus in ea Templum Domini, quod quidam ex antiquo nomine Salomonis appellant, non attendentes ipsam Iherusalem cum suo templo fuisse destructam. In quo dominus Soldanus oratorium sibi et suis sollempnissimum ordinavit, in quod cives ipsius civitatis omni sexta feria iubentur convenire et Mahummet adorare. Iuxta illud assignabatur nobis Probatica Piscina de qua Iohannes dicit: *Est autem Iherosolimis probatica piscina, que cognominatur hebraice Bethsaida, v porticus habens, etc.*[8]

Ex predicta eminentia Oliveti perspeximus Montem Syon, qui, ut ante tetigi, nunc includitur muris ipsius civitatis, [**30rb**] sed tempore passionis dominice excludebatur. In summo illius, quia latus est mons, habetur quoddam largum et pulcri aspectus cenobium, in quo manent etiam Suriani, Sarracenis tributarii, qui peregrinis illuc venientibus monstrant locum, in quo Dominus cenavit cum discipulis suis et mensam illam, in qua[h] idem Iesus Christus tradidit corporis et sanguinis sui misteria celebranda, et pelvem, vas, in quo Dominus lavit pedes discipulorum exemplum dans ministris, et sciens quid fecerit[i] eis. Et scitote, quia in Monte Syon erat hospitale sive domus illa, ad quam secundum librum Machabeorum, *vir*

---

[1] Part of the office hymn, *A solis ortus cardine*, sung at Lauds on Christmas Day.
[2] Matthew 27.7–8.   [3] First lines of the office hymn, *Quem terre pontus, aethera*, sung at Mattins on the feast days of the Blessed Virgin Mary.   [4] Matthew 21.1–2: *Bethphage ... castellum.*
[5] Cf. Matthew 21.1.   [6] Cf. Luke 22.44.   [7] Ephesians 4.8.   [8] John 5.2.

---

[a] tributarii *L*] tributari *P*.   [b] Matheus *L*] Marcus *P*.   [c] sepulcrum] *altered by copyist from* sepulturam *P, which is the word found in the Gospel text.*   [d] Nec *L*] Hec *P*.   [e] gutte *L*] gutta *P*.
[f] Sarracenus *L*] sarracenis *P*.   [g] inspicientes] inspitientes *P*.   [h] qua *L*] quo *P*.
[i] fecerit *L*] fecerim *P, following John 13.12:* Scitis quid fecerim vobis?

fortissimus Iudas collatione facta XII *milia dragmas argenti misit Iherosolimam offerri ea etc.*[1] In qua postmodum hospitale sancti Iohannis fuit edificatum. In hac etiam domo discipuli post passionem Domini latitantes et clausis foribus convenientes ipsum Dominum videre meruerunt teste Iohanne, qui dicit: *Cum esset sero die illo,*[a] *una sabbatorum, et fores essent clause, ubi erant discipuli pariter in eodem loco congregati propter metum Iudeorum, stetit Iesus etc.*[2] Iste etiam locus erat, in quo discipuli acceperunt Spiritum Sanctum. Unde Actus Apostolorum dicunt: *Cum complerentur dies pentecostes, erant omnes discipuli pariter in eodem loco. Et factus est sonus, etc.*[3] Illuc etiam aliud felix et immaculatum compactum corpus beate virginis Marie fuit resolutum, ubi eius felicissima et beata anima a corpore expirans ipsum ad tempus dereliquit. Quod postmodum, sicut supra tetigi, in valle Iosaphat fuit assumptum.

10. [I]nde venimus Bethaniam, quod est castellum parvum, duas habens ecclesias in se a Sarracenis observatas: Unam[b] in qua aliquando erat domus Symonis leprosi; in illa vi[**30va**] dimus locum, ubi Maria Magdalena, exemplum penitencie, amplexata pedes Domini gratiam quesivit et obtinuit. Alteram in qua erat ortus Marie et Marthe; in qua vidimus monumentum, a quo Dominus resuscitavit Lazarum. Iste ecclesie adeo vicine sunt, ut secundum meam opinionem Lazarus in orto vel curia Symonis fuerit sepultus.

Hec est illa Bethania, de qua Iohannes ait: *Erat quidam languens, Lazarus a Bethania, de castello Marie et Marthe, sororis eius.*[4] Et de ista ait Marcus: *Cum autem esset in Bethania, in domo Symonis leprosi, accessit ad eum mulier peccatrix etc.*[5] Hoc castellum distat a Iherusalem parvum miliare gallicum. Quod testatur evvangelista dicens: *Erat autem Bethania iuxta Iherusalem quasi stadiis* XV *etc.*[6]

11. Inde transeuntes viam difficilem et periculosam venimus Iherico. Quod est castellum parvum, destructos habens muros, a Sarracenis inhabitatum, cuius meminit Dominus, ubi dixit in parabola: *Homo quidam descendebat ab Iherusalem in Iherico, et incidit in latrones etc.*[7] Et vere ipsa via hodie periculosa est, multos habens latrones. De hac etiam Lucas ait: *Factum est autem, cum appropinquaret Ihesus Iherico, cecus sedebat secus viam mendicans etc.*[8] Et in Canticis: *Quasi palma exaltata sum in Cades et quasi plantacio rose in Iherico.*[9] Iuxta istam etiam vir, nomine Zacheus, desiderans videre Ihesum ascendit in arborem siccomorum et reliqua.[10] Et distat Iherico a Iordane duo parva miliaria, a Iherusalem XVI milia gallicana.

12. Et hinc paululum procedentes propter vallem planam et amenam venimus ad Iordanem, qui est fluvius admodum altus, altas et veloces habens aquas. De quo Matheus ait: [**30vb**] *Venit Ihesus a Galilea in Iordanem ad Iohannem, ut baptizaretur ab eo.*[11] Circa quem locum erat quedam ecclesia edificata, que nunc temporis fere tota est destructa, ubi, ut dicunt, ipse Iohannes baptista baptizavit baptismo penitencie. De isto etiam ait liber Regum: *Descendit* Naaman, princeps milicie, *et lavit in Iordane septies, et restituta est caro eius sicut caro pueri parvuli.*[12] Igitur et nos carnem interioris nostri hominis restitui et mundari

---

[1] Cf. 2 Maccabees 12.42–43.   [2] Cf. John 20.19, with the words *pariter in eodem loco* inserted from Acts 2.1.   [3] Acts 2.1–2.   [4] John 11.1.   [5] Cf. Mark 14.3: *Et cum esset Bethaniae in domo Simonis leprosi, et recumberet: venit mulier habens alabastrum unguenti nardi spicati pretiosi, et fracto alabastro, effudit super caput eius.* Luke 7.36–37: *Et ingressus domum Pharisaei discubuit. Et ecce mulier, quae erat in civitate peccatrix.*   [6] John 11.18.   [7] Luke 10.30.   [8] Cf. Luke 18.35. [9] Sirach (Ecclesiasticus) 24.18.   [10] Cf. Luke 19.2–4.   [11] Matthew 3.13.   [12] 2 Kings 5.14.

[a] die illo *L, following John 20.19*] dies illa *P, corrected by copyist from* dies ille.
[b] unam *L*] una *P.*

sperantes descendimus et lavabamur in eodem Iordane, sed ipsi Arabes nobis illudentes balneum et ipsum fluvium multi luti iniectione turbaverunt. Arabia enim illic usque ad Iordanem protenditur. Et scitote, quia non longe ab eo loco instat ipse Iordanis.

13. Inde venimus ad quoddam stagnum[a] fetidissimum infernalis nigredinis, tetrum habens odorem,[b] in quo Gomorram et Sodomam dicunt absorptas[c] fuisse. Iuxta illud etiam monstratur puteus Iacob. Sicut etiam in primo libro tractatum est, duo sunt fontes, Ior et Dan, qui oriuntur in pede Libani, et confluentes in unum Iordanem conficiunt.[d] Iuxta illum etiam locum vidimus desertum, de quo Matheus ait: *Ductus est Ihesus in desertum a Spiritu, ut temptaretur a diabolo etc.*[1]

14. Abhinc revertebamur Iherico, et non longe ab illa ascendimus quendam montem altissimum, in quo Dominus dicitur quadraginta ieiunasse diebus, a quibus ipse mons hodie Quarennia nuncupatur.

---

[1]   Matthew 4.1.

---

[a]   stagnum *L*] stangnum *P.*   [b]   odorem *L*] colorem *P.*   [c]   absorptas *L*] absortos *P.*
[d]   conficiunt] confitiunt *P.*

Frederick II's Arabic Inscription from Jaffa (1229)

Moshe Sharon

(The Hebrew University of Jerusalem, msharon@mscc.huji.ac.il)

with *Ami Schrager*

(The Hebrew University of Jerusalem, ami.schrager@gmail.com)

The Arabic inscription discussed below is attached to the sanctuary of Shaykh Murād near Jaffa (see Fig. 1). It is, without doubt, the twin inscription of a Latin one discovered at the end of the nineteenth century by Charles Clermont-Ganneau (see Fig. 6), both commemorating the works of Emperor Frederick II in Jaffa at the beginning of 1229. They were prepared on one or two blocks of marble, undoubtedly by two different carvers, and were probably set above the gate of the citadel of Jaffa or built into one of its walls. The discussion of the Latin fragment will follow a detailed study of the Arabic one.

There is a remote possibility that another piece of the Latin inscription was seen by someone in the nineteenth century, somewhere near the walls of Jaffa. Writing about an "alleged inscription" Clermont-Ganneau remarked:

> I was told of another fragment of an inscription built into the wall of the town, and from the description given me, I suspect it also to be mediaeval. Unluckily, however, I could not manage to test the truth of this statement. It may perhaps be a fragment that I found in 1881, referring to the King of England.[1]

At any rate, it is clear that the Arabic inscription reached Shaykh Murād with other building material gathered from around the ruins of Jaffa. In this way a fragment of a slab of veined white marble (70×50 cm, and only 5 cm thick) reached this local sanctuary with another Frankish Latin inscription surrounding a carved, bas-relief representation of a "mitred abbot or bishop," and other decorative elements. This, no doubt, had been the top cover of a clergyman's grave. Clermont-Ganneau read the date of 1258 in the inscription surrounding the central image. The back of the same fragment was used for an Arabic inscription, also read by Clermont-Ganneau,

---

We are deeply indebted to Professor Jeremy Johns, Director of the Khalili Research Centre and Professor of the Art and Archaeology of the Islamic Mediterranean, Oxford, for extending unreservedly invaluable help during the work on this article. Thanks are due to Israel Antiquities Authority (hereafter IAA) for the assistance during the work on the site, for putting at our disposal an excellent squeeze and archival photographs of the inscription and allowing us to use them. This research is carried out as part of the study of the Arabic inscriptions in Palestine sponsored by the Israel Academy of Sciences and Humanities and published by E. J. Brill, Leiden, in the series *Corpus Inscriptionum Arabicarum Palaestinae* (hereafter *CIAP*).

[1] Charles Clermont-Ganneau, *Archaeological Researches in Palestine during the years 1873–1874*, 2 vols. (London, 1896–99), 2:156 (hereafter *AR*).

Fig. 1   Shaykh Murād, 1932: inscription built upside down into the western wall
Photo: Israel Antiquities Authority

dated 736/1335–36, commemorating the building of a mosque. It was bought by
Baron Ustinov sometime before 1881 for his collection.[2]

Shaykh Murād: The Site and Its Inscriptions

Shaykh Murād is a small sanctuary of a local Muslim saint (*walīy*, colloq. *wilī*,
welī) otherwise unknown, built on a low hill some 2.5 kilometres to the east of
the walls of Jaffa.[3] The date of its establishment has nothing to do with the Arabic
inscription dated 736/1335–36, just mentioned, commemorating the building of
a mosque by the amīr Jamāl ad-Dīn somewhere in the Jaffa area. It must have
found its way to the hill where the sanctuary stands with other fragments. The
double-domed, two-roomed building of Shaykh Murād, such as one finds all over
the country and elsewhere in the Middle East, is not mentioned in Tewfik Canaan's
Saints and Sanctuaries in Palestine (1927).[4] It appears, however, that the Muslim
builders of the sanctuary mistook the Arabic inscription for some sacred Muslim

---

[2] Charles Clermont-Ganneau, in *Palestine Exploration Fund Quarterly Statement* (hereafter:
PEFQ) for 1874, 269ff.; idem, *AR*, 2:152–54 (only translation of the Arabic inscription); C. R. Conder
and H. H. Kitchener, *The Survey of Western Palestine*, vol. II: *Samaria* (London, 1882), pp. 275–78
(detailed report by Clermont Ganneau). See also H. C. Key in *PEFQ* for 1898, pp. 246–47; Denys
Pringle, *The Churches of the Crusader Kingdom of Jerusalem: A Corpus*, 4 vols. (Cambridge, 1993–
2009), 1:269, pl. cxc; Moshe Sharon, *CIAP, Addendum* (Leiden, 2007), pp. 113ff.

[3] See Andrew Petersen, *A Gazetteer of Muslim Buildings in Palestine* 1, British Academy
Monographs in Archaeology 12 (Oxford, 2001), p. 169.

[4] Tewfik Canaan, *Mohammedan Saints and Sanctuaries in Palestine* (Jerusalem, 1927).

Fig. 2   Inscription inserted into the southern wall of the western courtyard after repairs
          carried out ca. 1949
          Photo: Israel Antiquities Authority

text and attached it first upside-down to its western wall (Fig. 1) and then, when the
sanctuary was twice repaired in the mid-twentieth century (once just before 1949
and once again about thirty years later), in a different position and the right way up
(Fig. 2).

The first recorded mention of the inscription is found in a report of 13 June 1932 by
Jacob Ory, an inspector in the Department of Antiquities of the British Government
of Palestine. As can be seen in Figure 3, Ory added to his short description of the
inscription an exact drawing of its shape and the necessary measurements, indicating
"scale 1:10."[5] The report was accompanied by photographs showing the inscription
attached to the original building of the sanctuary, before its modern reconstruction.
The inscription can be seen built into the wall to the right of the lower remnants of
an arch partly blocked by a wall which had been built in it (see Fig. 1).

---

[5] Ref. Atq/40 No. S 1751.

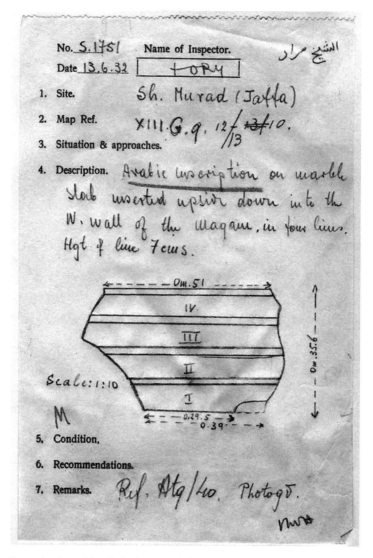

Fig. 3.   Reproduction of Jacob Ory's report (1932)
Courtesy Israel Antiquities Authority

In the IAA archival file on Jaffa there is a further report about the inspection of the place by Jacob Ory and Shmuel Yeivin in 1949. On 6 and 13 March 1949, Ory visited the sanctuary site again, searching for the inscription mentioned in Clermont-Ganneau's report published in the *Survey of Western Palestine*,[6] oblivious of the fact that it had left the country for Oslo with the collection of Baron Ustinov.

---

[6]   Conder and Kitchener, *Survey of Western Palestine*, 2:275–78.

He reported that the Mamlūk inscription was not found and seized the opportunity to describe the site which he had visited seventeen years earlier:

> the maqām contains two chambers. It has a domed roof and a small uncovered yard. One of the chambers contains a tomb and in the other one a recent tomb. The entrance to the maqām is through the yard. The height of the walls is 1.5 metres. At the western wall next to the corner, inserted into the wall is a slab of marble stone 34 × 60 cm., bearing an Arabic inscription with four lines. It seems to be an epitaph and it is not the Mamlūk inscription mentioned above.

It was L. A. Mayer who asked for the inspection of the site but he never followed up the investigation, probably accepting Ory's remark that the inscription "seemed like" a non-Mamlūk epitaph, and Yeivin's ruling that the inscription was "completely recent"; in other words of little interest.

There is no doubt that the inscription, first spotted and recorded in 1932, was not there in the late nineteenth century when Clermont-Ganneau carried out an intensive survey of the area, searching for inscriptions. He could not have missed it had it been attached at that time to the building of the sanctuary in such a prominent place. It was again photographed some time before 1970 by Barukh Sapir who described it as "an Arabic inscription from Shaykh Murād."[7] The mortar used to attach it to the wall is modern, which means that the inscription had been relocated to its present position not long before Sapir saw it, when the building was repaired for the second time. It is very possible that during these later repairs the inscription was not moved; only the wall around it was partially repaired with fresh cement.

In 1874 and 1881 Clermont-Ganneau surveyed the surroundings of Shaykh Murād and described his finds in detail.[8] He pointed out that the inhabitants of the small hamlet called Suknet Abū Kabīr, about 1 kilometre to the west of Shaykh Murād, were mostly quarrymen who dug building materials from ancient sites and ruins around Jaffa. In this way, this and other stones bearing bas-reliefs, fragments of sculpture, and inscriptions reached their village and its vicinity relatively far from their original sites.

The Arabic inscription discussed here, as well as other ancient fragments found by Clermont-Ganneau are, no doubt, only meagre remnants of what had been dug out by the villagers of Abū Kabīr and other quarrymen, and either reused as building material or burnt for lime. The present Arabic inscription almost miraculously found its way to the *welī* of Shaykh Murād. It was saved, but not before earlier hands had shaped it to serve some previous function. What remains is about one half of the original inscription.

---

[7] Barukh Sapir, "The Development of Building and Town Planning in Jaffa in the Crusader Period," (MA thesis in Sciences, submitted to the Technion, Israel Institute of Technology, Haifa, 1970), p. 41, fig. 50 (Hebrew).

[8] *AR*, 2:130ff.

Fig. 4   Arabic inscription of Frederick II (1229)
Photo 1949: Israel Antiquities Authority

It is very possible that the fragment of the Latin inscription of Frederick II (see Fig. 6), reconstructed and studied by Clermont-Ganneau, also came from Shaykh Murād or from the quarrymen in Abū Kabīr, who sold it to the Russian Archimandrite whose church was built nearby.[9] It seems almost certain that both the large block with the Arabic inscription and the small fragment of the Latin one were dug from the ruins of medieval Jaffa, probably during the reconstruction of its modern walls early in the nineteenth century.

The Arabic Inscription

A large fragment of a block of a grey marble 35.6 × 51 (56 cm max.) × 25 cm broken on all sides, with greater damage on the left and the top right, attached to the southern wall of the open courtyard in front of the gate of the sanctuary on the west (Fig. 2). Four lines in a unique style of *naskhī*, points, some vowels and signs; in relief (Figs. 4 and 5).

١)   [قيصر الم]ـعظم امبراطور رومية فر[دريك المنصور بالله مالك ألما
٢)   نيـ]ـة ولمبردية وتسقانة وإيطالية وا [نكبردة وقلورية وصقلية ومملكة
٣)   الشا]م القدسية معز إمام رومية الناصر للملة[المسيحية بشهر فورارو(؟)سنة ألف
٤)   وم‍]ـاتين وتسع وعشرين لتجسُّد سيدنا يسوع المسيح ...

---

⁹   *AR*, 2:155–56.

Fig. 5   Photograph of the squeeze of the Arabic inscription made in 2011
Courtesy Israel Antiquities Authority

1)   [The august Caesar], **Emperor of Rome, Fre**[derick, the victorious by (the help of)
     God, ruler of Germany (*almāniyah*)
2)   **and Lombardy, and Tuscany, and Italy, and** [Longobardia (*ankubardah*), and
     Calabria (*qalawriyah*) and Sicily and the Syrian kingdom
3)   **of Jerusalem; the fortifier of the *imām* of Rome, the protector of the Christian
     community,** [in the month of February(?) of the year one thousand
4)   **two hundred and twenty-nine of the incarnation of our lord Jesus Christ ...**

Fortunately it is possible to reconstruct this inscription *almost to the letter* by
comparing it to the preamble of a letter that Frederick II wrote in August 1229 to
his Muslim friend, Fakhr ad-Dīn Yūsuf b. Ṣadr ad-Dīn Shaykh ash-Shuyūkh, the
general and chief negotiator of al-Malik al-Kāmil Muḥammad, the Ayyūbid sultan
of Egypt, who had been responsible for the drafting of the treaty of Jaffa a few
months earlier. The opening of the letter contains the titles and the possessions of
the emperor in exactly the same order as they are given in the inscription, and they
both resemble the wording of similar texts of the Norman chancery in Sicily from
the time of Roger II onwards.[10] The text of the letter to Fakhr ad-Dīn contains the

---

[10]   These texts were studied by Jeremy Johns, "Le iscrizioni arabe dei re normanni di Sicilia: una
rilettura," (hereafter Johns [Italian]), in Maria Andaloro, ed., *Nobiles Officinae: perle, filigrane e trame
di seta dal Palazzo Reale di Palermo* (Catania, 2006), pp. 47–67; idem, "The Arabic Inscriptions of the

genealogy of Frederick II starting with his grandfather, Frederick I Barbarossa. This part could not have been included in the inscription, simply because there is not enough space for so much text in the first line.

The reconstruction of the inscription is based on the premise that most of the text (24–25 letters) is missing from the end of each line, whereas at the beginning of line 1 seven letters are missing, and at the beginning of lines 2–4 two to five letters are missing. In other words, the original inscription was double the size of the present fragment. Still, because we have the exact parallel in *at-Ta'rīkh al-Manṣūrī* and other parallels from similar documents from Sicily, the loss, though unfortunate, can be reconstructed as near as possible to the original. The only serious area of doubt concerns the month and the exact transliteration used for it.

The parallel passage in *at-Ta'rīkh al-Manṣūrī* presents the full text of Frederick II's letter in which he informs his friend Fakhr ad-Dīn about the situation which confronted him in Sicily and in his Italian domains on his return from the Holy Land (mainly, the invasion of the pope's army commanded by Frederick's father-in-law, John of Brienne) and his success in defeating all his enemies.

The letter begins with the preamble required by the rigid formulae employed both in the Islamic world and in the Norman chancery:

ثم دخلت سنة سبع وعشرين وستمائة
وفيها وصل بحران رسول الامبراطور إلى الكامل وعلى يده كتاب إلى فخر الدين بن شيخ الشيوخ بما نسخته:
بسم الله الرحمن الرحيم عنوانه ترجمته قيصر المعظم امبراطور رومية فردريك بن الامبراطور هنريك بن
الامبراطور فردريك المنصور بالله المقتدر بقدرته المستعلي بعزته مالك ألمانية ولمبردية وتسقانة وإيطالية وانكبردة
وقلورية وصقلية ومملكة الشام القدسية معز إمام رومية الناصر للملة المسيحية ...
[*Body of the letter*]
كتب [بـ]بِرلتَ(!) المَصُونة بتأريخ الثالث والعشرين من شهر أوسو ألأندقس الثاني[11]

In the year 627/1229 an ambassador to al-Kāmil came to Ḥarrān from the Emperor with a letter to Fakhr ad-Dīn, the son of Shaykh ash-Shuyūkh, which ran as follows:

In the name of Allah the compassionate the Merciful. Heading and Dedication:

The august Caesar, Emperor of Rome, Frederick, son of Emperor Henry (*Henrīk*, more like Heinrich. MS), son of Emperor Frederick, the victorious by (the help of) God, powerful in His might, exalted in His glory, ruler of Germany (*almāniyah*) and Lombardy and Tuscany and Italy and Longobardia (*ankubardah*) and Calabria (*qalawriyah*) and Sicily, and the Syrian kingdom of Jerusalem, the fortifier of the *imām* of Rome, the protector of the Christian community ...

[*Body of the letter*] ...

Written at (divinely) protected Barletta, 23 August of the second indiction (1229).[12]

Norman Kings of Sicily: A Reinterpretation" (hereafter Johns [English]), in Maria Andaloro, ed., *The Royal Workshops in Palermo during the Reigns of the Norman and Hohenstaufen Kings of Sicily in the 12th and 13th century* (Catania, 2006), pp. 324–37.

[11] al-Ḥamawī, Abū al-Faḍā'il Muḥammad b. ʿAlī, *at-Ta'rīkh al-Manṣūrī*, ed. P. A. Griaznevitch (Moscow, 1960), 187b–188a, 190a.

[12] See Francesco Gabrieli, *Arab Historians of the Crusades*, trans. from Italian by E. J. Costello (Berkeley and Los Angeles, 1984), pp. 280–81; David Abulafia, *Frederick II: A Medieval Emperor* (London, 1988), p. 197.

Apart from the list of the few titles at the beginning of the letter and the mentioning of the emperor's father Henry VI and his grandfather Frederick I (referred to by the words: *ʿunwānuhu tarjamatuhu*, rendered above as "heading and dedication"), the letter is identical with the inscription. However, the inscription most probably did not contain the *basmalah*, which figures twice in Frederick's letter (unless it is an addition of al-Ḥamawī, which we doubt). This verse, which opens 113 *Sūrahs* of the Qurʾān (except for *Sūrah* 9), entered into the Norman chancery directly from the Fāṭimid *diwān*, and appears in inscriptions as well.[13] The possibility that one line was lost from the inscription's top seems very remote, mainly because the letters in the first line are larger than those in the rest of the inscription and give the impression of constituting the first line of the inscription, which begins with the exact first words of the letter: "The august Caesar." The inclusion of the *basmalah* in a letter issued by Frederick's chancery to a Muslim friend is not surprising. It would be inappropriate, however, in an inscription above the gate of Jaffa's citadel to commemorate the work of a Christian ruler, and explicitly dated according to the Christian calendar.

Notes on the Text of the Inscription

Line 1

قيصر المعظم. – The glorified (or august, magnificent, resplendent etc.) Caesar. The top right corner of the inscription is more damaged than the rest of the right side. As pointed out, seven letters are missing; these are the four letters of *qayṣar* together with the three first letters of *al-muʿaẓẓam*. The word *qayṣar* is regarded to be a definite noun, like a proper name, and therefore – following the opening of the letter – does not need the article. There is a remote possibility that the inscription began with *al-malik al-muʿaẓẓam* – the glorified king, a title used by all the Norman kings and by Frederick II,[14] but in this case we have the letter to Fakhr ad-Dīn supporting our choice.

المنصور بالله – The number of the missing letters at the end of the line allows the insertion of this title, which is also found in other similar examples from the Norman chancery. Idrīsī refers to King Roger II by the titles *al-malik al-muʿaẓẓam Rujar al-muʿtazz bi-Allah al-muqtadir bi-qudratihi* – the august King Roger, the powerful through God and strengthened by His omnipotence.[15]

---

[13] Johns (Italian), p. 51; Johns (English), p. 326.

[14] Johns (Italian), p. 49; Johns (English), p. 325.

[15] al-Idrīsī, Abū ʿAbdallah Muḥammad b. Muḥammad. b. ʿAbd Allah, *Nuzhat al-Mushtāq fī Ikhtirāq al-ʾĀfāq* (Cairo, 1414/1994), 1:4. For more examples from the Norman chancery see Johns (Italian), p. 50; Johns (English), p. 325.

Line 2

لمبردية، تسقانة، إيطالية ... صقلية – The names of these four regions are perfectly transliterated.[16] Foreign names were always subject to strange transliterations in Arabic sources. Thus, for instance, Qalqashandī referring to Lombardy has its name transcribed: al-Lunbardiyyah (correct) "and it is also called (*wa yuqāl lahā*) an-Nūbaridiyyah wa-al-Anbaridiyyah."[17]

انكبردة، قلورية – This is the usual spelling in Arabic of the names of Longobardia and Calabria.[18] Qalqashandī transliterates Calabria as *Qalafriyah* which is quite close.[19] A particularly bad transliteration appears in the 1137–38 letter of the Fāṭimid Caliph al-Ḥāfiẓ (525–44/1131–49) to Roger II.[20]

Lines 2–3

مملكة الشام القدسية. – Literally, "the Jerusalemite kingdom of Syria." This term, which does not appear elsewhere, probably attempts to translate into Arabic the Latin "Ierosolimitanum regnum,"[21] emphasizing its geographic location in Syria or alluding to the "Surie" of the contemporary French texts, which denoted the Frankish possessions in Syria/Palestine.[22] Frederick became king of Jerusalem after his marriage to the child-queen Isabella II of Jerusalem in 1225. The queen died on 8 May 1228, soon after giving birth to their son Conrad IV. When Frederick finally went on crusade at the end of that year, his claim to rule the kingdom rested on being the guardian of his infant son.

Line 3

معز إمام رومية الناصر للملة المسيحية. – The fortifier (he who strengthens), the pope of Rome, the protector of the Christian community. These explicitly Christian titles appear from the very beginning of King Roger II's reign in 1130, when the *diwān*, the office of the chancery, was imported in full, most likely from the Fāṭimids.[23]

---

[16] See Idrīsī, 1:4.

[17] al-Qalqashandī, Abū al-ʿAbbās Aḥmad b. ʿAlī, *Ṣubuḥ al-Aʿshā fī Ṣināʿat al-Inshāʾ* (Cairo, 1305/1985), 5:415; Abū al-Fidāʿ, ʿImād ad-Dīn Ismāʿīl, *Al-Mukhtaṣar fī Akhbār al-Bashar* (Cairo, 1325/1907), 3:141.

[18] Idrīsī, ibid.; Michele Amari, *Le epigrafi arabiche di Sicilia* (Palermo, 1879), 2:87, 91. While Longobardia denoted south-eastern Italy, Lombardy was situated in its north-western part.

[19] Qalqashandī, 5:410.

[20] Johns (Italian), p. 50; Johns (English), p. 325; cf. also Abū al-Fidā·, 3:141.

[21] See, for instance, *Die Urkunden der lateinischen Könige von Jerusalem*, ed. Hans E. Mayer, 4 vols., MGH (Hanover, 2010), no. 654 (a. 1225).

[22] See, for instance, Filippo da Novara, *Guerra di Federico II in Oriente* (1223–1242), 3.1, 14.5, 23.1, 31.22, 39.1–5, c. 61, ed. and trans. Silvio Melani (Naples, 1994), pp. 68, 70, 78, 90, 100.

[23] Johns (English), p. 326. On the Fāṭimid chancery see Samuel M. Stern, *Fāṭimid Decrees. Original Documents from the Fāṭimid Chancery* (London, 1964).

These and similar designations remained as standard titles in the Muslim chancery for many generations. They represented the fact that the Muslims understood that the pope was "the caliph of the Christians" (*al-bābā khalīfat al-ifranj*). He was therefore the *imām* of the Christians. They knew that he resided in Rome and therefore designated him as "the Master of Rome" (*ṣāḥib rūmiyah*) or the *imām* of Rome.[24] They also knew the word *Papa* used by the *Ifranj* and transliterated it into Arabic as *bāba, pāpā* (with Persian *pa*), and *bāb*. Qalqashandī (d. 1412) offers detailed lists of the titles and honorary formulae used in the Muslim correspondence with the Christian rulers in his huge book, aimed at the education of perfect scribes, in which he included extensive material from earlier sources. These titles were particularly created for Christians, referring both to the pope and to the Christian community. The Europeans on their part, both in their correspondence with the Muslims and in translations of Muslim letters, also took care to use proper formulae even if the missionary tone would sometimes creep into their preambles. However, they never reached the resourcefulness of their Muslim counterparts, and in many cases they were unable to mask derogatory terminology and disrespect.[25]

The versatility of the usages invented by the Muslim bureaucrats in their *diwān* is remarkable.[26] Thus in addition to *muʿizz imām rūmiyah*, which is the standard usage in Sicily (as in the inscription and the letter), we have, for instance: *muʿizz al-bābā*; *ẓahīr al-bāb bābā rūmiya* – "The fortifier of the pope; The supporter of the *bāb* the pope of Rome." It is clear that the designation of *bāb* (gate) here is meant to ascribe an Arabic meaning to the word *bābā*.[27] Many titles were created with reference to the Christian community similar to the one in the inscription and in the letter. Hence we find among the many ingenious usages, titles like: *muʿayyid al-millah al-masīḥiyyah* – the support of the Christian community; *dhukhr al-millah an-naṣrāniyyah* – treasure of the Christian community, and a synonym of the latter: *kanz aṭ-ṭāʾifah aṣ-ṣalībiyyah* – the treasure of the community of the Cross, as well as *jamāl aṭ-ṭāʾifah aṣ-ṣalībiyyah* – the beauty of the community of the Cross; *nāṣir al-millah al-masīḥiyyah* – "protector of the Christian community," and so on. The titles were carefully categorized so that each Christian ruler is addressed with his properly designated title.[28] It should be pointed out, however, that the use of the adjectives *an-naṣrāniyyah*, and *aṣ-ṣalībiyyah* – literally: "The Nazarean" and "of the Cross" – have a derogatory side to them and, at least in the eyes of

---

[24] Ibn Wāṣil, Jamāl ad-Dīn Muḥammad b. Sālim, *Mufarrij al-Kurūb fī Akhbār Banī Ayyūb* (Cairo, 1372–95/1953–75), 4:248.

[25] See Benjamin Z. Kedar, "Religion in Catholic–Muslim Correspondence and Treaties," in *Diplomatics in the Eastern Mediterranean 1000–1500*, ed. Alexander D. Beihammer, Maria G. Parani, and Christopher D. Schabel (Leiden, 2008), pp. 409–10, 414.

[26] Qalqashandī, 6:77ff.

[27] Ibid., 6:89, 176, 178.

[28] Ibid, 6:94, 174–78. These were titles given by the Muslim chancery to the Christian rulers, not titles which these rulers chose for themselves. In other words, the Muslims created for the Christian kings, nobility, and clergymen a detailed titulature of which they became aware only when a letter arrived to them from the Muslim side.

Muslims, they are certainly less respectable than the adjective *masīḥī, masīḥiyyah* – Christian. However, the reference to *al-millah an-naṣrāniyyah* appears on the Christian side, both in the inscriptions of Roger II (1130–54) and in that decorating the alb of William II (1166–89),[29] which means that, in the Sicilian chancery, the term *naṣrāniyyah* was imported as an integral part of the royal titulature. In our inscription and the parallel letter *an-naṣrāniyyah* was avoided.

All these titles, whether in Egypt or Sicily, represented the rigid formulae of protocol and could not be changed, even if a given political situation might call for such a change. Thus the title "the defender of the pope of Rome" for the excommunicated Frederick II, who had to fight against the pope, seems completely out of place, and Gabrieli is justified when he remarked that this expression in the letter was "one of the ironies of protocol."[30] Only that in reality no irony was intended. The title of the "defender of the pope and of the Christian community" was not intended to represent facts; it was a fixed obligatory official formula which had to be followed strictly by the chancery scribes.

بِشهر فورارو(؟)سنة ألف ... – The number of missing letters in this line is also about 24, which allows the reconstruction of the end of line 3 with the suggested text. After the word *al-masīḥiyyah*, which is sure and can be copied from the letter, there is a place for the name of the month, most probably February, although we are not sure about how it was transliterated by the Sicilian scribes into Arabic letters. Tentatively we used the Sicilian name for February – *fivraru* – and offer very hesitantly this transliteration. We could not find a parallel text from Sicily with a date containing the name of February, the month in which the fortification of Jaffa was completed. The inscription could hardly have been made and fixed in place *after* the emperor had left the country.

Line 4

The date in this line is very clear and it represents the Arabic translation of *anno dominice incarnationis* …, which we read in the Latin inscription (below). In the documents and inscriptions from Sicily we find the usage of several calendars: according to the system of indictions (as in the letter), according to the Jewish calendar starting with the Creation of the World (for example, the year 4908 for AD 1148),[31] the usual Christian calendar since the birth of Christ (as in these documents) and the Muslim calendar of the Hijrah.[32] The date according to the Christian calendar was introduced by the formula: *wa-li-as-sayyid al-masīḥ* – "and to the lord the messiah (the year)."[33]

---

[29] Johns (Italian), pp. 49–50; Johns (English), pp. 325–26; Amari, 2:87, 91.

[30] Gabrieli, *Arab Historians of the Crusades*, p. 280, n. 5.

[31] Amari, *Le epigrafi arabiche di Sicilia*, 2:87–88.

[32] Cf. Johns (English), p. 326; Johns (Italian), p. 51; Amari, 2:91–92.

[33] Johns (English), p. 326; Johns (Italian), p. 51.

Incidentally, the Hijrī date has been in official use since the time of Roger II. He owned an elaborate royal mantle with a *ṭirāz* of an Arabic inscription bearing the Hijrī date 528/1133–34. Since he was crowned as king of Sicily on Christmas Day 1130, he could not have worn it for his coronation ceremony, but it was used in the coronation of the Holy Roman Emperors.[34] On the other hand, the inscription woven on the alb of William II (1166–89) reads: "... *sanat alf wa-mi'ah wa-aḥad wa-thamānīn li-ta'rīkh sayyidinā yasū' al-masīḥ*" – "the year one thousand and one hundred and eighty one (according) to the date of our lord Jesus the Messiah."[35]

The date in our inscription is similar but with special reference to "the *incarnation* of our lord Jesus the Messiah" which emphasizes its Christian character. Thus the inscription fits the mood of the time: the Holy Roman Emperor as the head of the crusade and the high Christian spirit of the crusaders which theoretically should have imbued him, the army, the pilgrims, and the military orders. On the other hand, it is clear that in the letter to Fakhr ad-Dīn, the neutral date of the indiction was chosen. In the chancery offices nothing was accidental.

The Script

The Arabic script of this inscription is unique. It is *naskhī*, but it does not resemble the *naskhī* script of the time in Syria and Egypt, of which there are examples in abundance, such as the numerous inscriptions of Saladin and al-Mu'aẓẓam 'Īsā.[36] It shows, however, some weak signs of the transition from the square script (wrongly called *kūfī*) to the round Ayyūbid one of the scribes, which happened about a century earlier in the eastern than in the western part of the Islamic lands. There is no doubt that the inscription was designed and composed in the emperor's chancery by the scribes who accompanied him. It had to be prepared quite quickly and fixed to its place in the wall above the gate of the citadel some time in February 1229 when the fortification works were completed, but when the emperor was still in the city, before leaving for Jerusalem in mid-March.

It was a monumental lintel, about 120 cm long and almost 50 cm wide. The text was engraved in flat relief in sunken fields created by wide bands also in relief which divided the lines. The script chosen by the artist who engraved the inscription represents an irregular style. The thickness of the letters is not uniform. The vertical lines of letters like *alif* or *lām* or parts of letters such as *ṭā'* and *ẓā'* are rather thick, while all the lines of the other letters are much thinner (except

---

[34] R. Bauer, "Zur Geschichte der sizilischen Gewänder, später Krönugsgewänder der Könige und Kaiser des Heiligen Römischen Reiches," in Wilfried Seipel, ed., *Nobiles officinae. Die Königlichen Hofwerkstätten zu Palermo zur Zeit der Normannen und Staufer im 12. und 13. Jahrhundert* (Milan, 2004), pp. 85ff., 115ff; Johns (Italian), p. 53; Johns (English), p. 327.

[35] Johns (Italian), p. 50, fig. 4.

[36] Max van Berchem, *Matériaux pour un Corpus Inscriptionum Arabicarum* (*CIA*), Deuxième partie: *Syrie du Sud, Jérusalem, "planches"* (Cairo, 1922; repr. Geneva, 2001), pls. xxxiii–xxxviii.

for some in the first line). In almost all the round letters a hole was bored in the middle of the letter. Sometimes such holes were drilled in unexpected places as well, such as in a diacritical point under the *yā'* in *iṭāliyah* (line 2) or in the *ʿayn* of *ʿishrīn* (line 4) and of *yasūʿ*. The holes are scattered all over the inscription and there is no doubt that they were meant to serve as a decorative element, the like of which is unknown to us from any other Arabic inscription. Since they resemble the drilled holes in western and Frankish inscriptions that denote the end of a word or a phrase, they suggest that Frederick's Arabic inscription is culturally western, and was not prepared by a culturally Ayyūbid mason.[37] Probably it was done by a Sicilian craftsman who accompanied the emperor.

In many cases letters were pushed up in the line and made smaller than the rest of the letters in the same line for no reason (such as *tusqānah* in line 2 and *rūmiyah* in line 2 and line 3). On close examination it becomes apparent that this was necessary to clear space for very pronounced diacritical points under the *yā'*. A strange feature is the insertion of the *shaddah* sign as a decorative element; it is in its correct place only once, in the word *al-qudsiyyah* (line 3). At any rate, the carver created an inscription of uneven quality. There are beautifully produced letters, as in line 4, and there are simple letters in the rest of the inscription. In a few cases some letters were almost "swallowed" by other letters attached to them. Thus in the word *wa-ʿishrīn* (l. 4) the *yā'* nearly disappears in the *nūn*, and in *lumbardia* (line 2) the *mīm* almost disappears in the previous *lām*. Having said that, it should be remembered that the inscription has suffered badly through the ages; when newly produced in its full length it must have been very impressive.

The Latin Fragment

The following is based on Clermont-Ganneau's description of the Latin inscription:

> A fragment of a marble block measuring 77 × 27 cm and 15 cm thick, which was used to cover a sewer in one of the streets at Jaffa. "The original was acquired by the Russian archimandrite. The characters are of the 12th or 13th century, and splendidly cut."[38]

Judging by the length of this small fragment (77 cm) the original inscription was at least as large as the Arabic one if not much larger, since it contained at least 80–85 letters out of which we have only 25.[39] The fragment (Fig. 6) allows for the following reconstruction:

---

[37] Professor Stefan Heidemann's suggestion.

[38] *AR*, 2:155.

[39] Or 26 including the reconstructions.

Fig. 6   Frederick II's Latin inscription

Fridericus Romanorum imperator semp]er **Augustus, Ie**[rusalem rex
anno Domi]**nice incarnatio**[nis[40]

This ties in with the emperor's official title at the time, *Fridericus Dei gratia* (or: *divina favente clementia*) *Romanorum imperator semper augustus Ierusalem et Sicilie rex* (Frederick, by the grace of God, emperor of the Romans always august, king of Jerusalem and Sicily).[41] This title appears also at the opening of the emperor's letter of 17 March 1229 to King Henry III of England, in which he informs him about the great achievements of his crusade, notably the recovery of Jerusalem.[42] The Arabic inscription allows us to surmise that the Latin one, too, spelled out the date 1229.

In 1229 or 1230, following the emperor's departure from the Holy Land on 1 May 1229, Gerold of Lausanne, patriarch of Jerusalem, strengthened the defences of Jaffa by building two towers on the castle's wall that faced Ascalon.[43] It is impossible, however, to assume (as Clermont-Ganneau did) that the Latin inscription commemorating the emperor's work was attached to them, or to other parts of Jaffa's new fortifications, by Patriarch Gerold, who bitterly opposed the emperor after his excommunication by the pope and the interdict on Jerusalem which he himself imposed. The Latin and Arabic inscriptions were attached to the new city fortress by Frederick II himself.[44] Following the practice in Norman Sicily, where multi-lingual texts were common, it suited Frederick to put up such a pair of monumental inscriptions in which his grandeur as the "emperor of the Romans and king of Jerusalem" is emphasized.

---

[40] *AR*, 2:156 (initially, on p. 155, Clermont-Ganneau proposed to reconstruct the third word of the first line as: I[mperator); Félix-Marie Abel, "Jaffa au moyen-âge," *Journal of the Palestine Oriental Society* 20 (1946), 24, n. 49; Sabino de Sandoli, *Corpus Inscriptionum Crucesignatorum Terrae Sanctae* (Jerusalem, 1974), p. 258, no. 347; Pringle, *The Churches*, 1:266.

[41] See, for instance, *Die Urkunden der lateinischen Könige*, ed. Mayer, nos. 654, 657, 659–62, 665–70, 673–77, 681, 686–87, 691.

[42] Matthew Paris, *Chronica Majora*, ed. Henry R. Luard, 7 vols., RS 57 (London, 1872–83), 3:173–76.

[43] Filippo da Novara, *Guerra di Federico II in Oriente*, c. 61, p. 146.

[44] Cf. Pringle, *The Churches* 1:265–66.

Frederick II and the Muslims

Both Muslim and Christian contemporaries assumed that Frederick was particularly well-disposed towards the Muslims.[45] His courtiers and many of his administrators were Muslims and his close relations with the sultan's court in Cairo continued a tradition which had existed since the time of the Hautevilles. Under him, these relations, which no doubt helped in the negotiations for the Treaty of Jaffa in 1229, developed almost into friendship that involved the exchange of expensive and unusual gifts, including exotic animals that enriched Frederick's menagerie.[46]

In the Arabic sources there is much sympathy for Frederick's person and his positive attitude to Islamic religion and holy places, particularly during his visit to Jerusalem (17–19 March 1229), after he had received the city from al-Malik al-Kāmil in the wake of the Treaty of Jaffa concluded a month earlier.[47] Muslims also appreciated the emperor's interest in science, logic and medicine (*muḥibban li-al-ḥikmah wa-al-manṭiq wa-aṭ-ṭibb*). Ibn Wāṣil, who mentions this, also indicates that "he was refined and learned (*fāḍil*) ... was favourable towards the Muslims because originally he grew up in the country of Sicily, and he, his father and his grandfather were its kings, and the inhabitants of that island are mostly Muslims."[48]

On the other hand, the Muslims who came into contact with him were not impressed by his looks, and Sibṭ Ibn al-Jawzī, who bitterly opposed the surrender of Jerusalem to the emperor, observes rather sarcastically that the "The emperor ... had a red skin, and was bald and short-sighted. Had he been a slave, he would not have been worth two hundred *dirham*." And referring to Frederick's convictions, the chronicler felt that he was materialistic (*dahrī*) and that his Christianity was like a game for him:[49]

قالوا وكان الإنبرطور أشقر أمعط في عينيه ضعف ، لو كان عبداً ما يساوي مائتي درهم. قالوا والظاهر من كلامه
أنه كان دهرياً وأنه كان يتلاعب بالنصرانية.[50]

Yet Muslims regarded Frederick's achievements with awe: "In fact no one in Christendom from the time of Alexander until today has ruled a kingdom the equal of his, particularly when one considers his power, his behaviour to their caliph, the

[45] Ibn Wāṣil, *Mufarrij al-Kurūb*, 4:243, 248.

[46] Ibid., 4:328.

[47] Sibṭ Ibn al-Jawzī, *Mirʾāt az-Zamān*, ed. James R. Jewett (Chicago, 1907), p. 434; also quoted in Maqrīzī, Taqī ad-Dīn Aḥmad b. ʿAlī, *as-Sulūk li-Maʿrifat Duwwal al-Mulūk* 1(1), ed. Muhammad M. Ziyadeh (Cairo, 1956), p. 231, n. 3 (trans. in Gabrieli, *Arab Historians of the Crusades*, pp. 274–75; see also Amin Maalouf, *Les croisades vues par les Arabes* (Paris, 1983), p. 263). René Grousset, *Histoire des croisades et du royaume franc de Jérusalem*, 3 vols. (Paris, 1934–36), 3:316, quotes al-ʿAynī.

[48] Ibn Wāṣil, *Mufarrij al-Kurūb*, 3:234; cf. Abū al-Fidāʾ, *Al-Mukhtaṣar fī Akhbār al-Bashar*, 3:141 repeating the same report.

[49] Gabrieli, *Arab Historians of the Crusades*, p. 275.

[50] Sibṭ Ibn āl-Jawzī, *Mirʾāt az-Zamān*, p. 433; Maqrīzī; *Sulūk*, 1(1).232 and note; Maalouf, *Les croisades*, pp. 263–64. Hans E. Mayer, *The Crusades*, trans. John Gillingham, 2nd ed. (Oxford, 1988), p. 235, reduces the original 200 *dirhams* of the Arabic source to 20.

pope, and his audacity in attacking him and driving him out."[51] The last part of this sentence refers to the victory of the emperor over the pope's army in the autumn of 1229.[52]

This reference to the vast lands under Frederick's rule is reflected by the enumeration of all these lands in the two letters he sent to Fakhr ad-Dīn. The same list of territories which appears in the opening of the letters also appears in our inscription. The enumeration of the imperial possessions does not appear in the Latin titles of the emperor even at the height of his achievements, but in the Arabic documents, and in this inscription, the influence of the Muslim chancery is very obvious. This influence began at the time of King Roger II, when the Norman administration flourished with the establishment of the royal *dīwān* – imported from Fāṭimid Egypt together with a complete system of titulature, which included the enumeration of the ruler's territorial possessions. The Arabic ceremonial style and the fixed formal parts regarding the addressees in every correspondence, as well as the preambles in every Arabic document issued by the *dīwān*, followed a very rigid pattern which formed the most important part in the education of the scribes.

Fortification of Jaffa

Jaffa, both before the First Crusade and under the first Frankish kingdom, was an important port and an emporium of Syria. The Arab geographers describe it as the harbour of Ramlah and admire its beauty and the strength of its fortifications.[53] Idrīsī, writing in 548/1154, describes Jaffa as the seaport (*furḍah*) of Jerusalem and refers to it, as well as to the other coastal towns, in positive terms.[54]

In July 1187, Saladin's brother al-ʿĀdil conquered Jaffa; in September 1191, Richard reconquered it and the town remained in Frankish hands until September 1197, when al-ʿĀdil heard about the arrival of German troops in Acre as part of a new crusade. ʿIzz ad-Dīn Ibn Shaddād (d. 684/1285), who wrote in 674/1275 a book on the rulers of ash-Shām and al-Jazīrah and dedicated a short description to the history of Jaffa, relates that al-ʿĀdil attacked Jaffa, which was defended by a small garrison of some forty horsemen. The city, which lacked a wall, fell quickly and after a short siege its citadel also fell. The garrison and the population were massacred; the city and castle were destroyed and their rubble thrown into the sea.[55] In 1204 the Franks regained Jaffa but the town remained deserted.

---

[51] *at-Taʾrīkh al-Manṣūrī*, 191a, trans. in Gabrieli, *Arab Historians of the Crusades*, p. 283.

[52] Mayer, *The Crusades*, p. 238.

[53] Sources gathered by Guy Le Strange, *Palestine under the Moslems, a Description of Syria and the Holy Land from AD 650 to 1500* (Boston, 1890), pp. 550–51, and A. S. Marmardjī, *Textes géographiques arabes sur la Palestine* (Paris, 1951), pp. 206–7.

[54] al-Idrīsī, *Nuzhat al-Mushtāq fī Ikhtirāq al-ʾĀfāq*, pp. 358, 364, 376.

[55] Ibn Shaddād, ʿIzz ad-Dīn Muḥammad b. ʿAlī al-Ḥalabī, *al-Aʿlāq al-Khaṭīrah fī Dhikr Umarāʾ ash-Shām wa-al-Jazīrah*, ed. Sāmī Dahhān (Damascus, 1387/1962), pp. 255, 256 and n. 2; 257.

The time for rebuilding Jaffa arrived after Frederick II landed in Acre. The crusader armies that preceded him engaged themselves in building Montfort, Sidon, and Caesarea. When the emperor declared his wish to rebuild Jaffa, his announcement was received with great enthusiasm. It had always been the feeling in the crusaders' camp that the fortification of Jaffa was a necessary step for achieving the real goal of returning to Jerusalem. They were not aware of the negotiations which had been in process between the emperor and al-Malik al-Kāmil via the good services of Fakhr ad-Dīn Yūsuf b. Shaykh ash-Shuyūkh, al-Kāmil's minister, who by then had developed friendly relations with the emperor. However, the fortification of Jaffa was also meant to add just the necessary pressure on the sultan not to drag out the negotiations.

Frederick's intention to refortify Jaffa was made public at the beginning of November 1228, a short while after his arrival in the Holy Land. The assembled army, now headed by the emperor, moved southwards and reached Jaffa on 15 November. The fortification works proceeded with great enthusiasm; the city, completely destroyed in 1197, began to reappear from the mountains of rubble which covered the foundations of its walls. The work of the fortifications concentrated on the city fortress. Its walls were built, strengthened by towers, and the moat was cleaned. The work was completed on 18 February 1229, and on that same day the armistice agreement (*hudnah*) between Frederick II and al-Malik al-Kāmil was signed in the city, for the duration of ten years, five months and forty days.

In addition to the peace treaty, which gained considerable territory for the crusaders, the refortification of Jaffa, to which Patriarch Gerold added the aforementioned two towers a short while later, was a great achievement for Frederick. Whereas in the Holy Sepulchre he took the opportunity to publish his imperial manifesto to the world, in building Jaffa he thought that he had left a monument for posterity.[56]

The two inscriptions – the Arabic and the Latin – bearing his name and enumerating his domains, were aimed at commemorating the work as much as his name in the Holy Land in a manner well known in Sicily but unique in Outremer. The Muslim scribes of his chancery, following a well-known formula and style, and co-operating with the workshop in which the inscriptions were prepared, composed the text of the Arabic inscription introducing only a few necessary amendments to it.

---

[56] The amount of source material and research dedicated to the fortification of Jaffa and to the events which preceded and followed it is vast. Here are only a few of the main works used for the above description: *Eracles* 33.7 in *RHC Oc* 2:372–73; Maqrīzī, *Sulūk*, 1(1):221 (Frederick and Fakhr ad-Dīn Yūsuf b. Shaykh ash-Shuyūkh in Sicily); Ibn Wāṣil, *Mufarrij al-Kurūb*, 3:233–34; Ibn al-Athīr, ʿAlī b. Muḥammad ʿIzz ad-Dīn, *al-Kāmil fī at-Taʾrīkh* (Beirut, 1982), 12:478ff.; Reinhold Röhricht, *Geschichte des Königreichs Jerusalem (1100–1291)* (Innsbruck, 1898), pp. 782–83; Grousset, *Histoire*, 3:304–6, 312–15; Steven Runciman, *A History of the Crusades*, 3 vols. (Cambridge, 1951–54), 3:171ff., 186, 187; Joshua Prawer, *Histoire du royaume Latin de Jerusalem*, 2 vols. (Paris 1969–70), 2:170ff., 195–97; Abulafia, *Frederick II*, pp. 185–91; Mayer, *The Crusades*, p. 234. For a lucid summary see Pringle, *The Churches*, 1:264–67.

Summary: The Epigraphic Context

Referring to the two centuries of Frankish presence in Palestine, Clermont-Ganneau wrote in 1874: "During all the years that I have hunted for inscriptions in this ungrateful soil I have met but five or six texts belonging to the period, and even they were for the most part fragmentary."[57] The number of such inscriptions has grown dramatically since his time,[58] but they are all in Latin or French. The only Arabic inscription from the crusader or Frankish side to have come down to us is the one discussed above.

Two Arabic inscriptions bear witness to the western activity in the country, but they come from places that were under Muslim control at the time they were written. The first, excavated in Ascalon, is dated 540/1150, bears the name of the Fāṭimid Caliph aẓ-Ẓāfir bi-Amr Allah (544/1149–549/1154), and commemorates the building of a tower in the walls that defended the city against the Franks. The tower was built about three years prior to the Frankish conquest of Ascalon in 1153. The city was destroyed and partly rebuilt by Richard the Lionheart,[59] destroyed again, and rebuilt by Richard of Cornwall in 1241. The Arabic inscription was then superimposed with five heraldic shields, three large and two small ones. The three large shields carry the blazon of the Wake family of Northampton. They were engraved over the Fāṭimid inscription of 1150 by Sir Hugh Wake who in 1240–41 took part in the crusade of Richard of Cornwall, and participated in the fortification of Ascalon in 1241.[60] The second inscription, dated 606/1210, comes from the village of Farkhah, between Jerusalem and Nābulus. It is a Muslim dedication text that contains details regarding the money devoted for the upkeep of a local mosque from the revenue of the *faṣal* of the village. This Arabic word is simply the transliteration of "vassal" and represents a system of Frankish taxation which continued to be used by the Muslims long after the Franks had left the village and even after they left the country altogether.[61]

As much as these two inscriptions are important, they are a far cry from the one that contains an Arabic text, backed by a Latin one, which attests to the brief yet eventful presence in the Holy Land of one of the great personalities of European history. It is a unique inscription which for the first time brings the research of the crusades physically in contact with an artefact bearing the fingerprints, so to speak, of a western ruler. Although an identical text exists in an Arabic manuscript, it is still breathtaking to witness its realization on stone.

---

[57] *PEFQ*, 1874, p. 269.

[58] See the more than 400 inscriptions assembled in de Sandoli's *Corpus Inscriptionum Crucesignatorum Terrae Sanctae* of 1974, and Denys Pringle, "Crusader Inscriptions from Southern Lebanon," *Crusades* 3 (2004), 131–51.

[59] Denys Pringle, "King Richard I and the Walls of Ascalon," *Palestine Exploration Quarterly* 116 (1984), 133–47.

[60] *CIAP*, 1:163ff.

[61] *CIAP*, 3:188–200; Moshe Sharon, "Vassal and Faṣal: The Evidence of the Farkhah Inscription from 608/1210," *Crusades* 4 (2005), 127–40. (The correct date is 606.)

Postscript, September 2012

The slab with the inscription (Fig. 7) has been detached from the wall and cleaned; it is now in the compound of the Israel Antiquity Authority in the Rockefeller Museum. The extrication has revealed that the inscription was engraved on a lintel. The measurements of the slab are 0.58 m × 0.35 m × 0.25 m; the original lintel must have been at least three times longer, that is, about 2.00 m.

Fig. 7   Block of marble, part of the original gate lintel engraved with the inscription

Two Crusaders out of Luck

Hans Eberhard Mayer

University of Kiel

> *R. B. C. Huygens amico fidelissimo*
> *anno a nativitate sua octogesimo.*
> In multitudine vitae tuae laborasti,
> non dixisti: Quiescam. (Isaiah 57.10)

The pilgrimage and captivity of Henry I of Mecklenburg and his servant Martin Bleyer has not received much attention from historians of the crusades, although Reinhold Röhricht – who else? – had already pulled together most of the hard charter evidence and assembled it conveniently in the *Meklenburgisches* (*sic*) *Urkundenbuch*.[1] Henry is not mentioned at all in Yvonne Friedman's book on captured crusaders.[2] It was not until 2009, more than a century after Röhricht had provided the references, that Nicholas Morton mentioned Henry's captivity,[3] but only in 25 lines, partly misinterpreting the relevant charters, and completely ignoring the evidence from chronicles. In the historiography of the medieval Baltic campaigns and of the Teutonic Order the case was only mentioned, as far as I can see, by William L. Urban.[4] In the regional historiography of Mecklenburg Henry did, of course, fare better.[5] For the benefit of students of the crusades the case is well worth rescuing from this partial oblivion because of the wealth of detail available.

---

[1] *RRH*, nos. 1492, 1501. Reinhold Röhricht, *Die Deutschen im Heiligen Lande* (Innsbruck, 1894), pp. 128–29.

[2] Yvonne Friedman, *Encounters between Enemies: Captivity and Ransom in the Latin Kingdom of Jerusalem*, Cultures, Beliefs and Traditions 10 (Leiden, 2002).

[3] Nicholas E. Morton, *The Teutonic Knights in the Holy Land, 1190–1291* (Woodbridge, 2009), p. 151.

[4] William L. Urban, *The Baltic Crusade*, 2nd ed. (Chicago, 1994), pp. 271, 307. Ernst Strehlke, *Tabulae ordinis Theutonici* (Berlin, 1869), p. 119, had referred to the case, but only in a footnote which went unnoticed.

[5] Ferdinand Heinrich Grautoff, *Beitrag zur Geschichte Heinrichs I. Fürsten von Mecklenburg* (Lübeck, 1826), reprinted in idem, *Historische Schriften* 1 (Lübeck, 1836), pp. 83–117; Franz Boll, "Des Fürsten Heinrich von Mecklenburg Pilgerfahrt zum Heiligen Grabe, 26jährige Gefangenschaft und Heimkehr," *Jahrbücher des Vereins für meklenburgische Geschichte und Alterthumskunde* 14 (1849), 95–105, 293–98; Friedrich Wigger, "Die Pilgerfahrt des Fürsten Heinrich I. von Meklenburg," *Jahrbücher des Vereins für meklenburgische Geschichte und Alterthumskunde* 40 (1875), 39–86. Wigger's article has been up to now the best and most detailed study of this topic. A brief sketch is found in Andreas Röpke, "Heinrich I," in *Biographisches Lexikon für Mecklenburg* 6 (Rostock, 2011), pp. 153–54; a few remarks in Wolfgang Huschner, "Heinrich II. (der Löwe)," in ibid., pp. 156–57. Conditions in Egypt during Henry's captivity have been investigated by Herbert Eisenstein, "Ägypten zur Zeit der Gefangenschaft Fürst Heinrichs I. (1272–1297)," *Mecklenburgische Jahrbücher* 116 (2001), 33–55. As far as Henry's captivity is concerned, Eisenstein follows Wigger. The same is true with exceptions in Anke and Wolfgang Huschner, "Wer regierte Mecklenburg? Konflikte um die Regentschaft während der Haft Heinrich I. in Kairo (1272–1298)," in *Land – Stadt – Universität. Historische Lebensräume*

The charters are supplemented by chronicles, mostly written in Middle High German or Low German. The earliest, and for this case by far the most reliable, is the chronicle which is generally quoted as that of Albrecht of Bardowik (†1310) who was chancellor of Lübeck.[6] He did not, in fact, write it but he caused it to be entered into a Lübeck cartulary compiled in 1298. The author was Alexander Huno (†1311), a notary and *Stadtschreiber* of Lübeck since 1289. In 1298 he met with Henry I in Rome when Henry was returning from his long captivity.[7] Alexander represented his city there in its long struggle against the bishop of Lübeck.[8] This means that Alexander's report on Henry's pilgrimage and captivity goes directly back to what Henry himself told him.

Henry I of Mecklenburg (1264–1302) ruled over territories inhabited by christianized Slavic Abotrites[9] and newly immigrated Germans and stretching from Gadebusch south-east of Lübeck to east of Wismar along the Baltic Sea. In a somewhat grandiose manner Mecklenburg was Grecized as Magnopolis or Megalopolis, when in fact the name was derived from *Mikilinburg* (now the village of Mecklenburg), the earlier residence of the Abotrite princes. Röhricht, Urban, and Morton prematurely called Henry duke of Mecklenburg but it was not until 1348 that Emperor Charles IV created a ducal title for the family. In his charters Henry styled himself lord or prince (*dominus*) of Mecklenburg.

Not long after his accession Henry I fought in 1268 near the Gulf of Finland against a Russian army from Novgorod under a son of Alexander Nevsky. There (*cum in peregrinationem versus Lyuoniam profecti essemus*) he was apparently thoroughly charmed by a little pagan girl of approximately three years of age (*ancillulam quandam multum tenere etatis, utpote triennem*). He had her baptized and then adopted her as daughter (*adoptavimus eam nobis in filiam*). Later on he seems to have had second thoughts on the matter or, perhaps, his wife Anastasia from the house of Pomerania-Stettin objected to the unusual addition to the family. In any case he did not bring her up in his household but on 8 July 1270 he presented her as an oblate to the Premonstratensian nuns at Rehna in a charter which told the earlier part of the story and by which he donated some land for her maintenance for life.[10]

---

von Ständen, Schichten und Personen, ed. Ernst Münch, Mario Niemann, and Wolfgang E. Wagner, Schriften zur Sozial- und Wirtschaftsgeschichte 14 (Hamburg, 2010), pp. 19–75.

[6] *Aufzeichnungen Albrechts von Bardowik vom Jahre 1298*, Die Chroniken der deutschen Städte 26 (Leipzig, 1899), pp. 285–316, cited hereafter as *Aufzeichnungen*. In his introduction to this chronicle (pp. 295–97) Karl Koppmann identified Alexander Huno as the author.

[7] *Detmar-Chronik von 1101–1395*, Die Chroniken der deutschen Städte 19 (Leipzig, 1884), p. 380. Detmar was a fourteenth-century Lübeck Franciscan. His chronicle exists in various versions.

[8] Wolf Dieter Hauschild, *Kirchengeschichte Lübecks* (Lübeck, 1981), pp. 84–86.

[9] He himself came from a family of Abotrite rulers. His great-great-grandfather's name was Pribislaw.

[10] *Meklenburger* (sic) *Urkundenbuch* [cited hereafter as *M. UB.*] 2 (Schwerin, 1864), p. 384, no. 1193.

Having repressed his brothers' claims to a share in his rule, he decided in the summer of 1271 to go to the Holy Land. He is last known to have been at home on 12 June 1271, when he issued a charter in his residential town of Wismar.[11] From a lost *Historia Iohannitarum* Steinmetz cited 13 June as the day of Henry's departure.[12] Almost a year later, on 1 May 1272, the archbishop of Magdeburg entered into an alliance with the *domini Slavie*, Henry I among them, against the margraves of Brandenburg.[13] From this, Anke and Wolfgang Huschner, followed by Röpke, concluded that Henry I was in Magdeburg on that day.[14] Consequently, they let Henry depart for the East only in June 1272. This charter does, however, not mean that Henry was still in Germany in May 1272. He was named because after his return, expected relatively soon, he would have to honour the agreement. In fact it is not certain that any one of the five *domini Slavie* listed here was present in Magdeburg on that day. They were not named among the witnesses, and not one of them sealed the charter; it was authenticated only by the seal of the archbishop and two more seals from the Magdeburg side. As the document is preserved in the archives of Schwerin it was obviously the written promise of the archbishop to the lord of Mecklenburg concerning his obligations in this alliance, even though the archbishop was careful enough to include the obligations of the *domini Slavie*. Probably all of them received such a charter from the archbishop. One may assume that counter-charters by the *domini Slavie* were issued to the archbishop, but, if so, we do not know at what date and under which seal. Even the seal of Henry I on such a counter-charter would not mean anything, because he did not take the matrix of his seal to the East, thus enabling his son Henry II to use his father's seal throughout his regency.[15] What we would have to expect if the *domini Slavie* including Henry I had been in Magdeburg on 1 May 1272 is shown in 1287 when a *Landfrieden* of 1283 was prolonged by the bishop of Schwerin and seven regional lords.[16] Seven of the eight sealed the charter; the seal of Henry I's son John had never been affixed, as was usual in his case.

There has been discussion whether Henry, later surnamed Henry the Pilgrim, went as a pilgrim or as a crusader, but he is said to have received the cross in the

---

[11] *M. UB.* 2, p. 414, no. 1231.

[12] Bernardus Latomus (= Steinmetz), *Genealochronicon Megalopolitanum*, in Ernst Joachim von Westphalen, *Monumenta inedita rerum Germanicarum* 4 (Leipzig, 1745), col. 238. But this was probably only an estimate based on Henry's last Mecklenburg charter from the day before. Dietrich Schröder, *Fünftes Alphabet der Mecklenburgischen Kirchengeschichte des papistischen Mecklenburg* (Wismar, 1739), p. 729, gives 13 July. Röhricht, *Die Deutschen*, p. 128, has 13 January, obviously a misprint for 13 June or July.

[13] *M. UB.* 2, p. 428, no. 1250.

[14] Anke and Wolfgang Huschner, "Wer regierte Mecklenburg?," pp. 21f.; Röpke, "Heinrich I.," p. 153.

[15] Anke and Wolfgang Huschner, "Wer regierte Mecklenburg?," pp. 64f.; Huschner, "Heinrich II.," p. 159.

[16] *M. UB.* 3 (Schwerin, 1865), p. 259, no. 1905.

Franciscan convent at Wismar.[17] As far as he was able to know, the kingdom of
Jerusalem was not in good shape and was suffering from the blows dealt by the
Mamluk sultan Baybars (1260–77). He must have known that the second crusade of
King Louis IX of France had collapsed when the king died in the camp at Tunis in
August 1270. The expedition of the Lord Edward, later King Edward I of England,
who landed in Acre in May 1271, came too late to influence Henry's decision.

We do not know how much of an entourage Henry had. Although none of
his vassals is known to have participated,[18] he would certainly not have gone by
himself. Only one man who accompanied him stands out because he shared his fate
and remained with Henry until the end: his squire, Martin Bleyer.[19] Martin became
the darling of the Lübeck and Mecklenburg chronicles. The faithful servant holding
out with his lord in captivity is a stock figure in crusader legends. Who would not
think of the minstrel Blondel finding and joining Richard the Lionheart in Austrian
captivity?[20] But unlike Blondel, Martin Bleyer is definitely not an invention of the
chroniclers, because we know from the *Wismarer Stadtbuch* that he bought a house
in Wismar between 1260 and 1271.[21]

Wigger lets Henry arrive in Acre in the fall of 1271; Röhricht, followed by
Morton, opted for June 1272; Röpke gives the end of 1272, as he must because he
believes Henry I to have still been in Germany in May 1272.[22] The end of 1272 is
hardly possible because in October shipping in the Mediterranean came to a halt
until March or April. The last big convoys left Europe in August to enable the
merchants to turn around in time in the East. Jacques de Vitry left Genoa for the
East in early October and his trip was far from pleasant.[23] The fall of 1271 is also
unlikely because Henry's departure in June or July 1271 made it impossible to catch
the Mediterranean eastbound sailings of August from Venice or Marseille.[24] Apart

---

[17] Schröder, *Papistisches Mecklenburg*, p. 730. Latomus, *Genealochronicon*, col. 238. The mere
fact of taking the cross is also mentioned in the *Detmar-Chronik*, p. 353.

[18] *Mecklenburgische Reimchronik des Ernst von Kirchberg*, ed. Christa Cordshagen and Roderich
Schmidt (Köln, 1997), p. 318, and Hermann Korner, *Chronica novella*, ed. Jakob Schwalm (Göttingen,
1895), p. 207, mention a considerable retinue but there is no hard evidence for this. The *Reimchronik*
was written in 1378 at the request of Henry's grandson; it was therefore a "house chronicle." Hermann
Korner (†1438) was a Lübeck Dominican.

[19] Martin is mentioned as Henry's man-servant in *Aufzeichnungen*, pp. 303, 306; in the *Annales
Lubicenses*, MGH SS 16, p. 417; in the *Detmar-Chronik*, p. 380; and in Kirchberg's *Reimchronik*, pp.
319, 321. Latomus, *Genealochronicon*, col. 238. Korner, *Chronica novella*, p. 207, some 150 years
removed from events, calls him Hermann in Ms. D, but Ms. B has the correct name.

[20] John Gillingham, *Richard I* (New Haven, 1999), p. 233.

[21] *M. UB.* 2, p. 165, no. 889.

[22] Wigger, "Pilgerfahrt," p. 57, who is followed by Eisenstein, "Ägypten," p. 39 (end of 1271);
Röhricht, *Die eutsche*, p. 128; Morton, *Teutonic Knights*, p. 151. Röpke, "Heinrich I.," p. 153. Urban,
Baltic Crusade, p. 271, has 1270, which, because of the charter evidence is out of the question.

[23] Jacques de Vitry, *Lettres*, ed. R. B. C. Huygens, 2nd edition, CCCM 171 (Turnhout, 2000), pp.
556, 560–61.

[24] Had he arrived in Acre in the summer or fall of 1271 he would certainly have participated in the
Lord Edward's military actions in July against Lydda and in late November against Qaqun. But in the
story told by Henry himself to Alexander Huno these events are not mentioned.

from travelling through one of these towns he could catch a sailing from Frisia at the end of March or in April 1272,[25] or he could sail from a Baltic to a Flemish port and travel from there to Marseille.[26] If, as is more likely, Henry arrived at Acre in the summer of 1272, he must have come with the European spring sailings of April or May after having wintered somewhere in Europe, while Mediterranean shipping was at a virtual standstill.[27]

By the summer of 1272 the situation in the East was essentially peaceful after a ten-year truce between Baybars and the Franks of Acre had been arranged in April of that year covering, aside from the city, only the plain of Acre and the pilgrim road to Nazareth.[28]

It seems that at Acre Henry lodged with the Teutonic Knights, at least they kept some valuables (*clenodia*) and money of his after misfortune had struck.[29] Rather than stay within the secure city walls Henry ventured out into the country and was taken prisoner with his companions by the Saracens. This is supposed to have happened on a 25 January (*am dage conversionis Pauly*).[30] In this case the year must have been 1273.[31] Given that under the terms of the truce of April 1272 he would have been safe in the plain of Acre and on the road to Nazareth, the incident must have happened at quite some distance from Acre. The best of the chronicles writes that he was captured on the way to the Holy Sepulchre.[32] It was a reckless undertaking, even if he travelled in disguise. The Church of the Holy Sepulchre, it is true, was in Christian hands[33] and it was not impossible for Christians to visit it upon payment of an admission fee of between 36 and 40 silver *gros tournois* per person,[34] but

---

[25] The sailings from there had to be earlier because of the longer route around the Iberian peninsula. In 1270 the Frisians assembled at the end of March, sailed from Borkum on 18 April, arrived in Marseille in early July and in Tunis after 25 August when Saint Louis had died.

[26] Kirchberg, *Reimchronik*, p. 318, says that he travelled via Marseille but this is not certain.

[27] The bishop of Linköping left Sweden in the summer of 1282, was in Bruges in September, made a will in Marseille in April 1283 and issued a charter in Acre in July 1283. He had probably wintered in Paris where he had once been a student; see Hans E. Mayer, "Ein Bischof geht einkaufen. Heinrich von Linköping im Heiligen Land," *Zeitschrift des Deutschen Palästina-Vereins* 124 (2008), 53–54.

[28] *Estoire de Eracles empereur*, RHC Oc 2, p. 462. "Annales de Terre Sainte," ed. Reinhold Röhricht, *AOL* 2ᵇ (1884), 455. Marino Sanuto the Elder, *Liber secretorum fidelium crucis*, in Jacques Bongars, ed., *Gesta Dei per Francos* 2 (Hanau, 1611), p. 224.

[29] See below, p. 169.

[30] Inscription on a memorial monument in the Franciscan church at Wismar, copied in the sixteenth century: Carl Ferdinand Crain, "Das Kirchenbuch des Grauen Klosters zu Wismar," *Jahrbücher des Vereins für meklenburgische Geschichte und Alterthumskunde* 6 (1841), 100. Latomus, *Genealochronicon*, col. 238.

[31] Albert Krantz, *Wandalia*, lib. VII c. 34 (Cologne, 1519, without foliation or pagination), gives the year as 1276 which is pure fantasy. Krantz (†1517) was a syndic of Lübeck.

[32] *Aufzeichnungen*, p. 302: *de ghevanghen wart over mere an pelegrimaze uppe dem weghe tho deme heylyghen grave.*

[33] Denys Pringle, *The Churches of the Crusader Kingdom of Jerusalem* 3 (Cambridge, 2007), pp. 32–33.

[34] Fidenzio of Padua, *Liber recuperationis Terre Sancte*, in Jacques Paviot, ed., *Projets de croisade (v. 1290–v. 1330)*, Documents relatifs à l'histoire des croisades 20 (Paris, 2008), p. 95. It was written 1290/1291.

under the truce the road to Jerusalem was unsafe for more than half the distance and, precisely because of the admission fee, the authorities at Acre had strictly forbidden Christians to visit Jerusalem as pilgrims. Menko (†1275/76), the abbot of the Premonstratensian house of Bloemhof in Wittewierum near Groningen, is explicit: only a few Christians then went to Jerusalem, because this had been prohibited under threat of excommunication, since it was felt that Christian expenditures in Jerusalem would enrich the Muslims and help to finance their anti-Christian war.[35] In spite of this, if we are to believe Menko, a few daredevils continued to go to Jerusalem then (*sepulchrum domini pauci visitabant*).

The story grew in the telling. A Franciscan inscription at Wismar (mentioned in n. 30) reports that Henry and Martin Bleyer were captured actually inside the Church of the Holy Sepulchre. Kirchberg says the same.[36] The inscription had it that Henry had more companions than just Martin at the time, who were immediately set free so that they might collect money in Mecklenburg for ransoming their lord (*de adel auerst des hern hinricj wurden wederumb gefort in dat ehre vaderlandt dat se versamleten eynen schatt tho ehres hern verlosinge*).[37] This is pure legend because it was not until 1287 that money was offered for Henry's liberation.

Henry and his servant Martin Bleyer were transferred to Cairo where they remained for a quarter of a century, probably in the citadel where prisoners were mostly being kept at this time.[38] High-ranking prisoners who might fetch a good ransom were, of course, not subjected to slave labour,[39] even though their lives were less than comfortable. Martin, it is said, learned to weave silk and sold it in town thus helping to feed his lord.[40] This freedom of movement is, at first sight, surprising. But it is known that, at least in the early fourteenth century, the captives were settled in the centre of the city together with the families they had been able to found by having married Christian women, probably Copts. There they even had

---

[35] *Menkonis Chronicon*, MGH SS 23, p. 558. This policy goes back to the crusade against Damietta; see Pope Honorius III for Genoa, dated 24 July 1217, ed. Christopher Schabel, *Bullarium Cyprium* 1, Texts and Studies in the History of Cyprus 44 (Nicosia, 2010), p. 183, no. c-3.

[36] Kirchberg, *Reimchronik*, p. 319. See also Latomus, *Genealochronicon*, col. 238.

[37] Crain, *Kirchenbuch*, p. 100. This was even topped in the eighteenth century when it was said that Jochen and Urban of Pritzbuer from a noble Mecklenburg family went to Acre with Henry in 1276 (!) but Urban died, while Jochen was made a knight of the Holy Sepulchre; [Joachim von Pritzbuer], *Index concisus familiarum nobilium ducatus Megalopolensis*, German trans. by Christoph Otto von Gamme (Neustrelitz, 1894), p. 148. Receiving the knighthood at the Holy Sepulchre did not become fashionable until well into the fourteenth century.

[38] *Aufzeichnungen*, p. 303: *unde ghevanghen lach 26 jar by Babelonie up eneme torne, de heet Kere.*

[39] The theologian Ibn Taymiyya who was imprisoned in the citadel of Cairo for a year and a half in 1307, complained in one of his letters: "The Christians are in a good prison ... If only our prison was the same kind as that of the Christians"; Ibn Taymiyya, *Lettre à un roi croisé*, trans. J. R. Michot (Louvain, 1995), p. 73. Those prisoners who had to do slave labour were mostly employed in building activities.

[40] *Annales Lubicenses*, p. 417: *famulus suus Martinus, qui tempore, quo esset dominus eius in diligenti custodia seratus, didicit contexere pannos sericos et totum pretium, quod a paganis deservivit, pro dicti domini sui exposuit nutrimento*; *Detmar-Chronik*, p. 380; Kirchberg, *Reimchronik*, p. 319; Korner, *Chronica novella*, p. 207; Latomus, *Genealochronicon*, col. 238.

their own church and lived mostly on making and selling wine and on providing "entertainment," which apparently was a euphemism for prostitution.[41] Weaving and selling silk, as Martin Bleyer did, is, therefore, not unlikely.

In Mecklenburg in the meantime, Henry's wife Anastasia acted as regent, later being replaced by her son Henry II, but with Henry I being absent, Mecklenburg sank into a chaos of feuds. No attempts were made until 1287 to liberate Henry, when he had already been a prisoner for fourteen years. By 1275 word had been received that Henry was in Muslim captivity. On 20 January 1275 *nos Anastasia domina Magnopolensis vicem dilecti domini et mariti nostri absentis fideliter gubernantes* donated a village to the Cistercian nuns of Sonnenkamp at Parchow.[42] This was done, she explained, because the nuns prayed for Henry's liberation (*ut deus ... propter iugem intercessionem earundem Christi ancillarum ... maritum nostrum dilectum dominum Hinricum Magnopolensem de vinculis paganorum, quibus includitur, salvum eripiat, ipsum nobis et pueris nostris ..., qui suum mestissime prestolantur reditum, ad propria remittat in solacium oportunum*). When in 1279 the deceased members of the princely family were listed, Henry was not among them.[43] But on 26 July 1286 Henry II flatly referred to his father as dead: *Hinrici patris nostri felicis recordationis.*[44] Rumours to this effect had probably reached Mecklenburg.

But it took more than just prayers to get Henry out of prison. More certain news of his fate apparently reached Mecklenburg in 1287. Now a serious effort to liberate him was begun. In December 1287 Anastasia and her son Henry II went to Lübeck and deposited with the city 2,000 marks of pure silver of the weight of Cologne, to be transferred to the Teutonic Order under their master Burchard of Schwanden. On 13 December 1287 the city issued a receipt for a deposit of *duo milia marcarum argenti puri de pondere Coloniensi* which had been received from Anastasia and Henry II as well as from another son, John. The city promised to hand over the money to the Order at Easter 1288 or later upon demand, provided that the receipt would be returned to the city along with an explanatory letter from the master.[45]

With such a deposit the city ran risks which it had excluded three days earlier. On 10 December 1287 Anastasia had issued a charter in Lübeck, sealed by her and Henry II, in which she and her two sons had promised that with regard to the 2,000 marks they would shoulder all deficiencies, damages, and risks from now on until, after the liberation of Henry I, the money would have been transferred to the Teutonic

---

[41] On Frankish prisoners in Cairo in the thirteenth and fourteenth centuries see the fine paper by Julien Loiseau, "Frankish Captives in Mamluk Cairo," *Al-Masaq. Islam and the Medieval Mediterranean* 23 (2011), 37–52. See also Eisenstein, "*Ägypten*," pp. 50–51.

[42] *M. UB.* 2, p. 506, no. 1353. A summary of a lost charter of Anastasia for the church of Schwerin says it was given *mit consens ihres vber See gefangenen Gemalss*; *M. UB.* 2, p. 462, no. 1294. It is dated 29 August 1273 but by this time news of Henry's misfortune could hardly have reached Mecklenburg. Wigger, "Pilgerfahrt," p. 67, n. 2, has shown convincingly that this piece belongs to 1275 or 1276.

[43] *M. UB.* 2, p. 612, no. 1506.

[44] *M. UB.* 3, p. 226, no. 1858.

[45] *M. UB.* 3, p. 285, no. 1935.

Knights and would have been transported at the expense and the risk of Anastasia to the city of Mechelen (near Antwerp) (*ex nunc quousque post liberacionem domini et patris nostri dictam pecuniam in civitate Lubicensi receperint et libere sub nostris expensis et periculis deduxerint in civitatem Mechele*).[46] Should they fail to meet their obligations for damages for more than two months after the Order had raised a claim, Anastasia's sons, along with ten of their knights, were required to come to Lübeck and remain in the city until such time when the Order should have been fully compensated for the damages incurred. Anastasia also promised that Henry of Werle (from a sideline of the family) would enter into the same obligations towards the Order as she was doing at this time.

It was a staggering amount of money. The mark silver of Cologne was a weight of 233 grams; 2,000 marks were, therefore, equivalent to 466 kilograms of silver.[47] In addition the Teutonic Order still held almost 300 marks of silver at Acre which Henry I had left there as a deposit and which could have been used for his release.[48] Being earmarked for the liberation of Henry I, the 2,000 marks were obviously intended to serve as ransom with, perhaps, a commission for the Order.[49] In order to strike a successful bargain in the East the Order had two possibilities. Either the silver could be shipped to Acre (but given the risks of this, it was only a theoretical option) or the Order could use it for its own purposes in Europe and advance the ransom in the East. It would seem that from the beginning this was the Order's plan because otherwise the transport to Mechelen does not make much sense. There the Teutonic Knights had a commandery in the castle of Pitsenburg within the city.[50] After slow beginnings in the years after 1220, the commandery embarked on a rapid expansion from 1270 onwards. In 1281 the pope had to protect it against local opposition.[51] In 1303 it needed a similar protection from the duke of Brabant. In 1287 even the founding family, the lords of Mechelen, had become slightly worried and came to an understanding with the Order, later not strictly observed, concerning its possessions in Mechelen.[52] Such expansion needed much money and it was perhaps for this reason that the Order intended to bring the silver from Lübeck to Mechelen.

---

[46] *M. UB.* 3, p. 285, no. 1934.

[47] In today's market (10 August 2011) this would fetch 391,000 Euro (+ modern sales tax, in Germany 19 per cent).

[48] See below, p. 169.

[49] Such commissions either in money or in kind were customary; see Friedman, *Encounters*, pp. 203f.

[50] On Pitsenburg see Karl Heinrich Lampe, "Zur Geschichte der Deutschordenskommende Pitzenburg und Mecheln," in *Preußenland und Deutscher Orden. Festschrift für Kurt Forstreuter*, Ostdeutsche Beiträge aus dem Göttinger Arbeitskreis 9 (Würzburg, 1958), pp. 225–54, especially p. 239; *De oorkonden van Pitsenburg, commanderij van de Duitse Ridderorde te Mechelen (1190–1794)*, ed. Alfred Jamees, 5 vols. (Antwerp, 1991–2000), was not available to me.

[51] Marian Tumler and Udo Arnold, *Die Urkunden des Deutschordenszentralarchivs in Wien. Regesten* 1, Quellen und Studien zur Geschichte des Deutschen Ordens 60/1 (Marburg, 2006), no. 868.

[52] On the last two charters see Lampe, "Pitzenburg," pp. 240–41.

If the money had remained and been used in Mechelen, the Order would have had to advance 2,000 marks in the East. But an advance of this magnitude was outside the Order's capacities. Its principal possession in the crusader states, the castle of Montfort, and the surrounding district had been severely curtailed in the truce concluded with Sultan Baybars in 1268. Only ten villages from now on belonged to the castle, the remainder had gone to the sultan.[53] In 1270 the Hospitallers had to allow the Teutonic Knights to sow and harvest for a year in the Hospital's *casal* of Manuet, around 20 kilometres north of Acre, "because of Montfort being in bad shape."[54] Apparently the Teutonic Knights could no longer provision their main castle. One year later the end of Montfort and the ten villages had come when Baybars took it. The Teutonic Knights were still able to buy real estate in the city of Acre shortly after this,[55] but we have no knowledge of such transactions after 1274. Whatever money was still available then to the Order at Acre went into taking over the lordship of Scandalion (Iskanderuna), around 12 kilometres south of Tyre.[56] In 1274 the Order guaranteed a loan of 2,000 bezants which the lady of Scandalion had received from a certain Jew by the name of Elias.[57] In 1280 her son stated that he was indebted to the Order in the amount of 17,400 bezants. The Order had loaned this amount to the lord of Scandalion and his mother, but had been forced to borrow it in turn from Jews and Sienese merchants at high interest (*sub gravibus usuris*).[58]

The Teutonic Knights at Acre were in decidedly straitened financial circumstances. They were quite unable to advance the ransom of Henry I of Mecklenburg from their own resources, and borrowing the advance from the moneylenders was a costly and risky business until the silver should have arrived at Mechelen – which it never did because it never left Lübeck. It was to remain there until after Henry had been set free. We do not know what the Teutonic Knights did, if anything, to achieve this.[59] Word that the silver had been deposited in Lübeck in December 1287 cannot have reached Acre before the spring sailings from Europe arrived in May or June 1288. After a year had elapsed, the Order on 14 August 1289, in good time for the autumn sailings from Acre to the West, conceded its defeat in the matter.

---

[53] Ibn al-Furat, *Ayyubids, Mamlukes and Crusaders* 2, trans. U. and M. C. Lyons (Cambridge, 1971), p. 130.

[54] *RRH*, no. 1374c.

[55] Marie-Luise Favreau-Lilie, "The Teutonic Knights in Acre after the Fall of Montfort (1271): Some Reflections," in *Outremer*, pp. 272–84. *RRH*, nos. 1388, 1390.

[56] Marie-Luise Favreau-Lilie, "Die Kreuzfahrerherrschaft Scandalion (Iskanderune)," *Zeitschrift des Deutschen Palästina-Vereins* 93 (1977), 18–29.

[57] *RRH*, no. 1399, last edited by Hubert Houben, "I Cavalieri Teutonici nel Mediterraneo orientale," in *I Cavalieri Teutonici tra Sicilia e Mediterraneo*, ed. Antonino Giuffrida, Hubert Houben, and Kristjan Toomaspoeg (Galatina, 2007), p. 71, no. 1.

[58] *RRH*, no. 1435, last edited by Houben, "Cavalieri Teutonici," p. 72, no. 2.

[59] At least on the Islamic side one normally worked through specialized agents, as we know from 1184, 1265, and 1270; Ibn Jobair, *Voyages*, trans. Maurice Gaudefroy-Demombynes, Documents relatifs à l'histoire des croisades 6 (Paris, 1958), p. 361; Makrizi, *Histoire des sultans Mamlouks de l'Egypte*, trans. Etienne Marc Quatremère 1/2 (Paris, 1840), pp. 25, 87.

Wirichus of Homberg, the preceptor of the Teutonic Knights in Acre deputizing for the master Burchard of Schwanden who was in Germany, instructed the city of Lübeck that the 2,000 marks of silver, deposited in Lübeck by Anastasia and her sons *pro redempcione domini ac patris eorum ... si ipsum potuissemus redemisse* [*sic*] should now be returned to Anastasia and her sons, since there was no hope of buying Henry's freedom from the Muslims (*cum proh dolor non sit spes, quod istis temporibus dominus Henricus de Mekelenburch a Sarracenorum vinculis redimatur*).[60] Wirichus expressed the hope that God in his compassion would find a different way to liberate Henry. He did, but it still took eight years.

We do not know exactly why efforts to liberate Henry II did not succeed or did not come about. As we have seen, the Order hardly had the money in the East to advance the ransom. Also there may have been an impending sense of doom. In April 1289 Sultan Qalawun, with whom such negotiations had to be conducted, had conquered Tripoli. A horrible massacre had ensued from which only a few people escaped. It may have been felt that given Qalawun's current disposition towards the Franks it was useless to even attempt to negotiate Henry's release. Finally, it is possible that internal dissent which had been developing among the Teutonic Knights since the last years of Master Hartmann of Heldrungen (1274–83), prevented any serious effort. Master Burchard of Schwanden precipitated a severe crisis in the Order. In March 1290 he was still in Germany.[61] Shortly thereafter he travelled to Acre where he caused a great scandal when he not only resigned the mastership but also joined the Hospitallers.[62] There was in these years a Palestinian party and a Prussian party in the Order.[63] Burchard of Schwanden was the leader of the "Palestinians," and apparently he despaired of his aim of concentrating the Order's resources on the Holy Land. In the turmoil following his resignation the other party triumphed. It was not very hard to see that the days of Frankish Acre were numbered and that the Order had more of a future in the Baltic region. The *Deutschmeister* Konrad of Feuchtwangen was elected to the mastership even though he was not present in Acre. Having been *Landmeister* of Prussia and Livonia in 1279–1280/81 he was the

---

[60] *M. UB.* 3, p. 354, no. 2030.

[61] Karl Heinrich Lampe, *Urkundenbuch der Deutschordensballei Thüringen* 1, Thüringische Geschichtsquellen N.F. 7 (Jena, 1936), p. 413, no. 478; p. 414, no. 479.

[62] Peter of Dusburg, *Chronicon terrae Prussiae*, ed. Max Töppen, in *Scriptores rerum Prussicarum* 1 (Leipzig, 1861), p. 205. The new Polish edition by Jaroslaw Wenta and Slawomir Wyszomirski (2007) was not available to me. Burchard is first found among the Hospitallers in 1296 as commander of Heimbach. Later on he held various offices for them in his native Switzerland; Dieter Wojtecki, *Studien zur Personengeschichte des Deutschen Ordens im 13. Jahrhundert*, Quellen und Studien zur Geschichte des östlichen Europa 3 (Wiesbaden, 1971), pp. 100f.

[63] Klaus Militzer, *Von Akkon zur Marienburg. Verfassung, Verwaltung und Sozialstruktur des Deutschen Ordens 1190–1309*, Quellen und Studien zur Geschichte des Deutschen Ordens 56 (Marburg, 1999), pp. 44–46; Udo Arnold, "Konrad von Feuchtwangen," *Preußenland* 13 (1975), 2–34, and esp. idem, "Deutschmeister Konrad von Feuchtwangen und die 'preußische Partei' im Deutschen Orden am Ende des 13. und zu Beginn des 14. Jahrhunderts," in *Aspekte der Geschichte. Festschrift für Peter Gerrit Thielen*, ed. Udo Arnold, Josef Schröder, and Günther Walzik (Göttingen, 1990), *passim*.

leader of the "Prussians." It was not in the interest of the "Palestinians" to contract heavy debts in the East for freeing Henry when the ransom money would be spent at Mechelen or elsewhere in Europe.

Internal strife paralysed the Order. While the fire was smouldering and shortly before the crisis exploded with the resignation of Burchard of Schwanden, the Teutonic Knights definitely closed their file on Henry I of Mecklenburg. In December 1289 the German king Rudolf of Habsburg held a court at Erfurt.[64] Burchard of Schwanden and Henry II of Mecklenburg attended and surely met. It must have been a painful interview. Burchard must have informed Henry II of the Order's failure to liberate his father and must have brought with him the original or a copy of the charter of Wirichus of Homberg of 14 August 1289, instructing the city of Lübeck to restore the 2,000 marks to Mecklenburg. In any case, on 23 December 1289 Burchard confirmed in Erfurt the action taken by Wirichus in Acre and also instructed Lübeck to hand the silver back to Henry II.[65] He also brought with him a few valuable items belonging to Henry I which the Order had kept for him for seventeen years. On 19 December 1289 Henry II issued a receipt to the Teutonic Knights for certain *clenodia* which his father had left at Acre with the Order. He listed a golden clasp (for closing a vestment), two belts and, somewhat enigmatically, four parts of a chalice or cup with two silver flasks (*quatuor partes calicis cum duabus ampullis argenteis*). Should his father, he said, happen to be liberated from Saracen bonds –a hope by now rather dim – and claim these items from the Order, it would not be held responsible.[66] In a separate charter of 23 December 1289 Henry II also stated to have received from Burchard of Schwanden what had remained of Henry I's travel budget – 296 marks of silver which he had left as a deposit with the Order at Acre.[67] On 20 January 1290 Henry II was in Lübeck and issued a receipt to the city that he had indeed received the 2,000 marks of silver, and on 1 February Anastasia followed suit with a similar receipt.[68]

Silence followed for another eight years during which two impostors, who were duly tried and executed, are said to have appeared in Mecklenburg claiming to be Henry I.[69] Surprisingly, Henry I and his servant Martin Bleyer were released from prison at some time in 1297, perhaps in December, by Sultan Husam al-Din Lajin

---

[64] Oswald Redlich, *Regesta imperii* 6/1 (Innsbruck, 1898), nos. 2261a, 2263a.

[65] *M. UB.* 3, p. 364, no. 2043.

[66] *M. UB.* 3, p. 363 no. 2042. Morton, *Teutonic Knights*, p. 151, completely misunderstands this charter, saying that Henry II gave the Order a number of valuables his father had taken on crusade and which the Order had tried to restore to Henry I, stipulating that the Order should restore these goods in the event of Henry's release! This is bad enough, but Kirchberg, *Reimchronik*, p. 318, was even worse, saying that Henry I had left 2,000 *florins* at Acre which Henry II recovered and then spent during his trip to Erfurt.

[67] *M. UB.* 25 A (1936), p. 33, no. 13794.

[68] *M. UB.* 3, p. 371, no. 2057; p. 374, no. 2059.

[69] Kirchberg, *Reimchronik*, p. 323. Latomus, *Genealochronicon*, col. 263.

(1296–99).[70] No ransom was paid because Henry II of Mecklenburg on 20 January 1298 still believed his father to be dead (*felicis memorie*).[71]

Maqrizi, who died in Cairo in 1442, reports in his enormously detailed chronicle that in October 1297 Lajin broke a hand and was confined to his Cairo palace for two months. When on 8 December 1297 he went downtown there was an enormous feast because he had recovered. He himself celebrated the occasion by setting free several prisoners.[72] Maqrizi does not name them, but Henry and his servant may have been among them. The real key to the matter, however, seems to have been that Henry had been chosen to bring a message from the sultan to the pope.[73] Ghazan, the Mongol Il-Khan of Persia (1295–1304), converted from Buddhism to Islam immediately after his accession. But the Mamluks of Egypt remained his principal foreign adversary, just as they had been to his predecessors, and he shared their aim of conquering Syria. This did not materialize until briefly during the campaign of October to December 1299, for which Ghazan had tried to enlist western help. This was not a new thing. Ghazan's father Arghun and his grandfather Abaqa had strongly lobbied all over Europe for an alliance with the West against the Mamluks. So did Ghazan, who repeatedly sent messages to the pope and the kings of France, England, and Cyprus.[74] Such activities did not, of course, go unnoticed in Cairo. They were worrisome and had to be counteracted. For Henry and Martin Bleyer it was a stroke of luck.

The two travelled home via the Morea and Rome. In the Morea Henry is supposed to have received horses, vestments, and money from Isabelle of Villehardouin, then ruling princess of Achaia.[75] On Pentecost (25 May) 1298 he was in Rome presenting himself to Pope Boniface VIII, to whom he delivered Lajin's message.[76]

---

[70] *Aufzeichnungen*, p. 303; *Annales Lubicenses*, p. 417. Kirchberg's story (*Reimchronik*, pp. 319–21) at this point turns more and more into a fairy tale: Lajin personally came to the prison and asked Henry if he should give him back his liberty in honour of Christ's birthday. Henry at first refused because he would not find his family still alive. But the sultan informed him that his wife was still living and his son was ruling. He himself, the sultan claimed, had been a servant of Henry's father. Then, finally, Henry I accepted liberation. At least the date given by Kirchberg (Christmas) tallies to some extent with the information supplied by Maqrizi (see below). It is either a serious mistake or a misprint in the article on Henry I in the *Allgemeine Deutsche Biographie* 11 (Leipzig, 1880), p. 541, that Henry was liberated as early as 1279.

[71] *M. UB.* 4 (Schwerin, 1867), p. 36, no. 2480.

[72] Makrizi, *Histoire* 2/2 (Paris, 1845), p. 54: *et mit en liberté plusieurs prisonniers*. From other Arab chronicles, Eisenstein, "*Ägypten*," p. 46, gives early September 1297 for the accident and 29 November for the feast.

[73] *Aufzeichnungen*, p. 303: *dar na cundyghede he deme pavese des soldanes bodeschap*.

[74] Felicitas Schmieder, *Europa und die Fremden. Die Mongolen im Urteil des Abendlandes vom 13. bis in das 15. Jahrhundert*, Beiträge zur Geschichte der Quellenkunde und des Mittelalters 16 (Sigmaringen, 1994), pp. 332–33. *Cronaca del Templare di Tiro (1243–1314)*, ed. Laura Minervini (Naples, 2000), p. 290, § 594: *Cestu Cazan ne layssa mye, pur ce que il estet sarazin, qui ne pensast tous jours de grever le soudan et les sarazins, et pour ce manda sovent mesages au roys crestiens, et les metet en boune esperanse de coure sus a soudan.*

[75] *Aufzeichnungen*, p. 303.

[76] *Aufzeichnungen*, p. 303; *Annales Lubicenses*, p. 417.

Doberan

In several charters dated 20 January 1298 Henry II was still the actual ruler of Mecklenburg.[77] But on 13 January 1299 Henry I had returned, resuming the rule after having been absent for 28 years.[78] Hermann Korner commented: *Qui perierat inventus est, qui mortuus putabatur revixit* (cf. Luke 15.24).[79] According to two sources Henry came back on the day of Saint Bartholomew (24 August 1298).[80] He is said to have brought with him a piece of the True Cross that he had received from the sultan, half of which he donated to the Franciscans in Wismar and half to the Cistercian monastery of Doberan, but there is no reliable evidence for this.[81] He found his family decimated. His wife and his son Henry II were still alive. But his son John had drowned at sea and his daughter Liutgard had been murdered by her own husband, the duke of Gniezno in Poland, which promptly earned her a reputation for sanctity among the Poles. Henry died on 2 January 1302 and was buried in Doberan.[82] He had been predeceased by his faithful servant Martin Bleyer who was buried in Wismar. "And so the story ends" (*aldus nymt de mere eyn ende*).[83]

---

[77] *M. UB.* 4, p. 36, no. 2479, 2480; p. 38, no. 2481; p. 40, no. 2482.

[78] *M. UB.* 4, p. 89, no. 2536.

[79] Korner, *Chronica novella*, p. 208.

[80] *Annales Lubicenses*, p. 417; *Detmar-Chronik*, p. 380. Latomus, *Genealochronicon*, col. 262, gives the day of Saint Pantaleon (28 July).

[81] Schröder, *Papistisches Mecklenburg*, p. 843; Latomus, *Genealochronicon*, col. 262.

[82] Friedrich Wigger, "Stammtafeln des Grossherzoglichen Hauses von Mecklenburg," *Jahrbücher des Vereins für meklenburgische Geschichte und Althertumskunde* 50 (1885), 153. On the burial see Kirchberg, *Reimchronik*, p. 326.

[83] *Aufzeichnungen*, p. 306, at the end of the report on the pilgrimage and captivity of Henry I of Mecklenburg.

Unpublished Notarial Acts on Tedisio Doria's Voyage to Cyprus and Lesser Armenia, 1294–1295

Antonio Musarra

Scuola Superiore di Studi Storici, Università degli Studi di San Marino,
Repubblica di San Marino
antoniomusarra@alice.it

Economic relations between Genoa and Cyprus began in the late twelfth century and increased considerably in the following decades.[1] Privileges received by the kings of Cyprus in 1218 and 1232 partially balanced Genoese losses following the appearance of the Latin Empire of Constantinople in 1204.[2] It is not possible to determine whether the Genoese took full advantage of the opportunities offered by the Cypriot privileges or not: notaries who worked in Genoa in the first half of the thirteenth century rarely specified the precise destination of investments in the Levant. We can only find records mentioning a generic *Ultramare* in *commenda* or sea loan contracts, less frequently *Cipro et ripariam Syrie* or merely *per riveriam*

I would like to thank, first and foremost, Steven A. Epstein, Enrico Basso, Giustina Olgiati, and the three anonymous readers for their helpful comments on this paper. Alfonso Assini, Michel Balard, Laura Balletto, Franco Cardini, Marina Montesano and Antony Molho read the manuscript and offered many useful suggestions. I would also like to thank Lorena Barale and Valentina Ruzzin for their meticulous proofreading. Alessandro Angelucci and Costanza Tognini helped me with the English text.

[1] Geo Pistarino, "Fonti documentarie genovesi per la storia medievale di Cipro," in idem, *Saggi e Documenti VI* (Genoa, 1985), pp. 339–75, and its extended version: "Maona e mercanti genovesi a Cipro," in idem, *Genovesi d'Oriente* (Genoa, 1990), pp. 423–35; Michel Balard, "Les Génois dans le royaume médiéval de Chypre," in *General History of Cyprus*, ed. Theodorus Papadopoullos (Nicosia, 1995), 4/1, pp. 259–332 [in Greek], reprinted in idem, *Les marchands italiens à Chypre* (Nicosie, 2007), pp. 13–18; Romeo Pavoni, "Liguri a Cipro tra i secoli XIII e XIV," in *Mediterraneo genovese. Storia e architettura*, *Atti del Convegno Internazionale, Genoa, 29 October 1992*, ed. Gabriella Airaldi and Paolo Stringa (Genoa, 1996), pp. 47–64; Michel Balard, "Les Génois à Famagouste (XIIIe–XVe siècles)," *Sources Travaux Historiques* 43–44 (1997), 85–93. See also David Jacoby, "The Rise of a New Emporium in the Eastern Mediterranean: Famagusta in the Late Thirteenth Century," *Μελέται και Υπομνήματα* 1 (1984), 145–79, reprinted in idem, *Studies on the Crusader States and on Venetian Expansion* (London, 1989), VIII; Nicholas Coureas, "Western Merchants and the Ports of Cyprus up to 1291," in *Cyprus and the Sea, Proceedings of the International Symposium, Nicosia, 25–26 September 1993*, ed. Vassos Karageorghis and Demetrios Michaelides (Nicosia, 1995), pp. 255–62; Catherine Otten-Froux, "Les Occidentaux dans les villes de province de l'Empire byzantine: le cas de Chypre (XIIe–XIIIe siècles)," in *Byzance et le monde extérieur. Contacts, relations, échanges*, *Actes de trois séances du XXe Congrès international des études byzantines, Paris, 19–25 août 2001*, ed. Michel Balard, Élisabeth Malamut, and Jean-Michel Spieser, Byzantina Sorbonensia 21 (Paris, 2005), pp. 27–44.

[2] *I Libri Iurium della Repubblica di Genova*, ed. Dino Puncuh (Genoa, 1996), I/2, docs. 348, 351. On these treaties, see most recently Laura Balletto, "Tra Genova e l'isola di Cipro nel Basso Medioevo," in *Genova. Una "porta" del Mediterraneo*, ed. Luciano Gallinari, 2 vols. (Cagliari, 2005), 1:32–33; and Nicholas Coureas, "Economy," in *Cyprus: Society and Culture 1191–1374*, ed. Angel Nicolaou-Konnari and Chris Schabel (Leiden and Boston, 2005), pp. 123–24.

Syrie.[3] Place names began to be specified around the middle of the century.[4] It was only when the Holy Land was lost by the Latins that Cyprus began to appear in sources frequently. In the so-called *terra Christianorum ultima* many westerners would establish themselves, mostly in Famagusta, in order to revive their activities.[5]

After 1258 Cypriot–Genoese relations began to steadily decline. In 1256 Genoa, Pisa, and Venice were engaged in the War of St. Sabas. During the conflict, Queen Plaisance, regent of the kingdom of Cyprus, chose to support the Venetians. This meant the start of a trend to foster Genoa's rivals which lasted throughout the following century: in the wars of 1294–99 and 1350–55 Cyprus favoured the Venetians.[6] However, just before the fall of Acre, in 1288, the Genoese merchant, diplomat, and admiral Benedetto Zaccaria obtained a new privilege from Henry II of Lusignan, which was rejected in 1292 by the Genoese government because – as Jacopo Doria wrote in his *Annales* – it was of no benefit to Genoa.[7] Business between Genoa and Cyprus, therefore, was taking a turn for the worse, so that a further treaty could not be concluded before 1329.[8] In 1299 the Genoese ambassadors Lanfranchino Spinola and Egidio di Quarto asked King Henry II for financial compensation for the damage Venetians caused the Genoese in his domain. The king refused, and the Genoese government proclaimed a trade blockade against the island. From 1 August all the Genoese had to leave the island, except for those

---

[3] See, for example, Otten-Froux, "Les Occidentaux," p. 42 (*Cipro et ripariam Syrie*); Laura Balletto, "Genova e la Sardegna nel secolo XIII," in *Saggi e documenti I* (Genoa, 1978), p. 106 (*per riveriam Syrie*).

[4] Geo Pistarino, "Miraggio di Terrasanta," in idem, *Genovesi d'Oriente*, pp. 70–71.

[5] Jacoby, "The Rise of a New Emporium," pp. 145–79; Balard, "Les Génois dans le royaume médiéval de Chypre," pp. 13–81; Coureas, "Economy," p. 128. How many of these were Franks and how many were *Suriens* (indigenous Levantine Christians) is unclear, see Peter W. Edbury, "Franks," in *Cyprus: Society and Culture*, pp. 98–100.

[6] Peter W. Edbury, "Cyprus and Genoa: The Origin of the War 1373–1374," in *Proceedings of the Second International Congress of Cypriot Studies*, ed. Theodorus Papadopoullos and Benedict Englezakis (Nicosia, 1986), pp. 109–26, reprinted in idem, *Kingdoms of the Crusaders. From Jerusalem to Cyprus* (Aldershot, 1999), XIV. On the War of St. Sabas see Antonio Musarra, *La guerra di San Saba* (Pisa, 2009). I am currently writing my Ph.D. thesis entitled "Prepotens Ianuensium Presidium. I genovesi, la crociata e la Terrasanta nella seconda metà del Duecento" (Università degli Studi di San Marino. Supervisor: Prof. Anthony Molho). Here I intend to reconsider the War of St. Sabas on the basis of some unpublished sources.

[7] Jacopo Doria, *Annales*, in *Annali genovesi di Caffaro e de' suoi continuatori*, ed. Cesare Imperiale di Sant'Angelo, 5 vols. (Genoa, 1929), 5:91 (*quia erat cum magnis expensis et detrimento comunis Ianue*); *I Libri Iurium della Repubblica di Genova*, ed. Eleonora Pallavicino (Genoa, 2002), I/8, doc. 1247. The agreement with the kingdom of Cyprus could undermine good relations with the Egyptian Sultanate: see Georg Caro, *Genova e la supremazia sul Mediterraneo (1257–1311)*, trans. Onorio Soardi, 2 vols. (Genoa, 1975), 2:129, 173 (= *Atti della Società Ligure di Storia Patria*, n.s., 14–15; originally published in 1895–99); Roberto S. Lopez, *Genova marinara nel Duecento. Benedetto Zaccaria ammiraglio e mercante* (Messina and Milan, 1933; repr. Florence, 1996), pp. 134–51, in particular pp. 143–45. In this refusal it is possible to see an attempt to better define and extend the rights granted to the Genoese by the charters of the first half of the century, in view of the importance that Cyprus would take after the fall of the Holy Land, see Balletto, "Tra Genova e l'isola di Cipro," pp. 37–39.

[8] *I* Libri Iurium, I/8, doc. 1265. In any case, the basic agreement remained the treaty of 1232.

who had resided there for a long time.[9] However, the Genoese presence in Cyprus in the late thirteenth and early fourteenth centuries was extensive enough. The gradual loss of the Latin coastal cities in Syria between 1263 and 1291 enhanced Famagusta's rise as an international trading port. The Genoese had held property there since 1218 but not a quarter with extra-territorial rights. Despite this, towards the end of the century – in particular after the fall to the Muslims of Marqab, Tripoli, and Botrun between 1285 and 1289 – many Genoese chose Famagusta as their residence.[10] According to David Jacoby and Nicholas Coureas, this choice may have resulted from the proximity of Famagusta both to Syria and to Lesser Armenia.[11] I think this is very plausible: Genoese merchants traded between Cyprus and Ayas – the chief commercial port of the Cilician kingdom – at least since the 1270s, as appears from the acts of Federico di Piazzalunga and Pietro di Bargone, both Genoese notaries resident there.[12]

The Genoese archives contain substantial notarial documentation relating to Genoese business in Cyprus and Lesser Armenia during these years. Most of the documents are written by the notary Lamberto di Sambuceto, who worked in Famagusta from around 1294 until 1307 as "notary and scribe of the commune of Genoa" or independently, using as his base some shops located on the water front, near the harbour and the Genoese loggia.[13] Lamberto's acts have been studied by

---

[9]   Caro, *Genova e la supremazia*, 2:295–99.

[10]   Additional Genoese refugees from Sidon, Tyre, and Tortosa reached Cyprus after their fall in 1291; the Genoese of Jubail only in 1300, see Jacoby, "The Rise of a New Emporium," pp. 156–61.

[11]   Jacoby, "The Rise of a New Emporium," pp. 153–54; Coureas, "Economy," p. 128.

[12]   Laura Balletto, *Notai Genovesi in Oltremare. Atti rogati a Laiazzo da Federico di Piazzalunga (1274) e Pietro di Bargone (1277, 1279). Le basi giuridiche* (Genova, 1989). See also Silvia Velle, "I Genovesi a Laiazzo sulla fine del Duecento," in *Saggi e Documenti III* (Genoa, 1983), pp. 79–115; Catherine Otten-Froux, "Ayas dans le dernier tiers du XIIIe siècle d'après les notaires génois," in *The Medieval Levant. Studies in Memory of Eliyahu Ashtor (1915–1984)*, ed. Benjamin Z. Kedar and Abraham L. Udovitch, Asian and African Studies 22 (Haifa, 1988), pp. 147–71; Pierre Racine, "L'Aïas dans la seconde moitié du XIIIe siècle," *Rivista di Bizantinistica* 2 (1992), 173–206; Catherine Otten-Froux, "Les échanges commerciaux," in *Le royaume arménien de Cilicie, XIIe–XIVe siècle*, ed. Claude Mutafian (Paris, 1993), pp. 119–26; Nicholas Coureas, "Lusignan Cyprus and Lesser Armenia, 1195–1375," Επετηρίδα του Κέντρου Επιστημονικών Ερευνών 21 (1995), 33–71; Catherine Otten-Froux, "Le commerce cilicien du XIIe ai XIVe siècle," in *Arménie entre Orient et Occident. Trois mille ans de civilisation, Catalogue de l'exposition de la Bibliothèque Nationale, 12 Juin–20 Octobre 1996*, ed. Raymond H. Kévorkian (Paris, 1996), pp. 134–38; eadem, "Les relations économiques entre Chypre et le royaume arménien de Cilicie d'après les actes notariés (1270–1320)," in *L'Arménie et Byzance. Histoire et Culture* (Paris, 1996), pp. 157–79; Laura Balletto, "Il commercio armeno-italiano (secoli XIII–XV)," in *Roma-Armenia*, ed. Claude Mutafian (Rome, 1999), pp. 184–88; David Jacoby, "Mercanti genovesi e veneziani e le loro merci nel Levante crociato," in *Genova, Venezia, il Levante nei secoli XII–XIV, Atti del Convegno Internazionale di Studi, Genova-Venezia, 10–14 marzo 2000*, ed. Gherardo Ortalli and Dino Puncuh, Atti della Società Ligure di Storia Patria, n.s., 41/1 (Genoa, 2001), pp. 240–41.

[13]   Cornelio Desimoni, "Actes passés à Famagouste de 1299 à 1301 par devant le notaire génois Lamberto di Sambuceto," *AOL* 2 (1884), 2–120, and *ROL* 1 (1893), 58–139, 275–312, 321–53; Laura Balletto, "Da Chiavari al Levante ed al Mar Nero nei secoli XIII e XIV," in *Atti del Convegno Storico Internazionale per l'VIII Centenario dell'urbanizzazione di Chiavari, Chiavari, 8–10 novembre 1978* (Chiavari, 1980), pp. 261–98; Valeria Polonio, *Notai genovesi in Oltremare. Atti rogati a Cipro da Lamberto di Sambuceto (3 luglio 1300–3 agosto 1301)* (Genoa, 1982); Romeo Pavoni, *Notai genovesi*

several scholars.[14] There are, however, other notarial acts, contained in *cartolare 147/I* (Archivio di Stato di Genova, *Notai antichi*, 147/I, *cartolare* attributed to Andreolo di Lanerio et al.), that have not yet been published. They were written by the notary Bonaiuncta di Savio between 2 December 1294 and 6 June 1295, and relate the voyage of Tedisio Doria, an important member of the Genoese nobility (he was the son of Lamba Doria, who would win the battle of Curzola against the Venetians in 1298),[15] to Cyprus and Lesser Armenia. Since documents are not catalogued by place in the inventory of *Cartolari notarili genovesi*, these acts have gone virtually unnoticed.[16]

---

in Oltremare. Atti rogati a Cipro da Lamberto di Sambuceto (6 luglio–27 ottobre 1301) (Genoa, 1982); Michel Balard, *Notai genovesi in Oltremare. Atti rogati a Cipro da Lamberto di Sambuceto (11 ottobre 1296–23 giugno 1299)* (Genoa, 1983); idem, *Notai genovesi in Oltremare. Atti rogati a Cipro da Lamberto di Sambuceto (31 marzo 1304–19 luglio 1305, 4 gennaio–12 luglio 1307) e da Giovanni de Rocha (3 agosto 1308–14 marzo 1310)* (Genoa, 1984); Romeo Pavoni, *Notai genovesi in Oltremare. Atti rogati a Cipro da Lamberto di Sambuceto (gennaio–agosto 1302)* (Genoa, 1987). The last remaining archival series of Lamberto will be published by Michel Balard.

[14] See in particular Michel Balard, "Génois et Pisans en Orient (fin du XIIIe–début du XIVe siècles)," in *Genova, Pisa e il Mediterraneo tra Due e Trecento: per il VII Centenario della battaglia della Meloria, Genova, 24–27 ottobre 1984*, Atti della Società Ligure di Storia Patria, n.s., 24/2 (Genoa, 1984), pp. 181–208, reprinted in idem, *La mer Noire et la Romanie génoise* (London, 1989), IV; idem, "I Piacentini in Cipro nel Trecento," in *Precursori di Colombo. Mercanti e banchieri piacentini nel mondo durante il medioevo, Atti del Convegno Internazionale di Studi, Piacenza, 10–12 settembre 1992* (Bologna, 1994), pp. 179–210; Peter W. Edbury, "Famagusta in 1300," in *Cyprus and the Crusades*, ed. Nicholas Coureas and Jonathan Riley-Smith (Nicosia, 1995), pp. 337–53; Nicholas Coureas, "The Genoese and the Latin Church of Cyprus, 1250–1320," in *Oriente e Occidente tra Medioevo ed Età Moderna. Studi in onore di Geo Pistarino*, ed. Laura Balletto (Acqui Terme, 1997), pp. 165–75; Catherine Otten-Froux, "Riches et pauvres en ville: le cas de Famagouste (XIIIe–XVe siècle)," in *Ricchi e poveri nella società dell'Oriente grecolatino*, ed. Chryssa Maltezou (Venice, 1998), pp. 331–49; Nicholas Coureas, "Commercial Relations between Cyprus and Florence in the Fourteenth Century," Επετηρίδα του Κέντρου Επιστημονικών Ερευνών 25 (1999), 51–68; idem, "Commercial Relations between Lusignan Cyprus and Venetian Crete in the Period 1300–1362," Επετηρίδα του Κέντρου Επιστημονικών Ερευνών 26 (2000), 141–55; idem, "Cyprus and Ragusa (Dubrovnik), 1280–1450," *Mediterranean Historical Review* 17/2 (2002), 1–13; idem, "Commercial Relations between Cyprus and Chios, 1300–1480," Επετηρίδα του Κέντρου Επιστημονικών Ερευνών 29 (2003), 51–68; Catherine Otten-Froux, "Chypre, un des centres du commerce catalan en Orient," in *Els Catalans a la Mediterrània oriental a l'edat mitjana, Jornadas Científiques de l'Institut d'Estudis Catalans, Secció Històrico-arqueològica, Barcelona, 16–17 novembre 2000*, ed. Maria Teresa Ferrer i Mallol (Barcelona, 2003), pp. 129–53; Nicholas Coureas, "Commercial Relations between Cyprus and the Genoese Colonies of Pera and Caffa, 1297–1459," Επετηρίδα του Κέντρου Επιστημονικών Ερευνών 30 (2004), 153–69; idem, "I mercanti genovesi ed i loro traffici a Nicosia dal marzo all'ottobre del 1297," in *Alle origini di Alessandria. Dal Gonfalone del Comune nella Lega Lombarda all'Aquila imperiale degli Staufen* (Alessandria, 2005), pp. 189–201; Steven A. Epstein, *Purity Lost: Transgressing Boundaries in the Eastern Mediterranean, 1000–1400* (Baltimore, 2006), pp. 81–90; Nicholas Coureas, "The Structure and Content of the Notarial Deeds of Lamberto di Sambuceto and Giovanni da Rocha," in *Diplomatics in the Eastern Mediterranean 1000–1500. Aspects of Cross-Cultural Communication*, ed. Alexander D. Beihammer, Maria G. Parani and Christopher D. Schabel (Leiden and Boston, 2008), pp. 223–34.

[15] Caro, *Genova e la supremazia sul Mediterraneo*, 2:230.

[16] Giorgio Costamagna, *Cartolari notarili genovesi (1–149). Inventario*, 2 vols. (Rome, 1956–61). Costamagna transcribed the name of the notary as *Bonaventura*. The name is in fact *Bonaiuncta*, as appears from fols. 15r, 16v, 26v.

The Manuscript

The *cartolare 147/I* consists of 150 folios (r–v) and contains acts by three notaries. The part attributed to Bonaiuncta di Savio is from fol. 1r to fol. 26v (2 December 1294 – 10 February 1302). The other folios are written by the notaries Giovanni di Avundo (fols. 27r–68r.) and Enrico di Recco (fols. 68r–150v) and contain various models of acts from 1294 to 1305.[17] Bonaiuncta's *quinternus* lacks a bookcover: the first act, at fol. 1r, lacks its beginning. However, his name appears in some acts written in Cyprus (fol. 15r), in a list of expenses made by him on the back of the *quinternus* (fol. 26r), and in a draft of his will composed at an unspecified time (fols. 16v–17r). The pagination of the folios is modern and each folio measures 240 × 325 mm; sheets that make up the *quinternus* are therefore of 480 × 650 mm. From page to page, measurements change by a few millimetres due to the erosion of the edges. However, Bonaiuncta's *quinternus* is generally well preserved and the pages are in good condition. The paper is thick, coarse and not filigree, as commonly used by medieval Genoese notaries.[18] Bonaiuncta's handwriting is the common Genoese notarial one in use during the thirteenth century. The ink is red-brown, sometimes black. In some cases it has faded so much that it was necessary to resort to ultraviolet light.

Bonaiuncta's acts cover a number of issues: loan contracts, wills, mandatory contracts, sales; yet economic contracts are the most important, and most of them are loan agreements. The notary was very close to the Doria family; several documents (not published here) refer to Tedisio Doria and his father Lamba. Some are written in Pegli, near Genoa, *in platea domus Thedixii Aurie*.[19] There are also some acts that have only been started, some without *invocatio* or with only the first words of the text. Bonaiuncta may have intended to complete them later, as he left a blank space, but he did not proceed to do so (fols. 5v, 9r, 10v). He did not always employ the whole page: he wrote two or three acts on each page and these do not always follow a chronological order. Folios 7v, 11r, 15v, 16r, 17v, 18r, 20v, 22r are completely blank (between fols. 8v and 9r there is a blank, non-numerated folio r–v); folios 9r, 10v, and 19v are almost entirely blank: there the notary began to draft an act, but did not complete; all other folios, except 1r–3v, 4v, 6r, 12v, 13v, 14v–15r, 21v, 22v, are only partially blank and contain completed, uncompleted and just started acts. For example, in doc. 22 we only read: *In nomine Domini, amen. Ego Petrus Abracinus confiteor tibi Iohannino de Savio me a te habuisse et recepisse mutuo gratis et amore libras 2000 ianuinorum ****.

---

[17] The presence in the *cartolare 147/I* of acts written by several notaries results from the bombardment of Genoa by a French fleet in May 1684, as punishment for Genoese support of Spain. The notarial archives were partly destroyed and the books were badly reassembled, see Giorgio Costamagna, *Il notaio a Genova tra prestigio e potere* (Rome, 1970), pp. 240–42.

[18] See Charles-Moïse Briquet, "Les papiers des Archives de Gênes et leurs filigranes," *Atti della Società Ligure di Storia Patria* 19 (1883), 292–97.

[19] AS GE, *Notai antichi*, 147/1, *cartolare* attributed to Andreolo di Lanerio et al., fols. 22v–25r.

The acts concerning Tedisio's voyage appear from fol. 1r to fol. 6r. They were written over a period of seven months. Bonaiuncta drew up the acts in different ports in which the galley docked. They are not sufficient in number in order to accurately track the voyage; however, many places reached by Tedisio's galley can be identified, including Messina, Reggio (and Capo dell'Armi), Kefalonia, Zakyntos, Ayas, Famagusta, Paphos and the *Montana Nigra*. The *insula Tarami* remains unidentified.[20] Documents are arranged chronologically: December: 5 acts; January: 1 act; February: no act; March: 4 acts; April: 4 acts; May: 3 acts; June: 4 acts. Sometimes the notary wrote several documents on the same day: 5 December 1294; 24 December 1294; 1 April 1295; 8 May 1295; 4 June 1295.

The notary uses the Genoese dating system: year of the Nativity, Genoese *indictio*, day of the month, time of day (*circa primam*; *ante*, *circa* or *post terciam*; *inter terciam et nonam*; *circa* or *post nonam*; *circa* or *post vesperas*; *post complectorium*); however, he does not mention any day of the week, or religious holidays.[21] In borders, internal or external, there is often an *F* (= *Factum*): this shows that the notary has issued a certified copy to the contractors (*mundum*) (docs. 3–13, 16, 17, 20). Document 19 was deleted with three pen strokes, indicating that the contract was cancelled by the contracting parties. However, I do not think that the notary always followed the commonly used triple editing system (*notula, cartolare, mundum*):[22] there are indeed many erasures, corrections and additions, especially in the part not edited here. Perhaps the notary sometimes wrote directly on *cartolare* without any previous *notula*; ever so often he used *formule ceterate* (fols. 9v, 1v, 11v–12v, 14r, 19r–20r, 21r, 24r–25r). He usually corrected or annulled the previous text with a pen stroke. The correction is generally inserted above the text. In one case additions appear in the external margin, with signs in reference to the text (doc. 13).[23]

The Text

Tedisio Doria's voyage probably began in Genoa in autumn, but we can follow it only from Messina. It is not at all strange to see a Genoese galley travelling by sea in winter. At the end of the thirteenth century the technological development and more sophisticated methods of navigation allowed risky voyages. This was, however,

---

[20] The reading of this word is uncertain. It may be also *Tarceni* or *Tarconi*. In medieval Genoese, *tarconus* meant "a shield," see Sergio Aprosio, *Vocabolario ligure storico-bibliografico*, 4 vols. (Saona, 2002), 1/2, p. 388.

[21] It is not at all strange to see a Genoese notary continuing the practice of noting the hour of the day even when so far from home. This was a common practice for all Genoese notaries since the early decades of the thirteenth century, see Costamagna, *Il notaio a Genova*, pp. 53–54.

[22] See Giorgio Costamagna, "*La triplice redazione dell'instrumentum genovese*," in idem, *Studi di paleografia e diplomatica* (Rome, 1972), pp. 237–302.

[23] Bonaiuncta is not a paragon of grammatical correctness. See docs. 1¹; 2¹; 2³; 3¹; 3²; 3³; 3⁴; 5²; 5³; 8¹; 8²; 9³; 9⁶; 9⁷; 12²; 13¹; 13³; 14²; 15¹; 15³; 15⁴; 16²; 19¹; 19²; 19³; 19⁶.

not the rule: generally there was a marked decrease in navigation from December to February and the majority of shipping sailed between spring and autumn.[24] In any case, Tedisio's galley moved for short distances from one port to another, and this could reduce the risk to passengers on board. Taking into account only the notarial acts drawn up on the galley, it is possible to obtain a partial list of these: Iacopo Grata di Voltri, Alamanino Brezolo di Voltri, Avenancio di Bulgaro, Oberto Pecholo, Palmerio Panzano, Galerino Becherio, Cechino *de Comis*, Pietro Guercio di Asti, Obertino di Portovenere, Oberto Bonaventura, Andrea Scarera, Ianino di Ancona, Thodanis di Romania, Iacopo *barberius* di Napoli, Iohannino Spaerio, Guglielmo Sarico di San Romolo, Iacopo Percenza di San Nazario, Raimondino di San Nazario, Bernardino Torsello, Guirardo Rubeo di Milano, Enrico *Alamanus*, Pietro Belbexino, Odino di Mondevich, Guglielmo Magdalena, Scireto di San Matteo, Obertino, figlio di Aldebrando di Maono, Bonino di Famagosta, Guglielmo, figlio di Vivaldo De Mari, Vignueleo di Marora, Guglielmo Sanco di San Romolo, Benedetto di Vexagna. Not all were merchants. Most were presumably members of the crew: among the notarial acts there are some petty loans, probably effected to meet the day-to-day requirements (see, for example, docs. 4, 5, 7). We have some information on a few of these people due to the acts of Lamberto di Sambuceto.

In Messina the galley was probably docked in the port. On 2 December 1294, the notary wrote one act *prope ecclesiam Sancti Salvatoris, in galea dicti Thedicii vocata Dominica*, probably an augurative name ("the Lord's ship"), although very particular and unusual.[25] It was evening; Mateino Vivaldi and Nicolò Spoleto were witnesses (doc. 1): the presence on Tedisio's galley of a member of the Vivaldi family (Mateino was the son of Gabriele, brother of Ugolino and Vadino Vivaldi) is of some importance. As is widely known, in 1291 Tedisio financed the expedition of the Vivaldi brothers *ad partes Indie*. Tedisio's uncle, Jacopo Doria, reports about the journey in his *Annales*. In May 1291 the Vivaldis headed towards the Atlantic in two galleys: they were never seen again, but at the time of Tedisio's voyage to the Levant in 1294–95 the two brothers were certainly alive in memory.[26]

The *Dominica* approached Calabria only a couple of days later. On 5 December, Iacopo Grata, from Voltri, a village west of Genoa, promises to pay all debts to Tedisio Doria. The amount is not specified. The notary refers only: *omne id et totum quod inveneris in cartularis tuis* (doc. 2). Other inhabitants of Voltri are mentioned in Bonaiuncta's acts, identified as originating *de Vulturo*: in addition to Iacopo Grata, these are Oberto Piloto (doc. 8), Oberto Bracho (doc. 17), Musso Moise

---

[24] See Michel Balard, *La Romanie Génoise (XII–début du XV siècle)*, 2 vols. (Rome and Genoa, 1978), 1:578–80. See also John Pryor, *Geography, Technology and War: Studies in the Maritime History of the Mediterranean, 649–1571* (Cambridge, 1988), pp. 88–89.

[25] It does not appear in the lists of Genoese ships published by Giovanna Petti Balbi, "I nomi di nave a Genova nei secoli XII e XIII," in *Miscellanea di storia ligure in memoria di Giorgio Falco* (Genoa, 1966), pp. 65–86, and by Benjamin Z. Kedar, *Merchants in Crisis: Genoese and Venetian Men of Affairs and the Fourteenth-Century Depression* (New Haven, 1976), pp. 142–55.

[26] According to Jacopo Doria, their voyage *mirabile fuit sed etiam non solum videntibus sed etiam audientibus*, see Jacopo Doria, *Annales*, 5:124.

(doc. 18), Nicolò Basso (doc. 21). I do not think they were part of the *Dominica*'s crew: all acts in which they are mentioned are from Famagusta. Probably they are Ligurian immigrants in Cyprus. The presence of *Riviera* inhabitants on the island is well documented by the notarial acts of Lamberto di Sambuceto and Giovanni *de Rocha*: according to calculations made by Michel Balard and Romeo Pavoni on the basis of notarial acts written between 11 October 1296 and 4 January 1307, Ligurians from the western *Riviera* were in the majority in Cyprus. Concerning the Voltri *Podesteria*, which included Voltri, Arenzano, Cogoleto, Sestri, Pegli, and Fegino (now incorporated in Genoa), the *Voltresi* were in first place.[27]

The act in which Iacopo Grata is mentioned was written *post nonam*. *Post vesperas* the *Dominica* was certainly at sea. Near Capo dell'Armi, the southern tip of the Italian Apennines, Tedisio asked for the services of Bonaiuncta: he appointed Palmerio Panzano, probably a member of the crew, as his attorney for settling his business. Palmerio belongs to a family who were well established in Cyprus and Ayas. In 1232 a relative named Bonifacio Panzano, admiral of a fleet, was sent by the Genoese government to Cyprus, in support of John of Ibelin, to fight against the forces of Frederick II.[28] From some acts of Lamberto di Sambuceto we also know that another relative, Tommaso Panzano, was, some time before 23 February 1301, the *potestas Ianuensium in partibus Cismarinis*. He was in charge of defending the interests of the Genoese in the Levant, particularly against Pisans and Venetians; to preside over the courts of justice for litigation among fellow citizens; to administer the Commune's properties; to be present at the drafting of commercial documents or wills.[29]

We cannot figure out when the *Dominica* began the sea route to the East. What is certain is that Tedisio was in Kefalonia by Christmas 1294. *Post complectorium* the notary Bonaiuncta wrote two petty loan agreements (docs. 4, 5). Leaving the port of Kefalonia, the *Dominica* arrived at Zakynthos around 27 December. At sea, Iacopo Percenza di San Nazario is said to have received in loan from Pietro Guercio di Asti of 5.5 white bezants of Cyprus, with a promise of repayment within a month (doc. 6). This is the highest amount of loan agreements: they range, in fact,

---

[27] Michel Balard, "La popolazione di Famagosta all'inizio del secolo XIV," in *La storia dei Genovesi IV* (Genoa, 1984), pp. 28–32; Romeo Pavoni, "Liguri a Cipro," pp. 56–57.

[28] *Annales*, 3:63–64.

[29] Polonio, *Notai genovesi in Oltremare. Atti rogati a Cipro da Lamberto di Sambuceto (3 luglio 1300–3 agosto 1301)*, docs. 236, 237, 242, 243, 260, 298, 300, 384; Pavoni, *Notai genovesi in Oltremare. Atti rogati a Cipro da Lamberto di Sambuceto (6 luglio–27 ottobre 1301)*, doc. 177; Balard, *Notai genovesi in Oltremare. Atti rogati a Cipro da Lamberto di Sambuceto (11 ottobre 1296–23 giugno 1299)*, doc. 90; idem, *Notai genovesi in Oltremare. Atti rogati a Cipro da Lamberto di Sambuceto (31 marzo 1304–19 luglio 1305, 4 gennaio–12 luglio 1307)*, doc. 31. See also Jacoby, "The Rise of a New Emporium," pp. 163–64. On functions of Genoese *consules* and *potestates* in the Levant, see Michel Balard, "Consoli d'oltremare (secc. XII–XV)," in *Comunità forestiere e nell'Europa dei secoli XIII–XVI*, ed. Giovanna Petti Balbi (Naples, 2002), pp. 83–94. Also surviving are a will and an inventory of goods of a man named Baliano Panzano dated 1277, see Balletto, *Notai genovesi in Oltremare. Atti rogati a Laiazzo da Federico di Piazalunga (1274) e Pietro di Bargone (1277, 1279)*, docs. 2, 4, 14; Otten-Froux, "L'Aïas dans le dernier tiers du XIIIe siècle," p. 170.

from a minimum of L 1, s. 1 of Genoa to maximum of 5.5 bezants of Cyprus. The interest for the money is never made explicit: probably it was included in the bill of payment.[30] After having passed, on 7 December, the unidentified *insula Tarami*, the ship's traces are lost. We find it again in Famagusta, on 10 March 1295, about to leave for Ayas, where Oberto di Bobiano, *de societate Scotorum*, by his own name and company, is said to have received from Oberto Pecholo 10,300 new Armenian *daremos*, with a promise of repayment s. 1, d. 1 of Genoa for each *daremus*, for a total of L 557, s. 18, d. 4 of Genoa, within fifteen days after submission of the document in Genoa to a shareholder of that company (doc. 9). Oberto di Bobiano and Oberto Pecholo are quite well known. The first was the agent of the bank of Scotti, an important Piacenzan company working in the Levant.[31] The second is an author of many money transactions. As we learn from the last edited act (doc. 23), he was a notary. On 26 April 1295, in Cyprus, *prope Salinas* (Larnaka), Tedisio Doria appointed Oberto Pecholo as his attorney for a year (doc. 13). This is interesting because on 8 April 1297, as we can read in an act by Lamberto di Sambuceto, Oberto Pecholo di Samo, *notarius*, on behalf of Tedisio Doria and Opezzino Ricio, receives from Lambertino, *habitator Nicossie*, the receipt for the payment of 60 white bezants: Oberto was therefore a reference man for Tedisio Doria in the Levant.[32]

The day after leaving Ayas, on 17 March 1295, the notary wrote an act *in Syria, in loco ubi dicitur Caroso*, near the *Montana Nigra* (the Amanus Mountains or Nur-Dağları), a ridge north of Antioch mentioned by Gerard of Nazareth, William of Tyre, and James of Vitry.[33] The place called *Caroso* is probably identifiable with the valley of the Karasu Çayı, a stream which flows into the ʿĀṣī river (although in that period it flowed into the lake of Antioch, in the depression known as al-ʿUmq), situated between the Amanus Mountains and the Kurd Dağ.[34] Here Francesco Nusia di Sagona is said to have received in loan from Iacopo Cluseterio di Sagona *libras duas et soldos decem ianuinorum*, with a promise to repay the same amount within two months (doc. 10). The loan agreement is made for a small sum: certainly

[30] See Laura Balletto, "Mutui ad interesse dichiarato nel traffico tra Genova e la Sardegna (sec. XIII)," *Archivio Storico Sardo di Sassari* 3/3 (1977), 99–128; Giovanna Petti Balbi, "Fenomeni usurai e restituzioni: la situazione ligure (secoli XII–XIV)," *Archivio Storico Italiano* 169/2 (2011), 199–220. According to some acts by Lamberto di Sambuceto, 1 bezant of Cyprus = 3 s., 6 d. of Genoa; see Balard, *Notai genovesi in Oltremare. Atti rogati a Cipro da Lamberto di Sambuceto (11 ottobre 1296–23 giugno 1299)*, docs. 135, 138, 158. See also Cornelio Desimoni, "Observations sur les monnaies, les poids et les mesures cités dans les actes du notaire gênois Lamberto di Sambuceto," *ROL* 3 (1895), 1–25.

[31] See Pierre Racine, "Marchands placentins à l'Aïas à la fin du XIII siècle," *Byzantinische Forschungen* 4 (1972), 195–205.

[32] Balard, *Notai genovesi in Oltremare. Atti rogati a Cipro da Lamberto di Sambuceto (11 ottobre 1296–23 giugno 1299)*, doc. 42.

[33] Gerard of Nazareth, "De conversacione virorum Dei in Terra Sancta morantium," ed. B. Z. Kedar, *Dumbarton Oaks Papers* 37 (1983), 73–74; WT 4.10, 15.14, pp. 247, 694; James of Vitry, *Historia Hierosolimitana*, in *Gesta Dei per Francos*, ed. Jacques Bongars (Hanau, 1611), 1:1069.

[34] See Angus D. Stewart, *The Armenian Kingdom and the Mamluks. War and Diplomacy during the Reign of Hetʿum II, 1289–1307* (Leiden, 2001), p. 49, n. 21.

it is not an evidence of trade with this area. Similarly, the mention of the *Montana Nigra* and the use of the term "Syria" do not mean trade with the Muslims: at that time the entire area had not yet fallen to the Muslims but was part of the kingdom of Lesser Armenia.[35]

Three days later the galley was back at sea. A man named Obertino, son of Adebrando di Maono, fell ill: on 20 March, *in mari, per miliaria XXXX, in galea vocata Dominica que est Tedicii Aurie*, he made a will (doc. 15).[36] On 1 April, the *Dominica* was in Paphos, where Ricobono di Diano and Obertino, son of Giovanni di Corsio, made loans (docs. 11, 12). From 26 April to 6 May the crew was in Famagusta, where Bonaiuncta drew up several notarial acts *in portu in galea Thedicii Aurie, ante* or *apud logiam Ianuensium; in domo hospitalis; in domo in qua habitat Iacobus taliator de Placentia; in domo in qua habitat societas Florentinorum* (docs. 13, 14, 16, 17, 18, 19, 20, 21, 23). Of some importance among these are the acts concerning Alegrino Fatinanti (doc. 14) and Tedisio Zaccaria (doc. 19), the latter through his servant Rizardo di Leone. Like Oberto Pecholo, Alegrino is also mentioned in many acts from the same period. According to an act by Lamberto di Sambuceto, we learn that he was *notarius, dragomanus* and *habitator Famaguste*.[37] On 28 April 1295 he gives *inter vivos* a white slave named Brancha to Oberto Pecholo (doc. 14).[38] Tedisio Zaccaria is probably the one who, in 1307, after the death of Benedetto Zaccaria, in disagreement with his cousin Benedetto II, hired the Catalan Company to occupy Phocea. But the occupation was short-lived: the Company was not able to defend its conquest, as they were too exposed to Turkish pirates.[39]

We do not know when Tedisio's voyage ended. Undoubtedly he returned to Cyprus between 1300 and 1301: the *cartolare 147/I* contains other notarial acts

---

[35]   Ibid., pp. 71–128.

[36]   Bonaiuncta adds in the text the words "in ialex," with a generic abbreviative mark. I was not able to solve this abbreviation. Probably he refers to *Alexandretta*, but this is just a hypothesis.

[37]   Polonio, *Notai genovesi in Oltremare. Atti rogati a Cipro da Lamberto di Sambuceto (3 luglio 1300–3 agosto 1301)*, docs. 25, 154, 289, 294, 349, 357, 358, 369, 375, 379; Pavoni, *Notai genovesi in Oltremare. Atti rogati a Cipro da Lamberto di Sambuceto (6 luglio–27 ottobre 1301)*, docs. 40, 51, 52, 71, 72, 106, 118, 119, 158a; Balard, *Notai genovesi in Oltremare. Atti rogati a Cipro da Lamberto di Sambuceto (11 ottobre 1296–23 giugno 1299)*, docs. 3, 16, 19, 154, 155, 156; idem, *Notai genovesi in Oltremare. Atti rogati a Cipro da Lamberto di Sambuceto (31 marzo 1304–19 luglio 1305, 4 gennaio–12 luglio 1307)*, docs. (I) 20, 29, 35, 68, 90, 99, 100, 175; (II) 5, 6, 18, 20, 68; Pavoni, *Notai genovesi in Oltremare. Atti rogati a Cipro da Lamberto di Sambuceto (gennaio–agosto 1302)* docs. 56, 58, 60, 65, 90, 91, 92, 117, 145, 176, 177, 198, 199, 199, 281.

[38]   On slaves in Cyprus see Angel Nicolaou-Konnari, "Greeks," in *Cyprus Society and Culture*, pp. 37–39.

[39]   At the bottom of this act (doc. 19) there is an order of cancellation by the contractor: *Cassa et vacua et nullius valoris de voluntate contrahencium in presenxia Oberti Pecholi et Guillelmi Balbi de Cellis eodem millesimo, die VI iunii, et inde cassa.* In the same paper, further down, there are these words: *Passio Domini nostri Ihesu Christi secundum Mateum. / In iillo tempore dissi Ihesu / discipulis suis satis quia pos<t> biduum pass<cha>* ***, partially the same as Matt. 26.1–2. It is not uncommon to find in the Genoese notarial cartularies such a note (but also recipes, spells, lists of expenditure, and so on).

written in Malvaxia, Ayas and Famagusta. These documents refer sometimes to acts of Lamberto di Sambuceto and provjde some information about the notary Bonaiuncta himself. He was ill during his voyages, or when he came back to Genoa: in fols. 16v–17r there is the draft of his will. The *quinternus* ends also with the list of expenses he had incurred, maybe in the Levant (fol. 26v).[40] The voyage of 1294–95 shows the reality of trading between Cyprus and Lesser Armenia in the aftermath of the fall of the crusader states. The peculiarity of these documents is that they are the oldest surviving regarding the presence of the Genoese in this area after 1291, preceding as they do the acts of Lamberto di Sambuceto. Although in 1290 the Genoese signed a pact with the sultan Qalawun according to which they could trade freely in the sultan's domains, this voyage can not be considered a medium-term consequence of this treaty: the area covered by Tedisio's galley lies mostly between Famagusta, Ayas, and the Gulf of *Alexandretta*.[41] No doubt at the end of the thirteenth century there were some business contacts between Cyprus and Muslim Syria: sometimes Lamberto di Sambuceto deliberately does not mention the destination of the investment, or gives it in a very general manner, probably to conceal trade with the Muslims, this being forbidden to western merchants under the terms of the papal embargo promulgated in 1292 and lasting until 1344.[42] Only at the beginning of the fourteenth century does trade between Genoa, the Genoese in Cyprus, and Muslim Syria seem to have been restored, albeit far less frequent than in the previous century.[43] In the same period, some important

---

[40]   See AS GE, *Notai antichi*, 147/1, fols. 14r–15r; 16v–17r; 21r; 26v. I intend to deal with these issues elsewhere. On the notary, see also Polonio, *Notai genovesi in Oltremare. Atti rogati a Cipro da Lamberto di Sambuceto (3 luglio 1300–3 agosto 1301)*, docs. 190, 235, 237, 253, 284, 300, 303, 305, 310, 311, 320, 325, 330, 341 (in the latter document Bonaiuncta is identified as the *scriba galee domini potestatis*); Pavoni, *Notai genovesi in Oltremare. Atti rogati a Cipro da Lamberto di Sambuceto (6 luglio–27 ottobre 1301)*, docs. 63, 170, 171, 183; Balard, *Notai genovesi in Oltremare. Atti rogati a Cipro da Lamberto di Sambuceto (11 ottobre 1296–23 giugno 1299)*, docs. 57, 117, 118, 137.

[41]   *Et precepit dominus Soldanus quod pro suo itu in exercitu in Siria vel in alia parte, nec per suos messaticos vel mercatores navigantes vel per aliquam aliam causam, non possit detineri vel impediri aliqua navis nec galea, nec alia ligna ullomodo non possint esse detenti*, see Belgrano, "Trattato del Sultano d'Egitto," p. 168. For a summary see Steven A. Epstein, *Genoa and the Genoese, 958–1528* (Chapel Hill, NC and London, 1996), p. 180.

[42]   See, for example, Desimoni, "Actes passés à Famagouste de 1299 à 1301," *AOL*, docs. 109, 143, 158, and *ROL*, docs. 391, 470, 474, 479, 487; Polonio, *Notai genovesi in Oltremare. Atti rogati a Cipro da Lamberto di Sambuceto (3 luglio 1300–3 agosto 1301)*, docs. 116, 148, 246, 247, 276, 307, 413; Pavoni, *Notai genovesi in Oltremare. Atti rogati a Cipro da Lamberto di Sambuceto (6 luglio–27 ottobre 1301)*, doc. 18; Balard, *Notai genovesi in Oltremare. Atti rogati a Cipro da Lamberto di Sambuceto (11 ottobre 1296–23 giugno 1299)*, doc. 149. See also Eliyahu Ashtor, *Levant Trade in the Later Middle Ages* (Princeton, 1983), pp. 17–22, 66–69.

[43]   For example, the Genoese Filippo di Nigro, owner of a galley, working in Famagusta, receives from Syria spices in 1300, see Pistarino, "Dal declino sul Mare di Levante," in idem, *Genovesi d'Oriente*, p. 116. Nicolò Fossatello, *draperius*, and Belengerio Lercario concluded a contract on 1 April 1312, according to which the first receives a sum of money from the second, promising to give him in exchange 2,700 Cypriot silver bezants when the galley of Manuel Maniavacha will reach *ad dictum locum Cipro, videlicet ad illum locum Sirie in quo dicta galea fecerit portum pro exonerando*, see Renée Doehaerd, *Les relations commerciales entre Gênes, la Belgique et l'Outremont, d'après les Archives*

Genoese families – among them the De Mari, Della Volta and De Camilla – began to promote commerce between Cyprus and the Genoese colonies of Pera and Caffa.[44] Slowly, Genoese trades moved further north, to the Black Sea, which was to become the main goal of the Genoese merchants in the fourteenth century.

---

notariales génoises aux XIIIe et XIVe siècles, 3 vols. (Brussels and Rome, 1941), vol. 3, doc. 1753. Nicolò Fossatello reached Syria in 1312 with lengths of scarlet cloth, and Iacopo Negrono did the same with lengths of French cloth in 1313, as well as Barnaba Benno, Raffael Fossatello, and Petrino di San Lorenzo in 1314, see Eliyahu Ashtor, *Levant Trade*, pp. 29–30; Doehaerd, *Les relations commerciales*, docs. 1809, 1813, 1820, 1831, 1847; Pistarino, "Dal declino sul Mare di Levante," pp. 116–17.

[44] An act of Lamberto di Sambuceto of 1 May 1297 alludes to a trading venture to Lesser Armenia, Sebasteia and Tabriz, see Balard, *Notai genovesi in Oltremare. Atti rogati a Cipro da Lamberto di Sambuceto (11 ottobre 1296–23 giugno 1299)*, doc. 94. See also Coureas, "Commercial Relations between Cyprus and the Genoese Colonies of Pera and Caffa," pp. 153–69; idem, "Economy," p. 154.

Transcription of AS GE, *Notai antichi*, 147/I, *cartolare* attributed to Andreolo di Lanerio et al., acts of Bonaiuncta *de Savio*, fols. 1r–6r

Brackets indicate deficiencies or the notary's omissions. Punctuation is modern. The notary's critical mistakes and oversights are pointed out.

1

2 December 1294, in the galley, in the port of Messina

The document has no beginning.

[…] instrumenta dicti debiti tibi do ad incidendum, volens quod sint cassa et irrito[1] et nullius valoris. Actum in portu Mesane, in galea dicti Thedicii vocata Dominica, prope ecclesiam Sancti Salvatoris, anno dominice nativitatis M°CC°LXXXXIIII, die II decembris, indictione VIIª, post vesperas. Testes Mateinus de Vivaldo et Nicolaus Spoletus.

[1] irrito: *sic*

2

5 December 1294, in Calabria, near Reggio

Iacopo Grata di Voltri promises to pay all debts to Tedisio Doria by 1 June 1295. Guarantor is Alamanino Brezolo.

In nomine Domini, amen. Ego Iacobus Grata de Vulturo promitto et convenio tibi Thedicio Aurie quod dabo et solvam et integrum restituam omne id et totum quod inveneris in cartulariis tuis me tibi dare debere, renuncians exceptioni et iuri et demum omni auxilio legum contra que venire possem, quos[1] tibi aud tuo certo noncio per me vel meum noncium omne quod tibi dare debuero dare et solvere promitto hinc ad kalendas iunii proximas, alioquin si contra fecero penam dupli dicte quantitatis cum restitucione dampnorum et expensarum tibi stipulanti promitto, et proinde omnia bona mea habita et habenda tibi pignori obligo. Insuper[2] Alamaninus Brezolus prebe[3] Vulturi de predictis omnibus observandis versus te dictum Thedicium principaliter intercessit et se et sua obligavit, abrenuncians iuri de principali, beneficio nove constitucionis de duobus reis et omni iuri. Actum in Calabria, prope Regium, anno dominice nativitatis M°CC°LXXXXIIII, die quinta decembris, indictione VIIª, post nonam. Testes Avenancius de Bulgaro et Obertus Pecholus.

[1] quos: *sic*   [2] *follows* ego *crossed out*   [3] prebe: *sic*

3

5 December 1294, in the galley, in Calabria, near Capo dell'Armi

Tedisio Doria, emancipated son of Lamba Doria, appointed as attorney Palmerio Panzano
for settling his business.

In the inner margin: "F[actum]."

In nomine Domini, amen. Ego Thedixius Auria, filius emancipatus Lambe Aurie, facio,
constituo et ordino meum certum noncium et procuratorem Palmerium Panzanum, absentem
tanquam presentem, ad petendum, exigendum et recipiendum pro me et meo nomine illos
bodronos quos ego possui[1] in dugana Neapolis aud procurator meus possuit et universa
alia debita mea quas[2] recipere debeo in Neapoli a galiotis fugitivis qui de galeis meis
aufugerunt seu a fideiubsoribus[3] ipsorum et a quacumque alia persona, corpore, colegio et
universitate, et ad vocandum quietum et solutum, [li]tem contestandum, testes et instrumenta
producendum, finem, remissionem et pactum faciendum et demum omnia facienda que in
predictis et circa <predicta> fuerint oportuna, dans et concedens predicto procuratori liberam
et generalem administracionem, promittens tibi notario infrascripto, stipulanti et recipienti
hanc confessionem nomine et vice illius vel illorum cuius vel quorum interest vel intererit,
me ratum et firmum prepetuo[4] habiturum quicquid per dictum procuratorem factum, gestum
seu procuratum fuerit in predictis et circa <predicta> et sub ypotecha et obligacione bonorum
meorum presencium et futurorum. Actum in Calabria, prope capud de Arma, in galea
dicti Thedicii vocata Dominica, anno dominice nativitatis M°CC°LXXXXIIII, die quinta
decembris, indictione VII[a]. Testes Gal(er)inus Becherius et Avenancius de Bulgaro, post
vesperas. /

---

[1] possui: *sic*   [2] quas: *sic*   [3] fideiubsoribus: *sic*   [4] prepetuo: *sic*

4

24 December 1294, in the galley, in the port of Kefalonia

Chechino de Comis, *living in* Domoculta, *said to have received in loan from Pietro Guercio
di Asti L 1, s. 1 of Genoa, with a promise of repayment within a month. Guarantor is Obertino
di Portovenere, nephew of Vassallino di Portovenere.*

In the external margin: "F[actum]."

[fol. 1v] In nomine Domini, amen. Ego Cechinus de Comis, qui sto in Domoculta, confiteor
tibi Petro Guercio de Ast me a te habuisse et recepisse mutuo gratis et amore libram[1] unam
et soldum unum ianuinorum, renuncians exceptioni non habite et non numerate peccunie et
omni iuri, unde et pro quibus tibi vel[2] tuo certo noncio per me vel meum noncium hinc ad
mensem unum proximum dare et solvere promitto, alioquin si contra fecero penam dupli
dicte quantitatis tibi stipulanti spondeo cum restitucione dampnorum et expensarum, credito
te de ipsis tuo simplici verbo sine testibus et iuramento, et proinde omnia bona mea habita
et habenda tibi pignori obligo. Insuper ego Obertinus de Portuveneris, nepos Vassallini de
Portuveneris, versus te dictum Petrum principaliter intercedo et me et mea solempniter obligo,
renuncians iuri de principali et omni iuri et sub ypotecha et obligacione bonorum meorum

presencium et futurorum. Actum in galea Thedixii Aurie vocata Dominica, in Zufaronia, in portu, anno dominice nativitatis M°CC°LXXXXV, die XXIIII decembris, indictione VIIᵃ, post complectorium. Testes Obertus Bonaventura et Andrea Scarera.

---

¹ libram: *first shortened and then written in full* ² *follows* vel *repeated*

5
24 December 1294, in the galley, in the port of Kefalonia

Ianino di Ancona said to have received in loan from Pietro Guercio di Asti L 1, s. 1 of Genoa, with a promise of repayment within a month. Guarantors are Thodanis di Romania and Iacopo barberius *di Napoli.*

In the external margin: "F[actum]."

In nomine Domini, amen. Ego Ianinus de Anchona confiteor tibi Petro Guercio de Ast me a te habuisse et recepisse mutuo gratis et amore libram¹ unam et soldum unum ianuinorum, renuncians exceptioni non habite et non numerate peccunie et omni iuri, unde et pro quibus tibi vel tuo certo noncio per me vel meum noncium hinc ad mensem unum proximum dare et solvere promitto, alioquin si contra fecero penam dupli dicte quantitatis tibi stipulanti spondeo cum restitucione dampnorum et expensarum, credito te de ipsis tuo simplici verbo sine testibus et iuramento et proinde omnia bona mea habita et habenda tibi pignori obligo. Insuper ego Thodanis de Romania et Iacobus barberius de Neapoli² versus te dictum Petrum principaliter intercedimus et nos et nostra solempniter obligamus, renunciantes iuri de principali et omni iuri et sub ypotecha et obligacione bonorum meorum³ presencium et futurorum. Actum in Zufaronia, in portu, in galea Thedixii Aurie vocata Dominica, anno dominice nativitatis M°CC°LXXXXV, die XXIIII decembris, indictione VIIᵃ, post complectorium. Testes Iohanninus Spaerius et Guillelmus Saricus de Sancto Remulo.

---

¹ libram: *first shortened and then written in full* ² ego – Neapoli: *sic* ³ meorum: *sic*

6
27 December 1294, in the galley, near Zakynthos Island

Iacopo Percenza di San Nazario, son of Arodi di Milano, said to have received in loan from Pietro Guercio di Asti 5.5 white bezants of Cyprus, with a promise of repayment within a month. Guarantor is Raimondino di San Nazario.

In the external margin: "F[actum]."

In nomine Domini, amen. Ego Iacobus Percenza de Sancto Nazario, filius quondam Arodi de Mediolano, confiteor tibi Petro Guercio de Ast me a te habuisse et recepisse mutuo gratis et amore bissancios albos de Cypro quinque et dimidium, renuncians exceptioni non habitorum et non receptorum bissanciorum et omni iuri, quos tibi vel tuo certo noncio per me vel meum noncium hinc ad mensem unum proxime venturum dare et solvere promitto, alioquin si contra fecero penam dupli dicte quantitatis tibi stipulanti spondeo cum restitucione dampnorum et expensarum, credito te de ipsis tuo simplici verbo sine testibus et iuramento, et proinde omnia bona mea habita et habenda tibi pignori obligo. Insuper ego Raymondinus de Sancto Nazario, qui prenominor Sosena, versus <te> / [**fol. 2r**] dictum Petrum principaliter intercedo et me et mea solempniter obligo, renuncians iuri de principali et omni iuri et sub ypotecha et obligacione bonorum meorum presencium et futurorum. Actum in galea Thedixii Aurie vocata Dominica, prope insulam Iazanti, anno dominice nativitatis M°CC°LXXXXV, die XXVII decembris, indictione septima, circa primam.[1] Testes Bernardinus Torsellus et Obertus Pecholus.

[1] *follows* The *crossed out*

7

7 January 1295, in the galley, near *Tarami* Island

Guirardo Rosso di Milano said to have received in loan from Enrico Alamanus s. 30 of Genoa, with a promise of repayment within three months.

In the inner margin: "F[actum]."

In nomine Domini, amen. Ego Guirardus Rubeus de Mediolano confiteor tibi Enrico Alamano me habuisse et recepisse mutuo gratis et amore soldos triginta ianuinorum, renuncians exceptioni non habitorum et non receptorum denariorum et omni iuri, quos tibi vel tuo certo noncio per me vel meum noncium hinc ad menses tres proxime venturos dare et solvere promitto, alioquin si contra fecero penam dupli dicte quantitatis tibi stipulanti spondeo cum restitucione dannorum et expensarum, credito te de ipsis tuo simplici verbo sine testibus et iuramento, et proinde omnia bona mea habita et habenda tibi pignori obligo. Actum in insula Tarami,[1] in galea Thedixii Aurie vocata Dominica, anno dominice nativitatis M°CC°LXXXXV, die VII ianuarii, indicione VII[a], post complectorium. Testes Petrus Belbexinus et Odinus de Mondevich.

[1] Tarami: *reading is uncertain*

8

10 March 1295, Famagusta

Oberto Piloto di Voltri said to have received in loan from Oberto Pecholo L 4 of Genoa, with a promise of repayment by 1 June 1295. Guarantor is Pietro Belbexino di Voltri.

In the inner margin: "F[actum]."

In nomine Domini, amem.[1] Ego Obertus Pilotus de Vulturo confiteor tibi Oberto Pecholo me a te habuisse et recepisse mutuo gratis libras IIII[or] ianuinorum, renuncians exceptioni non habite et non recepte peccunie et omni iuri, quas tibi vel tuo certo noncio per me vel meum noncium dare et solvere promitto in Ianua hinc ad kalendas menses[2] iunii proximas, alioquin si contra fecero penam dupli cum omnibus dampnis et expensis quas proinde feceris, tibi credito de ipsis tuo simplici verbo, sine testibus et iuramento et omni alia probacione. Insuper e<g>o Petrus Belbexinus de Vulturo versus te dictum Obertum principaliter intercedo et me et mea principaliter obligo, renuncians iuri de principali et omni iuri. Actum in Famagusta, anno dominice nativitatis M°CC°LXXXXV, die X marcii, indictione VII,[3] post terciam. Testes Gandaionus[4] de Cellis et Conradus de Albario.

[1] amem: *sic*   [2] menses: *sic*   [3] VII: *correct on* VIII[a]   [4] Gandaionus: G *correct on* F

9
16 March 1295, Ayas

Oberto di Bobiano of Piacenza, de societate Scotorum, by his own name and company, said to have received in loan from Oberto Pecholo 10.300 new Armenian daremos, with a promise of repayment s. 1, d. 1 of Genoa for each daremus, for a total of L 557, s. 18, d. 4 of Genoa, within fifteen days after submission of the document in Genoa to a shareholder of that company.

In the inner margin: "F[actum]."

In nomine Domini, amen. Ego Obertus de Bobiano, civis Placentie, de societate Scotorum,[1] meo proprio nomine et nomine sociorum dicte societatis, pro quibus promitto de rato habendo, confiteor tibi Oberto Pecholo me a te habuisse et recepisse in Layazo daremos novos de Ermenia decem milia trecentos, renuncians exceptioni non habitorum et non receptorum daremorum, doli mali, condicioni sine causa et omni iuri, unde et pro quibus ex causa cambii[2] promitto et convenio tibi meo propio[3] nomine et nomine sociorum dicte societatis dare et solvere in Ianua tibi vel tuo certo noncio / **[fol. 2v]** per me vel meum noncium aud per aliquem sociorum dicte societatis, ad racionem de soldo uno et denario uno ianuinorum pro quolibet daremo,[4] libras quingentas quinquaginta septem, soldos decem et octo et denarios IIII[or5] ianuinorum, infras[6] dies XV posquam[7] presens instrumentum presentatum fuerit in Ianua alicui sociorum dicte societatis, alioquin penam dupli dicte quantitatis cum omnibus dampnis et expensis propterea factis et faciendis tibi meo propio[3] nomine et sociorum[8] dicte societatis stipulanti spondeo, ratis manentibus supradictis, et pro hiis omnibus observandis omnia bona mea et sociorum dicte societatis, pro quibus promitto de rato et ubique nos cumveniri possimus, pignori obligo. Actum in Layazo, in logia Placentinorum, M°CC°LXXXXV, die XVI marcii, indicione VIII[a], circa vesperas. Testes Iohannes de Porta, civis Placentie, et Rogerius de Cornilianno, civis Placentie, et Belengerius de Montepesulano.

[1] de societate Scotorum: *above the line with cross-reference mark*   [2] ex causa cambii: *above the line with cross-reference mark*   [3] propio: *sic*   [4] pro quolibet daremo: *above the line with cross-reference mark*   [5] IIII[or]: *above the line with cross-reference mark*   [6] infras: *sic*   [7] posquam: *sic*   [8] sociorum: *above the line with cross-reference mark*

10

17 March 1295, in Syria, in the place called *Caroso*, near the *Montana Nigra*

Francesco Nusia di Sagona said to have received in loan from Iacopo Cluseterio di Sagona L 2, s. 10, with a promise of repayment within two months. Guarantor is Lanfranco Manencho di Sagona for s. 20 of Genoa.

In the external margin: "F[actum]."

In nomine Domini, amen. Ego Franciscus Nusia de Sagona confiteor me habuisse et recepisse a te Iacobo Cluseterio de Sagona mutuo gratis et amore libras II et soldos X,[1] renuncians exceptioni non numerate peccunie et non recepte et omni iuri, unde et pro quibus promitto[2] dare et solvere tibi vel tuo certo noncio libras duas[3] et soldos decem ianuinorum usque ad menses duos proximos, alioquin penam dupli dicte quantitatis tibi stipulanti promitto cum omnibus dampnis et expensis propterea factis et proinde omnia bona mea habita et habenda tibi pignori obligo. Insuper ego Lanfrancus Manenchus de Sagona pro dicto Francisco principaliter quantum pro soldis viginti ianuinorum intercedo versus te dictum Iacobum, promittens facere sic quod dictus Franciscus vobis solvet et atendet quantum pro dicta quantitate mihi pervenienti sub dicta pena et obligacione bonorum meorum. Actum in Syria, in loco ubi dicitur Caroso, prope Montano(n)i Nigram, anno dominice nativitatis M°CC°LXXXXV, indictione VII[a],[4] die XVII marcii, ante terciam. Testes Iohanninus Spaerius et Petrus de Rumbo de Cellis.

[1] II et soldos decem: *above the line on* IIII[or]   [2] *follows* tibi *crossed out*   [3] duas: *correct on* quatuor   [4] VII[a]: *correct on* VIII

11

1 April 1295, Paphos

Ricobono di Diano, nicknamed Pintardus, *said to have received in loan from Giovanni Lamberto di Ventimiglia L 2 of Genoa, with a promise of repayment within two months. Guarantor is Nicola Spoleto.*

In the external margin: "F[actum]."

In nomine Domini, amen. Ego Ricobonus de Diano, qui dicor Pintardus, confiteor me habuisse et recepisse a te Iohanne Lamberto[1] de Vintimilia mutuo gratis et amore libras duas ianuinorum, renuncians exceptioni non numerate peccunie et non recepte et omni iuri, unde et pro quibus promitto dare et solvere tibi vel tuo certo misso per me vel meum missum usque ad menses duos proxime venturos, alioquin si contra fecero penam dupli cum omnibus dampnis et expensis quas propterea feceris te credito de ipsis tuo solo verbo sine testibus et iuramento, et proinde omnia bona mea habita et habenda tibi pignori obligo. Insuper ego Nicolaus Spoletus de predictis pro dicto Ricobono principaliter intercedo versus te dictum Iohannem, promittens facere sic quod dictus Ricobonus vobis solvet et atendet sub ypotheca et obligacionem bonorum meorum, renuncians iuri de principali et omni iuri.[2] Actum in Baffa,[3] apud domum Costanci formaiarii, / **[fol. 3r]** anno dominice nativitatis

M°CC°LXXXXV, die prima aprilis, circa terciam, indictione VII[a]. Testes Lanfrancus de Seva de Sancta Agnete et Nicolaus Fatinanti, habitator Baffe.

[1] *follows* mutuo *crossed out*   [2] renuncians – iuri: *in the lower margin with cross-reference mark*   [3] Baffa: B *correct on* f

12
1 April 1295, Paphos

Obertino, son of Giovanni Corsi, said to have received in loan from Lanfranco di Seva di Sant'Agnete s. 36 of Genoa, with a promise of repayment within three months. Guarantors are Bonavia Suliano and Michael de Sancto Th(oma) filator.

In the inner margin: "F[actum]."

In nomine Domini, amen. Ego Obertinus, filius quondam Iohannis Corsi, confiteor tibi Lanfrancus de Seva de Sancta Agnete me a te habuisse et recepisse mutuo gratis soldos triginta sex ianuinorum, pro quibus tibi vel[1] tuo certo noncio per me vel meum noncium dare et solvere promitto usque ad menses duos proxime venturos soldos triginta sex ianuinorum, alioquin penam dupli cum omnibus dampnis et expensis, et proinde omnia bona mea habita et habenda tibi pignori obligo. Insuper nos Bonavia Sulianus et Michael de Sancto Th(oma) filator versus te dictum Lanfrancum pro dicto Obertino principaliter intercedimus, promittentes facere sic quod vobis solvet et atendet ut superius promisit, renuncians[2] iuri de principali, nove constitucionis pro quibus conveniri possimus. Actum in Baffa, prope domum Martini fabrii, anno dominice nativitatis M°CC°LXXXXV, die prima aprilis, post nonam, indictione VII[a]. Testes Thodanis de Romania et Venturinus de Cerialis.

[1] vel: v *correct on* s   [2] renuncians: *sic*

13
26 April 1295, in the galley, in Cyprus, near *Salinas*

Tedisio Doria appointed Oberto Pecholo as his attorney for a year.

In the inner margin: "F[actum]."

Ego Thedixius Auria facio, constituo et ordino meum certum noncium et procuratorem et loco meo pono Obertum Pecholum, presentem et recipientem, ad agendum, petendum, exigendum et recipiendum pro me et meo nomine id et totum quod recipere debeo seu debebo a quacumque persona, colegio sive universitate, quacumque occasione, tam in curia quam extra, et sub quocumque iudice tam ecclesiastico quam seculari, et ad vocandum se quietum et solutum, et ad cedendum iura et ad pacisendum,[1] compromittendum et transigendum, et ad acipiendum super me mutuo vel alio quoque titulo usque in quantitatem librarum mille ianuinorum qualitercumque, comodocumque et quandocumque sibi placuerit et videbitur,[2] et ad naulizandum pro me et meo nomine galeas mea[3] et ligna mea ad eundum quo voluerit et pro quo naulo voluerit et quandocumque ei placuerit et videbitur, et ad vocandum se quietum et solutum[4] de naulo, et ad acipiendum galiotos sive marinarios pro me et meo nomine usque in illam quantitatem quam sibi videbitur, et eorum salaria promittendum, et ad dandum et solvendum conductum ipsis vel cuilibet eorum, et ad accipiendum racionem a procuratoribus meis de eo quod receperint pro me et meo nomine, et ad vocandum se quietum et solutum ab eis et a quolibet eorum, et ad obligandum me et bona mea cui vel / [**fol. 3v**] quibus voluerit pro predictis decausis, et ad faciendum litem, questionem cui vel quibus voluerit, et ad deffendendum me et bona mea a quacumque persona que contra me vellet facere li[tem] seu questionem, et generaliter ad omnia et singula facienda que causarum merita postulant et requirunt et que egomet, si presens essem, facere possem, dans et concedens dicto procuratori meo liberam et generalem administracionem et potestatem faciendi in omnibus et singulis supradictis et circa predicta que per legitimum et generale<m> procuratorem fieri possint, et promitto tibi notario infrascripto, stipulanti et recipienti nomine et vice illius vel illorum cuius vel quorum interest vel intererit, habere et tenere ratum et firmum quicquid per dictum procuratorem factum fuerit seu gestum sub ypotheca et obligacione bonorum meorum. Hoc acto quod presens instr<umentu>m duret et locum habeat hinc ad annum unum proxime venturum. Actum in Cypri,[5] in galea predicti[6] Thedixii vocata Dominica, prope Salinas, anno dominice nativitatis M°CC°LXXXXV, die XXVI aprilis, indictione VII[a]. Testes Guillelmus Magdalena, cuxitor, et Sciretus de Sancto Matheo, circa tertiam.

[1] pacisendum: *sic*   [2] qualitercumque – videbitur: *in the external margin with cross-reference mark*
[3] mea: *sic*   [4] *follows* et solutum *crossed out*   [5] in Cypri: *above the line without cross-reference mark*   [6] predicti: *above the line with cross-reference mark*

14

28 April 1295, Famagusta

Alegrino Fatinanti, inhabitant of Famagusta, gives inter vivos *a white slave named Brancha to Oberto Pecholo.*

In nomine Domini, amen. Ego Alegrinus Fatinanti, habitator Famaguste, mera, pura donacione inter vivos dono tibi Oberto Pecholo quendam sclavum meum *** album vocatum nomine Brancham quem emi a Nicolao Nigrino, ut patet in instrumento scripto manu Gabrielis de Predono, notarii, M°CC°LXXXXIIII, die XIV septembris, quem sclavum mera et pura donacione inter vivos tibi dono et trado cum omni iure suo ad faciendum exinde quicquid volueris iure propietario sine contradicione mea vel heredum meorum, quem tibi promitto decetero non impedire nec subtrahere set ab omni persona legitime deffendere[1] et desbrigare et cui ipsum dederis sive vendideris per me vel heredes meos vel aliquam personam interpositam per me requisicio facta fiet; alioquin si contra fecero penam dupli de quanto nunc sclavus nonc[2] valet seu pro tempore valuerit tibi stipulanti promitto, abrenuncians legi que dicit donacione<m> ultra quingentos soldos vel aureos facta sine insinuacione[3] non valere et omni alii iuri; possessione<m> quoque et dominium dicti sclavi tibi confiteor corporaliter tradidisse et pro hiis omnibus observandis omnia bona mea habita et habenda tibi pigneri obligo. Actum in Cypro, in Famagusta, sub logia Ianuensium, anno dominice nativitatis M°CC°LXXXXV, die XXVIII aprilis, circa vesperas, indictione VII[a]. Testes Andrea Capcina et Franciscus Peragalus de Suxilia. /

[1] *follows* et auctorizare *crossed out*   [2] nonc: *sic*   [3] insinuacione: *in the text with generic abbreviation mark*

15

20 March 1295, in the galley, at 40 miles from the coast

Will of Obertino, son of Aldebrando di Maono.

[**fol. 4r**] In nomine Domini, amen. Ego Obertinus, filius Adebrandi de Maono, sane mentis existens, eger tamen corpore et in adversa valitudine positus, timens Dei iudicium intrare et ne intestatus decedam, mearum rerum taliter facio disposicionem. Primitus eligo corpus meum sepeliri apud ecclesia<m> Sancte[1] Luce de Lucha et ibi eligo pro exequis meis funeris soldos decem. Item eligo ad Sanctum Vitum de Bagnara soldos viginti.[2] Item eligo ad Sanctum Antonium de Ianua soldos decem. Item pro missis canendis ad Sanctum Vitum de Bagnara soldos viginti. Item volo et iubeo quod de dictis quos recipere debeo: ab Andrea Capcina de Naulo soldos XII, a Masculo de Marora soldos VIII, a Barlo de Marora soldos XXXV, a Francisco de Sagona, magistro axie, soldos viginti, detur et solvatur Lanceloto draperio, quos ei dare debeo, soldos quadraginta. Item recipere debeo a Guillelmo, filius[3] Vivaldi de Marora, turonenses centum quatuordecim. Reliquorum bonorum meorum mobilium et immobilium instituo mihi heredem Adebrandinum de Maono, patrem meum. Hec est mea ultima voluntas, que si non valet iure testamenti vel alterius iuris solempnitatis fueri<t> destituta, saltim vin[4] codicillorum obtineat seu alterius cuiuslibet ultime voluntatis; et si testamentum seu ultimam voluntatem hinc retro feci seu condidi, illud et illam casso et vacuo et nullius valoris seu momenti fore iubeo; istud in sua firmitate maneat. Actum in ialex,[5] in mari, per miliaria XXXX, in galea vocata Dominica que est Tedicii Aurie, anno dominice nativitatis M°CC°LXXXXV, die XX marcii, indictione VII[a]. Testes Boninus de Famagusta, Guillelmus Vivaldi de Mari, Vignueleus de Marora, filius Ravaschi, Guillelmus Sancus de Sancto Remulo et Benedictus de Vexagna, filius quondam Stephani, circa vesperas. /

---

[1] Sancte: *sic*   [2] viginti: *correct on* decem   [3] filius: *sic*   [4] vin: *sic*   [5] ialex: *in the text with generic abbreviation mark*

16

20 May 1295, Famagusta

Oberto di Finale, son of Vassallus Baffe, *said to have received from Francesco Vincenzo di Finale L 12, s. 12 of Genoa, with a promise of repayment within two months.*

In the external margin: "F[actum]."

[**fol. 4v**] In nomine Domini, amen. Ego Obertus de Finario, filius Vassalli Baffe, confiteor tibi Francisco Vicencio de Finario me habuisse et recepisse libras duodecim et soldos duodecim ianuinorum, renuncians exceptioni non numerate et non recepte sive non habite peccunie et omni iuri, unde et pro quibus tibi vel tuo certo noncio per me aud per meum noncium usque ad menses duos proximos[1] dare et solvere promitto, alioquin si contra fecero penam dupli cum omnibus dampnis et expensis que et quas pro hiis dictis exigendis feceris sub obligacione bonorum meorum suorum[2] presencium et futurorum, credito de hiis tibi tuo simplici verbo sine testibus et iuri et proinde omnia bona mea habita et habenda tibi pignori obligo. Actum in Famagusta, in portu, in galea Thedicii Aurie vocata Dominica, anno dominice nativitatis

M°CC°LXXXXV, die XX madii, circa nonam. Testes Ponzus de Vulturo, filius[3] Guillelmi Pona et Andrea Capcina, indictione VII[a].

[1] usque – proximos: *at the bottom with cross-reference mark*　　　[2] meorum suorum: *sic*
[3] filius: f *correct on abbreviation mark for* et

17

3 June 1295, Famagusta

Faciolo di Pietra said to have received from Oberto Pecholo L 3 of Genoa, with a promise of repayment within three months. Guarantor is Giovannino di Voltri, filius Berthori.

In the external margin: "F[actum]."

In nomine Domini, amen. Ego Faciolus de Petra confiteor tibi Oberto Pecholo me a te habuisse et recepisse libras tres ianuinorum, renuncians exceptioni non numerate peccunie et non acepte, doli mali, condicioni sine causa et omni iuri, pro quibus promitto tibi dare et solvere usque ad menses tres proximos, alioquin si contra fecero penam dupli cum omnibus dampnis et expensis que et quas feceris, credito tibi de hiis tuo simplici verbo sine testibus et iuri et proinde omnia bona mea habita et habenda tibi pignori obligo. Insuper ego[1] Iohanninus de Vulturo, filius Berthori, versus te dictum Obertum pro dicto Faciolo principaliter intercedo et me[2] et mea obligo, renuncians iuri de principali et omni iuri. Actum in Famagusta, in domo hospitalis, circa terciam, indictione VII[a], circa vesperas. Testes Nicolaus de Sancto Vicenzo et Obertus Brachus de Vulturo, M°CC°LXXXXV, die III iunii.

[1] ego: *above the line without cross-reference mark*　　　[2] me: *with abbreviation mark deleted*

18

4 June 1295, Famagusta

Obertino Ricolfo di San Romolo appointed Giovannino Bonolfo di San Romolo as his attorney.

In nomine Domini, amen. Obertinus Ricolfus de Sancto Remulo facio, constituo et ordino meum certum noncium et procuratorem Iohanninum Binolfum de Sancto Remulo, presentem et recipientem, ad petendum, exigendum et recipiendum quicquid recipere debeo et debebo a quacumque persona, quocumque modo et occasione, litem contentandum, testes et instrumenta producendum, opponendum, respondendum, defendendum et obligandum, contrahendum, iura cedendum, componendum, transigendum, instrumenta cassandum, liberandum, absolvendum quietum et solutum vocandum, dans dicto procuratori liberam licenciam et plenam administracionem petendi, exigendi recte omnia, demum faciendi iudicio et extra et quecumque ego facere possem si presens esse<m>, promittens tibi notario infrascripto stipulanti hanc confessionem nomine cuius vel quorum interest vel intererit ratum et firmum habere et tenere et in nullo contravenire dictus quicquid procurator[1] / [**fol. 5r**] fecerit in predictis et circa predicta sub ypotheca et obligacione bonorum meorum. Actum in Famagusta, ante logiam Ianuensium, anno dominice nativitatis M°CC°LXXXXV, die IIII iunii, indictione VII^a, post terciam. Testes Iohannes Spaerius et Mussus Moise de Vulturo.

^{1} *follows* procurator *repeated*

19
4 June 1295, Famagusta

Pietro Guercio di Asti said to have received from Rizardo di Leone, servant of Tedisio Zaccaria, some white bezants of the value of L 15, s. 7, d. 4 of Genoa, with a promise of repayment wherever Rizardo wants, if he will go away from Cyprus, or in Cyprus if Tedisio will decide to keep him.

The document is crossed with three lines.
In the bottom: "Cassa et vacua et nullius valoris de voluntate contrahencium in presencia Oberti Pecholi et Guillelmi Balbi de Cellis eodem millesimo, die VI iunii, et inde cassa."
In the bottom: "Passio Domini nostri Ihesu Christi secundum Mateum. / In iillo^1 tempore dissi^2 Ihesu / discipulis suis scitis quia pos<t> bibuum^3 pass<cha>."

Ego Petrus Guercius de Ast confiteor me habuisse et recepisse^4 a te Rizardo de Leone servitori Thedicii Zacharie tot bissancios albos de Cypri^5 qui valent a ianuinorum^6 libras XV, soldos VII, denarios IIII ianuinorum, renuncians exceptioni non numerate et non recepte peccunie et omni iuri, unde et pro quibus bissanciis promitto tibi dare et solvere ubicumque tibi placuerit posquam^7 de Cypro receseris, salvo si dictus Rizardus esset de voluntate dicti Thedicii quod remaneret dictus Petrus tenetur sibi dare bissancios supradictos, alioquin si contra fecerit penam dupli cum omnibus dampnis et expensis quas proinde feceris et proinde omnia bona mea habita et habenda tibi pignori obligo. Actum in Famagusta, in domo in qua habitat Iacobus, taliator de Placentia, apud logiam, anno dominice nativitatis M°CC°LXXXXV, indictione VII^a, die IIII iunii, circa nonam. Testes Iacobus Portaioa et Guillelmus Connius de Sagona et Ottoaldus Boninus. /

^{1} iillo: *sic* ^{2} dissi: *sic* ^{3} bibuum: *sic* ^{4} *follows* a te [...] *crossed out* ^{5} *follows* pro quibus a *crossed out* ^{6} a ianuinorum: *sic* ^{7} posquam: *sic*

20
8 May 1295, Famagusta

Pietro Belbexino di Voltri said to have received in loan from Ponzo di Voltri, son of Guglielmo Poncio, L 7, s. 7 of Genoa, with a promise of repayment within two months.

In the external margin: "F[actum]."

[**fol. 5v**] In nomine Domini, amen. Ego Petrus Belbexinus de Vulturo confiteor tibi Ponzo de Vulturo, filio Guillelmi Ponci, me^1 habuisse et recepisse mutuo gratis et amore libras VII et soldos duos ianuinorum, renuncians exceptioni non numerate peccunie et non recepte, doli mali, condicioni sine causa et omni iuri, unde et pro quibus et causa predicta promitto tibi usque ad menses duos proximos dare et solvere predictam quantitatem, alioquin penam dupli cum omnibus dampnis et expensis quas^2 propterea feceris, credito tibi de ipsis tuo simplici verbo sine testibus et iuramento et omni alia probacione et proinde omnia bona mea habita et habenda tibi pignori obligo. Actum in Famagusta, apud logiam Ianuensium, anno dominice nativitatis M°CC°LXXXXV, die VIIIᵃ, indictione VIIᵃ, madii,³ circa nonam. Testes Iohanninus Spaerius de Sagona et Iacobus, taliator, habitator Famaguste.

¹ me: *above the line on* mutuo *deleted*   ² quas: *with a generic abbreviation mark*   ³ indictione
VIIᵃ madii: *in the external margin*

21

8 May 1295, Famagusta

Vival Blancho di Arenzano said to have received in loan from Giovannino Spaerio di Sagona L 2, s. 8 of Genoa, with a promise of repayment within two months.

In nomine Domini, amen. Ego Vival Blanchus de Arenzano confiteor tibi Iohannino Spaerio de Sagona me a te habuisse et recepisse mutuo gratis et amore libras II, soldos VIII ianuinorum, renuncians exceptioni non numerate peccunie et non acepte et omni iuri, unde et pro quibus tibi vel tuo certo misso per me vel meum missum usque ad menses duos dare et solvere promitto, alioquin si contra fecero penam dupli cum omnibus dampnis et expensis quas proinde feceris et proinde omnia bona mea habita et habenda tibi pignori obligo. Actum in Famagusta, ante logiam Ianuensium. Testes Nicolaus Bassus de Vulturo et Ponzus de Vulturo, filius¹ Gullelmi Ponzi, anno dominice nativitatis M°CC°LXXXXV, die VIIIᵃ madii, circa tercia<m>, indictione VIIᵃ.

¹ *follows* qn *crossed out*

22

[…]

The document is interrupted.

In nomine Domini, amen. Ego Petrus Abracinus confiteor tibi Iohannino de Savio me a te habuisse et recepisse mutuo gratis et amore libras 2000 ianuinorum ***. /

23

6 June 1295, Famagusta

Francesco Fer di Durazzo said to have received in loan from Giovanni di Rubaldo L 11 of Genoa, with a promise of repayment within four years.

[**fol. 6r**] In nomine Domini, amen. Ego Franciscus Fer <de> Durazo confiteor tibi Iohanni de Rubaldo me habuisse et recepisse a te mutuo gratis et amore libras undecim ianuinorum, renuncians exceptioni non numerate peccunie et non recepte et omni iuri, unde et pro quibus et ex causa predicta promitto tibi dare et solvere aut tuo certo noncio per me vel meum noncium usque ad IIIIᵒʳ annos proximos, videlicet anuatim promitto dare libras tres ianuinorum et superfluum libras duas, alioquin si contra fecero penam dupli cum omnibus dampnis et expensis quas proinde feceris, credicto tuo¹ solo verbo sine testibus et iuramento et omni alia probacione et proinde omnia bona mea habita et habenda tibi pignori obligo. Actum in Famagusta, in domo in qua habitat societas Florentinorum, anno dominice nativitatis M°CC°LXXXXV, indictione VII^a, die VI iunii. Testes Obertus Pecholus notarius et Genoardus de Clapa, inter terciam et nonam. /

[1] tuo: *with abbreviation mark deleted*

Who's in Charge Here?
The Administration of the Church of Nicosia, 1299–1319

Chris Schabel

University of Cyprus
schabel@ucy.ac.cy

With the final fall of Acre and almost all the other Frankish towns on the Syro-Palestinian coast in 1291, Nicosia became the ecclesiastical capital of the Latin East. The inland city was already the seat of the archbishopric of the province of Cyprus, established by Pope Celestine III in 1196 with suffragan bishops in the coastal towns of Paphos, Limassol, and Famagusta. After 1291 the mendicant orders relocated their Holy Land headquarters to Nicosia, which also hosted a number of mainland refugees from the secular and regular clergy. Limassol became the new home of the Templars and the Hospitallers, while the population of Famagusta increased dramatically. Yet Cyprus's new importance also brought new anxiety, since along with the kingdom of Lesser Armenia it was the next target of Muslim aggression in the East. At the same time, the presence of the powerful military orders, the growing interest of the Italian trading communes, and the schemes of the Angevins further threatened the sovereignty of the Lusignan dynasty.[1]

The uneasy situation became critical in the first decade of the fourteenth century. Aside from the civil war between the Emperor Frederick II and the Ibelin family in 1228–33, the chroniclers of Frankish Cyprus concentrate on one brief period before the eventful reign of King Peter I (1359–69): the crisis of the years 1306–11, with Amaury de Lusignan's coup d'état against his brother, King Henry II, in 1306–10, and the arrest and trial of the Templars in 1308–11.[2] The Church played an important role in connection with these events, especially the latter, and yet throughout the decade there was no archbishop of Nicosia on the island, the local ecclesiastical leader being first absent, then suspended, and finally dead, with the disputed election of his successor remaining unresolved for several years. In the crucial negotiations between the spiritual and temporal authorities, then, the pope

I thank the three anonymous readers of *Crusades* for their suggestions, Constantinos Georgiou for printing out the unpublished letters of Pope John XXII, and William Duba for his description of the two *instrumenta*.

[1] On the political history of Cyprus in the thirteenth and fourteenth centuries, the standard works are Sir George Hill, *A History of Cyprus. Volume II: The Frankish Period 1192–1432* (Cambridge, 1948) and Peter W. Edbury, *The Kingdom of Cyprus and the Crusades, 1191–1374* (Cambridge, 1993). For the ecclesiastical history, see Nicholas Coureas, *The Latin Church in Cyprus, 1195–1312* (Aldershot, 1997) and *The Latin Church in Cyprus, 1313–1378* (Nicosia, 2010). For other topics, see Angel Nicolaou-Konnari and Chris Schabel, eds., *Cyprus: Society and Culture 1191–1374* (Leiden, 2005).

[2] On these years in general see especially Edbury, *The Kingdom of Cyprus*, pp. 101–40.

had to rely on legates, nuncios, and more minor local clerics. The daily diocesan administration continued, of course, and took in revenue, since the chapter (in Nicosia's case consisting of a dean, archdeacon, treasurer, cantor, and about a dozen canons) and secrète (administrative office) still functioned. Indeed, it has recently been argued that construction work on the cathedral, perhaps the greatest example of Gothic architecture in the Latin East, proceeded steadily in these years without a resident archbishop.[3] This article attempts to trace the history of the administration of the Church of Nicosia in these years, exploiting some recently published documentary evidence, passages in two unpublished papal letters, and two *instrumenta* from the Vatican Archives published here for the first time.[4]

The absence of the archbishop of Nicosia was nothing new in 1299. Following the death of the incumbent, disputed elections sometimes remained unresolved for years. At his election or appointment, the new archbishop might be abroad and required considerable time to arrive at his see. Troubles with the secular powers resulted in extended periods of exile for Archbishops Eustorge (1230s), Hugh (1250s and 1260s), and Ranulph (1280s), and the last two never returned. In these cases the archbishop usually appointed a vicar or vicars or, when there was no archbishop, the archbishop-elect or the cathedral dean or archdeacon might be given control of spiritual or temporal affairs or both.[5] In the early fourteenth century things were different.

Dean Gerard of the Church of Langres was appointed archbishop of Nicosia in the spring of 1295.[6] According to medieval chroniclers, Archbishop Gerard spent only two years in residence at his see.[7] This was probably between the spring of 1297 and the spring of 1299. He is attested in Cyprus on 1 May 1297 and again on 22 September 1298, when he held a provincial council at Limassol.[8] In a series of documents from 1299 relating to a dispute between the chapter of Nicosia and the

---

[3] Michalis Olympios, "Gothic Church Architecture in Lusignan Cyprus, c.1209–c.1373: Design and Patronage," (PhD thesis, University of London, 2010), Appendix V, pp. 354–83.

[4] The previous bibliography on this topic, always incomplete, is also often incorrect in many details. This article tacitly corrects the errors of previous scholarship.

[5] On the administration of the archbishopric in these years, see especially Louis de Mas-Latrie, "Histoire des Archevêques latins de l'île de Chypre," *AOL* 2 (1884), 211–328, esp. pp. 211–55; Coureas, *The Latin Church in Cyprus, 1195–1312, passim,* and *The Latin Church in Cyprus, 1313–1378, passim;* and Chris Schabel, "The Latin Bishops of Cyprus, 1255–1313, with a Note on Bishop Neophytos of Solea," *Επετηρίδα του Κέντρου Επιστημονικών Ερευνών* 29 (2004), 75–111, esp. pp. 77–96.

[6] *Bullarium Cyprium II: Papal Letters Concerning Cyprus, 1261–1314,* ed. Chris Schabel (Nicosia, 2010), no. o-6.

[7] Amadi, *Chroniques d'Amadi et de Strambaldi,* ed. René de Mas Latrie, vol. 1 (Paris, 1891), p. 233; *Cronaca del Templare di Tiro (1243–1314). La caduta degli Stati Crociati nel racconto di un testimone oculare,* ed. and Italian trans. Laura Minervini (Naples, 2000), p. 266, §314 (550).

[8] *The Cartulary of the Cathedral of Holy Wisdom of Nicosia,* ed. Nicholas Coureas and Chris Schabel (Nicosia, 1997), no. 90; *The Synodicum Nicosiense and Other Documents of the Latin Church of Cyprus, 1196–1373,* ed. and trans. Chris Schabel (Nicosia, 2001), no. G.a.

Franciscans of the capital, John de Nores, treasurer of Nicosia, probably along with Dean Nicholas de Camulio, are called vicars of Archbishop Gerard on 23 August, but Jean was not referred to thus on 4 April.[9] It is likely, then, that Gerard departed after 4 April and before 23 August 1299. A letter of Pope Boniface VIII dated 1 February 1301, concerning the disputed election to the Greek see of Solea, relates that the case was taken before the vicar (singular) of Archbishop Gerard, probably in late 1299 or in 1300. In another papal letter of 28 February 1301, describing the disputed election of the bishop of Limassol, it is stated that the archbishop's vicars (plural) confirmed the election of Anthony de Saurano, treasurer of Famagusta, probably in early 1300.[10] Finally, on 4 April 1302, when Boniface wrote concerning yet another disputed election, this time of the bishop of Paphos, two of the canons – allegedly excommunicates – were acting as the archbishop's vicars and confirmed the election of Peter de Montolif, probably in 1301.[11] It is unknown whether John and/or Nicholas remained Gerard's vicars and possessed benefices in Paphos in addition to their posts in Nicosia, although this would not have been unusual.

Neither was Gerard's absence very unusual. What happened next, however, was. During the great struggle between Pope Boniface VIII and King Philip IV the Fair of France, Gerard sided with the king. Accordingly, on 15 August 1303, Boniface suspended Gerard and, rather than replace him with another, assigned the administration over the goods and the spiritual and temporal affairs of the Church of Nicosia to the papal chaplain Henry de Gibelet (that is, the experienced archdeacon of Nicosia) and to Bishop Peter Erlant of Limassol.[12]

Henry and Peter remained in charge after Boniface's death on 11 October of that year and throughout Benedict XI's brief papacy until, shortly after his election in late 1305, Pope Clement V revoked Boniface's assignment and turned the administration over to Thomas de Morrovalle on 8 January 1306[13] – although according to documents surrounding Amaury's usurpation Peter Erlant and Henry de Gibelet were still in control in Nicosia on 14 May of that year,[14] so perhaps the news had not yet reached them. Thomas was the brother of Cardinal-bishop John (de Morrovalle) of Porto, and soon after Clement's assignment the pope decided to use the revenues of the Nicosia Church for his cardinals, giving half to John and the other half to Cardinal-deacon Peter Colonna.[15]

---

[9] Schabel, "A Neglected Quarrel over a House in Cyprus in 1299: The Nicosia Franciscans vs. the Chapter of Nicosia Cathedral," *Crusades* 8 (2009), 173–90, nos. 2–3.

[10] *Bullarium Cyprium II*, nos. o-50 and o-51.

[11] Ibid., no. o-56.

[12] Ibid., nos. o-62 and o-63.

[13] Ibid., no. q-1.

[14] Chris Schabel and Laura Minervini, "The French and Latin Dossier on the Institution of the Government of Amaury of Lusignan, Lord of Tyre, Brother of King Henry II of Cyprus," *Επετηρίδα του Κέντρου Επιστημονικών Ερευνών* 34 (2008), 75–119, at pp. 109a–110a and 119.

[15] Pierre-Vincent Claverie, *L'Ordre du Temple en Terre Sainte et à Chypre au XIIIe siècle*, 3 vols. (Nicosia, 2005), vol. 2, nos. 20–22; *Bullarium Cyprium II*, nos. q-73, q-74, and q-75.

In a document of 31 January 1307 concerning the usurpation, Henry is not mentioned, Peter is not called administrator, and now Philip of Assisi is called vicar of the Church of Nicosia, surely for Thomas de Morrovalle.[16] Three weeks later, on 20 February 1307, the see was termed vacant, and in a letter of 27 February 1308, Clement specifies that Archbishop Gerard had died.[17] What seems to have happened is that, at some point between 14 May 1306 and 31 January 1307, the news arrived in Nicosia that Archbishop Gerard had passed away, probably on 26 February 1306.[18] As we learn from much later letters of 10 May 1312 and 1 July 1313, Henry de Gibelet and Bishop Guy of Famagusta were elected archbishop of Nicosia in another disputed election, with Henry traveling to the papal curia to pursue his election. For seemingly unrelated reasons Henry was arrested instead, which explains why Clement did not put Henry back in charge of the administration of Nicosia. The election case remained pending until the 1312 letter, in which the pope appointed John of Conti.[19]

On 20 February 1307, with Peter Erlant in Cyprus, the see of Nicosia vacant, and Henry de Gibelet at or traveling to the papal curia, Pope Clement revoked his earlier decision in favor of Thomas de Morrovalle and the two cardinals and returned the spiritual and temporal administration of Nicosia to Peter Erlant alone, giving him the power to collect the revenues of the church that pertained to the archbishop's manse. These revenues, however, the pope assigned to James de Molay, the master of the Templars, and about 60,000 white bezants of Cyprus were turned over to the Templars on Cyprus from this source. After the arrest of the Templars, the pope ordered on 24 September 1309 that this money be given to Master Fulk de Villaret and the Hospitallers, to be put toward the expenses of a planned crusade. At the same time, Clement ordered that Peter Enlart provide a full financial account of his administration, both for the period he shared it with Henry de Gibelet and for the later time when he was alone in that position.[20]

These orders were given in letters to the papal legate, Bishop Peter (de Plaine-Chassagne) of Rodez, and the papal nuncio, Master Raymond de Pins, canon of Bazas and papal chaplain, who were to come to Cyprus in connection with the

[16] Schabel and Minervini, "The French and Latin Dossier," pp. 109b–110b.

[17] Claverie, *L'Ordre du Temple*, vol. 2, nos. 20–22; *Bullarium Cyprium II*, nos. q-27, q-73. q-74, and q-75.

[18] Mas Latrie, "Histoire des Archevêques," p. 254, quotes an earlier published document relating that an unnamed archbishop of Nicosia and former dean of Langres died on 26 February (IV Cal. Martii) and was buried in Paris. Without explanation, Mas Latrie asserts that the year was 1315.

[19] *Bullarium Cyprium II*, q-98 and q-103.

[20] Claverie, *L'Ordre du Temple*, vol. 2, nos. 20–22; *Bullarium Cyprium II*, nos. q-73, q-74, and q-75. Amadi actually covers some of this ground, and the new documents show just how much that chronicle could conflate various bits of information: *Innocent* V wrote a letter that was presented to the Nicosia chapter and Peter Enlart on 8 May *1308* making the latter vicar in spiritual and temporal affairs and ordering him to turn the incomes over to the *Hospitallers* for the conquest of Rhodes, transferring the *60* white bezants from the Templars to the Hospitallers (*Chroniques d'Amadi et de Strambaldi*, ed. Mas Latrie, vol. 1, pp. 280 and 283; cf. Mas Latrie, "Histoire des Archevêques," p. 253).

crises of the usurpation and the Templars.[21] A document dated Famagusta, 27 March 1310 (Instrumentum Miscellaneum 497 of the Vatican Archives, Appendix 1 below), concerns the Bishop Peter Erlant of Limassol's financial account:[22]

> Through this our present letter patent let it be clear to all that we, Peter, by the grace of God and the Apostolic See bishop of Limassol and administrator of the Church of Nicosia, at the insistence and request of the venerable man Lord Raymond de Pins, the chaplain and nuncio of our lord the highest pontiff, specially sent for the purpose of the below-written things along with the reverend in Christ father Lord Peter, by the grace of God bishop of Rodez and legate of the Apostolic See …

Peter promised to turn over or have turned over to Raymond or his deputy the remaining incomes of the Nicosia Church and whatever goods of the administration of the church remained in his hands, or had remained in his hands "at the time of the warning," or would remain in his or anyone else's hands while the account was being drawn up.

Peter Erlant was still administrator on 12 April and 19 June of 1310 during the trial of the Templars.[23] Raymond arrived in Cyprus in March and over the next couple of months he investigated and produced a document including, among other things, his report on Peter's financial dealings. Raymond found that 106,000 silver Tournois that were supposed to go the master of the Hospitallers had ended up with the Templars. Agents of the Peruzzi and Bardi banks had paid the Hospitaller master 4,000 bezants, but Raymond asked Amaury to force the agents to pay the master another 3,400 bezants. The bankers countered that they had received that last sum from Bishop Peter while acting on behalf of Cardinals Peter Colonna and John de Morrovalle, so presumably before early 1307. Raymond was not able to resolve this issue by the time he wrote his report. Nor did Peter Erlant's accounting go smoothly. Raymond remarks that he needed the account in order to pay the Hospitaller master, as Pope Clement had ordered. Raymond assigned some canons of Nicosia and "some other good men" to audit the account, and the men reported to Raymond and the legate that Bishop Peter had committed much fraud in his reckoning and much damage had been done to the Church of Nicosia. A few days later the bishop appeared before Raymond and the legate, but he refused to obey them. For this reason, and because of other things Raymond had discovered about the bishop, the nuncio excommunicated Peter. Peter appealed to the pope, but Raymond merely denounced Peter as excommunicate in public. At the time

---

[21] On Raymond, see Charles Perrat, "Un diplomate gascon au XIVe siècle: Raymond de Piis, nonce de Clement V en Orient," *Mélanges d'archéologie et d'histoire de l'École française de Rome* 44 (1927), 35–90; Chris Schabel, "Unpublished Documents from the Cypriot Activities of Papal Nuncio Raymond of Pins (†1311)," *Επετηρίδα του Κέντρου Επιστημονικών Ερευνών* 35 (2009–10), 53–64.

[22] Parchment, 16.6/16.9 cm long × 21.3/21.5 cm wide.

[23] Anne Gilmour-Bryson, *The Trial of the Templars in Cyprus. A Complete English Edition* (Leiden, 1998), pp. 43 (first page), 442 (last page), and *passim*.

Raymond was writing, the auditors were still claiming that Peter had deceived the pope and the Hospitaller master with his false account.[24]

It is unclear whether Peter Erlant was then removed from the administration of the Church of Nicosia. With the Templar trial, Amaury's murder on 5 June, Raymond's embassies to Armenia to secure the release of the exiled King Henry II, and Raymond's own death on 1 January 1311, replacing Peter may have been a low priority. The second document published below, Instrumentum Miscellaneum 528, dated Nicosia, 4 June 1311 (Appendix 2),[25] is addressed to "Peter de Brie, canon of Nicosia and vicar in the spiritual affairs of the same church, which see is vacant." Since the document does not mention the temporal affairs, nor does it refer to the administration,[26] there is no reason to assume thereby that Peter Erlant had been removed from the administration of Nicosia by mid-1311. Rather the pope, his representatives on Cyprus, or even the bishop of Limassol himself had assigned Canon Peter de Brie as vicar for the church's spiritual affairs. Thus Abbot Bartholomew of Episcopia (that is, Bellapais), at the request of Baldwin of Cyprus, who was only in minor orders, asked that Peter de Brie promote Baldwin to subdeacon and give him letters patent affirming this promotion. (Incidentally, this document is curious for another reason. The actor of the document is Abbot Bartholomew of Bellapais, but rather than a house of Augustinian or Premonstratensian canons, the document calls the abbey a monastery of the Cistercian Order.)[27]

There is evidence that Peter Erlant remained in place, even if Raymond had been keeping an eye on him in 1310. It was probably because the news of Raymond de Pins's death on 1 January had reached Avignon that, between March and August 1311, Pope Clement ordered Peter, Bishop Baldwin of Famagusta, and Master Dominic Leonardi, papal scribe, "to collect, seize, exact, and receive, with every care, diligence, and caution, all fruits, incomes, revenues, and rents" belonging to the archiepiscopal manse of the vacant see. They were to keep them for the Roman Church until the pope arranged otherwise. He also instructed them to do the same with anything received in the name of the pope or of the Roman Church

---

[24] Latin text in Perrat, "Un diplomate gascon," pp. 74–75.

[25] Parchment, 14.3/13.6 cm long × 21.0/21.6 cm wide.

[26] Contrary to various commentators (including me, "The Latin Bishops of Cyprus," p. 95, where I also give the date as January rather than June), based on the summary published in Regestum Clementis papae V (Rome, 1885–92), no. 10497.

[27] The history of the affiliation of Bellapais Abbey is complicated, since it seems to have begun in the 1190s as part of the order of Austin Canons, joined the Premonstratensians in the 1220s, but considered becoming Cistercian in the late 1230s: Bullarium Cyprium I: Papal Letters Concerning Cyprus, 1196–1261, ed. Chris Schabel (Nicosia, 2010), c-58, c-61, and d-8; Joseph-Marie Canivez, Statuta Capitulorum Generalium Ordinis Cisterciensis ab anno 1116 ad annum 1786, vol. 2 (Louvain, 1934), p. 193, no. 41. In 1308–11, it is still linked explicitly to the three different orders: Bullarium Cyprium II, nos. q-21, q-22, and q-23; the present document. It is possible that the canons used their distance from the West to maintain an unusual degree of independence from supervision, although eventually it seems to have become firmly Premonstratensian. Given the importance of the monastery for the ecclesiastical and architectural history of Cyprus, the projected study on the subject by Michalis Olympios will be valuable.

from 1 March 1311 to 1 March 1312. Afterwards, probably in early 1312, the pope granted these incomes to Cardinal James Colonna, although the cardinal had trouble getting the money and the pope had to send another letter to Peter, Baldwin, and Dominic on 13 August 1313.[28]

By then the cardinal's nephew, John del Conti, was archbishop. On 10 May 1312 Pope Clement transferred John from the archbishopric of Pisa, almost nine years since the previous archbishop had been suspended and thirteen years since the last archbishop was in residence. Yet one of the reasons for Clement's decision was to honor and supplement the income of the new archbishop's uncle, Cardinal James Colonna. Upon his election, Archbishop John agreed, or had to agree, to pay the cardinal half of the annual income of the Church of Nicosia after expenses, up to but not exceeding the amount of 5,000 gold florins, half on 1 June and the other half on 1 November or within four months of that date. The arrangement was to be perpetual, for the life of both cardinal and nephew, as long as John served as archbishop. Clement confirmed the arrangement on 8 February 1314.[29]

Nevertheless, the saga of the administration of the Church of Nicosia did not end there, for the archbishop's kinship with the cardinal did not cause him to give the money happily. On 25 June 1317 Pope John XXII addressed two letters on the matter to Bishop Baldwin of Famagusta and two others. One of the letters informs us that each year Archbishop John had been defrauding Cardinal James of his rightful half of the income of the Nicosia Church, holding in contempt the investigations undertaken and sentences passed by the executors and their sub-delegates that Pope Clement had assigned to the cardinal, and launching frivolous appeals. As a result, in the over three years since Clement's confirmation, the archbishop had paid his uncle only 1,350 florins, less than one-tenth of the estimated amount due. Indeed, Archbishop John was even claiming that the cardinal's share should be calculated from the time he received the papal letter, not from the date of the letter itself. Pope John himself complained that Archbishop John had not yet paid to the pope and cardinals the common services (that is, the income of the first year of vacancies filled by the papacy), although the archbishop had promised Pope Clement to do so and although the archbishop was certainly able to fulfill his obligations, since he had been receiving the revenues of the Church of Nicosia from the time of his transfer there two years before Clement's confirmation of the arrangement with Cardinal James.[30]

---

[28] *Bullarium Cyprium II*, no. q.-105; cf. q-86, q-87, and q-88, from August 1311, to the same addressees on other business.

[29] *Bullarium Cyprium II*, no. q-108; *Regestum Clementis papae V*, Appendix, no. 207, p. 243a.

[30] See *Bullarium Cyprium III: Lettres papales relatives à Chypre 1316–1378*, ed. Charles Perrat and Jean Richard with the collaboration of Chris Schabel (Nicosia, 2012), no. r-31, for the latest brief summary, but the full text of the new part of the *narratio* is worth quoting from Città del Vaticano, Archivio Segreto Vaticano, Reg. Vat. 66, fol. 56v, no. 3214: "Idem tamen archiepiscopus, processibus et sententiis variis per executores eiusdem cardinalis sibi per ipsius predecessoris litteras deputatos necnon et per subdelegatos ab eis specialiter promulgatis nequaquam obstantibus, sed potius vilipensis, et contra dictos processus et sententias per se et procuratores suos frivolis appellationibus interiectis, prefatum cardinalem medietate predicta singulis annis intollerabiliter defraudavit, ex eo videlicet quod

Naturally Pope John XXII ordered that Clement's arrangement be implemented, forcing the archbishop to pay arrears from the date of Pope Clement's confirmation. Yet the second letter reveals that the situation was still more complex. Despite the cardinal's many complaints about the archbishop, through their agents both nephew and uncle agreed to rent out the revenues of the Church of Nicosia for three years to the seneschal of Cyprus, Philip d'Ibelin, for a fixed price of 50,000 gold bezants annually, after the church's expenses. The money was to be divided equally between the cardinal and the archbishop, since 25,000 gold bezants did not reach the 5,000 gold florins of the previous agreement. The pope approved the rental arrangement. One assumes that Philip d'Ibelin continued to pay the rent until his death in October 1318 and that Cardinal James received the 25,000 gold bezants annually until his death in August of that year, although whether he succeeded in obtaining what had been owed to him for previous years is less certain.[31]

Archbishop John only arrived in Nicosia August of 1319, at which point the Church of Nicosia began functioning normally after twenty years of disruption. Chaotic as these two decades may have been at the top of the local Latin clerical hierarchy, however, central control from the papal curia and continuity in the lower ranks of the clergy in Nicosia ensured that the ecclesiastical machinery was in place to carry out daily administrative duties and even to meet the extraordinary crises that Cyprus faced in a period of grave uncertainty.

---

a tempore concessionis et donationis huiusmodi nisi mille trecentos quinquaginta florenos auri ratione dicte medietatis pro tribus annis iam transactis dicto cardinali prefatus archiepiscopus non persolvit. Propter quod oportuit cardinalem ipsum gravia subire onera debitorum. Dictus quoque archiepiscopus defraudatione huiusmodi non contentus, sed, ut dicti cardinalis gratiam magis semper attenuet, impudenter allegat cardinalem ipsum non a die date litterarum apostolarum super eadem facta sibi gratia confectarum, sed a die dumtaxat representationis ipsarum, ut fraudet eum fructibus medio tempore perceptis, debere medietatem percipere prelibatam. Et insuper ad contribuendum secum in solutione servicii in quo nobis et dictis nostris fratribus idem archiepiscopus est astrictus – ad cuius solutionem se infra certi temporis spacium iuxta morem curie ac mandatum predicto predecessori sub spiritualibus et temporalibus penis astrinxit, et constet eum per duos annos ante tempus huiusmodi facte dicto cardinali gratie ad dictam Nicosiensem ecclesiam fuisse translatum et percepisse pacifice fructus ex eadem, infra quos annos et ex quibus quidem fructibus prout tenebatur integre persolvere potuit servicium antedictum, <ut> cardinalis ipse [ipsum ms] asserit, obligatur."

[31] Ibid., no. r-30. Again, the full text of new part of the *narratio* is worthy of quotation from Città del Vaticano, Archivio Segreto Vaticano, Reg. Vat. 66, fol. 56v, no. 3213: "Nuper tamen, prelibatis cardinali et archiepiscopo, prout ex eiusdem cardinalis assertione didicimus, concorditer ordinantibus ut per procuratores eorum omnes fructus, redditus, et proventus eiusdem Nicosiensis <ecclesie> ad certi temporis spacium pro certo precio locarentur, et, deductis de dicto precio prefatis oneribus et expensis, medietas eius quod de nominato precio superesset dicto cardinali reliqua vero medietas eidem archiepiscopo traderentur, procuratores eorum habentes super hoc ab eis plenum et speciale mandatum prefatos fructus, redditus, et proventus eiusdem ecclesie dilecto filio nobili viro . . seneschallo regni Cipri usque ad triennium locaverunt. Ita videlicet quod idem seneschallus, ante omnia solutis per eum annuatim omnibus eiusdem ecclesie oneribus et expensis que predictum archiepiscopum subire oportet, solvere postmodum dictis procuratoribus predictorum cardinalis et archiepiscopi nomine ratione locationis eiusdem quinquaginta milia bisantiorum auri equis portionibus inter prelibatos cardinalem et archiepiscopum dividenda, quarum medietas summam quinque milium florenorum auri nequaquam attingit, annis singulis dicto durante triennio teneatur." On Philip d'Ibelin, see W. H. Rudt de Collenberg, "Les Ibelin aux XIIIe et XIVe siècles," Ἐπετηρίδα Κέντρου Ἐπιστημονικῶν Ἐρευνῶν 9 (1977–79), 117–265, at pp. 190–91.

Appendix 1
Archivum Secretum Vaticanum, Instrumentum Miscellaneum 497
Famagusta, 27 March 1310

Per has presentes nostras patentes litteras pateat universis quod nos, Petrus, Dei et Apostolice Sedis gratia episcopus Nimociensis et administrator Nicossiensis ecclesie, ad instantiam et requisitionem venerabilis viri domini Raymundi de Pynibus, domini nostri summi pontificis cappellani et nuntii, ad infrascripta omnia una cum reverendo in Christo patre domino Petro, Dei gratia episcopo Ruthenensi, Apostolicis Sedis legato, specialiter destinati cum illa clausula "ut vos vel alter vestrum," promisimus quod[1] domino Raymundo predicto vel eius mandato bene et legaliter consignabimus et consignari faciemus et in sua potestate ponemus ac poni faciemus quam citius fieri poterit absque mora omnes fructus, redditus, et proventus Nicossiensie ecclesie restantes et quicquid ad nos restat de bonis administrationis ecclesie supradicte vel restabat tempore monitionis et quicquid in futurum durante computo ad manus nostras vel alterius nostro mandato restabit, et quicquid sciverimus restare vel penes alium esse laborabimus bona fide recuperare et exigere et compellere debentes et reddere et restituere predicto domino Raymundo vel deputato ab eo. Et ad premissa omnia fideliter exequenda, iurare faciemus balivos et scrivanos nostros. Et fin<i>to computo, quicquid reperietur restare solvemus et trademus ipsi domino Raymundo vel deputato ab eo, omni mora et contradictione cessante, prius protestatione premissa per nos quod salvum sit nobis omne ius nostrum in expensis necessariis et utilibus per nos factis occasione administrationis Nicossiensis ecclesie, nec per predicta in ipsis nullum nobis preiudicium fieri intelligatur in dictis expensis. Cui protestationi dictus dominus Raymundus non consensit nisi in quantum iuxta predictum mandatum domini nostri summi pontificis ad ea tenetur.

In quorum omnium testimonium et evidentiam pleniorem presentes litteras fieri fecimus et nostri sigilli appensione muniri. Data et actum apud Famagustam, sub anno Domini MºCCCºXº, Indictione VIII, mensis Martii die XXVII.

---

[1] promisimus quod *mg. infra*

Appendix 2
Archivum Secretum Vaticanum, Instrumentum Miscellaneum 528
Nicosia, 4 June 1311

Venerabili et magne circumspectionis viro domino Petro de Bria, canonico Nicosiensi et eiusdem ecclesie sede vacante in spiritualibus vicario, frater Bartholomeus, permissione divina abbas monasterii beate Marie de Episcopia, Cysterciensis ordinis, honorem debitum cum salute.

Ad supplicationem Balduini de Cypro in civitate Nicosie domicilium obtinenti, omnes minores ordines iam adepti, quem examinatum et ad titulum bonorum ecclesie nostre de Episcopia, Nicosiensis diocesis, decenter attitulatum vobis transmittimus, amiciciam vestram requirimus et rogamus quatinus predictum Balduinum, exhibitorem presentium, ad prefatum titulum prout oportunum fuerit ad subdyaconatus ordines dignemini facere promoveri, concedentes pos<t>modum eidem Balduino vestras patentes litteras super promotione huiusmodi testimonium perhibentes.

In cuius rei testimonium sigillum nostrum presentibus est appensum.

Datum in domo nostra Nicosie, quarta die mensis Junii, anno a Nativitate Domini millesimo trecentesimo undecimo.

Pope Pius II and Crusading

Norman Housley

The University of Leicester
hou@le.ac.uk

Of all the popes who devoted time and energy to promoting the crusade in the late Middle Ages, only one has been accorded the stature enjoyed by the great crusading popes of the twelfth and thirteenth centuries. In 1992 I stated that "for all his faults, he was without doubt the greatest crusade pope since Gregory X [1271–76],"[1] and three years later James Hankins described him as "the greatest crusading pope of the fifteenth century."[2] The recipient of this high praise was Aeneas Sylvius Piccolomini,[3] whose short reign as Pius II (1458–64) was characterized by intensive efforts to organize a crusading response to the Ottoman Turks. Ludwig Pastor judged that "we cannot withhold our admiration and esteem from the untiring zeal with which, although feeble with age and tortured by bodily suffering, he laboured in what he must have felt to be the almost hopeless cause of the Crusade ... This alone will secure for him an honoured remembrance throughout all ages."[4] Cecilia Ady concurred with Pastor, "he died a martyr to a hopeless cause,"[5] while Kenneth Setton believed that "Pope Pius II's determination to go himself overseas on the crusade, come hell or high water, presents one of the nobler pictures of the Quattrocento."[6] The topos pervading these last three comments is that of heroic failure, and for some authors it interlocks with the search for the last crusade. For Johannes Helmrath the pope's death at Ancona on 14 August 1464 had a much broader significance: "his death signifies the final collapse of the crusade." Pius's demise sealed the fate not just of his own expedition but of crusading generally, because his 1464 campaign had been so vigorously promoted, had achieved a certain popular appeal, yet had ended in confusion and ignominy.[7] For the Germans in particular it was a turning

---

I am grateful to the journal's anonymous referees for their comments and suggestions, as well as to colleagues who responded to my arguments when I presented them at Amsterdam, Glasgow, Leicester and London.

[1] Norman Housley, *The Later Crusades, 1274–1580: From Lyons to Alcazar* (Oxford, 1992), p. 105.

[2] James Hankins, "Renaissance Crusaders: Humanist Crusade Literature in the Age of Mehmed II," *Dumbarton Oaks Papers* 49 (1995), 111–207, at pp. 129–30, words echoed by Nancy Bisaha, *Creating East and West: Renaissance Humanists and the Ottoman Turks* (Philadelphia, 2004), p. 140.

[3] I shall refer to him as Aeneas before his election, Pius after it, and in references that encompass both periods.

[4] Ludwig Pastor, *The History of the Popes,* trans. Frederick I. Antrobus, 5th ed., vol. 3 (London, 1949), p. 374.

[5] Cecilia M. Ady, *Pius II (Aeneas Silvius Piccolomini): The Humanist Pope* (London, 1913), p. 325.

[6] Kenneth M. Setton, *The Papacy and the Levant (1204–1571)*, Memoirs of the American Philosophical Society 114, 127, 161–62, 4 vols. (Philadelphia, 1976–84), 2:261.

[7] Johannes Helmrath, "Pius II. und die Türken," in *Europa und die Türken in der Renaissance*, ed. Bodo Guthmüller and Wilhelm Kühlmann, Frühe Neuzeit 54 (Tübingen, 2000) [hereafter *ETR*],

point. Many crusaders from southern Germany had been bitterly disappointed by their experiences in Hungary in 1456, and now their compatriots from the north suffered a similar disenchantment.[8] The process could not be repeated. Sir Steven Runciman contrasted Ancona in August 1464 with Clermont in November 1095 as a means of bringing his narrative survey of the crusades to a close: "The Crusading spirit was dead."[9] Both the last crusade idea and the heroic failure topos can be questioned. For various reasons the trajectory Clermont 1095 > Ancona 1464 is satisfying at an artistic level, but historically it is highly dubious: 1464 is no more defensible as an end date for crusading than 1291 or 1453.[10] There is artistry too in the topos, and it goes back a long way. It suffuses the self-construction of the pope's own *Commentarii*,[11] the letters and *Commentarii* composed by Jacopo Ammannati Piccolomini,[12] and the lives of Pius written by Giovanni Antonio Campano and Bartolomeo Platina.[13] Now that we are being made aware of how widespread and resonant crusading ideas were in fifteenth-century Europe,[14] it is time to reassess the reputation of their most brilliant and highly-regarded exponent. Does Pius II deserve the praise he has had showered on him?[15]

---

pp. 79–137, at pp. 136–37 ("Sein Tod bedeutet das endgültige Scheitern des Kreuzzugs").

[8] Thomas Vogtherr, "'Wenn hinten, weit, in der Turkei ...'. Die Türken in der spätmittelalterlichen Stadtchronistik Norddeutschlands," in *Europa und die osmanische Expansion im ausgehenden Mittelalter*, ed. Franz-Reiner Erkens, *Zeitschrift für historische Forschung*, Beiheft 20 (Berlin, 1997), pp. 103–25, at pp. 117, 120 ("eine einschneidende Erfahrung"), 121 ("Desaster von 1464").

[9] Steven Runciman, *A History of the Crusades,* 3 vols. (Cambridge, 1951–54), 3:468.

[10] Cf. Hans Eberhard Mayer, comp., *Bibliographie zur Geschichte der Kreuzzüge* (Hanover, 1960), p. xix: "Als zeitlichen Endpunkt für diese Bibliographie habe ich im allgemeinen die Eroberung Konstantinopels 1453 gewählt, weil mit diesem Ereignis die Kreuzzugsbewegung endgültig in die Türkenkriege umschlägt. Nachdem das Jahr 1291 als Schlußpunkt längst als aufgegeben gelten darf, bot erst wieder 1453 einen logischen Einschnitt, der allerdings ebensowenig befriedigt wie 1291"; Jonathan Riley-Smith, *What Were the Crusades?*, 4th ed. (Basingstoke, 2009), pp. 90–92; idem, *The Crusades, Christianity and Islam* (New York, 2008), pp. 45–61.

[11] *Pii II Commentarii rerum memorabilium que temporibus suis contigerunt*, ed. Adrian Van Heck, Studi e Testi 312–13, 2 vols. (Città del Vaticano, 1984). An excellent translation by Margaret Meserve and Marcello Simonetta is in progress in The I Tatti Renaissance Library: 2 vols. (bks. 1–4) to date.

[12] Jacopo Ammannati Piccolomini, *Commentarii*, in the Frankfurt 1614 ed. of Pius II's *Commentarii*; idem, *Lettere (1444–1479),* ed. Paolo Cherubini, Pubblicazioni degli Archivi di Stato, Fonti 25, 3 vols. (Rome, 1997), esp. 2:501–26, 614–22, 835–41, 885–92, nos. 74, 104, 192, 212.

[13] For Campano and Platina see *Le Vite di Pio II di Giovanni Antonio Campano e Bartolomeo Platina*, ed. Giulio C. Zimolo, RIS NS 3, pt. 3 (Bologna, 1964).

[14] Due above all to Daniel Baloup's project, "Les Croisades tardives: Conflits interconfessionnels et sentiments identitaires à la fin du Moyen Âge en Europe," ANR-06-CONF-020 (Université de Toulouse II / FRAMESPA - UMR 5136), the colloquia for which are generating an important series of collected essays.

[15] The bibliography is immense. For recent surveys see Helmrath, "Pius II. und die Türken"; Barbara Baldi, "Il problema turco dalla caduta di Costantinopoli (1453) alla morte di Pio II (1464)," in *La conquista turca di Otranto (1480) tra storia e mito,* ed. Hubert Houben, 2 vols. (Galatina, 2008), 1:55–76. The latter references most of the collections of essays resulting from conferences held to mark the sexcentenary of the pope's birth in 1405. Baldi's *Pio II e le trasformazioni dell'Europa cristiana* (Milan, 2006) is the most important study of Pius's ideology and policy in recent years.

Contextualizing Pius's Crusade Program

Pius's writings about crusading and the Turkish question exceed in both volume and diversity those of any other fifteenth-century pope or crusade enthusiast. He was already interested in the subject in the 1440s but his writings accelerated when he acted as secretary and envoy for Frederick III, especially in the series of imperial diets that followed the fall of Constantinople (1454–55). Thereafter it was one of his most consistent and heartfelt concerns. He approached the question from at least five different directions, and in each case his goal demanded its own style of writing. In the first place, there are the letters that he composed before the papal election in 1458. These form an ongoing commentary on contemporary crusading efforts that is unrivalled for its elegance, insight and wit.[16] Secondly, there is Aeneas writing at length in didactic mode, exemplified by his *De Europa* (1458), a bravura *tour d'horizon* in which classical learning and historical information are constantly enriched by personal experience.[17] Thirdly, and pivotally, there are the series of major orations and bulls in which, acting initially as imperial envoy and later as pope, Pius set himself the task of persuading the members of his audience to commit to undertaking a crusade, either as rulers or as individual Christians. Between 1458 and 1464 there are his many *brevi*, pithy and accessible letters written in his name to rulers and agents in which he attempted to shape, steer and safeguard his crusading enterprise. *Brevi* sent to collectors and even nuncios may have been written by third parties, but the ones intended for powerful lay figures like Francesco Sforza, Philip the Good of Burgundy, or the doge of Venice usually bear the hallmarks of the pope's dictation or at least revision.[18] Lastly, there are the *Commentarii*, his own reflective review of his goals and actions as pope, themselves the subject of much recent study which has highlighted their limitations and multi-functional character.[19] There is general agreement that Pius's approach towards crusading changed when he became pope and for tactical reasons shifted his emphasis from humanistic to religious values.[20] What is just as important about this extraordinary body of writings is its spectrum of purposes – to inform, amuse,

---

[16] Aeneas Sylvius Piccolomini, *Der Briefwechsel. III. Abteilung: Briefe als Bischof von Siena, vol. 1 (1450–1454)*, ed. Rudolf Wolkan (Vienna, 1918); Barbara Baldi, "La corrispondenza di Enea Silvio Piccolomini dal 1431 al 1454. La maturazione di un'esperienza fra politica e cultura," in *I confini della lettera. Pratiche epistolari e reti di communicazione nell'Italia tardomedievale,* ed. Isabella Lazzarini (Florence, 2009), = *Reti Medievali Rivista* 10, 1–22.

[17] Aeneas Sylvius Piccolomini, *De Europa*, ed. Adrian Van Heck, Studi e Testi 398 (Città del Vaticano, 2001); Barbara Baldi, "Enea Silvio Piccolomini e il *De Europa*: umanesimo, religione e politica," *Archivio storico italiano* 598 (2003), 619–83.

[18] For a good example, see Giovanni Battista Picotti, *La dieta di Mantova e la politica de' Veneziani*, facs. repr. of 1912 ed. (Trent, 1996), p. 417 (postscript in a letter to the doge, 25 August 1459).

[19] See esp. the essays by Jean Lacroix and Mario Pozzi in *Pio II e la cultura del suo tempo*, ed. Luisa Rotondi Secchi Tarugi (Milan, 1991).

[20] See, for example, Nancy Bisaha, "Pope Pius II and the Crusade," in *Crusading in the Fifteenth Century: Message and Impact*, ed. Norman Housley (Basingstoke, 2004) [hereafter *CFC*], pp. 39–52, 188–91, at pp. 43–44.

instruct, persuade, inspire, manage, interpret, record and, some would add, sanitize or mislead.

A few examples will illustrate how the abundance and prominence of Pius's writings have led historians to exaggerate his importance. The first relates to the debate about the origins of the Turks, which was significant because it keyed into the broader issue of the threat that they posed. It used to be thought that Pius played a central role in discrediting the notion that they were descended from the Trojans, because it bestowed on them undesirable nobility and validated their conquests from the Byzantines as vengeance. Rather they were ethnically Scythians; hence barbarians who hated learning and whose advance threatened civilized values as well as religious ones. Pius certainly took this position but so did many others.[21] Secondly, a good deal of the more radical promotion of the papal curia's involvement in crusading happened not under Pius but under his predecessor Calixtus III (1455–58). The idea of summoning a congress of powers, at which a crusade would be debated and bilateral agreements reached about contributions, was Calixtus's.[22] It was that pope's determination to create a papal crusade squadron that made possible the naval successes of 1456–57, despite the almost crippling expenses that they entailed.[23] And it was Calixtus who fully harnessed the services of the Franciscan Observants for crusade preaching and collection.[24] The establishment of a crusade treasure was certainly a notable achievement of Pius, not least because the group of cardinals entrusted with its management formed a crusading lobby which "carried the flame" after Pius's death in 1464. But he was developing an idea that had been hatched by Nicholas V ten years earlier.[25]

In general, the more detailed work is done on the period that stretched from the fall of Constantinople (1453) to that of Negroponte (1470), the more the contributions of others are being acknowledged. This is true above all of Cardinal Bessarion. Dan Ioan Mureşan noted Bessarion's "omnipresence" during the last phase of Pius's crusading program, and Iulian-Mihai Damian has eulogized him as "vero artefice ed ispiratore della crociata di Pio II."[26] It is likely that Bessarion exceeded Pius in his understanding of the military character of the Ottoman sultanate and his grasp of the strategic threat that it posed. But important contributions were also made by men like Rodrigo Sánchez de Arévalo, a Castilian who like the Valencian Calixtus

---

[21] Bisaha, *Creating East and West*, ch. 2; Margaret Meserve, *Empires of Islam in Renaissance Historical Thought* (Cambridge, MA, 2008), ch. 1 and *passim*.

[22] Benjamin Weber, "Lutter contre les Turcs. Les formes nouvelles de la croisade pontificale au XVe siècle" (thèse doctorat, Université Toulouse II Le Mirai, 2009), pp. 144–45.

[23] Ibid., pp. 117–19; Setton, *Papacy*, 2:184–90.

[24] Weber, "Lutter," pp. 259–61.

[25] Ibid., pp. 268–69.

[26] Dan Ioan Mureşan, "La croisade en projets. Plans présentés au Grand Quartier Général de la croisade – le Collège des cardinaux" (forthcoming), n. 61; Iulian-Mihai Damian, "La *Depositeria della Crociata (1463–1490)* e i sussidi dei pontefici romani a Mattia Corvino," *Annuario dell'Istituto Romeno di Cultura e Ricerca Umanistica di Venezia* 8 (2006), 135–52, at p. 144, and see also ibid., p. 139, "il vero ispiratore della crociata per la liberazione di Costantinopoli e della Chiesa d'oriente," and p. 149, "il vero genio della crociata tardiva."

brought an Iberian perspective to bear, much as Bessarion brought a Byzantine one, or Girolamo Lando that of his birthplace, Venice.[27] Pius of course had his own strengths: he knew the Holy Roman Empire well and could mesh his knowledge of German affairs with his refined understanding of Italian politics.[28] To a greater extent than Pius's voluminous writings reveal, his crusade was a collective enterprise, in which a group of like-minded enthusiasts pooled their strengths, debating issues, sharing responsibilities, and consoling each other when things went badly. As with any such enterprise there were also differences of opinion, focusing in this instance on how, when, and where to fight against the Turks.

A further point follows logically from this. It is futile to expect Pius's thinking about the crusade to be flawlessly coherent, not just because it was influenced by this exchange of ideas and information, but also because he was responding to multiple outside pressures and evolving circumstances. In Pius's own crusade writings, especially the letters, orations and *Commentarii*, the literary maestro transforms the battering effect of these pressures and changes into a plausible series of tactical maneuvers, designed to shelter his core aims and values. Reality was different. Both when he acted as Frederick's envoy at the 1454–55 diets, and during his reign as pope, Pius had to make do with compromises. Unwittingly, he provided a telling illustration of this. On 1 January 1454 he penned a swingeing critique of Nicholas V's ineffective response to the fall of Constantinople. The pope's actions had consisted largely of issuing crusading bulls without any diplomatic background work. How could anything be expected to happen in such a vacuum? "I ask you: who has seen a crusader? What army has set out? Surely it would have been a good idea to ensure that an army would assemble, and to ascertain its departure date? To avoid mockery, only then should indulgences have been granted." Much the same applied to Nicholas's clerical tenth. "Who is collecting? Who is paying? What nation is permitting it?"[29] This looks like fair comment, but exactly six years later *Ecclesiam Christi*, the crusade bull issued at the close of the Mantua congress, set out the indulgences to be earned by all who supported the crusade decreed there. And Pius was able to be no more specific in *Ecclesiam Christi* than Nicholas V had been. Anybody who took the cross in response to the bull would have had no idea what to do next. Mantua had produced no more than a list of promises whose implementation hinged on the arduous work of papal legates. So Pius's critical remarks of 1454 about Nicholas could with justice have been turned against him. Actually there were advantages to issuing bulls with generalized strategic

---

[27] Sánchez has not yet received the attention he merits, but for Lando see Dan Ioan Mureşan, "Girolamo Lando, titulaire du patriarcat de Constantinople (1474–1497), et son rôle dans la politique orientale du Saint-Siège," *Annuario dell'Istituto Romeno di Cultura e Ricerca Umanistica di Venezia* 8 (2006), 153–258.

[28] On Aeneas's German affinities see Erich Meuthen, "Ein 'deutscher' Freundeskreis an der römischen Kurie in der Mitte des 15. Jahrhunderts. Von Cesarini bis zu den Piccolomini," *Annuarium Historiae Conciliorum* 27/28 (1995/96), 487–542.

[29] *Aeneae Silvii Piccolomini Senensis opera inedita*, ed. Josephus Cugnoni (Rome, 1883, repr. Farnborough, 1968), no. xxxix, pp. 101–2.

templates, notably that they were easier to recycle. Hence *Ecclesiam Christi* was sent to Bosnia in November 1461, to be used in the event of a Turkish incursion.[30] The fact remains that what had seemed clear-cut to Aeneas Sylvius Piccolomini, bishop of Siena, was much less so to Pope Pius II. Except that even in 1454 he probably knew that things were not so cut and dried: he was writing to Juan Carvajal, a fellow crusading enthusiast, soon to become papal legate in Hungary. The simplified argument was tailored to its recipient.

Compromises were one thing: were there also inherent contradictions in Pius's position? Two contenders have to be considered. The first is the pope's famous letter to Mehmed II in 1461, in which he attempted to persuade the sultan to convert. The reasoned tone of the letter is wholly at odds with the violent attacks on Mehmed and his subjects in Pius's crusading output. On individual points this undoubtedly generated contradiction, most glaringly the pope's praise of the sultan and his Scythian forebears. The question of whether there was a broader, underlying contradiction cannot be answered without reference to Pius's purpose in writing the letter. One interpretation, advanced most recently by Nancy Bisaha, is that the letter was directed towards a European audience and that Pius had a mixture of goals: to shame rulers into supporting a crusade, to counter any revival of the conciliar lobby following the disappointing Mantua congress, and to reaffirm the capabilities of humanist, Catholic Europe vis-à-vis its challengers in the East.[31] The alternative, expounded in response to Bisaha by Benjamin Weber, treats the letter as genuine, laying emphasis on the medieval tradition of papal attempts to convert non-Christian rulers by epistolary persuasion.[32] For present purposes what matters is that neither interpretation is detrimental to Pius's reputation as a crusading pope, given that the tradition described by Weber had for generations coexisted with the curia's planning of crusades: he points out that for the period between 1199 and 1329 we have 23 conversion letters sent by the curia to Arabic, Turkish, and Mongol leaders.[33] The letter remains an eccentric member of the corpus of Pius's writings about crusading and the Turks; but given that scholarship has now moved away from the view that depicted most of what Pius did and wrote as dilettante and insincere, there is no reason why it should pose a major threat to his reputation.[34]

The other contender for inherent contradiction is Pius's co-ordination of his crusading program with other dominant strands of the curia's political activity.

---

[30] *Vetera monumenta historica historiam Hungariam sacram illustrantia*, ed. Augustin Theiner, 2 vols. (Rome, 1859–60), 2:366–69, no. 551.

[31] Nancy Bisaha, "Pope Pius II's Letter to Sultan Mehmed II: A Reexamination," *Crusades* 1 (2002), 183–200.

[32] Benjamin Weber, "Conversion, croisade et œcuménisme à la fin du Moyen-âge: encore sur la lettre de Pie II à Mehmed II," *Crusades* 7 (2008), 181–99, but note that on p. 197 Weber does not rule out a western audience too.

[33] Ibid., p. 187.

[34] The nineteenth-century German protestant historian Georg Voigt (*Enea Silvio de' Piccolomini, als Papst Pius der Zweite, und sein Zeitalter* [3 vols., Berlin, 1856–63]) was the principal proponent of the view that Pius was at root a shallow dilettante.

Surely, it could be argued, a pope who genuinely prioritized the war against the Turks would have been more conciliatory towards the Czech king George of Podiebrad (Poděbrady), Sigismondo Malatesta of Rimini, and the Angevin claim on Naples? Pius threatened Podiebrad with excommunication on the eve of his departure for Ancona in 1464. He also made war against Sigismondo into the autumn of 1463, and was unflinching in his support for Ferrante of Aragon. In a letter to Pius's nephew Francesco, written in the autumn of 1465, Ammannati recalled in some detail the debate that had taken place two years previously when the pope had sought advice on whether he should put on hold his preparations for a crusade in 1464 while settling matters with one of the most troublesome of the Papal State's lords, Everso dell'Anguillara.[35] Alienating the French was undoubtedly a dangerous strategy, driving them into Podiebrad's arms during the hectic diplomatic exchanges of 1463–64, and causing Louis XI to exert more pressure than he might have done on Philip the Good to pull out of Pius's crusading coalition. That was an issue of judgment. But when he proceeded with severity against heresy and threats to the security of the papacy's lands in central Italy from the likes of Sigismondo and Everso, Pius was acting in accordance with the deepest policy traditions at Rome. Every Renaissance pope took the same approach, following in the footsteps of their predecessors of the thirteenth and fourteenth centuries. Even Calixtus III, whose dedication to the cause of crusading against the Turks was as great as Pius's, declared a crusade against the condottiere Jacopo Piccinino in the summer of 1455.[36] In March 1457 Aeneas rejoiced to Alfonso of Aragon over the murder of Ulrich count of Cilli, four months earlier, by Ladislas Hunyadi, son of the hero of Belgrade. The son had performed a service to Christendom (*reipublicae Christianae*) that was no less admirable than the father's: "for Mehmed and the count alike were the foes of religion – the former external and the latter internal. What a year it has been, with the Turks driven back and the great count disposed of."[37] Or, in darker circumstances seven years later, when as pope he presided over a consistory that drew up a legal summons for Podiebrad two days before setting out for Ancona: "how can we wage war successfully abroad (*foris*), when we are wounded by those at home (*intus*)?"[38] Defeating, and if need be prioritizing the *hostis domesticus* was hardwired into the mental worldview of Pius II. While this approach had been dominant at the curia since Innocent III's reign, the urgency and proximity of the Turkish threat had the paradoxical effect of reinforcing it. For the

---

[35] Ammannati, *Lettere*, 2:815–25, no. 187. Peace with Sigismondo at this time was only concluded under strong pressure from Venice.

[36] Miguel Navarro Sorni, ed., "Breves del papa Calixto III en el 'Archivio di Stato' de Milán. (Año 1455)," *Anthologica annua* 44 (1997), 675–734, at p. 712, no. 23.

[37] *Opera omnia*, ep. 253, p. 785. For context, see Pál Engel, *The Realm of St. Stephen: A History of Medieval Hungary, 895–1526*, trans. Tamás Pálosfalvi, ed. Andrew Ayton (London, 2001), pp. 288–97.

[38] *Aeneae Silvii Piccolomini ... opera inedita*, no. lxxi, pp. 145–54, at p. 145. The citation was not sent: Pastor, *History*, p. 239. See also *Ungedruckte Akten zur Geschichte der Päpste vornehmlich im XV., XVI. und XVII. Jahrhundert, vol. 1: 1376–1464*, ed. Ludwig Pastor (Freiburg, 1904), no. 34, pp. 45–46 (Bartolomeo Visconti on Calixtus III and Piccinino, 1455).

sense of an embattled *Europa Christiana* was bound to heighten sensitivities about the enemy within.[39]

Thus far the logic of these opening remarks has been to strip away some of the exceptional character of Pius II's crusading program, by emphasizing his receptivity to the views of other crusading enthusiasts, his readiness to adapt in the face of change and failure, and his adherence to mainstream curial thinking on such core issues as conversion, heresy, and the defense of the Church against internal threats. This is starting to make the program sound unoriginal and drab, so by way of balance, it is useful to point out that one feature of Pius's approach was so boldly radical that it shocked contemporaries. This was his resolution to go on crusade in person. His announcement of his decision in a private address in March 1462 to the cardinals makes for one of the finest passages in the *Commentarii*. Pius describes the impasse reached since the close of the Mantua congress more than two years previously. The only way to generate action is for the pope to "lead from the front," and although the cardinals recognize that this is unprecedented, they applaud the proposal.[40] Crusading enthusiasts were naturally delighted: Bessarion would later tell Pius that the public announcement of papal leadership in October 1463 was the happiest day of his life.[41] But cardinals who did not attach supreme importance to the crusade must have been alarmed, fearing that they would be pressurized into accompanying the pope or, if they stayed behind, that the administration of the Church would become impossible without the pope. His death while on crusade would make for a chaotic conclave.[42] Outside the curia indignation in certain quarters was such that the pope devoted a whole section to the matter in his great crusade bull *Ezechielis* (22 October 1463). The pope, said his critics, was an old, ailing priest. He had no business fighting. Well, Pius would prefer not to, but these were desperate times, and Samuel and Elias furnished precedents. His commitment would inspire others to go, while his presence would raise morale in the field. Those cardinals who were strong enough would accompany the army, and other clerics would not just come but fight as well. Pius would be carrying out the Petrine brief of converting others by his example.[43] His equally spirited defense of his participation in the oration that he delivered before leaving Rome in June 1464 indicates that it remained highly contentious.[44]

It was contentious above all because of its political implications. If Pius went, all of Europe's stay-at-home rulers would lose face. "For what excuse can anybody

---

[39] For more on patterns of "turkishness" see Norman Housley, *Religious Warfare in Europe, 1400–1536* (Oxford, 2002), ch. 5.

[40] *Comm.* 7.16, ed. Van Heck, pp. 460–63.

[41] Ludwig Mohler, *Kardinal Bessarion als Theologe, Humanist und Staatsmann. Funde und Forschungen,* 3 vols. (Paderborn, 1923–42), 3:525.

[42] For example, *Ungedruckte Akten,* no. 153, p. 205.

[43] *Opera omnia*, pp. 914–23; also in *Vetera monumenta Slavorum meridionalium historiam illustrantia,* ed. Augustin Theiner, 2 vols. (Rome, 1863), vol. 1, no. 660, pp. 474–81.

[44] *Anecdota litteraria ex MSS codicibus eruta,* 4 vols. (Rome, 1772–83), 3:287–96, esp. pp. 287–88. Of course this was a make or break moment, when we would expect Pius to justify his stance.

have? An old, weak, sick man goes on campaign, while you, a young man, healthy and fit in body, skulk at home?" A crusading bull that circulated throughout Europe and was printed at Mainz in Latin and German,[45] accused Christendom's rulers of shirking their job: "Kings and princes, you do not recognize your duty."[46] The theme had been common currency in crusading orations and negotiations for decades, but this was the first time that it had been aired so bluntly and publicly. Nor was there any doubt that the ruler most under the spotlight was Louis XI of France. At 40 he was hardly young (though Philip the Good was 67 and Pius 58), but he was the Most Christian King and a descendant of St. Louis. He made no secret of his hostility towards his vassal Philip of Burgundy going on crusade and he was liaising with Podiebrad on an eccentric project for a form of crusade that would have barred the pope from anything but a peripheral role in the organization of Catholic Europe's defense against the Turks.[47] In much the same way that the pope's letter to Mehmed cannot be detached from the diplomatic situation prevailing in Europe in 1461, it is unrealistic to isolate Pius's decision to go on crusade from his ingrained hostility towards France and the anti-papal coalition that Podiebrad was constructing.[48] *Ezechielis* solemnly cursed those who stood in the way of Pius's crusade, and by denying Philip permission to go Louis XI placed himself in this position. By inference, the king of France joined the company of pirates and thieves.[49] Everybody knew that he was the source of the "wicked counsels" (*prava consilia*) that stopped Philip carrying out his vow.[50] Pius did not dare take direct action against Louis but his citation of Podiebrad to come to Rome to answer charges against him was, amongst things, a roundabout way of responding to the Burgundian debacle. The point about heretics, the citation declares, is that they wilfully exploit their contagiousness. "Not only do they destroy themselves and their souls; like diseased sheep they infect others in the Lord's sheepfold with whom they come into contact, applying all their efforts to spreading the poison of their madness throughout the Lord's flock."[51] This was surely a response to what Dan Ioan Mureşan has described as a "dangerous collusion between utraquism and gallicanism."[52] When Pius set out on crusade Franco-papal relations were probably

---

[45] Falk Eisermann, "The Indulgence as a Media Event: Developments in Communication through Broadsides in the Fifteenth Century," in *Promissory Notes on the Treasury of Merits: Indulgences in Late Medieval Europe* [hereafter *PN*], ed. R. N. Swanson, Brill's Companions to the Christian Tradition 5 (Leiden, 2006), pp. 309–30, at pp. 313–14.

[46] *Opera omnia*, p. 918.

[47] See, most recently, the essays by Jean-François Lassalmonie, Martin Nejedlý and František Šmahel in *La Noblesse et la croisade à la fin du Moyen Âge (France, Bourgogne, Bohême)*, ed. Martin Nejedlý and Jaroslav Svátek, Les Croisades tardives 2 (Toulouse, 2009).

[48] See Damian, "La *Depositeria della Crociata*," pp. 147–48.

[49] *Opera omnia*, p. 923.

[50] *Anecdota litteraria*, 3:290.

[51] *Aeneae Silvii Piccolomini ... opera inedita*, no. lxxi, pp. 145–54, at pp. 145–46.

[52] Mureşan, "La croisade en projets," at n. 78. Not to speak of schismatic tendencies within the college of cardinals: Baldi, *Pio II*, pp. 209–10.

worse than they had been at any point since the clash between Boniface VIII and Philip the Fair.

The controversy created by Pius's proactive behavior lasted beyond his death. In the final version of the oration that he had intended to present at Ancona before the assembled crusaders, Sánchez repeated the arguments that Pius had set out in *Ezechielis*.[53] Several letters written by Ammannati in 1465–66 reveal, albeit indirectly, the hostility that the pope had aroused. It is clear that Mantua and Ancona were lumped together as proof of Pius's neglect of the Church's vital interests, which required his residence at Rome. In January 1465 Ammannati wrote to another of Pius's intimates, Goro Lolli, mimicking those who were already criticizing the dead pope on account of his crusading endeavors: "such was the fruitlessness of the congress at Mantua, such the empty and pointless hope of setting out against the Turks ...."[54] At the beginning of autumn 1465 he wrote again to Lolli commending Campano's *Vita* as a fitting apologia for the maligned pope.[55] Most interesting is the letter written to Cardinal Francesco Piccolomini in 1466 in which Ammannati defended Pius against the charge of excessive absence from Rome. He argued that convening the Mantua congress had been essential to secure any progress on the crusade, while the journey to Ancona was undertaken to pressurize Philip of Burgundy into keeping his promise.[56] This was very much in line with the dead pope's own justification of his actions.

In the absence of surviving criticism it is hard to say how much of the post-mortem carping related to administrative issues, how much was based on the inherent inappropriateness of Pius's actions, and how far *Ezechielis* and the journey to Ancona were blended with his anti-French policy generally.[57] It is possible that the pope's actions in 1464 muddied the waters for the pro-crusade lobby, which had a tough enough task preserving Pius's crusade treasure without this complication. Within a generation, however, the contentious character of Pius's decision had faded away and it had come to be construed as an admirable and intensely personal deed, an offer of martyrdom. The kudos that it had built up was so powerful that others, most incongruously Alexander VI, paid it the compliment of imitation.[58] We have seen that it became the central image in the myth-making of Pius as the

---

[53] The oration remains unedited, but for a paraphrase see Wolfram Benziger, *Zur Theorie von Krieg und Frieden in der italienischen Renaissance. Die Disputatio de pace et bello zwischen Bartolomeo Platina und Rodrigo Sánchez de Arévalo und andere anläßlich der Pax Paolina (Rom 1468) entstandene Schriften* (Frankfurt am Main, 1996), pp. 154–58, esp. p. 157.

[54] Ammannati, *Lettere*, 2:614–22, no. 104, at p. 616.

[55] Ibid., *Lettere*, 2:835–41, no. 192, at pp. 836–37.

[56] Ibid., *Lettere*, 2:885–92, no. 212, at pp. 887–91.

[57] The most severe critique emanated from Francesco Filelfo in September 1464, but the text is so extreme that it is hard to see it as reflecting a broader reaction: see *Notes et extraits pour servir à l'histoire des croisades au XVe siècle*, ed. Nicolae Iorga, 6 series (Paris and Bucharest, 1899–1916), 4th ser., pp. 240–42.

[58] For example, *Vetera monumenta Poloniae et Lithuaniae gentiumque finitimarum historiam illustrantia*, ed. Augustin Theiner, 4 vols. (Rome, 1860–64), 2:269–76, no. 297, at pp. 273–74.

greatest crusading pope of his age. Irrespective of the contemporary response to his call to arms in 1463, he could not have devised a better way to impress posterity.

Language and Ideas

To make a full evaluation of the nature and especially the originality of Pius's crusade program, we have to pay close attention to the words that he employed and the ways that he hoped to use them to best effect. Pius cherished a strong belief in the persuasive power of eloquence, and few contemporaries could match him as an orator. Helmrath has described the impact made by the speeches that Aeneas gave at the three imperial diets of 1454–55, in particular *Constantinopolitana clades* (Frankfurt, 15 October 1454). People transcribed it immediately after its delivery, and at least two letters survive in which Aeneas promised to send copies. With fifty copies extant, *Constantinopolitana clades* "was one of the most widely copied orations from the last phase of manuscript production."[59] But as Pius himself was the first to admit, his most admired performances failed to produce action. The pope's letters, orations, and *Commentarii* were permeated by the theme that Christians were not as devout as they once had been, and as they needed to be if they were to save themselves by defeating the Turks. The theme took various forms, the most popular being unfavorable comparison with either or both of the Muslims and the first crusaders. In *Cum bellum hodie*, the oration that he delivered at Mantua in September 1459, Pius commented that if Godfrey, Baldwin, Eustace, Hugh, Bohemund, Tancred, and the other leaders of the First Crusade were present, they would by now be shouting "Deus vult!" rather than waiting for the pope's peroration.[60] This of course was rhetorical sleight of hand, given that a set-piece oration was not intended to arouse an audience but to convince it. But Pius wanted to make a point about the spontaneous enthusiasm of the first crusaders, perhaps contrasting it not so much with the audience listening to *Cum bellum hodie*, as with their sluggish assembly at Mantua, where the pope had waited throughout the summer months for their arrival.[61]

A few lines earlier in *Cum bellum hodie*, Pius had marked his place firmly in the line of distinguished crusading popes: like Urban, Eugenius, Innocent, Alexander, and others before him, Pius would "sign with the cross all Christians setting out on

---

[59] Johannes Helmrath, "The German *Reichstage* and the Crusade," in *CFC*, pp. 53–69, 191–203, at pp. 57–62.

[60] *Opera omnia*, pp. 905–14, at p. 914 (also available in Mansi, *Concilia* 32 [Paris, 1902], cols. 207–21); Helmrath, "The German Reichstage," pp. 63–64; more broadly Dieter Mertens, "*Claromontani passagii exemplum*: Papst Urban II. und der erste Kreuzzug in der Türkenkriegspropaganda des Renaissance-Humanismus," in *ETR*, pp. 65–78.

[61] The best analysis of the congress is Jocelyne G. Russell, "The Humanists Converge: The Congress of Mantua (1459)," in her *Diplomats at Work: Three Renaissance Studies* (Stroud, 1992), pp. 51–93.

this expedition."[62] Five years later he was himself to take the cross in St. Peter's before setting out for Ancona.[63] The bull *Ecclesiam Christi*, which followed *Cum bellum hodie* in January 1460, reiterated its message of fundamental continuity.

> In the first place, following the custom of our predecessors, who proclaimed general expeditions either to liberate the Holy Land, or against other unbelievers, we declare a general war and expedition against the very perfidious Turks, the most vicious of our God's enemies, a war that is to be taken up and fought by all Christ's faithful over a period of three years, and to which each and every Christian alike is summoned to contribute according to their ability.[64]

Yet this resounding passage contained a description of the war – *generale bellum atque expeditionem* – that would have sounded incongruous, even bland, to the predecessors referred to; they had shown a distinct preference for the terminology of cross and pilgrimage over that of warfare.[65] The linguistic shift that had occurred is registered most clearly in the *Commentarii*, which for all their demerits do have the advantage of showing us how Pius hoped that his crusade program would be remembered. Here the phrases used most frequently to describe the war against the Turks are neutral and classical: *bellum, expeditio* or *profectio, in, adversus* or *contra Turcos*.[66] At least twice the pope uses phrases emphasizing that this conflict is for the common good, *pro communi utilitate*.[67] Overt religious phraseology is used less frequently. We have a few instances of *res, causa, necessitas,* and *opus fidei* and *causa dei*.[68] Pius uses *bellum in hostes fidei*,[69] *conatus pro defensione fidei contra Turcos*,[70] *bellum pro fide catholica suscipere*,[71] *adversus fidei hostes*

---

[62] "Christianos omnes crucesignabimus in hanc expeditionem ituros": *Opera omnia*, p. 913. Urban II, Eugenius III, Innocent III, and Alexander III are surely the popes referred to.

[63] *Anecdota litteraria*, 3:287–96, esp. p. 287: "suscepturi hodie dominicae crucis, passionisque signum … ."

[64] "In primis generale bellum atque expedicionem contra perfidissimos Turcos dei nostri acerrimos hostes more predecessorum nostrorum, qui generales expediciones, vel ad liberandum [*sic*] terram sanctam, vel contra alios infideles indixerunt, ab omnibus christifidelibus triennio duraturum gerendum ac suscipiendum esse decernimus, omnes et singulos christianos ad presidium eius belli pariter pro viribus invitantes": *Vetera monumenta … Hungariam … illustrantia*, 2:367, no. 551.

[65] Riley-Smith, *What Were the Crusades?*, p. 2. This remained true even in the mid-thirteenth century: Caroline Smith, *Crusading in the Age of Joinville* (Aldershot, 2006), ch. 4.

[66] *Comm.* 3.32, 3.33 (×3), 7.16, 10.23, 12.31, 12.37, 13.1 (*bellum in Turcos gerendum, contra Turcos gerendum, adversus Turcos gerendum*); 12.15, 12.28 (*bellum adversus Turcos suscipere*); 1.26, 1.27 (×2), 3.13, 3.20, 3.36, 3.43, 5.4 (×2), 5.9, 5.11, 9.21, 12.14, 12.16, 12.42, 13.1 (*expeditio in Turcos, contra Turcos, adversus Turcos*); 1.27, 1.28 (×2), 1.29, 3.13, 3.31, 3.35, 6.1, 7.12, 7.16 (×2), 10.10, 12.30, 12.31, 12.34 (*bellum contra Turcos, in Turcos, adversus Turcos*); 2.1, 3.34, 3.35, 12.3, 12.31, 13.1 (*bellum in Turcos inferre*); 3.13, 6.1 (×2), 7.16, 12.28, 12.30, 12.35, 13.1 (*bellum Turcis indicendum*); 12.42 (*profectio in Turcos*).

[67] Ibid., 1.26, 5.4.

[68] Ibid., 4.4, 5.4, 5.8, 6.1, 9.21, 12.28.

[69] Ibid., 3.32.

[70] Ibid., 5.4.

[71] Ibid., 7.16.

... *bellum*,[72] and *sacre religionis defensio, defensio sacrosancti evangelii divineque legis*.[73] These references to the conflict's religious rationale confirm that Pius is not secularizing his planned crusade – that would undercut his own claims to initiate and control it. But the reflective and dispassionate treatment that he accords it is in line with his humanist convictions, besides replicating his model, Julius Caesar.[74]

One of the clearest ways in which Pius's predecessors had signaled the pilgrimage element in their crusading was through their use of the word *passagium*, and Pius's own use of *passagium* terminology is revealing about his evolving attitude toward crusading past and present. In letters written before he became pope Aeneas frequently used the word *passagium*,[75] and on at least one occasion he referred to a *generale passagium*.[76] What did he mean by this? One way to explore it is by reference to one of the very few instances of his use of the term in the *Commentarii*. Pius deployed the phase *generale passagium* in describing *Moyses vir dei*, the oration that he had given at Rome in April 1452 in which he had called for a crusade on behalf of Frederick III.[77] Aeneas used the opportunity to explain what the phrase signified, pointing out that *passagium* meant a passing over, or *transitus*. In recent history it had been applied to the crusades: "by calling something a *passagium* what we mean is an exceptionally large military expedition declared against unbelievers by Christians, who, if they take part as *cruce signati*, are entitled to the plenary remission of all their sins."[78] In a remarkable analogy, Aeneas likened these past *passagia* to the East to the seasonal migrations of birds. The word could, he wrote, be applied to any large-scale movement of peoples, like that of barbarians (Goths, Huns, and others) during the *Völkerwanderung*. Pedantically, he commented in passing that such migratory *passagia* had usually happened for motives of resettlement rather than warfare. The reason he used the phrase at Rome in 1452 was to make the point that the Turks owed their conquests only to their numbers. Man for man the Christians were militarily superior to the Muslims, who were also internally divided and demoralized by gloomy prophecies about the downfall of their faith. So provided an expedition was launched on the scale required – that is, of a *generale passagium* – the Turks could be defeated, just as they had been by the first crusaders. The obvious flaw in such an argument was that it called for a massive army: Aeneas referred to Otto of Freising's estimate

---

[72] Ibid., 3.5.

[73] Ibid., 12.28.

[74] The word constantly used in the dispatches of the Italian envoys is *impresa* (undertaking): *Ungedruckte Akten*, no. 65, p. 94, *et passim*.

[75] For example, Piccolomini, *Der Briefwechsel*, no. 112, p. 214, no. 194, pp. 377–78, no. 230, p. 418, no. 290, p. 490, no. 15 [*sic*], pp. 607–9.

[76] *Aeneae Silvii Piccolomini ... opera inedita*, no. xliii, p. 106.

[77] *Comm*. 1.24; *Opera omnia*, pp. 928–32.

[78] "passagii vocabulo nihil aliud designamus quam expeditionem militarem numerosissimam adversus infideles per Christianos indictam, quam si consequuntur cruce signati, plenariam peccatorum omnium remissionem merentur": *Opera omnia*, p. 929. Pius's distinction here between *crucesignati* and others who might take part in a *passagium* is a revealing one to which we shall return in the context of his 1464 expedition.

of 300,000 men on the First Crusade. He imagined his hearers exclaiming, when they heard his appeal for a *passagium*, "There you are! The old dream ... the old nonsense, the empty tales," and he had no answer for such skepticism apart from the unconvincing assertion "who doubts that a *passagium* can happen when it is summoned by papal authority and imperial mandate?" In short, Nicholas V could do nothing more useful or more glorious than support this *generale passagium*.[79] The same logic seems to lie behind his comment in a letter to Carvajal, in October 1454, that the pope should call a *general* assembly in order to launch a *general* passage.[80]

The argument that if a crusade was to succeed it would have to be a general passage, ideally conducted on the scale of the First Crusade, was a gift to skeptics, and over the course of time Pius learned to scale down his figures. At the Regensburg diet in the spring of 1454 he called for a German army 200,000-strong, which the German envoys who were present criticized as unrealistic.[81] By the time he spoke on behalf of the emperor at Wiener Neustadt in February 1455, the 200,000 had shrunk to 40,000. However, Aeneas hastened to add, this would just be the Germans: many other contingents would fight at their side. All would be well provided the crusaders did not allow the sin of pride to generate discord between the various contingents, as had happened on the Second Crusade.[82] At the close of the Mantua congress, by contrast, he regarded *overall* commitments totaling 70,000 as sufficient.[83] It was possible to justify these more realistic figures because Pius had already adjusted his argument about the opposition: speaking at Frankfurt in October 1454 he claimed that the Turks could muster no more than 15,000 decent soldiers.[84] It would be inaccurate to attribute his gradual discarding of *passagium* solely to greater realism about numbers, because he continued to believe in the central importance of a collective Christian effort. The shift in his thinking was probably broader. *Moyses vir dei* was a *pièce d'occasion*, one of a number of orations that Aeneas made on Frederick's behalf at Rome in the spring of 1452. Frederick had just been crowned emperor, so a clarion call to crusade was the order of the day. But he had also just married, and nobody really expected him to lead an army to save the Greeks, recover the Holy Land, and destroy Islam – the agenda set out for him in Aeneas's oration. The orator was flattering his most august listeners when he said that Europe would spring to arms at their command. It is revealing that he gave this speech only a few lines in the *Commentarii*.

Once Constantinople had fallen, on the other hand, it was impossible to treat the Turkish threat lightly. In strategic terms, too, the situation changed radically.

---

[79]   *Opera omnia*, pp. 930–32.

[80]   *Aeneae Silvii Piccolomini ... opera inedita*, no. xliii, p. 106.

[81]   *Deutsche Reichstagsakten unter Kaiser Friedrich III., fünfte Abteilung, erste Hälfte 1453–1454*, ed. Helmut Weigel and Henny Grüneisen, Deutsche Reichstagsakten 19.1 (Göttingen, 1969), pp. 277–79, 288–91, 294–300, 307–23.

[82]   *Pii II orationes*, ed. Joannes Dominicus Mansi, 3 vols. (Lucca, 1755–59), vol. 1, no. 14, pp. 287–306, at pp. 303–4.

[83]   Mansi, *Concilia* 35 (Paris, 1902), cols. 113–20, at col. 115.

[84]   *Opera omnia*, p. 685.

As Aeneas briefly explained in 1452, the language of the *passagium* was created in the circumstances of the seaborne expeditions to the Holy Land. It had enjoyed a prolonged lease of life thanks to being transferred to the Aegean world in the fourteenth century. The phased crusade, with a small or *particulare passagium* paving the way for a *generale passagium*, could be made to fit scenarios like the capture of the ports of Smyrna (Izmir) in 1344 and Alexandria in 1365. Through the concept of the bridgehead it reconciled the limited gains that could be got from such naval raids (booty, renown, deterrence) with the universality that had always lain at the heart of crusading's appeal. For a time the phased crusade even looked like the best way to ensure that the Greeks kept their promises about Church Union in return for military aid from the West.[85] After 1453 strategic debate about defensive crusading against the Turks continued to incorporate a strong naval element, though in general such an approach was less in the foreground under Pius than it had been under Calixtus or would be under Sixtus IV.[86] It became a truism that combined land and sea operations were essential to achieve maximum military impact on the Turks: "There is no point in conducting a naval war unless a land army also engages the Turks."[87] These operations could take place at some distance from Christian Europe: late in October 1454, for example, Aeneas was envisaging seaborne attacks on Greece and Asia, and a land war in Thrace or Macedonia.[88] But it was stretching language to describe such coordinated operations as *passagia* in the style that had been appropriate in the thirteenth or even fourteenth century. Both the meaning and historical origins of *passagium* no longer fitted the situation, with the result that the phraseology fell into disuse. Like most linguistic shifts, the process of abandonment was uneven. The peace terms concluded at Wiener Neustadt between Frederick III and Matthias Corvinus in July 1464 referred to a crusade against the Turks as both a "passagium generale" and an "expeditio generalis."[89] When referring to Sforza's contribution of 500 cavalry for Pius's crusade in 1464, Venice described the war as a "sancta expeditio contra Turcum," reserving the word *passagium* for the Adriatic crossing.[90] Pius's own move away from the term probably stemmed from several factors: the downsizing of numbers in the interests of realism; a weakening in his expectation of imperial leadership; greater attentiveness to the strategic realities that faced Christian Europe; and the inherent appeal of the more classical vocabulary to which he eventually gave full rein in the *Commentarii*.[91]

---

[85] Norman Housley, The *Avignon Papacy and the Crusades, 1305–1378* (Oxford, 1986), esp. pp. 149, 218–19.

[86] Weber, "Lutter," pp. 54–65.

[87] *Aeneae Silvii Piccolomini ... opera inedita*, no. liv, p. 119.

[88] Ibid., no. xlv, p. 109.

[89] Karl Nehring, *Matthias Corvinus, Kaiser Friedrich III. und das Reich. Zum hunyadisch-habsburgischen Gegensatz im Donauraum* (Munich, 1975), pp. 202–15; *Vetera monumenta ... Hungariam ... illustrantia*, vol. 2, no. 567, pp. 382–91, at p. 384.

[90] *Ungedruckte Akten*, no. 198, p. 310.

[91] Further on *passagium*, see Weber, "Lutter," pp. 378–79.

If the phrase *generale passagium* increasingly pointed to the past, the word *cruciata* was, in Pius's reign as pope, just entering its heyday. The word had been used for generations in various crusading contexts, especially the warfare in Iberia, but it was under the Valencian pope Calixtus III that it became commonplace in the documents emanating from the papal chancery. We have many of Calixtus's *brevi,* and *cruciata* is constantly employed.[92] Calixtus used the word to refer to the enterprise that he was trying to promote, but he also employed it, often in the same letter, in the narrower sense of crusade preaching and collection, the processes through which individuals took the cross to fight in person, or donated money or goods to the cause. Thus in a single letter to the collector Mariano da Siena, in July 1457, we find "cruciatam predicare," "elemosinas pro cruciata congregatas," and "ut ad cruciatam irent."[93] Pius's correspondence reveals that he took a similarly eclectic approach when the occasion called for it. In a *breve* dispatched to the same recipient almost two years later, we find "in vim cruciatae," "euntibus ad cruciatam," and "in cruciatae utilitatem."[94] It is quite possible that the same clerk composed both *brevi,* and in letters for which a stronger case can be made for the pope's involvement in the drafting process, his humanist training and outlook led him away from a word that had no classical origins or even frame of reference. But it would be wrong to read much into this. There was no question of Pius trying to camouflage what he needed to drive his program, in terms of individuals taking the cross or contributing in many other ways. His immediate response to Constantinople's fall in July 1453 included the expectation that legates dispatched by the pope "should preach the cross and promise remission of sins."[95] It was in this respect that the Church, acting under the curia's direction, continued to play its traditional role. Pius knew that his crusade would only materialize if he succeeded in creating and controlling an upsurge of popular devotion, and in common with his contemporaries and successors he made repeated reference to Capistrano's extraordinary achievement in raising and leading a volunteer army of *crucesignati* in 1456.[96] The challenge was to manage both aspects of the scenario: public and collective acceptance of the need for an *expeditio* or *bellum* against the Turks; personal and individual response to the preaching of the *cruciata.*

The message that Pius's mixed vocabulary had to convey oscillated between anxiety and assurance. This tension lay at the very heart of crusading and derived from its roots in the pilgrimage tradition. It was at its most evident when the fate of

---

[92] *Il "Liber brevium" di Callisto III. La crociata, l'Albania e Skanderbeg,* ed. Matteo Sciambra et al. (Palermo, 1968); *Acta Albaniae Vaticana. Res Albaniae saeculorum XIV et XV atque cruciatam spectantia,* ed. Ignatius Parrino, Studi e Testi 266 (Città del Vaticano, 1971). Cf. Weber, "Lutter," pp. 379–85.

[93] *Il "Liber brevium",* pp. 157–58.

[94] *Bullarium Franciscanum,* nova series, vols. 2–4, ed. Joseph M. Pou y Marti and Caesar Cenci (Quaracchi, 1939–90), vol. 2, no. 630, pp. 331–32.

[95] Piccolomini, *Der Briefwechsel. III. Abteilung ... vol. 1,* no. 112, pp. 204–15, at p. 214.

[96] Norman Housley, "Giovanni da Capistrano and the Crusade of 1456," in *CFC,* pp. 94–115, 215–224, esp. pp. 111–12.

Jerusalem, the location of Christ's suffering and resurrection, hung in the balance. But it was capable of being transferred to other theatres of crusading warfare because it hinged on the relationship between a just but merciful God and His sinning but chosen people. Making it work in the case of the Turks depended on showing that although they were a dangerous foe they could, nonetheless, be defeated. Pius did this most convincingly in *Constantinopolitana clades*. After opening with a brilliant passage on the fall of Constantinople, he conceded that a war against Mehmed II should only be started if it could be shown to be *iustum* (just), *utile* (advantageous), and *facile* (viable rather than easy). Aeneas then guided his audience through all three topics, interweaving biblical, classical and medieval precedents in a virtuoso display of his learning and rhetorical elegance. No war could be more just than one that was waged under proper authority for religion, homeland, and kinsmen. And a crusade, fought by all to protect all, offered the only prospect for both defeating the Turks and winning salvation.[97]

Constantinopolitana clades was directed at the Germans, so Aeneas made much play with the themes of imperial responsibility and German military prowess, but the threefold schema that he adopted when speaking as pope at Mantua, five years later, was not radically different from the one that he had devised for the envoys gathered at Frankfurt. *Causae* (causes), *facultates* (resources) and *praemia* (rewards) were natural successors to justice, advantage and viability. Pius described how, in accordance with Daniel's prophecy and Christ's injunction to his apostles, the Christian message had been carried throughout the world. But the spread of Islam had now driven it into Europe, a corner (*angulum*) of the world. It is likely that Aeneas borrowed the congestion argument from Flavio Biondo, who in his account of Urban II's Clermont sermon in the *Historiarum decades* took Robert of Reims's famous passage about population pressure and reformulated it in terms of Islamic conquest.[98] Aeneas argued that the capture of Constantinople had not sated but encouraged Mehmed's ambitions. Currently he was exerting pressure on Hungary, and if he succeeded in conquering that country he would not stop: Germany, Bohemia, Poland, and Italy were next on his agenda. In the five years since Frankfurt anxiety had increased, but so too had assurance. Thanks to the relief of Belgrade and the victories of Hunyadi and Skanderbeg, believers could not doubt that God would assist His people.[99]

The most significant feature of Pius's message was his adroit handling of the European theme.[100] This was fundamental in shaping the way he dealt with anxiety and assurance alike. At the start of *Constantinopolitana clades* Aeneas argued that the city's fall was unprecedented because it lay in Europe. Granted, the Turks had

---

[97] *Opera omnia*, pp. 678–89.

[98] Mertens, "*Claromontani passagii exemplum*," pp. 70–71.

[99] *Opera omnia*, pp. 905–14.

[100] This too was a borrowing from Biondo, bearing out Mertens's comment that "der fleißigste der frühen Leser Biondos war Enea Silvio Piccolomini": Mertens, "*Claromontani passagii exemplum*," p. 74, and see too pp. 71–72.

already reached Greece, the Tatars eastern Europe, and the Moors Spain; but none of these areas had possessed the strategic significance of Constantinople. Nor was it just a question of geo-politics. Constantinople had been the sole survivor of the Greek classical world, and now it had joined Thebes, Athens, Mycenae, Larissa, Sparta, and Corinth among the ranks of the departed. The Turks hated learning and in their sack of the city they had destroyed books as happily as relics. The resulting threat to the Catholic world was construed in much the same terms. For the time being, the Christian God was a European one, and the defense of His religion was the preservation of civilized values – above all humanist ones – across Europe. Admittedly, this was an elite culture, but it was important to everybody: soldiers might question why they should be concerned about the loss of book learning, but without the written word the memory of their deeds would die with them. The image was conjured up of a new wave of barbarians, successors to the Tatars, Magyars, Huns, Goths, and others, washing across central and western Europe, detained by neither human resistance nor natural barriers.[101] This emphasis on the threat to Christendom's interior explains Aeneas's assertion, in his first major written response to the fall of Constantinople in July 1453, that even the loss of Jerusalem, Acre, and Antioch was surpassed by that of Constantinople. On first reading this seems to be a hyperbolic if not shocking claim; but its rationale is that the earlier losses had not occurred on European soil. "Now," by contrast, "Mohammed reigns among us."[102]

But the *Europa* theme also boosted the grounds for hopes. For like other Asiatic would-be world conquerors before them, the strength of the Turks lay not in innate or acquired military virtues, but solely in their numbers, and a smaller but disciplined European army led by able commanders could defeat them. Ancient history shored up faith by corroborating the experience of the First Crusade: the new crusaders would follow in the footsteps of Alexander and Caesar as well as those of Godfrey of Bouillon.[103] In his concern to give assurance, Pius leaned too far in the direction of optimism. In particular, he constantly denigrated the military abilities of the Turks. At Wiener Neustadt in 1455 he wheeled in Aristotle to support this: "You will be fighting as well-armed against unarmed, trained against unskilled, bold against timid. For, as Aristotle attests, the Asians are unwarlike."[104] Later, the relief of Belgrade was used as evidence: if Capistrano's volunteers, "crusaders without arms or armor, equipped only with faith and protected only by heaven," could

---

[101]   *Opera omnia*, pp. 678–89.

[102]   Piccolomini, *Der Briefwechsel. III. Abteilung … vol. 1*, no. 109, pp. 189–202, at p. 201.

[103]   *Opera omnia*, pp. 905–14.

[104]   *Pii II orationes*, vol. 1, no. 14, p. 306. Surprisingly, the well-informed Bessarion took the same line, at least when trying to win over the envoys at Mantua: hence the vast majority of the Ottoman forces were "nudi, inermes, sine stipendio publico, absque omnibus opibus propriis, praeda duntaxat, et incursionibus viventes …" while "Italia sola … supra sexaginta militum millia et armis, et scientiae rei militaris … qui non modo Europa, sed tota Asia hanc immanissimam belluam repulissent, et Dominicum usque sepulchrum libere penetrassent." *Anecdota veneta nunc primum collecta ac notis illustrata*, ed. Joannes Baptista Maria Contareni, 1 (Venice, 1757), pp. 276–83, at p. 281.

defeat Mehmed, a professional army could achieve even more.[105] Provided they were combined with the penitence that had been displayed at Belgrade, European skill and discipline would prevail.

In his 1455 Wiener Neustadt address, Aeneas again relied on an Aristotelian argument to the effect that the 40,000-strong German force being proposed was the optimal size for effective deployment, supply and command. Indeed, in military terms this is Pius's most interesting oration: having already made the case for a crusade at the Regensburg and Frankfurt diets, he turned his attention to subjects like the maintenance of order and the treatment of captured Turks.[106] The argument about numbers was especially sensitive at the close of the Mantua congress, when Pius had managed to extract promises of only 70,000 troops. As we have seen, his conviction that the Turkish numbers did not give them military superiority enabled the pope to rationalize this disappointing outcome. The Romans, under commanders like Scipio Africanus, Pompey, and Julius Caesar, had also used small armies – in fact they had subdued the world with just four [sic] legions.[107] In 1453 he had argued that if Italy (that is, Rome) alone had conquered Greece, Asia, Libya and Egypt, what might not be achieved if the peninsula's resources were joined with those of Germany and France?[108]

Mobilizing Christian Europe

So the gist of Pius's message was that the Turks could be defeated: but this could only come about through a common effort on the part of Christian Europe. Bringing this effort into existence lay at the heart of Pius's crusading program, partly because, if all the Christian powers were involved, nobody could claim that their rivals were being favored. In the famous letter of July 1453 to Pope Nicholas V that set out his initial response to Constantinople's fall, Aeneas was already advocating a meeting of envoys: "your task now is to rise up, write to kings, send legates, give warning, and urge princes and communities to either attend or send [envoys] to a designated location."[109] But it is his critique of Nicholas V in January 1454 that best explains his reasoning. He listed Nicholas's crusading expenditures: 5,000 florins sent to Skanderbeg, 60,000 to the Knights of St. John, and 40,000 spent on shipping. There had been negotiations with Karaman, the Ottomans' Anatolian rival, and various Balkan peoples threatened by the Turks' advance had been encouraged to resist. But there was no underpinning strategy. Five galleys could do nothing against the Turks and 5,000 florins (which some said were only 3,000) would not

---

[105] Lodrisio Crivelli, *De expeditione Pii papae II*, in RIS NS 33, pt. 5, pp. 91–96 (*Vocavit nos Pius*), at p. 94. See Mansi, *Concilia* 35, cols. 113–20 (*Septimo iam exacto mense*), at col. 116.

[106] *Pii II orationes*, vol. 1, no. 14, pp. 304–5.

[107] Mansi, *Concilia* 35, cols. 113–20, at col. 116.

[108] Piccolomini, *Der Briefwechsel. III. Abteilung ... vol. 1*, no. 112, p. 215.

[109] Ibid., no. 109, p. 201.

go very far with Skanderbeg. What was needed was a *validissimum passagium* emulating the deeds of the great crusading leaders: Charlemagne, Godfrey, Conrad, Louis, and Frederick. The only way to bring that into being was through [inter-] national agreement (*nationum consensus*), which entailed summoning a *generalis congregatio*. The money spent on galleys would have been much better spent on the process of mobilization. Those who opposed such a gathering were afraid that critics of the curia would use it as a platform for their grievances, even demands for a general council. To that Aeneas had no convincing answer, but it is likely that he saw it as a risk that had to be taken.[110] The disappointments of the "Turkish diets" of 1454–55 only reinforced Aeneas's belief that a meeting of the powers or their envoys was essential if progress was to be made on a broad front.[111] And the unflagging energy of Calixtus III, which Pius much admired, only demonstrated the limits on what the most committed pope could achieve single-handed. *Vocavit nos Pius*, the bull in which Pius summoned his own congress in November 1458, added little of substance to the case that he had set out over four years previously. It is rich in Church history and biblical citations, but the only new element was the relief of Belgrade, that valuable morale-raiser. It showed what could be done, but Christians, Pius reminded his audience, must act "with pooled resources and strength," following "common counsel."[112]

We have seen that the idea of an assembly or congress, at which a collective approach would be agreed on, was far from original. It had been floated in 1451 by Philip the Good, who may have been thinking of something akin to the congress of Arras of 1435.[113] From the end of 1457 Calixtus had actively pursued it.[114] It is to Pius's credit that he brought the idea to fruition, and his approach towards his congress was influenced (mainly negatively) by the imperial diets that he had attended and (mainly positively) by the Italian league of 1455.[115] The greatest problem with his congress was that it possessed no juridical foundation. The impressive text dated 1 October 1459, and spelling out the procedure that was agreed with the Italian powers, dwelt on indissoluble obligations to God, Christ, angels, saints, and the entire heavenly court, an elaborate but in legal terms meaningless formula.[116] The pope's roll-call of the situation at the end of the Mantua congress was neatly divided into *certa promissa* and *sperata*, but in reality even the 70,000 troops listed under "certain promises" were far from guaranteed. Bessarion, who was given the thankless task of persuading the Germans to provide the 42,000 promised in the *Provisio Germaniae*, discovered during a frustrating

---

[110] *Aeneae Silvii Piccolomini ... opera inedita*, no. xxxix, pp. 99–102.

[111] Ibid., no. xliii, pp. 105–8.

[112] Crivelli, *De expeditione*, pp. 91–96.

[113] Jacques Paviot, *Les ducs de Bourgogne, la croisade et l'Orient (fin XIVe siècle – XVe siècle)* (Paris, 2003), p. 123 and n. 20.

[114] Cf. Baldi, "Il problema turco," p. 60.

[115] See Baldi, "Il problema turco," p. 70, for the diets and league as "points of reference." See also her *Pio II*, pp. 147–70.

[116] Picotti, *La dieta di Mantova*, p. 439.

legation in 1460 that the Germans did not regard the matter as settled; everything had to be renegotiated.[117] The empire's labyrinthine constitution certainly did not help matters, but even in the case of the other allegedly "certain" commitments, those of Burgundy and Hungary, the leverage that could be brought to bear was all indirect: Philip the Good's vow at the Feast of the Pheasant in February 1454, and Hungary's dependence on papal support, against Turks and Habsburgs alike.

Pius knew full well that his congress possessed no legal framework, a fact that he effectively acknowledged at the start of his closing address in January 1460 when he made the astonishing assertion that, instead of being dissolved, the assembly would accompany the pope and his curia, by being absorbed into his authority as pope. His argument was unconvincing: Pius had called the congress because of the need to secure the *nationum consensus*, but he was now asserting that papal authority by itself could move the crusade forward.[118] The explanation for this muddle was that Pius approached affairs not in juristic terms but in a way that fused aspiration with pragmatism – although an experienced politician and diplomat, he could not resist the allure of grand rhetoric. Sweeping and dogmatic statements about the appropriate way for the curia to proceed were therefore subjected to a radical overhaul when they failed to produce the hoped-for result; in Barbara Baldi's phrase, the result was "continui, faticosissimi aggiustamenti."[119] As wishful thinking, the conjuring trick that Pius performed on the Mantua congress was rivaled by the grandiose statements that he was prone to make in public documents about the reach of his authority in crusading matters. Two are particularly revealing, though it has to be added that in neither instance was the pope breaking new ground. In *Adversus impiam* (January 1460) he asserted that he had the authority to tax the laity for the cause of crusade without reference to their lay rulers: "We act in the place of he who is the lord of all, and since we are the head of the Church Militant, when urgent necessity dictates it, we could have ordered Christians to render assistance to their faith without obtaining anybody's agreement." Using such resounding phraseology in the mid-fifteenth century was mere bluff, as Pius acknowledged by immediately referring to the agreements that he had managed to reach with the Italians.[120] Even though he knew that papal *plenitudo potestatis* was dead, he could not resist the temptation to refer to it.

In a somewhat different vein, in *Ezechielis* (October 1463) Pius asserted that supporting the crusade in person or through contribution was *de necessitate salutis*, a universal Christian obligation that no believer could evade.[121] This claim went back at least as far as 1453, when Nicholas V had argued that the crisis caused by Constantinople's fall to the Turks was so grave that their defeat became a matter of faith: "since this is a moment of such necessity that nobody can legitimately excuse

[117] Mohler, *Kardinal Bessarion*, 1:292–303.
[118] Mansi, *Concilia* 35, cols. 113–20, at col. 113.
[119] Baldi, "Il problema turco," p. 68.
[120] Mansi, *Concilia* 32, cols. 265–66.
[121] *Opera omnia*, p. 922.

themselves from it."[122] It is possible to argue that in Pius's hands this indicated a shift in thinking about the crusade in terms of political identity, an identification of crusading duty with European citizenship that mirrored the anti-curial program which was being sponsored by Podiebrad's court in the early 1460s. But there is neither need nor justification for imposing such ways of thinking on Pius. It is more likely that the pope was simply exasperated by political opposition to his crusade, especially at the French court, and deployed this argument in the hope of quelling it. In other words, it arose not from any major shift in the way crusading was conceptualized, but from the needs of the hour. He may have hoped that his *de necessitate salutis* argument would make it easier to collect the lay thirtieth that he had decreed for the crusade, but this too did not hinge on any radical reformulation of what crusade entailed for the ordinary believer: Pius's thirtieth was just the latest in a series of papal attempts to impose a tax on the laity for crusading purposes that went back to Gregory IX and Gregory X in the thirteenth century. In other words, *De necessitate salutis* was close kin to *plenitudo potestatis*, and no more convincing.

In March 1462 Pius outlined to six trusted cardinals a shift in policy that amounted to a movement away from the *nationum consensus* approach. Mantua, he said, had shown the futility of congresses. The pope would therefore fall back on co-operation with those rulers and powers that either had a vested interest in resisting the Turks (notably Hungary) or (as in the case of Philip the Good) had taken a vow to help. There is no doubt that this contraction of scope and ambition constituted a personal blow for Pius: much of the work that had gone into Mantua had to be written off, though some (especially the proposed levies on the clergy, laity and Jews) was recycled within the new framework. The tone of his 1462 speech, which he reported in the *Commentarii*,[123] is emotional and almost desperate, as befits a personal commitment to crusade made in response to disappointment and a perceived lack of faith. In practice, taking into account Mantua's juridical vacuum and Louis XI's ability to sabotage anything that Pius tried to do in the broader arena, the shift from general to selective mobilization made a good deal of sense. Collaborating with interested parties had a very long pedigree at the curia: most recently the approach had been followed by Eugenius IV and Calixtus III, but it was solidly rooted in the naval leagues of the mid-fourteenth century.[124]

What Pius added to this tradition was his resolve to go on crusade in person. It remains an enigmatic decision. Possibly it reflected genuine shock at the apathetic response to his congress and at the extent to which this derived from suspicion of his motives.[125] It may have derived from hopes of replicating what Capistrano had achieved at Belgrade in 1456, and sharing that preacher's kudos. Even before

---

[122]   *Annales ecclesiastici*, ed. O. Raynaldus and G. D. Mansi, vol. 9 (Lucca, 1752), ad ann. 1453, nos. 9–11, at p. 617.

[123]   *Comm.* 7.16, ed. Van Heck, pp. 460–63.

[124]   Housley, *Avignon Papacy*, pp. 32–36.

[125]   Bisaha, "Pope Pius II and the Crusade," pp. 47–50.

1456 Pius had admired Capistrano greatly; in his Wiener Neustadt oration in 1455 he compared him to Jeremiah and John the Baptist as a preacher of repentance.[126] That said, we have seen that the personal commitment was probably also a political move, directed against the hostile Louis XI. The Milanese envoys at Rome in October 1463 were acute in connecting Pius's "ardor" for his forthcoming crusade with his need "to avoid the disgrace (*infamia*), which the French and many others have ascribed to him."[127] As the situation became increasingly unmanageable in 1464, Pius was caught between a rock (the Turks) and a hard place (the French). The crusade, which had already destabilized Italian politics to an alarming extent, could result in a military disaster, which would stimulate Ottoman ambitions. On the other hand, its abandonment would be a gift to the anti-curial lobby led by Louis XI, which would reap the harvest of carping and skepticism that formed the backcloth to Pius's activity during the winter of 1463–64.[128] There was a real threat that a council, probably convened at Lyons, would arraign the pope, inter alia, for failing to defend Christians and for wasting crusade funds.[129] In this regard Pius's record was not spotless: he had diverted crusading money to the Genoese to help them stave off the French.[130] When the full extent of the dilemma became apparent, in June 1464, the nervous strain caused even the urbane Pius to lose his temper with Sforza's envoy, abusing the French as empty-headed and volatile.[131] In late July the pope denied that he had any worries about the council that Louis kept floating, but his comment that if he wanted to he could stir up a magnate rebellion against the king was a sure sign that actually he was deeply troubled by the prospect.[132]

As things stood in the spring of 1462, the outcome of Pius's crusading resolution would likely have proved modest at best, but a year later Venice was plunged into war with Mehmed. Venetian resistance to commitment at Mantua had been both ingenious and notorious, giving rise to some of Pius's strongest criticism.[133] Working with the mercantile republic was trying and distasteful, and it carried the price of alienating Sforza, whom the pope longed to the end to bring into his project;[134] when attempting to persuade the duke to accept command of the crusade in September 1463, Pius resorted to the self-defeating argument that Sforza need not fear a Venetian attack on his lands during his absence because he would be working

---

[126] *Pii II orationes*, vol. 1, no. 14, p. 297.

[127] *Ungedruckte Akten*, no. 154, p. 210.

[128] Ibid., no. 179, pp. 267–73, no. 192, pp. 290–96, esp. pp. 292–93, no. 193, pp. 296–303, esp. p. 298; *Bullarium Franciscanum, Supplementum*, vol. 1, ed. Caesar Cenci (Rome, 2002), no. 1480, p. 687.

[129] *Ungedruckte Akten*, no. 188, pp. 282–86, esp. p. 285.

[130] Baldi, *Pio II*, pp. 189–91.

[131] *Ungedruckte Akten*, no. 193, pp. 296–303, esp. pp. 298–300 ("quelli cervelli francesi, pieni de legereza e de instabilità").

[132] Ibid., no. 199, p. 316.

[133] Picotti, *La dieta di Mantova; Comm.* 3.35, ed. Van Heck, pp. 223–24. Cf. Baldi, *Pio II*, pp. 241–43.

[134] *Ungedruckte Akten*, no. 171, pp. 245–54, and no. 187, pp. 281–82, are the clearest evidence of this.

for them![135] The Florentines and French were also scornful of the papal-Venetian partnership, though that mattered less since both Florence and Paris had become marginal to crusading.[136] But the benefits of Venetian commitment far outweighed the disadvantages. The transformation of the leading Mediterranean naval power from an opponent of crusading into one of its keenest exponents gave the pope's coalition major strike capacity. Energized by the Turkish conquest of Bosnia, which exposed both Venetian Dalmatia and south-western Hungary (Croatia-Slavonia) to attack, Pius's partners fashioned alliances that constituted far more sturdy frameworks for military action than the undertakings made at Mantua four years earlier.

Venice was the bridging power in the structure that resulted. On 12 September 1463 the Venetians and Hungarians entered an alliance at Petrovaradin that committed Venice to providing forty galleys carrying troops for operations in the Peloponnese and Dalmatia, while Matthias Corvinus undertook to attack by land. Hopes for papal involvement prompted the use of language that was heavily religious in character, notably that the alliance was formed "for the conservation of the most holy Christian religion."[137] On 19 October this involvement materialized, with the conclusion in Pius's palace at St. Peter's of a trilateral alliance between the pope, Venice, and Philip of Burgundy. The partners agreed to conduct hostilities for between one and three years, the clock starting when Philip arrived in Italy in May 1464. During that time none of the parties would make peace without the consent of the others. The Rome treaty was less specific than Petrovaradin had been: neither the individual contributions nor the field of operations were spelled out, though the influence of Venetian ambitions in the Peloponnese may be seen in the reiterated description of the sultan as "the occupier of Greece."[138] A few days later Pius gave in to Burgundian lobbying on Philip's contribution by stating that the duke was not obliged to fight for longer than two years, and that if ill-health stopped Philip coming in person, he could stay at home provided he sent the 6,000-strong contingent for which he had signed up at Mantua.[139]

For most of the period between these two treaties, 22 September to 21 October 1463, Pius conducted discussions at Rome with the envoys of the Italian powers about contributions towards his projected expedition. It was Mantua revisited, but confined to the peninsular powers and with an urgency springing from the pope's resolve to set out on crusade in 1464. The talks, brutally focused on "who, how much and how,"[140] were copiously reported in the envoys' dispatches, and anybody seeking evidence of cynicism in relation to Renaissance crusading need look no

---

[135] *Pii II orationes*, 3:113–14. Baldi, *Pio II*, p. 169 refers to Sforza as "il punto di riferimento fondamentale del pontefice," and his personal admiration complemented his commitment to the Milan–Rome–Naples axis: the problem was that this did not produce a crusade.

[136] For example, *Ungedruckte Akten*, no. 154, p. 210.

[137] *Vetera monumenta ... Hungariam ... illustrantia*, vol. 2, no. 566, pp. 380–82.

[138] Paviot, *Les ducs*, pp. 165, 321–27.

[139] Ibid., pp. 327–28.

[140] *Ungedruckte Akten*, no. 148, p. 190.

further. For example, in a long dispatch to Sforza on 24 September, Augustinus de Rubeis and Otto de Carretto provided a list of reasons that the duke could advance to explain why he could not help Pius: that the undertaking had inadequate support; that the duke's subjects would refuse to pay the taxes for three consecutive years; that there were unresolved issues of command as well as who would get the lands that the crusaders managed to conquer.[141] The envoys were intent on providing Sforza with a plausible fig leaf (*honestarse*), but they were still weighty points. Florence instructed its envoys to resist the idea that Italy should bear the burden of supporting the crusade; front-line nations like the Hungarians and Germans were under the illusion that "Italy is full of treasure," which they would insist on milking before moving an inch.[142] The reported talks show Pius at his most patient and accommodating. He badgered his compatriots to commit themselves on the grounds that it would be shameful if "our Sienese" failed to support a Sienese pope.[143] Facing the transparent Venetian goal of occupying the Peloponnese, he resorted to the pipe-dream that the republic might agree to hold it in vicariate from the Church.[144] Agreement was finally reached with Naples, Milan, Modena, Mantua, Bologna, and Lucca.[145] The Milanese envoys were impressed by the pope's achievement: a crusade that many had thought would "go up in smoke" had instead acquired sound foundations.[146]

Pius's last major crusade statement, *Ezechielis,* provides a useful overview of how he saw the situation at the close of these discussions. Deftly he outlined the partial mobilization that was in progress. The Christian coalition was powerful, and its efforts would be augmented by uprisings in Greece and Albania and by attacks in the rear by Muslim enemies of the Turks in Asia. Given the presence in the field of Burgundian and Hungarian troops, not to mention any soldiers that Skanderbeg managed to muster and bring to bear, one would expect *Ezechielis* to focus on collecting donations and encouraging spiritual support. So it is surprising to find that Pius directs much of his bull's content towards recruiting volunteers. It can even be construed as a second attempt at the general mobilization that Pius had failed to secure at Mantua, this time operating at the level of individuals and groups rather than states. "People should come in person if they are robust and readily able to do so," the pope wrote, specifying that departure would take place at Ancona on 5 June 1464. The Venetians would provide ships for the crossing and Pius undertook to ensure that crusaders would not be overcharged for it. At least six months' service was expected in exchange for the indulgence from anybody who accompanied Pius or attacked the Turks through Hungary or another route. There were the usual provisions for substitution and for donations (a week's household

---

[141] Ibid., no. 148, pp. 188–93.

[142] Ibid., no. 150, pp. 197–98, and see too no. 156, p. 214.

[143] Ibid., no. 153, p. 206, no. 173, pp. 256–57.

[144] Ibid., no. 154, p. 210.

[145] Ibid., no. 161, p. 226.

[146] Ibid., no. 163, p. 229. On the September–October 1463 talks see also Pastor, *History*, pp. 321–31.

expenses to be placed in collection chests). But it seems that Pius did expect his personal participation to generate sizeable groups of recruits, and that he welcomed them provided they were properly equipped.[147]

Both in conversation with Sforza's envoys and when writing to the duke himself a few weeks before the issue of *Ezechielis*, Pius expressed his hope that many people would come, and he accepted that the motivations of the volunteers would be as mixed as they always had been.

> More will come than we can credit. Zeal for the faith will bring some, greed for glory others, that and curiosity to see great events. Some who are unsafe at home will prefer honest exile, and others who are unwilling will be compelled by their kings to fight for the Lord, to stop them stirring up rebellion at home.[148]

It is possible that he was thinking above all of Germany: recollecting that country's enthusiastic response to Capistrano's crusade preaching in 1454–55, he may have hoped that *Ezechielis* would generate a similar wave of *crucesignati*, thereby circumventing the apathy consistently displayed by the German elites.[149] His timetable was workable, based on people taking the cross during the winter of 1463–64 and arriving for service in April and May. There was even a remarkable reversion in *Ezekielis* to the penitential theology that had underpinned early crusading, that of pilgrimage in arms: "so that as satisfaction for offences and the penances that would have been imposed, there functions the effort of the journey and the military service."[150]

This program of mobilization encountered a series of setbacks that culminated with the pope's death at Ancona on 15 August. To start with it was a plague year, which proved a handy excuse for Sforza to delay any preaching or collection in his lands.[151] In mid-January the Milanese envoy at Rome commented that, while the various naval contributions were set to reach an impressive total, progress in other respects was slow, in fact "this enterprise has not yet taken any form."[152] By

---

[147] *Opera omnia*, pp. 914–23, esp. pp. 920–22. This and cognate sources do not support Niccolo della Tuccia's assertion that Pius "voleva far denari per portare in quel paese, e non genti": "Cronaca di Viterbo," in *Cronache e statuti della città di Viterbo*, ed. Ignazio Ciampi, Documenti di storia italiana 5 (Florence, 1872), 1–272, at p. 269; see also Wadding's comment that the pope intended his preachers to raise money for wages, *Annales minorum*, 3rd ed., accuratissima auctior et emendatior ad exemplar editionis Josephi Mariae Fonseca ab Ebora, 25 vols. (Quaracchi, 1931–35), 13:308.

[148] *Pii II orationes*, 3:117 (quote); *Ungedruckte Akten*, no. 148, p. 189.

[149] Contrast Baldi, *Pio II*, p. 236, n. 20, who sees Pius effectively abandoning hope of a German contribution.

[150] "ita ut pro satisfactione delictorum et poenarum quae fuerant imponendae, succedat labor itineris atque militia": *Opera omnia*, p. 921. This is followed by the standard phraseology, raising the question of how those who did not go in person would earn the indulgence. There is an interesting discussion of *Ezekielis* and its background in Weber, "Lutter," pp. 183–89.

[151] *Ungedruckte Akten*, no. 179, p. 268.

[152] Ibid., no. 178, p. 266. Carretto reached a total of 27/28 galleys and 5/6 *nave*, but some of the contributions never materialized. Carretto reiterated his concerns a few days later: ibid., no. 179, pp. 268–69.

23 March Venice was concerned enough to make additional offers of assistance to Pius.[153] Then on 30 March, which appropriately was Good Friday, Pius received the shattering news of Philip the Good's withdrawal from the crusade. The secular leadership of Pius's crusade was now in abeyance, Sforza having rejected the poisoned chalice the previous autumn.[154] Pius's plan, as outlined in a letter that he had sent to Sforza on 19 March 1464, was to proceed from Ancona to Brindisi and from there to Albania: "there we shall take advice about where to proceed next."[155] Philip the Good's withdrawal caused the pope to contemplate sailing as far as Brindisi, and undertaking the crossing to Ragusa only if the situation justified it.[156] He was even receptive to Milanese suggestions of wintering at Brindisi and embarking on a campaign in 1465, which would delay failure and shift the burden of responsibility for it to Burgundy and France.[157] So the timetable slipped, and Pius only left Rome for Ancona on 18 June, 13 days *after* his scheduled embarkation date. By this time Venice was seriously worried that its own investment would be wasted and that Matthias Corvinus would give up on the campaign.[158] The king, whose concern was focused on the Turkish threat to Ragusa, complained in July that he had been seriously compromised by the slippage in the pope's timetable for the campaign.[159]

Meanwhile the *crucesignati* were arriving in Italy, and there was extraordinary confusion about where to assemble. *Ezekielis* directed *crucesignati* to make their way to Venice, but most appear to have gone straight to Ancona. Possibly they were attracted by the prospect of seeing the pope as soon as possible, but they (or their preachers) might also have been misled by the bull's phraseology, which could have been clearer. Maybe it was also the hope of seeing Pius that in late June brought several thousand German, Hungarian, and French volunteers to Rome, an unwise

---

[153] Ibid., no. 183, p. 277.

[154] *Opera omnia*, ep. 392, pp. 865–68, and see too ep. 393, pp. 868–69; Marcello Simonetta, "Pius II and Francesco Sforza. The History of Two Allies," in *Pius II 'el più expeditivo pontifice'. Selected Studies on Aeneas Silvius Piccolomini (1405–1464)*, ed. Zweder von Martels and Arjo Vanderjagt (Leiden, 2003), pp. 147–70, at pp. 164–66. D'Estouteville was placed in command of the crusaders and Forteguerri of the fleet: *Le Vite di Pio II*, p. 113 note.

[155] *Opera omnia*, no. 68, pp. 141–42 (also in *Aeneae Silvii Piccolomini ... opera inedita*, no. lxviii, p. 142). Presumably the advice would have been Skanderbeg's. See Damian, "La *Depositeria della Crociata*," pp. 144–45, for the most recent treatment of Pius's intentions.

[156] *Ungedruckte Akten*, no. 184, p. 278. In the (burlesque?) assault that he made on the deceased pope's crusading policy, Filelfo claimed that Pius had favoured Ragusa as a secure vantage point from which he could watch the Turks overrunning Hungary: *Notes et extraits*, 4th ser., p. 241.

[157] *Ungedruckte Akten*, no. 193, pp. 301–2, no. 196, p. 308, no. 199, p. 320 (the curia would move inland to more commodious Lecce).

[158] Ibid., no. 195, pp. 304–5. Matthias had 22,000 men under arms: *Mathiae Corvini Hungariae regis epistolae ad Romanos pontifices datae et ab eis acceptae 1458–1490* (*Mátyás Király levelezése a Római pápákkal*), Monumenta Vaticana Hungariae, ser. 1, vol. 6 (Budapest, 1891), pp. vii–viii; *Magyar Diplomacziai Emlékek. Mátyás Király Korából 1458–1490*, ed. Iván Nagy and Albert Nyáry, Monumenta Hungariae Historica, acta extera, vols. 4–7 (Budapest, 1875–78), vol. 1, no. 172, pp. 283–84.

[159] *Mátyás Király Levelei. Külügyi Osztály. Első Kötet. 1458–1479*, ed. Vilmos Fraknói (Budapest, 1893), no. 40, pp. 53–55, and cf. no. 39, pp. 52–53.

course of action given that Pius had already left and the Romans gave them their customarily inhospitable reception.[160] Those groups that arrived at Ancona in good time for the embarkation faced weeks of waiting in oppressive heat.[161] It is not surprising that fighting broke out between the various national groups, proving the wisdom of Aeneas's advice on this issue at Wiener Neustadt nine years previously.[162] Clearly Pius had mishandled this and his biographers Campano and Platina, eager to rescue the pope from posthumous criticism, shifted the blame to the volunteers. Campano claimed that the crusaders from France and Spain came expecting free shipping and supplies, and Platina wrote that many, above all the Germans, were unfit for military service or did not possess the financial reserves that the pope had specified in his bull.[163] It is true that while *Ezekielis* (in common with crusade bulls generally) had not entered into much detail, the possession of weapons, together with sufficient cash or credit for the minimum six months' service, was a reasonable expectation.[164] But it is possible that the high prices charged for food, lodging and stabling in the crowded port mean that well-equipped and funded volunteers ran through their cash reserves very quickly. A Mantuan envoy commented on 21 July that the crusaders at Ancona were "reasonably well-equipped with arms,"[165] while Ammannati made the telling observation that some men sold their weapons to raise cash for the journey home.[166]

The pope had anticipated some problems. On 11 April, for example, he asked Doge Cristoforo Moro to give Swiss crusaders, "with people, horses, possessions, arms and everything needed for the holy war," safe passage through Venetian lands.[167] A similar but more detailed request went to Sforza at Milan. Arriving crusaders were to be treated well, in particular their currency should be accepted at fair rates of exchange and prices for staples that they needed should not be raised; nor should they be subject to tolls.[168] But more broadly, was Pius aware, during the spring and summer months of 1464, that his bull had resonated as far afield as

[160] Guido Levi, ed., "Diario Nepesino di Antonio Lotieri de Pisano (1459–1468)," *Archivio della R. Società romana di storia patria* 7 (1884), 115–82, at pp. 139–40. Weber, "Lutter," p. 175, discovered that 597 *lettres de grâce* were given out to these volunteers at Rome.

[161] *Ungedruckte Akten*, no. 198, pp. 311–12: a vivid description, but coloured by the Mantuan envoy's intent to contrast conditions at Ancona with the excellent provision for visitors five years previously at the Mantua congress.

[162] Ibid., no. 198, p. 311; above, at n. 82.

[163] *Le Vite di Pio II*, p. 83 (Campano), p. 110 (Platina). Ammannati concurs with both (*Lettere*, 2:514, no. 74), and may have been their source of information. See too Johannes Simoneta, *Rerum gestarum Francisci Sfortiae Commentarii*, ed. G. Soranzo, RIS NS 21, pt. 2, pp. 477–78.

[164] These were the filtering criteria proposed by Venice in June 1464: *Ungedruckte Akten*, no. 195, pp. 305–6.

[165] *Ungedruckte Akten*, no. 198, p. 311.

[166] Ammannati, *Lettere*, 2:514, no. 74. Further details in Norman Housley, "Indulgences for Crusading, 1417–1517," in *PN*, pp. 277–307, at pp. 302–5, and Pastor, *History*, pp. 352–53.

[167] *Ungedruckte Akten*, no. 186, p. 281, with a rare reference to vicarious service: "ac gentes mittere et personaliter proficisci."

[168] *Opera omnia*, ep. 389, p. 864. Undated but sent *anno sexto* from Petriolo, where Pius was taking the waters in April 1464.

Poland and Crete,[169] and that Christian Europe was experiencing a significant surge of crusading fervor, bringing with it familiar problems of provisioning, muster, and the maintenance of public order? Listing his sources of recruitment, when he took the cross prior to departure on 18 June, the pope announced: "You can add the agitation of the faithful populace throughout Italy, Germany, and other provinces on the far side of the Alps, which our departure has generated. Unless we are mistaken, a great number of people will assemble."[170] Immediately after the pope's death Ammannati wrote a detailed account to Francesco Piccolomini of what happened between Pius's departure from Rome that same day and his death at Ancona;[171] it is tendentious but informative, especially when used in conjunction with the dispatches of Italian envoys.[172] Ammannati claimed that during his arduous journey to Ancona the pope was attentive to the needs of those who had assembled at the port.[173] It is safe to infer that he was receiving information about the movement of groups, though it is much harder to be certain about its extent or accuracy. Nor is it easy to be confident about how tough an approach he favored in distinguishing between combatants and others. In his April letter to Sforza, Pius wrote of "all the pilgrims (*peregrini*), whether *crucesignati* or not, who come to take part in this expedition." This intriguing phraseology could point towards the pope's willingness to accept a non-combatant element on his crusade, were it not that this would run counter to the military phraseology that he had consistently used in *Ezekielis*, and which he reiterated at the end of the April letter when he described "the faithful hurrying to this necessary war for Christ."[174] First Girolamo Lando, the versatile archbishop of Crete,[175] and then Cardinals Carvajal and d'Estouteville were given the demanding task of assessing the military capability of the volunteers who were assembling at Ancona; as Ammannati later observed, Carvajal in particular was well-suited for this given his Hungarian experience.[176] The line they followed was the traditional one of granting the crusader's indulgence to those whom they discharged.[177] An important role was also played by Rodrigo Sánchez, the Castilian diplomat and

---

[169] For Poland, see Jan Długosz, *Annals* (= *Annales seu cronicae incliti regni Poloniae*), trans. Maurice Michael, with a commentary by Paul Smith (Chichester, 1997), ad ann. 1464, p. 548 (reporting 20,000 recruits, though I have found no trace of them in the Italian sources); for Crete, see *Notes et extraits*, 4th ser., pp. 217–21.

[170] *Anecdota litteraria*, 3.290.

[171] Ammannati, *Lettere*, 2:501–24, no. 74.

[172] On these see esp. Pastor, *History*, pp. 354–70.

[173] Ammannati, *Lettere*, 2:507, no. 74.

[174] *Opera omnia*, ep. 389, p. 864.

[175] Mureşan, "Girolamo Lando," pp. 166–67.

[176] Ammannati, *Lettere*, 2:506, no. 74.

[177] *Le Vite di Pio II*, p. 110 and note; Ammannati, *Lettere*, 2:514, no. 74. Unsurprisingly, the discharged *crucesignati* still felt short-changed by their experience: by 1464 there were much easier ways to earn a plenary indulgence than traveling half-way across Europe, particularly if you were Lucchese (below, n. 209).

crusade enthusiast who wrote a commentary on *Ezechielis* and composed an oration for Pius to deliver to his crusaders at Ancona.[178]

It is tempting to ascribe this strong input by prominent members of the curia's crusading "team" to the pope's sickness, which was described as *febre fleumatica*.[179] We saw at the start that Pius's crusading policy was always a collective endeavor, but it is safe to assume that his ability to manage events was slipping. The situation that confronted him when he arrived at Ancona on 19 July was problematic, and it got worse over the weeks that followed as he impatiently waited for the Venetian fleet to arrive. Nothing could be done about the insufficiency of housing or water, and at the beginning of August plague broke out. The obvious solution was to get the volunteers out of Ancona as soon as possible. Before Pius's arrival Lando, worried that enforced idleness would aggravate desertion or disorder, suggested transporting some of the crusaders by sea to the Peloponnese.[180] The Venetians preferred their own paid troops and they were skeptical about the military worth of the volunteers. In April they claimed that their shipping was tied up in ferrying paid troops to the Peloponnese and Albania, and suggested that the *crucesignati* (whom they presumably anticipated arriving soon in Venice, as directed in *Ezechielis*), should proceed overland to help the Hungarians.[181] It was only reluctantly that they agreed on 21 June to use two available *naves* to transport 2,000 Saxon crusaders gathered at Ancona for service in the Peloponnese, after filtering out the "useless and unarmed."[182] A force several thousand strong assisted Malatesta in his unsuccessful siege of Mistra; they were the only crusaders recruited by Pius who saw action.[183]

Pius himself did not easily abandon the prospect of reaching the frontline. Ammannati tells a story, which although bizarre is supported by a Milanese dispatch, about the pope receiving news in the last days of July of a Turkish threat to lay siege to Ragusa. The port was inadequately provisioned to resist, and the pope made the audacious proposal, probably derived from hope of emulating Capistrano's relief of Belgrade in 1456, of sailing across in person with emergency supplies of grain. He argued that the Turks would not dare to besiege the port if they knew that Pius was there to rally its defense. Carvajal supported the idea, but to his own shame ("guided by the flesh rather than by the spirit"), Ammannati opposed it. The adventure did not go ahead because news arrived of a Turkish withdrawal.[184] By the

---

[178] Benziger, *Zur Theorie*, pp. 141–49, 154–58.

[179] *Ungedruckte Akten*, no. 201, p. 322.

[180] Ammannati, *Lettere*, 2:504, no. 74.

[181] *Ungedruckte Akten*, no. 185, pp. 280–81.

[182] Ibid., no. 195, pp. 305–6, and cf. no. 198, p. 310, on the two *naves*, which were still on offer for use by the Ancona *crucesignati* on 16 July. These Saxons were presumably the crusaders referred to by Lando. It is hard to piece together the scattered sources for events in 1464, but it is possible that there were two main waves of volunteers, first the Germans and later the Spanish and French.

[183] Giovanni Soranzo, "Sigismondo Pandolfo Malatesta in Morea e le vicende del suo dominio," *Atti e memorie della R. Deputazione di storia patria per le provincie di Romagna*, ser. 4, vol. 8 (1917–18), 211–80, esp. pp. 228–29.

[184] Ammannati, *Lettere*, 2:515–16, no. 74. See also *Ungedruckte Akten*, no. 201, p. 323 (dated 1 August).

time twelve Venetian galleys finally appeared at Ancona, on 12 August, the issue of destinations had become academic because the majority of the crusaders had dispersed.[185] As Ammannati admitted, by that point even those who had been well-supported had run out of patience.[186] The call to arms that was issued in *Ezekielis* had resulted in a debacle, one that was all too reminiscent of earlier crusades. But that does not detract from the fact that the bull itself was an attempt on Pius's part to extend the spiritual benefits of crusade as broadly as possible across Christian Europe, bringing as much military support as circumstances would permit to the campaign that he intended to accompany into Albania.

Resources and their Management

"Not the will but the means was lacking," Pius allegedly said to his six chosen cardinals in March 1462 in explanation of the lack of progress made on the crusade since the close of the Mantua congress. Pius went on to state that the resources of the Church of Rome itself were wholly inadequate for the task of responding to Ottoman aggression.[187] In a revealing report sent at this point to Sforza, Otto de Carretto, the Milanese envoy at the curia, wrote that the pope had put his annual income at no more than 150,000 ducats, including both spiritual and temporal sources.[188] When Pius addressed the whole college of cardinals on the crusade in September 1463, he doubled his earlier estimate, but immediately qualified this by saying that half of it was needed for ordinary expenses at Rome and in the Papal State.[189] So it is likely that in 1462–63 Pius was working on the basis of 150,000 ducats being at his disposal, a sum that would have paid for no more than a few galleys.[190] He had been aware of these constraints from his accession, having observed the enormous strain that inadequately funded crusading expenditure had entailed for the curia's finances under Calixtus III.[191]

Of course there were also extraordinary revenues that were traditionally associated with crusading. In his 1462 address to the cardinals Pius passed a judgment on the value of these that was bleak in its budgeting implications. If he tried to impose tenths, he complained, the clergy appealed against them to a future general council, while the preaching of indulgences in exchange for donations was popularly ascribed to curial greed. Both his address to the cardinals and his *tour d'horizon* of

---

[185] In his dispatch to Sforza on 11 August, reporting the arrival (finally) of the two Venetian *naves*, Stefano Nardini commented that "qui non ce sonno crucesignati, nè altra gente da passar": *Ungedruckte Akten*, no. 202, pp. 325–26.

[186] Ammannati, *Lettere*, 2:514, no. 74.

[187] *Comm.* 7.16, ed. Van Heck, pp. 460–61.

[188] *Ungedruckte Akten*, no. 125, p. 153.

[189] *Comm.* 12.31, ed. Van Heck, p. 770.

[190] For comparisons based on known expenditure see Setton, *Papacy*, 2:184 (150,000 ducats, 1456), 316 (over 144,000 florins, 1471–72).

[191] For example, *Opera omnia*, ep. 239, p. 780, ep. 272, pp. 798–99.

the European diplomatic scene in private discussion with Carretto show Pius at his most pessimistic.[192] The ordinary revenue of the curia was probably no higher than his estimate, but there were substantial proceeds from crusading sources, however great the storm of resentment and suspicion that accompanied them. Moreover, Giovanni de Castro's discovery in April 1461 of rich deposits of alum at Tolfa radically improved the curia's financial situation, once the *camera* had adjusted the excessively generous terms on which it initially sanctioned mining operations.[193] By 1465 contemporaries reckoned Tolfa to be yielding around 100,000 ducats p.a.[194] Despite the notorious difficulties thrown up by papal finance,[195] any assessment of Pius as a crusading pope must encompass his managerial approach towards this range of resources. We have seen that in his critique of Nicholas V in January 1454 he took that pope to task for the disappointing way he had used the money at his disposal. Was Pius's own track record any better?

In the mid-fifteenth century any return to general crusade preaching and clerical taxation, carried out solely under the aegis of papal authority, was inconceivable. The *nationum consensus* approach that underpinned the Mantua congress presupposed that financial contributions would stay with and be managed by rulers, notwithstanding the risks involved. This approach Pius consistently and sincerely adhered to.[196] Nobody would be expected to make a military contribution (for instance, one or more galleys), that exceeded the funding that could be raised in their territories.[197] What was to be done when there was a marked disparity between income and expenditure (as the Venetians claimed at Mantua), was not readily addressed.[198] In general, though, it would have been difficult to be more accommodating than Pius. He was happy for crusading funds to be spent on anything that suited the collecting authority, provided it also helped the crusade, "in galleys or provisions or armaments or whatever you like," as Siena's envoy reported in November 1463. Surely, the pope went on, if Siena provided the galley, sufficient adventurous, patriotic, and devout young men could be found to man it without expecting any payment beyond expenses?[199] At its best this approach produced results: Bologna paid for two galleys to be fitted out at Venice, sent contingents

---

[192] Baldi, *Pio II*, pp. 204–10. As she notes, the conversation was a kind of updated *De Europa*.

[193] Weber, "Lutter," pp. 232–34.

[194] Damian, "La *Depositeria della Crociata*," p. 141, n. 34.

[195] Peter Partner, "Papal Financial Policy in the Renaissance and Counter-Reformation," *Past & Present* 88 (1980), 17–62, esp. p. 53 on Pius II.

[196] For example, *Ungedruckte Akten*, no. 148, p. 192, "che de tali denaro non intendeva ... tochasse uno, nè per se, nè per alcuno de suoy, sed solum ciascunco principe nel dominio suo fecesse," no. 153, p. 206, no. 154, p. 209, no. 193, p. 303, no. 196, p. 307.

[197] *Ungedruckte Akten*, no. 159, p. 219.

[198] Picotti, *La dieta*, pp. 467–70, doc. no. XXX: asserting income from crusade sources of 87,000 ducats and outgoings of 810,000, the solution to which had to be assistance from the non-Italian powers.

[199] *Ungedruckte Akten*, no. 170, p. 241. Ibid., no. 184, p. 279, has similar suggestions for Florence. See also Setton, *Papacy*, 2:267, n. 123.

of volunteers, and appointed two captains to lead them.[200] Those elements of the crusade program for which papal sanction was needed, above all indulgences, would be handled either by indigenous clerics or by papal agents, and neither group could get anywhere without the full backing of the secular powers.

This decentralization markedly curtailed the pope's ability to contribute to the selective crusade program that his failure at Mantua forced him to pursue from 1462 onwards. Amongst the powers that came together in the coalition of 1463–64, Hungary was a net importer of subsidies. Burgundy and Venice allowed both crusade preaching and taxation within their lands but the proceeds did not find their way to Rome. As he complained in March 1464, Pius could rely only on taxes collected in Italy. Outside Italy (Pius was thinking mainly of France and Germany), clerics were being shielded from payment by their rulers. Against such resistance the pope had no recourse but to refer the authorities to God's judgment; it was an astonishing admission of the constraints within which the curia now operated, and strikingly at odds with the bold assertions of papal authority that we noted earlier.[201] Nor could the proceeds from indulgences replace taxes. "With the people's charity cooling, and various men of ill-will obstructing matters," the profits were usually disappointing. Pius's bureaucrats no doubt knew that at the rate of a half-florin, the bargain basement figure required for many indulgences, a full 900 would have been needed to equip a single galley for a month.[202]

Paradoxically, the two territories that Pius fell back on for much of his own crusade funding were the furthest away and the closest to home. In the Scandinavian lands the authorities permitted clerical tenths and indulgences for Rome's benefit, in exchange for a percentage of the proceeds, and an active process of collection took place.[203] Pius made use of the services of an able and energetic collector called Marinus de Fregeno, a Parma subdeacon whose surviving accounts and indulgence receipts form useful evidence for the ground-level preaching of the crusade.[204] But a more important source of crusade income was the Papal State. The lands of the Church, with certain adjacent territories such as Lucca, became the most reliable areas for crusade revenues. It was a development that mirrored their assumption of the central position in providing yields from ordinary revenues, and the reason was surely their susceptibility to control and supervision, coupled with the relative

---

[200] *Corpus chronicorum bononensium*, RIS NS 18, pt. 1, pp. 321, 326–29; *Cronica gestorum ac factorum memorabilium civitatis Bononie*, ed. A. Sorbelli, RIS NS 23, pt. 2, p. 97; *Della historia di Bologna parte terza del R.P.M. Cherubino Ghirardacci*, ed. A. Sorbelli, RIS NS 33, pt. 1, pp. 185–86. Also on Bologna see Baldi, *Pio II*, p. 235, n. 19.

[201] *Aeneae Silvii Piccolomini ... opera inedita*, no. lxix, pp. 142–44.

[202] Weber, "Lutter," p. 221, and see pp. 120–21 for Pius's naval preparations.

[203] See *Diplomatarium svecanum, appendix, Acta pontificum svecica, I, Acta cameralia, vol. II ann. MCCCLXXI–MCDXCII*, ed. L. L. Bååth (Stockholm, 1957).

[204] Janus Møller Jensen, *Denmark and the Crusades 1400–1650*, The Northern World 30 (Leiden, 2007), pp. 93–96; Klaus Voigt, "Der Kollektor Marinus de Fregeno und seine '*Descriptio provinciarum Alamanorum*'," *Quellen und Forschungen aus italienischen Archiven und Bibliotheken* 68 (1968), 148–206, at pp. 160–62; Weber, "Lutter," pp. 250–53.

ease with which collected funds could be transferred to Rome. This dependence on the lands over which the curia exercised direct lordship became apparent in the strenuous revenue-raising of Calixtus III. His bulls and *brevi* show a remarkable degree of micro-management of the Franciscan Observants on whose services he principally relied both to collect tenths and to preach the *cruciata*.[205] Pius's curia showed some flair in the way it handled the preaching in 1463–64, specifying attendance at preaching in detail. In November 1463 collectors in the Papal State were instructed that the resident bureaucracy from provincial governor downwards (castellans excepted) were to be present at their preaching, and that they should compel the populace, including the Jews, to attend. While preaching was in progress all hostelries and apothecaries were to be closed under penalty of a fine which the authorities would share with the *camera apostolica*. The entire clergy should also be at the preaching, separated from the laity.[206] Such compulsion proved insufficient. Neither in central Italy nor in the lands of the far north was collection a straightforward matter. Collectors proved fraudulent or inefficient, or at least (as in the case of Marinus de Fregeno) fell under suspicion of such failings.[207] And there was protracted and often ingenious resistance from the local clergy towards paying. What was effectively a tax revolt took place at Perugia, where in spring 1464 the pope was reduced to making sweeping threats of excommunication, interdict, and heavy fines if money and corn that had been promised were not forthcoming.[208] Pius even resorted to offering the indulgence in exchange for simply paying the lay thirtieth. And in the case of Lucca, where it was agreed that tenth, twentieth and thirtieth would be handed over to the civic authorities in exchange for their fitting out a single galley, the whole population was promised the indulgence, conditional on their rulers keeping their side of the bargain.[209]

In such agreements Pius can be seen scrambling for cash, and even more so ships, during the hectic early months of 1464. The bureaucracy throughout the Papal State was asked to contribute 20 per cent of their salaries; 2,000 ducats were expected from the officials in the small town of Recanati.[210] Even bishops coming to Rome to pay their common services were expected to contribute towards the forthcoming crusade.[211] On the eve of his departure for Ancona Pius sold a number of fortresses in the Papal State, a sure sign of financial exigency given the normal tendency to

---

[205] For example, *Bullarium Franciscanum*, vol. 2, no. 215, p. 119, no. 230, p. 123, no. 249, pp. 131–32, nos. 275–78, pp. 144–45, no. 323, pp. 162–63, nos. 341–42, p. 176.

[206] Ibid., vol. 2, no. 1177, pp. 609–10.

[207] *Diplomatarium svecanum*, nos. 1359–60, 1362, pp. 501–5.

[208] *Opera omnia*, ep. 391, pp. 864–65.

[209] Ibid.; also in *Bullarium Franciscanum*, vol. 2, no. 1220, pp. 631–32. The ruling (April 1464) is a good example of Pius putting results before equity: it seems that any Lucchese who refused to pay the tax would still get the plenary indulgence.

[210] Damian, "La *Depositeria della Crociata*," p. 140.

[211] *Bullarium Franciscanum, Supplementum*, ed. Caesar Cenci, 1 (Rome, 2002), no. 2263, p. 968, no. 2322, p. 984, no. 2483, p. 1027, no. 2637, p. 1064.

prioritize the security of the Church's lands.[212] Pius's lack of cash was the natural consequence of the curia losing any chance of quarrying substantial sums out of the areas that in the past had been Christendom's crusading heartlands. It was galling that England, France, and Germany provided virtually nothing for the cause. The pope's comment in March 1462 about his attempts to levy tenths being countered by appeals to a future general council echoed the harsh exchanges that had taken place between his legate Bessarion and the envoys at the 1460 diets. In point of fact, Bessarion denied any intention of imposing a tenth, and he assured the Germans that any money granted for the crusade would stay in the empire, whose crusaders it would be used to fund. He argued, surely correctly, that the crusade entailed a net outflow of money for the curia, for reasons that included the heavy cost of legations like his own. But he had not managed to reassure the Germans.[213] Their suspicion of Rome had become too powerful, remaining a leitmotif of German response to crusading calls through to the Reformation.[214]

Boxed in by these circumstances, Pius was much helped in the last months of his reign by the income stream from Tolfa. He had done his best to maximize profits by establishing a monopoly; in the Maundy Thursday prohibition list (*In coena domini*) of April 1463 a ban was placed on the import of alum from the East, justified by reference to the crusade.[215] Concurrently, Pius carried forward the work of his predecessors that aimed to separate off crusade revenue from other papal income. In November 1463 the pope appointed his kinsman and *cubicularius* Niccolò di Piccoluomo Piccolomini as *depositarius sancte cruciate*, with the job of monitoring and safeguarding all revenues collected for the purpose of the crusade (the *camera sancte cruciate*). The register that Niccolò initiated on 15 November, known as the *Liber sancte cruciate*, was the logical culmination of papal consolidation of the *cruciata* as a network of directly managed fiscal devices and procedures, which had been promoted so forcefully by Calixtus III. What persuaded Pius to go further than Calixtus had done was, first, the desirability of monitoring as closely as possible the heavy expenses associated with his participation in the 1463 coalition and, secondly, the need to create a financial mechanism that was independent of the *camera apostolica*, so that it could accompany the pope on crusade.[216] In a sense therefore Niccolò's appointment was an acknowledgement of defeat. It signaled Pius's acceptance that instead of presiding over a collective Christian effort, the curia had to be content with membership of an alliance system, operating within its own budget.

---

[212] Weber, "Lutter," p. 226.

[213] The most important texts are in Mohler, *Kardinal Bessarion*, 3:376–403.

[214] Erich Meuthen, "Reiche, Kirchen und Kurie im späteren Mittelalter," *Historische Zeitschrift* 265 (1997), 597–637.

[215] Weber, "Lutter," pp. 235–37.

[216] Weber, "Lutter," pp. 267–306, is now the definitive study of the *camera/depositeria* from Pius to Sixtus IV. Weber plans an edition with commentary of the *Liber sancte cruciate* (Archivio di Stato di Roma, Cam. I, vol. 1233).

The compensation was that the *camera sancte cruciate* gave the curia's crusade lobby a sort of rallying point; from the start it could be anticipated that, should Pius die and his crusade collapse, attempts would be made to raid the *camera* for other papal projects. Enthusiasts for the crusade wanted to avoid a repetition of what had happened in 1458, when little of the money painstakingly assembled by Calixtus III for crusading purposes had been available for Pius's use.[217] This tactical consideration almost certainly shaped Pius's own thinking in the autumn of 1463 when he set up the *camera*, and immediately after the election of Paul II the new pope, under pressure from the pro-crusade lobby, set up a permanent commission (*congregatio*) of cardinals to manage its funds. Pius's *camera sancte cruciate* was now rebranded as the *depositeria della crociata*, and its financial resources were regularized and substantially enhanced by designating it as the normal recipient of funds from the alum mines. The commission was made up of the most fervent supporters of Pius's crusade, Bessarion and Carvajal, together with Guillaume d'Estouteville.[218] Their combined experience and authority were formidable, and before the year was out they had produced a robust new crusade program to carry forward the dead pope's work.[219]

The accounts of the *Liber sancte cruciate* help us to quantify Pius's major expenditures in 1463–64, which included spending on shipping, arms, supplies, and recruitment. It was undoubtedly heavy. In January 1464, when Venice lobbied for a papal subsidy of 100,000 ducats for Hungary, the response was that outlays for the pope's own contribution to the crusade were expected to reach 214,000 ducats before Pius even embarked at Ancona.[220] Following the pope's death the commission decided that the galleys, arms, and provisions raised for the crusade should be assigned to Venice while the remaining cash in the *camera* should go to Hungary. Pius might have looked askance at subsidizing the Venetians, whose delay in July–August he regarded as fatal to his venture, but he would have approved of the 40,314 ducats that went to support Matthias Corvinus.[221] For he was a firm believer in the strategic significance of Hungary as Christian Europe's leading *antemurale* state. As he put it to Alfonso of Aragon in 1457, it was "our religion's wall," and if it fell the Turks would pour through Carniola and Friuli into Italy.[222] In 1455 he sympathized with the casualties sustained by the Hungarians during their 70-year struggle against the Turks, asserting hyperbolically that

---

[217] Damian, "La *Depositeria della Crociata*," p. 139.

[218] Ibid., pp. 137–43; Ammannati, *Lettere*, 2:683–88, no. 132. Paul's choice of d'Estouteville, who was less of an enthusiast for crusading than Bessarion or Carvajal, may have been an attempt to placate the French.

[219] Mureşan, "La croisade en projets," at n. 69, and *annexe*: an important redating of a project that was previously ascribed to 1471. Further on the commission's activity, see Ammannati, *Lettere*, 2:572–78, no. 88, pp. 683–88, no. 132.

[220] *Ungedruckte Akten*, no. 177, pp. 263–64. See also Damian, "La *Depositeria della Crociata*," p. 141.

[221] Ibid., p. 143.

[222] *Opera omnia*, ep. 266, p. 791.

during the country's two most recent campaigns every household of note had lost a soldier.[223] But, as so often, he could not follow rhetoric with action. At Mantua he declared himself willing to match any manpower that Hungary provided to the crusade, but he had to withdraw the offer in 1460 when it was clear that he could not afford it.[224] Nonetheless, the posthumous *camera* payment initiated a flow of subsidies to Matthias Corvinus which continued into the reign of Paul II. As with the alliances of 1463–64, there was nothing original in such a subsidy system, but Pius does deserve credit for recognizing the pivotal significance of Hungary. With great difficulty he succeeded in balancing his loyalty towards Frederick III with his support for Matthias Corvinus.[225] He also maintained the curia's strong support for Skanderbeg, an approach that presented fewer problems since it fitted his diplomatic schema, given the Albanian leader's close ties with Aragonese Naples.[226]

Conclusion

Pius II does not rank with the most creative crusading popes, Urban II and Innocent III, but then no other pope does. His contribution does, however, stand up to scrutiny when compared with notable predecessors other than these two giants, that is with popes who either brought new elements of thinking and practice to bear, or who energized their contemporaries and inspired their successors. It helps to take these two areas separately. In terms of new elements, there is a strong case for arguing that, through his writings and orations before his election and his pronouncements after it, Pius played the central role in shaping the character of crusading against the Ottoman Turks. This may be defined as a war of self-defense waged by a European community that was both Christian and civilized, against an implacably aggressive and uncivilized Islamic power. In this process Pius's humanist training and outlook were naturally crucial, and the more the crusading ideas of other humanists like Benedetto Accolti, Flavio Biondo, and Francesco Filelfo are examined, the more they are shown to have had in common with those of Pius.[227] The difference lay in the influence that Pius could bring to bear as pope, his success in merging his humanism with his spiritual authority and responsibility, in particular with the entrenched ways of managing the crusade that characterized the bureaucracy with which he had to work. It was a remarkable achievement of synthesis, with substantial implications for the formation of a European identity. And it would be quite wrong to undervalue that achievement because contemporaries like Calixtus III and Bessarion are accorded the credit due to their

---

[223] Ibid., ep. 398, pp. 923–28, at p. 926.

[224] *Vetera monumenta ... Hungariam ... illustrantia*, vol. 2, no. 536, pp. 356–57, no. 544, p. 362, no. 545, p. 363. But Matthias was sent a generous subsidy: Mohler, *Kardinal Bessarion*, 3:394.

[225] For example, *Vetera monumenta ... Hungariam ... illustrantia*, vol. 2, no. 498, p. 325.

[226] *Acta Albaniae Vaticana*, nos. 364–527, pp. 88–133.

[227] Bisaha, *Creating East and West*; Meserve, *Empires of Islam*.

new ideas and approaches. That said, Pius's attempt to carry his synthesis into the realm of action, in the shape of the Mantua congress, could not work because it was at odds with the political realities of the day. Christian Europe shared certain religious and cultural values, but it was no longer possible to translate these into collective military action under the papal aegis. Pius's successors made attempts to convene similar congresses, usually as a way of fending off calls for a general council. Innocent VIII succeeded in presiding over a congress at Rome in 1490, but it was a lackluster affair from which nobody seriously expected an outcome.[228] In practice, crusading against the Turks continued to assume the two formats that Pius had reluctantly fallen back on: ad hoc coalitions and leagues, and the channeling of financial support to hard-pressed front-line states.

Pius's goal throughout his reign was to generate action by appealing to Christian unity, and he tried this initially through exhortation and then through personal example. These were contrasting approaches, but both impressed contemporaries. Lodovico Foscarini sent a report of the pope's performance at Mantua which gives a compelling impression of his skills as speaker and negotiator.[229] And reading the reports of Italian envoys that were written in 1463–64, one encounters an acceptance, sometimes grudging, sometimes enthusiastic, of the pope's altruism and dedication.[230] Pius may have been misguided, particularly in his ingrained hostility towards France,[231] but he did not arouse the suspicion, bordering on contempt, that corrupt nepotists like Sixtus IV and Alexander VI engendered when they tried to don the crusading mantle. Pius's resolve to lead his crusade in person was not just asserted: it was followed through. Like Gregory X, whose Lyons council of 1274 in some respects bears comparison with Pius's Mantua congress, Pius attracted respect; Gregory had been to Palestine before his election, while Pius proved that he was willing to accompany his crusade against the Turks. What would have happened if he had not died at Ancona? We have seen that Pius was attracted by the idea of postponing the 1464 campaign to 1465, building this on the flimsy foundation of Philip the Good finally appearing with his contingent.[232] If he had decided to go ahead in 1464, it is likely that the outcome would have been neither a triumph nor a disaster, but a face-saving exercise. At best Pius might have engaged in a naval foray in the eastern Mediterranean, like Cardinal Trevisan's in 1456–57 and Cardinal Carafa's in 1472.[233] More likely he would simply have crossed to Ragusa, a substantial port where he would have been fêted, and hopefully held high-profile discussions with either or both of Matthias Corvinus and Skanderbeg,

[228] Setton, *Papacy*, 2:413–16.

[229] Picotti, *La dieta di Mantova*, pp. 474–76, doc. no. XXXIIII [*sic*]. Cf. Russell, "The Humanists Converge," pp. 74–82.

[230] *Ungedruckte Akten*, no. 170, p. 243, no. 175, p. 260, no. 176, pp. 261–63, no. 199, p. 320.

[231] In his crusading exhortations to Louis XI, notably *Opera omnia*, ep. 387, pp. 861–62, Pius was content to rehearse traditional arguments about French participation.

[232] *Aeneae Silvii Piccolomini ... opera inedita*, no. lxv, p. 138.

[233] Setton, *Papacy*, 2:184–90, 316–18.

before returning to Brindisi.[234] More than that was not practicable, given that Venice did not want an ambitious and interventionist pope like Pius. The republic insisted on being in charge of its own war. It wanted Pius to confine his efforts to mobilizing the Balkan powers in its support, and providing support when its Christian rivals took advantage of its exposed position to attack its *terraferma*.[235] The Hungarian position was a little more accommodating, but not dissimilar. In the circumstances of the times it made no difference whether Pius was directing from Rome, managing from Mantua, or leading from Ancona. He could achieve nothing on a large scale. As Pius knew, typically expressing it better than anybody else, pope and emperor alike had lost too much authority to head up the military efforts of Catholic Europe.[236] But, for his commitment and resilience, as well as the novel ways of thinking about crusade that underpinned them, he deserves the reputation that he has come to enjoy.

---

[234] This was the itinerary predicted by the well-informed Otto de Carretto on 2 May: Baldi, *Pio II*, p. 259, n. 22.

[235] For example, *Ungedruckte Akten*, no. 177, pp. 263–64.

[236] *Opera omnia*, ep. 127, pp. 654–57, trans. Setton, *Papacy*, 2:153.

REVIEWS

Le comté de Tripoli: état multiculturel et multiconfessionnel (1102–1289), ed. Gérard Dédéyan and Karam Rizk, with a preface by Jean Richard. Paris: Librairie orientaliste Paul Geuthner, 2010. Pp. 242. ISBN 978 2 7053 3839 8.

It has been over sixty-five years since the publication of Jean Richard's original and as yet unsurpassed monograph on the county of Tripoli, and as the great historian himself acknowledges in this new collection of papers on the subject, a lot has changed since then. New sources for the county have become available, not least with Richard's publication of the relevant documents of the Porcelet archives. Furthermore, the explosion of secondary works on the crusades and the Latin East – including Richard's various publications concerning Tripoli specifically – has revolutionized the historiographical landscape. More subtle but equally profound are the shifts in terminological nuance: 1945's "état franc/provençal" has become 2010's "état multiculturel."

Indeed, it is the "multiculturalism" of the county throughout the two centuries of Frankish rule that serves as the unifying theme of this collection of thirteen research papers, originally given at the ninth "Sommet de la Francophonie" held in Beirut in October 2002. The collection is a collaborative effort between the Université Paul Valéry-Montpellier III and the Université Saint-Esprit de Kaslik, as personified by the two editors, Gérard Dédéyan and Karam Rizk respectively, although a range of other, mostly francophone institutions are represented amongst the contributors. The papers are all presented in French with the exceptions of one in Arabic and one in English.

Unsurprisingly, Richard's influence is keenly felt throughout all the papers in this collection; the appendix even includes reproductions of maps found in Richard's original monograph. Richard provides not only a preface, but also a full paper in which he elaborates the basic hypothesis developed throughout his various publications on the topic: that the county's feudal landscape reflected largely the needs and preferences of the ruling dynasties, from the confidence of the early "dynastie toulousaine" to the divisive "dynastie antiochénienne." Richard combines the incisive analysis of his earlier studies with new and improved sources and insights. The paper offers no fundamental revision of Richard's earlier conclusions, but its real merit lies in consolidating an unparalleled six decades of research.

Many of the other papers make important contributions to an overall understanding of the county's history. Jean Charaf's article is particularly outstanding, offering a persuasive and revisionist argument that the Lebanese Christian allies of the Franks of Tripoli were probably not the Maronites of Lebanon proper, as traditionally believed, but rather the Jacobites and Nestorians of the littoral-facing foothills. Charaf argues that the prevailing assumption that the Maronites were the Franks' indigenous allies is largely the product of an apologist elaboration of William of Tyre's chronicle by the Maronite patriarch and historian, Istafan al-Duwayhi (1630–1702).

Another strong contribution is provided by Gérard Dédéyan, a respected specialist in Armenian history, who provides a paper surveying the experiences of the Armenians in and around the county, spanning the late Byzantine, crusader and early Mamluk periods. Other useful papers include Isabelle Augé's reassessment of relations between the county of Tripoli and Byzantium throughout the Komnenian period, which improves upon Richard's original assessment in 1945 by utilizing more recent secondary works, and by elaborating more upon events during the reign of Manuel Komnenos. Meanwhile, Antoine Doumit's contribution aims to provide an overview of two centuries of trade in and through the county, placed within the context of Levantine and Mediterranean trade more generally. The main shortcoming with this paper is its presentation in Arabic; an abstract in French would have facilitated its wider dissemination.

Élias Kattar and Ahmad Hoteit provide general overviews of the various indigenous communities of the county, whilst Olivia Olmo does something very similar, albeit restricted to the Christian sects. The similarity of these three papers in theme, content, and approach unfortunately creates a sense of redundancy here, revealing a structural weakness in the collection overall. It must also be said that at times the level of analysis appears shallow. Nevertheless, these articles do make use of Arabic sources and secondary works that may otherwise be obscure and inaccessible to historians working in the West.

The collection contains many valuable archaeological studies, and the abundance of plates and figures alone is worthy of praise. The most illuminating of the archaeological papers is Balazs Major's assessment of above-ground remains in the northern half of the former county, now located within the Republic of Syria. The paper serves as a welcome complement to the work on rural settlement patterns carried out for the kingdom of Jerusalem by Ronnie Ellenblum and Denys Pringle. Jean-Claude Voisin provides a paper on defensive structures that in some ways supplements Major's by covering in greater depth the southern half of the county, now in the Republic of Lebanon. The accompanying photographic plates somewhat compensate for the regrettable brevity of Voisin's paper.

Lévon Nordiguian provides a detailed survey of the remains of one particular crusader-era chapel: the evocatively named Sayyīdat al-Kharāʾib ([Our] Lady of the Ruins), in a village near Batrūn (crusader Botron). The chapel is of great interest, not only for its fragmentary wall paintings (full-colour pictures kindly provided), but for its double-naved structure, reminiscent of similar churches in the kingdom of Jerusalem and on Cyprus, which Pringle first suggested may have been shared by two distinct confessional groups.

Brunehilde Imhaus analyses the funerary monuments of two members of the Visconte family, who left the county for Cyprus in the thirteenth century. The epitaphs of these two monuments – now preserved in Nicosia – are transcribed and images of both provided, whilst a third fragmentary monument preserved at Limassol is also described. Imhaus's study is complemented here by Marie-Adélaïde Nielen's meticulous genealogical reconstruction of the same Visconte family, based largely upon the *Lignages d'Outremer* and sigillographic evidence.

In summary, this collection offers a much appreciated overview of current research into the often neglected county of Tripoli. Some of the papers serve as useful introductions to the sources available for the county, especially in regard to the Arabic literature. Others constitute useful case studies. A handful provide genuinely profound and far-reaching reinterpretations of key issues. Most encouragingly, the collection showcases the increasing vibrancy of domestic scholarship in the regions once occupied by the county, with a number of contributors based in Lebanon. It is to be hoped that recent events in the region will not curtail further developments in this direction.

KEVIN JAMES LEWIS
MERTON COLLEGE, OXFORD

Crusading and Chronicle Writing on the Medieval Baltic Frontier. A Companion to the Chronicle of Henry of Livonia. ed. Marek Tamm, Linda Kaljundi and Carsten Selch Jensen. Farnham and Burlington, VT: Ashgate, 2011. Pp. xxxiii, 484. ISBN 978 0 7546 6627 1 (hardback), 978 1 4094 3396 5 (ebook).

The chronicle of Henry of Livonia, written in the late 1220s, is a record of the beginning of the final phase of christianization of the Baltic area. These campaigns, which were regarded by the participants, if not initially by the popes, as crusades, established the bishopric of Riga, and prepared the ground for the thirteenth-century campaigns of the Teutonic Order, which arrived in Prussia in 1230. In spite of the importance of this arena of crusade, it has been relatively neglected by English-speaking scholars. This volume represents the work of scholars from Estonia, Latvia, Denmark, and Germany as well as contributions from North America and the United Kingdom and is a welcome addition to the research currently available in English. Its importance lies not just in the fact that it assembles an overview of current research in the area from a variety of perspectives, but also that it situates the chronicle in the wider setting of the state of religious warfare and conversion in the Baltic in the thirteenth century, giving an overview of issues such as the legitimacy and justification of the wars, the practicalities of warfare, and the reception of the chronicle itself.

The introduction, by James Brundage, the author of the only English-language translation of Henry's chronicle, gives a broad introduction not only to the chronicler, but to the wider context of the circumstances and politics of the christianization of the eastern Baltic. The rest of the book is divided into three sections. The first, "Representation," deals with the chronicler's construction of the events he is describing. Christopher Tyerman sets the work within the context of crusading ideology and a detailed discussion of the development of a crusading ideology specific to the Baltic, while Jaan Undusk and Carsten Selch Jensen look at the theological context of the chronicle. Alan V. Murray investigates the practicalities of how communication with the local peoples across multiple languages may have been managed during the process of conversion, while Jüri Kivimäe evaluates the chronicle as a source for the names of the local peoples in his article on ethnography. Finally, Marek Tamm and Torben Kjersgard Nielsen discuss the chronicle's perspective on death and the wilderness respectively. Tamm's contribution focuses on the rhetorical function of "good" and "bad" deaths in the chronicle and their sources in traditional motifs and patristic literature, while Nielsen's examines the antithesis in the chronicle represented by Christian "order," exemplified by roads and cultivation, and pagan "deviance," as represented by the wilderness.

The second section of the book, "Practices," focuses on the practicalities of warfare and uses archaeology and studies of weaponry to give a fascinating account of the reality of siege warfare during this period. Kurt Villads Jensen traces the social and economic changes which in turn changed the way campaigns were fought and fortifications built. Ain Mäesalu contributes a detailed chapter on weaponry in the early thirteenth century, discussing the use of horses, crossbows, and trebuchets. Valter Lang and Heiki Falk develop some of these themes, showing how recent archaeology has enabled scholars to refine their understanding of the chronicle and shed light on the practicalities of warfare. Marika Mägi's article uses archaeological findings to give a more nuanced understanding of the importance of the island of Ösel in the early thirteenth century, and in so doing also gives the modern reader an insight into the strategic importance of the eastern Baltic for trade with Russia and the East. Finally, Iben Fonnesberg-Schmidt and Nils Holger Petersen discuss the practicalities of conversion. Petersen introduces the reader to the nature and scope of liturgical plays during this period, while Fonnesberg-Schmidt traces the importance of papal interventions and shows how, in the early stages at least, the locals' understanding of their activities in the eastern Baltic were often at odds with official papal policy. It was not until the papacy of Honorius III, she suggests, that crusades here were given parity with crusades in the East, resulting in a tension between Henry's depictions of the wars and the official papal view of them.

The final section, "Appropriations," reviews the reception of Henry's chronicle. Although now widely regarded as an important source for the history of the early thirteenth century, Anti Selart demonstrates that it was not widely disseminated during that time because the events it described came to be eclipsed in importance by the conflict between the Teutonic Order and the bishops and archbishops of Riga. Only one manuscript survives from the thirteenth century, and it itself did not become known to scholars until 1862. The first modern scholarly edition of the chronicle based on all known texts was compiled in 1955. The contributors show how the chronicle was interpreted according to the prevailing beliefs and ideologies of the time. Stefan Donnecker discusses the humanist interpretations, and shows how it was used during the Enlightenment, somewhat problematically, as an illustration of a people moving from a primitive "state of nature" to that of an organized commonwealth. Tiina Kala revisits some of these ideas and goes on to show how different nationalities interpreted the chronicle according to their own priorities. The contribution of the chronicle to modern Estonian nationalism is taken up and expanded in Linda Kaljundi's final, thought-provoking contribution. This strand of thought has not been much explored by west European researchers and could usefully be applied to other key works from this period.

As a whole, the volume is both accessible and authoritative. The maps are essential for students new to this region and period and the difficult problem of place-names has been dealt with elegantly and effectively. This volume will be used both by students as a reliable and up-to date introduction to the crusades in the Baltic and to Henry's chronicle, and by researchers who do not have access to the range of languages and literature represented here.

Mary Fischer

Edinburgh Napier University

Nicholas Coureas, *The Latin Church in Cyprus, 1313–1378* (Cyprus Research Centre Texts and Studies in the History of Cyprus, 65). Nicosia: Cyprus Research Centre, 2010. Pp. 557. ISBN 978 9 9630 8119 6.

The flowering of recent research on Cyprus by scholars such as Angel Nicolau-Konnari, Peter Edbury, Gilles Grivaud, Christopher Schabel, and Nicholas Coureas has meant that crusader historians have every reason to integrate the Lusignan kingdom more fully into their understanding of eastern Mediterranean politics, society, and culture in the thirteenth to fifteenth centuries. Nicholas Coureas has been at the forefront of bringing previously little-known source material to the attention of historians, notably in his and Schabel's edition of the Cartulary of the Cathedral of St. Sophia, Nicosia, in his translation of Cypriot Orthodox monastic rules, and in articles on various aspects of Cypriot ecclesiastical and political history from 1191 onwards. The present book is a sequel to his earlier *Latin Church in Cyprus, 1191–1312* (1997). That it is much fuller and more detailed than his previous survey of the Latin Church is in large measure a reflection of the greater volume of source material available for the later period. Most of this material comes from the published *acta* and letters of the Avignon popes, though Coureas has also used the principal documents produced by the ecclesiastical institutions of Cyprus, namely the cartulary of St. Sophia and the *Synodicum Nicosiense*, in addition to the evidence of western pilgrims in Cyprus, the chronicles of Amadi, Makhairas, and Stephen de Lusignan, who, though writing in the fifteenth century, preserve valuable information on the Lusignan period.

The Latin Church in Cyprus can be viewed in a number of different, but overlapping registers, and the organization of Coureas's book reflects the complexity of the subject matter and the intertwined nature of the evidence. Successive chapters examine the papacy and secular church in Cyprus and dealings with Cypriot lay society; the role of the Latin Church in crusading in the fourteenth century; the categories of people who staffed the Cypriot Church; the finances and internal governance of the Cypriot Church; the mendicant orders in Cyprus; monasteries and the military orders; and finally, the relations between the Latin Church and non-Latins. Within each chapter the material is organized comprehensively and largely according to chronology.

Underlying the commendably full and detailed research in the book is a paradox that Coureas himself acknowledges implicitly. The Latin Church in Cyprus was a "minority" institution, largely catering for and representing the interests of the Lusignan nobility and non-Cypriot merchant communities. The majority of the population of the island belonged to the Orthodox Church which, following the provisions of the Bulla Cypria of 1260, preserved its own episcopal and parochial structures and its own monastic institutions. We meet a few notable Greek converts to Catholicism, such as Thibaud Belfarage, a *familiaris* of Peter I, and John Laskaris, but these anomalous examples show Greeks wanting to get ahead professionally. The story of the Latin Church can much more readily be told in the coherent fashion presented here than is the case for the Orthodox Church and people, for which the institutional evidence is much less secure.

The major theme dominating the book is the position of Cyprus as a hinge of eastern Mediterranean Christendom. Thus, although Coureas devotes a single chapter to crusading, the role of Cyprus as a bulwark of western Christian power in a Mamluk world is inescapable when he examines matters such as sources of finance and papal relations with the crown and ecclesiastical establishment. For example, the settlement of the Latin patriarchate of Jerusalem in Cyprus after 1291 meant that there was a constant need to finance its operations by finding sources of income and property on the island. A good deal of papal correspondence with the crown dealt with this issue. Yet there seems to have been little questioning of the continuing need for the patriarchate; on the contrary, the role of Cyprus as an active crusading power in the fourteenth century confirmed it. The naval league formed by John XXII in 1331 resulted in the conquest of Smyrna from the Turks in 1344, and during the 58 years that the city remained in Christian hands it had to be administered as part of Latin Christendom. Similarly, the capture of Adalia in Asia Minor by Peter I in 1361 – a precursor to his more celebrated conquest of Alexandria in 1365 – made necessary detailed provision for the establishment of priests and churches, responsibilities which fell to the Cypriot Church.

Frankish Cypriot society was a small and closed world. A surprising amount of papal correspondence is devoted to dispensations for nobles to marry within the prohibited degrees of consanguinity, so as to maintain noble status and to avoid intermarriage with the indigenous people. A related problem emerges when Coureas examines the personnel of the Cypriot Church. Because few Latin Cypriots went into the Church, almost all of the higher clergy were émigrés, mostly French or Italian. One of the distinctive features of the Cypriot Church, therefore, was its internationalism. Whereas the use of provisions by the papacy aroused hostility in other western kingdoms, it does not seem to have been controversial in Cyprus, where there were not enough native Frankish clergy to fill the available benefices. The friars arrived early in Cyprus, and three of the four major orders – Franciscans, Dominicans, and Carmelites – had settled there by the mid-thirteenth century. The fortunes of the mendicant orders differed according to circumstance, but all were influential during the fourteenth century, for the reasons given above. The Carmelites enjoyed particular favour under Peter I because of the close relations established with Peter Thomas, the pro-crusading Carmelite papal legate in the 1360s. On the other hand, the Franciscans suffered from the hostility of Hugh IV, who suspected their complicity in his quarrel with Ferrand of Majorca. Hugh even accused his daughter of adultery when she wanted to confess to Franciscan friars.

This thoroughly researched book adds to the growing body of substantial publications on Cypriot medieval history by the Cyprus Research Centre. It will surely serve as the standard reference work on the subject for the foreseeable future.

ANDREW JOTISCHKY
LANCASTER UNIVERSITY

Fortresses of the Intellect: Ismaili and Other Islamic Studies in Honour of Farhad Daftary, ed. Omar Ali-de-Unzaga. London: IB Tauris, 2011. Pp. xvi, 600. ISBN 978 1 8488 5626 4.

Farhad Daftary has, for the last three decades, been one of the foremost figures in Ismaili studies in the medieval period. Many readers will be familiar with his magnum opus *The Ismāʿīlīs: Their History and Doctrine* (2007), although this is only one of a number of ground-breaking works which he has written, a full bibliography of which is recorded at the beginning of this festschrift.

The volume, published in conjunction with the Institute of Ismaili Studies in London, of which Daftary is a senior member, contains 22 articles written by some of the foremost scholars of medieval Islamic studies, including Carole Hillenbrand, C. Edmund Bosworth, Patricia Crone and Wilferd Madelung. The study covers almost the whole sweep of the medieval period, from Hamid Algar's study of the mid-eighth-century imam Jaʿfar al-Ṣādiq to Andrew Newman's examination of subalterns in seventeenth-century Safavid Iran. The volume's scope of subject is equally impressive, covering history, religion, politics, literature and linguistics. Such a wide remit reflects Daftary's own research interests.

Many of the articles in this volume will prove useful for scholars of the crusades. While only one study, that by Hillenbrand, deals directly with the crusading period, many others consider issues of direct relevance to understanding Muslim reactions to the Franks, especially Ismaili reactions which, in the crusading period, signifies the Fatimids of Egypt and the Nizaris (Assassins) in Syria.

Hillenbrand's article examines the killing of Gervase of Basoches by Tughtegin, atabeg of Damascus, in 1107/8, shedding light both on why he may have done so and the symbolic nature of Tughtegin's scalping of Gervase and turning his head into a drinking cup, which she demonstrates are remnants of pre-Islamic Turkic culture. Delia Cortese provides a thoughtful glimpse into Arabic historiography through an examination of the use of the dream motif in Arabic historical writing; Wilferd Madelung and Paul Walker give a useful window into the ideas behind Ismaili missionary activity through an edition and translation of the missionary text attributed to the ninth-century Ismaili ʿAbdān; Ismail Poonawala gives an assessment of some of the works of the qadi al-Nuʿmān, the foremost Fatimid jurist and the founder of the Ismaili school of jurisprudence; and two articles examine the Ikhwān al-Ṣafāʾ, an important secret Ismaili group from the ninth or tenth centuries, whose ideas influenced later Ismaili thought on a plethora of issues.

As can be expected from such a host of top academics, the scholarship is of the highest standard, being intelligent and lucid, while the subject matter of each contributes usefully to a fuller understanding of the medieval Middle East in general. This volume would consequently be a useful addition to any library.

ALEX MALLETT

ROYAL HOLLOWAY, UNIVERSITY OF LONDON

Matthew Gabriele, *An Empire of Memory: The Legend of Charlemagne, the Franks, and Jerusalem before the First Crusade*. Oxford: Oxford University Press, 2011. Pp. xii, 202. ISBN 978 0 1995 9144 2.

This efficiently argued and interesting book is an informed and thoughtful discussion of the ideas and associations that attached themselves to the memory of Charlemagne between the reign of his successor Louis the Pious and the First Crusade. Gabriele perceives a progressive intensification and deepening of the cultural resonances that Charlemagne stimulated, and, as a corollary, a broadening of the range of related associations, with the result that the "Franks" and Frankishness as a transcendent quality increasingly came to participate as sites of value and meaning in the myths that circulated around the emperor himself. Various literary incarnations of Charlemagne feature in Gabriele's careful analysis: Charlemagne as legendary founder of monasteries, Charlemagne as supposed pilgrim, Charlemagne as defender of the Holy Places, and Charlemagne as leader of the Christian people under arms. The book ends with the First Crusade, enthusiasm for which is seen in terms of the narratives of self-fashioning that those who responded to Pope Urban II's call to arms extrapolated from the current ideas of Frankishness that were in their turn outgrowths of the core Charlemagne myth. As Gabriele suggestively argues, such narratives had the power to collapse what we, from a modern historical perspective, tend to assume were considerable chronological and geographical spaces. Central to the book's argument is the interesting distinction between "memory" and "history" as strategies for negotiating the past and configuring its relationships to the present and future. While "memory" encapsulates expectations of continuity, "history" disjunctively promotes the opposite, emphasizing the feeling of difference between observer and observed. Much, indeed most, central medieval engagement with the past leans towards "memory" as so defined. This is a fruitful perspective and it perhaps could have been developed further. In addition, the author has interesting and pertinent things to say about the artificiality of the time-honoured distinction between "historical" and "poetic," or literary, sources; and his advocacy of an interdisciplinary methodology is welcome. In a book of this length, the argument is necessarily rather compact and consequently can tend towards the neatly teleological as it builds towards the climax in the form of the response to the First Crusade. One would have liked more discussion of the loose ends, the internal contradictions and the inconsistencies in the source base: these would not necessarily invalidate Gabriele's thesis, but would perhaps introduce more cultural "white noise" than he allows for. That said, this is a valuable and insightful book, and it is an important contribution to the study of the intellectual background to the First Crusade.

MARCUS BULL
UNIVERSITY OF NORTH CAROLINA AT CHAPEL HILL

Identities and Allegiances in the Eastern Mediterranean after 1204, ed. Judith Herrin and Guillaume Saint-Guillain. Farnham and Burlington, VT: Ashgate, 2011. Pp. xv, 347. ISBN 978 1 4094 1098 0.

Derived from a conference convened under the aegis of the project "Prosopography of the Byzantine World" (PBW), this collection might be considered a companion volume to *Byzantine and Crusaders in Non-Greek Sources, 1025–1204*, ed. Mary Whitby (Oxford, 2007). The latter is concerned principally with surveying the sources needed to chart prosopographically an expanding Byzantine World (no longer simply the Byzantine Empire), while the volume under review is devoted to various parts of the Byzantine World that remained bound by cultural ties as the empire fragmented following the Fourth Crusade. Most chapters provide a prosopographical appendix or contain specific prosopographical content.

The first part of the book, which comprises half the volume, addresses the western and core parts of the former empire, in turn the polities of Achaea, Constantinople, Nicaea, Epirus, Bulgaria, and Serbia in the period 1204–61. Teresa Shawcross examines the immediate impact of the Fourth Crusade on the inhabitants of the former imperial provinces of Hellas and Peloponnesos, which had experienced unprecedented growth and prosperity through the twelfth century, boasting more than sixteen main cities, and which fell under the sway of the Villehardouin rulers of Achaea and Morea. Most attention is paid to Michael Choniates (and the evidence of his letters), who doggedly persisted with administration. Shawcross offers as a prosopographical digest a list of 93 individuals of Greek origin named in regional sources for the period 1204–22. Michael Angold's chapter concludes that marriage strategies between Latin and Greek aristocrats in the Latin empire of Constantinople were generally less successful than one might have imagined, given the number and significance of such marriages prior to 1204. The failed policy of Henry of Hainault to establish a dynastic framework for the Latin succession ensured that Latins were regarded as "alien intruders." Vincent Puech explores Byzantine aristocratic support for, and opposition to, the emperors of Nicaea, focusing on various families: for example, the enduring importance of the Mouzalon clan, who were not lacking in *eugeneia* as Pachymeres claimed. Günter Prinzing's paper on Epiros offers a most original and insightful prosopographical contribution: a hitherto overlooked necrology contained in Oxford MS Cod. Cromwell 11, written in Ioannina in 1225, which provide the names of 39 individuals (23 men, 16 women), several of which had names that have not before been recorded in medieval Greek. Prinzing posits cleverly that the group may have been a confraternity, perhaps devoted to the Theotokos Eleousa. Dimiter Angelov provides a useful historical summary of events in Bulgaria from 1204 to 1261, coupled with some insights into the sources and their utility as sources for prosopographical data and indicators of ethnic sentiment. Ljuobmir Maksimovic provides a rather more schematic treatment of Serbia in the same period, with no specific prosopographical contribution. The first part of the book concludes with a short but richly illustrated paper by numismatist Cécile Morrisson, on thirteenth-century "metallic identities." This shows that the reformed currency of the Comnenian period provided the model for all coins struck by the empire's various successors until 1261, but that each distinguished itself through the use of titles, nomenclature, and dynastic and iconographic signifiers (various saints, but also winged emperors, the Archangel Michael, and the Theotokos). A useful table summarizes the observations, which are demonstrated by twenty-two illustrations of coins and seals. These are the volume's only figures, but there are six excellent regional maps.

The book's second part turns to the eastern fringes of Byzantium, beginning with Rustam Shukourov's substantial paper on Trebizond and the Seljuk Sultanate in Anatolia. The Trapezuntine section centres on the Acts of Vazelon, a cartulary beginning in 1245, the first part of which preserves more than a hundred names that might be dated before 1261. Shukurov focuses attention on ethnicity, demonstrating that 60 per cent of those named may not have been Greek. Through lexicographical and etymological analysis, he highlights first Laz and then Latin individuals, the latter apparently living as naturalized and Orthodox inhabitants of the Pontos region many decades before the accepted date for the Genoese and Venetian settlement. The second part of the paper addresses Greeks in Muslim Anatolia. Robert Thomson's paper contains a vignette that will fascinate crusade historians: although Armenian historians generally ignore, or occasionally misdate, the events of 1204, a colophon written into a commentary on Luke by the scribe Grigor at Hromkla offers a contemporaneous and sympathetic treatment of the Latins. Tassos Papacostas was given the brief, at the conference, to address Cyprus and the crusader states of Syria-Palestine in 1204–61. But for reasons he sets out clearly, he believes much of this material does not belong in the PBW, and his focus falls squarely on Cyprus, where there is a relative dearth of information. Colophons and marginal notes in manuscripts provide little, and inscriptions in stone and on seals tend to duplicate names already known. A short list of painted dedicatory inscriptions in churches, on the other hand, all belong to individuals who are otherwise unknown.

The collection's third and shortest substantive section concerns western interests. Catherine Otten-Froux provides useful lists of Pisans, collated from documents listing persons and their property in Constantinople shortly before the Fourth Crusade. Information is far scarcer after 1204, and scarcer still for the Genoese, who appear to leave the city for other locations, for example Thessalonike and the islands, notably Lesbos. Guillaume Saint-Guillain addresses Venetian historiography, ostensibly as a source of prosopographical data, with as highlights the anonymous *History of the Doge of Venice*, which names 150 individuals, and the histories of Martino de Canal that name more than 400. Finally, Sally McKee returns to ethnicity, seeking to "unsettle common assumptions" by arguing from one document from Venetian Crete that certain designations, here "Greek," are too inflexible to be meaningful. Section four comprises two short conclusions, by Judith Herrin, who offers reflections on refugees, and by Catherine Holmes, who summarizes the volumes main findings and points in relation to the PBW, complementing Charlotte Roueché's introduction.

PAUL STEPHENSON
UNIVERSITY OF DURHAM

Jacques de Vitry, *Histoire orientale. Historia orientalis*, ed. and trans. Jean Donnadieu (Sous la règle de saint Augustin, 12). Turnhout: Brepols, 2008. Pp. 562. ISBN 978 2 5035 2521 1.

Les historiens le savent depuis Jacques Bongars, il s'agit là d'une œuvre majeure et d'une source capitale: celle d'un acteur et témoin essentiel de la Cinquième croisade, étudiant à Paris, chanoine à Oignies, prédicateur aux côtés du légat Robert de Courson ou d'Olivier de Paderborn, sacré évêque d'Acre par Honorius III le 31 juillet 1216, avant de gagner la Terre sainte quelques semaines plus tard et d'accompagner en 1218 les croisés en Égypte jusqu'à Damiette. Il participe alors à l'interminable siège jusqu'à la prise de la ville le 5 novembre 1219 et y réside au moins jusqu'en avril 1221, le désastre étant consommé le 29 août de la même année.

Outre une rare correspondance qui relate cette dernière phase, mais pas la reddition (éd. R. B. C. Huygens, 1960, trad. G. Duchet-Suchaux-J. Longère, 1998), et à côté de sa prédication aux pèlerins et aux croisés dont il reste des modèles de sermon (C. T. Maier, 1994 et 2000), le tableau historico-géographique qu'il dresse de l'histoire et de la situation en Orient comme en Occident forme un monument à vrai dire composite et largement plus complexe qu'on ne l'imaginerait.

Ce qui explique peut-être, malgré l'édition latine ancienne de ses parties relatives à l'Orient, reprise par Dom Martène (1717) et, sur la base de celle de Bongars (1611), sa traduction en français par François Guizot (1825), ses extraits par J.-F. Michaud et J.-T. Reinaud (1829) ou sa traduction anglaise par Aubrey Stewart (1896), sa quasi absence des *Recueils des Historiens des Croisades* qui l'avaient pourtant inscrit à leur programme: seuls quatre chapitres isolés d'une traduction médiévale fragmentaire (manuscrit de Troyes) y ont été publiés, au milieu de *narrationes minores*. Texte d'autant plus difficile d'accès que sous un titre commun, *Historia Hierosolymitana abbreviata*, se rattachent plusieurs volets: un Livre I *Historia orientalis*, dont il est ici principalement question, mais aussi un Livre II *Historia occidentalis*, complétés par un Livre III "revenant d'Occident en Orient" sur les événements plus proches et qui s'achève avant même la reprise de Damiette. L'attribution à Jacques de Vitry de ce dernier livre a été discutée depuis le XIXe siècle au moins (P. Meyer) sur le critère essentiel d'une démarque d'Olivier de Paderborn. Assorti d'un Prologue indiquant les circonstances, les intentions et le contenu de l'ouvrage, cet ensemble a fait l'objet d'approches dissociées au gré des intérêts des éditeurs – les uns davantage polarisés par l'Orient que par l'Occident, ou inversement – et suivant la composition même des manuscrits, qui comprennent tout ou partie de ces livres. Les travaux récents de Jessalynn Bird (2003–2006) vont même, contre toute attente, jusqu'à inverser la place des deux premiers livres, seuls reconnus pour authentique.

Des 124 manuscrits latins subsistants du Livre premier, Jean Donnadieu a choisi de s'appuyer sur un témoin unique qu'il confronte seulement à dix autres manuscrits: l'*editio princeps* publiée à Douai en 1596–1597 (réimpr. 1971) par François Moschus, fournit en effet la copie d'un manuscrit aujourd'hui disparu et alors obtenue du prieur de Saint-Nicolas d'Oignies avec lequel Moschus était en relation. L'examen attentif est convaincant: il montre bien qu'il s'agit là d'une version initiale, la plus complète et, de surcroît, datée de 1224. L'évocation des dissensions entre Génois et Pisans en 1222 (chap. 64) semble corroborer cet élargissement de la période de rédaction dont le début, à s'en tenir aux seuls éléments internes du livre (chap. 77 et 80) et au rapprochement avec les lettres de Jacques de Vitry, peut être situé en 1219–1221, au moment de son séjour en Égypte.

Jacques de Vitry est un témoin direct: ainsi son épiscopat à Acre et sa tournée prédicatrice de Césarée à Tripoli en passant par Margat et le Crac des Chevaliers, l'ont porté à l'observation et à l'information directe auprès des habitants de toutes confessions et cultures "j'ai vu," "je me suis informé auprès d'un moine syrien" (chap. 53), "j'ai observé moi-même," "comme je cherchais à savoir" (chap. 76). De même, à côté des références scripturaires (dont l'usage mériterait une analyse fouillée, on songera aux Maccabées par exemple), ses emprunts sont multiples, à la dimension de son projet proto-encyclopédique: les historiens de la première croisade, Foucher de Chartres notamment, Guillaume de Tyr, les Itinéraires (Fretellus, Burchard), Eusèbe de Césarée, Hégésippe, saint Jérôme, Pline, Solin, Isidore de Séville, Marbode, Hugues de Fouilloy, Jean Damascène,

Pierre le Vénérable. Ceux du Pseudo-Callisthène, de Julius Valerius ou du Roman d'Alexandre sont bien relevés. De même, les "anciennes histoires des Orientaux" que J. de Vitry avoue avoir consultées (chap. 11), textes grecs, syriaques en particulier (à propos d'Abgar, chap. 31) ou arabes où l'on reconnaîtra, en autres, des emprunts à al-Tabarî ou à al-Kindî et certaines versions apocryphes des évangiles. Jacques de Vitry les confronte, les précise, loin d'être un compilateur servile. Aussi, les informations qu'il transmet sont souvent plus que précieuses: sur l'histoire et la perception de l'Islam dont il marque une réfutation mais non la condamnation des Sarrasins ("malheureux abusés," p. 114–15), sur les diverses "nations" d'Orient et en particulier les Maronites dont il livre une des toutes premières descriptions connues (chap. 78), sur l'état du clergé (chap. 71–72), les ordres hospitaliers et militaires (chap. 74–76) mais sans mention des lépreux de Saint-Lazare, sur les langues (chap. 76), la culture (où il atteste la lecture des *Libri naturales* par certains savants musulmans en contradiction avec la loi de Mahomet et, de ce fait amenés, à se convertir (chap. 6), les croyances et pratiques religieuses, y compris celles de l'Orient plus lointain, ses "créatures fabuleuses" et la religion des brahmanes (Hindouisme) sur laquelle retranscrit les lettres à Alexandre (chap. 92). On lui doit une des toutes premières occurrences du mot "coton" (chap. 86) et la première trace écrite de la boussole aimantée et de son utilisation pour la navigation (chap. 91). Ses observations actualisent la littérature alors disponible: sur le paysage, l'économie, la géographie des cités, l'hydrographie, le climat, la faune, la flore, l'alimentation (où il découvre entre autres – et nous aussi – la banane! chap. 86), les mœurs et en particulier le comportement des "Poulains" (chap. 68 et 73) qu'il dénonce vivement, sans oublier la forte présence des colons italiens (chap. 67). Sa correspondance envoyée de Damiette constitue l'esquisse de biens des traits rapportés et des sentiments de J. de Vitry: le fait aurait pu être souligné davantage qu'en un court paragraphe de l'introduction (p. 9).

L'appareil critique de cette publication est d'une grande richesse: il est hélas reporté (mais c'est la loi fort incommode de la collection dans laquelle paraît l'ouvrage) en fin de volume (notes, pp. 465–522). Dans ces notes, on est toutefois étonné de voir l'éditeur affubler les chanoines du Saint-Sépulcre du qualificatif impropre de *fratres cruciferi* (p. 493, LVIII, 2) ou encore préciser à propos d'Azot (l'actuelle Ashdod) que Jacques de Vitry situe "non loin de la mer" (p. 196–97, 5) qu'"il ne s'agit pas d'une cité côtière" (p. 489, XLI, 1 et non placée sur la carte, p. 83). La relativisation des interdits du vin (p. 479, VI, 31) semble oublier les prescriptions formelles du *Coran* 2, 216 et 5, 92 tout comme la guérison des lépreux et la résurrection de Lazare relèvent de *Coran*, 5, 110 exclusivement et non jusqu'au verset 114 (p. 479, VI, 31) et l'on regrettera que ce chapitre ne fasse pas l'objet d'une confrontation plus systématique avec les sources polémiques. Les *indices* biblique et onomastique (p. 525–47) sont bien venus, malgré la frustration de ne point disposer d'un toujours utile *index rerum*. Quelques inévitables coquilles ("Poche-Orient" pour Proche-Orient, p. 82) ou un décalage de la numérotation des notes (p. 502, LXXII) ne sauraient contrevenir à la qualité de la traduction, hormis l'emploi répété du terme familier "coins" (p. 221 ou p. 263) pour *partibus*, "régions" ou "parties du monde."

Faut-il s'en tenir là? Une bonne transcription de l'*editio princeps* et des variantes des dix manuscrits sélectionnés (sans liste plus complète), une traduction, qu'avait précédée celle de Guizot (rééd. Paléo, 2005) ou plus récemment celle de Marie-Geneviève Grossel (2005), sont-ils suffisants pour saisir le projet de Jacques de Vitry, l'économie de l'œuvre dans sa totalité? Peut-on si facilement évacuer le Prologue et le Livre III (qui ne sont certes pas dans l'édition de Moschus) par un déni d'attribution, fût-elle, pour ce dernier, l'objet de discussions fort anciennes (Introduction, p. 9)? Ou au prétexte d'une recomposition et de compléments indépendants de Jacques de Vitry? Jusqu'à quel point? L'ensemble figure pourtant bien avec le Livre II dans l'un des témoins originaux les plus anciens, daté de la première moitié du XIIIe siècle (Paris, BNF, ms lat. 16 079): un manuscrit parfaitement contemporain de l'auteur devenu cardinal de Tusculum (1229) et envoyé par le pape pour négocier avec Frédéric II, sitôt son propre retour d'Acre et le rêve accompli de retrouver Jérusalem – à un prix sans doute insatisfaisant et précaire (le traité de Jaffa). Suffit-il d'arguer des emprunts, voire d'une simple copie de l'*Historia Damiatina* d'Olivier de Paderborn que J. de Vitry a pu fréquenter dès ses années de jeunesse, puis croiser en permanence: à Paris, lors de ses missions de prédication contre les Albigeois, pour la Cinquième croisade, à Acre et Damiette? Olivier le devançant même à la Curie romaine. En quoi serait-il gênant que son récit de l'expédition en Égypte, répondant au vœu même de Jacques de Vitry, qui n'avait plus guère le loisir de parachever son dessein, ou qui avait pu l'abandonner comme il s'était démis de sa charge d'évêque à Acre pour rentrer en Europe, ait trouvé ici sa place? Une rédaction à plusieurs mains, sous-traitée par des secrétaires ou chapelains qui entourent le prélat? L'hypothèse d'un enrichissement progressif à la façon de dossiers tour à tour intégrés (comme la juxtaposition sans transition du traité des sacrements dans le Livre II le laisse penser) doit-elle être écartée?

On ne voit pas que le Prologue, donné pour écrit sur les rives du Nil après la prise de Damiette (5 novembre 1219), et qui accompagne les manuscrits latins les plus anciens autant que ses traductions médiévales vernaculaires (C. Buridant, 1986), contrarie les vues énoncées dans la correspondance comme dans le corps ou la composition des trois livres: celles d'un témoin désabusé, parcouru de nostalgie et de désillusion face à la somme des obstacles et à la répétition des échecs. Cela méritait bien un aussi vaste panorama inscrit dans le plan du salut: la définition des adversaires, la récapitulation des forces et la dénonciation des faiblesses du monde chrétien d'Orient comme d'Occident, à commencer par celles du clergé. Que l'enquête ainsi proposée (*Historia*) se présente aujourd'hui sous une apparence hétérogène, voire hétéroclite, n'est-ce pas le propre de tout inventaire … en cours? Et que l'ampleur nécessaire à la démonstration et le besoin permanent de son actualisation ajoutés aux circonstances instables de la rédaction aient eu pour conséquence de la laisser inachevée ou interrompue (*abbreviata*) n'en sont-ils pas l'essence même? Sans nuire pour autant à sa diffusion large et durable.

Cette édition du premier Livre vient compléter, mais sûrement pas achever, la redécouverte. Elle doit ouvrir à une reconsidération plus que jamais indispensable à sa compréhension d'ensemble.

FRANÇOIS-OLIVIER TOUATI
UNIVERSITÉ DE TOURS

The Proceedings Against the Templars in the British Isles. Volume 1: The Latin Text; Volume 2: Translation, ed. and trans. Helen J. Nicholson. 2 vols. Farnham and Burlington, VT: Ashgate, 2011. Pp. xl, 432 and lx, 653. ISBN 978 1 4094 3650 8 and 978 1 4094 3652 2.

The Templars' responses to the charges that had led to their arrest in October 1307 are to be found in surviving descriptions of testimony recorded at the enquiries into their behaviour and into that of the Order as a whole. The first group of these comprise an investigation by the papal inquisitor in Paris and episcopal enquiries in Normandy, Champagne, and Languedoc and Provence during the nine months after the arrests. This period culminated in depositions made before the pope at Poitiers and a team of cardinals at Chinon in the summer of 1308. Rather later come the records of investigations in Britain, Clermont, Nîmes, Mainz and Trier, the Papal States, Tuscany, Cesena, Apulia, Sicily, Portugal and Castile, Roussillon, Aragon and Navarre, and Cyprus. Meanwhile a papal commission charged with investigating the order was sitting in Paris from 1309 to 1311. The accounts began to be published from the seventeenth century onwards. Recent editions include those by Anne Gilmour-Bryson (the Papal States), Roger Sève and Anne-Marie Chagny-Sève (Auvergne), Francisco Tommasi (Cesena), and Josep Maria Sans i Travé (Castile). Barbara Frale discovered the original report of the meeting with the cardinals at Chinon, although this adds little of substance to Finke's 1908 edition of a later redaction.

There is a definite need to revisit some of the earlier editions, which are obsolescent, and Helen Nicholson deserves the highest praise for tackling the records of the enquiries in the British Isles. Using Bodleian Library MS Bodley 454, the fullest and most wide-ranging version, as a base text, she has collated it with British Library Cotton MS Julius B xii, which contains testimonies from the province of Canterbury. In separate sections she has added materials from the Cotton MS that have no parallels in the Bodley MS; Vatican MS Armarium XXXV, 147, which appears to be a summary of the proceedings sent for use at the Council of Vienne; and fragments in British Library Cotton MS Otho B iii, collated with a transcript in British Library Additional MSS 5244, which may be all that survives from a summary written for a provincial council that met in London in 1311. She provides a translation into English. Appendices list the Templars and their properties referred to in the proceedings, the locations of the enquiries and the prisons in which the brothers were held. The work Dr. Nicholson has put into these two volumes is immense. Since she had to cope with difficult texts that are very highly abbreviated she has indicated in every case her reading of the abbreviation concerned. The monumentality of the effort and concentration required will be clear to anyone who makes use of her edition.

In her introduction to the volume of Latin text, Dr. Nicholson describes the manuscripts in detail and explains the editorial conventions she has used. Her introduction to volume 2 contains a description of the enquiries, a discussion of the value of the testimonies as historical evidence, and a description of the way she has approached the translation. It is a pity that, in common with many English-speaking historians of the Templar process, she continues to employ the word "trial" when referring to enquiries. This criticism is not pedantry. Although inquisitorial procedures could lead to trials, the forensic methods employed and the freedoms given to the interrogators were distinct. She herself stresses the care which the inquisitors took, even going to the lengths of checking evidence given when it referred to events abroad. This is not, of course, to deny that there were presumptions of guilt, which were hardly surprising considering the speed with which the most senior Templars in France had confessed to blasphemy within a week or two of their arrests. Secondly, like many of her colleagues she refuses to believe that even a proportion of the more serious charges – in particular a rite of passage involving the denial of Christ – could have taken place and goes to great lengths to demonstrate that the use, or threat, of torture invalidates all the evidence presented to the enquiries. The case for scepticism has been recently argued by Dr. Alan Forey in an article in *Viator* 42 (2011), but Dr. Nicholson is less restrained than he was. She asserts several times that all the Templars in France were tortured and then has to explain away the testimony of those who specifically stated that they had not been. She even goes so far as to end by asserting that "these trial proceedings reveal how a large-scale heresy trial in the British Isles was organised and recorded, but may tell us virtually nothing about the Order of the Temple." A natural reaction would be to ask why as a historian of the military orders she has bothered to edit the material at all, but her assertion should not be taken seriously, because, leaving aside the value or otherwise of the witnesses' testimony in relation to the charges, the rest of the evidence they provided is fascinating and there are no grounds for disbelieving everything they said about themselves and their careers. The misfortune into which they had fallen generated an almost unique body of material, which is far more extensive than anything we have in relation to other religious orders of the central Middle Ages. Nowhere else do we find so many details about the lives of the brothers, the houses in which they resided, and workings of their Order's administration. So my advice is to ignore Dr. Nicholson's self-deprecation. She has edited very important texts – and, what is more, she has translated them – and her contribution is a very substantial one.

JONATHAN RILEY-SMITH
EMMANUEL COLLEGE, CAMBRIDGE

Jürgen Sarnowsky, *Die Templer*. Munich: C. H. Beck, 2009. Pp. 128. ISBN 978 3 4065 6272 3.

This erudite and short monograph on the Templars is the middle volume of Jürgen Sarnowsky's trilogy on the three major military-religious orders, preceded by a work on the Teutonic Order (*Der Deutsche Orden*, 2007) and succeeded by one on the Hospitallers (*Die Johanniter*, 2011), published in C. H. Beck's "Wissen" series and intended for the general readership. To explain the Templars' significance in world history, Sarnowsky shows how the Order participated in the fight for the Holy Land during the era of the crusades, contributed to the origins of the banking system, and became an object of fascination for esoteric circles in modern times.

In his introduction (pp. 6–7), Sarnowsky argues that the Order's sudden demise in the early fourteenth century gave rise to Templarism ("Templerismus"), namely an ongoing fascination with anything "Templar," but cautions that mythopoetic discourse reveals little about the Order's actual history. The book's first part addresses the Templars' origins and rise to prominence. The reader becomes acquainted with the crusading movement, the Augustinian ideas concerning "just" war, the Christianization of the European knighthood, and the pilgrimage movement. According to Sarnowsky, the pilgrims' needs were met by three groups: the canons of the Holy Sepulchre who saw to their spiritual care; the Hospitallers who tended to their physical well-being; and the Templars who ensured their safety while traveling in the Holy Land. Yet, the Templars' unprecedented combination of monastic and knightly ideals proved to be a major obstacle. This was not overcome by the Order's Rule, drafted by the Council of Troyes (1129), but, rather, by Bernard of Clairvaux's explanation of their existence in the form of his famous defense of the Templars as "the new knighthood" in *De laude novae militae* (1136/1137), as well as Pope Innocent II's bull *Omne datum optimum* (1139). Donations to the Order followed in both West and East, and the Templars soon found themselves defending and building castles; transferring and administrating their own assets, as well as the assets of others; and arguing with ecclesiastical and secular rulers about their rights and obligations. Sarnowsky concludes his first part with a discussion of the Templars' catastrophic losses at the Battle of Hattin (1187), which necessitated the development of even stronger ties between the Order's headquarters in the East and its supply bases in the West.

In the second part, Sarnowsky elucidates a variety of aspects pertaining to the Order's history in the twelfth and thirteenth centuries. He traces the evolution of the Templars' normative texts, addresses recruitment, membership, hierarchy, offices, and leadership structures (acknowledging the flexibility and adaptability of these structures) and provides examples for their ongoing military engagement, their blossoming naval activities, and their "network" in and around the Mediterranean world. In a sub-chapter on the Templars' spirituality and contributions to cultural history, Sarnowsky draws attention to the assessment of the Order's main accomplishments by the last Templar master, James of Molay, who ranked the

Templars' liturgy and divine service first, their alms-giving second, and their defense of Christendom third. The book's final part describes the Order's demise. Sarnowsky's narrative makes clear that the Order's sudden downfall was not a foregone conclusion, that in the course of the thirteenth century the Order even expanded its activities to include Frankish Greece and eastern Europe and that the Order forcefully argued against a merger of the existing military-religious orders. However, Sarnowsky also states (pp. 103–4) that, unlike the Hospitallers and the Teutonic Order, the Templars were unable to find new tasks ("neue Aufgabenfelder") for themselves after the fall of Acre (1291), which is why the arrests of 1307 caught them unprepared. This may ring true enough in hindsight; however, whether the other orders were really engaged in anything truly "new" is debatable. The Hospitallers' attack on Rhodes (1306) was viewed (at least by contemporaries) in the context of the Templars' occupation of Ruad (1300–1302); and the Teutonic Knights had, in fact, been in Prussia for decades. This notwithstanding, Sarnowsky's sub-chapter on the proceedings against the Templars (1307–14) includes a balanced discussion of what might have motivated King Philip IV to turn against the Order, shows that the Templars ultimately found themselves caught in a tug-of-war between the French king and pope, and stresses that the Council of Vienne dissolved the Order not because its guilt had been proven, but because its reputation had been damaged beyond repair. In his conclusion, Sarnowsky demonstrates that the Templars continue to feature prominently in all sorts of mythopoetic discourse. The book also contains a bibliography, a list of Templar masters, an index, two excellent maps, and several illustrations.

Given the volume's publisher-imposed brevity, it would be pointless to dwell on what else could have been included. What is here is impressive indeed. Above all, it must be emphasized that this book is not a mere sketch of the Templars' history in broad brushstrokes. Utilizing quotes from a wide range of primary sources, Sarnowsky brilliantly and stylishly alternates between "big picture" tapestries and "focused" vignettes. For example, when discussing the evolution of the Templars' normative texts, Sarnowsky seizes the opportunity to point out that the respective manuscripts' sections on "how to admit members into the Order" show clear traces of heavy use, which renders absurd the accusation (made during the proceedings against the Order in the early fourteenth century) that the Templars had secret and heretical initiation rituals. Examples for similar attention to detail include the author's account of the challenges of transporting horses by sea (pp. 70–74), his description of the inner workings of Templar houses in different parts of Europe (pp. 74–78) and his explanation that the Templars had a head start on the Italian bankers because of their network of commanderies all over Latin Christendom (pp. 80–81). In sum, not just the general readership will benefit from Sarnowsky's synthesis of current scholarship on the Templars; it is also recommended reading for students and scholars of the crusades and military-religious orders.

Jochen Burgtorf
California State University, Fullerton

Miriam Rita Tessera, *Orientalis ecclesia. Papato, Chiesa e regno latino di Gerusalemme (1099–1187)* (Bibliotheca erudita. Studi e documenti di storia e filologia, vol. 32). Milan: Vita e pensiero, 2010. Pp. x, 660. ISBN 978 8 8343 1849 2.

Despite the vast literature on the papacy and the crusading movement, and the significance of the papacy in studies of the Church in the crusader states, we have until now lacked a monograph specifically on papal relations with the crusader states. Such a lacuna is now well and truly filled by this massive examination of the topic from the time of Gregory VII (the first date in the title is rather misleading) until the issue of the encyclical *Audita tremendi* by Gregory VIII in the immediate aftermath of the defeat of 1187. The approach is essentially narrative; after an introductory chapter on crusading ideas immediately before 1099, relations between the papacy, the Latin Church in the crusader states (for Antioch plays a significant part in her discussion) and the Frankish rulers are then discussed in six chronological chapters, and finally two more are devoted to the papacy and the evolution of the Church in the kingdom of Jerusalem and the dispute between the patriarchs of Antioch and Jerusalem over the province of Tyre. This last considerably extends, not least chronologically, the well-known study on this issue by John Rowe written more than fifty years ago.

Tessera can certainly not be faulted on grounds either of scholarship or thoroughness. Her discussion is based firmly on the sources, both narrative and documentary, which are examined exhaustively, while she has also profited from a mastery of the secondary literature, and especially that in German and English. (This last is not always the case with Italian scholars, at least those writing on the history of their own country, who are often surprisingly ill-informed about the relevant Anglophone literature.) All of this is greatly to be commended. Tessara begins by locating the origin of the crusades firmly within the ideology of the Gregorian reform, and papal concern with the "imitation of Christ." She is (rightly) clear that the recovery of Jerusalem was always the intention behind the First Crusade. She then proceeds to a very detailed discussion of the ecclesiastical politics of the kingdom of Jerusalem, and to some extent also of the other crusader states, and the papal role therein. There is much here of interest. She stresses, for example, the role played by the canons of the Holy Sepulchre in the disputes about the patriarchate during the reign of Baldwin I, indeed the power and significance of these canons is one of the major themes of this book, on which a great deal of emphasis is laid, especially in the penultimate chapter. Tessara views Daimbert of Pisa not as an ambitious and self-interested prelate, but as a sincere reformer anxious to fulfil the aims of the Gregorian movement. In the discussion of Baldwin II's reign, she underlines the importance of the Council of Nablus as showing what could be achieved by the co-operation of *regnum* and *sacerdotium*, and sees the Patriarch Warmund as an ally, not an opponent, of Baldwin II. She later describes this period as "a phase of profound institutional and disciplinary reform" (p. 470). She stresses the significance of Calixtus II as an ally of the kingdom, not least in encouraging the Venetian Crusade of 1122; and she emphasizes too the importance of Honorius II's bull of May 1128 confirming the legitimacy of Baldwin's rule, and encouraging the measures that the king was taking to ensure the succession.

Tessera continues to examine the role played by the crusader states in the 1130 papal schism, stressing the importance to both popes of claiming the Holy Land's support, and why by 1132 Innocent II had been recognized there, and skilfully interweaves this with a discussion of the relations of Genoa and Pisa with the Holy Land. (Here she expands her brief discussion in *Crusades* 9 (2010), 1–12.) She goes on to look at Innocent's relations with Antioch during the brief but turbulent patriarchate of Ralph of Domfront, and with the Byzantine Emperor John Komnenos threatening to take over the principality. The chapter on the Second Crusade and its consequences is one of the most interesting parts of the book, although the examination of the crusade itself – a notably well-balanced one – strays from the papacy and the kingdom of Jerusalem into a more general discussion of the papacy and the crusades. But there are some interesting and novel insights here – that Eugenius III was as concerned with the reunion of the Church as he was with the recovery of Christian territory, and that a section of the kingdom's bishops (and perhaps Baldwin III) were looking to Frederick Barbarossa as a potential overlord of the Holy Land in the mid-1150s. Tessera suggests too that, during this decade, Eugenius III and Adrian IV actively supported the claims of monasteries and military orders, appealing to Rome after a series of local disputes with the episcopate, in an attempt to curb the independence of the Holy Land patriarchs and prelates.

In contrast to what happened after 1130, Tessera argues that the 1159 schism did not have significant consequences for the Church in the crusader states, although Alexander III made the most of his more or less immediate recognition by the churches of the region, at the Council of Nazareth in the summer of 1160. There is, again, a good and clear discussion of the complex diplomacy of the 1160s and 1170s, during which it is suggested that the kingdom of Jerusalem, during the minority of Baldwin IV, once again made overtures to Frederick Barbarossa (and while he was still in conflict with the papacy). But inevitably papal concern with the Holy Land became more and more bound up with the problems of its defence, as the threat from Nur-ed-Din and Saladin grew, and appeals for aid became more frequent. The various attempts to bring help to the East, or to begin a new crusade, are discussed in detail, as well as the immediate reaction to the disaster at Hattin.

Papal involvement in the internal affairs of the Church of Jerusalem is covered in the last two chapters, perhaps the most interesting part of the book. Tessera cogently describes and explains the slow and complicated evolution of the ecclesiastical structure in the kingdom, in which the attempt by successive patriarchs to create a viable and properly canonical episcopal network was often delayed, and sometimes entirely frustrated, by vested interests, notably those of the canons of the Holy Sepulchre, the monks of Mount Tabor, and the bishops of Bethlehem – these last keen to prevent a separate bishopric being established at Ascalon. The popes to a considerable extent remained impotent spectators; thus, despite Alexander III encouraging the Patriarch Amalric to make further changes to the Church's structure in 1168, few of the measures proposed then were achieved, apart from the creation of the two southern sees of Hebron and Petra (something already agreed, and which the king and the local lords supported). But at the same time the pope reinforced further the rights of the Holy Sepulchre, which were often invoked to frustrate patriarchal reforms, notably to prevent the establishment of a bishopric at Jaffa. Similarly, with the dispute between the two patriarchates over the province of Tyre, ringing statements of papal authority, such as that made by Innocent II in July 1138, were hardly carried through in practice, while the archbishops of Tyre defended their interests every bit as single-mindedly as other churches of the kingdom – Tessera indeed suggests that Archbishop William I sought for his province to become an exempt one, directly dependent on the papacy and independent of both patriarchates, while William II (the celebrated historian) revived the whole issue in the 1180s, looking to subject his province to Antioch rather than to his hated rival the Patriarch Heraclius.

While the examination of the internal development of the Church (naturally) draws heavily on the work of Mayer and Hamilton, Tessera weaves her analysis into a very clear and effective study of its evolution. The chapter on the Tyre problem also goes well beyond the earlier study of Rowe, particularly in examining the ecclesiology of the dispute, as also its revival in the early 1180s. Indeed, throughout the book her detailed discussion of the theological underpinnings and implications of papal bulls is one of its most impressive features. Yet while her touch on ecclesiastical issues is sure, that on lay politics is perhaps less so. She assumes, for example, that Baldwin II faced significant opposition from within his baronage throughout his reign, and that the legitimacy of his rule remained uncertain, at least for a considerable period. She follows Alan Murray in interpreting Galbert of Bruges's story about an offer of the crown to Charles of Flanders as an attempt to unseat the king. But, if this offer took place, was it anything more than a "plan B" in case Baldwin, who had no male heir, did not return from his captivity in the north in 1122–24? Similarly, she refers to "the revolt of the barons" in 1134 (even though she has read Mayer's revisionist comments on this incident), and she tends to be relatively uncritical when discussing factional dispute in the reign of Baldwin IV, although she is clearly aware of the cautionary view of Peter Edbury on this issue. It is a pity too that some minor slips with regard to the Church in the West have not been corrected: Angoulême was not an archbishopric, for example: Gerard of Angoulême was archbishop of Bordeaux (pp. 176–77).

Inevitably, much of Tessera's discussion covers well-tilled ground, but this important and ambitious book offers a powerful and insightful re-examination of a topic of great importance for crusader studies. Serious scholars will doubtless quarry its chapters to refine and rethink their own work. But how much impact it will have in the wider Anglophone world of students of the crusades is a good question: given the length of this volume a full English translation is probably unlikely. The author has, however, published articles in English. One would encourage her to consider preparing a briefer and more analytical version of this work for an English-speaking audience, which would certainly profit from reading it.

G. A. LOUD
UNIVERSITY OF LEEDS

Susanna A. Throop, *Crusading as an Act of Vengeance, 1095–1216*. Farnham and Burlington, VT: Ashgate, 2011. Pp. ix, 232. ISBN 987 0 7546 6582 3.

It seems intuitive that vengeance would have motivated crusaders to fight. Indeed, the warrior culture of the high Middle Ages demanded that family members and vassals of mistreated or murdered nobles take revenge on the perpetrators. Previous scholars have emphasized this fact in relation to the attitudes of early crusaders. However, in this present work Susanna A. Throop demonstrates how the idea of the crusades as vengeance evolved in the twelfth century from the combination of religious, legal, and social values. She shows how writers and propagandists appealed to the idea of vengeance to evoke a powerful emotional response from their readers or hearers in favor of the crusades. The author embarks on an analysis of significant "crusading texts" from three major chronological periods from 1095 to 1216. These texts include chronicles, narratives, letters, histories, sermons, songs, and poetry. In so doing, Throop integrates linguistic analysis, religious and crusades studies, and the growing field of the study of human emotion.

In the first chapter Throop analyzes the meaning and historical use of the words, *vindicta*, *ultio*, and *venjance* in medieval texts. Based on this investigation, she produces a "working definition" of the medieval understanding of vengeance as "violence (both physical and nonphysical) driven by a sense of moral authority, and in certain cases divine approbation, against those who are believed to question that authority and/or approbation" (p. 12). Throop also identifies the process that led to acts of vengeance. This began with an injury that led to shame, and lastly vengeance. While this cycle of vengeance took place routinely in knightly culture, Throop demonstrates how religious writers specifically connected that idea of vengeance to justice. When the proper authorities called for vengeance or carried it out, it became not only licit, but virtuous.

Chapter two focuses on the early years of the central texts associated with the First Crusade and the early twelfth century. While some early texts mentioned the concept of vengeance in relation to the First Crusade, vengeance did not play a major role in any of the eyewitness accounts of the crusade. These accounts emphasized pilgrimage and the glory of martyrdom. According to Throop, the later histories of the First Crusade, written by non-participants, did identify righteous vengeance as a significant motivational factor. These writers, such as Guibert of Nogent and Robert of Rheims, concentrated on God's just punishment and the social obligations of *auxilium* and *caritas* enhanced by the religious dimensions of the First Crusade.

Lastly, she points out possible, but not explicit, connections between anti-Jewish violence as revenge for the crucifixion and the First Crusade.

In the following two chapters Throop analyzes a large number of texts associated with the crusades from 1138 to 1216. She asserts that the idea of crusade as an act of vengeance became more prevalent during this period until in culminated in the reign of Innocent III. Generally, Throop's analysis of the legal, theological, and historical texts demonstrates a greater emphasis on the papacy as a legitimate authority to call for divine vengeance. Additionally, theological and devotional texts, vernacular poetry, and Hebrew sources show the growing focus on the relationship between Christ's crucifixion, the crusades, and the enemies of the cross, namely, Muslims, Jews, and heretics. However, Throop points out that no twelfth-century popes referred to crusading as an act of vengeance from 1138 to 1197 in their correspondence, while Innocent III used the idea incessantly.

After the analysis of the idea of crusades as an act of vengeance, Throop investigates the use of the word *zelus* in the twelfth and early thirteenth centuries. Zeal was the emotion that connected love for God and righteous anger at his enemies. Throop demonstrates how medieval religious writers cited zeal for God or righteous causes as an expression of good intention, even when one's actions were suspect or committed out of ignorance. Ultimately, zeal for God's love inspired the crusader to imitate Christ through acts of self-sacrifice. Building on the theories of recent scholars on the relationship of anger and vengeance to medieval social relationships, Throop asserts that crusading as an act of vengeance followed the pattern of the "script" of injury, shame, zealous anger, and vengeance in medieval society. Specifically, the emotion of zeal for God's cause affirmed the crusader's actions as morally justified.

Throop's examination of the idea of vengeance and its emotional and intellectual appeal to crusaders is significant. She has used an impressive number of sources from various genres, including Latin, Hebrew, and vernacular texts. Two appendices contain short discussions of modern historiography and medieval sources respectively. Her close textual analysis of specific terms and their specific cultural context is solid scholarly work. While providing some interpretation, she focuses intently on the sources and their explanations regarding vengeance and the crusades. Throop also understands the ongoing dialogue of scholarship by suggesting further study of particular topics.

The manner by which the author integrates the study of the crusades with other fields further expands the field of crusades studies. Throop demonstrates how the crusades reflected the theological and devotional developments and emphases of the twelfth and thirteenth centuries. For instance, she discusses how a greater amount of devotion to the crucified Christ, the importance of Jerusalem as a geographical location and a spiritual ideal, and God's retribution against the enemies of the cross inspired the rhetoric of crusading in this period. This integration of theological ideas also led to a conflation of Jews, Muslims, and heretics as those who not only rejected the theology of Christ's redemption but actually mistreated the relics of the True Cross and crucifixes. Additionally, the author integrated research from the still evolving field of the history of human emotion in relation to medieval knightly culture.

Despite its many positive qualities, Throop's work does exhibit a few flaws. First, this book was poorly edited in certain places. The most obvious example appeared on pages 106 and 107, where Throop cites the same quote within three paragraphs. The final chapter on zeal seems a bit out of place. If this emotional connection played such a major role in understanding crusading as an act of vengeance, then it should have been examined earlier in the book. Lastly, while Throop does mention the loss of the relic of the True Cross at Hattin in 1187, she does not connect this event sufficiently with her overall theme. Coupled with the loss of Jerusalem, the loss of this holy relic played a central role in the propaganda for the Third Crusade and early thirteenth-century crusades. Henry, the Cardinal Bishop of Albano and the pope's designated preacher for the Third Crusade, exhorted potential crusaders to avenge the injury to the True Cross. Alan of Lille, the famous Parisian theologian who also preached a sermon for the Third Crusade, encouraged his hearers to vindicate Christ's injuries as they sought to regain the Holy Land and the relic of the True Cross. These sources (which she did not cite) would have added to Throop's central argument about the increasing use of the rhetoric of just vengeance against the enemies of the cross in the late twelfth and early thirteenth centuries.

C. MATTHEW PHILLIPS
CONCORDIA UNIVERSITY, NEBRASKA

Christopher Tyerman, *The Debate on the Crusades* (Issues in Historiography). Manchester and New York: Manchester University Press, 2011. Pp. xii, 260. ISBN 978 0 7190 7320 5 (hardback), 978 0 7190 7321 2 (paperback).

A monograph on the historiography of the crusades has long been overdue. Even though the history of the debate about the crusades has been the subject of several specialist articles, chapters, and books focusing on particular aspects or periods of crusade historiography, Christopher Tyerman's new book is the first comprehensive treatment of the matter. In essence it is a long version of Tyerman's earlier summary of crusade historiography in Part 3 of his *The Invention of the Crusades* (1998). As befits the subject, Tyerman works his way through the periods chronologically, beginning with a chapter on medieval views of the crusades followed by a chapter each on the sixteenth and seventeenth centuries, the Enlightenment, the early nineteenth century, and the late nineteenth century. The final three chapters are devoted to what one might call the history of modern crusade studies, tracing respectively the growing influence of professional academe during the first half of the twentieth century, the influence of Carl Erdmann and Steven Runciman on modern crusade studies, and the most recent developments within the contemporary scene of crusade scholarship.

The opening chapter, entitled "Medieval Views," is perhaps the least focused part of the book. Here Tyerman employs a very wide definition of historiography, discussing a great number of different genres of texts, from the chronicles of the First Crusade to vernacular chansons, canon law tracts, and the so-called "recovery" literature, to name just a few. It is of course difficult to do justice in but 25 pages to 400 years of records by authors who commented on the crusades as history-in-the-making. Unfortunately, Tyerman makes no particular effort to impose a clear analytical framework or at least formulate some lead questions as guidance through this jungle of evidence. He rightly stresses the fact that medieval historiography was by its very nature favouring a diversity of views and visions, being "less concerned to recite information than in illustrating didactic lessons conjured from an invented universe of optimism, virtue, evil, punishment for sin, reward for goodness: a world defined by memories of past glory" (p. 32). Still, a clearer focus, perhaps on the question of the development of medieval conceptualizations of the crusade, would have been welcome.

For the early modern period the historiography of the crusades is easier to grasp, and in consequence, from Chapter 2 onwards the book becomes more focussed. The fifteenth and sixteenth centuries for the first time produced a number of books which attempted to view the crusades – or rather the holy wars as they were more commonly called at the time – in terms of history proper: that is, events of a past that was perceived as clearly distanced from the present and which called for judgment. Tyerman competently shows how the confessional divide in Europe produced sympathy and antipathy for the Catholic crusades according to the authors' confessional stance, and how emerging historical professionalism led to the first systematic collections of crusade texts and documents which formed the basis for the writing about the crusades for centuries to come. Far from simply setting the stage for controversy and debate about the good and evil of the crusades, this period selected the crusades as a subject of serious intellectual pursuit. Here, as in the remainder of the book, Tyerman displays his great knowledge and his gift for dense commentary in a pleasantly flowing narrative, speckled with interesting asides, that never fails to engage the reader's attention.

Next Tyerman safely navigates his readers through the thundering commentaries of the great Enlightenment thinkers who, from their rationalist premise, never tired of condemning the barbarism of backward medieval crusaders. As Tyerman shows, their moral judgments were far from simplistic. On the contrary, some influential writers such as William Robertson and later on Edward Gibbon also saw the crusades as an unintended turning point towards progress away from feudalism and superstitious religion towards civil society and greater cultural refinement. However, the crusades were no "big topic" during the Enlightenment period. This changed in post-Napoleonic times. Tyerman's two chapters on the nineteenth century trace the rise of crusade history in the wake of a renewed interest in the medieval period, fuelled by the perceived historical parallels between the crusades and contemporary orientalism and colonialism. Nationalism played a role in this, as did romanticism. The nineteenth century is the period of crusade heroes, partisan nationalistic versions of crusade history, and a largely positive vision of the superiority of western Christian civilization projected back onto the medieval crusades. Again Tyerman is a reliable and sure-footed guide through the vastly expanded field of nineteenth-century histories of the crusade.

The last three chapters describe the genesis of modern crusade studies. The first half of the twentieth century can be characterized as featuring new people and new methods. As history departments in universities across the globe became more prominent, the writing of academic history was further professionalized. With the growth of interest in medieval history, especially in the United States, and with crusader history forming part of the budding Israeli concern with writing their own version of the history of the Holy Land, the diversity and volume of crusade history increased significantly. Tyerman devotes a separate chapter to two of the century's most prominent crusade historians, Carl Erdmann and Steven Runciman. Erdmann represents what one might call – although Tyerman does not – a new structural approach, breaking the predominance of political and military history and opening up crusades studies towards other areas of medieval history. As Erdmann is arguably the single most influential crusade historian of the twentieth century, Tyerman is right in examining his contribution in detail. Steven Runciman did not change the direction of scholarly crusade studies but has nonetheless been one of the most influential crusade historians of all times. Tyerman's assessment of Runciman's influence as a writer as much as an historian, and for the general public rather than the professional historian, is superb and assigns Runciman the place in the pantheon of crusade historians he deserves.

Unfortunately, Tyerman's take on the most recent developments in crusade studies is flawed by his own partisan stance. The great divide he constructs between generalists/traditionalists and pluralists, following Giles Constable's terminology, is of far smaller significance than Tyerman makes it out to be, and his insistence on the divide serves him ill for explaining where crusade studies are heading today. The allegedly great rift between a narrower and a wider vision of crusades – that is, whether crusades were primarily expeditions to the Holy Land or not – was exaggerated beyond reasonable proportions at a conference in Cardiff in 1983, in which Tyerman took part. The course of the debate there must have shaped Tyerman's outlook profoundly, but for the majority of younger crusade historians, as well as many of Tyerman's contemporaries, the obsession with "true crusades vs. aberrations" is not really the central question. This is not to say that the issue of defining the crusade is no longer relevant; it will engage historians' efforts for a long time to come for the simple reason that the medieval sources struggled with the concept. But crusade studies nowadays have embraced a host of exciting new issues – from prosopography to gender issues, finance to liturgy and theology, to name just a few – which counteract traditional, more limited approaches to crusade history. Tyerman knows this, but some parts of his final chapter read like the continuation of a petulant squabble which contributes little towards explaining the direction of modern crusade studies.

Inevitably, a book such as this raises more questions than it answers, but this can be taken as a sign of its quality. Throughout, the book is scratching the surface of a story which calls for further investigation. Not only each chapter, but also many of the writers mentioned in this book deserve full-length studies of their own. It is Christopher Tyerman's great achievement to have given us a coherent narrative which spans the very beginnings of recording the First Crusade to today's analytical approaches to a medieval movement which has fascinated different ages for different reasons.

CHRISTOPH T. MAIER
UNIVERSITÄT ZÜRICH

James Waterson, *The Ismaili Assassins – A History of Medieval Murder*. Barnsley, UK: Frontline Books, 2008. Pp. xxl, 227. ISBN 978 1 8483 2505 0.

To date Waterson has written three books on aspects of medieval Islam, of which *The Ismaili Assassins* is the second. Introduced by a bibliographical comment from David Morgan, it is divided into nine chapters, complemented by a timeline of key events; genealogical/succession tables for Assassin Grand Masters, various Caliphates and Sultanates, "The House of the Prophet," and the Great Khans; two maps; 35 illustrations (16 in color); suggestions for further reading; and a useful index. The text is enlivened by many quotations, primarily drawn from Islamic historians.

Morgan's foreword characterizes Waterson's work as "up to date, informative, and in no way difficult to read or understand." This latter assertion is less true of the first two chapters, which trace Islamic history from the time of Mohammad into the late eleventh century, than of the latter parts of the work. In fairness to Waterson, it is very difficult to summarize struggles over lordship and orthodoxy within Islam from the seventh to the eleventh century, and considerable backing and filling is needed to position the Ismaili branch of Shiite belief within the larger story and to explain the emergence of the Assassin sect from its ranks in the late eleventh century. The second chapter focuses primarily on the Fatimid Caliphate that ruled Egypt after 960. The creation of that Shiite realm, along with the Buyid occupation of Iraq in 945, initiated the "Shiite century," but each regime espoused a different Shiite branch. The Persian Buyids were tolerant, while the Fatimids, seeing themselves as destined to rule *Dar al-Islam*, established the House of Propaganda in Cairo, where *dais*, itinerant missionaries for Ismaili Shiism, were trained and sent to other Muslim realms. The Saljuq Turks, who embraced Sunni beliefs, brought the Shiite century to a close. Shortly after supplanting the Buyids in 1055, the Saljuqs initiated three decades of war with the Fatimids for control of Syria, during which Hasan-i-Shabbah, a Fatimid missionary, successfully propagated Ismaili beliefs in northern Persia.

Hasan and the followers he recruited were already established in fortified strongholds in northern Persia, one of which was Alamut, when he broke with the Fatimids. In 1094 the Egyptian *wazir* interfered in the succession to the caliphate, disinheriting and murdering the caliph's eldest son Nizar, whom Hasan characterized as the rightful Imam. About this time, under attack from the Saljuqs, Hasan developed strategic assassination as a tactic to protect and promote his sect's cause. He recruited zealots, his *fidai'in*, who willingly gave their lives as they carried out Hasan's orders in defense of their Nazari Ismaili sect. Hasan trained them in dissimulation and disguise, so they could position themselves to ply daggers against any he ordered to be publically assassinated. Their earliest triumph was the 1092 killing of Nizam al-Mulk, the Seljuq *wazir*, while Turkish forces were besieging Alamut. As it happened, the Sultan Malikshah died soon thereafter, and without Nizam al-Mulk's guiding hand the succession struggle led to virtual dissolution of the Saljuq realm. Subsequent high-profile assassinations cast a shadow of fear, and established the master of the order as a major political force.

The Ismaili Assassins is replete with fascinating details as it traces the succession of Grand Masters after Hasan, under whose guidance the order's fortunes rose and fell. Their emergence in Persia was only a few years before the First Crusade, and by undermining the Saljuqs the Assassins unintentionally set the stage for crusade successes, and through the two centuries that Franks occupied territory in Outremer they interacted with the Assassins, sometimes as allies.

Waterson's canvas is far broader than Palestine and Syria, and rightly so, for the order became a territorial state in northern Persia, with important enclaves in Syria, and functioned as a major power within Islam, inspiring fear and coercing alliances and tribute through notorious murders. Its victims included Sunni religious leaders, wazirs, Saljuq and Mamluk emirs and sultans, Frankish princes and kings, and both Fatimid and Abbasid caliphs. The Assassin fortresses protected the Grand Masters and their devotees through the twelfth century and beyond, but they were brought down when their blades were turned against the Mongols. When Chinggis Khan's army entered Islamic territory in 1219 the Assassins offered submission, even assisting as the Mongols hunted down the Khwarazm Shah's would-be successors, and the Mongols bypassed the Assassins as they moved into Azerbaijan and Anatolia. Ala al-Din (Assassin Grand Master 1230–55) reversed course in 1253, dispatching 400 *fidai'in* to murder Mongke Khan. The Mongols discovered the plot, however, and Mongke sent his brother Hulegu to both extirpate the Assassins and bring the remnants of *Dar al-Islam* into the Mongol Empire. Alamut surrendered in 1256, and the Mongols rounded up all Nizari Ismailis they could, killing them and their Imam, Rukh al-Din, the last Grand Master. After the fall of Baghdad two years later it seemed the Muslim world would perish, but the Mamluks defeated the Mongols at Ain Jalut in 1260, signaling the limit of Mongol expansion. Ultimately the Mongol rulers of Persia and Anatolia, like their kinsmen in the Golden Horde, converted to Islam.

The fall of Alamut was not the end of the Ismaili Shiism or of the Assassins. Some devotees escaped the Mongols, making their way to India, where missionaries had earlier spread their beliefs, and the Assassin enclaves in Syria survived into the fifteenth century, subjected to the Mamluks. No longer a major power, they survived because useful to the Mamluks, who could order *fidai'in* sent to dispose of rivals. Although their glory days were over, the Assassins had already become legendary figures in European and Islamic literature. Waterson's book will give readers a thorough introduction to the sect and its history. If asked, I would probably recommend beginning with Bernard Lewis, *The Assassins. A Radical Sect of Islam* (1967, reprinted 2002), but Waterson's book is also worthwhile, and abounds in detail that more than merely supplements Lewis. It is heavy going in places, but worth the effort.

JAMES D. RYAN
CITY UNIVERSITY OF NEW YORK (EMERITUS)

John Zimmer, Werner Meyer and Letizia Boscardin, *Krak des Chevaliers in Syrien. Archäologie und Bauforschung 2003 bis 2007* (Veröffentlichungen der Deutschen Burgenvereinigung, Reihe A: Forschungen, 14). Braubach: Deutsche Burgenvereinigung e.V., 2011. Pp. 400. ISBN 978 3 9275 5833 5.

Although a comprehensive volume on the same topic was published only recently, the work under review opens up a new chapter in the investigation of the Crac des Chevaliers, regarded by T. E. Lawrence as the "most wholly admirable castle in the world." The book is presented in a stable slipcase together with a box of 31 large-scale folding plans. The lavishly illustrated book is divided into two principal sections: the first one on the findings of the survey and excavation campaigns conducted by the authors in 2003–2007 ("Die Befunde"), and the second one on interpretations ("Die Deutungen"), comprising a chapter dealing with the history of the site from the very beginning to the present day. Summaries in German and English (a French edition of the book is being prepared), maps of the crusader domains and a bibliography complement the contents. Regrettably, an index is missing.

The campaigns were conducted as a joint mission of the Syrian Directorate of Antiquities, the Service des sites et monuments nationaux of Luxemburg, and the University of Basel, Switzerland. They were aimed at reinvestigating the site on a much broader scale than the German team which worked here in 1988–2003, following the original investigations by Paul Deschamps and his team in the 1930s. The three authors, who had participated in the German campaigns, came to the conclusion that, without excavations, the building history of the castle could not be determined properly. Their approach offers new perspectives resulting in a much better understanding of the development of the site, based on more substantial evidence. The spectrum of methods was further extended to include palaeobiological investigations, X-ray fluorescence spectrometry (ED-XRF) of ceramic glazes, and radiocarbon dating of selected finds.

In the introduction, the authors specify the castle's building phases, thus anticipating the major outcome of their investigations. They suggest dividing the building history into three main periods: period I starts ca. 980, when the castle was founded, and ends in 1170, when the first castle on the site was totally destroyed by an earthquake; period II comprises the Hospitaller phases (1170–1271); and period III covers the Mamluk reconstructions and additions after the conquest of 1271. In the subsequent chapter, following a suggestion from the reviewer, a series of photographs of the castle by Louis de Clercq, who accompanied Emmanuel G. Rey in 1859, are presented.

The excavations comprised small-scale soundings at five different spots and the exposure of four larger areas, which gave reason to expect intact stratigraphic sequences despite the extensive cleaning work by Deschamps during the 1930s. The most interesting findings were scant remains of the first castle, which, according to the archaeological evidence, was founded in the last decades of the tenth century, probably around 980. A further objective was to clarify the nature of the triangular elevation to the south of the castle, which is surrounded by a rock-cut ditch. This having been regarded as an outwork of the Hospitaller castle by other scholars, the authors now suggest that it was part of the pre-crusader fortification. Their view is shared by the reviewer who in the 1980s still saw remains of a wall of poor masonry on the edge of the slope and openings of rock-cut cisterns – features which probably do not correspond to a later outwork but are likely to belong to an earlier fortification.

The rich body of archaeological finds (pp. 84–168) is presented in an exemplary manner. For their classification, supported by Denys Pringle, other find complexes from the region were consulted for comparison. Palaeobiological analyses provide a vivid picture of the nutrition and food situation through the centuries. Interestingly, the occurrence of pig and boar, dominating the period before 1170, decreases significantly in the post-1170 period in favour of caprine.

The architectural investigations yielded a wealth of information on the building history of the castle. The presentation and discussion of the results, together with those of the survey, take up the largest and most important part of the book (pp. 173–344). The different building periods are excellently presented, offering insightful detailed views as well as ground and elevation plans of the structures. Each principal building phase is completed by a full-page reconstruction drawing in perspective, perfectly visualizing the architecture of the respective building phase. In addition, the drawings of all these phases are again presented in a synopsis at the end of the book (pp. 378–79), forming a highly illustrative depiction of the development of the castle. Furthermore, answers to previously open questions are presented, and some controversial issues are cleared up. The first Hospitaller building phase, constitutive of all later construction, is a good example. The soundings revealed that, after the earthquake of 1170, the ground was thoroughly cleared of the debris it had left, providing a sound basis and ample material for comprehensive rebuilding. This first Hospitaller castle on site could be determined convincingly. Soundings also allowed fixing the building sequence of the north-west tower of the main ward. Initially a simple rectangular salient with its field-side front flush with a feeble forewall, it was later dismantled and rebuilt as a much larger latrine tower with a portal at the north-eastern flank. However, to identify this tower as the *barbacane* mentioned in the inscription in the new outer wall remains questionable. The portal, which allowed communication with the outer ward, may have been no more than a postern, typically located in the flanks of towers. The term *barbacane*, originally designating a forewall, obviously refers to the new outer wall, where the inscription is located, even though it might not be in situ.

Chapters on construction technologies, on military and sacral aspects, on daily life, on water supply and waste disposal, and on the figural sculpture of the castle complete this section. The last part of the book is devoted to the history of the site (pp. 345–73). Not only are the known facts concerning the castle proper presented there, but also the historical framework. One small amendment must, however, be allowed: It is not true that there were no attempts to come to terms on the border zone after the conquest of Tripoli in 1109 (p. 348). There was a treaty later that year between Tancred, prince of Antioch, and the emir of Damascus, putting this borderland between Homs and Tripoli under Frankish control, and forcing the inhabitants of *Ḥiṣn al-Akrād* (the later Crac) to pay tribute.

Although some of the findings have already been published (*Der Crac des Chevaliers*, ed. T. Biller, 2006), the book breaks new ground in the exploration and understanding of the castle. The results presented there are a good example of how minimally invasive but well-planned archaeological investigations, combined with exact surveying and scrutinizing analyses of the standing structures, yield a maximum of information on historic architecture. What may be missing is the placing of the findings into the context of contemporary fortification architecture of the region, which obviously was not within the scope of this study. Nevertheless, the new findings, based on a state-of-the-art scientific approach, an excellent presentation, in particular the large-scale folding plans, and the wide range of topics treated make the book a work of reference for many years to come.

MATHIAS PIANA
AUGSBURG

Short Notices

Julian Chrysostomides, *Byzantium and Venice, 1204–1453*, ed. Michael Heslop and Charalambos Dendrinos (Variorum Collected Studies Series, CS972). Farnham and Burlington, VT: Ashgate, 2011. Pp. xvii, 294. ISBN 978 1 4094 2370 6.

This collection unites ten articles by Julian Chrysostomides previously published elsewhere and one unpublished paper. One article has been translated from the original Greek. The articles are preceded by a preface by the editors, a list of Chrysostomides' publications and two maps. There is an index of persons and places following the articles: "John V Palaeologus in Venice (1370–1371) and the Chronicle of Caroldo: a Re-interpretation" (1965); "Studies on the Chronicle of Caroldo, with Special Reference to the History of Byzantium from 1370 to 1377" (1969); "Venetian Commercial Privileges under the Palaeologi" (1970); "Corinth 1394–1397: Some New Facts" (1975); "An Unpublished Letter of Nerio Acciaiuoli (30 October 1384)" (1975); "Italian Women in Greece in the Late Fourteenth and Early Fifteenth Centuries" (1982); "Was Neri Acciaiuoli Ever Lord of Vostitsa and Nivelet?" (1988); "Merchant versus Nobles: a Sensational Court Case in the Peloponnese (1391–1404)" (1992); "Glimpses of Wealth and Poverty in Greece during the 14th and 15th Centuries as seen in Venetian documents" (originally in Greek; 1998); "Symbiosis in the Peloponnese in the Aftermath of the Fourth Crusade" (2003); "Tenedos 1376 Revisited" (previously unpublished; 2005).

Crusades – Medieval Worlds in Conflict, ed. Thomas F. Madden, James L. Naus and Vincent Ryan. Farnham and Burlington, VT: Ashgate, 2010. Pp. xiii, 212. ISBN 978 1 4094 0061 5.

The twelve studies collected in this volume originated as papers read at a conference of the same title in February 2006 at Saint Louis University. The volume is divided into four parts with an introduction and an index: *Part I. The Crusades and Conflicting Worlds of Sanctity*: "*Jihad* Poetry in the Age of the Crusades" by Carole Hillenbrand; "Crucified with Christ: The Imitation of the Crucified Christ and Crusading Spirituality" by C. Matthew Phillips; "Brothers in Arms: *Hermandades* among the Military Orders in Medieval Iberia" by Sam Zeno Conedera. *Part II. The Crusades and Contested Worlds of Ideas*: "The Classical Author Portrait Islamicized" by Robert Hillenbrand; "Alfonso I and the Memory of the First Crusade: Conquest and Crusade in the Kingdom of Aragón-Navarre" by Jennifer Price; "*Crucesignatus*: A Refinement or Merely One More Term among Many?" by Walker Reid Cosgrove. *Part III. The Crusades and the Byzantine World*: "God's Will or Not? Bohemund's Campaign Against the Byzantine Empire (1105–1108)" by Brett Edward Whalen; "'Like an Ember Buried in Ashes:' The Byzantine-Venetian Conflict of 1119–1126" by Thomas Devaney; "John II Comnenus and Crusader Antioch" by David Parnell. *Part IV. The Crusades and the World of Louis IX*: "Saints and Sinners at Sea on the First Crusade of Saint Louis" by Caroline Smith; "Louis IX, Charles of Anjou, and the Tunis Crusade of 1270" by Michael Lower; "The Place of the Crusades in the Sanctification of Saint Louis" by M. Cecilia Gaposchkin.

On the Margins of Crusading. The Military Orders, the Papacy and the Christian World, ed. Helen J. Nicholson (Crusades – Subsidia, 4). Farnham and Burlington, VT: Ashgate, 2011. Pp. xiii, 209. ISBN 978 1 4094 3217 3 (hardback), 978 1 4094 3218 0 (e-book).

This volume contains eleven papers presented at the seventh conference of the Society for the Study of the Crusades and the Latin East at Avignon on 28–31 August 2008, preceded by the editor's introduction and followed by an index: "A Jerusalem Indulgence: 1100/3" by Anthony Luttrell; "Fulfilling a Mediterranean Vocation: *The Domus Sancte Marie Montis Gaudii de Jerusalem* in North-West Italy" by Elena Bellomo; "Templar Liturgy and Devotion in the Crown of Aragon" by Sebastián Salvadó; "Gerard of Ridefort and the Battle of Le Cresson (1 May 1187): The Developing Narrative Tradition" by Peter Edbury; "Clement V and the Road to Avignon, 1304–1309" by David Morrow Bryson; "'Vox in excelso' Deconstructed. Exactly What Did Clement V Say?" by Anne Gilmour-Bryson; "Myths and Reality: The Crusades and the Latin East as Presented during the Trial of the Templars in the British Isles, 1308–1311" by Helen J. Nicholson; "La Réforme de l'Hôpital par Jean XXII: Le Démembrement des Prieurés de Saint-Gilles et de France (21 juillet 1317)" by Jean-Marc Roger; "The Search for the Defensive System of the Knights in the Dodecanese (Part I: Chalki, Symi, Nisyros, Tilos)" by Michael Heslop; "Kronobäck Commandery: A Field Study" by Christer Carlsson; "Crisis? What Crisis? The 'Waning' of the Order of St. Lazarus after the Crusades" by Rafaël Hyacinthe.

La Papauté et les croisades / The Papacy and the Crusades. Actes du VIIe Congrès de la Society for the Study of the Crusades and the Latin East / Proceedings of the VIIth Conference of the Society for the Study of the Crusades and the Latin East, ed. Michel Balard (Crusades – Subsidia, 3). Farnham and Burlington, VT: Ashgate, 2011. Pp. xii, 301. ISBN 978 1 4094 3007 0 (hardback), 978 1 4094 3008 7 (e-book).

Following an introduction by the editor, this volume contains twenty papers presented at the seventh conference of the Society for the Study of the Crusades and the Latin East at Avignon on 28–31 August 2008, divided into four sections and followed by an index: *Part I: Les Mots/Terminology*: "Nouveau mot ou nouvelle réalité? Le terme *cruciata* et son utilisation dans les textes pontificaux" by Benjamin Weber; "Le varie ragioni per 'assumere la croce': Il senso di un arruolamento in più direzioni" by Giulio Cipollone; "The French Recent Historiography of the Holy War" by Michel Balard. *Part II: L'Occident/The West*: "Louis VII, Innocent II et la Seconde Croisade" by Monique Amouroux; "'Smoking sword': le meurtre du légat Pierre de Castelnau et la première croisade albigeoise" by Marco Meschini; "Casting Out Demons by Beelzebul: Did the Papal Preaching against the Albigensians Ruin the Crusades?" by Karl Borchardt; "The Papal 'Crusade' against Frederick in 1228–1230" by G. A. Loud; "When Ideology Met Reality: Clement V and the Crusade" by Sophia Menache; "1308 and 1177: Venice and the Papacy in Real and Imaginary Crusades" by David M. Perry; "Papal Claims to Authority over Lands Gained from the Infidel in the Iberian Peninsula and Beyond the Straits of Gibraltar" by Alan Forey; "The Papacy and the Crusade in XVth Century Portugal" by Luis Ado De Fonseca, Maria Cristina Pimenta, Paula Pinto Costa. *Part III: L'Orient/The East*: "The Papacy and the Fourth Crusade in the Correspondence of the Nicaean Emperors with the Popes" by Aphrodite Papayianni; "A Vacuum of Leadership: 1291 Revisited" by James M. Powell; "Crusading in a Nearer East: The Balkan Politics of Honorius III and Gregory IX (1221–1241)" by Francesco Dall'Aglio; "La Politique de soutien pontifical aux lignages nobiliaires moréotes aux XIIIe et XIVe siècles" by Isabelle Ortega; "La Papauté et les Hospitaliers de Rhodes aux lendemains de la chute de Constantinople (1453–1467)" by Pierre Bonneaud; "Papauté, Latins d'Orient et Croisés sous le regard de l'archevêque de Tarse, Nersês Lambronatsi" by Isabelle Augé; "Le rôle de la papauté dans la politique arménienne des Hospitaliers au XIVe siècle" by Marie-Anna Chevalier. *Part IV: L'Europe du Nord et de l'Est/Northern and Eastern Europe*: "Poland and the Papacy Before the Second Crusade" by Darius von Güttner Sporzynski; "Politics and Crusade: Scandinavia, the Avignon Papacy and the Crusade in the XIVth Century" by Janus Moller Jensen.

Jürgen Sarnowsky, *On the Military Orders in Medieval Europe. Structures and Perceptions* (Variorum Collected Studies Series, CS992). Farnham and Burlington, VT: Ashgate, 2011. Pp. xii, 360. ISBN 978 1 4094 2326 3.

Of the twenty-two articles originally published between 1989 and 2010 and collected in this volume, four have been translated from the original German into English, two are published here for the first time, and six are in German. The collection is divided into four sections: *General Aspects of the History of the Military Orders*: "Identity and Self-perception of the Military Orders" (trans.; 1998); "The Statutes of the Military Orders" (trans.; 2010); "Historical Writing in Military Orders / 12th–16th centuries" (2009); "Der Johanniterorden und die Kreuzzüge" (1999); "The Late Medieval Military Orders and the Transformation of the Idea of Holy Wars" (first publication). *Administration, Internal Government*: "The Oligarchy at Work: The Chapters General of the Hospitallers in the XVth Century (1421–1522)" (1996); "'The Rights of the Treasury': The Financial Administration of the Hospitallers on Fifteenth-century Rhodes (1421–1522)" (1998); "Kings and Priors: The Hospitaller Priory of England in the Later Fifteenth Century" (1999); "The Convent and the West: Visitations in the Order of the Hospital of St. John in the Fifteenth Century" (2007). *"Order States", Foreign Policies*: "Military Orders and

Power – Teutonic Knights, Hospitallers, and their 'Order State'" (first publication);
"Ritterorden als Landesherren: Münzen und Siegel als Selbstzeugnisse" (2005);
"*Pragmaticae Rhodiae*. The Territorial Legislation of the Hospitallers on Rhodes"
(trans.; 2002); "Die Kirche auf Rhodos im 15. Jahrhundert" (1997); "The Military
Orders and their Navies" (2008); "Ein Streit der Marienburger Großschäfferei mit
den Grafen von Northumberland am Anfang des 15. Jahrhunderts" (1989); "The
Teutonic Order confronts the Mongols and Turks" (1994). *Life within the Orders*:
"Hospitaller Brothers in 15th-century Rhodes" (2006); "The Priests in the Military
Orders – a Comparative Approach on their Standing and Role" (in press); "Der Tod
des Großmeisters der Johanniter" (1993); "The Legacies and the Bequests of the
Masters in the Military Orders" (trans.; 2008); "Gender-Aspekte in der Geschichte
der geistlichen Ritterorden" (2003).

SOCIETY FOR THE
STUDY OF THE CRUSADES
AND THE LATIN EAST

BULLETIN No. 32, 2012

Contents

Editorial

Voici le nouveau *Bulletin*, n° 32, 2012. Il est le complément de la revue *Crusades*, son support, son vivier d'auteurs, de chercheurs et, ne l'oublions pas, de ceux qui, à travers le monde, exercent aussi bien souvent la lourde tâche de susciter la relève auprès de plus jeunes. Enseigner. Il forme un outil essentiel pour suivre, au fil des années, les avancées et les projets, la réflexion sans cesse renouvelée autour des croisades et de l'Orient latin, pour cerner ses évolutions historiographiques. Les publications sont plus nombreuses que jamais: leur recension dépasse de dix pages cette année le précédent Bulletin! Beau dynamisme: le reflet de la vie de notre Société, la SSCLE.

Les données rassemblées sont issues des renseignements fournis par chacun: certains ont choisi de ne les transmettre que tous les deux ans, quelques-uns oublient d'envoyer leurs fiches, d'autres enfin récapitulent l'ensemble de leur riche production. Il faut alors harmoniser, trier, ordonner. Malgré l'ampleur du travail d'édition, je dois dire le plaisir de cette mise à jour et de découverte de vos travaux. Merci à tous les membres qui font l'effort d'envoyer leurs données de bien vouloir suivre la présentation et la forme typographique ici employée (sélection en "langue anglaise").

Le *Bulletin de la SSCLE* est un lien précieux pour la communauté des chercheurs à l'échelle internationale. Il rassemble les adresses des membres, signalant les nouveaux arrivants (*): 30 cette année (33 en 2011)! Il est aussi une base de données scientifiques, rare et appréciée. Il recense les données bibliographiques les plus récentes des adhérents, leurs conférences et communications lors des congrès, thèses et travaux en cours, thèmes de recherche, projets multiples, informations variées sur les évènements scientifiques, colloques, expositions, etc. Le site web informatique est actuellement en cours de profondes transformations: il devrait bientôt permettre une plus grande interactivité, d'accès plus immédiat pour nos membres et au-delà, peut-être faire évoluer cette publication elle-même? Tout repose sur vos informations, vos cotisations et abonnements. Ma précision dépend de la vôtre, parfois aussi de la lisibilité de vos manuscrits. Je reste à votre disposition.

L'attrait pour les ordres religieux militaires se confirme fortement encore cette année. De même, l'intérêt déjà signalé autour de la guerre et de la paix, les guerres et les paix: thème central de notre Congrès de Cáceres. Aux côtés de l'Archéologie, la réflexion historiographique, les travaux sur l'économie et la monnaie annoncent des renouvellements prometteurs. J'ai hâte de vous lire!

François-Olivier Touati

Message from the President

Dear Fellow Members,

Under the terms of the new Constitution, elections were held in January for the officers of the Society. The following were re-elected for a further four-year term: Professor Luis Garcia-Guijarro as Secretary; Professor François-Olivier Touati as Bulletin Editor; Professor Jonathan Phillips as Officer for Postgraduate Members, and myself as President. Two new officers were elected: Professor Thomas F. Madden succeeds Dr Zsolt Hunyadi as Webmaster; and Dr Jon M.B. Porter succeeds Dr James D. Ryan as Treasurer. The General Meeting of the Society held at Cáceres on 29 June ratified these appointments.

Dr Ryan did not stand for re-election. He has held the office of Treasurer since 2005 and the Society is greatly indebted to him, because he took over at a time of crisis arising from a discontinuity in the work of his two predecessors. As a former Treasurer of the Society I can say from experience that on a day-to-day level the smooth running of the Society depends on the work of the Treasurer, who doubles his financial function with that of membership secretary. Dr Ryan has carried out his duties in an exemplary way, and under his direction the Society's membership has grown and its finances have prospered. He has also been a valued member of the Committee for his considered and helpful advice. I offer him on behalf of the Society our sincere thanks for his work on our behalf and our good wishes for the future.

The Society's year 2011–12 began with a Conference on "The Crusades, Islam and Byzantium", held at the German Historical Institute in London on 8–9 July 2011. This was a new initiative, devised by Professor Jonathan Phillips the Officer for Postgraduate Members, with the help of Dr Jochen Schenk and Dr William Purkis. Apart from three keynote speakers, all the communications were given by and monitored by postgraduate and postdoctoral members of the Society. The Conference was well attended and the general standard of the papers given was high. This occasion was warmly welcomed by the participants, and it is hoped to hold another Conference of this kind within the next three years. Following the precedent set by Michael Carr and Nikolaus Chryssis in 2010, a group of postgraduate and postdoctoral members, led by Jan Vandeburie, assisted by Liz Mylod, Guy Perry and Thomas Smith, organized a two-day Conference at the University of Kent, Canterbury from 13–14 April 2012. This attracted an international response and the proceedings will be published by Ashgate in the Crusades Subsidia series. I give advanced notice that Jan Vandeburie is organizing a new Conference on "Crusade Preaching and Propaganda: A workshop on Primary Sources", which will be held at the University of Kent on 29–30 March 2013, under the sponsorship of our Society.

The highlight of the past year was, of course, the Eighth Quadrennial Conference of the Society, which met at Cáceres in Spain from 25–29 June 2012. The theme was "Warfare and Peace at the Time of the Crusades". I wish on your behalf to thank Professor Luis Garcia-Guijarro and Professor Manuel Rojas for the time and effort which they have given to organizing this Conference over the past four years, and particularly for their success in overcoming the not inconsiderable problems arising from the ongoing Spanish economic crisis. A total of sixty papers was given at the Conference, covering a wide spectrum of crusading history, and the Proceedings will be edited by Professor Manuel Rojas and published by the Extremadura University Press.

At the General Meeting of the Society held at Cáceres on 29 June it was agreed that the theme of the next Quadrennial Conference in 2016 would be "The Baltic Crusades", and Professor Kurt Villads Jensen of the University of Southern Denmark was appointed our new Conference Secretary.

The General Meeting also made one technical constitutional change. Noting that the office of Vice-President does not exist in the Society, the meeting agreed that it was anomalous to style former Presidents Honorary Vice-Presidents and ruled that in future they should be called Honorary Presidents.

The Society's year ended in July with a Round Table at the Leeds International Conference, hosted by our new Conference Secretary on the theme of Crusading Studies in the New Millennium.

I wish to thank all the members of the Committee for their support and commitment during the past year, and to wish all our members a happy and successful year in 2012–13.

Bernard Hamilton

Practical information

Succeeding Prof. James D. Ryan, **Dr Jon M.B. Porter** is our new Treasurer. If you have any queries concerning your subscriptions and payments, please contact him at the following address: **Global Historical Program, Butler University, 4600 Sunset Avenue, Indianapolis IN 46208, USA; jporter1@butler.edu**

The *Bulletin* editor would like to remind you that, in order to avoid delays, he needs to have information for the Bulletin each year at an early date, usually in January or February. Please ensure that the presentation of your information conforms to the typographical model of this Bulletin. It is preferable that you send this as an email attachment when you subscribe. My address is: **Prof. François-Olivier Touati, La Croix Saint-Jérôme, 11 allée Émile Bouchut, 77123 Noisy-sur-École, France;** email: **francoistouati@aol.com**

I want to thank all members who provide me with bibliographical data. In order to make the *Bulletin* more useful for you, it would be helpful if those members who edit proceedings or essay volumes could let me know not only about their own papers but also on the other papers in such volumes. You are encouraged to supply any information via email.

Professor Thomas F. Madden is **webmaster** for our official website: **http://sscle.slu.edu.** There you can find news about the SSCLE and its publications as well as bibliographical data and links to related sites.

Our journal entitled *Crusades*, now no. 11, 2012, allows the Society to publish articles and texts; encourages research in neglected subfields; invites a number of authors to deal with a specific problem within a comparative framework; initiates and reports on joint programmes; and offers reviews of books and articles.

Editors: Benjamin Z. Kedar and Jonathan Phillips; Associate Editors: William J. Purkis; Reviews Editor: Christoph Maier; Archaeology Editor: Denys R. Pringle.

Colleagues may submit papers for consideration to either of the editors, Professor Benjamin Z. Kedar and Professor Jonathan Phillips. A copy of the style sheet is to be found in the back of this booklet.

The journal includes a section of book reviews. In order to facilitate the reviews editor's work, could members please ask their publishers to send copies to: **PD Dr Christoph T. Maier, Reviews editor, *Crusades*, Sommergasse 20, 4056 Basel, Switzerland; ctmaier@ hist.uzh.ch**. Please note that *Crusades* reviews books concerned with any aspect(s) of the history of the crusades and the crusade movement, the military orders and the Latin settlements in the Eastern Mediterranean, but not books which fall outside this range.

The cost of the journal to individual members is £25, $46 or €32; the cost to institutions and non-members is £65, US$130 or €93. **Cheques in these currencies should be made payable to SSCLE. For information on other forms of payment contact the treasurer.**

Members may opt to receive the *Bulletin* alone at the current membership price (single £10, $20 or €15; student £6, $12 or €9; joint £15, $30 or €21). Those members who do not subscribe to the journal will receive the Bulletin from the Bulletin Editor.

List of abbreviations

Avignon SSCLE 7: La Papauté et les Croisades, *The Papacy and the Crusades*, VIIe Congrès international de la SSCLE, proceedings of the VIIth Conference of the SSCLE, Avignon, 27–31 August 2008, ed. Michel Balard, Crusades-Subsidia 3, Farnham: Ashgate, 2011.

Caceres SCCLE 8: *War and Peace during the Crusades/Guerre et paix à l'*époque des Croisades. VIIIth International Conference of the SSCLE, Cáceres, June 2012.

DTT: *The Debate on the Trial of the Templars (1307–1314)*, ed. Jochen Burgtorf, Paul F. Crawford, and Helen Nicholson, Farnham and Burlington, Ashgate, 2010, xxv+399p.

ICMS (following the year): International Congress of Medieval Studies, Kalamazoo, USA.

IMC (following the year): International Medieval Congress, Leeds, UK.

IMO: Conference *Islands and the Military Orders*, organized by: University of the Aegean und Forth Ephorate of Byzantine Antiquities on Rhodes, 27–29 April, 2011, ed. Simon D. Phillips and Emanuel Buttigieg.

MO5: *The Military Orders: Politics and Power*, 5th Conference on the Military Orders, Cardiff University, 3–6 September 2009, ed. Peter Edbury, Farnham: Ashgate.

OM16: *Die Ritterorden in Umbruchs- und Krisenzeiten/The Military Orders in Times of Change and Crisis, Ordines militares: Colloquia Torunensia Historica XVI (2009)*, edition: Toruń, 2011.

OM17: *Die Ritterorden in Krieg und Frieden*. 17th Conference Ordines Militares, Colloquia Torunensia Historica, Uniwersytet Mikolaya Kopernica, Toruń, Poland, 22–25 September 2011.

Palmella 2012: *As ordens militares. Freires, guerreiros, cavaleiros, Actas do VI Encontro sobre Ordens Militare (2010)*, ed. I.C.F. Fernandes, Palmela, 2012.

Studi per Franco Cardini: "Come l'orco della fiaba". Studi per Franco Cardini, a cura di M. Montesano, Firenze, 2010.

1. Recent publications

AILES, Marianne, *The History of the Holy War: Ambroise's "Estoire de la Guerre Sainte"*), translated Marianne Ailes, notes by Marianne Ailes and Malcolm Barber, Woodbridge: Boydell & Brewer, 2011, xvi + 214 p. (original hardback, 2003).

BALARD, Michel, dir., SSCLE Avignon (*La papauté et les Croisades*), Farnham: Ashgate, 2011; "1261. Genova nel mondo: il trattato di Ninfeo", in *Gli anni di Genova*, Bari: Laterza, 2010, pp. 39–68; "Voltaire et le Proche-Orient des croisades", in B. Bernard, J. Renwick, N. Cronk and J. Godden, eds., *Voltaire. Essai sur les mœurs et l'esprit des nations*, t. III, Oxford, 2010, pp. XXXVII–XLVII; "L'historiographie des croisades en France au XXe siècle", in M. Montesano, ed., *Studi per Franco Cardini*, Florence, 2010, pp. 17–35; "Il regno nell'orizzonte mediterraneo", in P. Cordasco and F. Violante, eds., *Un regno nell'impero. I caratteri originari del regno normanno nell'età sveva: persistenze e differenze (1194–1250)*, Bari, 2010, pp. 31–48; "Mediterraneo, Levante e Mar nero", in *La Società ligure di Storia Patria nella storiografia italiana 1857–2007*, Atti della Scietà Ligure di Storia patria, n.s., L/1, 2010, pp. 331–348; "La guerre sainte musulmane du Moyen Age à nos jours", *Bulletin de la Société des Amis de Vincennes*, 61, 2010, pp. 41–44; "Le grand commerce", "Les possessions des Occidentaux à Byzance", in A. Laiou and C. Morrisson, eds., *Le monde byzantin*, t. III, Paris: Presses Universitaires de France, 2011, pp. 117–127 and 401–427; "Les actes notariés génois au Moyen Age", *Le Gnomon. Revue internationale d'histoire du notariat*, 168, July–September 2011, pp. 17–24.

BARBER, Malcolm, "The Challenge of State Building in the Twelfth Century: the Crusader States in Palestine and Syria", *Reading Medieval Studies*, 36, 2010, pp. 7–22; "The Military Orders and Egypt in the time of king Amlric", *Deus Vult. Miscellanea di studi sugli Ordini militari*, ed. C. Guzzo, 2011, vol. 1, pp. 9–19.

BAYDAL, Vicent, *La croada d'Almeria, 1309–1310. La host de Jaume II i el finançament de la campanya*, Saarbrücken: Lambert Academic Publishing, 2012, 208 p.; "La història política del regne de València baixmedieval. Renovació i propostes", *Calp. Institut d'Estudis Calpins*, 6, 2012, pp. 4–12; "Peites, qüesties, redempcions d'exèrcit i subsidis. La naturalesa i l'evolució dels principals tributs reials directes a la Corona d'Aragó des de Jaume I fins a Alfons el Benigne (1213–1336)", in M.T. Ferrer i Mallol, ed., *Jaume I. Commemoració del VIII centenari del naixement de Jaume I*, Barcelona: Institute of Catalan Studies, 2011, vol. 1, pp. 259–286; "A figura de Francesc de Vinatea no reino de València. Da crônica real aos documentos arquivísticos (1331–1332)", *Mirabilia*, 13, 2011, pp. 214–237; "La señera de Valencia y el pendón de San Fernando. Dos banderas para dos conmemoraciones diferentes: el 9 de octubre y el 23 de noviembre", *Banderas. Boletín de la Sociedad Española de Vexilología*, 118, 2011, pp. 1–14; *Seifukuou Jaume issei Kunkouroku. Rekonkisuta senki wo yomu*, coed. with A. Ozaki, Kyoto, Kyoto daigaku shuppankai, 2010, 608 p.; "El *Llibre dels fets* de Jaume I, a pams del sol naixent", *Afers*, 65, 2010, pp. 205–220; "Santa Tecla, San Jorge y Santa Bárbara: Los monarcas de la Corona de Aragón a la búsqueda de reliquias en Oriente (siglos XIV–XV)", *Anaquel de Estudios Árabes*, 21, 2010, pp. 153–162; "Monedatge", "Pecha", "Peita", "Qüestia", entries of *Les mots de l'impôt dans l'Occident méditerranéen. Base de données critique de fiscalité médiévale*, CNRS – CSIC, 2010 [http:// www.mailxxi.com/fiscalitat/index.htm/]; "Los primeros hechos del levantamiento mudéjar de 1276 en el reino de Valencia", *Actas del XI Simposio Internacional de Mudejarismo*, Teruel, Centre of Mudejar Studies, 2009, pp. 727–737; "'Que vengués a emparar et reebre los dits regnes e terres sues'. La naturaleza diversa de los pactismos territoriales de la Corona de Aragón a la llegada al trono de Jaime II (1291–1293)", *Actas IV Simposio Internacional de Jóvenes Medievalistas. Lorca*, Murcia: University of Murcia, 2009, pp. 27–38; "'Tan grans messions'. La financiación de la cruzada de Jaime II de Aragón contra Almería en 1309", *Medievalismo*, 19, 2009, pp. 57–154; "Fitant els termes entre Banyeres, Serrella i Bocairent en l'any 1265. En quina llengua parlava aquella gent?", *Barcella*, 38, 2009, pp. 110–112; *La senyoria de Beniparrell (1258–1419): Dels Romaní als Escrivà de Romaní*, Beniparrell: Beniparrell Council, 2008, 265 p.; "El naixement de l'impost del morabatí al regne de Valencia (1265–1266)", *Anales de la Universidad de Alicante. Historia medieval*, 15, 2008, pp. 141–164

BELLOMO, Elena, "Riflessioni e metodi d'indagine sulla milizia templare in Italia nord-occidentale (1142–1308)", *Rivista di Storia della Chiesa in Italia*, 64, 2010, pp. 11–37; "Fulfilling a Mediterranean Vocation: The *Domus Sancte Marie Montis Gaudii de Jerusalem* in North-west Italy", in H. Nicholson, ed., *On the Margins of Crusading: The Military Orders, the Papacy and the Christian World*, Farnham and Burlington: Ashgate, 2011, pp. 13–29.

BERKOVICH, Ilya, "The Battle of Forbie and the Second Frankish Kingdom of Jerusalem", *Journal of Military History*, 75, 2011, pp. 9–44.

BOAS, Adrian J., "The Ecology of Crusading: Investigating the Environmental Impact of Holy War and Colonisation at the Frontiers of Medieval Europe", with Aleksander Pluskowski and Christopher Gerrard, *Medieval Archaeology*, 55, 2011, pp. 192–225; "Frankish Jaffa", in Aaron Burke and Martin Peilstocker, eds., *The History and Archaeology of Jaffa 1*, Los Angeles, 2011, chapter 10, pp. 121–126.

BOMBI, Barbara, "Gli archivi dei procuratori di curia all'inizio del XIV secolo", in A. Kehnel, C. Andenna, C. Caby and G. Melville, eds., *Paradoxien der Legitimation. Ergebnisse einer deutsch-italienisch-französischen Villa Vigoni-Konferenz zur Macht im Mittelalter*, Micrologua Library, 35, 2010, pp. 295–306.

BONNEAUD, Pierre, "La Papauté et les Hospitaliers de Rhodes aux lendemains de la chute de Constantinople (1453–1467)", Avignon SSCLE 7.

BORCHARDT, Karl, *Documents concerning Cyprus from the Hospital's Rhodian Archives: 1409–1459*, ed. with Anthony Luttrell and Ekhard Schöffler, Cyprus Research Centre, Texts and Studies on the History of Cyprus 66, Nicosia, 2011; "Zucker und Mohren: Zur Krise der Johanniter auf Zypern im 15. Jahrhundert", OM16, pp. 191–212; "Casting Out Demons by Beelzebul: Did the Papal Preaching against the Albigensians Ruin the Crusades?", Avignon SSCLE 7, pp. 77–89.

BURKIEWICZ, Łukasz, *Na styku chrześcijaństwa i islamu. Krucjaty i Cypr w latach 1191–1291*, Historia Iagiellonica, Kraków 2008, 170 p.; "Polityka Wschodnia Fryderyka II Hohenstaufa ze szczególnym uwzględnieniem jego stosunku do Królestwa Cypru (w świetle kroniki Filipa z Novary)", in *Prace Historyczne Uniwersytetu Jagiellońskiego*, Jagiellonian University Press, 2006, z. 133, pp. 7–29; "Podróż króla Cypru Piotra I z Lusignan po Europie w latach 1362–1365 i jego plany krucjatowe", *Studia Historyczne*, 2007, R.L., Z. 1, 197, pp. 3–29; "The Cypriot Jews under the Venetian Rule (1489–1571)", *Scripta Judaica Cracoviensia*, Jagiellonian University Press, 2008, 6, pp. 49–61, and in Επετηρίς της Κυπριακής Εταιρείας Ιστορικών Σπουδών, 2010, 9, pp. 51–66; "Templariusze i ich wpływ na politykę wewnętrzną Królestwa Cypru w przededniu kasaty zakonu", *Studia Historyczne*, 2009, R.LII., Z. 1 (205), pp. 3–18; "Salomon Aszkenazy – dyplomata i lekarz. Pomiędzy Cyprem, Turcją a Polską", *Portolana. Studia Mediteranea*, 2010, vol. 4, pp. 161–175; "Królestwo Cypru jako obiekt zainteresowań państw śródziemnomorskich w latach 1192–1489. Próba zarysowania problem", *Prace Historyczne Uniwersytetu Jagiellońskiego*, 2010, z. 137, pp. 27–42; "Polityka egipskiego sułtanatu mameluków wobec łacińskiego Królestwa Cypru w XV wieku", in *Zeszyty Naukowe Towarzystwa Doktorantów Uniwersytetu Jagiellońskiego – Nauki Społeczne*, 2011, nr 2 (1/2011), pp. 7–22.

Buttigieg, Emanuel, *Nobility, Faith and Masculinity: The Hospitaller Knights of Malta, c.1580–c.1700*, London and New York, Continuum, 2011, 336 p.; "Chastity, Bachelorhood and Masculinity in early modern Europe: The case of the Hospitaller Knights of St John (c.1520–c.1650)", in Carla Salvaterra and Berteke Waaldijk, eds., *Paths to Gender: European Historical Perspectives on Women and Men*, Pisa: PLUS, 2009, pp. 209–24.

Bysted, Ane L., with Carsten Selch Jensen, Kurt Villads Jensen and John H. Lind, *Jerusalem in the North: Denmark and the Baltic Crusades (1100–1522)*, Turnhout: Brepols, 2012, xiv + 393 p.; "The Ideology of Mission and the Wendish Crusade of 1147" in Birgitte Fløe Jensen and Dorthe Wille-Jørgensen, eds., *Expansion – Integration? Danish-Baltic contacts 1147–1410 AD*, Museerne.dk, 2, Vordingborg: Danmarks Borgcenter, 2009, pp. 9–14; "Crusading Ideology and *Imitatio Christi* in Anders Sunesen, Bernard of Clairvaux and Innocent III", in T.M.S. Lehtonen and É. Mornet, eds., *Les élites nordique et l'Europe occidentale (xiie–xve siècles)*, Paris: Publications de la Sorbonne, 2007, pp. 127–138.

Carraz, Damien, *"Pro servitio maiestatis nostre.* Templiers et hospitaliers au service de la diplomatie de Charles Ier et Charles II", in Zoltán Kordé and István Petrovics, eds., *La Diplomatie des États Angevins aux XIIIe et XIVe siècles*, actes du colloque international de Szeged-Visegrád-Budapest, 13–16 September 2007, Rome and Szeged: Accademia d'Ungheria in Roma, 2010, pp. 21–42; "Églises et cimetières des ordres militaires. Contrôle des lieux sacrés et *dominium* ecclésiastique en Provence (XIIe–XIIIe siècle)", *Lieux sacrés et espace ecclésial (IXe–XVe siècle), Cahiers de Fanjeaux*, Toulouse, 2011, 46, pp. 277–312; with Sophie Aspord-Mercier, "Le programme architectural d'un pôle seigneurial: la commanderie de Montfrin (Gard)", in Y. Mattalia, ed., *Organiser l'enclos: sacré et topographie dans les maisons hospitalières et templières du Midi de la France, actes du séminaire Terrae, Toulouse, 24 avril 2009, Archéologie du Midi médiéval*, 28, 2010, pp. 297–316.

Cassidy-Welch, Megan, "Refugees: Views from 13th-Century France", in C. Chazelle, F. Lifshitz, S. Doubleday and A. Remensnyder, eds., *Why the Middle Ages Matter: Medieval Light on Modern Injustice*, Routledge, 2011, pp. 141–53; "Incarcération du corps et libération de l'esprit: un motif hagiographique", in I. Heullant Donat, E. Lusset and J. Claustre, eds., *Enfermements: Le cloître et la prison (Vie–XVIIIe siècle)*, Paris: Publications de la Sorbonne, 2011, pp. 57–70; "Images of Blood in the Historia Albigensis of Pierre les Vaux de Cernay", *Journal of Religious History*, 35:4, 2011, pp. 478–491.

Cerrini, Simonetta, *La Rivoluzione dei Templari*, Milano, Arnoldo Mondadori Editore, 2008; *La Révolucion de los Templarios*, Buenos Aires: El Ateneo, 2008; *Misterul calugarilor razboinici*, Litera International, 2010; "I Templari, i religiosi e gli intellettuali nel XII secolo. Alcuni spunti", in Palmela 2012. 1, pp. 339–354; "I templari, la regola e il cavallo sacrificato", in F. Cardini and L. Mantelli, eds., *Cavalli e cavalieri. Guerra, gioco, finzione*, Atti del Convegno internazionale di Studi Certaldo Alto, 2010, Pisa: Pacini, 2011, pp. 87–108; "Orders, Military: Levantine Orders", in *The Oxford Encyclopedia of Medieval Warfare*, ed. C.J. Rogers, Oxford University Press, 2010, 3, pp. 78–83.

Chevalier, Marie-Anna, *Les ordres religieux-militaires en Arménie cilicienne. Templiers, hospitaliers, teutoniques et Arméniens à l'époque des croisades*, Paris: Éditions Geuthner, Collection Orient chrétien médiéval, 2009, 890 p.; *Sur l'histoire des relations de l'Arménie cilicienne avec les ordres religieux-militaires*, Académie nationale de la République d'Arménie. Institut d'Histoire, Éditions de l'Université d'État d'Erevan, Erevan, 2007, 118 p.; "Les ordres militaires et la mer en Arménie cilicienne (milieu XIIe–fin XIVe siècle)", in M. Balard (dir.), *Les ordres militaires et la mer*, éditions du CTHS (Comité des travaux historiques et scientifiques), 2009, CD-Rom (publication en ligne sur internet: http://cths.fr/ed/edition.php?id=4254); Notices "Meleh", "Hét'oum Ier", "Zapêl", "Saint-Blaise d'Arménie (ordre de)", "Édesse (comté d')", "La Roche Guillaume", "Ayas" et "Port-Bonnel", in N. Bériou and Ph. Josserand (dir.), *Dictionnaire européen des ordres militaires au Moyen Âge*, Paris: Fayard, 2009; "L'ordre de l'Hôpital en Arménie cilicienne du début du XIIe siècle à la fin du règne de Hét'oum Ier", in G. Dédéyan and I. Augé (dir.), *L'Église arménienne entre Grecs et Latins (fin XIe–milieu XVe siècle)*, Paris: Éditions Geuthner, 2009; dir., *La fin de l'ordre du Temple*, Paul Geuthner, 2012.

CHRISSIS, Nikolaos, G., Review of Julian Chrysostomides, *Byzantium and Venice, 1204–1453: Collected Studies*, ed. Michael Heslop and Charalambos Dendrinos, Farnham: Ashgate, 2011, in *The Anglo-Hellenic Review* 44, 2011, pp. 31–32.

CHRIST, Georg, *Trading Conflicts. A Venetian Consul in Mamlûk Alexandria at the Beginning of the 15th Century*, The Medieval Mediterranean 93, Leiden: Brill, 2012, 366 p.; "Eine Stadt wandert aus. Kollaps und Kontinuität im spätmittelalterlichen Alexandria", *Viator* 42, multilingual, 2011, pp. 145–168.

CHRISTIE, Niall, "Ali b. Tahir al-Sulami," in *Christian-Muslim Relations: A Bibliographical History, Volume 3 (1050–1200)*, ed. David Thomas et al., Leiden: E.J. Brill, 2011, pp. 307–11.

CLAVERIE, Pierre-Vincent, "Une source méconnue sur la bataille de La Mansourah: la chanson de Guillaume Longue-Épée, in U. Vermeulen and K. D'hulster, eds., *Egypt and Syria in the Fatimid, Ayyubid and Mamluk Eras*, t. VI, Louvain, 2010, pp. 49–61; "Les relations islamo-chrétiennes à l'aune du récit de pèlerinage de Jacques de Vérone (1335)", ibid., pp. 191–205; "La contribution des sources diplomatiques à l'histoire ecclésiastique de Tyr durant les Croisades", in J. Aliquot, P.-L. Gatier and L. Nordiguian, eds., *Tyr dans les textes l'Antiquité et du Moyen Âge*, Damas: Institut Français du Proche-Orient, 2011, pp. 201–219; "Un patriarche latin d'Antioche méconnu: Grazia de Florence (1219)", *Le Moyen Age*, CXVII, 2011, fasc. 1, pp. 81–90; "Les templiers informateurs de l'Occident à travers leur correspondence", in Palmela, 2012, II, pp. 715–735.

CONNELL, Charles W., "Origins of Medieval Public Opinion in the Peace of God Movement", in Albrecht Classen and Nadia Margolis, eds., *War and Peace. Critical Issues in European Societies and Literature 800–1800*, Gottingen: De Gruyter, 2011, pp. 171–92.

COSTA, Paula Pinto, with Luís Adão da Fonseca and Maria Cristina Pimenta, "The Papacy and the Crusades in XVth Century Portugal", Avignon SSCLE 7, pp. 141–154; "Amândio Tavares. IX Reitor da Universidade do Porto desde 1946 a 1961", in: *Os Reitores da Universidade do Porto: 1911–2011*, Porto: Universidade do Porto / Fundação Eng° António de Almeida, 2011, pp. 159–167; *D. Maria, a "Formosíssima" Maria*. Lisboa: Academia Portuguesa da História e Quid Novi, 2011, 80 p.; with Maria Cristina Pimenta), "A cruzada e os objectivos fundacionais das Ordens Religioso-Militares em Portugal", in *Revista Portuguesa de História*, Universidade de Coimbra, 40, 2009, pp. 273–284.

COUREAS, Nicholas S., "Medieval Sources of a Diplomatic and Ecclesiastical Nature edited and published in Cyprus", in P. Krafln, ed., *Almanach medievisty-editora*, Prague, 2011, pp. 71–76.

CRAWFORD, Paul F., "Four Myths about the Crusades", in *Intercollegiate Review*, 46:1, 2011, pp. 13–22; article on "Malicide not Homicide: The Military Religious Orders" and sidebar on "Bernard of Clairvaux's In Praise of the New Knighthood", *World History Encylopedia* in the medieval volume, ed. Alfred Andrea, ABC-Clio, 2011.

DEMPSEY, John A., "Ideological Friendship in the Middle Ages: Bonizo of Sutri and his Liber ad amicum", in Albrecht Classen and Marilyn Sandidge, eds., *Friendship in the Middle Ages*, Berlin and New York: De Gruyter, 2011, pp. 395–427; "From Holy War to Patient Endurance: Henry IV, Matilda of Tuscany and the Evolution of Bonizo of Sutri's Response to Heretical Princes", in Nadia Margolis and Albrecht Classen, eds., *War and Peace: New Perspectives in European History and Literature*, Berlin: De Gruyter, 2011; "Bonizo of Sutry", in *International Encyclopedia of the Middle Ages*, UCLA, Online, 2012.

DIVALL, Richard, "Some aspects of the Music on Malta during the Rule of The Order of St. John. Nicolò Isouard and Michel'Angelo Vella: Recent research and discoveries", *Journal of the Monastic Military Orders*, June 2010, 3, pp. 1–16; ed., Michel'Angelo Vella. (1710–1792), *Sonatas for Three Traverso Flutes. Nos. 7–12, and 13–24*, Melbourne: Lyrebird Press, 2011 and 2012.

DOUROU-ELIOPOULOU, Maria, *The crusading dominions in Romania (13th–15th centuries). History and institutions*, Athens, 2011, 212 p.; "The Angevins of Sicily and the principality of Achaea", *Proceedings of the Greco-Italian Congress for Achaea and South Italy, Aeghion, 6–9 July 2006*, Athens 2011, pp. 298–305; "The latin church in New Patras during the Catalan period", *Proceedings of the Congress for the history of the Church in Hypati, Hypati, 8–10 May, 2009*, Athens 2011, pp. 313–321; "Latin settlement in Greek lands after the 4th crusade", *Moira and Myra, Honorary Volume for Professor Voula Lambropoulou*, Athens, 2011, pp. 183–190.

EDBURY, Peter, "Machaut, Mézières, Makhairas and *Amadi*: Constructing the reign of Peter I (1359–1369)", in Renate Blumenfeld-Kosinski and Kiril Petkov, eds., *Philippe de Mézières and his Age: Piety and Politics in the Fourteenth Century*, Leiden: Brill, 2011, pp. 349–358; "Gerard of Ridefort and the battle of Le Cresson (1 May 1187): the developing narrative tradition", in H. Nicholson, ed., *On the Margins of Crusading: the Military Orders, the Papacy and the Christian World*, Farnham: Ashgate, 2011, pp. 45–60; ed., *The Military Orders: Politics and Power* (Military Orders Conference, Cardiff, September 2009), Farnham: Ashgate, 2012 [MO5].

EDGINGTON, Susan, [with Carol Sweetenham], *The* Chanson d'Antioche: *An Old French Account of the First Crusade*, Crusade Texts in Translation, 22, Farnham: Ashgate, 2011, 440 p.; "Matilda of Canossa (1046–1115)" and "Bouillon, Godfrey de (ca. 1060–1100)" in *The Encyclopedia of War*, ed. G. Martel, New York: Blackwell, 2011; "Walter the Chancellor", in A. Mallett et al., eds., *Christian-Muslim Relations: A Bibliographical History. Volume Two: 900–1200 CE*, Leiden: Brill, 2011, pp. 379–82.

EKDHAL, Sven, "Aufmarsch und Aufstellung der Heere bei Tannenberg/Grunwald (1410). Eine kritische Analyse", in Jan Gancewski, ed., *Krajobraz grunwaldzki w dziejach polsko-krzyżackich i polsko-niemieckich na przestrzeni wieków. Wokół mitów i rzeczywistości*, Biblioteka Mrągowski Studiów Humanistycznych, Historia, 1, Olsztyn: ElSet, 2009, pp. 31–103 and 3 supplementary maps; "Die Söldnerwerbungen des Deutschen Ordens für einen geplanten Angriff auf Polen am 1. Juni 1410. Ein Beitrag zur Vorgeschichte der Schlacht bei Tannenberg", in Bernhart Jähnig, ed., *Beiträge zur Militärgeschichte des Preußenlandes von der Ordenszeit bis zum Zeitalter der Weltkriege*, Tagungsberichte der Historischen Kommission für ost- und westpreußische Landesforschung, 25, Marburg: N.G. Elwert, 2010, pp. 89–102; "Diplomatie und Söldnerwerbung vor der Schlacht bei Žalgiris", *Lietuvos istorijos studijos*, 25, 2010, pp. 48–61; "The Turning Point in the Battle of Tannenberg (Grunwald/Žalgiris) in 1410", *The Lithuanian Quarterly Journal of Arts and Sciences*, 56:2, Summer 2010, pp. 53–72; *Das Soldbuch des Deutschen Ordens 1410/1411. Die Abrechnungen für die Soldtruppen, II: Indices mit personengeschichtlichen Kommentaren*, Veröffentlichungen aus den Archiven Preußischer Kulturbesitz, Vol. 23, II, Köln: Böhlau,

2010, 408 p.; "Bitwa pod Grunwaldem/Tannenbergiem w polsko-niemieckiej historii na przestrzeni dziejów", in Katarzyna Murawska-Muthesius, ed., *Jana Matejki Bitwa pod Grunwaldem: Nowe spojrzenia*, Warszawa: Muzeum Narodowe w Warszawie, 2010, pp. 9–25; "The Battle of Grunwald/Tannenberg and its political and symbolic Interpretations in Poland and Germany through the Centuries", in Katarzyna Murawska-Muthesius, ed., *Jan Matejko's Battle of Grunwald: New Approaches*, Warsaw, The National Museum in Warsaw, 2010, pp. 9–25; "Das politische Umfeld und die Schlacht von Tannenberg", in *Tannenberg/Grunwald 1410. Gesammelte Beiträge*, Miscellanea Ordinis Teutonici, 1, Wien: Amt des Hochmeisters, 2010, pp. 18–28; "'Lietuvių pabėgimas' iš Žalgirio mūšio/'Ucieczka Litwinów' spod Grunwaldu/The 'Lithuanian retreat' from the Battle of Grunwald", in *Kaip tai atsitiko Didžiajame mūšyje ... Žalgirio atodangos/ Jako to było podczas Wielkiej Bitwy ... Odsłony Grunwaldu/How this happened in the Great Battle ... Exposé of Grunwald (Tarptautinės parodos katalogas/Katalog międzynarodwej wystawy/International Exhibition Catalogue)*, sud./opr./ed. Vydas Dolinskas, Birutė Verbiejūtė, Lietuvos didžiųjų kunigaikščių rūmū katalogai, IV tomas/Katalogi Pałacu Wielkich Książąt Litewskich, tom IV/ Catalogues of the Palace of the Grand Dukes of Lithuania, Volume IV, Vilnius, 2010, pp. 33–43; "1410. Die Schlacht bei Tannenberg. 600. Gedenkjahr", in Ernst Gierlich, ed., *Ostdeutsche Gedenktage 2010. Persönlichkeiten und Historische Ereignisse*, Bonn: Kulturstiftung der deutschen Vertriebenen, 2010, pp. 288–298; "Бітва пад Танэнбергам і яе значэнне ў гісторыі ордэнскай дзяржаы", БЕЛАРУСКІ ГІСТАРЫЧНЫ АГЛЯД / *Belarusian Historical Review*, 17, 1–2, 2010, pp. 3–41; "Набор наемников перед Грюнвльдской битвой 1410 гв контексте политики и дипломатии эпохи", *Studia Slavica et Balcanica Petropolitana*, 2010, 2, pp. 17–24; *Grunwald 1410. Studia nad tradycją i źródłami*. Tłumaczenie Maciej Dorna, Kraków: Avalon, 2010, pp. 349; "'In crastino, die sancti Procopii'. Überlegungen zu einer falsch interpretierten Datumsangabe in der Cronica conflictus", in T. Grabarczyk, A. Kowalski-Pietrzak and T. Nowak, eds., *In tempore belli et pacis. Homines – Loca – Res / Ludzie-Miejsca-Przedmioty* [Book in honour of Professor Jan Szymczak], Warszawa: Wydawnictwo DiG, 2011, pp. 561–568; "Polnische Söldnerwerbungen vor der Schlacht bei Tannenberg (Grunwald)", in O. Ławrynowicz, J. Maik and P.A. Nowakowski, eds., *Non sensistis gladios* [Book in honour of Professor Marian Głosek], Łódz: Instytut Archeologii Uniwersytetu Łódzkiego, 2011, pp. 121–134.

FAVREAU-LILIE, Marie-Luise, "Die italienischen Seestaedte und die islamische Levante (Aegypten und Syrien) im Zeitalter der Kreuzzuege (12./13.Jh.)", in Stefan Leder, ed., *Crossroads between Latin Europe and the Near East. Corollaries of the Frankish Presence in the Eastern Mediterranean (12th–14th centuries)*, Istanbuler Texte und Studien, Orient-Institut Istanbul, vol. 24, Würzburg: Ergon, 2011, pp. 147–177.

FISHHOF, Gil, "Saint-Hilaire at Semur-en-Brionnais and the Meaning of Models in 12th-century Burgundian Architecture", *Arte Medievale*, 2008/2, pp. 25–46; "Political Intentions and Romanesque Portal Iconography: Saint-Hilaire in Semur-en-Brionnais, Saint Hugh of Cluny and the Dynastic Strategies of the Lords of Semur", *Mediaevistik. International Journal of Interdisciplinary Medieval Research*, 23, 2010, pp. 11–48.

FLORI, Jean, *Prêcher la Croisade, XIe–XIIIe siècle. Communication et propagande*, Paris: Perrin, 2012.

FOREY, Alan J., "Were the Templars Guilty, even if they were not Heretics or Apostates?", *Viator*, 42, 2011, 2, pp. 115–141; "Papal Claims to Authority over Lands gained from the Infidel in the Iberian Peninsula and beyond the Straits of Gibraltar", Avignon SSCLE 7, pp. 131–139; "A Hospitaller *Consilium* (1274) and the Explanations advanced by Military

Orders for Problems confronting them in the Holy Land in the Later Thirteenth Century", in *Die Ritterorden in Umbruchs- und Krisenzeiten/ The Military Orders in Times of Change and Crisis*, Torun: Nicolaus Copernicus U.P., 2011, pp. 7–17.

GABRIELE, Matthew, "Translation of Charlemagne's Pilgrimage from Benedict of Monte Soratte's *Chronicon*", in Brett Whalen, ed., *Pilgrimage in the Middle Ages*, Toronto: University of Toronto Press, 2011, pp. 124–125.

GAPOSCHKIN, Cecilia, "Place, Status and Experience in the Miracles of Saint Louis", *Cahiers de recherches médiévales et humanistes*, Orléans, 19, 2010, pp. 249–266; "The Role of the Crusades in the Sanctification of Louis IX of France", in T. Madden, ed., *Crusades: Medieval Worlds in Conflict*, Farnham: Ashgate, 2011, pp. 195–209.

GEORGIOU, Stavros G., "Studies on the Court Hierarchy of the Komnenian Era II: The Title of Pansebastohypertatos", *Vyzantinos Domos*, 17–18, 2009–2010, pp. 527–536 [in Greek with a summary in English]; "The Bishopric of Tamasos", in Vasiliki Lysandrou, ed., *Mnimeia Mitropolis Tamasou kai Oreinis. Naoi kai xoklisia*, Nicosia 2011, pp. 9–14 [in Greek]; "The Attribution of the titles of Sebastohypertatos and Despotes to the Archon of Nauplion Leo Sgouros (ca. 1200–1208)", in Th. Korres, Polymnia Katsoni, I. Leontiadis and A. Gkoutzioukostas, eds., *Filotimia. Timitikos tomos gia tin Omotimi Kathigitria Alkmini Stavridou-Zafraka*, Thessalonica, 2011, pp. 205–220 [in Greek with a Summary in English].

GILLINGHAM, John, "Christian Warriors and the Enslavement of Fellow Christians", in M. Aurell and C. Girbea, eds., *Chevalerie et christianisme aux XIIe et XIIIe siècles*, Rennes: Presses universitaires de Rennes, 2011, pp. 237–256.

GOURDIN, Philippe, "Des 'latins de cour' dans la Tunisie hafside du XVe siècle", in *IBLA* (Institut des Belles Lettres Arabes), Tunis, 72–1, 2009, pp. 83–105; ed. with Monique Longerstay, *De Tabarka aux 'Nouvelles Tabarka': Carloforte, Calasetta, Nueva Tabarca. Histoire, environnement, préservation*, Tunis, Finzi, 2011, 244 p.

HAMILTON, Bernard, "Why did the Crusader States produce so few Saints?", in P. Clarke and T. Clayton, eds., *Sainthood and Sanctity*, Studies in Church History, 47, The Boydel Press, 2011, pp. 103–111; "Latins and Georgians and the Crusader Kingdom", *Al-Masāq*, 23 (ii), 2011, pp. 103–111.

HANSON, Chris, *The Mongol Siege of Xianyang and Facheng*, Lance and Longbow society, The Hobilar, 2007.

HARRIS, Jonathan, "Greeks at the papal curia in the fifteenth century: the case of George Vranas, bishop of Dromore and Elphin", in Martin Hinterberger and Chris Schabel, eds., *Greeks, Latins, and Intellectual History 1204–1500*, Leuven: Peeters, 2011, pp. 423–438.

HARSCHEIDT, Michael, see: www.harscheidt.de

HESLOP, Michael, co-edition of *Byzantium and Venice, 1204–1453, Collected Studies of Julian Chrysostomides*, Farnham: Ashgate, 2011, 314 p.; "The search for the defensive system of the knights in the Dodecanese (I: Chalki, Symi, Nisyros and Tilos)", in H. Nicholson, ed., *On the Margins of Crusading: The Military Orders, the Papacy and the Christian World*, Crusades Subsidia, vol. 4, Farnham: Ashgate, 2011, pp. 139–165.

HINZ, Felix, *Wechselwirkungen und Anpassungsprozesse in der Geschichte – Spanischer Kolonialismus (+ Wahlmodul Kreuzzüge), Geschichte und Geschehen Themenheft Oberstufe*, Leipzig, Ernst-Klett-Verlag, 2012, 132 p., http://www.klett.de/produkt/isbn/3-12-430079-3; "The crusades myth in historical novels written in German" for Edumeres, december 2011, Georg-Eckert-Institut, Braunschweig: http://www.edumeres.net/publikationen/details/d/european-receptions-of-the-crusades-in-the-nineteenth-century-franco-german-perspectives/p/the-crusades-myth-in-historical-novels-written-in-german-work-in-progress.

html; "Saladin und der Alte vom Berge. Geschichtsdidaktische Zugriffe auf Islambilder in parabolischen westlichen Kreuzzugsromanen", in *Historische Sozialkunde. Geschichte – Fachdidaktik – Politische Bildung* 4, 2010, pp. 49–56, http://vgs.univie.ac.at/_TCgi_Images/vgs/20110207152119_ZHSK_4_2010_Fachdidaktik.pdf.

HOLMES, Catherine, "Provinces and Capital", in L. James, ed., *A Companion to Byzantium*, Oxford: Blackwell, 2010, pp. 55–67; "Political Literacy", in P. Stephenson, ed., *The Byzantine World*, London: Routledge, 2010, pp. 137–48; "Concluding remarks", in J. Herrin and G. Saint-Guillain, eds., *Identities and Allegiances in the Eastern Mediterranean after 1204*, Farnham: Ashgate, 2011, pp. 309–314.

HUNT, Lucy-Anne, "A Deesis mould in Berlin: Christian–Muslim cultural interchange between Iran, Syria and Mesopotamia in the early Thirteenth Century", *Islam and Christian–Muslim Relations*, 22 (2), April 2011, pp. 127–45; "Marking Presence: Art, Ritual and Pilgrimage in the Eastern Mediterranean in the Crusader Period", in *Ritual and Space in the Middle Ages; Proceedings of the 2009 Harlaxton Symposium*, ed. Frances Andrews, Harlaxton Medieval Studies XXI, Donington, Shaun Tyas, 2011, pp. 61–70; "The Wallpainting Programme at the Church of Mar Tadros, Behdaidat: Art Historical Aspects in the Light of the current conservation Project", in Isabelle Doumet Skaf and Giorgio Capriotti, eds., *Conservation of 13th Century Mural Paintings in the Church of St. Theodore, Behdaidat, Bulletin d'Archéologie et d'Architecture Libanaises* 13, 2011 (labelled 2009), pp. 274–88; "Sinai Icons from the "Eastern" Perspective: Hybridity and Polyculturalism during the Period of the Crusades", Communication at the Round Table "Sinai through the Ages: a Place of Cult and Pilgrimage", Archaeology and History Section (RT21), *Proceedings of the 22nd International Congress of Byzantine Studies*, Sofia, 22–27 August 2011, vol. II *Abstracts of Round Table Communications*, Sofia: Bulgarian Heritage Foundation, p. 144; "Eastern Christian Art and Culture in the Ayyubid and early Mamluk periods: Cultural convergence between Jerusalem, Greater Syria and Egypt", in R. Hillenbrand and S. Auld, eds., *Ayyubid Jerusalem: The Holy City in Context 1187–1250*, London: Altajir Trust, 2009, pp. 327–347.

HOWE, John, "Did St Peter Damian die in 1073? A new Perspective on his Final days", *Analecta Bollandiana*, 128, 2010, pp. 67–86; "Reforging the 'Age of Iron', Part I The Tenth Century as the End of the Ancient World?", *History Compass*, 8/8, 2010, pp. 866–887; "Part II: The Tenth Century in a New Age", ibid., 8/9, 2010, pp. 1000–1022.

JACOBY, David, "Benjamin of Tudela and his *Book of Travels*", in Klaus Herbers and Felicitas Schmieder, eds., *Venezia incrocio di culture. Percezioni di viaggiatori europei e non europe a confronto. Atti del convegno Venezia, 26–27 gennaio 2006*, Centro Tedesco di Studi Veneziani, Ricerche, 4, Roma, 2008, pp. 135–164; "Caviar Trading in Byzantium", in Rustam Shukurov, ed., *Mare et litora. Essays presented to Sergei Karpov for his 60th Birthday*, Moscow: Indrik, 2009, pp. 349–364; "The Economy of Byzantine Constantinople, ca. 850–1453", in *From Byzantium to Istanbul. 8000 Years of a Capital*, Exhibition catalogue, Sabanci University, Sakip Sabanci Museum, Istanbul, 2010, pp. 92–101, 248–249 (endnotes); "Thirteenth-Century Commercial Exchange in the Aegean: Continuity and Change", in Ayla Ödekan, Engin Akyürek and Nevra Necipoglu, eds., *Change in the Byzantine World in the Twelfth and Thirteenth Centuries*, First International Sevgi Gönül Byzantine Studies Symposium, Istanbul: Vehbi Koç Vakfi, 2010, pp. 187–194; "Mediterranean Food and Wine for Constantinople: The Long-Distance Trade, Eleventh to Mid-Fifteenth Century", in E. Kislinger, J. Koder and A. Külzer, eds., *Handelsgüter und Verkehrswege. Aspekte der Warenversorgung im östlichen Mittelmeerraum (4. bis 15. Jahrhundert)*, Österreichische Akademie der Wissenschaften, Philosophisch-historische Klasse, Denkschriften, 388. Band, Wien, 2010, pp. 127–147; "Jews and Christians in Venetian Crete: Segregation, Interaction, and Conflict", in U. Israel, R. Jütte and R.C. Mueller, eds., *"Interstizi"*: *Culture ebraico-cristiane a Venezia e nei suoi domini dal medioevo all'età modern*, Centro Tedesco di Studi veneziani, Ricerche, 5, Roma, 2010, pp. 243–279; "Candia between Venice, Byzantium and the Levant: the Rise of a Major Emporium to the Mid-Fifteenth Century", in Maria Vassilaki, ed., *The Hand of Angelos: an Icon-Painter in Venetian Crete*, exh. cat., Benaki Museum, London and Athens, 2010, pp. 38–47; "Acre-Alexandria: A Major Commercial Axis of the Thirteenth Century", in *Studi per Franco Cardini*, pp. 151–167; "Oriental Silks go West: a Declining Trade in the Later Middle Ages", in C. Schmidt Arcangeli and G. Wolf, eds., *Islamic Artefacts in the Mediterranean World: Trade, Gift Exchange and Artistic Transfer*, Venice: Marsilio, 2010, pp. 71–88; "The Operation of the Cretan Port of Candia in the Thirteenth and First Half of the Fourteenth Century: Sources, Speculations, and Facts", *Thesaurismata*, 39/40, 2009/2010, pp. 9–23; "Western Merchants, Pilgrims and Travelers in Alexandria in the Time of Philippe de Mézières (c. 1327–1405)", in R. Blumenfeld-Kozinski and K. Petkov, eds., *Philippe de Mézières and His Age: Piety and Politics in the Fourteenth Century*, Leiden and Boston: Brill, 2011; "The Jews in the Byzantine Economy (Seventh to Mid-Fifteenth Century)" in R. Bonfil, O. Irshai, G.G. Stroumsa, R. Talgam, eds., *Jews in Byzantium: Dialectics of Minority and Majority Cultures*, Leiden and Boston: Brill, 2012, pp. 219–255.

JENSEN, Carsten Selch, *Crusading and Chronicle Writing on the Medieval Baltic Frontier, A Companion to the Chronicle of Henry of Livonia*, ed. Marek Tamm, Linda Kaljundi and Carsten Selch Jensen, Farnham: Ashgate 2011, 487 p.; "'Verbis non verberibus': The Representation of Sermons in the Chronicle of Henry of Livonia", in Marek Tamm, Linda Kaljundi and Carsten Selch Jensen, eds., *Crusading and Chronicle Writing on the Medieval Baltic Frontier, A Companion to the Chronicle of Henry of Livonia*, Farnham: Ashgate, 2011, pp. 179–206.

JENSEN, Kurt Villads, *Korstog ved verdens yderste rand. Danmark og Portugal ca.1000 til ca. 1250*, Odense: Syddansk Universitetsforlag, 2011. 611 p. [Crusading at the edge of the World. Denmark and Portugal, c. 1000–c. 1250].

JORDAN, William Chester, "The Priory of Deerhurst and the Treaty of Paris (1259)", *Thirteenth Century England*, 13, 2011, pp. 133–40; "The Ardennais Monastery of Élan in the Late Twelfth and Early Thirteenth Century", Cîteaux, Commentarii cistercienses, 61 (2010): pp. 127–40.

JOSSERAND, Philippe, *Les Templiers en Bretagne*, Paris: Gisserot, 2011, 32 p.; with Carlos de Ayala Martínez, "La actitud de los freiles de las órdenes militares ante el problema de la muerte en Castilla (siglos XII–XIV)", *Deus vult. Miscellanea di studi sugli ordini militari*, 1, 2011, pp. 53–67; "Les croisades de Terre sainte et les ordres militaires dans les chroniques royales castillano-léonaises (milieu XIIe–milieu XIIIe siècle)", in Matthias Tischler and Alexander Fidora, eds., *Christlicher Norden – Muslimischer Süden. Ansprüche und Wirklichkeiten von Christen, Juden und Muslimen auf der Iberischen Halbinsel im Hoch- und Spätmittelalter*, Münster, 2011, pp. 433–443; "Le procès des Templiers dans le royaume de Castille", in Marie-Anna Chevalier, ed., *La fin de l'ordre du Temple*, Journée d'études réunie à Montpellier le 28 janvier 2011), Paris: P. Geuthner, 2012; "Frontière et ordres militaires dans le monde latin au Moyen Âge", in Michel Catala, Dominique Le Page and Jean-Claude Meuret, eds., *Frontières oubliées, frontières retrouvées. Marches et limites anciennes en France et en Europe*, Rennes, 2011, pp. 189–197; "De l'arrière au front: perspectives croisées, perspectives comparées. Regards sur la logistique des ordres militaires au Moyen Âge", in Palmela, 2012, II, pp. 683–703; "O processo da Ordem do Templo em Castela", in José Albuquerque Carreiras and Giulia Rossi Vairo, eds., *Actas do I Colóquio internacional. Cister, os Templarios e a Ordem de Cristo*, Tomar, 2012, pp. 141–157.

Jubb, Margaret A., Entries on the "Chronique d'Ernoul et de Bernard le Trésorier"; "Estoires d'Outremer et de la naissance Salehadin" and "William of Tyre", in *Encyclopedia of the Medieval Chronicle*, ed. R.G. Dunphy, Leiden: Brill, 2010, pp. 335, 586–7 and pp. 1515–16.

Kedar, Benjamin Z., "The Latin Hermits of the Frankish Levant Revisited", in *Studi per Franco Cardini*, pp. 185–202; "Haim Beinart", *Speculum*, 56, 2011, pp. 860–863; "The Eastern Christians in the Frankish Kingdom of Jerusalem: An Overview", in Marián Gálik and Martin Slobodník, eds., *Eastern Christianity, Judaism and Islam between the Death of Muhammad and Tamerlane (632–1405). Proceedings of the Humboldt-Kolleg, June 25–28, 2008, Dolná Krupá, Slovakia*, Bratislava, 2011, pp. 143–153; "Muslime in den fränkischen Burgen des Königreichs Jerusalem", *Burgen und Schlösser*, 52, 2011, pp. 210–218.

Kolia-Dermitzaki, Athina, Entries in *Christian–Muslim Relations. A Bibliographical History*, vol. 1 (600–900), ed. David Thomas and Barbara Roggema, Leiden: Brill, 2009: "The forty-two martyrs of Amorion by Sophronios, archbishop of Cyprus", pp. 675–678, "by Michael the Synkellos", pp. 628–632, "by Euodius the Monk", pp. 844–847, BHG 1212 και BHG 1214c, pp. 636–641

Lapina, Elizabeth, "Anti-Jewish Rhetoric in Guibert of Nogent's *Dei Gesta Per Francos*", *Journal of Medieval History*, 35, 2009, pp. 239–253; "La représentation de la bataille d'Antioche (1098) sur les peintures murales de Poncé-sur-le-Loir", *Cahiers de Civilisation Médiévale*, 52, 2009, pp. 137–157.

Ligato, Giuseppe, "'Uomo a terra!'. Il disarcionamento del 'miles' medievale nella tattica e nella mentalità cavalleresche", in *Cavalli e cavalieri. Guerra, gioco, finzione*, Convegno internazionale del Centro Europeo di Studi sulla Civiltà Cavalleresca, Certaldo, 16–18 settembre 2010, a cura di F. Cardini, L. Mantelli, Pisa, 2011, pp. 109–136; *L'ordalia della fede. Il mito della crociata nel frammento di mosaico pavimentale recuperato dalla basilica di S. Maria Maggiore a Vercelli*, Spoleto 2011; "Un documento della letteratura cavalleresca caro a Carducci: l'*Epistola epica* di Rambaldo de Vaqueiras", in *Suol d'Aleramo. Studi su Carducci e il Monferrato*, Atti della giornata di studio, Bologna, 17 ottobre 2009, a cura di R. Maestri e A. Settia, Alessandria 2011, pp. 61–95; "La crociata a Damietta tra legato papale, profezie e strategie", in *San Francesco e il sultano*, Giornata di studio, Firenze, 25 settembre 2010, in *Studi francescani*, 108, 2011, pp. 427–476; "Il drago nel mosaico di Bobbio: transizione di un simbolo dall'Europa romanobarbarica al movimento crociato", in *Pellegrinaggi e monachesimo celtico. Dall'Irlanda alle sponde del Mediterraneo*, Giornata di studio, Genova, 14 ottobre 2010, a cura di M. Montesano e F. Benozzo, Alessandria, 2011, pp. 127–167.

Lobrichon, Guy, "L'*Apocalypse* en débat: entre séculiers et moines au XIIe siècle (v. 1080–v. 1180)", in *L'Apocalisse nel Medioevo*, a cura di Rossana Guglielmetti, Firenze, SISMEL – Edizioni del Galluzzo, 2011, pp. 403–426; "The early schools, c. 900–1100", *The New Cambridge History of the Bible. From 600 to 1450*, ed. Richard Mardsen and E. Ann Matter, Cambridge, Cambridge University Press, 2012, pp. 536–554.

Luchitskaya, Svetlana, *Homo legens. Styles and practices of Reading: Comparative Analysis of Oral and Written Traditions in the Middle Ages*, dir. with M.-C.Varol, Turnhout: Brepols, 2010, 230 p.; Introduction (with M.-C.Varol), ibid., pp. 1–25; "'Veoir' et 'oïr', *legere* et *audire*: reflexions sur les interactions entre traditions orale et ecrite dans les sources relatives a la Premiere croisade", ibid., pp. 89–127.

Luttrell, Anthony, "Prolusione", in *Cavalieri di San Giovanni in Liguria e nell'Italia settentrionale: Quadri regionale, Uomini e Documenti*, ed. J. Costa Restagno, Genoa-Albenga, 2009, pp. 13–21; "Preface", in *Prier et Combattre: Dictionnaire europeen des*

Ordres Militaires au Moyen Age, ed. N. Beriou, P. Josserand, Paris, 2009, pp. 15–16; "West–East Attitudes and Ambiguities: the Hospitallers of Rhodes after 1306", in E. Farrugia, ed., *Dies Amalphitana: Pontificio Istituto Orientale*, Rome, 2009, pp. 55–68; "Juan Fernandez de Heredia's History of Greece", *Byzantine and Modern Greek Studies*, 54, 2010, pp. 330–337; "Los Origines de la Encomienda templaria en el Occidente latino", in J.M. Sans Travé and J. Serrano Daura, *Actes de les Jornadas internacionals d'Estudi sobre els Origensi l'Expansio de l'Orde del Temple a la Corona d'Arago: 1120–1200*, Tarragona, 2010, pp. 55–68; "The Election of the Templar Master Jacques de Molay", in DTT, pp. 21–31; "La Chapelle de Frere Guillaume de Reillanne à Sainte-Eulalie de Larzac", *Bulletin de la Société de l'Histoire et du Patrimoine de l'Ordre de Malte*, 23, 2010, pp. 61–66; "The Amalfitan Hospices in Jerusalem", in E. Farrugia, ed., *Amalfi and Byzantium*, Orientalia Christiana Periodica, 287, Rome, 2010, pp. 105–122; "Juan Fernandez de Heredia and the Compilation of the Aragonese Chronicle of the Morea", in C. Guzzo, ed., *Deus Vult: Miscellanea di Studi sugli Ordini Militari*, 2010, 1, pp. 69–134; "Il Cavallo nell'Ordine dell'Ospedale a Rodi dopo il 1306", in F. Cardini and L. Mantelli, eds., *Cavalli e Cavalieri: Guerra, Gioco, Finzione*, Pisa, 2010, pp. 205–215; "A Jerusalem Indulgence: 1100/3", in H. Nicholson, ed., *On the Margins of Crusading: the Military Orders, the Papacy and the Christian World*, Farnham: Ashgate, 2011, pp. 5–11; *Documents Concerning Cyprus from the Hospital's Rhodian Archives: 1409–1459*, ed. with K. Borchardt and E. Schoffler, Nicosia, 2011, Xli–550 p.; "Rhodes and Cyprus: 1409–1459", ibid., pp. xliii–xciii.

MADDEN, Thomas F., ed., *Crusades: Medieval Worlds in Conflict*, Farnham: Ashgate, 2011.

MATA, Joel Silva Ferreira, "A educação das freiras do Mosteiro de Santos", *VI Encontro sobre Ordens Militares*, Palmela,2011, pp. 557–566; "A Visitação à Igreja Paroquial de Nossa Senhora da Oliveira, de Canha, em 1565", *Revista População e Sociedade*, CEPESE, Porto, 2010, pp. 183–201.

MAYER, Hans Eberhard, "Zur lage der Kirche St. Andreas in Akkon", *Zeitschrift des Deutschen Palästina-Vereins*, 126, 2010, pp. 140–152.

MENACHE, Sophia, "Papal Attempts at a Commercial Boycott of the Muslims during the Crusader Period", *Journal of Ecclesiastical History*, 63–2, 2012, pp. 1–24.

MITCHELL, Piers D., "The spread of disease with the crusades", in B. Nance and E.F. Glaze, eds., *Between Text and Patient: The Medical Enterprise in Medieval and Early Modern Europe*, Florence: Sismel, 2011, pp. 309–330; (with Anastasiou, E., and Syon D.), "Human intestinal parasites in crusader Acre: evidence for migration with disease in the medieval period", *International Journal of Paleopathology*, DOI: 10.1016/j.ijpp.2011.10.005; (with Wagner, T.G.), "The illnesses of King Richard and King Philippe on the Third Crusade: an understanding of arnaldia and leonardie", *Crusades*, 10, 2011, pp. 23–44.

MORTON, Nicholas, "*In subsidium*: The declining contribution of Germany and Eastern Europe to the crusades to the Holy Land, 1187–1291", *German Historical Institute Bulletin*, 2011, pp. 33–66.

MUSARRA, Antonio, "Le vie dell'immaginario: dal Mediterraneo all'Atlantico", in *Pellegrinaggi e monachesimo celtico. Dall'Irlanda alle sponde del Mediterraneo*, ed. Francesco Benozzo and Marina Montesano, Alessandria, Edizioni dell'Orso, 2011, pp. 39–58 (= "Studi Celtici", numero speciale [2010]); *Roma, Santiago, Gerusalemme. Vie e luoghi dell'incontro con Dio*, Catalogo della Mostra, Roma, Palazzo delle Esposizioni, 2–21 novembre 2010 (with Franco Cardini and Marina Montesano), Rimini, Il Cerchio, 2010, pp. 230–73; *Gli Annali di Ogerio Pane (1197–1219) e di Marchisio Scriba (1220–1224)* (with Marina Montesano), Genova, Frilli Editori, 2010, pp. 219; *Gli Annali di Ottobono Scriba*

(1174–1196) (with Marina Montesano), Genova, Frilli Editori, 2010, pp. 144; *La guerra di San Saba*, Pisa: Pacini, 2009, pp. 93.

MYLOD, Liz, ed. with Zsuzsanna Reed Papp, *Postcards from the Edge: European Peripheries in the Middle Ages, Bulletin of International Medieval Research*, vol. 15–16 for 2009–2010, Leeds, 2011, 205 p.

NICHOLSON, Helen, *The Proceedings against the Templars in the British Isles*, Farnham: Ashgate, 2011, vol. 1, *The Latin Edition*: xl + 432 p., vol. 2, *The Translation*: ix + 653 p.; "The role of women in the Military Orders", in *Militiae Christi: Handelingen van de Vereniging voor de Studie over de Tempeliers en de Hospitaalridders vzw*, Jaargang 1, 2010, 210–219; "Have the Knights Templar and the Knights Hospitaller had a positive impact on Wales?", in *The Western Mail*, 24 March 2011, also available online at: http://www.walesonline. co.uk/news/welsh-history/articles/2011/03/22/have-the-knights-templar-and-the-knights-hospitaller-had-a-positive-impact-on-wales-91466-28383041/; "Itinerarium peregrinorum et Gesta Regis Ricardi (Journey of the crusaders and deeds of King Richard)", in *Encyclopedia of the Medieval Chronicle*, ed. Graeme Dunphy, Leiden: Brill, 2010, 1, pp. 890–891.

NICOLAOU-KONNARI, Angel, "Apologists or Critics? The Reign of Peter I of Lusignan (1359–1369) Viewed by Philippe de Mézières (1327–1405) and Leontios Makhairas (ca. 1360/80–after 1432)", in Renate Blumenfeld-Kosinski and Kiril Petkov, eds., *Philippe de Mézières and His Age: Piety and Politics in the Fourteenth Century*, The Medieval Mediterranean 91, Leiden and Boston: Brill, 2012, pp. 359–401; "'A poor island and an orphaned realm…, built upon a rock in the midst of the sea…, surrounded by the infidel Turks and Saracens': The Crusader Ideology in Leontios Makhairas's Greek *Chronicle* of Cyprus", *Crusades*, 10, 2011, pp. 119–145.

NICOLLE, David, *Ottoman Fortifications 1300–1710*, Oxford: Osprey, Fortress 95, 2010, 64 p.; *Cross & Crescent in the Balkans: The Ottoman Conquest of Southeastern Europe*, Barnsley: Pen & Sword, 2010, 256 p.; *Saladin*, Oxford: Osprey, Command series 12, 2011, 64 p.; *The Great Chevauchée. John of Gaunt's Raid on France 1373*, Oxford: Osprey, Raid series 20, 2011, 80 p.; *European Medieval Tactics (1) The Fall and Rise of Cavalry 450–1260*, Oxford: Osprey, Elite 185, 2011, 64 p.; *Late Mamlūk Military Equipment*, Collection Travaux et Études de la Mission Archéologique Syro-Française, Citadelle de Damas (1999–2006): Volume III, IFPO, Damascus, 2011, 396 p.; *The Fourth Crusade 1202–04, The Betrayal of Byzantium*, Oxford: Osprey, Campaign 237, 2011, 96 p.; "Le Guerrier; la guerre au service de la politique", in *Saladin et son Temps. Histoire Antique & Médiévale*, Hors-serie, 25, Décembre 2010, pp 32–35.

O'MALLEY, Gregory John, "The Hospitaller Preceptory of St John in Ards or Castleboy – a preliminary survey of the medieval documentary evidence", *Journal of the Upper Ards Historical Society*, 35, 2011, pp. 19–21.

OMRAN, Mahmoud Said, *Coin of The Middle Ages in Europe* [in Arabic], Dar al-Maarifah al-Gamieya, Alexandria, Egypt, 2011, 375 p.

ORTEGA, Isabelle, "Geoffroy de Briel, un chevalier au grand cœur", *Byzantinistica*, III, Spolète, 2001, pp. 329–341; "Quelques réflexions sur le patrimoine des lignages latins dans la Principauté de Moréeé, *Byzantinistica*, VII, Spolète, 2005, pp. 159–180; "L'inventaire de la bibliothèque de Léonard de Véroli. Témoignages des influences occidentales et orientales dans la principauté de Morée (fin XIIIᵉ siècle)", in *L'autorité de l'écrit au Moyen Âge (Orient–Occident), XXXIXᵉ Congrès de la SHMESP (Le Caire, 30 avril–5 mai 2008)*, Paris, 2009, pp. 196–201; "Permanences et mutations d'une seigneurie dans la principauté de Morée: l'exemple de Corinthe sous l'occupation latine", *Byzantion*, LXXX, 2010, pp. 308–332;

"Les mariages indigènes des nobles moréotes (XIIIᵉ–XVᵉ siècle), ou comment transgresser les frontières établies?", in *Textes et frontières, Actes du colloque International (Nîmes, 9–11 juin 2009)*, ed. J. Raimond, J.-L. Brunel, Nîmes, 2011, pp. 233–254; "La politique de soutien pontifical aux lignages nobiliaires moréotes (XIIIᵉ–XVᵉ siècle)", Avignon SSCLE 7, pp. 185–202.

PARKER, Kenneth Scott, with Christian Jörg, Nina Pleuger, Christofer Zwanzig, "Soziale Konstruktion von Identität. Prozesse christlicher Selbstvergewisserung im Kontakt mit anderen Religionen", in M. Borgolte, J. Dücker, M. Müllerburg and B. Schneidmüller, eds., *Integration und Desintegration der Kulturen im europäischen Mittelalter*, Berlin: Akademie Verlag, 2011, pp. 17–102.

PASTORI RAMOS, Aurelio, "*Las Cruzadas, 1095–1291*", in Gerardo Rodriguez (dir.), *Cuestiones de Historia Medieval*, vol. 1., Buenos Aires: Selectus, 2011, pp. 393–429; "*Navigare necesse, vivere non necesse*? El estudio de la Historia Medieval en el Uruguay, comparado con los países limítrofes. Balance y desafíos", in D. Arauz Mercado, ed., *Pasado, presente y porvenir de las humanidades y las artes*, III, Mexico: AZECME, 2011, pp. 343–358.

PAVIOT, Jacques, "L'idée de croisade à la fin du Moyen Âge", in *Académie des Inscriptions et Belles-Lettres, Comptes rendus des séances de l'année 2009*, Paris: Diffusion De Boccard, 2009, pp. 865–875.

PERRA, Photeine V., "Leo of Armenia Minor and the 'lion' of Venice. Relations between Leo II the Great and the Venetian Republic, at the beginning of the 13th c", Βυζαντιακά, 28, 2009, pp. 263–278 [in Greek]; "The image of the other during the Middle Ages. Aspects of the relations between Greeks and Latins (10th–15th c.)", in *Culture and diversity: We and the others*, Thessaloniki: Ant. Stamoulis Publ., 2011, pp. 106–117 [in Greek].

PERRY, Guy, " 'Scandalia … tam in oriente quam in occidente': the Briennes in East and West, 1213–1221", *Crusades* 10, 2011, pp. 63–77.

PHILLIPS, Jonathan, *Heiliger Kreig: Eine neue Geschichte der Kreuzzüge*, Munich: Deutsche-Verlags-Anstalt, 2011; *Sacri Guerrieri: La straordinaria storia delle crociate*, Bari: Laterza, 2011.

PHILLIPS, C. Matthew, "Crucified with Christ: The Imitation of the Crucified Christ and Crusading Spirituality", in T.F. Madden, J.L. Naus and V. Ryan, eds., *Crusade. Medieval Worlds in Conflict*, Farnham: Ashgate, 2010, pp. 26–33.

PIANA, Mathias, "Die Wehrarchitektur der Kreuzfahrer zwischen Tradition und Innovation: die Frage nach den Einflüssen", *Burgen und Schlösser*, 52/4, 2011, pp. 240–55.

PIMENTA, Maria Cristina, *Santa Joana*, Academia Portuguesa da História, Vila do Conde: Quid Novi, 2011; *D. Isabel de Trastâmara*, Academia Portuguesa da História, Vila do Conde: Quid Novi, 2011; "As Ordens Militares de Avis e de Santiago e o Rei D. Manuel I (1495–1521): algumas notas de reflexão", *Revista de las Órdenes Militares*, Real Consejo de las Órdenes Militares, 6, 2010, pp. 225–274; with Luís Adão da Fonseca and Paula Pinto Costa, "The Papacy and the Crusade in Fifteenth Century Portugal", Avignon SSCLE 7, pp. 141–154; with Luís Adão da Fonseca and Paula Pinto Costa, "Military Orders in the fifteenth century", in J. Mattoso, M. De L. Sousa, B. Vasconcelos and M.J. Branco, eds., *The Historiography of Medieval Portugal (c. 1950–2010)*, Lisbon: Instituto de Estudos Medievais of the New University of Lisboa, 2011, pp. 440–457

POLEJOWSKI, Karol, "Report on Conference Islands and the Military Orders", in: *Zapiski Historyczne*, Torun, t. LXXVI, 2011, z. 3, pp. 161–165; "Ród Brienne w kronice Jana de Joinville (The Briennes in the Chronicle of Jean de Joinville)", in J. Sochacki and A.

Teterycz-Puzio, eds., *A Pomerania ad ultimas terras. Studia ofiarowane Barbarze Popielas-Szultce w 65 rocznicę urodzin i 40 lecie pracy naukowej*, Słupsk, 2011, pp. 427–439.

PORTNYKH, Valentin, with G. Pikov and T. Miakin, *The Deeds of the Franks and the other pilgrims to Jerusalem. Commented Russian translation*, Novosibirsk University Press, 2010, 252 p. [in Russian], located in free access on the site of Moscow State University: http://www.hist.msu.ru/ER/Etext/Franks.pdf; *"De conversione Sarracenorum nulla scriptura loquitur*: Humbert of Romans' Viewpoint on the Perspectives of the Conversion of Saracens", in *Vestnik of the Novosibirsk State University. History and Philology*, 2011, vol. 10, ed. 1: History, pp. 157–164 [in Russian]; "The Symbolism of the Sign of the Cross in the XIIIth Century Crusader Sermons", ibid., vol 10, pp. 13–21 [in Russian].

RICHARD, Jean, "Papacy and Cyprus", Introduction to *Bullarium Cyprium*, ed. Ch. Schabel, Nicosie, I, 2010, pp. 1–65; "Chypre vue par les voyageurs occidentaux au temps de la domination franque", in *Hellenisme et contacts de langue, d'histoire et de culture*, Strasbourg, 2010, pp. 79–86.

RIST, Rebecca, "Pope Gregory IX and the Grant of Indulgences for Military Campaigns in Europe in the 1230s: A Study in Papal Rhetoric", *Crusades* 10, 2011, pp. 79–102; "The Baltic Crusades (11th–15th Century)", in *The Encyclopedia of War*, ed. G. Martel, Oxford, 2011, vol. 1, pp. 231–237.

ROCHE, Jason T., "The Causes of the Crusades to the Holy Land and Egypt, ABC-CLIO Database: *World at War: Understanding Conflict and Society*, 2011; "The Consequences of the Crusades to the Holy Land and Egypt", ibid.; "Surveying the Aspect of the Medieval West Anatolian Town", *Al-Masāq: Islam and the Medieval Mediterranean*, 22 iii (2010), pp. 249–257; "In the Wake of Mantzikert: the First Crusade and the Alexian Reconquest of Western Anatolia", *History: The Journal of the Historical Association*, 94, 2009, pp. 135–153; "Niketas Choniates as a Source for the Second Crusade in Anatolia", in Ebru Altan et al., eds., *Prof. Dr. Işýn Demirkent Anýsýna / In Memory of Prof. Dr. Işýn Demirkent*, Istanbul, 2008, pp. 379–388.

RODRÍGUEZ GARCÍA, José Manuel, "Entre violencia sagrada y guerra sacralizada. Las Cruzadas", with A. Echevarría Arsuaga, in *Guerra Santa. Guerra Justa, Revista de Historia Militar*, special issue, Madrid, 2009, pp. 113–139; "De vueltas con la conexión alemana de la Orden de Calatrava. De Thymau a Bebenhaussen", in *Homenaje al profesor Benito Ruano*, Madrid, SEEM, 2010, t. II, pp. 671–681.

ROGER, Jean-Marc, "De Rhodes à Malte: quelques notes sur Philippe de Villiers l'Isle-Adam" in *De Rhodes à Malte. Le grand maître Philippe de Villiers de L'Isle-Adam (1460–1534) et l'ordre de Malte*, 2004, pp. 28–49; "La fondation de la chapelle du Saint-Nom-de-Jésus en l'église du Temple de Paris par le grand maître Philippe de Villiers l'Isle-Adam", ibid., pp. 54–61; "F. Robert de Saint-Riquier, lieutenant au prieuré d'Aquitaine (1367–1368)", *Revue historique du Centre-Ouest*, t. V, 1er sem. 2006, 2007, pp. 31–64; "Louis Fradin de Belabre, consul et antiquaire, et son *Rhodes of the Knights*, 1908", ibid., pp. 113–155; "Nouveaux regards sur des monuments des Hospitaliers à Rhodes. Bartholino da Castiglione, architecte de Pierre d'Aubusson: monuments dépendant de la langue de France; loge; chapelle Saint-Michel", in *Journal des savants*, 2007, pp. 113–170 and pp. 359–433; "Les sceaux de l'Hôpital en Champagne jusqu'à l'"oppugnation' de Rhodes (1253–1522)", in *Les sceaux, sources de l'histoire médiévale en Champagne, Actes des tables rondes de la Société française d'héraldique et de sigillographie (Troyes, centre universitaire, 14 septembre 2003, Reims, demeure des comtes de Champagne, 9 octobre 2004)*, Paris, 2007 [2008], X, pp. 53–83; "Le prieuré de Saint-Jean-en-l'Île-lez-Corbeil", in *Paris et Ile-de-France*,

Mémoires, t. 60, 2009, pp. 177–291; "La prise de possession par l'Hôpital de maisons du Temple en Poitou et en Bretagne (mai 1313)", *Revue historique du Centre-Ouest*, t. VII, 2ᵉ sem. 2008, 2009, pp. 215–243; "F. Jean de Nanteuil, prieur d'Aquitaine, amiral de France", ibid., pp. 245–286; "F. Jean de Vivonne, prieur d'Aquitaine (1421–1433)", ibid., pp. 287–400; *Nouveaux regards sur des monuments des Hospitaliers à Rhodes (II). Les auberges, le bailliage du commerce, la maison de f. Hieronimo de Canel*. Poitiers, 2010, viii + 149 p.; "Les commandeurs de Troyes au xivᵉ siècle", *Mémoires de la Société académique de l'Aube*, t. CXXXIV, 2010, pp. 145–179; "La réforme de l'Hôpital par Jean XXII: le démembrement des prieurés de Saint-Gilles et de France (21 juillet 1317)", in Nicholson, H., ed., *On the Margins of Crusading: The Military Orders, the Papacy and the Christian World*, Farnham: Ashgate, 2011, pp. 101–137; "Les biens de l'Hôpital au bailliage de Troyes en 1333: la prisée de 1333, la déclaration de Coulours de 1338", *Mémoires de la Société académique de l'Aube*, t. CXXXV, 2011, pp. 243–297; "Service de Dieu, service du prince. Le lignage des Giresme, Giresme, chevaliers du prieuré de France (xivᵉ–xviᵉ siècles)", in *Hommes, cultures et sociétés à la fin du Moyen Âge*. Liber discipulorum *en l'honneur de Philippe Contamine*, 2012, pp. 315–340.

Santi, Francesco, "Dante in gara con la Bibbia?", in *La Bibbia di Dante. Esperienza Mistica, Profezia e teologia biblica in Dante*, Atti del Convegno internazionale di Studi Ravenna, 7 novembre 2009, a cura di Giuseppe Ledda, Bologna, Longo, 2011, pp. 217–232; *Gabriele M. Allegra, Scintille dantesche. Antologia dai diari*, introduzione, edizione e commento, Bologna, Edizioni Dehoniane, 2011, 395 p.: "L'insegnamento di Claudio Leonardi", in *L'esperienza intellettuale di Claudio Leonardi*, Firenze, Sismel, 2011, pp. 31–41 (and introduction to the book, pp. IX–X); *L'età metaforica. Figure di Dio e letteratura latina medievale da Gregorio Magno a Dante*, Spoleto, Fondazione Centro Italiano di Studi sull'Alto Medioevo, Uomini e mondi medievali 25, 2011, xviii + 404 p., fig. 1; "L'insegnamento di Claudio Leonardi", in *Il rischio della fede nell'epoca delle idolatrie* = *Parola e Tempo*, Annale dell'Istituto Superiore di Scienze religiose A. Maravelli, vol. 9, 2010, pp. 402–407, Rimini, Pazzini Editore, 2010; "Un'interpretazione di Dante, nello specchio delle lacrime", in *Studi per Franco Cardini*, pp. 554–570; "Domenico di Caleruega, Tommaso d'Aquino e la profezia nell'Ordine dei Predicatori", *Bollettino delle suore domenicane Unione S. Tommaso d'Aquino*, 39, 1, 2010, pp. 47–55.

Sarnowsky, Juergen, *Die Johanniter. Ein geistlicher Ritterorden in Mittelalter und Neuzeit*, München, Beck Wissen, 2011, 128 p.; *On the Military Orders in Medieval Orders in Medieval Europe. Structures and Perceptions*, Variorum Collected Studies Series, 992, Farnham: Ashgate 2011, xii + 360 p. (with three articles not printed before and four articles newly translated into English); "Die Hanse und der Deutsche Orden. Eine ertragreiche Beziehung", in Gisela Graichen, Rolf Hammel-Kiesow, *Die deutsche Hanse. Eine heimliche Super-macht*, Reinbek bei Hamburg: Rowohlt 2011, pp. 163–81; "Herausforderung und Schwäche: die Johanniter und die Anfänge der äußeren Bedrohung von Rhodos, 1428–1464", in *Ordines militares. Yearbook for the Study of the Military Orders*, 16, 2011, pp. 125–140; editor of *Ordines militares. Yearbook for the Study of the Military Orders*, 16, 2011.

Shotten-Hallel, Vardit, "A Graffito of a Nineteenth-Century Armed Ship from Akko, Israel", with Y. Kahanov and D. Cvikel, *The Mariner's Mirror*, 94.4, 2008, London, Cambridge University Press, pp. 388–404; "Reconstructing the Hospitaller Church of St. John, Acre, with the Help of Gravier d'Ortières' Drawing of 1685–87", *Crusades*, 9, 2010, pp. 185–198.

Sweetenham, Carol, *The Chanson d'Antioche: an Old French account of the First Crusade*, trans. with Susan Edgington, Farnham: Ashgate, 2011.

Throop, Susanna, *Crusading as an Act of Vengeance, 1095–1216*, Farnham: Ashgate, 2011, 232 p.

Touati, François-Olivier, "Mahomet, Charlemagne et la Corse : quels enjeux entre Francs et Musulmans au haut Moyen Âge ?", in Michel Vergé-Franceschi (dir.), *La Corse, la Méditerranée et le monde musulman*, Douzièmes Journées Universitaires de Bonifacio, Ajaccio, 2011, pp. 89–106; "Croisades: la guerre des médecins", *L'Histoire*, n° 367, September 2011, pp. 76–80; review of T.G. Wagner, *Die Seuchen der Kreuzzüge. Krankheit und Krankenpflege au den bewaffneten Pilgerfahrten ins Heilige Land*, Würzburg: Königshausen & Neumann (Würzburger Medizinhistorische Forschungen, 7), 2009, in *Revue de l'Institut français d'Histoire en Allemagne*, 2011, pp. 367–369.

Tsurtsumia, Mamuka, "The Evolution of Splint Armour in Georgia and Byzantium: Lamellar and Scale Armour in the 10th–12th Centuries", *Byzantina Symmeikta*, 21, 2011, pp. 65–99; "The Helmet from the Wawel Royal Castle Museum and its Place in the Evolution of Oriental Helmet", *Acta Militaria Mediaevalia*, 7, 2011, pp. 79–103.

Tyerman, Christopher, ed., *The Debate on the Crusades*, Manchester University Press, 2011, 260 p.; trad., *Chronicles of the First Crusade*, London, Penguin Classics, 2011.

Upton, Todd P., "*Hostis Antiquus* Resurgent: A Reconfigured Jerusalem in Twelfth-Century Latin Sermons about Islam", *Quidditas*, 32, Dec., 2011; online journal, pp. 30–71.

Vaivre, Jean-Bernard, de, "Notes sur la commanderie de Bellecroix (Saône-et-Loire) du XIIIᵉ au XVᵉ siècle", *Bulletin de la Société nationale des Antiquaires de France*, 2009, [published in 2012]; "L'Ordre de Saint-Jean de Jérusalem dans le Dodécanèse", *Archivum Heraldicum*, II, 2011; with L. Vissière, "*Car je vueil que soit ung chef d'euvre*, instructions de Guillaume Caoursin pour réaliser le manuscrit enluminé de ses œuvres (vers 1483)", *L'Art de l'Enluminure*, 40, mars–avril–mai 2012; "L'enfeu du tombeau de Pierre d'Aubusson, grand maître de Rhodes", *Monuments Piot*, 90, 2011; "Les canons de Rhodes offerts à Napoléon III", *Cahiers de la Villa Kérylos*, 22 (Actes du XXIᵉ colloque de la Villa Kérylos, 8–9 octobre 2010, *Histoire et archéologie méditerranéennes sous Napoléon III*), éd. A. Laronde (†), P. Toubert, J. Leclant, Paris: De Boccard, 2011.

Weber, Benjamin, "La bulle Cantate Domino (4 février 1442) et les enjeux éthiopiens du concile de Florence", *Mélanges de l'École Français de Rome*, CXXII-2, 2010, pp. 435–443; "Existovaly v 15. století papežské projekty křížoúych uýprav?" ["Were there any papal crusading projects in the fifteenth century?"], in P. Sokup and J. Svatek, eds., *Křížové uýpravy v pozdním středověku*, Prague, 2010, pp. 34–46.

Wilskman, Juho, "The Campaign and Battle of Pelagonia 1259", Βυζαντινός Δόμος, 17–18, 2009–2010, pp. 131–174.

2. Recently completed theses

Anckaer, Jan, *The political and economical relations between Belgium and the Ottoman Empire (1830–1865)*, PhD, 2011.

Barbé, Hervé, *Le château de Safed et son territoire durant la période des croisades*, PhD, Hebrew U of Jerusalem, directed by Prof. Benjamin Z. Kedar and Nicolas Faucherre, 2011.

Baydal, Vicent, *Els fonaments del pactisme valencià. Sistemes fiscals, relacions de poder i identitat col·lectiva en el regne de Valencia (c. 1250 – c. 1365)*, PhD in Medieval History awarded with a European Doctorate Certificate, Pompeu Fabra University of Barcelona.

Bishop, Adam, *Criminal law the development of the assizes of the crusader Kingdom of Jerusalem in the twelfth century*, University of Toronto, 2011.

BURKIEWICZ, Łukasz, *Polityczna rola Królestwa Cypru w XIV-wiecznej Europie [The Political role of the kingdom of Cyprus in the Fourteenth Century Europe]*, PhD, Jagiellonian University, 2011.

CALZADO SOBRINO, *Maria Pilar, Tumbo Menor de Castilla y Tumbo Menor de León: Estúdio histórico, codicológico, diplomático y paleográfico de las primeras recopilaciones documentales de la Orden Militar de Santiago*. PhD, Universidad de Castilla La Mancha, 2011.

CARR, Michael, *Motivations and Response to Crusades in the Aegean: c.1300–1350*, PhD, Royal Holloway, University of London, 2011, supervised by Prof. Jonathan Harris.

COSTA, Diana Daniela Ladeira da, *As práticas assistenciais da Ordem Militar e Religiosa do Hospital*, MA, Faculty of Arts, Porto University, 2011, supervised by Pr Paula Pinto Costa.

CIUDAD RUIZ, Manuel, *Los freiles clérigos de la Orden de Calatrava en la Edad Media. Organización y forma de vida*, PhD, Universidad de Castilla La Mancha, 2011.

FROUMIN, Robin, *Continuation or non-continuation of Pilgrimage in the Holy Land; Churches from the Crusader Period built on the remains of Byzantine Churches*, MA, Haifa University, supervised by Professor Adrian Boas, 2011.

HENRIQUES, Pedro Nuno Medeiros de, *Os Portugueses e as cruzadas (séculos XII–XIV)*, MA, Faculty of Arts, Porto University, 2011, supervised by Pr Paula Pinto Costa.

PASTORI RAMOS, Aurelio, *La idea de guerra santa en la obra de Bernardo de Claraval*, PhD, Facultad de Filosofía y Letras, Universidad de Buenos Aires, 2011.

PORTNYKH, Valentin, *Le Traité d'Humbert de Romans, O.P., De la prédication de la sainte croix contre les Sarrasins (XIIIe siècle). Analyse historique et édition du texte*, PhD, Université Lumière Lyon 2 (France) and Novosibirsk State University (Russia), supervised by Nicole Bériou and Gennady Pikov, 2011.

SIMSONS, Raitis, *Senprūšu sabiedrības sociālo un politisko struktūru atainojums Elbingas vārdnīcā [The representation of the social and political structures of Old Prussian society in Elbing Vocabulary]*, MA, University of Latvia, supervised by Andris Šnē.

TSOUGARAKIS, Nickiphoros I., *The Western Religious Orders in Medieval Greece*, PhD, Institute for Medieval Studies, University of Leeds, 2008.

WILSKMAN, Juho, *Bysanttilaisten ja Akhaian ruhtinaskunnan väliset sotatoimet 1259–83: Tapaustutkimus myöhäis-bysanttilaisesta sodankäynnistä [War between Byzantines and the Principality of Achaia 1259–83: A Case Study in Late Byzantine Warfare]*, MA, University of Helsinki, 2007.

YOLLES, Julian, *The Rhetoric of Simplicity: Faith and Rhetoric in Peter Damian*, M.A., Theology, Utrecht University, 2009.

3. Papers read by members of the Society and others

ANTAKI-MASSON, Patricia, "Archéologie, étude du bâti et patrimoine mobilier", "Ora est hora: un cadran solaire au monastère Notre Dame de Balamand", "Un legs des tailleurs de pierre de Belmont: que nous révèlent les marques lapidaires?", at: the seminar *Le monastère Notre Dame de Balamand*, Balamand University (Lebanon), December 2010.

BALARD, Michel, "Voltaire et les croisades", communication présentée au 136e Congrès des Sociétés historiques et scientifiques, Perpignan, mai 2011; "La piraterie dans la Méditerranée médiévale", conclusions du colloque *Piraterie im Mittelmeerraum*, Bochum, mai 2011; "Amalfi nel Mediterraneo medieval", rapport présenté au colloque international *Interscambi socio-culturali ed economici fra le città marinare d'Italia e l'Occidente dagli osservatori mediterranei*, Amalfi, mai 2011.

BELLOMO, Elena, "Islands as strongholds for the defense of Christendom: The case of the Order of Our Lady of Betlehem", at: *Islands and the Military Orders*, Rhodes, 28–29 April 2011.

BIRD, Jessalynn, "The Role of Prophecy during the Fifth Crusade and the Crusade of Frederick II, at: Meeting of the Medieval Academy of America, 2012; "Preaching the Fifth Crusade: The Sermons of BN nouv. acq. lat. 999", at: ICMS, Kalamazoo, 2012.

BONNEAUD, Pierre, "Negociations and warfare: The Hospitallers of Rhodes around and after the fall of Constantinople (1440–1480)", at: *Colloquia Torunensia Historica*, XVIth Conference: The Military Orders in War and Peace, Torun, Sept. 2011.

BORCHARDT, Karl, "Hans Prutz Revisited: On the Causes for the Suppression of the Templars", at: Eighth Biennial Conference of the Australian and New Zealand Association for Medieval and Early Modern Studies, Dunedin / New Zealand, 2011 February 2–5; "A Fifteenth-Century Innovation: Humanistic Script on Hospitaller Rhodes", at: IMO.

BUTTIGIEG, Emanuel, "The Maltese Islands and the Religious Culture of the Hospitallers: Isolation and Connectivity c.1540s–c.1690s", at: IMO.

BYSTED, Ane L., "The Preaching of the Cross in Denmark and Sweden at the time of the Fifth Crusade" at: SCCLE 8 Caceres.

CARR, Michael, "Angevin Attempts to Re-establish the Latin Empire of Constantinople", at: the conference *Between Worlds: The Age of the Angevines*, Targoviste, Romania, October 2011; "The Hospitallers of Rhodes and their Alliances Against the Turks", at IMO; "Crusade and Commercial Exchange Between Christians and Muslims in the Aegean", at: *Late Medieval History Seminar*, Institute of Historical Research, London, March 2011; "The Influence of Papal Policy on the Italian Merchants and Turkish Maritime Emirates in the Aegean: 1300–1350", at: the conference *Union in Separation: Trading Diasporas in the Eastern Mediterranean (1200–1700)*, University of Heidelberg, February 2011; "Turkish Pirates and Italian Merchants in the Fourteenth-Century Aegean", at: History Department Seminar Series, Royal Holloway, November 2010; "Trade or Crusade? The Genoese, Venetians and Crusades against the Turks: 1300–1350", at: *Crusades and the Latin East Seminar*, Institute of Historical Research, May 2010.

CASSIDY-WELCH, Megan, "Emotion and memory at the tomb of King Louis IX of France", at: *Emotions in the Medieval and Early Modern World*, Australian Research Council Centre for the History of Emotions conference, University of Western Australia, June 2011; "O Damietta: Egypt and thirteenth-century war memory", at: *Places of Memory in Medieval and Early Modern Europe* symposium, State Library of Victoria, Sept–Oct. 2011.

CHEVALIER, Marie-Anna, "Aperçu des caractéristiques défensives des forteresses des ordres militaires en Arménie" at: *Terrae sur "Les châteaux, d'ici et d'ailleurs"*, Université de Toulouse-Le Mirail, UMR 5608 Traces (France), 19 février 2010; Organisation de la journée d'études sur *La fin de l'ordre du Temple*, Université Montpellier 3, France, Introduction de la rencontre et communication intitulée "De la prise d'Acre au procès chypriote: les conditions de la survie et du déclin des templiers en Orient", 28 janvier 2011; "La perception du Caucase à travers les récits des voyageurs occidentaux (XIIIe–XIVe siècle)", at: Colloque international *L'Europe et le Caucase – Relations interrégionales et la question de l'identité*, l'Université d'Etat Ilia, Tbilissi (Géorgie), *27–31 octobre 2011*.

CHRISSIS, Nikolaos, "Re-integrating the European Middle Ages in Greek university history teaching: the crusades as a case-study" [in Greek], at: the Academic Workshop *Medieval and*

Early Modern European History in Greek Universities: Research and Teaching, University of Crete, 25–27 November 2011; "Of heretics and Christian brothers: Pope Gregory IX (1227–41) and the Greek East", at: 22nd International Congress of Byzantine Studies, Sofia, 22–27 August 2011.

CHRISTIE, Niall, "The Crusades: What were they and why are they still relevant?", at: Simon Fraser University Seniors Forum, Simon Fraser University, Vancouver, Canada. Video available on the Internet at: <http://www.sfu.ca/cstudies/seniors/forums0911.htm>, September 2011; "Imaginary Journeys to the Lands of the Franks: Some Instances from the *Arabian Nights*", at: 20th Colloquium on the *History of Egypt and Syria in the Fatimid, Ayyubid and Mamluk Eras*, University of Ghent, Belgium, May 2011.

CIPOLLONE, Giulio, "Il *signum* dei Trinitari. Al tempo di crociate e gihad: originalità iconografica e innovazione estetica", at: Congresso internazionale *Colori e significati. Una 'croce disarmata' tra crociata e gihad*, Roma, Pontificia Università Urbaniana, 26–28 Gennaio 2011.

CLAVERIE, Pierre-Vincent, "Notes sur l'onomastique franque durant les croisades et quelques énigmes prosopographiques", at: 20th Colloquium on the *History of Egypt and Syria in the Fāṭimid, Ayyūbid and Mamlūk Eras* (CHESFAME), Ghent University, 13 May 2011; "L'ordre du Temple dans l'Europe des croisades (1120–1312)", 30 September 2011 at: the I Colóquio internacional *Cister, os Templários e a Ordem de Cristo*, Tomar (Portugal); "Un siècle et demi de relations barcelono-chypriotes (1291–1435)", Centre de Recherches Historiques sur les Sociétés Méditerranéennes (CRHiSM), Université de Perpignan, 15 December 2011.

CONNELL, Charles W., "The Erotic Nature of the Antichrist in 12th and 13th century Europe",18th Annual ACMRS Conference in Tempe, AZ, 16–18 February 2012.

COUREAS, Nicholas S., "Foreign Soldiers in 13th and 14th Century Cyprus according to the Chronicles" at: The Medieval Chronicle, VIth International Congress, University of Pécs, Hungary 25–29 July 2011; "Greeks for Rome: The Split in the Greek Church caused by the Latin Conquest of Cyprus" at: The 22nd International Congress of Byzantine Studies, University of Sofia, Bulgaria 22–27 August 2011; "Participants or Mediators: The Hospitallers and the Wars involving 15th century Lusignan Cyprus" at: OM 17.

EDGINGTON, Susan, "Regulations for the administration of the hospital of St John in Jerusalem, c1180", at: *International Network for the History of Hospitals conference*, University of Evora, Portugal, 8 April 2011; "The capture of Acre, 1104, and Baldwin I's conquest of the littoral", at: *Crusades and the Latin East Seminar*, IHR London, 13 June 2011; "Why Did the Franks of Outremer Express such Admiration of Oriental Medicine?", at: Second Biennial Conference of the Society for the Medieval Mediterranean, Southampton University, 5 July 2011; "The *Gesta Francorum Iherusalem expugnantium* of Bartolf of Nangis", at: Medieval Chronicle Society Congress, University of Pécs, Hungary, 26 July 2011.

EKDAHL, Sven, "Neue Forschungen über die Schlacht bei Grunwald/Tannenberg", at: Institute of History, Adam Mickiewicz-University, Poznań, 27 April, 2010; "Eine verlorene Schlacht und deren Bewältigung", at: *Grunwald/Žalgiris/Tannenberg. 600 Jahre historischer Mythos*, Societas Jablonoviana, Leipzig, 7 May, 2010; "Das politische Umfeld und die Schlacht von Tannenberg", at: *Tannenberg 1410, Amt des Hochmeisters*, Wien, 20 May, 2010; "Neue Forschungen über die Schlacht bei Tannenberg 1410", Deutschordensmuseum, Bad Mergentheim, 25 June, 2010; "Probleme und Perspektive der Grunwaldforschung", at: *Grunwald, Tannenberg, Žalgiris 1410–2010*, Malbork (Marienburg), 20 September, 2010; "Das politische Umfeld und die Schlacht von Tannenberg", at: Conveniat oft the Teutonic Order's Komturei "An Elbe und Ostsee", Łagów (Poland), 2 October, 2010;

"Quellenaussagen über die Taktik in der Tannenbergschlacht", at: *Žalgiris-Grunwald-Tannenberg 1410: Krieg und Frieden im späten Mittelalter*, University of Vilnius, 23 October, 2010; "1410 – Die Schlacht bei Tannenberg und ihre Folgen für das Deutschordensland", at: Kulturhistorisches Seminar der Landsmannschaft Ostpreußen, Bad Pyrmont, 9 November, 2010; "Neue Forschungen über die Schlacht bei Tannenberg 1410", at: Westpreußisches Bildungswerk Berlin-Brandenburg, Berlin, 2 December, 2010; "Die Grunwaldschlacht 1410 im Spiegel neuerer Forschungen", at: Institute of History, University of Warsaw, 7 March, 2011; "Battlefield Archaeology at Tannenberg (Grunwald, Žalgiris): Physical Remains of the Defeat of the Teutonic Order in Prussia in 1410", at: 6th International Fields of Conflict Conference, University of Osnabrück, 17 April, 2011; "Der erste Thorner Frieden (1411) im Spiegel der Söldnerfrage", at: OM17; "Jan Matejko's Gemälde 'Die Schlacht bei Grunwald (Tannenberg) 1410", Entstehung-Symbolik-Rezeption, at: *Die Landschaft nach der Schlacht. Jan Matejkos Bild "Schlacht bei Tannenberg" als politisches Symbol*, Deutsches Kulturforum östliches Europa, Vertretung des Freistaates Sachsen beim Bund, Berlin, 6 October, 2011; "Bronzezeitliche Petroglyphen mit Waffendarstellungen in Schweden", at: Ars et Arma. 3rd Scholars in Arms Meeting, University of Łódź, 2 December, 2011.

FAVREAU-LILIE, Marie-Luise, "Machtstrukturen und Historiographie im Koenigreich Jerusalem: Die Chronik Wilhelms von Tyrus", at: *Macht und Spiegel der Macht. Herrschaft in Europa im 12.und 13. Jahrhundert vor dem Hintergrund der Chronistik*, Internationale Tagung, Deutsches Historischen Institut Warschau/Historisches Seminar der Universitaet Hamburg, Warszawa, 10–13 March 2011; "Strategien der mittelalterlichen Seerepubliken im Kampf gegen Seeraub: Zur Bedeutung von Diplomatie und Rechtsbildung", at: *Piraterie im Mittelmeerraum-Gefaehrdete Konnektivitaet [Piracy in the Mediterranean – Endangered Connectivity]*, Internationale Tagung, Zentrum für Mittelmeerstudien (ZMS) an der Ruhr-Universitaet, Bochum, 5–7 May, 2011.

FOREY, Alan J., "The Participation of Military Orders in Truces with Muslims in the Holy Land and Spain during the Twelfth and Thirteenth Centuries", at: OM17.

FRANKE, Daniel, "England and the Crusade in the 'Long' Fourteenth Century: Lay Response and Impact", at: *The Crusades, Islam and Byzantium: An Interdisciplinary Workshop and Conference*, London, July 2011.

GABRIELE, Matthew, "The Chosen Peoples of the 11th & 21st Centuries", at: *Revisiting the "Judeo-Christian" Tradition*, Virginia Tech, October 2011; "Reorienting the Medieval West around the Millennium: Thinking from Past to Future", at: Symposium *The Making of Religion? Re-Describing Religious Change in Pre-Modern Europe*, Harvard University, April 2011.

GEORGIOU, Constantinos, "Propagating the Hospitallers' *Passagium*: Crusade Preaching and Liturgy in 1308–1309", at IMO.

GEORGIOU, Stavros G., "The Saved Testimonies fot the Byzantine Karpasia (4th–12th Centuries)" [in Greek], at: 2nd Scientific Congress for Karpasia, Limassol, Cyprus, 19 June 2011.

HALL, Martin, "Translating Caffaro", at: IMC Leeds, 2011.

HAMILTON, Bernard, "An Anglican view of the Crusades: Thomas Fuller's The Historie of the Holy Warre", at: The Ecclesiastical History Society's summer Conference, Oxford, August 2011.

HARRIS, Jonathan, "The role of Greek émigrés in East–West cultural communication before and after the fall of Constantinople", at: International Conference on *Mediterranean Cities: Civilisation and Development*, Institut d'Estudis Catalans and Institut Europeu de la Mediterrània, Barcelona, November 2011; "Constantinople as City State, 1403–1453", at: IMC Leeds, 2011; "Victims and Victors: The Historiography of Byzantium and the Crusades" (plenary lecture), at: *The Crusades, Islam and Byzantium*, German Historical Institute and Institute of Historical Research, London, July 2011; "The Antiquary, the Scribe and the Pirate: the Perils of Ancient Greek in fifteenth-century England", First Annual Classical Legacy Lecture, Center for Interdisciplinary Renaissance Studies, University of Massachusetts, December 2010.

HESLOP, Michael, "Fear and Ingenuity in the Byzantine Dodecanese: the Flight to safety on Tilos (c. 650–1306)", at: The XLIV Spring Symposium of the Society for the Promotion of Byzantine Studies, Newcastle University, 8–10 April 2011; "Byzantine Defences in the Dodecanese Islands: planned or improvised?", at: 22nd International Congress of byzantine Studies, Sofia, 22–27 August 2011.

HOWE, John, "Attaining the Piligrim's Goal: Urban II's Spiritual reward for the First Crusade", at: *Crusades: Medieval Worlds in Conflict*, Saint Louis University, 17–20 February 2010.

JOSSERAND, Philippe, "L'Espagne et la croisade: le mot et la chose", at: *Le terme "croisade" et ses emplois dans la péninsule Ibérique (XIIIe–XIVe siècles). La naissance d'une catégorie langagière*, Journée d'études du 12 janvier 2012 à l'Univeristé de Toulouse-II Le Mirail; "Las cruzadas de Tierra Santa y las órdenes militares en las crónicas reales latinas de Castilla y León (siglos XII–XIII)", at: Congreso internacional para el aniversario de la batalla de Las Navas de Tolosa, Jaén, 10–12 avril 2012.

KEDAR, Benjamin Z., "True Cross, miraculous fire, Holy Resurrection", at Notre Dame University, 7 April 2011; "The harbour chain in Mediterranean history", at : the conference on the *Mediterranean as a cultural bridge*, Haifa University, 5 May 2011; "Cultural persistence despite total political collapse", at: the annual conference of the World History Association, Beijing, July 8, 2011.

KOLIA-DERMITZAKI, Athina, "Holy war" in Byzantium twenty years later: a question of term definition and interpretation, at: *Die Kriegsideologie der Byzantiner zwischen römischer Reichsidee und christlicher Religion*, Vienna 19–21 May 2011.

LAPINA, Elizabeth, "Gaming and Gambling on the Crusades", at: IMC Leeds, 2011; "The Narratives of Intervention of Saints in the Battle of Antioch: the Norman Background", at: Institute of Historical Research (IHR), University of London, January 2011.

LEWIS, Kevin James, "Countess Hodierna of Tripoli: from crusader politician to 'princesse lointaine'", at: *Shield Maidens and Sacred Mothers*, Cardiff University, 7 October 2011; "The Gold of Tripoli: the economy of the County of Tripoli in the early thirteenth century", at: IMC Leeds, 2011; "Tripoli and Transnationalism: networks linking East and West in the age of the Crusades", at: *History Lab Annual Conference 2011*, Institute of Historical Research, London, 22 June 2011; "A Templar's belt: the oral and sartorial transmission of memory and myth in the Order of the Temple", at: *Myths, Legends and Folklore*, Cardiff University, 17 May 2011; "Shifting Borders: The ambiguous status of the county of Tripoli", at: *Graduate Medieval History Conference*, University of Oxford, 18 March 2011.

LIGATO, Giuseppe, "Nicola de Hanapes, patriarca di Gerusalemme e legato pontificio, alla caduta di S. Giovanni d'Acri", at: *Legati, delegati e impresa d'Oltremare*, Convegno internazionale di studio, Università Cattolica, Milano, 9–11 marzo 2011; "Guglielmo il Vecchio alle crociate, in Ranieri di Monferrato e i poteri signorili tra Novi e Oltregiogo", Atti della giornata di studi, Novi Ligure, 17 settembre 2011.

LUCHITSKAYA, Svetlana, "Treason and traitors as mirrored by the chansons de geste of the XII–XIIIth cc.", at: Russian Academy of Sciences, Moscow, April 2011; "The *Assizes of*

Jerusalem and the judicial practice of the XIIIth century in the Latin kingdom of Jerusalem", at: Institut für europaische Rechtsgeschichte, Frankfurt am Main, April 2010.

MADDEN, Thomas F., "Rivers of Blood: A New Analysis of the Conquest of Jerusalem during the First Crusade in 1099", Keynote Address at: Il Simposio Internacional de Estudios Medievales, Gabriela Mistral University, Santiago, Chile, 29 September 2011; "The Crusades and the Modern World", at: Escuela Militar, Las Condes, Chile, 28 September 2011; "The Life, Death, and Resurrection of the Knights Templar", at: Centro de Estudios Medievales, Gabriela Mistral University, Santiago Chile, 27 September 27, 2011; "Spouse of the Sea: The Republic of Venice and the Crusades", at: Escuela Naval de Valparaíso, Valparaíso, Chile, September 26, 2011; "Excavating a Venetian Version of the Fourth Crusade", at: IMC Leeds, 2011; "Changing Perspectives on the Fall of Constantinople in 1204", Keynote Address at: *The Crusades, Islam, and Byzantium: An Interdisciplinary Conference*, German Historical Institute in London, 8–9 July, 2011; "Competing Narratives of the Fourth Crusade in Late Medieval Venice", at: ICMS Kalamazoo 2011; "Did the Plunder of the Fourth Crusade Include the Shroud of Turin?", at: 86th Meeting of the Medieval Academy of America, Arizona State University, 16 April 2011.

MILITZER, Klaus, Kommunikations- und Verständigungsprobleme vor und nach der Schlacht bei Tannenberg; Bildung und Ausbildungsstand der Brüder im Deutschen Orden während des Mittelalters; Der Deutsche Orden in seinen Balleien im Deutschen Reich; Das Echo der Schlacht bei Tannenberg in deutschen Städten und auf deutschen Reichstagen.

MITCHELL, Piers D., "Trauma in the crusades and its medical treatment", at: Second International Conference on Biomedical Sciences and Methods in Archaeology, Kusadasi, Turkey, 15–18 September 2011; "Human intestinal parasites in Acre: stories from a crusader cesspool", at: 13th Annual Conference of the British Association for Biological Anthropology and Osteoarchaeology, University of Edinburgh, 2–4 September 2011.

MUSARRA, Antonio, "Memorie di Terrasanta. Reliquie, traslazioni, culti e devozioni a Genova tra XII e XIV secolo", at: *Come a Gerusalemme. Evocazioni, riproduzioni e imitazioni dei luoghi santi tra Medioevo ed Età Moderna*, XV Seminario del Centro Internazionale di studi "La Gerusalemme di San Vivaldo", Montaione, 30 June–2 July 2011.

NICHOLSON, Helen J., "The Knights Hospitaller in Wales", at: the Planed Heritage Day, Stackpole Centre, Pembrokeshire, 6 November 2010; "'La Damoisele del chastel': women's role in the defence and functioning of castles in medieval writing from the twelfth to the fourteenth centuries", at: *Medieval Frontiers at War*, 8–14 November 2010, University of Extremadura, Cáceres, Spain; "The historiography of the Templars' trial", at: Monmouth School, 8 February 2011; "Heroes and villains? Christians and Muslims in crusade narratives", at: 2011 Staff-student colloquium, Gregynog, 1 March 2011; "Treading on sensitive toes: communicating the history of the Knights Templar and crusades outside the University environment", at: the "Voice of Humanities" day conference at the Graduate Centre, Cardiff University, 17 March 2011; "The Knights Hospitaller", at: the Church of St Augustine, Hackney, 17 May 2011; "The Hospitallers' and Templars' involvement in warfare on the frontiers of the British Isles" at: OM16; "The Third Crusade", at: Historical Association, Shrewsbury School History Society, 14 October 2011.

NICOLAOU-KONNARI, Angel,"The Cypriot Dialect during the Latin Rule", at: *Cypriot Dialect: A Cultural Heritage, Celebrations of the European Day of Languages*, The European Commission Delegation in Cyprus, Department of Byzantine and Modern Greek Studies, University of Cyprus, Nicosia, 13 October 2011; "Melodramatic Perceptions of History: Caterina Cornaro Goes to the Opera", at: Cyprus Music Institute, *Second Biennial Euro-*

Mediterranean Music Conference, University of Cyprus and University of Nicosia, 8–10 September 2011; "Cultural Interaction and Ethnic Identity in Lusignan Cyprus", *Byzantium Without Borders*, 22nd Congress of Byzantine Studies, Round Table "Cyprus Between East and West", Sofia, 22–27 August 2011; "Chypre médiévale (1191–1571), lieu de production et d'inspitation musicale", Projet de recherche ms Torino J.II. 9, Table Ronde, Université Paul Valéry, Montpellier III, 23 May 2011;

NICOLLE, David, "'Take shavings of rawhide': Mamluk examples of al-Tarsusi's style of hardened leather helmet from the Citadel of Damascus", at: the 20th CHESFAME Colloquy, Ghent, May 2011; "Myth, Tradition and Reality in the Presentation of Middle Eastern Military Equipment at the Time of the Crusades", at: *L'Historiographie de la guerre dans le Proche-Orient médiéval (Xe–XVe siècles)*, IFPO, Damascus, 3–4 December 2010.

OMRAN, Mahmoud Said, "Mongol Paper Money", at: The Forth International Symposium of Printing and Publishing in The Language and Countries of The Middle East, Biblotheca Alexandria-Egypt, 27–29 September 2011.

PARK, Danielle, "Behold here are two swords; is it enough?: Defending Those Left Behind – the Co-operation of Papal and Secular Crusade Protection in Practice", at: *The Crusades, Islam and Byzantium Workshop*, IHR, London, July 2011; "Diplomats and Diplomatic: New Directions in the Use of Charter Evidence – the Concept and Consequences of the Crusades in the Charters of Crusade Regents", IMC Leeds, July 2011; "'To Act After the Manner of the King': French Royal Crusade-Regencies – the Practice and Practicalities of their Power", at: Crusades and the Latin East Seminar, IHR, London, 21 November 2011.

PARKER, Kenneth Scott, "The Indigenous Christians of Bilād al-Shām and Egypt and the Crusade of Alexandria, 1365", at: *The Crusades, Islam and Byzantium Workshop*, IHR, London, July 2011; "Coptic Language and Identity in Fatimid and Ayyūbid Egypt", at: *Cultures, Communities, and Conflicts in the Medieval Mediterranean*, Society for the Medieval Mediterranean, University of Southampton, July 2011; "The indigenous Christian minorities of Ayyūbid Egypt and Syria in the thirteenth century", at: History Colloquium, Byzantinistik, Johannes Gutenberg Universität Mainz, 14 June 2011; "Coptic Views of Muslims and Arabs in the Middle Ages", at: *The European Middle Ages in Global Entanglement*, SPP1173: Integration und Desintegration der Kulturen im europäischen Mittelalter, Berlin, 25–28 May 2011; "The Indigenous Christians of the Near East: the Black Death, the Rescript of Sultan aṣ-Ṣāliḥ Ṣāliḥ, and the Crusade of King Peter of Cyprus (1347–67)", at: Crusades Centre, University of Cardiff, 5 April 2011; "'The enemy is in your midst, under your rule – it is the Christians'.The indigenous Christian minorities of the Bilād al-Shām and Egypt between the Fifth and the Eighth Crusades (1218–70)", at: *Crusades Seminar*, IHR, London, 7 March 2011; "The Copts of Egypt in the 1320s according to European Travelers", at: *Coptic Workshop*, Johannes Gütenberg Universität Mainz, Department of Byzantine Studies, 1 February 2011.

PERRA, Photeine V., "Aspects of the relations between the Hospitallers Knights of Rhodes and the Republic of Venice: Contacts and collaboration during the Second Venetian Ottoman War (1499–1502/3)", at: IMO.

PHILLIPS, Jonathan, "Holy Warriors: Christian and Muslim Views of the Crusades", at: St Bonifatiuscollege, Utrecht, November 2011.

PHILLIPS, Simon D., "The Hospitallers and Concepts of Island Existence", at: IMO.

PIANA, Mathias, "How ancient theatres became medieval castles – examples from the Middle East", at: *20th Colloquium on the History of Egypt and Syria in the Fatimid, Ayyubid and Mamluk Eras (10th–15th centuries)*, Ghent University, 11–13 May 2011.

POLEJOWSKI, Karol, "Teutonic Order after the fall of Acre – a few remarks about the activities of Charles of Trier in the years 1291–1312", at MO16; "Hospitallers of Rhodes and attempts of the family of Brienne to reclaim the Duchy of Athens", at: IMO.

PORTNYKH, Valentin, "Humbert of Romans' treatise about the preaching of the holy cross: The viewpoint on the perspectives of conversion of the Saracens", at: *The Crusades, Islam and Byzantium*. An Interdisciplinary Workshop and Conference, German Historical Institute, London, 8–9 July 2011; "Preaching the Holy Cross: Humbert of Romans' Manual and Its Reception", at: IMC Leeds 2011; "The Treatise 'About the Preaching of the Holy Cross against Saracens' as a Historical Source for the History of the Western Christianity", at: *Contemporary Problems of the Church History Studies*, Moscow State University, 7–8 November 2011 [in Russian]; "The discussions around the book "Aristote au mont Saint-Michel" by Sylvain Gouguenheim", at: *Siberia at the Crossroads of the World Religions*, Novosibirsk State University, 1 November 2011 [in Russian].

PURKIS, William J., "Early Crusaders and their Relics", at: ICMS 2011; "Rewriting the History Books: The First Crusade and the Past", at: *Historiography, Memory and Transmission: New Approaches to the Narratives of the Early Crusade Movement*, University of Liverpool, 20 May 2011; "From Divine Body Marks during the Crusades to the Stigmata of St Francis", at: *Into the Skin: Identity, Symbols and History of Permanent Body Marks*, Pontificia Università Urbaniana, Vatican City, 6 December 2011.

ROCHE, Jason T., "Poverty and Disorder on the Second Crusade", at: IMC Leeds, 2011; "Constantinople before Çelebi's Istanbul: the views of western travellers", at: Symposium in honour of the 400th anniversary of the Evliya Çelebi, Fatih University, Istanbul, March 2011; "Crusading armies and their violence across medieval frontiers"; at *Medieval Frontiers at War*, University of Extremadura, Cáceres, Spain, November 2010; "Medieval military demography: problems and potential solutions", at: IMC Leeds, 2010; "*De Profectione Ludovici VII in Orientem* and the conventional notion that *Alemanni praecedentes omnia perturbant*: a calculated subplot of Odo of Deuil's Second Crusade narrative?'"; Avignon SSCLE 7.

RODRÍGUEZ GARCÍA, José Manuel, "Consideraciones geoestratégicas y militares de la guerra cruzada. Una visión comparativa entre la Península Ibérica, Tierra Santa y el Báltico", at: *VI seminario de Historia Medieval. Guerra Santa y Cruzada en la Edad Media*. Segovia, UNED, September 2011; "La imagen de las OOMM en el s. XIII en los reinos de Castilla y León", at: *Jornadas sobre las Cruzadas y Órdenes Militares en la Península Ibérica*, UAM/ Museo Cerralbo, November 2010); "The Teutonic Order in the Kingdoms of Spain, 13th– 18th centuries", at: *Kolloquium: Forschungskolloquium zur mittelalterlichen Geschichte*, University of Bochum-Rhur, Germany, November 2011.

ROGER, Jean-Marc, "En hommage à Joseph Delaville Le Roulx (1855–1911). Aux origines de deux maisons de l'Hôpital ancien: Bourganeuf et Lureuil", at: Société des Antiquaires de l'Ouest, Poitiers, 16 novembre 2011.

ROMINE, Anne, "Travel, Crusade and Pilgrimage in the Fourteenth-Century Knightly Career", at: IMC, 2010; "Chivalry and the Fortunes of War in Fourteenth-Century England" ICMS, 2010; "Visionary Intellectual or Ordinary Knight? The Early Career of Philip of Mézières", at: Second International Symposium on Crusades Studies, Saint Louis University, 2010; "Philip of Mézières: Knightly Career and Crusade in the 14th Century", at: Saint Louis University Graduate Research Symposium, 2010; "When Constantinople Didn't Fall: Marshal Boucicaut's Expedition of 1399", at: ICMS, 2008.

RUBIN, Jonathan, "Benoit d'Alignan and Thomas Agni: Two Frankish Intellectuals and the

Study of Oriental Christianity in 13th-century Kingdom of Jerusalem", at: *The Crusades, Islam and Byzantium: An Interdisciplinary Workshop and Conference*, German Historical Institute, London, July 2011.

RYAN, James D., "European popular religion, ecclesiastical reform, and the launching of the First Crusade", at: Sewanee Medieval Colloquium, The University of the South, Sewanee, Tennessee, 30 March 2012.

SHOTTEN-HALLEL, Vardit, "Dilemmas in Reconstructing Crusader Elements: Reconstruction of a Construction Site, Works carried out in the Hospitaller Compound of Akko", at: *Holy War: the Past and Present: the Crusader Phenomenon and its Relevance Today*, Jerusalem, Israel, June 2008.

SMITH, Thomas, "Papal-Imperial Relations and the Crusade under Honorius III (1216–27)", at: Central Medieval Workshop, University of Cambridge, 20 October 2011; "Did a Papal Crusade Policy Exist under Honorius III (1216–1227)?", at: IMC Leeds 2011.

THROOP, Susanna, "Christian Society on the Second Crusade: Religious Practices in the *De expugnatione Lyxbonensi*", at: *Charles Homer Haskins Society Annual Conference*, Boston College, November 6, 2011; "Crusading as Vengeance and the Motif of the Crucifixion", at: ICMS 2011.

TOKO, Hirofumi, "The chartophylakeion of St Sophia", at: Monthly Meeting of the Historical Association of Tokai University, Tokai University, Hiratsuka, 22 February 2011.

TOUATI, François-Olivier, "Lepers and Leprosy: Connections between East and West in the Middle Ages", Key-Lecture, at: *Leprosy, Language and Identity in the Medieval World*, King's College, Cambridge, 12–13 April 2011; "Au-delà des croisades, l'Orient latin", at: *Rendez-vous de l'Histoire*, Blois, 13 October 2011; "L'Or de l'Orient. Le cas du Moyen Âge" et "L'Orient en Occident", *Rendez-vous de l'Histoire*, Blois, 14 October 2011; "Soigner et se soigner au XIIe siècle à Jérusalem", at: Journée d'étude *Prendre soin de soi, Prendre soin d'autrui. Histoire, sociologie, anthropologie*, UMR CNRS Citères/ Cost-EMAM, Axe transversal "Corps, solicitude, santé", Tours, 17 November 2011; "De la Renaissance médicale carolingienne à la renaissance du XIIe siècle: de Raban Maur à Constantin l'Africain", Séminaire du Centre d'Études Supérieures de la Renaissance, Tours, 18 November 2011; "Les mots arabes dans la pharmacopée et l'alimentation au Moyen Âge", Alma Mater Studiorum, Bologna (Italy), 17 January 2012; "Sir Thomas Lawrence et les débuts de l'historiographie anglaise des États latins, un enjeu politique", at: *Écrire l'histoire des croisades (III): la Méditerranée, une historiographie européo-centrée?*, Journée d'Étude, Université François-Rabelais, EMAM, Tours, 23 March 2012.

TSOUGARAKIS, Nickiphoros I., "Οι Δεσμοί πατρωνίας των δυτικών μοναχικών ταγμάτων στη λατινοκρατούμενη Ελλάδα", at: "Μοναστήρια, οικονομία και πολιτική από το μεσαίωνα στους νεότερους χρόνους", University of Crete, December 2009; "Franciscan Inquisitors and Franciscan Heretics in Medieval Greece", at: Medieval Seminars series of the School of History, University of Leeds, November 2009; "The Franciscans as defenders of Catholic Orthodoxy in Medieval Greece', at IMC 2009.

UPTON, Todd P., "*Revertamur Jerusalem*': Perceptions of Community and Liminality in the Scholastic Age", at: ICMS 2012.

De VAIVRE, Jean-Bernard, "Les commémorations par Pierre d'Aubusson du siège de Rhodes de 1480", at: Société nationale des Antiquaires de France, Paris; (with L. Vissière), "Les manuscrits de Guillaume Caoursin", Académie des Inscriptions et Belles-Lettres, Paris.

VANDEBURIE, Jan, *"Est autem in Babylonia alia Bestia": Animals of the Holy Land. The Bestiary in Jacques de Vitry's "Historia Orientalis"*, at: IMC 2011.

WEBER, Benjamin, "Role and perception of non-professional warriors in the crusades against the Turks", at: IMC 2011; "La *camera sancte cruciate* e la gestione dell'allume", at: Congress *I papi e l'allume: alle origini del monopolio commerciale (XV–XVI secolo)*, University La Sapienza/École Française de Rome, Roma, December 2010; "Unione religiosa, unità politica, alleanza militare. I legati pontefici in Oriente al tempo del concilio di Firenze e le loro mission", at: *L'Italia e la frontiera orientale dell'Europa*, Academia di Romania, Roma, November 2010.

WILSON, Ian, "Cowardice, Chivalry and the Crusades", at: IMC, 2011.

WILSKMAN, Juho, "Avoiding pitched battles in Byzantine warfare against the Latins during the thirteenth century: Benefits and drawbacks", at: *22nd International Congress of Byzantine Studies*, Sofia 25 August 2011; "Infantrymen in the Latin 'Romania': Fourth Crusade and after", at: IMC, 2011.

4. Forthcoming publications

ANDREI, Filippo, "The Variants of the *Honestum*: Practical Philosophy in the *Decameron*", Papio, Michael and Elsa Filosa, ed., *Boccaccio in America: Proceedings of the 2010 International Boccaccio Conference at The University of Massachusetts Amherst*, The University of Massachusetts, Amherst, April 30 – May 1, 2010. Longo Editore, series: "Memoria del Tempo"; Ps.-Romualdus, *Glosula super Psalmos*, critical edition to be published in the series *Corpus Christianorum Continuatio Mediaevalis*, Turnhout, Brepols.

ANTAKI-MASSON, Patricia, "Les marques lapidaires de l'abbaye de Belmont", "Les linteaux en bâtière: des marqueurs chronologiques", "L'heure de la prière au cadran canonial de l'abbaye de Belmont", Université de Balamand, 2011; "Les fortifications de Tyr à travers les sources médiévales", in J. Aliquot, P.-L. Gatier and L. Nordiguian, eds., *Tyr dans les textes antiques et médiévaux*, Beyrouth: Presses de l'Université Saint-Joseph, 2011.

ATTIYA, Hussein, *A History of the Crusades*, Alexandria, Dar AL- Maareifa Al Jameiya September 2012

BALARD, Michel, *La Méditerranée au Moyen Age*, Paris: Hachette, 2012.

BARBER, Malcolm, *The Crusader States in the Twelfth Century*, London: Yale University Press, 2012.

BAYDAL, Vicent, "El cabeçatge, un desconegut servei de les Corts valencianes de 1301–1302", *Anales de la Universidad de Alicante. Historia Medieval*, 18, 2012; "El record personal i familiar: la memòria (1604–1627) de Pere Escrivà i Sabata", with V.J. Escartí, *Afers*, 70, 2012; "Cambistas, fiscalidad y linajes dominantes en la ciudad de Valencia (c. 1260– c. 1370)", in *En busca de Zaqueo. Los recaudadores de impuestos en las épocas medieval y moderna*, Madrid, Institute of Fiscal Studies; "'Contra barbaras nationes'. La justification de la guerre entre chrétiens et musulmans dans la croisade castillane-aragonaise contre l'Émirat de Grenade en 1309", in *Faire la guerre, faire la paix*, París, Comité des travaux historiques et scientifiques; *Els fonaments del pactisme valencià. Sistemes fiscals, relacions de poder i identitat col·lectiva en el regne de Valencia (c. 1250–c. 1365)*, Barcelona, Noguera Foundation; *Els orígens de la revolta de la Unió al regne de València (1330–1348)*, Valencia, University of Valencia; *Les relacions epistolars del Consell municipal de Barcelona (1381– 1566)*, Barcelona, Barcelona Historical Archives, 2013.

BELLOMO, Elena, new Latin edition and translation into Italian of Caffaro, *Ystoria captionis Almarie et Turtuose, De liberatione civitatum Orientis Liber* and anonymous *Regni*

Ierosolimitani brevis hystoria, in Caffaro, *Opere*, in collaboration with Antonio Placanica, Edizione Nazionale dei Testi Mediolatini, Società Internazionale per lo Studio del Medioevo Latino (SISMEL) [2011–2012]; "The Temple, the Hospital and the Towns of North and Central Italy: *Status Quaestionis* and Lines of Future Research", in D. Carraz, ed., *Les Ordres religieux militaires dans la ville medievale. 1150–1350*; "The Spanish Military Orders in Italy: Initial Remarks on Patronage and Settlement (XII–XIV Centuries)", in MO5; "Gerusalemme, la Terrasanta e la crociata nelle memorie agiografiche delle città marinare (1098–c.1135). Le traslazioni dei santi Nicola, Isidoro e Giovanni Battista", *Quaderni di storia religiosa*, 17 (2010) [2011]; "A neglected source for the History of the Hospital: The Letter of Master Jobert (1171/72–1177) to the Citizens of Savona".

BERKOVICH, Ilya, "Templars, Franks, Syrians and the Double Pact of 1244", in: MO5.

BIDDLECOMBE, Steven, The *Historia Ierosolimitana* of Baldric of Bourgueil – a Scholarly Edition in Latin and Critical Analysis, Boydell and Brewer (2012); "Baldric of Bourgueil and the *Familia Christi*", in *Proceedings of the Crusade Narrative Conference in Liverpool, 2011*, Boydell and Brewer, 2012.

BIRD, Jessalyn, Crusade and Christendom: Innocent III to the Fall of Acre, Annotated Documents in Translation, 1187–1291, University of Pennsylvania Press, 2013, a sourcebook in collaboration with Edward Peters and the late James Powell; Entries on "Oliver of Paderborn and his works" for *Christian–Muslim Relations: A Bibliographical History*, Brill.

BOMBI, Barbara, "An archival Network: the Teutonic Knights in the thirteenth and fourteenth centuries", in *Proceedings of the Anglo-Scandinavian Conference*, Studies in Church History, Subsidies, Boydel.

BOAS, Adrian J., *Montfort Castle: The Western Ward and the Great Hall*, monograph published by the Zinman Institute of Archaeology, January 2012; The first volume of publications by the Montfort Castle Project – *Montfort 1: past History, Early Research and Recent Studies* – planned for publication in 2012; *Acre-East 1999, 2000: Two Seasons of Excavations in the Estate of the Teutonic Order in Acre* – monograph (with Georg Philipp Melloni) planned for publication in 2012; "The Location of the Teutonic House in Akko", (with Georg Philipp Melloni) in J. France, ed., *The Sieges of Acre*, Farnham: Ashgate; "The First Four Years of Renewed Research at Montfort Castle".

BONNEAUD, Pierre, "Success and Failure in the practice of power by Pere Ramon Sacosta, Master of the Hospital (1461–1467)", MO5, 2012; "La crise financière des Hospitaliers de Rhodes au quinzième siècle (1426–1480)", *Anuario de Estudios Medievales*, 42/2, Barcelona, June 2012; "Les Hospitaliers Catalans entre Rhodes, l'Italie et la Catalogne (1420–1480)", Élites et Ordres militaires au Moyen-Âge, Collection de la Casa Velasquez, Madrid, 2012; "The Influential Community of Western Merchants in Hospitaller Thodes during the Fifteenth Century (1421–1480)", in *International Conference Union in Separation, Trading Diasporas in the Eastern Mediterranean (1200–1700)*, University of Heidelberg, 2013.

BORCHARDT, Karl, *Die geistlichen Ritterorden in Mitteleuropa: Mittelalter*, Rytířské duchovní řády ve střdní Europě: Středověk, ed. Karl Borchardt, Libor Jan (Matice Moravska) [Proceedings of the Čejkovice conference], Brno 2012

BURKIEWICZ, Łukasz, "Polski epizod w cypryjskich dążeniach do zrzucenia zwierzchnictwa sułtanatu mameluków", *Studia Gdańskie*, 2011; *Sylwetka o. Antonio Possevino SJ, [w:] Życie i dzieło o. Antonio Possevino SJ*, Kraków 2012 (Jesuit University Press); *Aleksandria 1365*, Warszawa 2012 (Bellona S.A.).

BUTTIGIEG, Emanuel, *Nobility, Faith and Masculinity: The Order of Malta c.1580–c.1700*, London: Continuum.

CARR, Michael, "Trade or crusade? The Zaccaria of Chios and crusades against the Turks", in Mike Carr and Nikolaos Chrissis, eds., *Contact and Conflict in Frankish Greece and the Aegean, 1204–1453: Crusade, Religion and Trade between Latins, Greeks and Turks*, Farnham: Ashgate, 2013.

CARRAZ, Damien, "La territorialisation de la seigneurie monastique. Les commanderies provençales du Temple (XIIe–XIIIe siècle)", in G. Castelnuovo and A. Zorzi, eds., *Les pouvoirs territoriaux en Italie centrale et dans le Sud de la France. Hiérarchies, institutions et langages (12e–14e siècles): études comparées*, actes de la table-ronde de Chambéry (4 mai 2007), *Mélanges de l'École française de Rome-Moyen Âge* (publication: 2011); "La spiritualité de la chevalerie au regard du cartulaire du Temple de Richerenches", in *Le XIIIe siècle, entre Provence et Dauphiné*, ed. M. Bois, actes du colloque de Lachau, 25–27 septembre 2009, Pont-Saint-Esprit (publication: 2012); "Aux origines de la commanderie de Manosque. Le dossier des comtes de Forcalquier dans les archives de l'Hôpital (début XIIe–milieu XIIIe siècle)", in M. Olivier and Ph. Josserand, eds., *La mémoire des origines propres chez les ordres religieux militaires au Moyen Âge*, actes du colloque de Göttingen, juin 2009, Münster, Vita regularis, 2012; "Expériences religieuses en contexte urbain. De l'*ordo monasticus* aux *Religiones novæ*: le jalon du monachisme militaire", in D. Carraz, ed., *Les ordres religieux militaires dans la ville médiévale (1100–1350)*, actes du colloque de Clermont-Ferrand, 26–28 mai 2010, Clermont-Ferrand, Presses universitaires Blaise-Pascal, 2012; "Les commanderies dans l'espace urbain. Templiers et Hospitaliers dans les villes de l'Occident méditerranéen (XIIe–XIIIe siècle)", in C. Caby, ed., *Espaces monastiques et espaces urbains de l'Antiquité tardive à la fin du Moyen Âge*, *Mélanges de l'École française de Rome-Moyen Âge*, 2012; "Le monachisme militaire, laboratoire de la sociogenèse des élites laïques dans l'Occident medieval?", in N. Bériou, Ph. Josserand and L.F. Oliveira, eds., *Élites et ordres militaires au Moyen Âge*, actes du colloque de Lyon, 21–23 octobre 2009, Madrid, Casa de Velázquez 2013; "Les Templiers de Provence et la Terre Sainte: mobilité et carrières (XIIIe–XIVe siècle)", in I.C. Fereira Fernandes, ed., *Freires, Guerreiros, Cavaleiros, VI Encontro sobre Ordens Militares. Palmela, 10 a 14 de março de 2010* (publication: 2013).

CERRINI, Simonetta, *L'Apocalisse dei Templari*, Milano, Mondadori [book]; "Rangs et dignités dans l'ordre du Temple au regard de la règle", in N. Bériou, Ph. Josserand and L.F. Oliveira, eds., *Élites et ordres militaires au Moyen Âge. Rencontre en l'honneur d'Alain Demurger*, Lyon, 21–23 octobre 2009; "La règle de l'ordre et la hiérarchie templière", in Catalogue de l'exposition *Templiers. De Jérusalem aux commanderies de Champagne*, ed. A. Baudin, G. Brunel, N. Dohrmann, Paris, Somogy éditions d'art/Archives départementales de l'Aube, Troyes.

CHEVALIER, Marie-Anna, "Le rôle de la papauté dans la politique arménienne des hospitaliers au XIVe siècle", in Michel Balard (dir.), *La Papauté et les Croisades*; "L'implantation des ordres religieux-militaires sur le littoral arméno-cilicien et ses répercussions économiques et militaires", Actes du séminaire *L'espace économique de la Méditerranée* (2008–2010), dir. D. Coulon, A. Nef, Ch. Picard et D. Valérian, Saint-Denis: Éditions Bouchène, 2011–2012; "Les réactions des ordres religieux-militaires face au déferlement mongol au Proche-Orient", Actes du colloque du CNRS, *Le Bilad al-Sham face aux mondes extérieurs. La perception de l'autre: approches textuelles et iconographiques*, Damas, 17–19 décembre 2009, dir. D. Aigle; "Les ordres religieux-militaires et les pouvoirs arméniens en Orient (XIIe–XIVe siècles)", Actes du colloque international de Lyon Élites et ordres militaires au Moyen Âge, 21–23 octobre 2009, Madrid, Collection de la Casa de Velázquez; "La correspondance entre les élites arméniennes et la papauté pendant le règne de Lewon Ier", in *Correspondances diplomatiques et traités de chancellerie*, *Eurasian Studies*, sous la direction de D. Aigle et M.

Bernardini, 2012; "L'ordre de l'Hôpital et la défense de l'Arménie: enjeux d'une présence et moyens mis en œuvre", in Actes du colloque international *La Méditerranée des Arméniens (XIIe–XVe siècles)*, Jérusalem, 1er–3 juillet 2009; "Une approche de l'historiographie et des sources de l'histoire de l'Arménie cilicienne", in *Armenian History Handbook*, coll. Handbuch der Orientalistik, Brill.

CHRISSIS, Nikolaos, "The City and the Cross: the image of Constantinople and the Latin Empire in papal crusading rhetoric in the thirteenth century", *Byzantine and Modern Greek Studies*, 35, 2012; *Crusading in Frankish Greece: a Study of Byzantine–Western Relations and Attitudes, 1204–1282*, Turnhout, Brepols, 2012; "Crusades and crusaders in Medieval Greece", in P. Lock and N. Tsougarakis, eds., *A Handbook of Medieval Greece*, Leiden: Brill, 2012; "Gregory IX and the Greek East", in C. Egger and D. Smith, ed., *Pope Gregory IX*, Farnham: Ashgate, 2012; "New Frontiers: Frankish Greece and crusading in the early 13th century", in N. Chrissis and M. Carr, eds., *Contact and Conflict in Frankish Greece and the Aegean, 1204–1453: Crusade, Religion and Trade between Latins, Greeks and Turks*, Farnham: Ashgate, 2013.

CHRIST, Georg, "Contrebande, vin et révolte: lecture critique d'un conflit inter-culturel à l'ombre des rapports officieux entre Venise et Alexandrie à l'époque medieval", in C. Décobert, ed., *Alexandrie médiévale 4*, Études alexandrines, Le Caire: IFAO; "Quelques observations concernant la navigation vénitienne à Alexandrie à la fin du Moyen Âge", in S.G Franchini and G. Toscano, eds., *Venise et la Méditerranée*, Paris and Venice: INP, Istituto Veneto; "Sliding Legalities: Venetian Slave Trade in Alexandria and the Aegean", in Ch. Cluse and R. Amitai, eds., *Slavery and the Slave Trade in the Mediterranean Region During the Medieval Period (1000–1500)*; "Mapping change: A Collaborative GIS-based Cue Card System for the Humanities", in *Proceedings of the SCCH09—Scientific Computing & Cultural Heritage November 16th–18th 2009*, ed. M. Winckler and H. Mara, Heidelberg, Springer; "Filippo di Malerbi – un spécialiste du transfert clandestin en Égypte au début du 15ème siècle", in D. König, Y. Benhima, R. Abdellatif and É. Ruchaud, eds., *Acteurs des transferts culturels en Méditerranée médiévale*, Paris: DHIP; "Einrichtungen zur Gefangenenbefreiung und zur Bewältigung anderer Folgen der Piraterie im spätmittelalterlichen Mittelmeerraum", in N. Jaspert and S. Kolditz, eds., *Gefährdete Konnektivität. Piraterie im Mittelmeerraum*; "Czu vortribin di seeroubir, di Gotis und allir werlde finde", Piratenbekämpfung durch Hanse und Deutschen Orden (1370–1400)", in A. Brendecke and T. Weller, eds., *Fließende Grenzen. Abgrenzungspraktiken auf See. (15.–18. Jahrhundert)*; "Section: Mediterranean Economies / Chapter: Materials, products and services of exchange", in A. Nichols Law, ed., *Mapping the Medieval Mediterranean, c. 300–1550*, Leiden: Brill.

CHRISTIE, Niall G. F., *The Book of the Jihad of 'Ali ibn Tahir al-Sulami (d. 1106): Text, Translation and Commentary*, Ashgate, 2012, viii + 377 p.; "Noble Betrayers of their Faith, Families and Folk: Some Non-Muslim Women in Mediaeval Arabic Popular Literature", *Folklore*; "The Great Mice at Cordoba: De-Mythologising and Re-Mythologising Religious Imagery in David Petersen's *Mouse Guard*", *Journal of Religion and Popular Culture*, "'Curses, Foiled Again!' Further Research on Early Use of the '*Hadalahum Allah*' Invocation during the Crusading Period", *Arabica*; "Paradise and Hell in the *Kitab al-Jihad* of 'Ali b. Tahir al-Sulami (d. 500/1106)", in S. Günther and T. Lawson, eds., *Roads to Paradise: Eschatology and Concepts of the Hereafter in Islam*, Leiden: Brill; Chapter: "Europe seen from the Muslim World", in János M. Bak, ed., *Medieval Narrative Sources: A Chronological Guide*, Turnhout: Brepols.

CLAVERIE, Pierre-Vincent, "Mythes et réalités de la présence templière à Famagouste", in M. Walsh, P. Edbury and N. Coureas, eds., *Medieval and Renaissance Famagusta: History and Monuments*, Farnham: Ashgate 2012; *Honorius III et l'Orient (1216–1227)*, Leiden: Brill, 2012; "Pierre de Blois et la légende dorée de Renaud de Châtillon", in U. Vermeulen and K. D'hulster, eds., *Egypt and Syria in the Fatimid, Ayyubid and Mamluk Eras, VIII.*, Louvain, 2012; "La politique orientale du Saint-Siège à l'avènement d'Honorius III (1216)", ibid.; "Un siècle et demi de relations barcelono-chypriotes (1291–1435)", *Επετηρίδα του Κέντρου Επιστημονικών Ερευνών*, XXXVIII, 2012; "Essai sur l'historiographie templière et ses déclinaisons culturelles depuis le XIVᵉ siècle", *Le Moyen Age*, CXVIII, 2012; "L'ordre du Temple dans l'Europe des croisades (1120–1312)", in J. Albuquerque Carreiras, ed., *I Colóquio Internacional Cister, os Templários e a Ordem de Cristo*, Tomar, 2012, pp. 69–89; "L'évolution des réseaux d'information de l'Orient latin durant les croisades (fin XIᵉ–début XIVᵉ siècle)", in Ch. Picard, ed., *Espaces et Réseaux en Méditerranée, VIᵉ–XVIᵉ siècles*, III, *Les réseaux à l'épreuve du temps*, Paris, 2012; "Les relations du Saint-Siège avec les ordres militaires sous le pontificat d'Honorius III (1216–1227)", in Ph. Josserand and N. Bériou, eds., *Élites et ordres militaires au Moyen Âge. Colloque de Lyon, 21–23 octobre 2009*, Lyon, 2012; "Les tribulations orientales du seigneur Gonfroy II de Marquise (1096–1138)", in U. Vermeulen and K. D'hulster, eds., *Egypt and Syria in the Fatimid, Ayyubid and Mamluk Eras*, IX, Louvain, 2013; "Les difficultés de l'épigraphie franque de Terre sainte aux XIIᵉ et XIIIᵉ siècles", *Crusades*, XII, 2013.

CONNELL, Charles W., "The Tin Ear of 19thc. Medievalism", in Anne Scott and Cynthia Kosso, eds., *An anthology on the Poor and Poverty in the Middle Ages and early Modern Era*, Leiden: Brill, 2012.

CONSTABLE, Giles, *William of Adam. How to Defeat the Saracens*, Washington, D.C., 2012.

COSTA, Paula Pinto, "The Role of the Order of St John in Pilgrimage and Politics: The Case of the North of Portugal", in Antón M. Pazos, ed., *Pilgrims and Politics*, Farnham Ashgate, 2012; "As visitações: as Ordens Militares portuguesas entre poderes?", in Palmela, 2010, pp. 415–437; "As Ordens Militares: entre a História e a Historiografia", in R. Nascimento, ed., *Entre a História e a Historiografia*, Goiânia, Pontifícia Universidade Católica de Goiás, 2011; "Da fronteira à consolidação do território: o contributo das Ordens Militares nos séculos XII–XIII para o processo de territorialização", in S. Boisselier, ed., *Les territoires frontaliers entre Chrétienté et Islam, IX–XVe siècles, nouvelles approches: la territorialisation, de la guerre à la paix*, Turnhout: Brepols, 2011.

COUREAS, Nicholas S., "Taverns in Medieval Famagusta", in M. Walsh, P. Edbury and N. Coureas, eds., *Medieval and Renaissance Famagusta: History and Monuments*, Ashgate, 2012; "Commercial Relations between Genoese Famagusta and the Mamluk Sultanate, 1374–1464", in U. Vermeulen and K. D'Hulster, eds., *Egypt and Syria in the Fatimid, Ayyubid and Mamluk Eras 7, Proceedings of the 16th, 17th and 18th HES*, Leuven, 2012; "Losing the War but Winning the Peace: Cyprus and Mamluk Egypt in the Fifteenth Century", ibid.; "The Tribute Paid to the Mamluk Sultanate, 1426–1517: The Perspective from Lusignan and Venetian Cyprus", ibid.; "The Third Crusade according to Greek Sources from Cyprus", *The Medieval Chronicle*, 8, 2012; "King James II of Cyprus and the Hospitallers: Evidence from the *Livre des Remembrances*", MO5, 2012; "Friend or Foe? The Armenians in Cyprus as others saw them in the Lusignan Period", in G. Dédéyan and C. Mutafian, eds., *The History of the Armenian Mediterranean 12th to 15th Centuries*, Paris, 2012; "The Use of the Arabic Language in Lusignan and Venetian Cyprus: 1200–1570", in U. Vermeulen and K. D'Hulster, eds., *Egypt and Syria in the Fatimid, Ayyubid and Mamluk Eras 7, Proceedings of the 19th and 20th HES*, Leuven: Peeters, 2013; "Envoys between the Mamluk Lands and Lusignan Cyprus: Evidence from the Cypriot Chronicle of Leontios Makhairas", ibid.; "Cultural Brokers at the Court of Cyprus", in N. Jaspert, J. Oesterle and M. von der Hoh, eds., *Cultural Brokers between Religions: Border-Crossers and Experts at Mediterranean Courts*, Mediterranean Studies Series, Ruhr University; "Hospitaller Estates and Agricultural Production on 14th and 15th Century Cyprus", in E. Buttigieg and S. Phillips, eds., *Islands and Military Orders, c.1291–c.1798*, Farnham: Ashgate; "Religion and Ethnic Identity in Latin Cyprus: How various Groups regarded themselves and how others viewed them", in T. Papacostas and G. Saint-Guillain, eds., *Identity/Identities in Late Medieval Cyprus*, Nicosia, 2013.

DANSETTE, Béatrice, ed., Bernard de Breydenbach, *Voyage en Terre sainte et en Égypte*, transcription, traduction et notes sous la direction du Professeur Jean Meyer, collectif.

DEMURGER, Alain, "Étourdis ou petits malins? Pourquoi les Templiers n'ont-ils pas eu de légende d'origine?", in *La mémoire des origines dans les ordres religieux militaires au Moyen Âge*, actes du colloque de la Mission Historique Française en Allemagne des 25 et 26 juin 2009, éd. Ph. Josserand et M. Olivier, *Vita Regularis. Ordnungen und Deutungen religiosen Lebens im Mittelalter*; "Subsidium Terrae sancte et ordres religieux-militaires", in Palmela, 2010.

DOSTOURIAN, Ara, *Armenia and the Crusades: The Chronicle of Matthew of Edessa*, 2nd ed., paperback, Armenian Heritage Press, National Association for Armenian Studies and Research, 2012.

EDGINGTON, Susan, "Pagans and Others in the *Chanson de Jérusalem*", in S. Lambert, E. James and H. Nicholson, eds., *Languages of Love and Hate*, Turnhout: Brepols, 2012; Paperback translation of Albert of Aachen's *Historia*, Ashgate, 2013.

EHLERS, Axel, "Indulgentia und Historia. Die Bedeutung des Ablasses für die spätmittelalterliche Erinnerung an die Ursprünge des Deutschen Ordens und anderer Gemeinschaften", in *Mémoire des origines dans les ordres religieux-militaires au Moyen Âge*, ed. P. Josserand and M. Olivier, *Vita Regularis. Ordnungen und Deutungen religiosen Lebens im Mittelalter*, 2012.

EKDAHL, Sven, "Politics, Diplomacy and the Recruitment of Mercenaries before the Battle of Tannenberg-Grunwald-Žalgiris in 1410", MO5, 2012; "The Battle of Tannenberg and its political circumstances", *Journal of the Monastic Military Orders*, Malta, ed. Dane Munro, 5, 2012; "W przededniu bitwy grunwaldzkiej. Dyplomacja i werbowanie żołnierzy zaciężnych w czerwcu 1410 r.", in J.M. Piskorski, ed., Średniowieczne bitwy i wojny. *Rzeczywistość i narodowy mit. Wokół bitwy pod Grunwaldem i jej życia pośmiertnego/Medieval Battles and Wars. Reality and the National Myth. The Battle of Grunwald and its Posthumous Life*, Warsaw: Bellona, 2012; "Quellenaussagen über die Taktik in der Tannenbergschlacht", in G. Vercamer, ed., Žalgiris – Grunwald – Tannenberg 1410: Krieg und Frieden im späten Mittelalter, Quellen und Studien, Warschawa: Deutsches Historisches Institut, 2012 [also translation into Lithuanian in a book published by the University of Vilnius, ed. Rimvydas Petrauskas, 2012]; "Probleme und Perspektiven der Grunwaldforschung", in K. Ożóg et al., eds., *Grunwald-Tannenberg-Žalgiris 1410–2010. Historia-Tradycja-Polityka / Geschichte-Tradition-Politik*, Malbork [Marienburg]: Muzeum Zamkowe Malbork, 2012; "Der erste Thorner Frieden (1411) im Spiegel der Söldnerfrage", in R. Czaja, Krzysztof Kwiatkowski, ed., *Die Ritterorden in Krieg und Frieden*, Ordines Militares, 15, Toruń: Wydawnictwo Uniwersytetu Mikołaja Kopernika, 2012; "Battlefield Archaeology at Tannenberg (Grunwald, Žalgiris): Physical Remains of the Defeat of the Teutonic Order in Prussia in 1410", *Journal of Conflict Archaeology*; *Bitwa pod Grunwaldem: nowe spojrzenie* [Polish translation of a lecture held in 2010], Poznań, University of Poznań, 2012; *Jana Długosza*

"Banderia Prutenorum" [Polish translation of a book published in Göttingen in 1976: *Die "Banderia Prutenorum" des Jan Długosz*], Olsztyn, ElSet, 2012.

FRANKE, Daniel, "War, Crisis, and East Anglia, 1334–1340: Towards a Reassessment", in Donald Kagay and L.J. Andrew Villalon, eds., *The Hundred Years War III*, Leiden: Brill, 2011.

GABRIELE, Matthew, "On the Language of Christian Violence in Contemporary American Society: From Iraq to Virginia Tech", in Theo Riches and Gerd Althoff, eds., *Denkmuster christlicher Legitimation von Gewalt*, Bonn: Ergon Verlag, 2012.

GAPOSCHKIN, Cecilia, "Origins and Development of the Pilgrimage and Cross Blessings in the Roman Pontificals of the Twelfth and Thirteenth Centuries", *Medieval Studies* 73, PIMS, 2011; "From Pilgrimage to Crusade: Liturgy, Devotion, and Ideology", *Speculum*; "The Role of Jerusalem in Western Crusading Rites of Departure (1095–1300)", *The Catholic Historical Review*, 2013; *Blessed Louis, Most Glorious of Kings: Texts relating to the Cult of Louis IX of France*, Notre Dame University Press.

GEORGIOU, Constantinos, "Propagating the Hospitallers' *Passagium*: Crusade Preaching and Liturgy in 1308–1309", in IMO.

GEORGIOU, Stavros G., "The Anonymous Kamytzes of Pentekontakephalon of Saint Neophytos the Recluse", *Hellenica*, 62, 2012 [in Greek]; "The Office of Kourator of Cyprus during the Eleventh and Twelfth Centuries", *Vyzantina*, 31, 2011 [in Greek, Summary in English]; "The Saved Historical Testimonies for the Foundation of Astromeritis and the Honour of Saint Auxibios", in P. Lazarou, ed., *O Agios Afxivios Protos Episkopos Solon*, Evrychou 2012 [in Greek]; "The History of the Bishopric of Tamasos", in Volume for the *History and the Monuments of the Holy Bishopric of Tamasos and Oreinis, Holy Bishopric of Tamasos and Oreinis*, Bank of Cyprus Cultural Foundation, Nicosia 2012 [in Greek]; "The Saved Testimonies for the Byzantine Karpasia (4th–12th Centuries)", in P. Papageorgiou, ed., *Karpasia. Praktika Defterou Epistimonikou Synedriou "Eis gin ton Agion kai ton Iroon", Kyriaki 19 Iouniou 2011, Xenodocheio Navarria, Lemesos*, Limassol 2012 [in Greek]; "The Bishopric of Keryneia and the Notitia Episcopatuum no. 3", *Epetirida Kentrou Meleton Ieras Monis Kykkou*, 10, 2012 [in Greek]; "Notes on the Byzantine Cyprus II", *Epetirida Kentrou Meleton Ieras Monis Kykkou*, 10, 2012 [in Greek]; "Limassol during the Proto-Christian and Byzantine Periods. The Saved Testimonies for the City and the Local Church", in M. Sophocleous, ed., *Praktika tou Pemptou Epistimonikou Symposiou Proforikis Istorias, "I Lemesos tou politismou: Prosopa, gegonota, fainomena kai thesmoi stin politistiki tis istoria", Lemesos, Paraskevi, Savvato kai Kyriaki, 27–29 Noemvriou 2009, Dimos Lemesou*, Limassol 2012 [in Greek]; "The Office of the Rebel Rapsomatis in Cyprus (ca. 1091–1092)", in A.A. Demosthenous, ed., *Sevasti. Timitikos tomos stin Kathigitria Vyzantinis Istorias tou Aristoteleiou Panepistimiou Thessalonikis k. Vasiliki Nerantzi-Varmazi*, Thessalonica 2012 [in Greek].

GILCHRIST, Marianne, "Getting Away with Murder: Runciman and Conrad of Montferrat's Career in Constantinople", *The Mediaeval Journal*, 2, 1, St Andrews, May 2112.

HALL, Martin, "An academic call to arms in 1252: John of Garland's crusading epic *De triumphis Ecclesiae*", *Caffaro, Genoa and the Crusades*, with Jonathan Phillips, Crusade Texts in Translation: an annotated English translation of all Caffaro's works and other texts relevant to Genoa's role in the Crusades and the Holy Land to 1200, with historical introduction, Farnham: Ashgate.

HAMILTON, Bernard, with Andrew Jotischky, *Latin and Orthodox Monasteries in the Crusader States*, CUP, 2012.

HARRIS, Jonathan, (with Dmitri Tolstoy), "Alexander III and Byzantium", in Peter D. Clarke and Anne J. Duggan, eds., *Pope Alexander III (1158–81)*, Farnham: Ashgate, 2012; "Constantinople as City State", in C. Holmes, E. Russell and J. Harris, eds., *Byzantines, Latins and Turks in the Eastern Mediterranean World after 1150*, Oxford University Press, 2012; "Collusion with the infidel as a pretext for western military action against Byzantium (1180–1204)", in S. Lambert and H. Nicholson, eds., *Languages of Love and Hate: Conflict, Communication and Identity in the Medieval Mediterranean*, Turnhout: Brepols, 2012.

HARSCHEIDT, Michael, Additional chapters of the *Knights Templar project*: "Rosslyn Chapel", "Shroud of Turin", "Anthroposophical Templar Theories", "Grail", "Treasure Fantasies", "Larmenius thesis", "Templarian Gothique Thesis".

HOLMES, Catherine, *Byzantines, Latins and Turks in the Eastern Mediterranean world after 1150*, ed. with J. Harris and E. Russell, Oxford Studies in Byzantium, Oxford, 2012, which includes a 30 p. introduction and an individual study, "Shared Worlds: a question of evidence. Compilation literature and Byzantine political culture in the tenth and eleventh centuries", *Dumbarton Oaks Papers*, 64, 2012, 24 p.; "Basil II, Bulgaroktonos and the 1014 blinding of Bulgarian prisoners-of-war: mutilation and surrender in the Middle Ages", in H. Afflerbach and H. Strachan, eds., *How Fighting Ends. A History of Surrender*, Oxford, 2012; "Archbishop Eustathios of Thessaloniki's 'Capture of Thessaloniki' as a lens for east–west encounters in the twelfth- and thirteenth-century east Mediterranean world", in E. Georganteli, ed., *Encounters in the Balkans, east Mediterranean and Black Sea, 12th–15th c.*, Leiden: Brill.

HUNT, Lucy-Anne, "Skin and the Meeting of Cultures: Outward and Visible Signs of Alterity in the Medieval Christian East", in *Images of Alterity in East and West*, Conference Proceedings, University of Heidelberg: Cluster of Excellence, Asia and Europe in a Global Context, 17–19 June 2010, ed. L.E. Saurma-Jeltsch and A. Eisenbeiß, Munich: Deutscher Kunstverlag; "Ceiling and Casket at the Cappella Palatina and Christian Arab Art between Sicily and Egypt in the Twelfth and Thirteenth Centuries", in D. Knipp, ed., *Siculo-Arabic Ivories and Islamic Painting, 1100–1300: Proceedings of the International Conference, Berlin, 6–8 July 2007*, Römische Forschungen der Biblioteca Hertziana, 36, Munich: Hirmer Verlag, pp. 170–197.

JOSSERAND, Philippe, dir. with M. Olivier, *La mémoire des origines dans les ordres religieux militaires au Moyen Âge (Actes du colloque de la Mission Historique Française en Allemagne des 25 et 26 juin 2009)*, Dresde, *Vita Regularis. Ordnungen und Deutungen religiosen Lebens im Mittelalter*, 2012; "L'ordre de Santiago face au récit de ses origines au tournant du Moyen Âge et de l'époque moderne: variations sur l'espace et le temps", ibid.; dir. with N. Bériou et L.F. Oliveira, *Élites et ordres militaires au Moyen Âge. Rencontre en l'honneur d'Alain Demurger (Actes du colloque international réuni à Lyon les 21, 22 et 23 octobre 2009)*, Madrid, Casa de Velázquez, 2012; "Portrait de maître en héros croisé: la chronique perdue de Pelayo Pérez Correa", in M. Nejedly et J. Svatek, eds., *Histoire et roman de croisades à la fin du Moyen Âge (Prague, 2008)*, Toulouse, 2012; "Troubles and Tensions before the Trial: the Last Years of the Castilian Templar Province", MO5; "De l'arrière au front. Perspectives croisées, perspectives compares", rapport général de la cinquième session "Oriente e Ocidente", Palmela, 2010; "Frontière et ordres militaires dans le monde latin au Moyen Âge", in M. Catala, D. Le Page et J.-C. Meuret, eds., *Frontières oubliées, frontières retrouvées. Marches et limites anciennes en France et en Europe (Châteaubriant, 30 septembre–2 octobre 2010)*, 2012; "Las órdenes militares en discurso cronístico castellano-leonés en época de Fernando III", in M. Ríos Saloma et C. de Ayala Martínez, eds., *Fernando III, tiempo de cruzada*, colloque international, México, 24, 25 et 26 août 2011; "Grenze(n) und geistliche Ritterorden in der lateinischen Welt des Mittelalters", OM 17; "O processo do Templo no reino de Castela", in J. Albuquerque Carreiras et I.C. Ferreira Fernandes, eds., *I Colóquio internacional. Cister, os Templarios e a ordem de Cristo. Da ordem do Templo à ordem do Cristo: os anos de transição*, Tomar (Portugal) les 30 septembre, 1er et 2 octobre 2011, 2012; "Prier et combattre hors du Temple", in G. Brunel et A. Baudin, eds., *Templiers. De Jérusalem aux commanderies de* Champagne, 2012.

JOTISCHKY, Andrew, "Ethnic and Religious Categories in the Treatment of Jews and Muslims in the Crusader States", in J. Renton and B. Giddins, eds., *Antisemitism and Islamophobia*, Bloomington: Indiana University Press, 2012; "Pope Eugenius III and the Latin Church in the Crusader States", in Iben Fonnesberg-Schmidt and Andrew Jotischky, eds., *Pope Eugenius III*, Farnham: Ashgate; with Bernard Hamilton, *Monasticism in the Crusader States*, Cambridge, CUP, 2012.

KEDAR, Benjamin Z., "Emicho of Flonheim and the Apocalyptic Motif in the 1096 Massacres: Between Paul Alphandéry and Alphonse Dupront", in a Festschrift; "Prolegomena to a World History of Harbor and River Chains", in a Festschrift.

KOLIA-DERMITZAKI, Athina, "'Holy war' in Byzantium twenty years later: a question of term definition and interpretation", in Proceedings of the Conference *Die Kriegsideologie der Byzantiner zwischen römischer Reichsidee und christlicher Religion*, Vienna 19–21 May 2011, pp. 1–15; "The pressure from the West: the Crusades", in T. Lounghis and E. Kislinger, eds., *Byzantium. History and Civilization* [in Greek], pp. 1–33.

KOSTICK, Conor, Review: Malcolm Barber and Keith Bate, "Letters from the East", *Journal of Military History*, 2011.

LIGATO, Giuseppe, *La "Torre di Davide": rocca, immagine e idea della Gerusalemme dei crociati*.

MADDEN, Thomas F., *Venice: Islands of Honor and Profit*, New York, Penguin/Viking, 2012; "The Venetian Version of the Fourth Crusade: Memory and the Conquest of Constantinople in Medieval Venice", *Speculum*, 2012; "Alexander III and Venice", in Peter D. Clarke and Anne J. Duggan, eds., *Pope Alexander III (1159–81)*, Farnham: Ashgate, 2012; "Triumph Reimagined: The Golden Gate and Popular Memory in Byzantine and Ottoman Constantinople", in R. Gertwagen and Elizabeth Jeffreys, eds., *Shipping, Trade and Crusade in the Medieval Mediterranean*, Farnham: Ashgate, 2012.

MENACHE, Sophia, "From Unclean Species to Man's Best Friend – Dogs in the Biblical, Mishnah, and Talmud Periods", in R. Zalashik and P. Ackerman Lieberman, eds., *Jew's Best Friend?: The Image of the Dog Throughout Jewish History*, Brighton, Sussex; "*Studium, Regnum* and *Sacerdotium* in the Early Avignon Period: The University of Paris", in S. Noakes, ed., *Petrarch's Babylon: Cultural Intercourse in Papal Avignon*, Minneapolis: Minnesota University Press; "In Pursuit of Peace in a Conflicted Area: The Israeli Contribution to the Study of the Crusades", *Proceedings of the Terruel Conference*, ed. L. Garcia Guijarro; "Emotions from the Holy Land – The First Crusader Kingdom", *Proceedings of the Huesca Conference*, ed. L. Garcia Guijarro; "Self-Image and 'the Other' in the Second Crusader Kingdom: 1187–1291", in S. Luchitskaya, K. Levinson, et al., eds., *Obrazi proshlogo (Images of the Past). Studies in Medieval Culture in Honour of Aaron Gurevitch*; articles "Communications" and "Clement V", in *European Dictionary of the Military Orders*.

MILITZER, Klaus, *Herrschaft, Netzwerke, Brüder. Der Deutsche Orden in Mittelalter und Früher Neuzeit*, Quellen und Studien zur Geschichte des Deutschen Ordens, 2012; *Regesten der Urkunden des Deutschordenshauses in Köln*, 2012; Die Übersiedlung Siegfrieds von Feuchtwangen in die Marienburg, OM16, pp. 47–61.

MITCHELL, Piers D., with Millard, A.R., "Approaches to the study of migration during the crusades". *Crusades*; "Medical and nursing care in the military orders", in W.T. Reich, and J.S.C. Riley-Smith eds., *Chivalry, Honor and Care*, Washington, Georgetown University Press; "Violence and the crusades: warfare, injuries and torture in the medieval Middle East", in M. Smith and C. Knüsel, eds., *Traumatised Bodies: an Osteological History of Conflict from 8000BC to the Present*, New York: Routledge, Taylor & Francis; "The crusades middle east migration", in *Encyclopedia of Global Human Migration*, D.I. Ness, New York: Wiley-Blackwell; with D. Syon, E. Stern, "Water installations at Crusader 'Akko'", *Atiqot*.

MUSARRA, Antonio, "Memorie di Terrasanta. Reliquie, traslazioni, culti e devozioni a Genova tra XII e XIV secolo", in *Come a Gerusalemme. Evocazioni, riproduzioni e imitazioni dei luoghi santi tra Medioevo ed Età Moderna*, XV Seminario del Centro Internazionale di studi *La Gerusalemme di San Vivaldo*, Montaione, 30 giugno–2 luglio 2011, ed. A. Benvenuti, Firenze, Società Internazionale per lo Studio del Medioevo Latino (SISMEL), 2012.

NICHOLSON, Helen J., "Myths and Reality: the Crusades and the Latin East as presented during the Trial of the Templars in the British Isles, 1308–1311", in *On the Margins of Crusading: The Military Orders, the Papcy and the Christian World*, SSCLE Crusades Subsidia Vol. 4, Farnham: Ashgate, 2011; with S. Lambert, eds., *Languages of Love and Hate: Conflict, Communication, and Identity in the Medieval Mediterranean* World, Turnhout: Brepols, 2012; "Love in a hot climate: gender relations in *Florent et Octavien*", ibid.

NICOLAOU-KONNARI, Angel, "Alterity and Identity in the Work of Philippe de Mézières (1327–1405) and Leontios Makhairas (ca. 1360/80–after 1432)", in *Identity / Identities in Late Medieval Cyprus*, Proceedings of the Joint Newton Fellowship and Annual ICS Byzantine Colloquium, Centre for Hellenic Studies, King's College London and Cyprus Research Centre, 13–14 June 2011, Nicosia, 2012; "Melodramatic Perceptions of History: Caterina Cornaro Goes to the Opera", in *Cyprus and Venice in the Era of Caterina Cornaro*, Institute for Interdisciplinary Cypriot Studies, University of Münster, Venice, German Centre for Venetian Studies, 16–18 September 2010, 2012; "The Fascinating Journey of a Pioneer: Louis de Mas Latrie (1805–1897) and the Medieval History of Cyprus" [in Greek], in *Aspects of Clio: Historiography of Cyprus*, University of Cyprus, Nicosia, 2012; "Review: *Bullarium Cyprium*, vol. I, *Papal Letters Concerning Cyprus 1196–1261*, vol. II, *Papal Letters Concerning Cyprus 1261–1314*, ed. Chris Schabel, intr. J. Richard, Cyprus Research Centre, Texts and Studies in the History of Cyprus LXIV, Nicosia, 2010", in *Kypriakai Spoudai* Nicosia, 2012; "Review: Philip of Novara, *Le Livre de Forme de Plait*, ed. and trans. P.W. Edbury, Cyprus Research Centre, TSHC LXI, Nicosia, 2009", ibid.

NICOLLE, David, *European Medieval Tactics (2) From Chivalry to Professionalism, AD 1260–1500*, Oxford, Osprey, Elite, 2012, 64 p.; *The Fall of English France (1449–1453)*, Oxford, Osprey, Campaign Series, 2012.

O'MALLEY, Gregory John, "Procedure, Political Influence and Preceptorial appointments in the Hospitaller Priory of England: the Templecombe Disputes of 1463–79", MO5

ORTEGA, Isabelle, "L'onomastique au service des lignages nobiliaires moréotes", in G. Grivaud, dir., *Stratégies familiales dans le monde gréco-latin des XIIIᵉ–XVIᵉ; Les lignages nobiliaires dans la Morée latine du début du XIIIᵉ siècle au milieu du XVᵉ siècle. Permanences et mutations*, Turnhout: Brépols, 2012.

PASTORI RAMOS, Aurelio, *Algunas reflexiones sobre la relación entre los poderes político y eclesiástico a comienzos de la Edad Media: el uso del término "bellum" en la correspondencia de Gregorio Magno*, Historias del Orbis Terrarum, Santiago, Chile, 2011

PAVIOT, Jacques, "Les croisades tardives (XIVᵉ–XVIᵉ s.): bilan historiographique et état de la recherche: France et Angleterre", in *Les croisades tardives (XIVe–XVIe s.): bilan historiographique et état de la recherche*. Actes du colloque de Toulouse, 22–23 mars 2007, Toulouse, 2012; "Inciter le roi de France à partir à la croisade: Le sermon *Exaltavi lignum humile* de Pierre de La Palud (1332) et le *Discours du voyage d'outre-mer* de Jean Germain (1451)", in *Croisade et discours de guerre sainte à la fin du Moyen Âge. Légitimation, propagande, prosélytisme*, Actes du colloque de Toulouse, 27–28 mars 2008, Toulouse, 2012; ed. *Projets de croisades, XIIe –XVIIe s.*, Actes du colloque de Paris, juin 2009, Toulouse, 2012; "Faire la paix pour faire la guerre. Paix et guerre dans la croisade", in Gisela Naegle, ed., *Frieden schaffen und sich verteidigen im Spätmittelalter / Faire la paix et se défendre à la fin du Moyen Âge*, Pariser Historische Studien, 98; "La croisade: guerre juste, guerre sainte?", in *Guerre juste et juste guerre*, Actes du colloque de Créteil, octobre 2009, Paris, 2012.

PERRA, Photeine V., "Aspects of the Messenian history during Latin domination. The case of Navarino/Port de Jonc", in *Messenia. A contribution to its history and civilization*, Athens, Papazisis Publ., 2012. [in Greek].

PETRE, James, *Crusader Castles of Cyprus. The Fortifications of Cyprus under the Lusignans, 1191–1489*, Nicosia, Cyprus Research Center.

PHILLIPS, Jonathan, "Ibn Jubayr, Saladin and the 'unification' of the Muslim Near East", in K.V. Jensen, K.L. Salonen and H. Vogt, eds., *Cultural Encounters During the Crusades*, University Press of Southern Denmark, 2012; "Caffaro of Genoa and the Motives of the Early Crusaders", in P. Ingesman, ed., *Religion as an Agent for Change*, Aarhus University Press, 2012–13; with Martin Hall, Translation, introduction and notes to: *Caffaro, Genoa and the Crusades*, Crusader Texts in Translation series, Farnham: Ashgate.

PIANA, Mathias, with Christer Carlsson, ed., *Architecture and Archaeology of the Military Orders*, Ashgate, 2012; "A Bulwark Never Conquered: the Fortifications of the Templar Citadel of Tortosa on the Syrian Coast", ibid.

PIMENTA, Maria Cristina, A Ordem de Santiago em Portugal: fidelidade normativa e autonomia política", in Palmela, [2010], 2012, pp. 397–414.

POLEJOWSKI, Karol, "The counts of Brienne and Military Orders in the XIIIth century", MO5, Ashgate 2012; "Teutonic Order's propaganda in France during the wars against Poland and Lithuania (XV century)", in *Die geistlichen Ritterorden in Mitteleuropa*, Brno, 2012; *Hrabiowie Brienne w Grecji frankijskiej: między realizacją a upadkiem rodowych ambicji (do 1311 r.) (The Counts of Brienne in Frankish Greece: between realization and fall of the dynastic politics (till 1311)*, Gdansk Medieval Studies, 2012.

PRINGLE, Denys, "The Order of St Thomas of Canterbury in Acre", MO5; "Crusader Castles and Fortifications: The Armenian Connection", in G. Dédeyan and C. Mutafian, eds., *La Méditerranée des Arméniens, XIIe–XVe siècles*, Lisbonne: Fondation Calouste Gulbenkian.

PURKIS, William J., "Crusading and Crusade Memory in Caesarius of Heisterbach's *Dialogus miraculorum*", *Journal of Medieval History*, 2013; "Rewriting the History Books: The First Crusade and the Past", in Marcus Bull and Damien Kempf, eds., *Narrating the First Crusade: Historiography, Memory and Transmission in the Narratives of the Early Crusade Movement*, Boydell & Brewer, 2013.

RIST, Rebecca, *The Cathars and the Albigensian Crusade: A Sourcebook*, ed. and trans. with C. Léglu, and C. Taylor, Longman, 2012.

ROCHE, Jason T., ed. with Janus Møller Jensen, *The Second Crusade: Holy War on the Periphery of Latin Christendom*, Turnhout, 2012; "The Second Crusade: Main Debates and

New Horizons", ibid.; "King Conrad III of Germany in the Byzantine Empire: a Foil for Native Imperial Virtue", ibid.

RODRÍGUEZ GARCÍA, José Manuel, *La cruzada en tiempos de Alfonso X el Sabio*, Silex, Madrid, 2012; *La ideología de cruzada en el s. XIII. Una visión desde Castilla*, Actas, Madrid, 2012; "La predicación de cruzada y yihad. Una aproximación comparativa", in *Guerra santa peninsular y peregrinaje Mediterráneo en la Edad Media*, Anales de la Universidad de Alicante, 2011; "Existieron ejércitos cruzados en la época de Fernando III", in *Fernando III, tiempo de cruzada*, Silex-UAM, 2012.

RUBIN, Jonathan, "John of Ancona's *Summae*: A Neglected Source for the Juridical History of the Latin Kingdom of Jerusalem", *Bulletin of Medieval Canon Law*, 29, 2011.

SIMSONS, Raitis, "Prūšu *nobiles* Dusburgas Pētera *Chronicon Terrae Prussiae* un to loma prūšu sabiedrībā" ("Prussian nobiles in *Chronicon Terrae Prussiae* by Petri de Dusburg and their probable political role in the Prussian community"), University of Latvia, Scientific Papers University of Latvia, No 764 – History, 2012.

SLACK, Corliss, *Historical Dictionary of the Crusades*, revised edition, Lanham, Maryland and Oxford: Scarecrow Press, 2012.

SMITH, Thomas, "Honorius III and the Crusade: Responsive Papal Government versus the Memory of his Predecessors", in Peter Clarke and Charlotte Methuen, eds., *Studies in Church History*, 49, 2013.

STAPEL, Rombert, "Power to the educated? Priest-brethren and their education, using data of the Utrecht bailiwick of the Teutonic Order, 1350–1600", MO5.

STOHLER, Patrick, "Wahrnehmung und Traditionsbildung in einem Traktat des 14. Jh."; "Das 18. Jahrhundert und 'der Kreuzzug': Genese und Entwicklung eines Konzepts".

SWEETENHAM, Carol, "Crusaders in a Hall of Mirrors: the portrayal of Saracens in Robert the Monk's *Historia Iherosolimitana*", in S. Lambert, E. James and H. Nicholson, eds., *Languages of Love and Hate*, Turnhout: Brepols, 2012.

TEBRUCK, Stefan, "Die sizilischen Klöster S. Maria Latina und S. Maria in Valle Josaphat", in E. Bünz and W. Huschner, eds., *Italien-Mitteldeutschland-Polen. Internationale Tagung der Universität Leipzig*, Schriften zur sächsischen Geschichte und Volkskunde; "Crusades, Crusaders I. Christianity", in *Encyclopedia of the Bible and its Reception*, Berlin and New York, De Gruyter, 2012.

TOUATI, François-Olivier, "Pertes et profits des Croisades".

TSOUGARAKIS, Nickiphoros I., *The Latin Religious Orders in Medieval Greece, 1204–1500*, Turnhout: Brepols, 2012; co-ed., *A Companion to Medieval Greece*, Leiden: Brill, 2013; "Religious Patronage in Medieval Greece", in *Monasteries on the Borders of Medieval Europe: New Perspectives*, Turnhout: Brepols.

TSURTSUMIA, "Mamuka, τριβόλος: A Byzantine Landmine", *Byzantion*, 82, 2012.

TYERMAN, Christopher, "New wine in old skins? The Crusade and the Eastern Mediterranean in the later Middle Ages", in C. Holmes and J. Harris, eds., *Byzantines, Latins and Turks in the Eastern Mediterranean World after 1150*, Oxford Byzantine Studies, OUP, 2012.

De VAIVRE, Jean-Bernard, "Guillaume Caoursin et ses silences. Prolégomènes à une édition des récits de Rhodes assiégée", *Comptes-rendus de l'Académie des Inscriptions et Belles-Lettres*, Paris; *"Tous les deables de l'Enfer", Relations du siège de Rhodes par les Ottomans en 1480*, Éditions Droz.

VANDEBURIE, Jan, "Chroniclers during the Fifth Crusade in the Middle between the Muslim East and the Christian West: The Works of Jacques de Vitry and Oliver of Paderborn Bridging

Latin and Arabic Historiography", *Carnival: Journal of the International Students of History Association*, 13.

WEBER, Benjamin, "Gli Etiopi a Roma nel Quattrocento. ambasciatori politici, negoziatori religiosi o viaggiatori peregrini?", in *Dall'Archivio Segreto Vaticano. Miscellanea di testi, saggi e inventari*, 2012; "Nouveau mot ou nouvelle réalité? Le terme *cruciata* et son utilisation dans les textes pontificaux", Avignon SSCLE 7.

WILSKMAN, Juho, "A conflict (and some co-habitation) in Crusader Greece – Morea 1264 and the Battle of Makry-Plagi", *CEU Crusades* (working title)

5. Work in progress

ANTAKI-MASSON, Patricia, Crusader fortifications of Beirut; Crusader topography and fortifications of Tyre; Medieval sundials of Lebanon; History of the Cistercian abbey of Belmont (Tripoli-Lebanon); Cistercian abbeys of Lebanon.

BALARD, Michel, La Méditerranée au Moyen Age [book].

BAYDAL, Vicent, The Union revolt in the kingdom of Valencia in 1347 [book]; research on the Aragonese crusade against Almeria in 1309; prosopographical study of the composition of the army of James II.

BELLOMO, Elena, "Diplomazia e Crociata nel Mediterraneo di inizio Trecento: il Francescano savonese Filippo Brusserio"; "I Sentieri della memoria: crociata e reliquie oltremarine in un'anonima cronaca monferrina medievale" [articles]; The Spanish military Orders in Italy (XIII–XV centuries); The Italian maritimes cities and the first crusades: a study on motivation and propaganda.

BIDDLECOMBE, Steven, A translation into English of Baldric of Bourgueil's *Historia Ierosolimitana* – a collaborative project with Dr Susan B. Edgington; "Fellow Travellers" – the Texts Chosen by Medieval Manuscript Commissioners to Accompany Baldric's *Historia* – What can they tell us about the context in which First Crusade narratives were received and transmitted?

BIRD, Jessalynn, The *"History of the West" (Historia Occidentalis) of Jacques de Vitry*, Liverpool University Press, translation with critical introduction and notes; *Women and the Crusades*, London Books; *An English translation of the letters and Historia Orientalis of James of Vitry*; Articles on James of Vitry and Oliver of Paderborn on Islam and Eastern Christians; An article on prophecy, the crusade, and the circle of Peter the Chanter.

BOAS, Adrian J., *Montfort One: History, Early Research and Recent Studies*.

BOMBI, Barbara, Preaching in the canon law commentaries of the early 13th century.

BORCHARDT, Karl, with Damien Carraz, edition of: *Comptes de la commanderie de l'Hôpital de Saint-Gilles pour les années 1283 à 1290*, Institut de recherche de d'histoire des textes.

BUTTIGIEG, Emanuel, with Dr Simon Phillips of the University of Cyprus, organised a conference on Rhodes between 27 and 29 April 2011 on the theme of "Islands and the Military Orders". The plenary speakers were Anthony Luttrell and Victor Mallia-Milanes. Now in the process of collecting and editing the contributions with the intention of publishing the proceedings.

CARR, Michael, *Crusades in the Aegean from the Fall of Acre to the Black Death: 1291–1351* [monograph]; "Papal trade licences, Italian merchants and the changing perceptions of the Mamluks and Turkish *beyliks* in the fourteenth century" [article]; "The Hospitallers of Rhodes and their Alliances Against the Turks" [article]; "Humbert of Vienne and the Crusade of Smyrna: A Reconsideration", [article].

CARRAZ, Damien, "Les Templiers de Provence et la Terre Sainte: mobilité et carrières (XIIIe–XIVe siècles)", in Palmela 2010; "Pour une approche globale des novæ religiones: en Basse-Provence aux XIIe–XIIIe siècles", in Journée d'étude en l'honneur du Professeur D. Le Blévec, Université de Montpellier, 3 février 2011; "Les établissements des ordres militaires dans l'espace urbain au XIIIe siècle. État de la question (Orient/Occident)", in Espaces monastiques et espaces urbains, ed. C. Caby, Mélanges de l'École française de Rome-Moyen Âge; "Templars and Hospitallers as peacemakers in feudal and princely conflicts in Occitania during the twelfth and thirteenth centuries", MO17; "Paix et trêve entre Xe et XIIe siècles", La réforme "grégorienne" dans le Midi (milieu XIe–fin XIIe siècle), 48e colloque de Fanjeaux, juillet 2012.

CASSIDY-WELCH, Megan, "War and memory in European culture: a long perspective", funded by the Australian Research Council through a Future Fellowship, 2011–2015

CHEVALIER, Marie-Anna, Participation au programme de recherches sur La paix. Concepts, pratiques et systèmes politiques, sous la responsabilité de Denise Aigle (UMR 8167 "Orient et Méditerranée"), Michele Bernardini (Université de Naples), Stéphane Péquignot (EPHE), Frédéric Bauden (Université de Liège), Nicolas Drocourt (Université de Nantes).

CHRISSIS, Nikolaos, publication of the proceedings of the conference organised with Mike Carr (RHUL), under the auspices of the SSCLE, entitled: "Contact and conflict in Frankish Greece and the Aegean: crusade, trade and religion amongst Latins, Greeks and Muslims, 1204–1453", 9 July 2010, Institute of Historical Research, London. The volume will include contributions on Byzantine, crusade and Ottoman history, by Prof. Bernard Hamilton (Nottingham), Prof. Peter Lock (York St John), Dr. Evrim Binbaş (RHUL), Mike Carr (RHUL), Dr. Nikolaos Chrissis (RHUL), Dr. Rhoads Murphey (Birmingham), Dr. Teresa Shawcross (Amherst), and Dr. Judith Ryder (Wolfson College, Oxford).

CHRIST, Georg, ed. with Alexander Daniel Beihammer, Stefan Burkhardt, Franz Julius Morche, Wolfgang Kaiser, Wolfgang, Roberto Zaugg, Union in Separation – Trading Diasporas in the Eastern Mediterranean (1200–1700), Heidelberg: Springer; Cretan Wine between Cairo, Venice and London 1200–1700: Multilateral Trading Systems Revisited; "Portugese Ships in India and Rotting Pepper in Alexandria. News Management and Self-Fullfilling Supply Crisis (1503–1505)".

CHRISTIE, Niall G.F., Muslims and Crusaders: Christianity's Wars in the Middle East, 1095–1291, from the Islamic Sources [book to be published by Pearson]; Preaching Holy War: Crusade and Jihad, 1095–1105, with Deborah Gerish [book to be published by Ashgate].

COLEMAN, Edward, "Ireland and the Crusades. A survey of the evidence"; "The Italian city communes and the Crusades in the twelfth century" [articles].

CONNELL, Charles W., Public Opinion in the Middles Ages [book]; article on the dehumanization of the Saracen in crusade rhetoric, forthcoming in an anthology of articles resulting from the 2010 ACMRS conference; articles on "public opinion", "Foreigners and Fear", and "sermons" in Medieval Culture: a Compendium of Critical Topics in the series Fundamental Aspects and Condtions of the European Middle Ages, ed. Albrecht Classen, Berlin and New York: de Gruyter.

COSTA, Paula Pinto, member of several teams: project Eurocore Cuius Regio. An analysis of the cohesive and disruptive forces destining the attachment of groups of persons to and the cohesion within regions as a historical phenomenon (CURE), by European Science Foundation (2010–2013); project Comendas das Ordens Militares: perfil nacional e inserção internacional – projecto n° FCOMP-01-0124-FEDER-010538 (Refª. FCT PTDC/HIS-HIS/102956/2008, by FCT – 2010–2013); project "A cultura dos pazos en Galicia:

o pazo de Tovar (CULTURPAZ)", Dirección Xeral de Investigación, Desenvolvimento e Innovación de la Xunta de Galicia – 10SEC606033PR (CSIC de Santiago de Compostela, since January 2011); *Medieval Europe – Medieval Cultures and Technological Resources*, COST Action (since 2011).

CRAWFORD, Paul F., A translation of the *Passio Reginaldis* and other documents relating to Renaud of Châtillon (as per *Crusades* 9).

DANSETTE, Béatrice, La *Peregrinatio in terram sanctam* de Bernhard von Breidenbach, édition critique sous la direction du Pr. Jean Meyer.

DEMPSEY, John A., Entry on "Medieval Papacy", De Gruyter's Shorter Handbook on Medieval Studies, ed. Albrecht Classen.

DEMURGER, Alain, *Les hospitaliers de Saint-Jean de Jérusalem (XIe–début du XIVe siècle)*; *Le peuple templier: prosopographie des Templiers d'après les procès-verbaux des interrogatoires des templiers au cours des process*, Catalogue alphabétique électronique et introduction sous forme de livre.

DICKSON, Gary, Charisma, Medieval and Modern [Essay].

DIVALL, Richard, Music Edition from Archives of Malta and Wignacourt Museum, Works by Michel'Angelo Falosi and Don Michel'Angelo Vella (18th Century).

DOUROU-ELIOPOULOU, Maria, Research program of the University of Athens: The Aragonese policy in Greece in the 14th century based on unpublished archival material from Barcelona.

EDBURY, Peter, Critical edition of the Chronicle of Ernoul and Old French Continuations of William of Tyre (with Massimiliano Gaggero), Brill; with Nicholas Coureas, *Chronique d'Amadi* (annotated translation), Cyprus Research Centre.

EDGINGTON, Susan, Guido da Vigevano's *Regimen sanitatis*: edition, translation and commentary; Paperback translation of Albert of Aachen's *Historia* (for Ashgate).

FAVREAU-LILIE, Marie-Luise, *Italien und der islamische Orient zur Zeit der Kreuzzüge*; *Merkantile Expansion und historische Selbstdarstellung der itallienischen Seestädte* [book].

FISHHOF, Gil, "The Crusader Capitals of Nazareth Revisited: Historiography and New Suggestions".

FOLDA, Jaroslav, Study of the Origins and Development of Chrysography in Byzantine, Crusader, and Italian painting.

FONSECA, Luís Adão da, Coordinator of the research project Comendas das Ordens Militares: perfil nacional e inserção internacional (FCT-Portugal-2010–2013) [Commanderies of the Military Orders: national profile and international setting].

FOREY, Alan J., The Papacy and the Spanish Reconquest; Western Converts to Islam; Paid Troops in the Service of Military Orders; Visitations in the Military Orders (Twelfth and Thirteenth Centuries).

FRIEDMAN, Yvonne, Book: *Interludes of Peace*.

GABRIELE, Matthew, Prophecy, Apocalypse, and the Intellectual Transformation of the Medieval West; *The Legend of Charlemagne in Latin Culture*, ed. with William Purkis, Rochester, NY: Boydell and Brewer; *Exegesis in Practice, Prophecy Come True: Pope Urban II, the Arc of Sacred History, and the Language of Christian Reconquest*.

GAPOSCHKIN, Cecilia, *Crusade, Liturgy, Ideology and Devotion*, 1050–1350 [book].

GILCHRIST, Marianne M, Biographical research on Conrad of Montferrat.

GOURDIN, Philippe, "Les relations entre l'Italie tyrrhénienne et le Maghreb, et les Italiens dans l'Empire hafside au XVe siècle", *BEFAR*.

GRASSO, Christian, *Papauté et croisade entre le IVᵉ Concile du Latran et le Iᵉʳ Concile de Lyon (1216–1245)*, thèse de Post-doctorat, École pratique des hautes études, Paris.

HALL, Martin, New critical edition of John of Garland's *"De triumphis Ecclesiae"*, based on a new transcription of the manuscript, and an English translation, to be published respectively in the series *Corpus Christianorum, Continuatio Medievalis* and *Corpus Christianorum in translation*, Turnhout: Brepols Publishers)

HAMILTON, Bernard, *The Crusades and a Wider World*, Continuum Books.

HANSON, Chris, Synchrony – the significance of the horse as herd animal in medieval steppe warfare and horse archery.

HARRIS, Jonathan, Research into the last 150 years before the fall of Constantinople.

HINZ, Felix, ed., Kreuzzüge des Mittelalters und der Neuzeit. Realhistorie – Geschichtskultur – Didaktik (Crusades of the Middle Ages and in the Modern Era: History – Reflections – Teaching), Hildesheim, Georg-Olms-Verlag, 2013; Mythos Kreuzzüge. Selbst- und Fremdbilder in historischen Romanen (The crusades myth in historical novels). (publisher not yet clear) 2013; http://www.felixhinz.de/Plakat-Hinz-A0.pdf.

HOLMES, Catherine, ed. with B. Weiler, J. Van Steenbergen and J.Shepard, *Political Culture in Three Spheres. Byzantium, the Islamic World and the West.*

HOSTEN, Jan, Research on Gerard de Ridefort.

IRWIN, Robert, Book on Hamilton Gibb and Bernard Lewis; Twelfth-century Arabic poetry with reference to the Crusades; The Mamluk army in thirteenth-century Syria.

JORDAN, William Chester, Aspects of the court circle of Louis IX.

JOTISCHKY, Andrew, *The cult of St Katherine of Alexandria across the Norman diaspora*, to be published in a collection of essays co-edited by Keith Stringer as part of the AHRC-funded "Norman Edge" research project at Lancaster University; a short book for the general reader on the Crusades in the *Beginners Guide* series in 2011/12.

JUBB, Margaret A., Article on a prose version of the *Ordre de Chevalerie* interpolated after Book 21, Chapter 27, in two manuscripts of the *Eracles*, Baltimore, Walters Art Gallery, ms.137 and Épinal, Bibliothèque municipale, ms. 45.

KANGAS, Sini, *Children in Holy War, c. 1100–1300*, Helsinki Collegium for Advanced Studies.

KEDAR, Benjamin Z., *A cultural history of the Kingdom of Jerusalem* [book]; Inventio patriarcharum – part 2 [article]; The battle of Arsuf, 1191[article]; Inventio patriarcharum – part 2, [article].

LEONARD Jr., Robert D., Gold Coins of Crusader States of Jerusalem and Tripoli.

LOWER, Michael, "Gregory IX and the Crusades", book chapter for *Pope Gregory IX (1227–1241)*, Ashgate, 2012; *The Tunis Crusade of 1270* [book].

LUCHITSKAYA, Svetlana, Images of Saracens in the *Bibles* moralisées [series of articles].

MADDEN, Thomas F., A monograph on Venice and the crusades.

MENACHE, Sophia, "Love your neighbour"? Changing attitudes to the Moslems in the Crusader Period.

MITCHELL, Piers D., Analysis of a latrine at the crusader castle of Saranda Kolones at Paphos, Cyprus for evidence of intestinal parasites in the garrison; Research on the human skeletal remains excavated from the crusader castle of Blanchegarde, Israel (Tell es-Safi).

MÖHRING, Hannes, *Saladin und seine Nachfolger. Die Geschichte der Aiyubiden* [book].

MUSARRA, Antonio, "Abbandonare Acri? Guglielmo Boccanegra e la guerra di San Saba,

1256–1258"; "Benedetto Zaccaria e la caduta di Tripoli. Nuove evidenze documentarie dall'Archivio di Stato di Genova"; "Vita quotidiana di un notaio genovese in Oltremare, 1294–1301" [articles]; "Acri, 1291. La caduta"; "Praepotens Genuensium Praesidium. I Genovesi, la crociata e la Terrasanta nel XIII secolo"; "The Italian Maritimes Cities and the Fall of the Crusader States, 1244–1291" [books]; "AS GE, ms. 62, Nicolai De Porta, quondam Mathaei, notarii quarti clerici Ianuensis, *Historia translationis beati Ioannis Baptiste ad Civitatem Ianue compilata per Nicolaum qondam Matthei de Porta notarium quartum clericum Ianuensem*" [edition].

NICHOLSON, Helen J., The Knights Templars' English and Welsh Estates, 1308–13, a transcription and analysis of the inventories and accounts of the Templars' properties in England and Wales during the trial of the Templars – as described in Bulletin no. 29.

NICOLAOU-KONNARI, Angel, *La Culture du Locus. De l'Espace géographique à l'Espace utopique (1200–1650)*, Colloque International, Université de Chypre – Sapienza Università di Roma (Nicosia, 6–7 May 2011), ed. with Evelien Chayes, Rafaella Anconetani, Sonia Gentili; Research programme "Digital Library of Sources on Medieval Cyprus", in collaboration with King's College, London, UK; Research programme "Prosopography of Medieval Cyprus", in collaboration with King's College, London, UK; Research programme "New edition of Ms Torino J.II. 9", in collaboration with the Université Paul Valéry, Montpellier III, France; *History of Limassol*, co-editor with Chris Schabel, Medochemie Series 2, 2009/10; with C. Schabel, "Frankish and Venetian Limassol", ibid.; *Two Cypriots of the Diaspora : Works and Days of Pietro and Giorgio de Nores* [Cyprus Research Centre] Nicosia, 2010; *Medieval Famagusta*, co-editor with G. Grivaud, C. Otten-Froux, C. Schabel, and A. Weyl Carr; "Women and Family Life (in Lusignan and Venetian Famagusta)", ibid.

NICOLLE, David, Un pari manqué: La seconde croisade et le siège de Damas en 1148, co-authored with Yann Kervran; *Portuguese Forces in the Age of Discovery, mid-14th to mid-17th centuries*, Oxford, Osprey, Men-at-Arms series, 2012–2013); A Preliminary Report on the Mamluk military equipment found in Tower 4 of the Citadel of Damascus, for the Council for British Research in the Levant Bulletin.

PASTORI RAMOS, Aurelio, Violence in Medieval Hagiography: the *Vita Sancti Stephani Obazinensis*, and the *Vita Sancti Malachiae* (St. Bernard of Clairvaux).

PHILLIPS, Christopher Matthew, Book on *Crusade Preaching, Doctrine of Redemption, Devotion to the Cross*.

PHILLIPS, Jonathan, Saladin: A Medieval and Modern Hero; Flanders and the Third Crusade.

PHILLIPS, Simon D., The Hospitallers on Cyprus and Rhodes in the Late Middle Ages; The Hospitaller Priory at Clerkenwell and the local community 1400–1540; The Military Orders and Island History.

POLEJOWSKI, Karol, *The Briennes and the Mediterranean World in the XIIIth and XIVth centuries; The Teutonic Order in the XIIIth and XIVth centuries*.

PORTNYKH, Valentin, Humbert of Romans' treatise "De praedicatione sanctae crucis contra Saracenos": critical edition.

PURKIS, William J., *Bearers of the Cross* [book]: a study of the materiality of belief and religious material culture associated with crusading; *Charlemagne in Latin* (book): a collection of essays, co-edited with Matthew Gabriele.

REYNOLDS, Burnam W., *The Prehistory of the Crusades: Missionary War and the Baltic Crusades*, London, Continuum Press, 2013.

RICHARD, Jean, *Bullarium Cyprium*, t. III (Jean XXII–Grégoire XI).

RIST, Rebecca, Book on *The Papacy and the Jews in the Central Middle Ages.*

ROCHE, Jason T., *The Crusade of King Conrad III of Germany: Warfare and Diplomacy in the Byzantine Empire, Anatolia and Outrémer, 1145–1149*; "King Louis VII of France and the Second Crusade in Anatolia".

RODRIGUEZ GARCIA, José Manuel, *The Teutonic Order and the Kingdoms of Spain* (13th–18th centuries) [book]; The way of preaching the Crusade and Jihad in Castile and Leon (1140–1340) [article].

RUBENSTEIN, Jay, Holy War and History: The First Crusade at the End of the Time.

SARNOWSKY, Juergen, Die Schuldbücher und Rechnungen der Großschäffer und Lieger des Deutschen Ordens in Preußen, Bd. 2: Großschäfferei Königsberg II (Ordensfoliant 142–149) (Quellen und Darstellungen zur hansischen Geschichte N.F. LIX,2 = Veröffentlichungen aus den Archiven Preußischer Kulturbesitz 62, 2), Köln, Weimar, Wien: Boehlau.

SCHRYVER, James G., with Tasha Vorderstrasse, A study of the Port St. Symeon ware from Hama, in the National Museum of Copenhagen.

SIDSELRUD, Kaare Seeberg, The Sonnenburg Collection of Armorial Achievements of the Johanniter Orden, Balley Brandenburg – containing Coat of Arms of Knights of the Order from the late Middle Ages to the dawn of WWI.

SLACK, Corliss, A History of British Crusade Sites.

STANTCHEV, Stefan, *Spiritual Rationality: Papal Embargo as Cultural Practice, 1150–1520* (Book); "The Medieval Origins of Embargo as a Policy Tool".

STOHLER, Patrick, History of Armenia.

SWEETENHAM, Carol, Translation of the *Chanson des Chétifs* and *Chanson de Jérusalem* for Ashgate's Crusade Texts in Translation series.

TEBRUCK, Stefan, Aufbruch und Heimkehr. Jerusalempilger und Kreuzfahrer aus dem sächsisch-thüringischen Raum, 1100–1300 (Vorträge und Forschungen – Sonderbände, hg. vom Konstanzer Arbeitskreis für mittelalterliche Geschichte; zugl. Habilitationsschrift Friedrich-Schiller-Universität Jena 2007), Ostfildern 2013, in print.

THROOP, Susanna, "Christian Community and the Crusades: Religious Practices in the *De expugnatione Lyxbonensi*" [article]; "Text, Image and Ideology: The Crucifixion and the First Crusade in a Late Medieval Manuscript (BNF fr. 352)" [article].

TOUATI, François-Olivier, *Les actes et documents relatifs à Saint-Lazare de Jérusalem (Orient-Occident)*, édition.

TSOUGARAKIS, Nickiphoros I., "Freedom and Servitude in the Crusader States of Greece".

TSURTSUMIA, Mamuka, Crusaders' commemorations in the manuscripts of the Monastery of the Holy Cross in Jerusalem.

TYERMAN, Christopher J., Book on *Crusade.*

UPTON, Todd P., *Sacred Topography: Western Sermon Perceptions of Jerusalem, the Holy Sites, and Jews during the Crusades, 1095–1193* [book]; "'*Revertamur Jerusalem*' : Transformed Perceptions of Jerusalem and the *Loca Sancta* by the Third Crusade" [article].

De VAIVRE, Jean-Bernard, Rhodes aux XIVe–XVe et début du XVIe siècle; Fortifications des Hospitaliers en Dodécanèse; Chypre, iconographie à la fin du XIVe siècle.

VILLEGAS-ARISTIZABAL, Lucas, "The Failed Attempt to Conquer Lisbon c. 1142 as described by the Historia gothorum and De expugnatione Lyxbonensi"; "The Annals of Emon of Florudus Hortus and the Fifth Crusade"; "Did Salveric of Maleon Participate in the Failed

Attempt on Caceres of Alfonso IX"; "The decline of the Anglo-Norman Involvement in the *Reconquista* after the Second Crusade c. 1150–1248".

WEBER, Benjamin, Edition and comment of the *Liber Sancte Cruciate*, book of account of Pius II's crusade in 1464.

WILSON, Ian, Tancred and the Laws of War.

WILSKMAN, Juho, Periodical article "The Battle of Prinitsa in 1263"; Periodical article "The conflict between the Angevins and the Byzantines in Morea in 1267–1289: A Late Byzantine endemic war".

YOLLES, Julian, Critical edition of the third book of Achard and Geoffrey's poem on the Templum Domini, which constitutes a versification of Hegesippus' paraphrase of Josephus' *Jewish War*.

6. Theses in progress

BALDWIN, Philip B., *Pope Gregory X and the Crusades*, PhD, Queen Mary, University of London.

BARBU, Diana Cornelia, The Anjou Dynasty, the Order of Saint George and the links with the rulers of Wallachia, PhD, Valahia University of Targoviste, Romania.

BARREIRO, Poliana Monteiro, *As instituições da Ordem de Santiago em Setúbal entre a Medievalidade e a Modernidade*. PhD, Porto University, supervised by Pr Paula Pinto Costa.

BERNER, Alexander, *Crusaders from the Lower Rheinland*, PhD, Bochum University, supervised by Pr. Nikolas Jaspert.

BINYSH, Betty, *Peace-making in the Latin East between 1099 and 1291*, PhD, Cardiff University, supervised by Dr Helen Nicholson.

BLEY, Matthias, *Purity, Reform and the Other*, PhD, Bochum University, supervised by Prof. Nikolas Jaspert.

BRACHTHÄUSER, Urs, *The Crusade against Mahdia in 1390*, PhD Thesis, Bochum University, supervised by Pr. Nikolas Jaspert.

BUCK, Andrew David, *The Crusader principality of Antioch as a frontier society, 1130–1201*, PhD, Queen Mary, University of London, supervised by Dr. Tom Asbridge.

BUCKINGHAM, Hannah, Identity and archaeology in everyday life: the material culture of the Crusader states, PhD, Cardiff University, supervised by Denys Pringle.

CARR, Michael, Motivations and Response to Crusades in the Aegean: c.1302–1348, PhD, Royal Holloway, University of London, supervised by Pr. Jonathan Harris.

CHRIST, Georg, *Trade Embargos. Barriers, Taxes and Evasion Practices in Maritime Trade in the Realm of the Hanseatic League and the Eastern Mediterranean (1200–1400)*, Universität Heidelberg, Habilitation/second book.

COSGROVE, Walker Reid, *Clergy and Crusade: the Church of Languedoc during the Albigensian Crusade*, PhD, Saint-Louis University, USA.

DACHELET, Joffrey, *Les Scandinaves et la Méditerranée au Moyen Âge*, PhD, Université François-Rabelais, Tours, supervised by Pr. François-Olivier Touati ?

DIVALL, Richard, *The Complete Sacred Music of Nicolò Isouard [1773–1818]*. An edition and thesis, PhD in Theology, Catholic Theological College, Melbourne as part of Melbourne College of Divinity University.

DURKIN, Frances, Crusade Preaching: Origins, Evolution and Impact, PhD, University of Birmingham, supervised by Dr. William Purkis.

DONNACHIE, Stephen, *Reconstruction and Rebirth: The Kingdom of Jerusalem, 1187–1233*, PhD, Swansea University, supervised by Pr. John France and Daniel Power.

GEORGIOU, Constantinos, *Crusading preaching during the 14th century*, PhD, University of Cyprus, supervised by Christopher Schabel.

GOURINARD, Henri, *Levantine Towns in the* itineraria *of the 14th–17th Centuries*, PhD, The Hebrew University of Jerusalem, supervised by Pr. Benjamin Z. Kedar.

GUTGARTS-WEINBERGER, Anna, *Jerusalem in the Twelfth Century – A Systematic Analysis of a Developing Urban Landscape*, PhD, The Hebrew University of Jerusalem, supervised by Pr. Ronnie Ellenblum and Dr. Iris Shagrir.

HALL, Martin, "John of Garland's '*De triumphis Ecclesiae*': critical edition with translation and historico-literary analysis", PhD, Royal Holloway, University of London, supervised by Pr Jonathan Phillips.

HOBBS, Chris, *A Study of the Historia Byzantina of Doukas*, MPhil/PhD, Royal Holloway, University of London, supervised by Pr. Jonathan Harris.

IKONOMOPOULOS, Konstantinos, *Byzantium and Jerusalem, 9th–13th Centuries*, PhD, Royal Holloway, University of London, supervised by Pr. Jonathan Harris.

JOHN, Simon A., *Godfrey of Bouillon: The development of a First Crusade hero, c.1100–1325*, PhD, Swansea University, supervised by Pr. John France and Pr. Daniel Power.

KOOL, Robert, *The Circulation and Use of Coins in the Latin kingdom of Jerusalem, 1099–1291*, PhD, Hebrew U of Jerusalem, supervised by Pr. Benjamin Z. Kedar co-directed with Michael Metcalf.

LEWIS, Kevin James, *A study of the internal aspects of the county of Tripoli during the twelfth century*, PhD, Oxford University, supervised by Dr Christopher Tyerman.

LINCOLN, Kyle C., *The Bishops and Church of the Kingdom of Castile during the reign of Alfonso VIII*, PhD, University of St.Louis, USA.

MUSARRA, Antonio, *Praepotens Genuensium Praesidium. Genova, la crociata e la Terrasanta nella seconda metà del Duecento, 1244–1301*, PhD, Scuola Superiore di Studi Storici, Università degli Studi di San Marino, supervised by Pr. Anthony Molho.

MYLOD, Liz, *Pilgrimage in the Holy Land, 1187–1291*, PhD, Institute for Medieval Studies, University of Leeds.

PARK, Danielle, "Under Our Protection, That of the Church and Their Own" – Papal and Secular Protection of the Families and Properties the Crusaders Left Behind, *c.* 1095–1254, PhD, Royal Holloway College, University of London.

PARKER, Kenneth Scott, *The Indigenous Christians of Bilād al-Shām and Egypt in an Age of Crusaders, Mamlūks, and Mongols (1244–1366)*, PhD, Royal Holloway, University of London, supervised by Pr. Jonathan Harris.

POLEJOWSKI, Karol, *Fidelis pugil Ecclesiae? The Briennes and their Mediterranean World in the XIIIth and XIVth centuries*, habilitation thesis, University of Gdansk, Faculty of History, 2012.

RAJOHNSON, Matthieu, PhD, *The Image of Jerusalem in the West, from 1187 to the end of the 14th Century*, Université Paris Ouest – Nanterre La Défense (France).

ROMINE, Anne, *Crusade and Chivalry in the Fourteenth Century: Philippe de Mézières and the Order of the Passion*, PhD, Saint Louis University, supervised by Pr. Thomas F. Madden.

RUBIN, Jonathan, *Intellectual Activities and Intercultural Exchanges in Frankish Acre,*

1191–1291, PhD, Hebrew University of Jerusalem, supervised by Prof. Benjamin Z. Kedar, co-directed with Laura Minervini.

RUSSELL, Eugenia, Encomia to St Demetrius in Late Byzantine Thessalonica, PhD, Royal Holloway, University of London, supervised by Pr. Jonathan Harris.

RYAN, Vincent, The Cult of the Virgin Mary and the Crusading Movement during the High Middle Ages, PhD, Saint Louis University.

SMARANDACHE, Bogdan C, *Frankish-Muslim Relations in the Latin Kingdom of Jerusalem, 1099–1291*, MPhil, St. Catharine's College, University of Cambridge.

SHOTTEN-HALLEL, Vardit, *The Churches of the Latin Kingdom of Jerusalem: Medieval Building Technologies and Architecture in the Frankish Levant and in Europe*, PhD, Hebrew University of Jerusalem, supervised by Pr. Benjamin Z. Kedar.

SMITH, Thomas, *Pope Honorius III and Crusading to Egypt and the Holy Land, 1216–1227*, PhD, Royal Holloway, University of London, supervised by Pr. Jonathan Phillips.

STAPEL, Rombert, *Cronike van der Duytscher Oirden* ["Jüngere Hochmeisterchronik"], PhD, Leiden University/Fryske Akademy.

STOHLER, Patrick, *Europa: Konflikt, Kontakt, Konstrukt. Europäisierung und Nationenbildung im Mittelalter. Die Kreuzzüge im Spannungsfeld zeitgenössischer Wahrnehmung*, PhD, University of Basel, supervised by Pr. Dr. Achatz Freiherr von Müller.

TAMMINEN, Miikka, *Ad crucesignatos et crucesignandos*. Constructing "the True Crusader" in the Crusade Model Sermons of the 13th Century, PhD, University of Tampere, Finland.

TSURTSUMIA, Mamuka, *Medieval Georgian Army: Organisation, Tactics, Equipment*, PhD, Ivane Javakhishvili Tbilisi State University.

VANDEBURIE, Jan, *The Background, Sources and Composition of Jacques de Vitry's* Historia Orientalis *and its Influence in Western Europe and on the Later Crusades*, PhD, University of Kent.

WEBB, Daniel, "Henry VI, Empire, and Crusade", PhD, Saint Louis University, supervised by Pr. Thomas F. Madden.

WHELAN, Mark, *Outside expertise in the Turkish wars of the kings of Hungary, 1396–1460*, PhD, Royal Holloway, University of London, supervised by Pr. Jonathan Harris;

WILSKMAN, Juho, *Comparing "Military Cultures": Warfare in the Aegean Region from the Fourth Crusade to the Early Fifteenth Century*, PhD, University of Helsinki.

WORTH, Meghan Holmes, *"To Write About Kings": The Creation of Kingship in Outremer*, PhD., Knoxville, University of Tennessee.

ZELNIK, Joseph, *Silent enim leges inter arma*?: Laws of War in the Latin Kingdom of Jerusalem, PhD, Bar-Ilan University, Israel, supervised by Professor Yvonne Friedman.

7. Fieldwork planned or undertaken recently

ANTAKI MASSON, Patricia, The crusader fortress of Beirut: recent discoveries; Masons' marks of the Cistercian abbey of Belmont (Tripoli); Medieval sundials of the county of Tripoli.

ATTIYA, Hussein, Muslims and Crusaders as viewed by each other at the time of the first crusade.

BADER, Fady Georges, Independent Scholar, research based on the contribution of Templars in the Lebanese medieval history.

BAYDAL, Vicent, transcripts a register of the royal chancery of James II of Aragon in which most of the members of the army that attacked Almeria in 1309 were listed.

BIDDLECOMBE, Steven, is producing a new edition of Baldric's *Historia* a total (so far) of 23 manuscripts containing a copy of Baldric's text have been found. This compares to the seven used by the editors of the *Recueil* edition.

BOAS, Adrian J., The first season of excavations by the Montfort Castle Project took place in August–September, 2011. The excavations were located in the castle's Great Hall. A second season in the outer ward on the northern slope is planned for the spring of 2012 and conservation work as well as a third summer season are planned for 2012.

BURKIEWICZ, Łukasz, Battle of Nicopolis 1396.

COSTA, Paula Pinto: Participate in the Annual Meeting of CARMEN Co-operative for the Advancement of Research through a Medieval European Network (Centro de Ciencias Humanas y Sociales – CSIC de Madrid; Instituto Empresa University de Segóvia, 9 e 11 de Setembro de 2011).

DIVALL, Richard, Concert and CD: The Sacred Music of Nicolò Isouard. St John's Co-Cathedral, Valletta, Malta, December 2011; Concert: Maltese Sacred Music. St John's Co-Cathedral, Valletta, Malta, June 2012.

HARSCHEIDT, Michael, Webmaster activities: www.templaria.de; www.osmth-moenchengladbach.de

HUNT, Lucy-Anne, 2010–2011: visits to the church of Mar Tadros, Behdaidat, Lebanon working as the art historian with the team, under the directorship of Isabelle Doumet-Skaf, conserving the 13th-century wallpaintings at the church of Mar Tadros, Behdaidat, Lebanon.

KEDAR, Benjamin Z., Coordinating excavations in Acre's Genoese quarter.

LEWIS, Kevin James, is of planning a research trip to North Lebanon in Summer/Autumn 2012 to conduct a preliminary survey of crusader rural settlements in the vicinity of Tripoli.

LIGATO, Giuseppe, Researches concerning the *kazaghand* and other items of Islamic armor.

MUSARRA, Antonio, Gli Italiani e la Terrasanta (XII e XIII secolo); Guglielmo Boccanegra e la Genova del Duecento; Iacopo Doria, Iacopo da Varagine e l'Oriente latino; Benedetto Zaccaria: nuove evidenze documentarie sul commercio in Oltremare dall'Archivio di Stato di Genova.

NICOLLE, David, Continuing research into the Mamluk military equipment found in Tower 4 of the Citadel of Damascus, as and when circumstances allow; A proposed attempt to determine the precise route taken by King Louis' contingent across western Anatolia during the Second Crusade.

PETRE, James, Survey of the site now known as Prophitis Elias in the Pentadaktilos Mountayns.

PORTNYKH, Valentin, The Bible and the Crusades

POLEJOWSKI, Karol, History of the French families, especially the Briennes, in the XIII and first half of the XIV century in the Mediterranean region (Outremer, Greece, Italy).

TEBRUCK, Stefan, Crusaders in the Holy Roman Empire during 11th to 13th centuries – comparative studies on social, economic, political and spiritual aspects of crusading in different territories – this research is planned to be a project of the Chair of Medieval History at the University of Gießen.

De VAIVRE, Jean-Bernard, Rhodes au temps des Hospitaliers; L'ordre de Saint-Jean de Jérusalem, XIIIe–début XVIe siècles.

WEBER, Benjamin, Uses and meanings of the word "crusade" in the Middle Ages. Western contacts with Ethiopia in the Middle Ages

8. News of interest to members

a) Conferences and seminars

Crusades of the Middle Ages and in the Modern Era: History – Reflections – Teaching, conference organized by Dr Felix Hinz, Hildesheim (Germany) 16/17.12.2011); http://www. uni-hildesheim.de/index.php?id=7566

"Écrire l'histoire des croisades (III): L'économie des Croisades et des États latins", Journée d'Étude, org. by Pr. François-Olivier Touati, Université François-Rabelais, Tours, 23 March 2012.

Contextualising the Fifth Crusade: An Interdisciplinary Colloquium on the Crusading Movement in the First Half of the 13th Century, University of Kent, Canterbury, 13–14 April 2012. Organising Committee: Liz Mylod (University of Leeds), Guy Perry (University of Leeds), Thomas Smith (Royal Holloway, University of London), Jan Vandeburie (University of Kent).

International conference *Die Kreuzzugsbewegung im römisch-deutschen Reich (11.–13. Jahrhundert)* organized by Prof. Dr. Nikolas Jaspert, Ruhr-Universität Bochum, and Prof. Dr. Stefan Tebruck, Justus-Liebig-Universität Gießen, 2012, June 21–23.

2ème volet du colloque international sur "L'Europe et le Caucase – Relations interrégionales et la question de l'identité, septembre 2012, Université Montpellier 3, France; contact : Dr Marie-Anna Chevalier.

Colloque international L'économie templière en Occident: patrimoines, commerce, finances, Troyes (Aube), Centre Universitaire-Ville-sous-la-Ferté (Aube), Abbaye cistercienne de Clairvaux, 24 au 26 octobre 2012; contact: Dr Dammien Carraz.

Kevin James Lewis convenes the Oxford Crusades Graduate Reading Group, which meets multiple times during term and discusses a variety of broad issues relating to the crusades. Past topics have included disability, Mediterranean history, neo-Frankish identity, and relations with Byzantium. The group is aimed primarily at graduate students at Oxford University who have an interest in crusade history, but the meetings are open to everyone; contact him for further information.

The *Crusades Studies Forum* at Saint Louis University meets ten to twelve times annually to hear lectures from scholars worldwide or discuss recent publications in the field. All members of the SSCLE are cordially invited to attend. The Crusades Studies Forum at Saint Louis University is a venue for the presentation of current research, the discussion of recent scholarship, and the exploration of new directions in topics relating to the Crusades. Participants include those local to the Saint Louis region as well as distinguished scholars from across the globe. All are welcome to attend and participate in the forum. During the 2011–2012 academic year, CSF presenters include Robert Somerville (Columbia University), Laurence Marvin (Berry College), John France (Swansea University), and Brenda Bolton (Retired, University of London). For more information see the website at http://crusades.slu. edu. Or our colleague, Pr. Thomas Madden.

Information for the annual SSCLE Dinner at Kalamazoo can be found at http://sscle.slu.edu.

ANZAMEMS – Ninth Biennial Conference 2013 Melbourne Australia. Theme: "Cultures in Translation", Monash University, Caulfield Campus, Melbourne, Australia. We have had a number of sessions on crusades and crusading organised under auspices of SSCLE at ANZAMEMS conferences in 2008 (Tasmania) and 2011 (New Zealand). ANZAMEMS [Australian & New Zealand Association for Medieval & Early Modern Studies Inc] announced that their next conference will be held 12–16 February 2013 at Monash University,

Melbourne, Australia. Contact: Dr Darius von Guettner; http://arts.monash.edu.au/history/conferences/anzamems-2013/

29–30 March 2013, University of Kent, Canterbury: "Crusade Preaching and Propaganda": A Workshop on Primary Sources; contact: j.vandeburie@kent.ac.uk

9–12 May 2013, 48th International Congress on Medieval Studies, Kalamazoo: "Jacques de Vitry: His Career, Writings, and Impact"; contact: jessalynn.bird@iname.com

1–4 July 2013, International Medieval Congress, Leeds: "Ad Crucesignatos – Crusade Preaching and Propaganda"; contact: j.vandeburie@kent.ac.uk.

The sixth International conference of the London Centre for the Study of the Crusades, the military religious orders and the Latin East will be held at St John's Gate, London, 5–8 September 2013. Contact: Michael Heslop.

9. Members' queries

NICOLLE, David: Does anyone know of a study, completed, recent, forthcoming or incomplete, concerning the medieval Byzantine road system in Anatolia?

WOLKOMIR, Alfred F., Aside from one hopitaller document regarding "La Platta" and a few documents in RRH, are there any other primary source documents regarding the lordship of Marash (1098–1149)? What do we know about the "Medaille" struck by the Crusader Kingdom?

10. Income and expenditure for the SSCLE from 1 October 2010 to 30 September 2011

This report shows SSCLE assets in separate columns, totaling the amount in each of the three currencies in which these funds are held. Whenever notes that follow refer to the total assets or liabilities of the society, these are totaled and reported in sterling followed by the equivalent amount in dollars and in euros. In each case these are computed using the prevailing rates as of 30 September 2011 (i.e.: £1 = $1.5585 = €1.1641), rounded to the nearest whole unit.

Using these currency equivalencies, on 1 October 2010, the total of SSCLE funds equaled £26,584 (or $41,431 or €30,947). On 30 September 2011 the society's assets totaled £25,259 (or $39,365 or €29,404). 363 subscriptions were paid or prepaid for 2010–2011, the majority of which (275) were for membership with the journal (Crusades Vol. 10). Additional funds were received for back issues of the journal and as prepayment for future subscriptions. Because the society is billed for the journal only after it is published, and since Crusades Vol. 10 was published October 2011, after the period covered by this report had closed, the bill for that volume, which totaled £5,340 (or $8,322 or €6,216), must be considered as pending charges against SSCLE assets. In addition approximately £1,580 (or $2,462 or €1,839) has been collected in prepayments for future issues of the journal, and must also be considered as pending charges. These liabilities are roughly equal to 26% of the society's funds on deposit as of the close of the reporting period. The expenditure of funds for the journal reported above (£5,460) was in payment for Crusades Vol. 9 (for 2010), which was mailed out in November 2011, and in payment for various back-issues of Crusades during the reporting period.

Notable expenses for this period include £3,770 ($5,875, €4,389), partially repayment to members of the Executive Committee for their out-of-pocket expenses incurred when they assembled in London in June 2011. In addition, funds were expended to partially reimburse the SSCLE's organizer and representative at the CISH/ICHS conference/quadrennial meeting in Amsterdam. Funds (£250) were also allocated to help defray the costs of the July one-

	U.K. Accounts (£)	U.S. Accounts ($)	Euro Accounts (€)
BALANCES CARRIED FORWARD, 1 OCTOBER 2010	**£12,347.66**	**$15,481.94**	**€5,008.15**
INCOME			
Subscriptions, etc., received	£2,177.50	$7,572.93	€2,488.00
Interest received	£4.76	$19.35	
Total income	**£2,182.26**	**$7,592.28**	**€2,488.00**
EXPENDITURES			
Journal	£5,460.00		
Executive Committee meeting	£49.40	$4,934.07	€645.49
Expenses, CISH meeting	£630.44		
Postage, supplies, etc.	$430.03		
Editing expenses			€ 40.00
Conference subvention	£250.00		
Bank charges		$25.55	
Total expenditures	**£6,389.84**	**$5,389.65**	**€ 685.49**
SURPLUS OF INCOME OVER EXPENDITURES	£4,207.58	$2,202.63	€1,802.51
TRANSFER OF FUNDS BETWEEN CURRENCIES			
to UK£ £3,128.72	from US$ $5,000.00		
BALANCES ON HAND, 30 SEPTEMBER 2011	**£11,268.80**	**$12,684.57**	**€ 6,810.66**

day postdoc seminar in London (organized by Jonathan Phillips under SSCLE auspices). Lastly, support was provided to the editor of the transactions of the 2008 SSCLE meeting in Avignon to reimburse extraordinary editing expenses. It should also be noted that the item bank charges does not include fees levied by Paypal, which collects between 2 and 4% of the value of each transaction, fees which are consistent with those charged by banks/credit card companies to commercial vendors.

Concerning Paypal, it appears that the funds lost to Paypal fees are a relatively small cost offset by the convenience for members in non-euro/dollar/sterling areas who save very significant amounts over the cost of transferring funds through bank cheques or money orders. In the 2011 reporting period 67 members paid using Paypal, netting subscriptions totaling $3,328.65. Fees lost to collect those funds equal approximately $102, or 3% (+/−) of the net collected. The SSCLE partially recovers the funds lost to Paypal's fee through savings on postage and traditional bank fees. The service fees lost to Paypal are not computed precisely herein because, since the SSCLE now accepts such payments in dollars, sterling or euro, and Paypal's fees are collected as a percentage in each currency before converting the payment into dollars, computing the exact total of these relatively slight amounts is not required for the purposes of this report. It does appear that the SSCLE garners more members and subscriptions by using Paypal, and that it is well worth the minor costs of the service.

In summary, our society's funds decreased slightly last year, despite a modest rise in the number of subscribers, primarily because of extraordinary expenditures, several of which were unique events, while others (such as the postdoc conference and the committee meeting) are intermittent expenditures. Your Treasurer is confident that, as a consequence of the reform in the method of computing dues and the separation of journal subscriptions from dues collections, the SSCLE's core funds will continue to grow in future years. At the time of this writing it appears certain that revenues for 2012 have increased. It has been my primary goal to restore ample reserve funding to the SSCLE's treasury, which was sorely depleted when I took office seven years ago. As the membership has already been informed, my term will expire in 2012, and I am not standing for reelection. I will take particular pleasure, when I hand over my duties to my successor, from the fact that the fiscal health of the society has been restored, and the knowledge that the reserves in place will ensure the solvency of the society and its ability to carry out its mission for years to come. This has only been made possible by the generous cooperation of the membership. I again express gratitude to my colleagues in the SSCLE for their support, encouragement and unfailing courtesy.

Respectfully submitted,

James D. Ryan, Treasurer

11. List of members and their addresses

(* Recorded as new member)

Dr David S.H. Abulafia, Gonville and Caius College, Cambridge, CB2 1TA, ENGLAND, UK

Dr Marianne Ailes, 48 Melrose Avenue, Reading, RG6 7BN, ENGLAND, UK; marianne.ailes@bristol.ac.uk

Brian Allison Lewis, c/o Sabic, PO Box 5101, Riyadh 11422, SAUDI ARABIA

Dr Martín Alvira Cabrer, Universidad Complutense de Madrid, Facultad de Geografía e Historia, Departamento de Historia Medieval, C/Profesor Aranguren, s/n, 28040-Madrid (Spain); malvira@ghis.ucm.es

Prof. Reuven Amitai, The Eliyahu Elath Chair for the History of the Muslim Peoples, Institute of Asian and African Studies, Hebrew Univ., Jerusalem 91905, ISRAEL; r_amitai@mscc.huji.ac.il

Dr Monique Amouroux, 2, Avenue de Montchalette, Cassy, 33138 Lanton, FRANCE; monique.amouroux@aliceadsl.fr

Dr Jan Anckaer, Avenue du Roi Albert 126, B-1082 Brussels, BELGIUM; jananckaer@yahoo.com

Prof. Alfred J. Andrea, 161 Austin Drive, Apartment 3, Burlington VT 05401, USA; aandrea@uvm.edu

*Juanita Andrea, 161 Austin Drive, #3 Burlington VT 05401, USA; aandrea@uvm.edu

Dr Filippo Andrei, 1644 Oxford Street, Apt. 5, Berkeley CA, 94709, USA; filandrei@berkeley.edu

Patricia Antaki-Masson, Rés. La Palisse Bât B., 5 rue du 21 juin 1940, 64100 Bayonne, Bayonne, France; patriciaantaki@yahoo.com

Spyridon Antonopoulos, 112 Yarmouth Road, Norwood MA 02062, USA; spyridonantonopoulos@yahoo.com

Dr Benjamin Arbel, School of History, Tel-Aviv Univ., Tel-Aviv 69978, ISRAEL; arbel@post.tau.ac.il

Dr Marco Arosio, Università del Sacro Cuore, Milano, ITALY; marco_arosio@tin.it

Dr Thomas S. Asbridge, Dept. of History, Queen Mary and Westfield College, Univ. of London, Mile End Road, London E1 4NS, ENGLAND, UK; t.s.asbridge@qmul.ac.uk

Prof. Zubaida Atta, 19 Sphinx Building – Sphinx Square, Apartment 85, Muhandessin, Cairo, EGYPT; prof.zatta@yahoo.com

Prof. Hussein M. Attiya, 20 Ahmed Sidik Street, Sidi Gaber El-Sheik, apartment 4, Alexandria, EGYPT; husseinattiya@hotmail.com

Marc J. Ayers, 2593 Inverness Point Dr., Birmingham AL 35242, USA; mayers@babc.com

Prof. Taef Kamal el-Azhari, International Affairs Dept., Qatar Univ., Faculty of Arts, 2713 Doho, QATAR; taef@gega.net

Dr Mohammed Aziz, PO Box 135513, Beirut, LEBANON

*Fady Georges Bader, Level 2, Karam Building, Next to Ogero, Brummana, Metn, LEBANON; fadygbader@gmail.com

Dr Xavier Baecke, Louis-Roelandplein 29, 9000 Gent, BELGIUM; xavierbaecke@hotmail.com

Dr Dan Bahat, PO Box 738, Mevasseret Zion 90805, ISRAEL; danbahat@gmail.com

Archibald Bain, Dufftown, Banffshire AB55 4AJ, SCOTLAND, UK; ArchieBain@aol.co.uk or gilliesbeag@yahoo.co.uk

Prof. Michel Balard, 4, rue des Remparts, 94370 Sucy-en-Brie, FRANCE; Michel.Balard@univ-paris1.fr

Prof. Susan Balderstone, Adjunct Professor in Cultural Heritage, Deakin Univ., Melbourne, AUSTRALIA; susan.balderstone@bigpond.com

Philip B. Baldwin, RR 2, 5738 County Road 1, Consecon, Ontario, K0K 1T0, CANADA; pipbb@yahoo.com

Laura Balletto, Via Orsini 40/B, 16146 Genova, ITALY; Laura.Balletto@lettere.unige.it

Prof. Malcolm Barber, Dept. of History, Univ. of Reading, PO Box 218, Whiteknights, Reading RG6 6AA, ENGLAND, UK; m.c.barber@reading.ac.uk

Diana Cornelia Barbu, Calea Martirilor no.60, sc.A, Apt.32, Timisoara 300719, ROMANIA; dia.704@gmail.com

Dr Michael Bardot, Dept. Behavioral and Social Sciences, Lincoln Univ., 820 Chestnut Street, Room 310 Founders Hall, Jefferson City MO 65102, USA; Bardotm@lincolnu.edu

Prof. John W. Barker, 5611 Longford Terrace, Madison WI 53711, USA; jwbarker@wisc.edu

Dr Sebastian Bartos, 319 Oak Center Place, Valdosta GA 31602, USA; sebartos@hotmail.com

*Dr Vicent Baydal, Manuel Candela, 65, 2–4ª, 46021-Valencia, SPAIN; vicentbaydal@harca.org

Prof. George Beech, 1745 Hillshire Drive, Kalamazoo MI 49008, USA; george.beech@wmich.edu

Dr Gregory D. Bell, Duke Univ., History Dept., Durham NC 27708, USA; gdb@duke.edu

Dr Elena Bellomo, via dei Rospigliosi 1, 20151 Milano, ITALY; elena.bellomo@libero.it

Colin Bennett, 6212 Pumpernickle Lane, Monroe NC 28110, USA; colinb.writer@gmail.com

Matthew Bennett, 58 Mitchell Avenue, Hartley Wintney, Hampshire RG27 8HG, ENGLAND, UK; matthew.bennett970@mod.uk

Stephen Bennett, Langelandsgade 128, 8000 Århus, DENMARK; bennett_stephen876@btinternet.com

Dr Nora Berend, St Catharine's College, Cambridge CB2 1RL, ENGLAND, UK; nb213@cam.ac.uk

Ilya Berkovich, Peterhouse, Cambridge CB2 1RD, ENGLAND, UK; ib275@cam.ac.uk

Dr Steven Biddlecombe, 65 Conybeare Road, Canton, Cardiff CF5 1GB, WALES, UK; sjbidleuk@yahoo.co.uk

Betty Binysh, 1 The Paddock, Cowbridge, Vale of Glamorgan, CF71 7EJ, WALES, UK; binyshe@cardiff.ac.uk

Jessalynn Bird, 1514 Cortland Drive, Naperville IL 60565, USA; jessalynn.bird@iname.com

Prof. Nancy Bisaha, Vassar College, History Department, Box 711, 124 Raymond Avenue, Poughkeepsie NY 12604, USA; nabisaha@vassar.edu

Adam Bishop, 14 rue Léon Blum, 44000 Nantes, FRANCE; adam.bishop@univ-nantes.fr

Charl Blignaut, PO Box 566, Ventersdorp 2710, North-West Province, SOUTH AFRICA; charlblignaut777@yahoo.com

Prof. John R.E. Bliese, Communication Studies Dept., Texas Tech Univ., Lubbock TX 79409, USA.

Prof. Adrian J. Boas, 10 HaRav Berlin Street, Jerusalem 92503, ISRAEL; adrianjboas@yahoo.com

Prof. Mark S. Bocija, Columbus State Community College, 550 E. Spring Street, Columbus OH 43216-1609, USA; mbocija@cscc.edu

Louis Boisset, Louis Boisset, Curia Generalizia della Compagnia di Gesù, Borgo S. Spirito 4, 00193 Roma, ITALIA; louis.boisset@gmail.com

Brenda M. BOLTON, 8 Watling Street, St Albans AL1 2PT, ENGLAND, UK; brenda@bolton.vianw.co.uk

Dr Barbara BOMBI, School of History, Rutherford College, Univ. of Kent, Canterbury CT2 7NX, ENGLAND, UK; bb55@kent.ac.uk

Myra BOM, 306 Glade Street, Chapel Hill NC 27516, USA; myrambom@gmail.com

Pierre BONNEAUD, Chemin des chênes verts, Pont des Charrettes, 30700 Uzès, FRANCE; pierre.bonneaud@orange.fr

Prof. Karl BORCHARDT, c/o Monumenta Germaniae Historica, Ludwigstraße 16, 80539 München, for letters: Postfach 34 02 23, 80099 München, GERMANY; karl.borchardt@mgh.de

Prof. Charles R. BOWLUS, History Dept., Univ. of Arkansas, 8081 Mabelvale Pike, Little Rock AR 722091099, USA; Haymannstraße 2A, 85764 Oberschleißheim, GERMANY; crbowlus@ualr.edu

Prof. Charles M. BRAND, 180 South 38th Street, Boulder CO 80305, USA; cmbrand@indra.com

Dr Cristian BRATU, Baylor University, One Bear Place #97392, Waco TX 76798-7392, USA; Cristian_Bratu@baylor.edu

Dr Michael BRETT, School of Oriental and African Studies, Univ. of London, Malet Street, London WC1E 7HP, ENGLAND, UK

Keagan BREWER, 3/51–55 Frances St, Lidcombe, NSW, 2144, AUSTRALIA; keaganjoelbrewer@hotmail.com

Heidi BRIDGER, The Old Station House, Kedington Road, Sturmer, Essex CB9 7XR, ENGLAND, UK; hbridger@hotmail.com

Robert BRODIE, Saint Agnes Lodge, 16 High Saint Agnesgate, Ripon, North Yorkshire HG4 1QR, ENGLAND, UK; robertbrodie@btinternet.com

Dr Judith BRONSTEIN, Ilanot 29/2, Haifa 34324, ISRAEL; Judith_bronstein@hotmail.com

Prof. Elizabeth A.R. BROWN, 160 West 86th Street PH4, New York NY 10024, USA; earbrown160@aol.com

Prof. James A. BRUNDAGE, 1102 Sunset Drive, Lawrence KS 660444548, USA; jabrun@ku.edu

David BRYSON, 1935 Westview Drive, North Vancouver, BC, Canada V7M3B1; dbryson1935@telus.net

Andrew David BUCK, Hartley Corner, 6a Old Lodge Lane, Purley, Surrey, CR8 4DE, ENGLAND, UK; ledzep_4_ever_69@hotmail.com

Dr Marcus G. BULL, Dept. of Historical Studies, Univ. of Bristol, 13–15 Woodland Road, Clifton, Bristol BS8 1TB, ENGLAND, UK; m.g.bull@bris.ac.uk

Prof. Jochen BURGTORF, California State Univ., Dept. of History, 800 North State College Boulevard, Fullerton CA 92834, USA; jburgtorf@fullerton.edu

*Dr Łukasz BURKIEWICZ, ulica Krótka 6/8, Kraków 31–149, POLAND; lukasz.burkiewicz@uj.edu.pl

Prof. Charles BURNETT, The Warburg Institute, Univ. of London, Woburn Square, London WC1H 0AB, ENGLAND, UK; charles.burnett@sas.ac.uk

The Rev. Prof. Robert I. BURNS, 300 College Avenue, Los Gatos CA 95030, USA.

Dr Peter BURRIDGE, Harmer Mill, Millington, York YO4 2TX, ENGLAND, UK.

Dr Emanuel Buttigieg, 110, Palm Street, Paola, PLA 1412, MALTA; emanuel_buttigieg@yahoo.co.uk

Ane Lise Bysted, Tyvdalen 12, 21 DK 8940 Randers SV, DENMARK; ane.bysted@mail.dk

Christer Carlsson, Litsbyvägen 66, 18746 Täby, SWEDEN; cc-archaeologist@yahoo.se

Dr Annemarie Weyl Carr, 608 Apple Road, Newark DE 19711, USA; acarr@smu.edu

Michael Carr, Flat 4, 11 Rochester Terrace, Camden, London, NW1 9JN, ENGLAND, UK; m.carr@rhul.ac.uk

Dr Damien Carraz, 14, rue François Arago, 84000 Avignon, FRANCE; damien.carraz@wanadoo.fr

Marc Carrier, 1038 Péladeau, St-Jean-sur-Richelieu, Québec, J3A 2A2, CANADA; marctcarrier@yahoo.ca

Dr Megan Cassidy-Welch, School of Historical, Philosophical and International Studies, Monash University, Clayton Victoria 3800, AUSTRALIA; megan.cassidy-welch@monash.edu

Prof. Brian A. Catlos, Dept. of History, Univ. of California Santa Cruz, Stevenson Academic Center, 1156 High Street, Santa Cruz CA 95064-1077, USA; bcatlos@ucsc.edu

Prof. Fred A. Cazel Jr., 309 Gurleyville Road, Storrs Mansfield CT 06268-1403, USA

Dr Simonetta Cerrini, Via Carducci 68A, 15076 Ovada (Alessandria), ITALY; alloisiocerrini@inwind.it

William Chapman, 68 Carisbrooke Gardens, Yeovil, Somerset BA20 1BY, ENGLAND, UK; bill-chapman@pilgrim-env.co.uk

Dr Martin Chasin, 1125 Church Hill Road, Fairfield CT 06432-1371, USA; mchasin@att.net

*Dr Marie-Anna Chevalier, 180 rue Fabri de Peiresc Résidence Le Parc des Arceaux Bât. A7. 34080 Montpellier, FRANCE; ma_chevalier@yahoo.fr

Dr Nikolaos G. Chrissis, Flat 16, Victoria House, South Lambeth Road, SW8 1QT, London, UK; N.Chrissis@rhul.ac.uk or nchrissis@yahoo.co.uk

Georg Christ, Friedrich-Ebert-Anlage 39, 69117 Heidelberg, GERMANY; Georg.christ@uni-heidelberg.de

Dr Katherine Christensen, CPO 1756 Berea College, Berea KY 40404, USA; katherine_christensen@berea.edu

Dr Niall G.F. Christie, Corpus Christi College, 5935 Iona Drive, Vancouver, BC, V6T 1J7, CANADA; niallchristie@yahoo.com

Ioanna Christoforaki, Centre for Byzantine and Post-byzantine Art, Academy of Athens, Anagnostopouloy 14, GR-106 73 Athens, GREECE or Heracleous 6, GR-152 34 Halandri, Athens, GREECE; ichristoforaki@yahoo.co.uk

Prof. Giulio Cipollone, Piazza S. Maria alle Fornaci 30, 00165 Roma, ITALY; cipolloneunigre6009@fastwebnet.it

Dr G.H.M. Claassens, Departement Literatuurwetenschap, Katholieke Universiteit Leuven, Blijde Inkomststraat 21, Postbus 33, 3000 Leuven, BELGIUM

Dr Pierre-Vincent Claverie, 9 rue du Bois-Rondel, 35700 Rennes, FRANCE; pvclaverie@yahoo.fr

David J. Clover, 5460 Ocean View Drive, Oakland CA 94618, USA; rollsroyceggm24@yahoo.com

Paul M. Cobb, Dept. of Near Eastern Languages & Civilizations, University of Pennsylvania, Philadelphia PA 19104, USA; pmcobb@sas.upenn.edu

Dr Penny J. Cole, Trinity College, 6 Hoskin Avenue, Toronto, Ontario M5S 1HB, CANADA; pjcole@trinity.utoronto.ca

Dr. Edward Coleman, Dept. of History and Archives, Faculty of Arts and Celtic Studies, University College Dublin, Belfield, Dublin 4, IRELAND; Email: edward.coleman@ucd.ie

Prof. Eleanor A. Congdon, Dept. of History, Youngstown State Univ., 1 University Plaza, Youngstown OH 44555, USA; eacongdon@ysu.edu

Prof. Charles W. Connell, PO Box 6023, Dept. of History, Northern Arizona Univ., Flagstaff AZ 86011-6023, USA; charles.connell@nau.edu

Prof. Robert Connor, Triton College, River Grove IL; 53 Lakebreez Ct, Lake Zurich IL 60047, USA; rconnor1@triton.edu

Prof. Giles Constable, Institute for Advanced Study, 506 Quaker Road, Princeton NJ 085 40, USA.

Prof. Olivia Remie Constable, Dept. of History, Univ. of Notre Dame, Notre Dame IN 46556-0368, USA; constable.1@nd.edu

James Conway, 30 Park Drive, Little Paxton, St. Neots, Cambridgeshire, PE19 6NT, ENGLAND, UK; penny.conway@ntlworld.com

Prof. Robert F. Cook, French Language and General Linguistics Dept., Univ. of Virginia, 302 Cabell Hall, Charlottesville VA 22903, USA.

Barry Cooper, Loretto School, Linkfield Road, Musselburgh, East Lothian EH7 5HE, SCOTLAND, UK; bcooper@loretto.com, ec53cooper@loretto.com

Prof. Rebecca W. Corrie, Phillips Professor of Art, Bates College, Lewiston ME 04240, USA; rcorrie@bates.edu

Walker Reid Cosgrove, History Dept., Saint Louis Univ., 3800 Lindell Boulevard, Saint Louis MO 63108, USA; cosgrowr@slu.edu

Prof. Paula Maria de Carvalho Pinto Costa Faculdade de Letras da Universidade do Porto, Via Panorâmica, s/n, 4150-564 Porto, PORTUGAL; ppinto@letras.up.pt

Dr Nicholas S. Coureas, PO Box 26619, Lykarittos, 1640 Nicosia, CYPRUS; ncoureas@moec.gov.cy or ncoureas@hotmail.com

The Rev. H.E.J. Cowdrey, 19 Church Lane, Old Marston, Oxford OX3 0NZ, ENGLAND, UK; fax (0)1865 279090

Prof. Paul F. Crawford, 5 Mum Drive, Washington PA 15301, USA; crawford_p@calu.edu or paul.f.crawford@gmail.com

Dana Cushing, 201 N Garden Avenue, Sierra Vista AZ 85635, USA; dana.cushing@alumni.utoronto.ca

David M. Cvet, 822-18 Concorde Pl., Toronto, ON, M3C 3T9, CANADA; david.cvet@gmail.com

Charles Dalli, Dept. of History, Faculty of Arts, Univ. of Malta, Msida MSD06, MALTA; cdalli@arts.um.edu.mt

Philip Louis Daniel, Archivist, Equestrian Order of the Holy Sepuchre of Jerusalem, 37 Somerset Road, Meadvale, Redhill, Surrey RH1 6LT, ENGLAND, UK; fax 01737-240722

Dr Béatrice Dansette, 14 rue Georges Ville, 75116 Paris, FRANCE; beatricedansette@orange.fr

*Michael De Nève, Gritxnarstrasse, D-12163Berlin, GERMANY; michaeldeneve@gmx.de

Eugene De Rass, Po Box 35043, Ottawa ON K1Z 1A2, Canada; eugene959@gmail.com

Americo De Santis, 88 East Main Street, Box Number 141, Mendham NJ 07945, USA; ricodesantis@hotmail.com

Prof. Bernhard Demel O.T., Leiter des Deutschordenszentralarchivs, Singerstraße 7, 1010 Wien, AUSTRIA; tel. 513 70 14

John A. Dempsey, 218 Edgehill Road, Milton MA 02186, USA; jdempsey@westfield.ma.edu

Dr Alain Demurger, 5, rue de l'Abricotier, 95000 Cergy, FRANCE; ademurger@orange.fr

Prof. George T. Dennis, S.H. Jesuit Center, 300 College Avenue, Los Gatos CA 95031, USA; gdennis@calprov.org

Kelly DeVries, Department of History, Loyola College, 4501 N Charles Street, Baltimore MD 21210-2699, USA; kdevries@loyola.edu

Dr Gary Dickson, School of History, Classics and Archaeology, University of Edinburgh, Doorway 4, Teviot Place, Edinburgh EH8 9AG, SCOTLAND, UK; garydickson1212@blueyonder.co.uk

Frà Prof. Richard Divall AO OBE, 301 Arcadia, 228 The Avenue, Parkville, Vic Australia 3052, AUSTRALIA; maestro@spin.net.au

Dr Erica Cruikshank Dodd, 4208 Wakefield Place, Victoria, B.C. V8N 6E5, CANADA; edodd@uvic.ca

*James Doherty, Apt. 4, Union Forge, 33 Mowbray Street, Sheffield. S3 8ER, ENGLAND, UK; j.doherty@lancaster.ac.uk

César Domínguez, Universidad de Santiago de Compostela, Facultad de Filologia, Avda. Castealo s/n, 15704 Santiago (La Coruna), ESPAÑA

Cristina Dondi, 128 Berkeley Court, Glentworth Street, London NW1 5NE, ENGLAND, UK; christina.dondi@history.ox.ac.uk

*Stephen Donnachie, 29 Bryn Road, Swansea, SA2 0AP, WALES, UK; 294772@swansea.ac.uk

Dr John Doran, Dept of History and Archaeology, University of Chester, Parkgate Road, Chester, CH1 4BJ, ENGLAND, UK; j.doran@chester.ac.uk

Ara Dostourian, Box 420, Harmony RI 02829, USA; aradostourian@yahoo.com

Maria Dourou-Eliopoulou, Kephallenias 24, Althea 19400, Attiki, GREECE; mdourou@arch.uoa.gr

Janet Draheim, 732 W Happfield Dr., Arlington Heights IL 60004-7100, USA; jandra818@comcast.net

Andrew Dunn, 229 W 60th Street, Apt. 4T, New York NY 10023, USA; aggdunn@yahoo.com

John Durant, 32 Maple Street, PO Box 373, West Newbury MA 01985, USA.

Frances Durkin, 16 Billington Road, Leighton Buzzard, Bedfordshire, LU7 4TH, ENGLAND, UK; frankie_durkin@hotmail.com

Dr Valerie Eads, 308 West 97th Street, New York NY 10025, USA.

Prof. Richard Eales, School of History, Univ. of Kent, Canterbury CT2 7NX, ENGLAND, UK; r.eales1@btinternet.com

Ana Echevarría Arsuaga, Facultad de Geografía e Historia, Departimento de Historia Medieval, Av. Conde de Aranda 1, 3° E, 28200 San Lorenzo del Escorial (Madrid), ESPAÑA; anaevjosem@hotmail.com

Prof. Peter W. EDBURY, School of History and Archaeology, Cardiff University, Humanities Building, Colum Drive, Cardiff CF10 3EU, WALES, UK; edbury@cf.ac.uk

Dr Susan B. EDGINGTON, 3 West Street, Huntingdon, Cambs., PE29 1WT, ENGLAND, UK; s.b.edgington@btinternet.com

Dr Axel EHLERS, Gehägestraße 20 N, 30655 Hannover, GERMANY; aehlers1@gwdg.de

Prof. Sven EKDAHL, Sponholzstraße 38, 12159 Berlin, GERMANY; Sven.Ekdahl@t-online.de

Dr Ronnie ELLENBLUM, 13 Reuven Street, Jerusalem 93510, ISRAEL; msronni@pluto.mscc.huji.ac.il

Prof. Steven A. EPSTEIN, History Dept., Univ. of Kansas, Lawrence KS 66045-7590, USA; sae@ku.edu

Dr Helen C. EVANS, The Medieval Dept., The Metropolitan Museum of Art, 1000 Fifth Avenue, New York NY 10028, USA; helen.evans@metmuseum.org

Michael EVANS, 301 West Broomfield, Kewardin 10-03, Mount Pleasant MI 48858, USA; evans2m@cmich.edu

Prof. Theodore EVERGATES, 146 West Main Street, Westminster MD 21157, USA

Nicolas FAUCHERRE, 4, rue de l'Hôtel de Ville, 44000 Nantes, FRANCE; n.faucherre@wanadoo.fr

Prof. Marie-Luise FAVREAU-LILIE, Kaiser-Friedrich-Straße 106, 10585 Berlin, GERMANY; mlfavre@zedat.fu-berlin.de

Dr Gil FISHHOF, Department of Art History, Tel Aviv University, Tel Aviv 69978, ISRAEL; fishhofg@post.tau.ac.il

Dr Jean FLORI, 69, rue Saint Cornély, 56340 Carnac, FRANCE; flori.jean@wanadoo.fr

Prof. Jaroslav FOLDA, 112a Hanes Art Center, Dept. of Art, Univ. of North Carolina, Chapel Hill NC 27599-3405, USA; jfolda@email.unc.edu

Dr Michelle FOLTZ, M.D., PMB 33, PO Box 1226, Columbus MT 59019, USA; mfoltz@imt.net

Dr Iben FONNESBERG SCHMIDT, Dept. of History, Aalborg Univ., Fibgerstraede 5, 9220 Aalborg, DENMARK; imfs@ihis.aau.dk

Luis Adão DA FONSECA, Rua do Revilão 521, 4100-427 Porto, PORTUGAL; luisadaofonseca@netcabo.pt

Harold FORD, PO Box 871009, Stone Mountain GA 30087, USA; tsh212511@aol.com

Dr Alan J. FOREY, The Bell House, Church Lane, Kirtlington, Oxon. OX5 3HJ, ENGLAND, UK; foreys@somail.it

Edith FORMAN, 38 Burnham Hill, Westport CT 06880, USA

Barbara FRALE, via A. Gramsci 17, 01028 Orte (VT), ITALY; barbara-frale@libero.it

Dr John FRANCE, Department of History and Classics, Swansea University, SA2 8PP, WALES, UK; j.france@swansea.ac.uk

Daniel FRANKE, University of Rochester, Department of History, 364 Rush Rhees Library, Rochester NY 14627, USA; danielfranke79@gmail.com

Prof. Yvonne FRIEDMAN, Department of General History, Department of Land of Israel Studies and Archeology, Bar-Ilan University, Ramat-Gan 52900, ISRAEL; yfried36@gmail.com

Robin FROUMIN, PO Box 9713, Hadera 38541, ISRAEL; robin_fr@zahav.net.il

Michael and Neathery FULLER, 13530 Clayton Road, St Louis MO 63141, USA

Michael S. FULTON, 272 Sydenham St., Kingston, Ontario, CANADA; michael.fulton@tricolour.queensu.ca

Prof. Matthew GABRIELE, Dept. of Interdisciplinary Studies, Virginia Tech, 342 Lane Hall (0227), Blacksburg VA 24061-0227, USA; mgabriele@vt.edu

Cecilia GAPOSCHKIN, 6107 Carson Hall, History Department, Dartmouth College, Hanover NH 03755, USA; m.c.gaposchkin@dartmouth.edu

Prof. Luis GARCÍA-GUIJARRO, Facultad de Ciencias Humanas, Plaza de la Constitución s/n, 22001 Huesca, SPAIN; luguijar@unizar.es

Sabine GELDSETZER, M.A., Westheide 6, 44892 Bochum, GERMANY; sabine.geldsetzer@ruhr-uni-bochum.de

Constantinos GEORGIOU, 3 Thessalonikis Street, Flat 201, Strovolos, 2020, Nicosia, CYPRUS; grconsta@hotmail.com

Dr Stavros G. GEORGIOU, PO Box 25729, 1311 Strovolos, CYPRUS; stggeorgiou@yahoo.gr

Dr Ruthy GERTWAGEN, 30 Ranans Street, PO Box 117, Qiryat Motzkin 26317, ISRAEL; ruger@macam.ac.il

Dr Marianne McLeod GILCHRIST, Flat 10, 13 Kelvin Drive, Glasgow G20 8QG, SCOTLAND, UK; docm@silverwhistle.free-online.co.uk

Prof. John B. GILLINGHAM, 49 Old Shoreham Road, Brighton, Sussex BN1 5DQ, ENGLAND, UK; johnbgilli@gmail.com

Prof. Anne GILMOUR-BRYSON, 1935 Westview Drive, North Vancouver, B.C. V7M 3B1, CANADA; annegb@telus.net

Charles R. GLASHEEN, 4300 Yacht Club Road, Jacksonville FL 32210, USA; rglashee@comcast.net

Prof. Dorothy F. GLASS, 11 Riverside Drive, Apartment 6-OW, New York NY 10023, USA; dglass1@att.net

Miguel GOMEZ, Department of History, 6th Floor Dunford Hall, University of Tennessee, Knoxville TN, 37996, USA; Mgomez3@utk.edu

Prof. Philippe GOURDIN, 11, avenue du général de Gaulle, 91000 Évry, FRANCE; philgourdin@yahoo.fr

Dr Christian GRASSO, via Colucci 30, 83048 Montella, ITALY; Ciham-UMR 5648 Université Louis-Lumière-Lyon 2, 18 Quai Claude Bernard, 69365 Lyon Cedex 07, FRANCE; chrisgrasso@iol.it

Prof. Gilles GRIVAUD, 8, rue du Général de Miribel, 69007 Lyon, FRANCE

The Rev. Joseph J. GROSS, Holy Trinity Monastery, 8400 Park Heights Avenue, PO Box 5742, Baltimore MD 21282, USA; jjgross@trinitarianhistory.org

Dr Darius von GUETTNER, School of Historical Studies, Univ. of Melbourne, Victoria 3010, AUSTRALIA; d.guttner@unimelb.edu.au

*Anna GUTGARTS-WEINBERGER, 9 Shprinzak st., apartment 3, Tel-Aviv, ISRAEL, 64738; a_gutgarts@yahoo.com

Prof. Klaus GUTH, Greiffenbergstraße 35, 96052 Bamberg, GERMANY; klaus.guth@uni-bamberg.de

Rachel HADDAD, 5 avenue de Verdun, Mont de Gif, 95200 Sarcelles, FRANCE; haddadrachel@yahoo.fr

Dr Brian J. HALE, 4228 Nebel Street, Stevens Point WI 54481, USA; bhaleuwsp.edu

Martin HALL, 8 Stanhope Place, London, W2 2HB, ENGLAND, UK; martin.allan.hall@gmail.com

Benjamin HALLIBURTON, 4020 Lindell Blvd. #216, St. Louis MO 63108, USA; bhallibu@slu.edu

Adina HAMILTON, 469 Albert Street, Brunswick, West Victoria 3055, AUSTRALIA or History Dept., Univ. of Melbourne, Parkville, Victoria 3052, AUSTRALIA

Prof. Bernard HAMILTON, 7 Lenton Avenue, The Park, Nottingham NG7 IDX, ENGLAND, UK; bernhamilt@yahoo.com

Dr Mona HAMMAD JAHAMA, Hollins University, Box 9586, Roanoke VA 24020, USA; monahammad@hotmail.com

Philip David HANDYSIDE, 1555 S. Ridgewood Avenue, DeLand FL 32720, USA; phandysi@stetson.edu

* Chris HANSON, 3000 S. Higgins Avenue # i12, Missoula MT 59801, USA; shurite7@yahoo.com

Peter HARITATOS Jr., 1500 North George Street, Rome NY 13440, USA.

Prof Jonathan HARRIS, Dept. of History, Royal Holloway, Univ. of London, Egham, Surrey TW20 0EX, ENGLAND, UK; jonathan.harris@rhul.ac.uk

Kathryn D. HARRIS, 6 Gallows Hill, Saffron Walden, Essex CB11 4DA, ENGLAND, UK; lfiddock@ntlworld.com

Dr. Michael HARSCHEIDT, Dellbusch 229, D-42279 Wuppertal, GERMANY; office@harscheidt.de

Jeffrey HASS, Ave Maria University, 2395 Naples Trace Creek # 3, Naples FL 34109, USA; jeffrey.hass@avemaria.edu, or jd-hass@yahoo.com

Prof. Eva HAVERKAMP, Rice Univ., History Dept. MS 42, for letters PO Box 1892, Houston TX 77251-1892 or for packages 6100 Main Street, Houston TX 77005, USA; haver@rice.edu

David HAY, 164 McCaul Street, Apartment 1, Toronto, Ontario M5T 1WA, CANADA.

Prof. Thérèse de HEMPTINNE, Universiteit Gent, Faculteit van de Letteren, Vakgroep Middeleeuwse Geschiedenis, Blandijnberg 2, 9000 Gent, BELGIUM

Michael HESLOP, The Old Vicarage, 1 Church Street, Lower Sunbury, Middlesex TW16 6RQ, ENGLAND, UK; michaelheslop@ntlworld.com

Dr Paul HETHERINGTON, 15 Luttrell Avenue, London SW15 6PD, ENGLAND, UK; phetherington@ukonline.co.uk

Prof. Rudolf HIESTAND, Brehmstraße 76, 40239 Düsseldorf, GERMANY

Charles A. HILKEN, PO Box 4825, St Mary's College, Moraga CA 94575, USA; chilken@stmarys-ca.edu

Dr George HINTLIAN, Armenian Patriarchate, PO Box, Jerusalem 14001, ISRAEL

*Dr. Felix HINZ, Universität Hildesheim, Institut für Geschichte, Marienburger Platz 22, 31141Hildesheim, GERMANY; felix.hinz@uni-hildesheim.de

Dr Martin HOCH, Konrad-Adenauer-Stiftung, Rathausallee 12, 53757 Sankt Augustin, GERMANY; Lobebaer@gmail.com

Dr Natasha HODGSON, Dept. of History, Heritage and Geography, Nottingham Trent Univ., Clifton Campus, Nottingham NG11 8NS, ENGLAND, UK; natasha.hodgson@ntu.ac.uk

Laura H. HOLLENGREEN; Univ. of Arizona, School of Architecture, 1040 North Olive, PO Box 210075, Tucson AZ 85721-0075, USA; laurah@u.arizona.edu

Dr Catherine HOLMES, University College, Oxford OX1 4BH, ENGLAND, UK; catherine. holmes@univ.ox.ac.uk

John D. HOSLER, Dept. of History and Geography, Morgan State University, 325 Holmes Hall, Baltimore MD 21251, USA; john.hosler@morgan.edu

Jan HOSTEN, Kaaistraat 12, 8900 Ieper, BELGIUM; jan.hosten@leicon.be

Dr C. Patrick HOTLE, Culver-Stockton Coll., N° 1 College Hill, Canton MO 63435, USA; photle@culver.edu

Prof. Norman J. HOUSLEY, School of Historical Studies, The Univ. of Leicester, Leicester LE1 7RH, ENGLAND, UK; hou@le.ac.uk

Prof. John HOWE, Texas Tech Univ., Dept. of History, Box 41013, Lubbock TX 79409-1013, USA; John.Howe@ttu.edu

Lubos HRADSKY, Svermova 23, 97404 Banska Bystrica, SLOVAK REPUBLIC; lubohradsky@centrum.sk

Prof. Lucy-Anne HUNT, MIRIAD, Manchester Metropolita University, Righton Building, Cavendish Street, Manchester M1 5 6BG, ENGLAND, UK; l.a.hunt@mmu.ac.uk

Dr Zsolt HUNYADI, 27 Szekeres u., 6725 Szeged, HUNGARY; hunyadiz@hist.u-szeged.hu

Sheldon IBBOTSON, PO Box 258, Rimbey, Alberta T0C 2JO, CANADA; bronwen@ telusplanet.net

Robert IRWIN, 39 Harleyford Road, London SE11 5AX, ENGLAND, UK; irwin960@ btinternet.com

John E. ISLES, 10575 Darrel Drive, Hanover MI 49241, USA; jisles@hughes.net

Prof. Peter JACKSON, Department of History, University of Keele, Keele, Staffs. ST5 5BG, ENGLAND, UK; p.jackson@his.keele.ac.uk

Martin JACOBOWITZ, The Towers of Windsor Park, 3005 Chapel Avenue — 11P, Cherry Hill NJ 08002, USA

Prof. David JACOBY, Dept. of History, The Hebrew Univ., Jerusalem 91905 ISRAEL ; jacobgab@mscc.huji.ac.il

Colin Wheldon JAMES, 30 Hendrefoilan Avenue, Sketty, Swansea, SA2 7LZ, WALES, UK; col.james@ymail.com

Prof. Nikolas JASPERT, Ruhr-Univ. Bochum, Historisches Institut – Lehrstuhl Mittelalter II, Universitätsstraße 150 (GA 4/31), 44801 Bochum, GERMANY; nikolas.jaspert@rub.de

Carsten Selch JENSEN, Department of Church History, Faculty of Theology, University of Copenhagen, Koebmagergade 44–46, 1150 DK-Copenhagen, DENMARK ; csj@teol.ku.dk

Dr Janus Møller JENSEN, Dept. of History and Civilization, Univ. of Southern Denmark, Campusvej 55, 5230 Odense M, DENMARK; jamj@hist.sdu.dk or : mailto:jamj@hist.sdu. dk

Prof. Kurt Villads JENSEN, Dept. of History and Civilization, Univ. of Southern Denmark, Campusvej 55, 5230 Odense M, DENMARK; kvj@hist.sdu.dk

Lady JILL, Duchess of HAMILTON, 52, Elm Park Gardens, Chelsea, London, SW10 9PA, ENGLAND, UK

Luc JOCQUÉ, c/o Corpus Christianorum, Sint-Annaconvent, Begijnhof 39, B-2300 Turnhout, Belgium

Simon A. JOHN, Simon John, 245 Mansel Road, Bonymaen, Swansea, SA1 7JT, WALES, UK; s.a.john.308858@swansea.ac.uk

Prof. William Chester JORDAN, Dept. of History, Princeton Univ., Princeton NJ 08544, USA; wchester@princeton.edu

Dr Philippe JOSSERAND, 14, rue du roi Albert, 44000 Nantes, FRANCE; ph.josserand@wanadoo.fr

Dr Andrew JOTISCHKY, Dept. of History, Lancaster Univ., Lancaster LA1 4YG, ENGLAND, UK; a.jotischky@lancaster.ac.uk

Dr Margaret A. JUBB, Dept. of French, Taylor Building, Univ. of Aberdeen, Old Aberdeen, AB15 9NU, SCOTLAND, UK; m.jubb@abdn.ac.uk

Dr Elena KAFFA, 2B Thivon, Kaimakli 1026, Nicosia, CYPRUS; niryida@yahoo.com

Prof. Sophia KALOPISSI-VERTI, Kronou 30, Palaio Faliro, GR-175 61 Athens, GREECE; skalop@arch.uoa.gr

Dr Sini KANGAS, Department of Philosophy, History, Culture and Art Studies, POBox 59, Unioninkatu 38 A, 00014 University of Helsinki, FINLAND; shkangas@mappi.helsinki.fi

Dr Fotini KARASSAVA-TSILINGIRI, Th. Kairi 14, Nea Smyrni, Athens 17122, GREECE; ptsiling@teiath.gr

Tatiana KARTSEVA, 73–50 Vavilova Street, Ap. 50, Moscow 117335, RUSSIA; tvkartseva@hotmail.com

Anna-Maria KASDAGLI, 59 Stockholmis Street, 85100 Rhodes, GREECE.

Prof. Benjamin Z. KEDAR, Dept. of History, The Hebrew Univ., Jerusalem 91905, ISRAEL; fax (home) 972-8-970-0802, bzkedar@huji.ac.il

Alexander KEMPTON, Skøyenveien 30, 0375 Oslo, NORWAY; alexansk@student.hf.uio.no

Prof. Nurith KENAAN-KEDAR, Dept. of Art History, Tel-Aviv Univ., Tel-Aviv 69978, ISRAEL; kenaank@post.tau.ac.il

Prof. Sharon KINOSHITA, Associate Professor of Literature, Humanities Academic Services, Univ. of California Santa Cruz, Santa Cruz CA 95064, USA; sakinosh@ucsc.edu

Dr Klaus-Peter KIRSTEIN, Frankenstraße 251, 45134 Essen, GERMANY; k.kirstein@r25.de

David KLOSTER, 7914 7th Street, Downey CA 90241, USA; jesushunter22@yahoo.com

Dr Michael A. KOEHLER, Hertogenlaan 14, 1970 Wezembeek-Oppem, BELGIUM; koehler.family@pandora.be

Prof. Athina KOLIA-DERMITZAKI, Plateia Kalliga 3, Athens 11253, GREECE; akolia@arch.uoa.gr

Miha KOSI, Zgodovinski institut ZRC SAZU, Novi trg 2, p.p. 306, 1000 Ljubljana, SLOVENIA; kosi@zrc-sazu.si

Philip KOSKI, 1310 Jersey Avenue N, Golden Valley MN 55427, USA; pkoski@slu.edu

Dr Conor KOSTICK, 31, Ashington Gardens, Navan Road, Dublin 7, IRELAND; kosticc@tcd.ie

Thomas KRÄMER, Friedrich-Franz-Straße 18, 12103 Berlin, GERMANY; thomas_kraemer@yahoo.com

Dr James G. KROEMER, 9440 N. Bethanne Dr., Brown Deer WI 53223, USA; jameskroemer@gmail.com

Prof. Jürgen KRÜGER, Steinbügelstraße 22, 76228 Karlsruhe, GERMANY; krueger-kunstgeschichte@t-online.de

Suha Kudsieh, Box: 19027, 360 A Bloor Street W., Toronto, ON, M5S 3C9 CANADA; kudsieh@gmail.com

Türk Tarih Kurumu, Kizilay Sokak, no. 1, Sihhiye 06100, Ankara, TURKEY.

Dr Malcolm David Lambert, Flat 3, 3 Queens Road, Worthing, BN11 3LX, ENGLAND, UK.

Mark Lambert, 515, North High, Kirksville MO 63501, USA; mml184@truman.edu, or marklambert@gmail.com

Sarah Lambert, 35 Cromer Road, London SW17 9JN, ENGLAND, UK; slambert@gold. ac.uk

The Rev. William Lane, Brooke Hall, Charterhouse, Godalming, Surrey GU7 2DX, ENGLAND, UK; wjl@charterhouse.org.uk

Elizabeth Lapina, Department of History, 43 North Bailey, Durham, DH1 3EX, ENGLAND, UK; ealapina@yahoo.com

Stephen Lay, c/o Dept. of History, Monash Univ., Melbourne, AUSTRALIA

Armelle Leclercq, 36, rue de l'Orillen, 75011 Paris, FRANCE; armelle73@yahoo.com

Eric Legg, PSC 98 Box 36, Apo AE 09830, USA; ericlegg@hotmail.com

Robert D. Leonard Jr., 1065 Spruce Street, Winnetka IL 60093-2169, USA; rlwinnetka@ aol.com

Richard A. Leson, 2720 St Paul Street, Apartment 2FF, Baltimore MD 21218, USA; ral2@ jhunix.hef.jhu.edu

Dr Yaacov Lev, PO Box 167, Holon 58101, ISRAEL; yglev@actcom.net.il

Kevin James Lewis, Merton College, Merton Street, Oxford, OX1 4JD, ENGLAND, UK; kevin.lewis@history.ox.ac.uk or kevin.j.lewis@hotmail.co.uk

Dr Christopher G. Libertini, Dominican College, 470 Western Highway, Orangeburg NY 10962, USA; christopher.libertini@de

Dr Tom Licence, Magdalene College, Cambridge, CB3 0AG, ENGLAND, UK; tol21@cam. ac.uk

Laura S. Lieber, Dept. of Religion, Middlebury College, Middlebury VT 05753, USA; llieber@middlebury.edu

Dr Giuseppe Ligato, Viale San Gimignano 18, 20146 Milano, ITALY; giuseppeligato@ virgilio.it

Prof. Ralph-Johannes Lilie, Kaiser-Friedrich-Straße 106, 10585 Berlin, GERMANY; lilie@ bbaw.de

Dr Ora Limor, 5b Elroey Street, Jerusalem 92108, ISRAEL; orali@openu.ac.il

*Kyle C. Lincoln, 3000 Lafayette Ave., Apt. 2A, St. Louis MO, 63104, USA, klincoll@ slu.edu

Prof. Guy Lobrichon, 4, Impasse Caillod, 84000 Avignon, FRANCE; guy.lobrichon@univ-avignon.fr; guy.lobrichon@numericable.fr

Prof. Peter W. Lock, 9 Straylands Grove, Stockton Lane, York YO31 1EB, ENGLAND, UK; ptrlock425@googlemail.com

Scott Loney, 4153 Wendell Road, West Bloomfield MI 48323, USA; scottloney@live.com

Albert G. Lopez, 277 Patterson Avenue, Stratford CT 06614, USA; aglopez46@snet.net

Prof. Graham A. Loud, School of History, Univ. of Leeds, Leeds LS2 9JT, ENGLAND, UK; g.a.loud@leeds.ac.uk

Prof. Michael LOWER, 1814 N. Lincoln Park West, # 1, Chicago IL 60614, USA; mlower@umn.edu

Zoyd R. LUCE, 2441 Creekside Court, Hayward CA 94542, USA; zluce1@earthlink.net

Dr Svetlana LUCHITSKAYA, Institute of General History, Leninski pr. 89-346, Moscow 119313, RUSSIA; svetlana@mega.ru

Andrew John LUFF, Flat 3, The Hermitage, St Dunstans Road, Lower Feltham, Middlesex TW13 4HR, ENGLAND, UK; andrew@luffa.freeserve.co.uk

Dr Anthony LUTTRELL, 20 Richmond Place, Bath BA1 5PZ, ENGLAND, UK; margaretluttrell@gmail.com

Christopher MACEVITT, Dumbarton Oaks, 1703 32nd Street NW, Washington DC 20007, USA

Dr James B. MACGREGOR, Dept. of History, Philosophy, and Geography, Missouri Western State Univ., 4525 Downs Drive, Saint Joseph MO 64501, USA; macgregor@missouriwestern.edu

Dr Merav MACK, The Van Leer Jerusalem Institute, 43 Jabotinsky Street, Jerusalem, 91040, ISRAEL; merav.mack@gmail.com

Dr Alan D. MACQUARRIE, 173 Queen Victoria Drive, Glasgow G14 7BP, SCOTLAND, UK [See also MC]

Prof. Thomas F. MADDEN, Center for Medieval and Renaissance Studies, Saint Louis Univ., 3800 Lindell Boulevard, PO Box 56907, Saint Louis MO 63108, USA; maddentf@slu.edu

Ben MAHONEY, 131 High Street, Doncaster, Victoria 3181, AUSTRALIA; bmahoney@abl.com.au

Dr Christoph T. MAIER, Sommergasse 20, 4056 Basel, SWITZERLAND; ctmaier@hist.uzh.ch

Christie MAJOROS, 215 W. 7th St., #14, Long Beach CA 90813, USA; c_majoros@yahoo.com

Prof. Lucy DER MANUELIAN, 10 Garfield Road, Belmont MA 02478, USA; lucy.manuelian@tufts.edu

Roben McDonald MARLOW, 36 Burton Old Road West, Lichfield, Staffordshire, WS13 6EN, ENGLAND, UK; roben@mac.com

Prof. Laurence W. MARVIN, History Dept., Evans School of Humanities, Berry College, Mount Berry GA 30149-5010, USA; lmarvin@berry.edu

Dr Federica MASÈ, 100 rue de la Roquette, 75011 Paris, FRANCE; f.mase@free.fr

Prof. Hans Eberhard MAYER, Historisches Seminar der Universität Kiel, 24098 Kiel, GERMANY.

Robert MAYNARD, The Old Dairy, 95 Church Road, Bishopsworth, Bristol BS13 8JU, ENGLAND, UK; maynard966@btinternet.com

Brian C. MAZUR, 718 W. Webster, Royal Oak MI 48073, USA; bcmazur1066@yahoo.com

Roben McDONALD MARLOW: see to Roben McDonald MARLOW

Dr Marianne McLeod GILCHRIST: see to Dr Marianne M. GILCHRIST

M. McNAUGHTON, The Old Rectory, River Street, Pewsey SN9 5DB, ENGLAND, UK; pewsey_books@hotmail.com

Gerald P. McOSKER, Salve Regina Univ., 100 Ochre Point Avenue, Newport RI 06240, USA; gerald.mcosker@salve.edu

Sean Robert MARTIN, 74 Electric Avenue, West Seneca NY 14206, USA; Seanmart32482@gmail.com

*Joel Silva Ferreira MATA, Rua João Domingos Bontempo, 11, 4445-476- Ermesinde, PORTUGAL; joelsmata@gmail.com or joel.mata@oninet.pt

Prof. Sophia MENACHE, Department of History, University of Haifa, Haifa 31905, ISRAEL; menache@research.haifa.ac.il

Marco MESCHINI, Via alle Cascine 37/B, 21100 Varese, ITALY; marco.meschini@unicatt.it

Dr Benjamin MICHAUDEL, IFPO, POBox 344, Damascus, SYRIA; benjamin_michaudel@hotmail.com

Prof. Klaus MILITZER, Winckelmannstraße 32, 50825 Köln, GERMANY; klaus.militzer@uni-koeln.de

Greg MILLER, 105 Valley Street, Burlington IA 52601, USA; greg.miller@lpl.com

Jane MILLIKEN, 26 Emmetts Farm Road, Rossmore NSW 2557, AUSTRALIA; jane.milliken@swahs.health.nsw.gov.au

Dr Paul Richard MILLIMAN, 107 E Custis Avenue, Alexandria VA 22301; USA; prmilliman@gmail.com

Peter John MILLS, 3 Huxley Road, Leyton, London E10 5QT, ENGLAND, UK; petermills@lireone.net

Prof. Laura MINERVINI, Dipartimento di Filologia Moderna, Università di Napoli Federico II, Via Porta di Massa 1, 80133 Napoli, ITALY; laura.minervini@unina.it

*Vincenzo Felice MIRIZIO, Via Manzoni nr.5, 73039 Tricase, Province of Lecce, ITALY; vincenzomirizio@email.it

Dr Piers D. MITCHELL, Department of Archaeology and Anthropology, University of Cambridge, The Henry Wellcome Building, Fitzwilliam Street, Cambridge CB2 1QH, ENGLAND, UK; pdm39@cam.ac.uk

PD Dr Hannes MÖHRING, Wilhelm-Bode-Straße 11, 38104 Braunschweig, GERMANY; hannes_moehring@web.de

Prof. Johannes A. (Hans) MOL, Grote Dijlakker 29, 8701 KW Bolsward, THE NETHERLANDS; hmol@fryske-akademy.nl

Dr Kristian MOLIN, 38 Vessey Terrace, Newcastle-under-Lyme, Staffordshire ST5 1LS, ENGLAND, UK; kristian.molin@nottingham.ac.uk

Dauvergne C. MORGAN, 235 Tooronga Road, Glen Iris, Melbourne, Victoria 3142, AUSTRALIA

Jonathan C. MORGAN, 19 Elia Street, Islington, London N1 8DE, ENGLAND, UK; jonathan.morgan@whb.co.uk

J. Diana MORGAN, 64 Victoria Avenue, Swanage, Dorset BH19 1AR, ENGLAND, UK.

Hiroki MORITAKE, Kami-Ono 371, Hiyoshi-mura, Kitauwa-gun, Ehime-ken 798-1503, JAPAN; jerus@hiroshima-u.ac.jp

April Jehan MORRIS, 1710 Sam Bass Boulevard, Apt. 724, Denton TX 76205, USA; ajehanmorris@gmail.com

The Rev. Prof. Colin MORRIS, 12 Bassett Crescent East, Southampton SO16 7PB, ENGLAND, UK; cm5@soton.ac.uk

Dr Rosemary MORRIS, Dept. of History, Univ. of York, York YO10 5DD, ENGLAND, UK; rm22@york.ac.uk

Michael Morton, 19 Bruce Street, Even Swindon, Swindon, Wiltshire SN2 2El, ENGLAND, UK; michaelmorton37@hotmail.co.uk

Dr Nicholas Morton, School of Arts and Humanities, Nottingham Trent University, Clifton Lane, Nottingham, NG11 8NS, ENGLAND, UK; nicholas.morton@ntu.ac.uk

Suleiman Ali Mourad, Smith College, Dept. of Religion, Wright Hall 114, Northampton MA 01063, USA; smourad@smith.edu

Dr Alan V. Murray, International Medieval Institute, The University of Leeds, Parkinson 103, Leeds LS2 9JT, ENGLAND, UK; a.v.murray@leeds.ac.uk

Stephen R.A. Murray, Apartment 351, 176 The Esplanade, Toronto, Ontario M5A 4H2, CANADA; sramurray@hotmail.com

*Antonio Musarra; Via Romagnoli 6/4, 16144, Genova, ITALY; antoniomusarra@alice.it

Claude Mutafian, 216, rue Saint-Jacques, 75005 Paris, FRANCE; claude.mutafian@wanadoo.fr

Liz Mylod, Institute for Medieval Studies, University of Leeds, Leeds, LS2 9BE, ENGLAND, UK; e.j.mylod@leeds.ac.uk

Dr. Abdollah Naseri Taheri, P.O Box 19935-581, Tehran, IRAN; a.naseri@tarikhnevesht.com & naseri_na@yahoo.com

James Naus, Dept. of History, Saint Louis Univ., 3800 Lindell Boulevard, Saint Louis MO 63108, USA; nausjl@slu.edu

Alan Neill, 13 Chesham Crescent, Belfast BT6 8GW, NORTHERN IRELAND, UK; neilla@rescueteam.com

Dr Helen J. Nicholson, Cardiff School of History, Archaeology and Religion, Cardiff University, Humanities Building, Colum Drive, Cardiff CF10 3EU, WALES, UK; nicholsonhj@cardiff.ac.uk

Angel Nicolaou-Konnari, PO Box 54106, 3721 Limassol, CYPRUS; an.konnaris@cytanet.com.cy or gpkonari@ucy.ac.cy

Dr David Nicolle, 67 Maplewell Road, Woodhouse Eaves, Leicestershire LE12 8RG, ENGLAND, UK; david.c.nicolle@btinternet.com

J. Mark Nicovich, 119 Short Bay Street, Hattiesburg MS 39401, USA; mnicovich@wmcarey.edu

Prof. Torben Kjersgaard Nielsen, Institute for History, International and Social Studies, Aalborg Univ., Fibigerstraede 5, 9220 Aalborg OE, DENMARK; tkn@ihis.aau.dk

Yoav Nitzen, 4 H'Adereth Street, Jerusalem 92343, ISRAEL; raem@bezeqint.net

Leila Norako, 1415 Clover St., Rochester NY 14610, USA; lknorako@gmail.

Dr Randall L. Norstrem, 28822 Pacific Highway S., Federal Way WA 98003, USA; templariidvm@yahoo.com

Elvor Andersen Oftestad, Faculty of Theology, Postboks 1023 Blindern, 0315 Oslo, NORWAY; e.a.oftestad@teologi.uio.no

Dr Gregory O'Malley, 4 Holly Bank, Hugglescote, Leicestershire LE67 2FR, ENGLAND, UK; gregoryomalley@btinternet.com

Prof. Mahmoud Said Omran, History Dept., Faculty of Arts, Univ. of Alexandria, Alexandria, EGYPT; msomran@dataxprs.com.eg; Web Site: www.msomran.com

Col. Erhard (Erik) Opsahl, 5303 Dennis Drive, McFarland WI 53558, USA; epopsahlw@aol.com

Jilana ORDMAN, 2525 W Cortex St., Apartment 2, Chicago IL 60622, USA; jordman@luc.edu

*Dr Isabelle ORTEGA, 1573 avenue de la Pompignane, 34000 MONTPELLIER, France ; isabelle.ortega@cegetel.net

Rhiain O'SULLIVAN, Second Floor Flat, 116–117 Saffron Hill, London EC1N 8QS, ENGLAND, UK; rhiainaroundtheworld@hotmail.com

Catherine OTTEN, 9, rue de Londres, 67000 Strasbourg, FRANCE; otten@umb.u-strasbg.fr.

Marcello PACIFICO, Corso Pisani 274, 90120 Palermo, ITALY; marcellopacifico@unipa.it

Dr Barbara PACKARD, 35 Marnham Crescent, Greenford, Middlesex UB6 9SW, ENGLAND, UK; bcpackard@yahoo.co.uk

Dr Johannes PAHLITZSCH, Parallelstraße 12, 12209 Berlin, GERMANY; pahlitz@zedat.fu-berlin.de

Dr Aphrodite PAPAYIANNI, 40 Inverness Terrace, London W2 3JB, ENGLAND, UK; aphroditepapayianni@hotmail.com

Danielle PARK, 2 Blagrave Rise, Tilehurst, Reading, Berks RG31 4SF, ENGLAND, UK; Danielle.Park.2007@live.rhul.ac.uk

Kenneth Scott PARKER, History Dept., Royal Holloway, Univ. of London, Egham, Surrey TW20 0EX, ENGLAND, UK; Kenneth.Parker.2007@live.rhul.ac.uk; parkerk@uni-mainz.de; kscottparker@gmail.com

*Matthew PARKER, 3615 Olive Street, #305, St. Louis MO 63108, USA; mparke26@slu.edu

Dr Peter D. PARTNER, Murhill Farmhouse, Murhill, Limpley Stoke, Bath BA2 7FH, ENGLAND, UK; pdp4@aol.com

Aurelio PASTORI RAMOS, 8424 NW 56th. Street, Suite MVD 05249, Miami FL 33166, USA; apastori@correo.um.edu.uy

Martin PATAIL, 2211 South West First Avenue Unit 102, Portland OR 97210, USA; patailm@pdx.edu

Dr Nicholas L. PAUL, Department of History, Fordham University, Dealy Hall, 441 E. Fordham Road, Bronx NY 10458, USA; npaul@fordham.edu

Prof. Jacques PAVIOT, Faculté des Lettres, Langues et Sciences humaines, Université de Paris-Est Créteil, 61, avenue du Général de Gaulle, F-94010 Créteil Cedex, FRANCE; paviot.jacques@wanadoo.fr

Michael J. PEIXOTO, 168 East 82nd Street, Apartment 5B, New York NY 10028-2214, USA.

Peter Shlomo PELEG, 2 Mordhai Street, Kiryat Tivon 36023, ISRAEL; fax 972 4 9931 122; ppeleg@netvision.net.il

Stelios Vasilis PERDIOS, 1344 Walton Dr., app. 206, Ames IA 50014, USA; sperdios3@gmail.com

Christopher PERKINS, 137 Adrian Drive, Stockbridge GA 30281, USA; gop7384@yahoo.com

Dr Photeine V. PERRA, Hexamilia Corinth, Corinth 201 00, GREECE; fperra@otenet.gr

Prof. David M. PERRY, Assistant Professor, Dept. of History, Dominican Univ., 7900 Divistion Street, River Forest IL 60305, USA; dperry@dom.edu

Dr Guy PERRY, School of History, University of Leeds, Leeds, LS2 9JT, UK; G.J.M.Perry@leeds.ac.uk

Nicholas J. PERRY, PO Box 389, La Mesa NM 88044, USA; nicholasperry@earthlink.net

James PETRE, The Old Barn, 8A Church Road, Stevington, Bedfordshire MK43 7QB, ENGLAND, UK; jamespetre@btinternet.com

Theodore D. Petro, New England College, 98 Bridge Street, PO Box 74, Henniker NH 03242, USA; tpetro@ccsnh.edu

Natalia I. Petrovskaia, Peterhouse, Cambridge, CB2 1RD, ENGLAND, UK; np272@cam.ac.uk

Dr Christopher Matthew Phillips, Social Science Dept., Concordia Univ., 800 N. Columbia Avenue, Seward NE 68434, USA; Matthew.Phillips@cune.edu

Prof. Jonathan P. Phillips, Dept. of History, Royal Holloway Univ. of London, Egham, Surrey TW20 0EX, ENGLAND, UK; j.p.phillips@rhul.ac.uk

Dr Simon D. Phillips, 15 Parthenonos Street, Apt. 202, Strovolos 2020, CYPRUS; simondph@ucy.ac.cy

Dr Mathias Piana, Benzstraße 9, 86420 Diedorf, GERMANY; mathias.piana@phil.uni-augsburg.de

Dr Maria Cristina Pimenta, Rua Costa Cabral, 1791 1º, 4200-228 Porto, PORTUGAL; cristina_pimenta@sapo.pt

Marion Pincemaille, 15 rue des Rossignols, 67320 Ottwiller, FRANCE; marion.pincemaille@gmail.com

Paula Maria de Carvalho Pinto Costa, see: Costa.

Dr Karol Polejowski, Ul. Wadowicka, 1B/12, 80-180 Gdansk, POLAND; kpolejowski@interia.pl

Cleber Da Silva Pontes, Rua Silva Rosa, nº 261/ apt. 402, Maria da Graça, Rio de Janeiro – RJ 21050-650, BRASIL; cl-pontes@hotmail.com

Jon Porter, Global Historical Program, Butler University, 4600 Sunset Avenue, Indianapolis IN 46208, USA; jporter1@butler.edu

Dr Valentin Portnyckh, 2 Pigorov Street, 630090, Novosibirsk, RUSSIA; valport@list.ru

Prof. James M. Powell, 5100 Highbridge Street, Apartment 18D, Fayetteville NY 13066, USA; mpowell@dreamscape.com

Dr Amanda Power, Department of History, University of Sheffield, Sheffield, S 10 2TN, UK; a.power@sheffield.ac.uk

Prof. R. Denys Pringle, School of History and Archaeology, Cardiff Univ., PO Box 909, Cardiff CF10 3EU, WALES, UK; pringlerd@cardiff.ac.uk

Dragan Prokic, M.A., Rubensallee 47, 55127 Mainz, GERMANY; dragan.prokic@o2online.de

Prof. John H. Pryor, Centre for Medieval Studies, Univ. of Sydney, John Wolley Building A20, Sydney, New South Wales 2006, AUSTRALIA; john.pryor@usyd.edu.au

Dr Emmanuelle Pujeau, Ca Antica d'En Duras, Chemin de Fregouville, 32200 Maurens, France; emmanuelle.pujeau@wanadoo.fr

Dr William J. Purkis, School of History and Cultures, Univ. of Birmingham, Edgbaston, Birmingham B15 2TT, ENGLAND, UK; w.j.purkis@bham.ac.uk

Rachael Pymm, 4 Beechtree Avenue, Englefield Green, Egham, Surrey TW20 0SR, ENGLAND, UK; peruvian_explorer@hotmail.com

*Matthieu Rajohnson, 19 rue des Gobelins, 75013 Paris, FRANCE; matthieu.rajohnson@gmail.com

Gary Ramsell, 25 Kings Road, East Sheen, London, SW148PF, ENGLAND, UK; gary@ramsell.com

Prof. Pierre Racine, 8, rue Traversière, 67201 Eckbolsheim, FRANCE; racine.p@evc.net

Yevgeniy / Eugene Rasskazov, Worth Avenue Station, PO Box 3497, Palm Beach FL 33480-3497, USA; medievaleurope@apexmail.com

Burnam W. Reynolds, Department of History, Asbury University, Wilmore KY 40390, USA; burnam.reynolds@asbury.edu

Prof. Jean Richard, 12, rue Pelletier de Chambure, 21000 Dijon, FRANCE

Maurice Riley Esq., 2 Swallow Court, Winsford, Cheshire CW7 1SR, ENGLAND, UK; rileymaurice@yahoo.com

Prof. Jonathan S.C. Riley-Smith, The Downs, Croxton, St Neots, Cambridgeshire PE19 4SX, ENGLAND, UK; jonathan.rileysmith@btinternet.com

Dr Rebecca Rist, 64, Blenheim Gardens, Reading, RG1 5QG, ENGLAND, UK; r.a.c.rist@reading.ac.uk

Daniel Roach, 7 Waverley Avenue, Exeter, Devon EX4 4NL, ENGLAND, UK; dr229@ex.ac.uk

Prof. Louise Buenger Robbert, 709 South Skinker Boulevard Apartment 701, St Louis MO 63105, USA; lrobbert@mindspring.com

Dr Jason T. Roche, Manchester Metropolitan University, Geoffrey Manton Building, All Saints, Manchester, M15 6BH, ENGLAND, UK; j.t.roche@mmu.ac.uk

José Manuel Rodríguez García, Despacho 506b, Departamento de Historia Medieval, Facultad de Geografía e Historia, Universidad Nacional de Educación a Distancia, C/ Senda del Rey, 7 (Edif. Humanidades), 28040 Madrid, ESPAÑA; jman.rodriguez@geo.uned.es

Keoen Roelandts, 2393 Spring Mill Estates Dr., Saint Charles MO 63303, USA; kroeland@slu.edu

Jean-Marc Roger, 14 rue Jean Jaurès, 86000 Poitiers, FRANCE; j-m.roger@wanadoo.fr

Prof. Manuel Rojas, Departamento de Historia, Facultad de Filosofía y Lettras, Universidad de Extremadura, 10071- Càceres, SPAIN; mrojas@unex.es

Anne Romine, Saint Louis University, Department of History, 3800 Lindell Boulevard, Saint Louis MO 63108, USA; aromine@slu.edu

Prof. Myriam Rosen-Ayalon, Institute of Asian and African Studies, The Hebrew Univ., Jerusalem 91905, ISRAEL

Prof. John Rosser, Dept. of History, Boston College, Chestnut Hill MA 02467, USA; rosserj@bc.edu

Shirley Rossi-Rivera, 2205 Roslyn Ln, Lakeland FL 33812, USA; rossirivera@rocketmail.com

Jesse S. Rouse, 8001 160th Ave, Bristol WI 53104, USA; sikkibahm@hotmail.com

Prof. Jay Rubenstein, Dept. of History, Univ. of Tennessee, 6th Floor, Dunford Hall, Knoxville TN 37996-4065, USA; jrubens1@utk.edu

Jonathan Rubin, Elazar Hamodai 12, Jerusalem 93671, ISRAEL; jonathan.rubin1@mail.huji.ac.il

Prof. Frederick H. Russell, Dept. of History, Conklin Hall, Rutgers Univ., Newark NJ 07102, USA; frussell@andromeda.rutgers.edu

Prof. James D. Ryan, 100 West 94th Street, Apartment 26M, New York NY 10025, USA; james.d.ryan@verizon.net

Vincent RYAN, Dept. of History, Saint Louis Univ., 3800 Lindell Boulevard, Saint Louis MO 63108, USA; ryanv@aquinascollege.edu

Sebastian SALVADO, 308 Gateway Drive, Apt. 236, Pacifica CA 94044, USA

*Francesco, SANTI, via Bartolini, 25 I – 59100 Prato or S.I.S.M.E.L., Certosa del Galluzzo, I – 50124 Firenze, ITALY; frsanti@conmet.it direzione@sismelfirenze.it

Dr Andrew J. SARGENT, 33 Coborn Street, Bow, London E3 2AB, ENGLAND, UK; asargent164@gtinternet.com

Prof. Juergen SARNOWSKY, Historisches Seminar, Universität Hamburg, Von-Melle-Park 6, 20146 Hamburg, GERMANY; juergen.sarnowsky@uni-hamburg.de

Christopher J. SAUNDERS OBE, Watery Hey, Springvale Road, Hayfield, High Peak SK22 2LD, ENGLAND, UK; cjs@sandtassetmanagement.com

Prof. Alexios G.C. SAVVIDES, Aegean Univ., Dept. of Mediterranean Studies, Rhodes, GREECE; or: 7 Tralleon Street, Nea Smyrne, Athens 17121, GREECE; savvides@rhodes. aegean.gr

Dr Christopher SCHABEL, 728 Linn St., Boone IA 50036, USA and Dept. of History and Archaeology, Univ. of Cyprus, PO Box 20537, 1678 Nicosia, CYPRUS; schabel@ucy.ac.cy

Dr Jochen SCHENK, German Historical Institute London, 17 Bloomsbury Square, London WC1A 2NJ, ENGLAND, UK; schenk@ghil.ac.uk

Dr James G. SCHRYVER, Univ. of Minnesota Morris, HUM 104, 600 East 4th Street, Morris MN 56267, USA; schryver@morris.umn.edu

Warren C. SCHULZ, De Paul Univ., Dept. of History, 2320 Kenmore, Chicago IL 60614, USA; wschultz@depaul.edu

DR Beate SCHUSTER, 19, rue Vauban, 67000 Strasbourg, FRANCE; beaschu@compuserve. com

Prof. Rainer C. SCHWINGES, Historisches Institut der Universität Bern, Unitobler – Länggass-Straße 49, 3000 Bern 9, SWITZERLAND; rainer.schwinges@hist.unibe.ch

Einat SEGAL, 20 Neve Rehim Street, Ramat Hasharon, ISRAEL; eisegal@netvision.net.il

Iris SHAGRIR, Dept. of History, The Open Univ. of Israel, PO Box 808, Ra'anana 43107, ISRAEL; irissh@openu.ac.il

Joseph SHANNON, 269 Lawson Street, Saline MI 48176, USA; salinecett@yahoo.com

Prof. Maya SHATZMILLER, 19 King Street, London, Ontario N6A 5N8, CANADA; maya@ uwo.ca

Dr Teresa SHAWCROSS, Trinity Hall, Cambridge CB2 1TJ, ENGLAND, UK; teresa. shawcross@googlemail.com

Dr Jonathan SHEPARD, Box 483, 266 Banbury Road, Oxford OX2 7DL, ENGLAND, UK; nshepard@easynet.co.uk

Vardit SHOTTEN-HALLEL, 14 Alon Street, Timrat, ISRAEL 36576; shotten-hallel@012.net.il

William SHULL, 481 Barham Avenue, Henderson TN 38340, USA; wshull@gmail.com

Dr Elizabeth J. SIBERRY, 28 The Mall, Surbiton, Surrey KT6 4E9, ENGLAND, UK; elizabeth. siberry@gmail.com

Kaare Seeberg SIDSELRUD, Granebakken 9, 1284 Oslo, NORWAY; kss@sidselrud.net

Raitis SIMSONS, Konsula 15A-1, Riga 1007, LATVIA; raitiss@btv.lv

Micaela Sɪɴɪʙᴀʟᴅɪ, School of History, Archaeology and Religion, Cardiff University, Humanities Building, Colum Drive, Cardiff CF 10 3EU, WALES, UK; sinibaldim@cardiff.ac.uk

Dr Corliss K. Sʟᴀᴄᴋ, History Department, Whitworth University, Spokane WA 99205, USA; cslack@whitworth.edu

*Bogdan C. Sᴍᴀʀᴀɴᴅᴀᴄʜᴇ, St. Catharine's College, Cambridge CB2 1RL, ENGLAND, UK; b.smarand@gmail.com

Rima E. Sᴍɪɴᴇ, 25541 Altamont Road, Los Altos Hills CA 94022, USA.

Dr Caroline Sᴍɪᴛʜ, 551, 47th Road, 3L, Long Island City NY 11101, USA; caroline.a.smith@gmail.com

Thomas Sᴍɪᴛʜ, Department of History, Royal Holloway, University of London, Egham, Surrey, TW20 0EX, UK; thomas.smith.503@gmail.com

Simon Sᴏɴɴᴀᴋ, 658 Canning Street, North Carlton, 3054 Victoria, AUSTRALIA; ssonnak@bigpond.net.au

Arnold Sᴘᴀᴇʀ, 8 King David Street, Jerusalem 94104, ISRAEL; hui@spaersitton.co.il

Dr Alan M. Sᴛᴀʜʟ, 11 Fairview Place, Ossining NY 10562, USA; amstahl@optonline.net

Stefan Sᴛᴀɴᴛᴄʜᴇᴠ, 18007 N 88th Dr., Peoria AZ 85382, USA; stefan.stantchev@asu.edu

Rombert Sᴛᴀᴘᴇʟ, Fryske Akademy, Postbus 54, 8900AB, Leeuwarden, The Netherlands / home: Koolgracht 33, 2312PD, Leiden, The Netherlands; rstapel@fryske-akademy.nl / r.j.stapel@hum.leidenuniv.nl

Rodney Sᴛᴀʀᴋ, 170 Camino Rayo del Sol, Corales NM 87048, USA; rs@rodneystark.com

Patrick Sᴛᴏʜʟᴇʀ, Oetlingerstraße 192, 4057 Basel, SWITZERLAND; Patrick.Stohler@unibas.ch

Dr Myra Sᴛʀᴜᴄᴋᴍᴇʏᴇʀ, 171 North Hamilton Road, Chapel Hill NC 27517, USA; struckme@alumni.unc.edu

Jace Sᴛᴜᴄᴋᴇʏ, Louisiana Tech Univ., History Dept., PO Box 8548, Rushton LA 71272, USA; jstuckey@marymount.edu

*Carol Sᴡᴇᴇᴛᴇɴʜᴀᴍ, 7 Betty Lane, Oxford, OX1 5BW, ENGLAND, UK; carol@sweetenham.org

Miikka Tᴀᴍᴍɪɴᴇɴ, Kaarina Maununtyttären tie 1142, 36200 Kangasala, FINLAND; miikka.tamminen@uta.fi

Prof. Dr. Stefan Tᴇʙʀᴜᴄᴋ, Historisches Institut der Justus-Liebig-Universität Gießen, Otto-Behaghel-Str. 10 C, D-35394 Gießen, Germany; Stefan.Tebruck@geschichte.uni-giessen.de

Miriam Rita Tᴇssᴇʀᴀ, via Moncalvo 16, 20146 Milano, ITALY; monachus_it@yahoo.it

Prof. Peter Tʜᴏʀᴀᴜ, Historisches Institut, Univ. des Saarlandes, for letters Postfach 15 11 50, 66041 Saarbrücken, for packages Im Stadtwald, 66123 Saarbrücken, GERMANY; p.thorau@mx.uni-saarland.de

Susanna Tʜʀᴏᴏᴘ, Ursinus College, History Department, PO Box 1000, Collegeville PA 19426-1000, USA; sthroop@ursinus.edu or susannathroop@gmail.com

Dr Steven Tɪʙʙʟᴇ, Copsewood, Deadhearn Lane, Chalfont St Giles, Buckinghamshire HP8 4HG, ENGLAND, UK; steve.tibble@btinternet.com

Prof. Hirofumi Tᴏᴋᴏ, 605-3 Kogasaka, Machida, Tokyo 194-0014, JAPAN; htoko@mtd.biglobe.ne.jp

Prof. John Victor Tolan, Département d'Histoire, Université de Nantes, B.P. 81227, 44312 Nantes, FRANCE, or: 2, rue de la Chevalerie, 44300 Nantes, FRANCE; john.tolan@univ-nantes.fr

Ignacio de la Torre, Saxifraga 9, 28036 Madrid, ESPAÑA; ide@profesor.ie.edu

Prof. François-Olivier Touati, Département d'Histoire et d'Archéologie, Université François-Rabelais, 3 rue des Tanneurs, B.P. 4103, F-37041 Tours Cedex 1, or: La Croix Saint-Jérôme, 11, allée Émile Bouchut, 77123 Noisy-sur-École, FRANCE; francoistouati@aol.com

*Nickiphoros I. Tsougarakis, 21 Otterburn Gardens, Isleworth, Middlesex, TW7 5JL, ENGLAND, UK; nickytsougarakis@hotmail.com

*Mamuka Tsurtsumia, Arakishvili 1st Alley 8, Tbilisi, 0179, GEORGIA; mkhedari@mkhedari.ge

Dr Christopher J. Tyerman, Hertford College, Oxford, Catte Street, Oxford OX1 3BW, ENGLAND, UK; christopher.tyerman@hertford.ox.ac.uk

*Dr Todd P. Upton, PO Box 270813, Littleton CO 80127, USA; tj_upton@me.com

Dr Judith M. Upton-Ward, 6 Haywood Court, Reading, Berks., RG1 3QF, ENGLAND, UK; juptonward@btopenworld.com

Jean-Bernard de Vaivre, Vieux Château, Le Bourg, 71800 Amanze, FRANCE; jbv@100cibles.fr

Toon Van Elst, Prof. Piccardlaan 32, 2610 Wilrijk, BELGIUM; toonvanelst@hotmail.com

Jan Vandeburie, De Gribovalstraat 9, 8550 Zwevegem, BELGIUM; j.vandeburie@kent.ac.uk

Dweezil Vandekerckhove, Talybont South, Trotman Dickinson Place, House 20/0/1-4, Cardiff C14 3UU, WALES, UK; vandekerckhoved@cardiff.ac.uk

Øyvind Fossum Vangberg, Engveien 10, 1920 Sørumsand, NORWAY; ofvangberg@live.no

Theresa M. Vann, Hill Monastic Manuscript Library, St John's Univ., Collegeville MN 56321, USA; tvann@csbsju.edu

Rafael Velázquez Parejo, c/ Villa de Rota, n°2, 4° F, 14005 Córdoba, ESPAÑA; mariceli50@hotmail.com

Dr Lucas Villegas-Aristizabal, 11 Sutton Court Road, Chiswick, London, W4 4NN, ENGLAND, UK; lucasvillegasa@gmail.com

Fiona Weir Walmsley, 41 Broomley Street, Kangaroo Point, Queensland 4169, AUSTRALIA; f.walmsley@optusnet.com.au

Laura Wangerin, 811 W. Belden Avenue, Chicago IL 60614, USA; lwangerin@latinschool.org

Dr Marie-Louise von Wartburg Maier, Paphosprojekt der Universität Zürich, Karl Schmid-Strasse 4, CH-8006 Zürich; ml.v.wartburg@access.uzh.ch

Michael Wasson, PO box 940, Randwick PO Randwick N.S.W. 2031, AUSTRALIA; mwasson7@bigpond.com

*Daniel Webb, 3800 Lindell Blvd, room 137, St. Louis MO 63108, USA; dwebb11@slu.edu

Benjamin Weber, 31, avenue Étienne Billières, 31300 Toulouse, FRANCE; benji.tigrou@gmail.com or benjamin-weber@laposte.net

Steven A. Weidenkopf, 6814 Barnack Drive, Springfield VA 22152, USA; steve@ourcatholichistory.com

Dr Mark WHITTOW, St Peter's College, Oxford OX1 2DL, ENGLAND, UK; mark.whittow@ st-peters.oxford.ac.uk

Raymond WIESNER, 1725 Graham Avenue, Apartment 409, St. Paul MN 55116-3280, USA; raymondwiesner@yahoo.com

Timothy WILKES, A.H. Baldwin & Sons Ltd., 11 Adelphi Terrace, London WC2N 6BJ, ENGLAND, UK; timwilkes@baldwin.sh

The Rev. Dr John D. WILKINSON, 7 Tenniel Close, London W2 3LE, ENGLAND, UK; johnwilkinson@globalnet.co.uk

Dr Ann WILLIAMS, 40 Greenwich South Street, London SE10 8UN, ENGLAND, UK; ann. williams@talk21.com

Prof. Steven James WILLIAMS, Dept. of History, New Mexico Highlands Univ., PO Box 9000, Las Vegas NM 87701, USA; stevenjameswilliams@yahoo.com

*Juho WILSKMAN, Tupalantie 19 D 29, 04400, Järvenpää, Finland; juho.wilskman@helsinki. fi

Ian James WILSON, 1 Freeman Close, Hadleigh, Suffolk, IP7 6HH, England, UK; ian. wilson@btopenworld.com

*Samuel James WILSON, 46 Spalding Road, Nottingham, NG3 2AZ, UK; samuel. wilson2007@my.ntu.ac.uk

Peter van WINDEKENS, Kleine Ganzendries 38, 3212 Pellenberg, BELGIUM; wit.hus@ skynet.be

Prof. Johanna Maria VAN WINTER, Keizerstraat 35 A, NL-3512 EA Utrecht, NETHERLANDS; j.m.vanwinter@uu.nl

Ashley Sarah WINTERBOTTOM, 158 Broadway, Chadderton, Oldham. OL9 0JY, ENGLAND, UK; ashley.winterbottom@hud.ac.uk

Dr Noah WOLFSON, 13 Avuqa Street, Tel-Aviv 69086, ISRAEL; noah@meteo-tech.co.il

*Alfred F. WOLKOMIR, 1 Markwood Lane, Rumson NY 07760, USA; afwmir@aol.com

*Meghan Holmes WORTH, 225 Brancroff Cir., Knoxville TN 37920, USA; mworth1@ tennessee.edu

*Wang XIANG PENG, School of History and Culture, Northeast Normal University, 5268 Renmin Street, Changchun, Jilin Province, Popular Republic of CHINA; fantasywxp123@ hotmail.com

*Xu Jia-ling, School of History and Culture, Northeast Normal University, 5268 Renmin Street, Changchun, Jilin Province, Popular Republic of CHINA, xujl270@nenu.edu.cn

Prof. Shunji YATSUZUKA, 10–22 Matsumoto 2 chome, Otsu-shi, Shiga 520, JAPAN; shunchan@mub.biglobe.ne.jp

*Dr Julian YOLLES, 20 Calvin St, Apt 2, 02143 Somerville MA, USA; jjtyolles@gmail.com

William G. ZAJAC, 9 Station Terrace, Pen-y-rheal, Caerphilly, CF83 2RH, WALES, UK.

Prof. Ossama Zaki ZEID, 189 Abd al-Salam Aref Tharwat, Alexandria, EGYPT; ossama_ zeid@hotmail.com

Joseph ZELNIK, 25 Wingate Street, Ra'anana 43587, ISRAEL; jzelnik@galilcol.ac.il

Ann ZIMO, 2809 Pleasant Avenue, Apt. 106, Minneapolis MN 55408, USA; zimox001@ umn.edu

Institutions subscribing to the SSCLE

Bibliothécaire Guy Cobolet, Le Bibliothécaire, École Française d'Athènes, 6, Didotou 10680 Athènes, GREECE

Centre de Recherches d'histoire et civilisation de Byzance et du Proche-Orient Chétien, Université de Paris 1, 17, rue de la Sorbonne, 75231 Paris Cedex, FRANCE

Centre for Byzantine, Ottoman and Modern Greek Studies, Univ. of Birmingham, Edgbaston, Birmingham B15 2TT, ENGLAND, UK

Corpus Christianoru, Brepols Publishers, Sint-Annaconvent, Begijnhof 39, 2300 Turnhout, BELGIUM

Couvent des Pères Dominicains, Saint-Étienne, Bibliotèque, PO Box 19053, 91 190, Jerusalem, ISRAEL

Deutsches Historisches Institut in Rom, Via Aurelia Antica 391, 00165 Roma, ITALY

Deutschordenszentralarchiv (DOZA), Singerstraße 7, 1010 Wien, AUSTRIA

Dumbarton Oaks Research Library, 1703 32nd Street North West, Washington D.C. 20007, USA

Europäisches Burgeninstitut, Schlossstraße 5, 56338 Braubach, GERMANY; ebi@deutsche-burgen.org

Germanisches Nationalmuseum, Bibliothek, Kornmarkt 1, 90402 Nürnberg, GERMANY

History Department, Campbell College, Belfast, BT4 2 ND, NORTHERN IRELAND, UK

The Jewish National and University Library, PO Box 34165, Jerusalem 91341, ISRAEL

The Library, The Priory of Scotland of the Most Venerable Order of St John, 21 St John Street, Edinburgh EH8 8DG, SCOTLAND, UK

The National Library of Israel, Periodical Department, PO Box 39105, 91390 Jerusalem, ISRAEL

The Stephen Chan Library, Institute of Fine Arts, New York Univ., 1 East 78th Street, New York NY 10021-0102, USA

Metropolitan Museum of Art, Thomas J. Watson Library, Serials Dept., 1000 Fifth Avenue, New York NY 10028-0198, USA

Museum and Library of the Order of St John, St John's Gate, Clerkenwell, London EC1M 4DA, ENGLAND, UK

Order of the Temple of Jerusalem, Priory of England and Wales, c/o Mr. John Reddington, 2 Alberta Gardens, Coggeshall, Coldchester, Essex CO6 1UA, ENGLAND, UK

Serials Department, 11717 Young Research Library, Univ. of California, Box 951575, Los Angeles CA 90095-1575, USA

Sourasky Library, Tel-Aviv Univ., Periodical Dept., PO Box 39038, Tel-Aviv, ISRAEL

Teutonic Order Bailiwick of Utrecht, Dr John J. Quarles van Ufford, Secretary of the Bailliwick, Springweg 25, 3511 VJ Utrecht, THE NETHERLANDS

Türk Tarih Kurumu [Turkish Historical Society], Kizilay Sokak No. 1, Sihhiye 06100 Ankara, TURKEY

Eberhard-Karls-Universität Tübingen, Orientalisches Seminar, Münzgasse 30, 72072 Tübingen, GERMANY

University of California, Los Angeles Serials Dept. / YRL, 11020 Kinross, Box 957230, Los Angeles CA 90 095-723, USA

University of London Library, Periodicals Section, Senate House, Malet Street, London, WC1E 7HU, ENGLAND, UK

University of North Carolina, Davis Library CB 3938, Periodicals and Serials Dept., Chapel Hill NC 27514-8890, USA

Universitätsbibliothek Tübingen, Wilhelmstraße 32, Postfach 26 20, 72016 Tübingen, GERMANY

University of Reading, Graduate Centre for Medieval Studies, Whiteknights, PO Box 218, Reading, Berks., RG6 6AA, ENGLAND, U.K

University of Washington, Libraries, Serials Division, PO Box 352900, Seattle WA 98195, USA

University of Western Ontario Library, Acquisitions Dept., Room M1, D.B. Weldon Library, London, Ontario N6A 3K7, CANADA

The Warburg Institute, Univ. of London, Woburn Square, London WC1H 0AB, ENGLAND, UK. [John Perkins, Deputy Librarian, jperkins@a1.sas.ac.uk]

W.F. Albright Institute of Archaeological Research, 26 Salah ed-Din Street, PO Box 19096, Jerusalem 91190, ISRAEL

12. Officers of the Society

President: Professor Bernard Hamilton.

Honorary Presidents: Professor Jean Richard, Professor Jonathan Riley-Smith, Professor Benjamin Z. Kedar, Professor Michel Balard.

Secretary: Professor Luis García-Guijarro Ramos.

Assistant Secretary: Professor Adrian Boas.

Conference Secretary: Professor Kurt Villads Jensen

Editor of the Bulletin: Professor François-Olivier Touati.

Officer for Postgraduate Members: Professor Jonathan Phillips

Treasurer: Dr. Jon M.B. Porter.

Website: Professor Thomas F. Madden.

Committee of the Society: Professor Antonio Carile (Bologna), Professor Hans Eberhard Mayer (Kiel).

Guidelines for the Submission of Papers

The editors ask contributors to adhere to the following guidelines. Failure to do so will result in the article being returned to the author for amendment, or may result in its having to be excluded from the volume.

1. Submissions. Submissions should be sent as email attachments to one of the editors. Papers should be formatted using MS Word, double-spaced and with wide margins. Times New Roman (12 pt) is preferred. Remember to include your name and contact details (both postal and email addresses) on your paper.

2. Peer Review. All submissions will be peer reviewed. They will be scrutinized by the editors and sent to at least one outside reader before a decision on acceptance is made.

3. Length. Normally, the maximum length of articles should not exceed 6,000 words, not including notes. The editors reserve the right to edit papers that exceed these limits.

4. Notes. Normally, notes should be REFERENCE ONLY and placed at the end of the paper. Number continuously.

5. Style sheet. Please use the most recent *Speculum* style sheet (currently *Speculum* 75 (2000), 547–52). This sets out the format to be used for notes. Please note that this is not necessarily the same format as has been used by other edited volumes on the crusades and/or the Military Orders. Failure to follow the Speculum format will result in accepted articles being returned to the author for amendment. In the main body of the paper you may adhere to either British or American spelling, but it must be consistent throughout the article.

6. Language. Papers will be published in English, French, German, Italian and Spanish.

7. Abbreviations. Please use the abbreviation list on pp. xi–xiii of this journal.

8. Diagrams and Maps should be referred to as figures and photographs as plates. Please keep illustrations to the essential minimum, since it will be possible to include only a limited number. All illustrations must be supplied by the contributor in camera-ready copy, and free from all copyright restrictions.

9. Italics. Words to be printed in italics should be italicized if possible. Failing this they should be underlined.

10. Capitals. Please take every care to ensure consistency in your use of capitals and lower case letters. Use initial capitals to distinguish the general from the specific (for example, "the count of Flanders" but "Count Philip of Flanders").

11. Summary of Article. Contributors will be required to provide a 250 words summary of their paper at the start of each article. This will be accompanied by the author's email address. The summary of the paper is to be in English, regardless of the language of the main article.

Editors

Prof. Benjamin Z. Kedar
Department of History
The Hebrew University of Jerusalem
Jerusalem 91905, Israel
bzkedar@huji.ac.il

Prof. Jonathan Phillips
Department of History
Royal Holloway, University of London
Egham
Surrey TW20 0EX
U.K.
J.P.Phillips@rhul.ac.uk

SOCIETY FOR THE STUDY OF THE CRUSADES AND THE LATIN EAST
MEMBERSHIP INFORMATION

The primary function of the Society for the Study of the Crusades and the Latin East is to enable members to learn about current work being done in the field of crusading history, and to contact members who share research interests through the information in the Society's Bulletin. There are currently 467 members of the SSCLE from 41 countries. The Society also organizes a major international conference every four years, as well as sections on crusading history at other conferences where appropriate.

The committee of the SSCLE consists of:
Prof. Bernard Hamilton, *President*
Prof. Jean Richard, Prof. Jonathan Riley-Smith, Prof. Benjamin Z. Kedar and Prof. Michel Balard, *Honorary Presidents*
Prof. Luis García-Guijarro Ramos, *Secretary*
Prof. Adrian Boas, *Assistant Secretary*
Prof. Kurt Villads Jensen, *Conference Secretary*
Dr. Jon M. B. Porter, *Treasurer*
Prof. Jonathan Phillips, *Officer for Postgraduate Members*
Prof. François-Olivier Touati, *Bulletin Editor*
Prof. Thomas F. Madden, *Website*

Current subscription fees are as follows:
* Membership and Bulletin of the Society: Single £10, $20 or €15;
* Student £6, $12 or €9;
* Joint membership £15, $30 or €21;
* Membership and the journal *Crusades*, including the Bulletin: £25, $46 or €32.